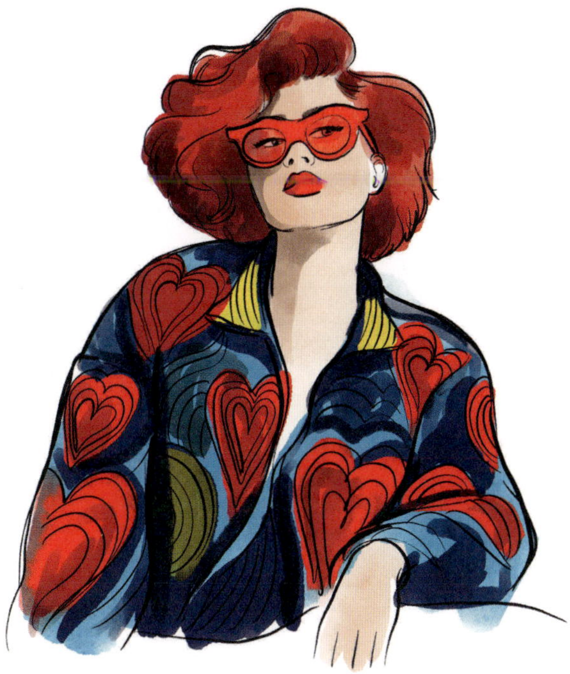

SKETCH YOUR Amazing STYLE

Conceived, designed, and produced by
The Bright Press,
an imprint of the Quarto Group,
1 Triptych Place, London SE1 9SH,
United Kingdom
T (0)20 7700 6700
www.Quarto.com

ISBN: 978-1-4197-7464-5

Authors: Justine Lecouffe and Chloe Takahashi

Part opener images on pages 10–11, 50–51, 190–191 © Shutterstock
Fabric swatch images on pages 29, 54, 58, 62, 66, 70, 74, 78, 83, 86, 90, 96, 100, 105, 108, 113, 116, 120, 124, 128, 132, 139, 142, 147, 150, 154, 159, 162, 167, 172, 176, 180, 184, 192, 196, 200, 204 © Shutterstock

For The Bright Press:
Publisher: James Evans
Editorial Director: Anna Southgate
Art Director: James Lawrence
Senior Designer: Emily Nazer
Managing Editor: Jacqui Sayers
Senior Editor: Dee Costello
Project Editor: Jen Moore
Design: Clare Barber

MIX
Paper | Supporting responsible forestry
FSC® C016973

For Abrams:
Editor: Shawna Mullen
Design Manager: Danny Maloney
Managing Editor: Kayla White
Production Manager: Larry Pekarek

Library of Congress Control Number has been applied for and may be obtained from the Library of Congress.

Published in 2024 by Abrams Image, an imprint of ABRAMS.

Printed and bound in China
10 9 8 7 6 5 4 3 2 1

ABRAMS The Art of Books
195 Broadway, New York, NY 10007
abramsbooks.com

A BODY-POSITIVE GUIDED SKETCHBOOK FOR DRAWING DREAM WARDROBES

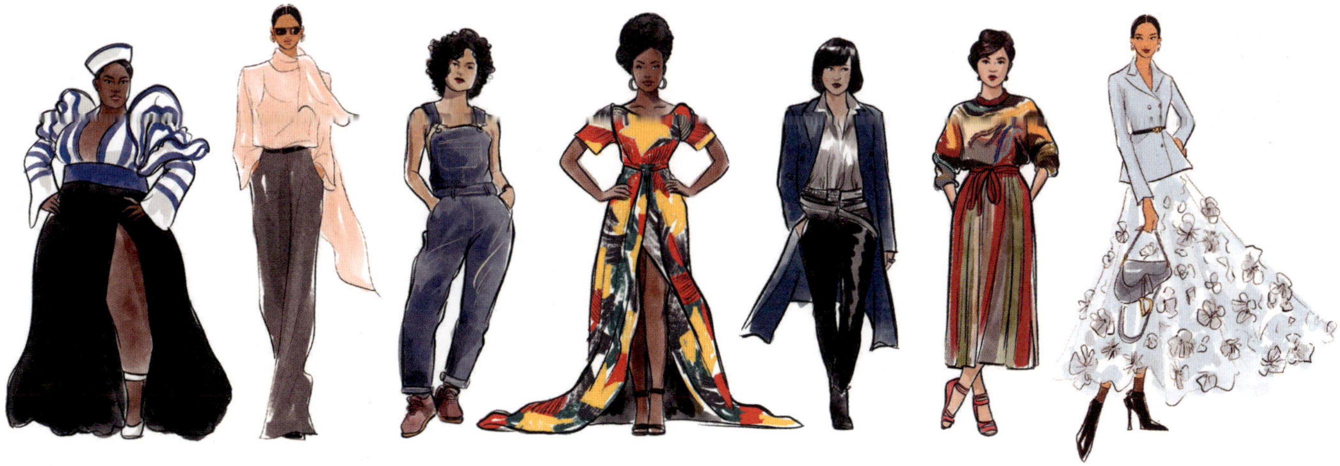

SKETCH YOUR *Amazing* STYLE

JUSTINE LECOUFFE & CHLOE TAKAHASHI

Abrams Image, New York

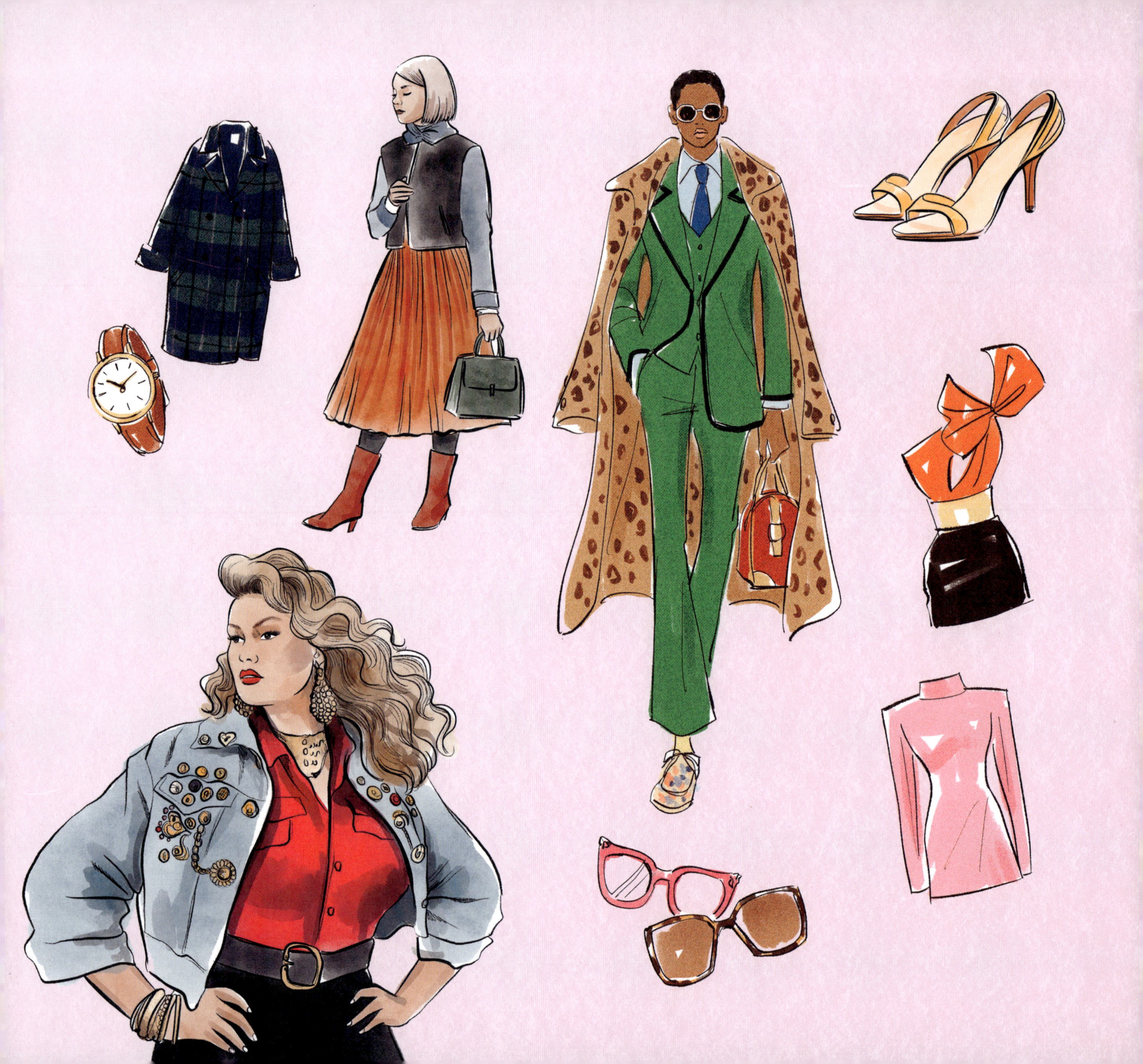

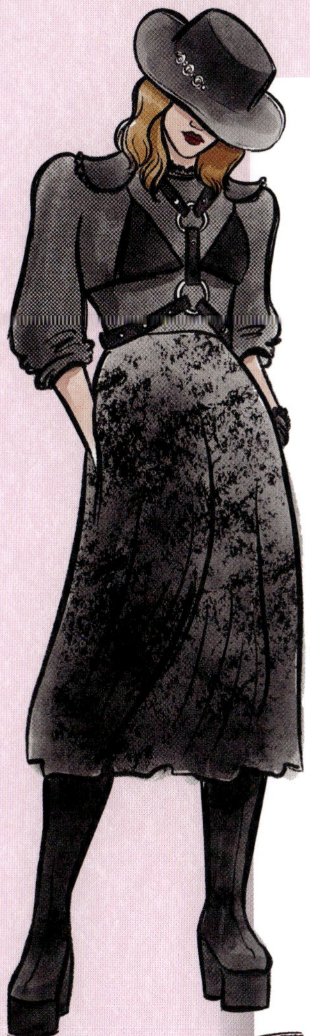

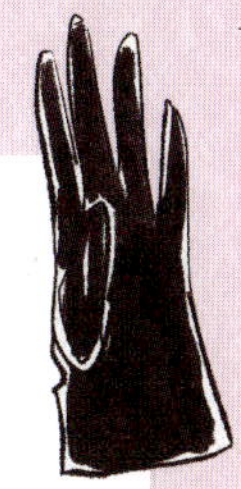

Contents

Introduction 6
How to Use This Book 8

Part One: STYLE SKETCHING 11
Tools and Techniques 12
How to Draw a Croquis 14
Know Your Body Shape 16
Adding Details to Your Figures 22
How Fabric Works 26
Using Color 28
Visual Glossary 32

Part Two: STYLE INSPIRATION 51
Style Inspiration Themes 52
Timeless Classics 54
Wild Imagination 82
Haute Couture 116
Street Style 142
Global Twist 172

Part Three: STYLE JOURNAL 191
Spring 192
Summer 196
Fall 200
Winter 204

About the Authors 208

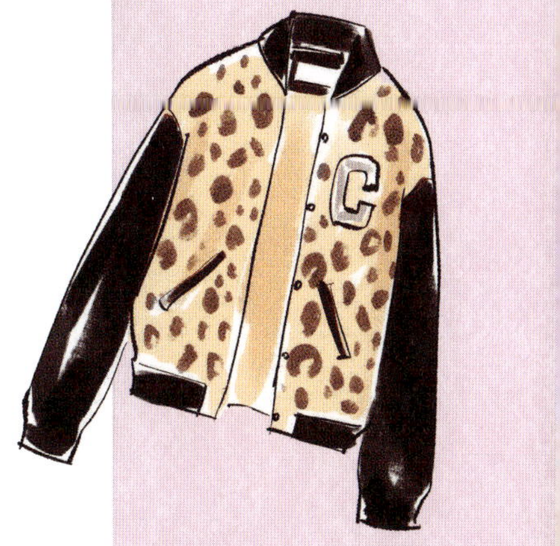

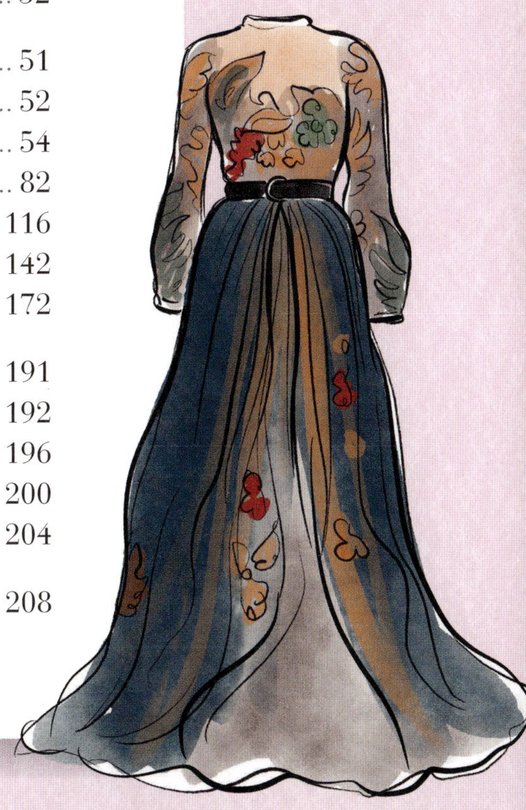

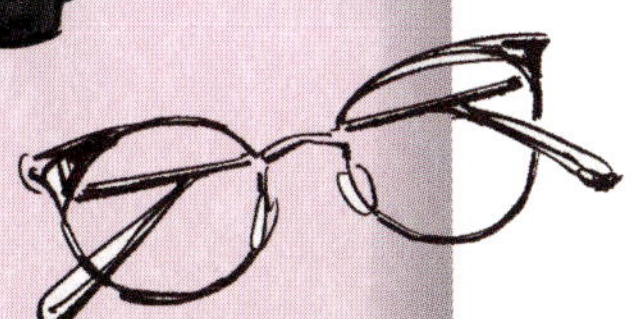

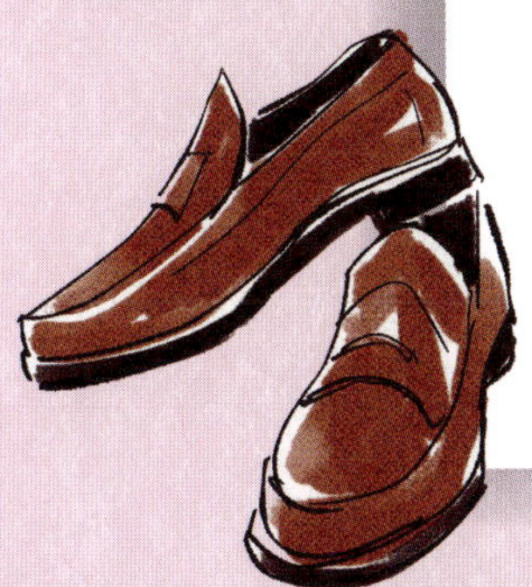

Introduction

Welcome to the world of amazing style! I'm Chloe Takahashi (@chloetakahashi_illustrator), co-authoring this book with Justine. I am a Manhattan-based fashion illustrator from Japan, mainly working with fashion and beauty brands. I also teach fashion illustration online through in-depth video tutorials.

This book, *Sketch Your Amazing Style*, is a bundle of fun—it not only covers the basics of figurative drawing and the chic, dazzling world of fashion, but also celebrates body positivity and diversity. By using the informative and inspirational material within, you can create your own dream wardrobe and "amazing" style! As you learn the concepts and tackle the DIY pages, I want you to enjoy creating, soak in inspiration, and embrace what you like and who you are—your own unique style and love for fashion are what make a great fashion sketch. In my earlier career, I was in a completely different field. I started drawing just a few years ago, but believing in the above principles truly made my dream job come true. I hope this book will guide you on your own exciting journey!

Chloe Takahashi

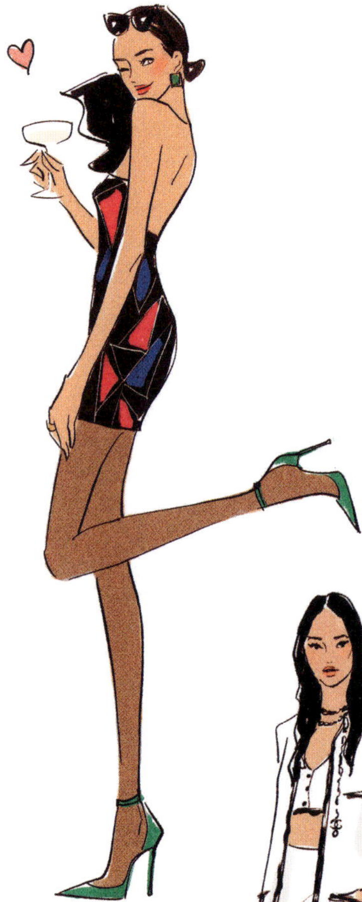

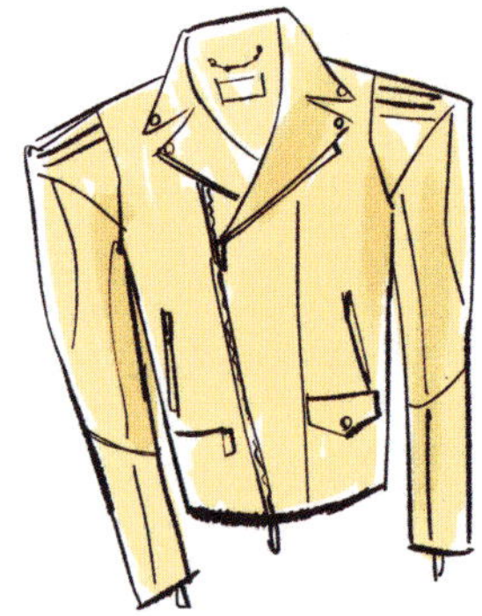

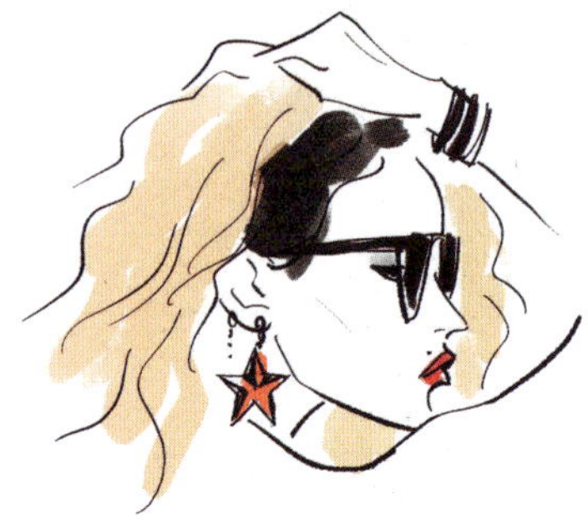

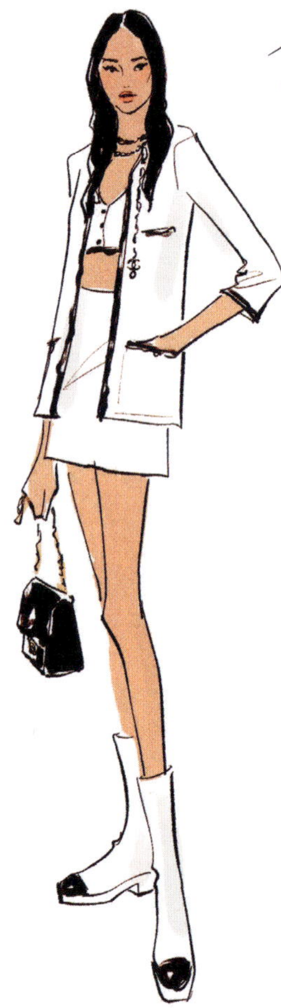

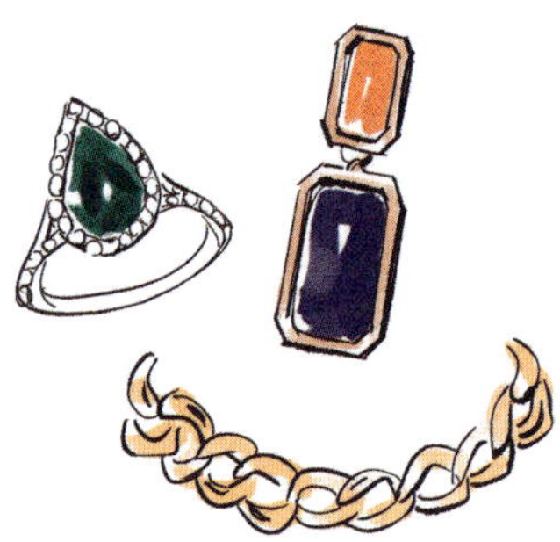

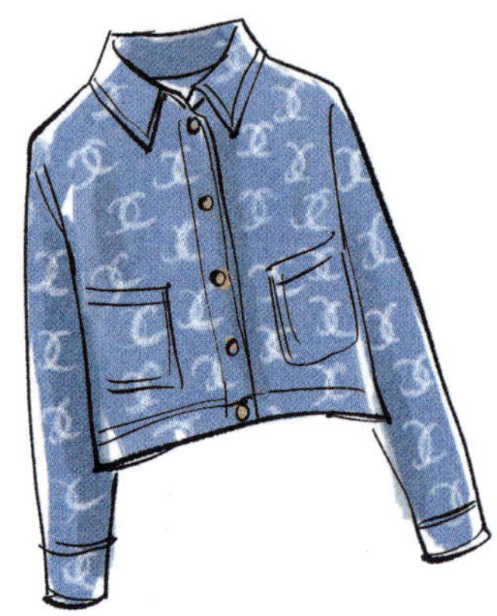

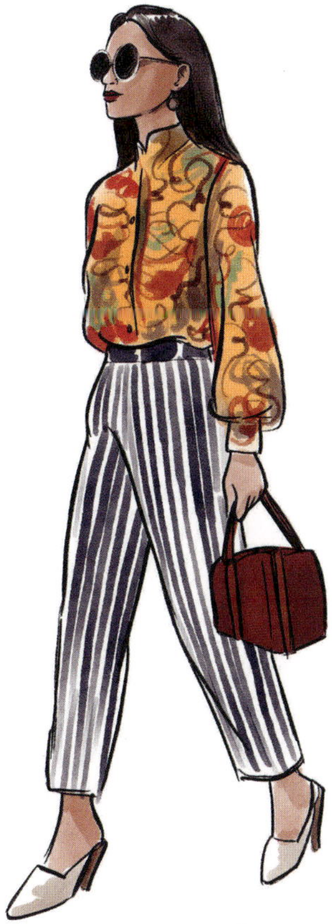

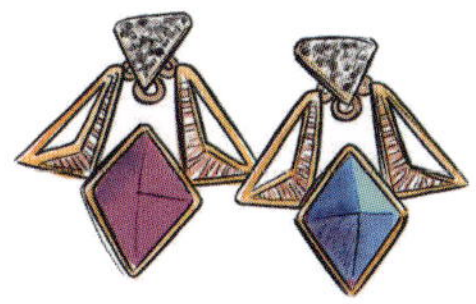

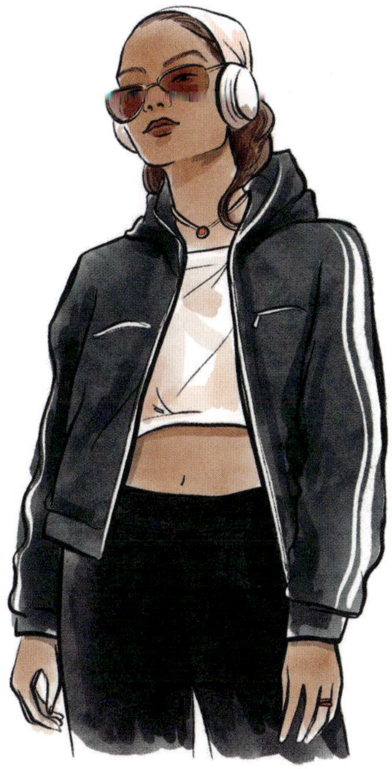

Hello, and welcome to the vibrant world of sketching your amazing style, where fabric meets fantasy, pencils meet stitches, and style becomes a language.

My name is Justine. I am a French illustrator living in Ireland and I'm delighted to be co-authoring this book with Chloe. From children's books to editorial illustrations, I've had the chance to explore various styles, mediums, and techniques through my work. But fashion has always had a special place in my heart. I love how a pencil stroke can capture the essence of elegance, movement, and couture.

Through this book you will get the chance to explore the interplay of colors, experiment with diverse mediums, and embrace the fusion of traditional and digital looks. Join me in unlocking the secrets of sketching runway-ready designs, and translating imagination onto paper. *Sketch Your Amazing Style* is more than a book, it's an invitation to unleash your artistic potential and become a maestro of fashion illustration.

Bring your own artistic flair and perspective, and contribute to the vibrant landscape of fashion illustration!

Justine Lecouffe

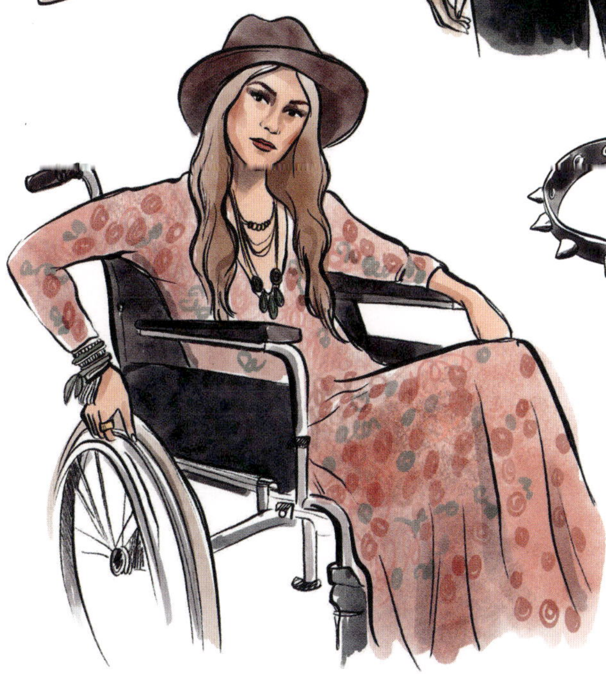

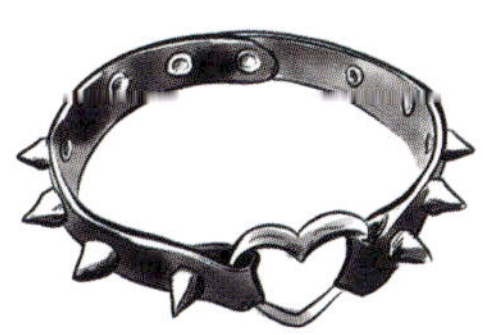

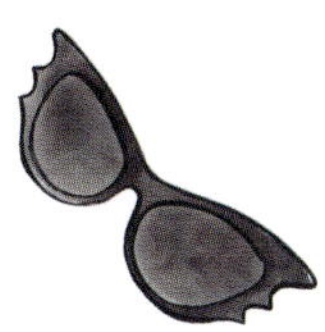

How to Use This Book

We've designed this book to be an inspirational and educational experience for aspiring artists or fashion enthusiasts looking to hone their skills. Here's a guide to help you make the most of your fashion sketching book.

In **Part One: Style Sketching,** we look at the basic tools, drawing techniques, and finishing methods you need to begin your sketching journey. You will find step-by-step instructions to help you practice each technique and build proficiency. This chapter also contains a Visual Glossary, which is a quick reference guide to key wardrobe pieces like skirts, pants, jackets, and accessories. Try different styles, mediums, and approaches, and allow yourself to make mistakes. They're part of the learning process!

Once you understand the basics, you can start having fun creating your own designs. Exploring fashion trends is a fantastic way to infuse your designs with freshness and relevance. In **Part Two: Style Inspiration,** we let creativity flow by seeking inspiration from various sources—fashion shows, nature, art, or even everyday life. This will allow you to incorporate elements that inspire you, from wild trends to timeless classics, into your sketches. We look at the work of haute couture designers who have left their mark on the world of fashion—innovators who changed the rules with their forward-thinking designs and opened our eyes to different ways of dressing—as well as global traditional fashion, celebrating the uniqueness of different cultures.

Part One contains templates and exercises that will teach you the basics of fashion illustration. You'll learn how to draw and dress your croquis, and hone your unique sketching style.

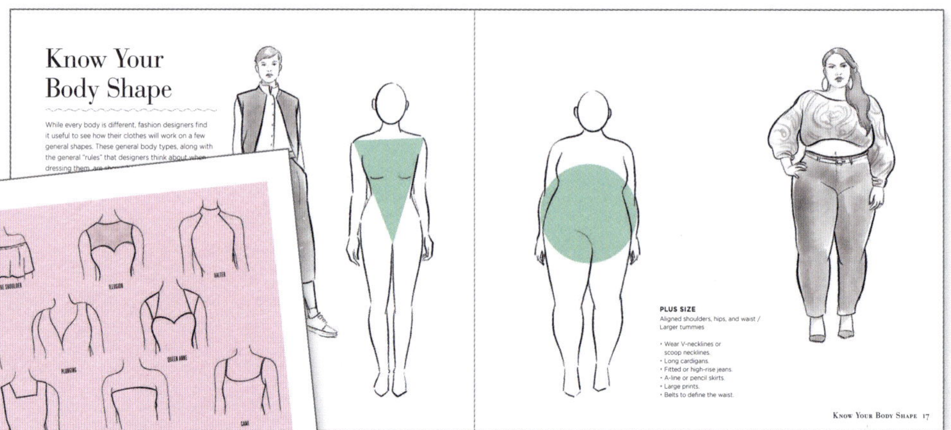

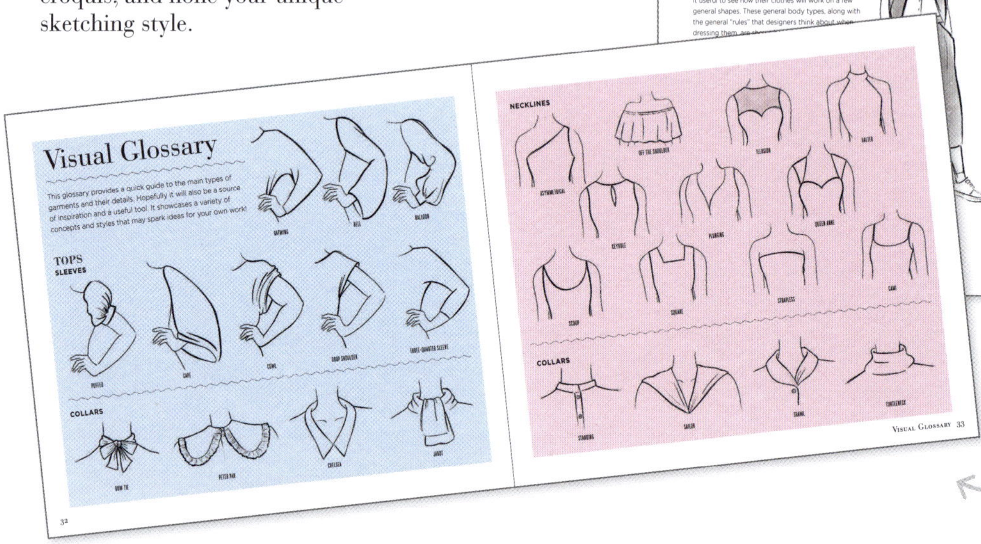

You'll also find a Visual Glossary packed with inspiration!

Contemporary designers often draw inspiration from heritage fashion, infusing traditional elements into modern clothing. This fusion gives rise to innovative designs that blend the richness of heritage with current fashion sensibilities. Remember, while trends provide a framework for fashion sketching, your unique perspective and creative interpretation are what will make your designs stand out. Let your imagination and originality shine through in your creations. **Part Three: Style Journal,** will encourage you to explore and refine your personal style while documenting your fashion journey. Feel free to use your journal to experiment with new styles, combinations, or accessories. Step out of your comfort zone and note down your experiences. This style journal is a personal space for exploration, expression, and refining your unique fashion identity.

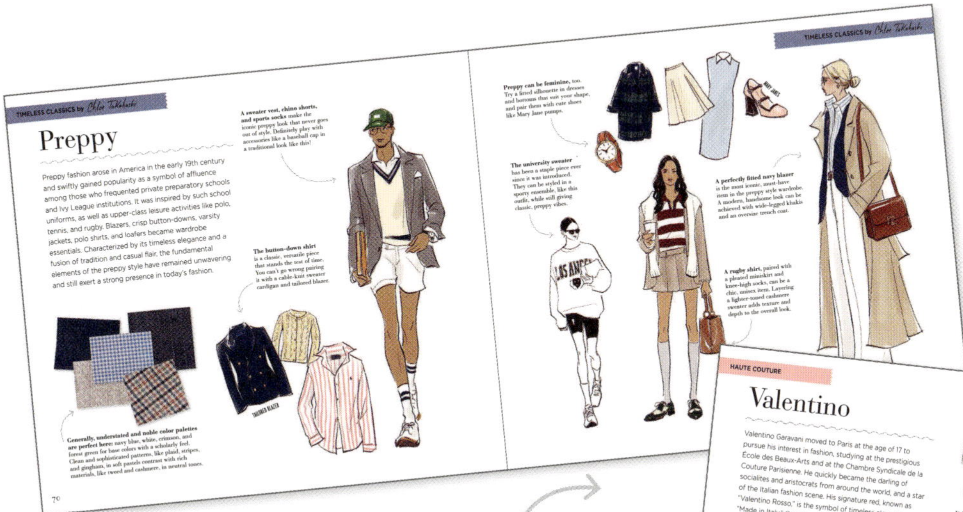

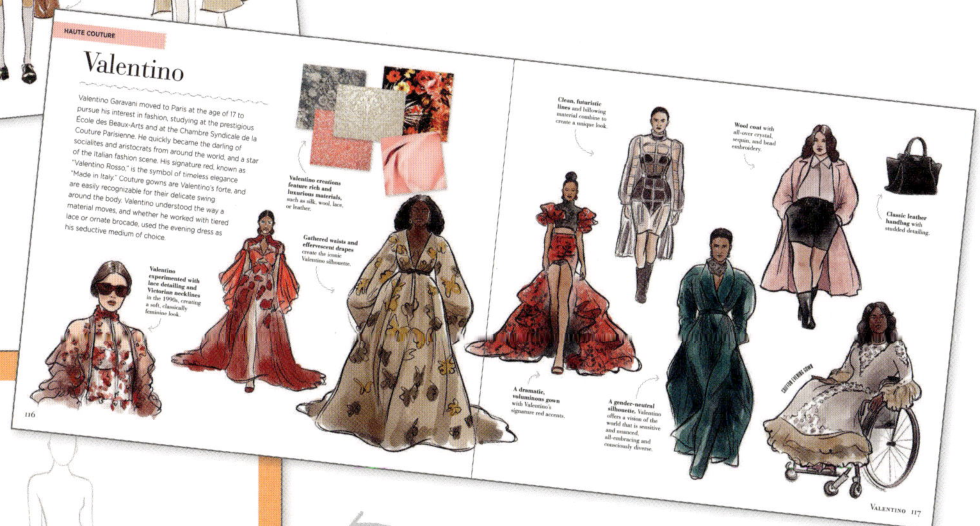

Part Two is organized by theme, from designers who have stood the test of time to the latest fashion trends.

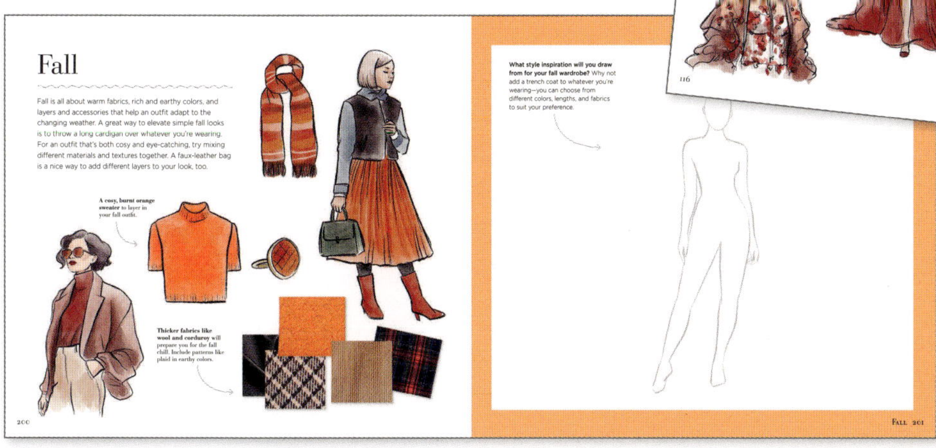

Part Three offers fashion inspiration for every season, as well as journal pages so that you can keep track of your favorite outfits!

PART ONE

STYLE SKETCHING

Sketching fashion can be fun and easy! This chapter will teach you how to draw the outline of a human figure and how to add clothes and accessories to the figure you have drawn. First, you will learn to create a croquis—the base of your sketch—and how to represent the proportions and pose of your model. You will need a pencil, an eraser, and some colored pencils or markers. Templates are included to help you practice. Next, try your hand at dressing the croquis. This is the fun part, where you can add your own ideas for clothes and accessories! You'll learn how to draw fabric to change the look and structure of garments, and then how to liven them up with color and patterns. The Visual Glossary is a quick reference guide to key wardrobe pieces and also includes tips on how to create details like pleats and darts.

Tools and Techniques

You can use any medium you like to draw with—pencil, felt-tip, marker, or ballpoint—or even experiment with the effects of different media in a single sketch.

Trace a loose outline of your garment with soft pencil lines.

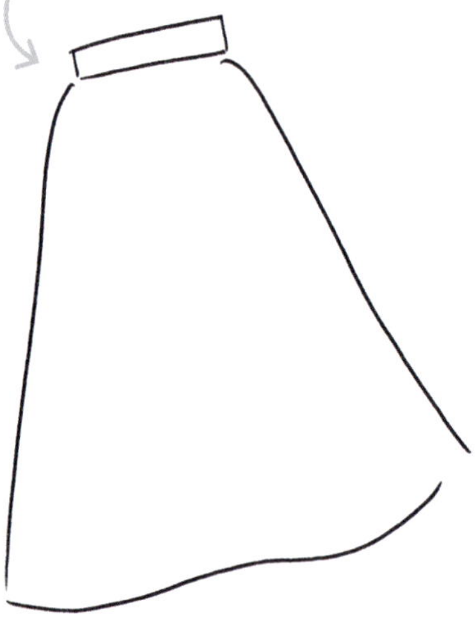

Sharpen up your outline and add details, like the folds of the skirt and a belt.

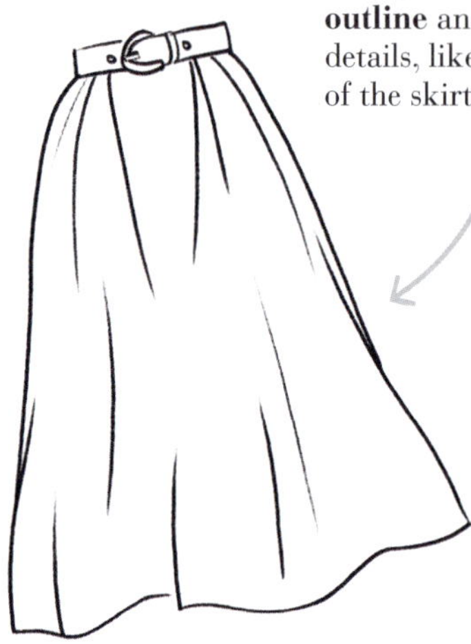

Add some shading to your drawing with the tip of your pencil.

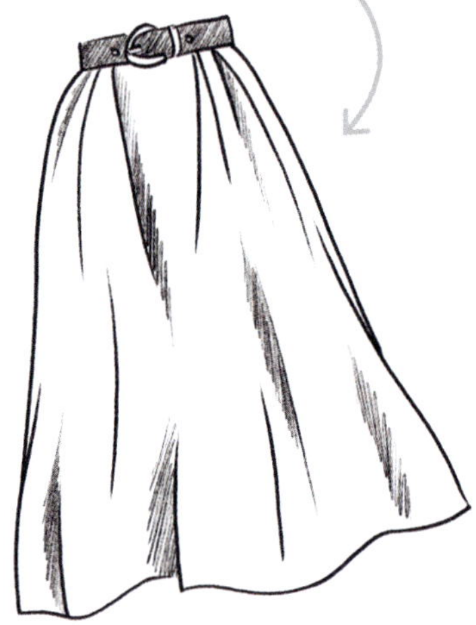

Cross-hatching is another technique to show areas of shading. Create it with the point of a ballpoint, fine pen, or pencil.

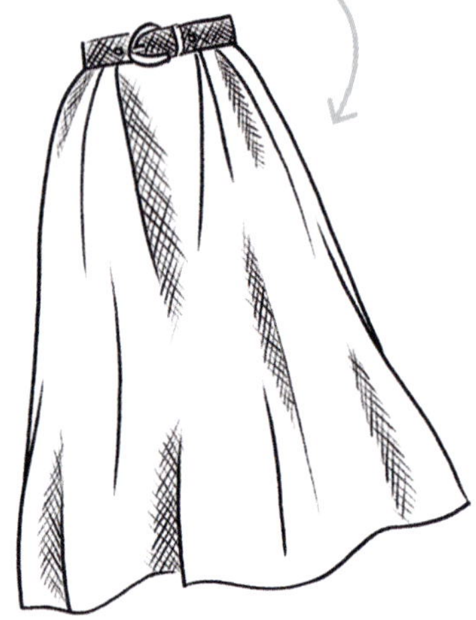

For soft coloring, try using pencils. You don't have to color in neatly; keeping it rough will give your drawing a distinctive style.

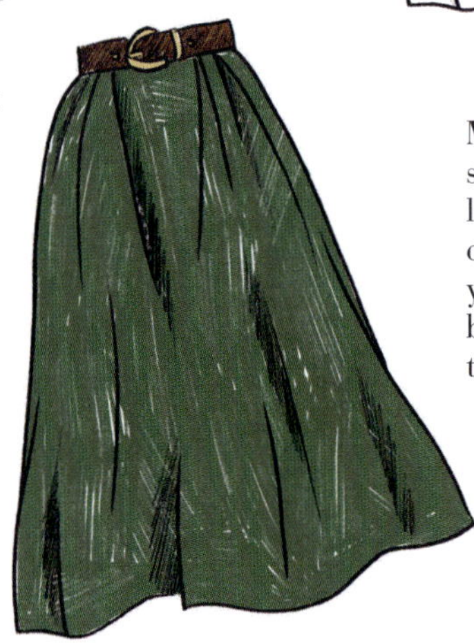

Markers are ideal for bold strokes and shading. Try using light colors at first to build up confidence. To add impact to your colored illustration, use a black marker to sharply define the outline of your garment.

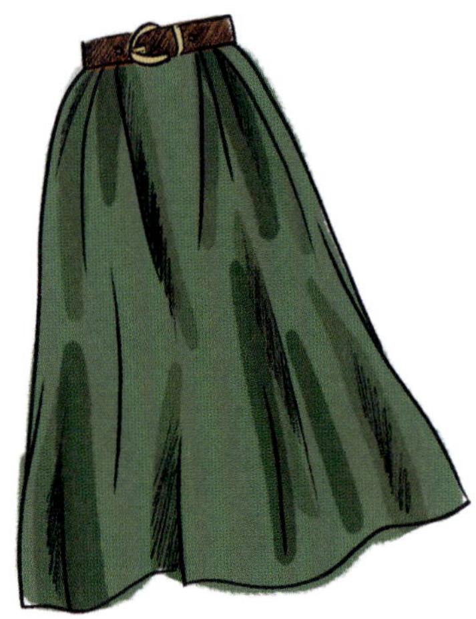

If you're just starting out, using a pencil will allow you to adjust your sketch as you go. A hard lead (H) pencil makes light, sketchy marks that are easy to erase.

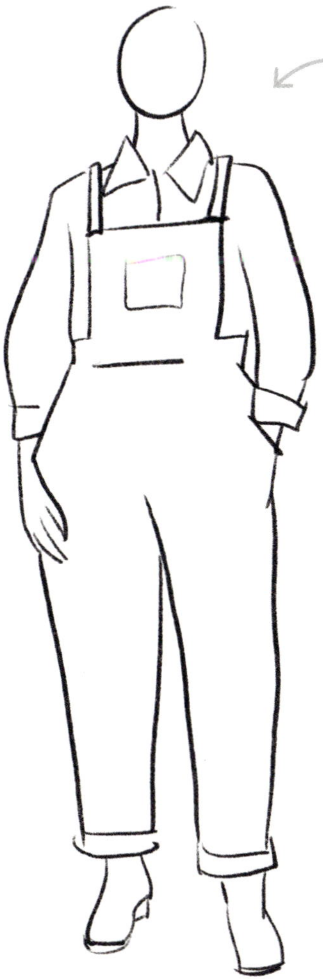

1. Vary the thickness of your lines to add character and energy to your illustration. Experiment with leaving them somewhat loose, too, including gaps and overlaps rather than joining everything precisely.

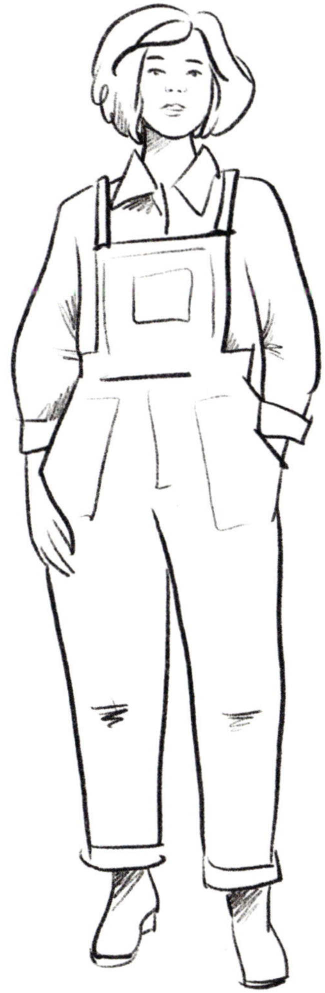

2. Next, add shading to give your figure and clothing some contrast.

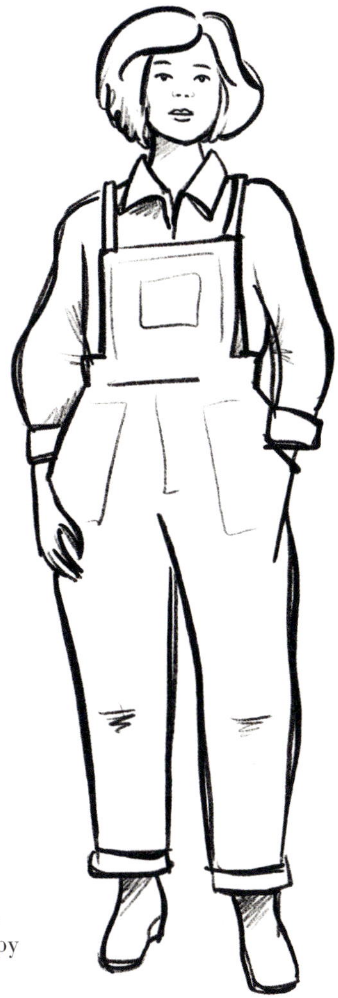

3. Strengthen up the lines once you're happy with your design.

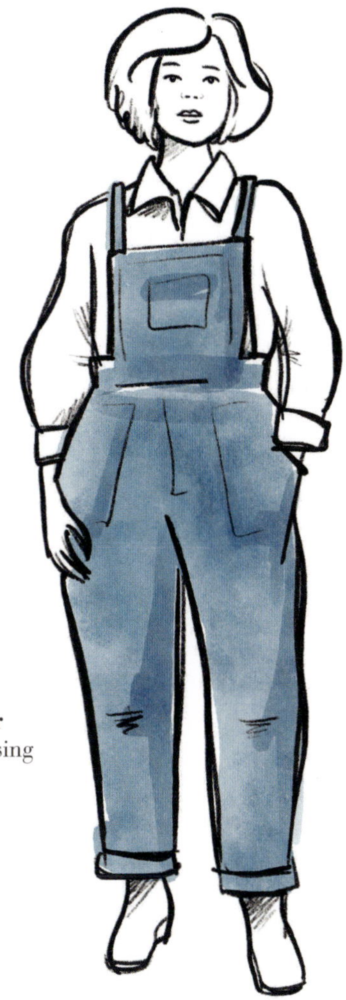

4. Finally, finish off your sketch by adding color, using shading to add depth.

How to Draw a Croquis

A croquis is a figure template onto which you can draw your own fashion sketches. Don't be afraid to explore different body shapes and poses—from there, you'll find your own signature croquis style.

HOW MANY HEADS HIGH ARE YOU?

The standard figure is 8 heads high. Designers use a 7-head model for petite figures. How many heads high are you?

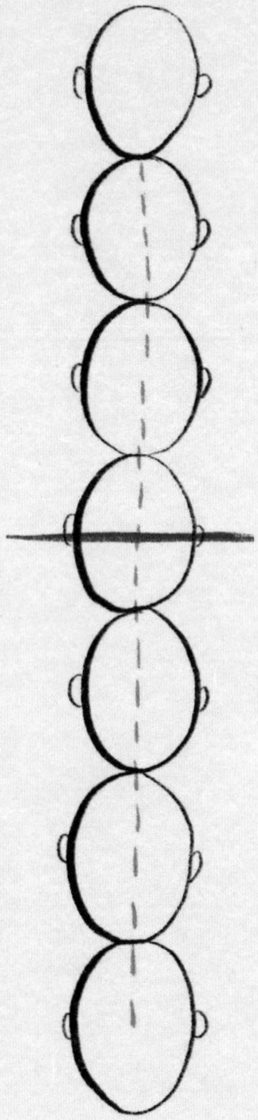

PROPORTIONING YOUR CROQUIS

1. Draw the head, then measure roughly 6 heads down from the chin to the toes.

2. The halfway point between the top of the head and the toes is where the legs start. This will help you work out where the different parts of the body should go.

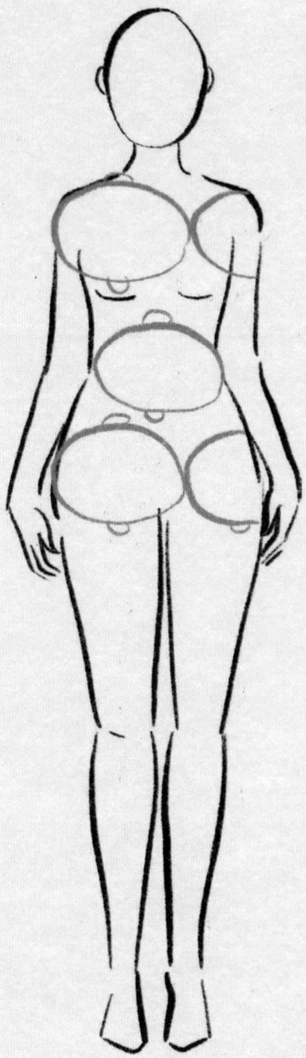

7-HEAD

The width of the figure is measured by head lengths. As a rough guide:

- Shoulders = 1½ heads.
- Waist = 1 head.
- Hips = 1½ heads.

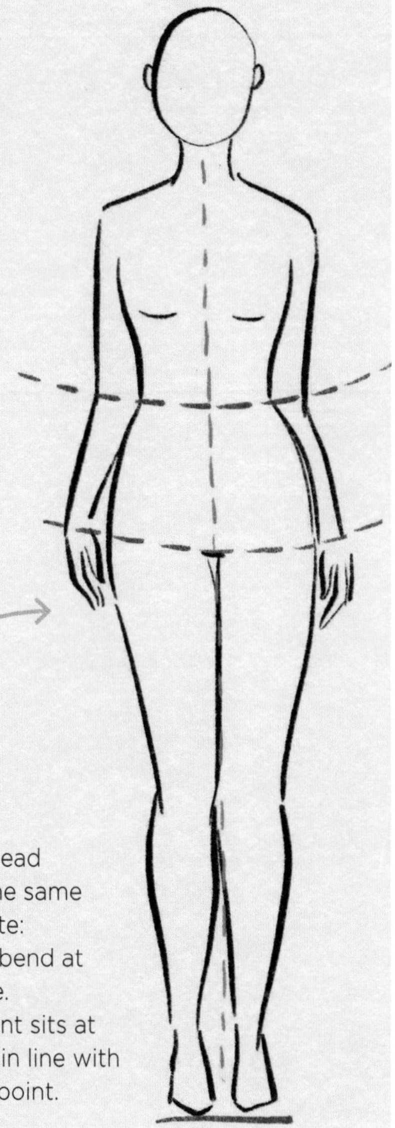

7½-HEAD

Here is a 7½-head figure using the same technique. Note:

- The elbows bend at the waistline.
- The wrist joint sits at crotch level, in line with the halfway point.

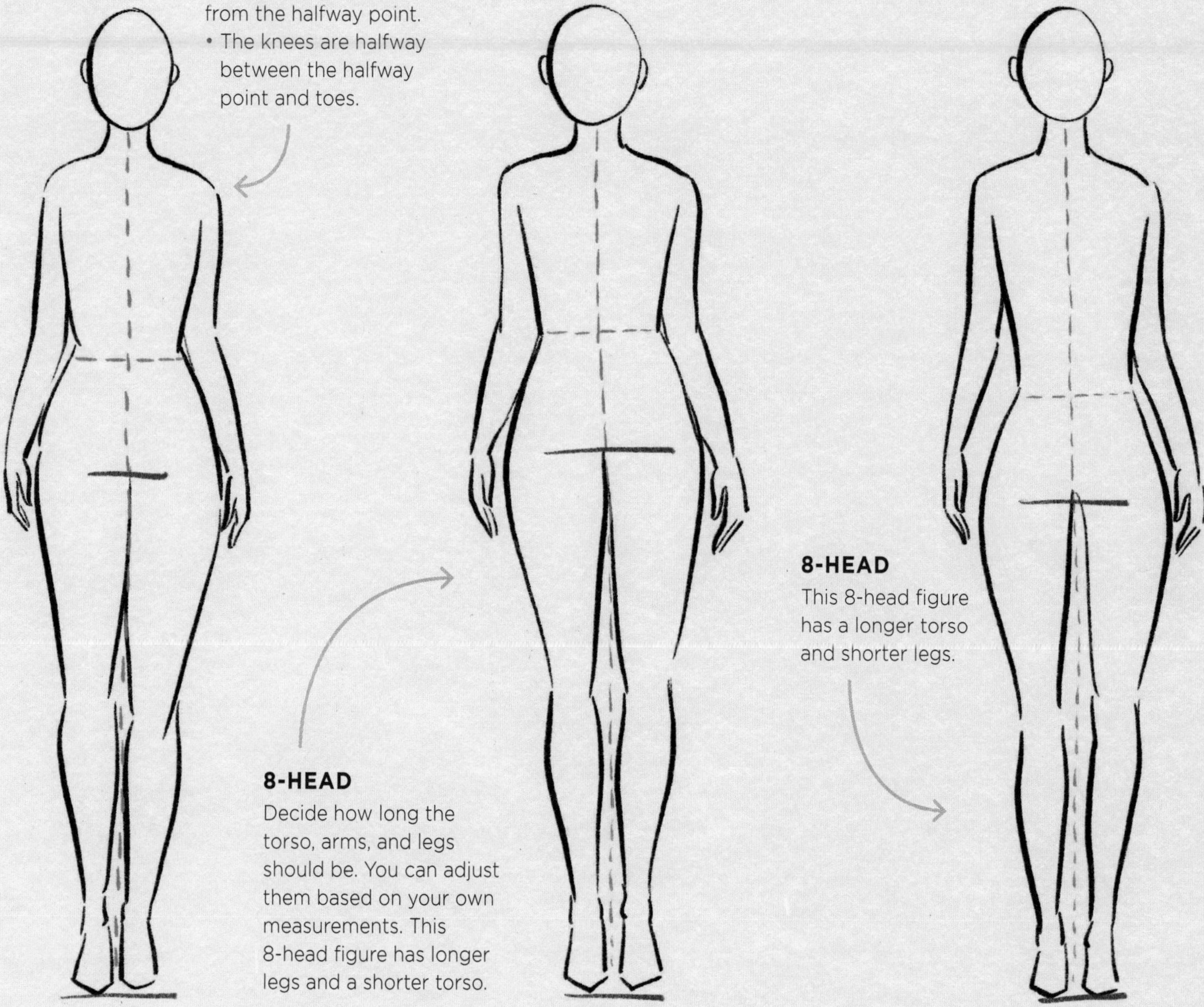

8-HEAD

The waistline is 1 head up from the halfway point.

- The knees are halfway between the halfway point and toes.

8-HEAD

Decide how long the torso, arms, and legs should be. You can adjust them based on your own measurements. This 8-head figure has longer legs and a shorter torso.

8-HEAD

This 8-head figure has a longer torso and shorter legs.

Know Your Body Shape

While every body is different, fashion designers find it useful to see how their clothes will work on a few general shapes. These general body types, along with the general "rules" that designers think about when dressing them, are shown here. Keep them in mind when you're sketching your own croquis—but also remember that these rules aren't hard and fast, and there's nothing to stop you from experimenting in your own designs. At the end of the day, whatever makes you feel good is what suits your body!

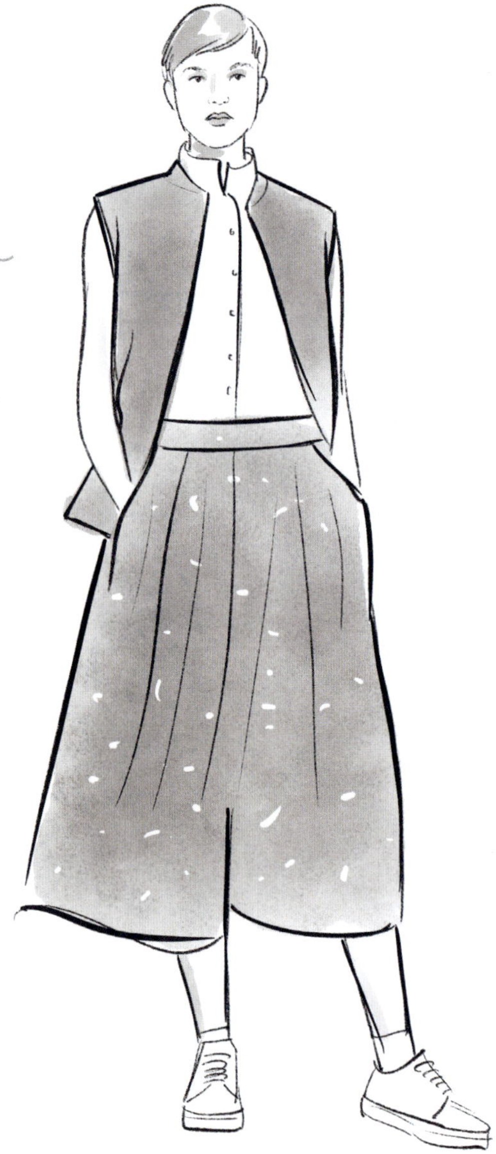

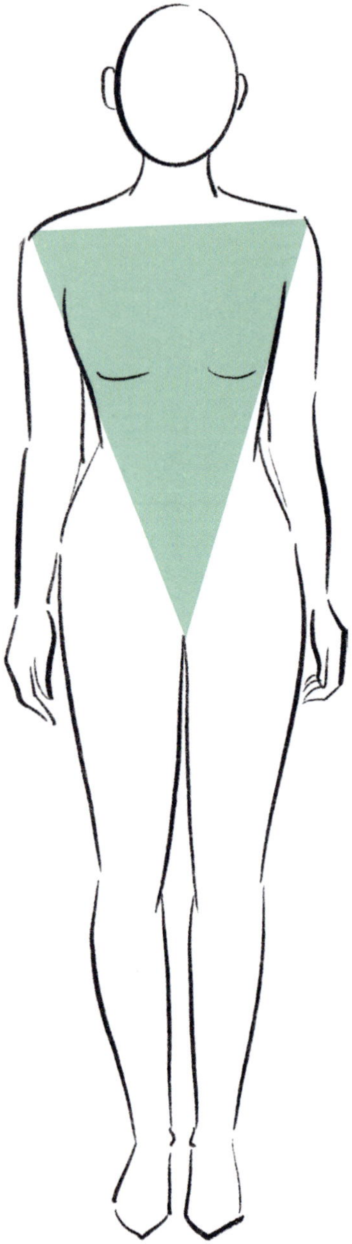

INVERTED TRIANGLE

Strong shoulder / Wide back / Slim lower body

- Go for jackets with structure and fitted shoulders, plus flared pants for balance.
- Full and A-line skirts.
- Boot-leg or wide-leg pants.

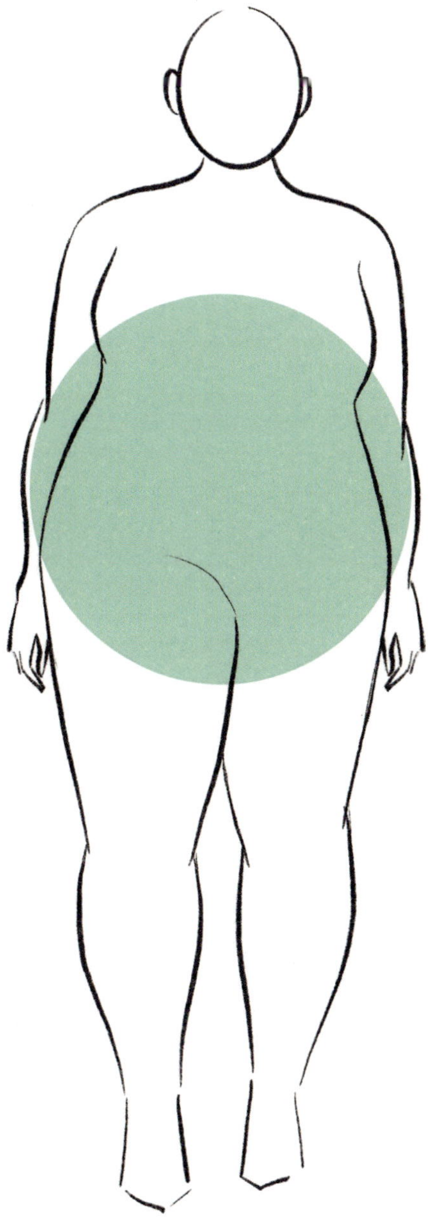

PLUS SIZE

Aligned shoulders, hips, and waist / Larger tummies

- Wear V-necklines or scoop necklines.
- Long cardigans.
- Fitted or high-rise jeans.
- A-line or pencil skirts.
- Large prints.
- Belts to define the waist.

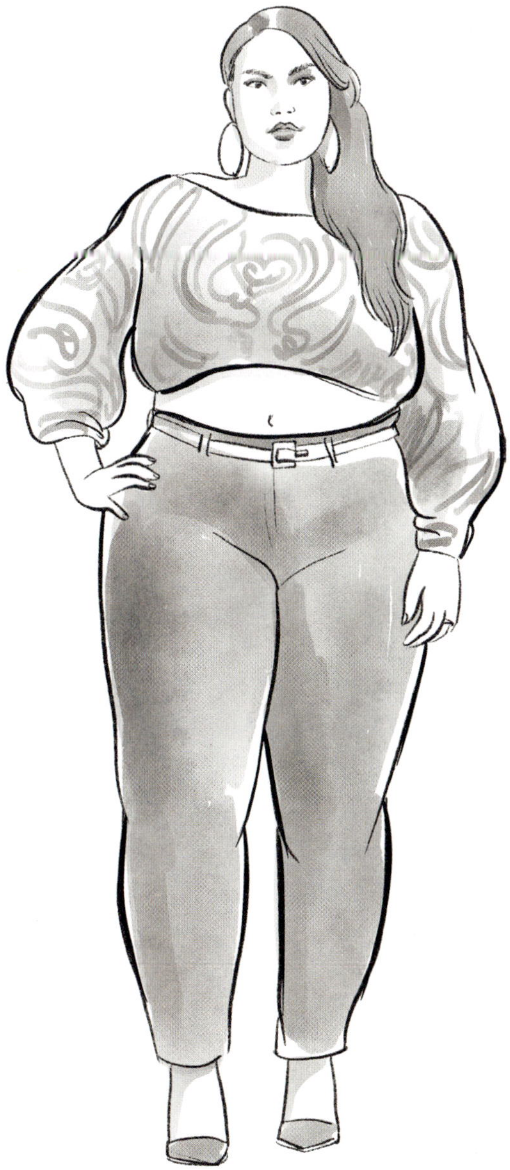

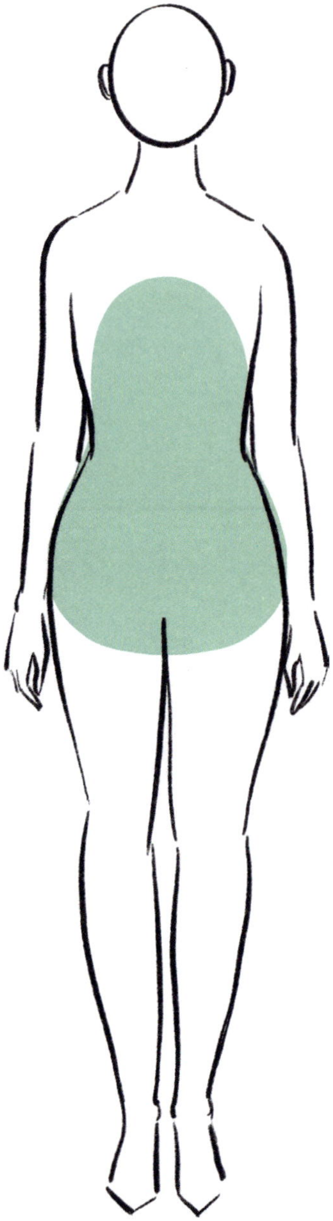

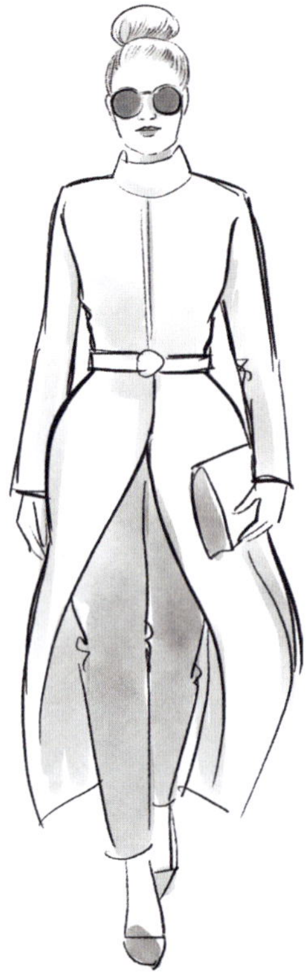

PEAR

Narrow shoulders / Well-defined waist / Lower body wider than upper body / Full hips and thighs

- Enhance the waistline and add volume to the shoulders for a balanced silhouette.
- Wide V- or U-necklines.
- High-waisted pants and skirts.
- A-line dresses.
- Straight-leg jeans.
- Layer jackets and gilets.
- Statement necklace.
- Shoulder bag.

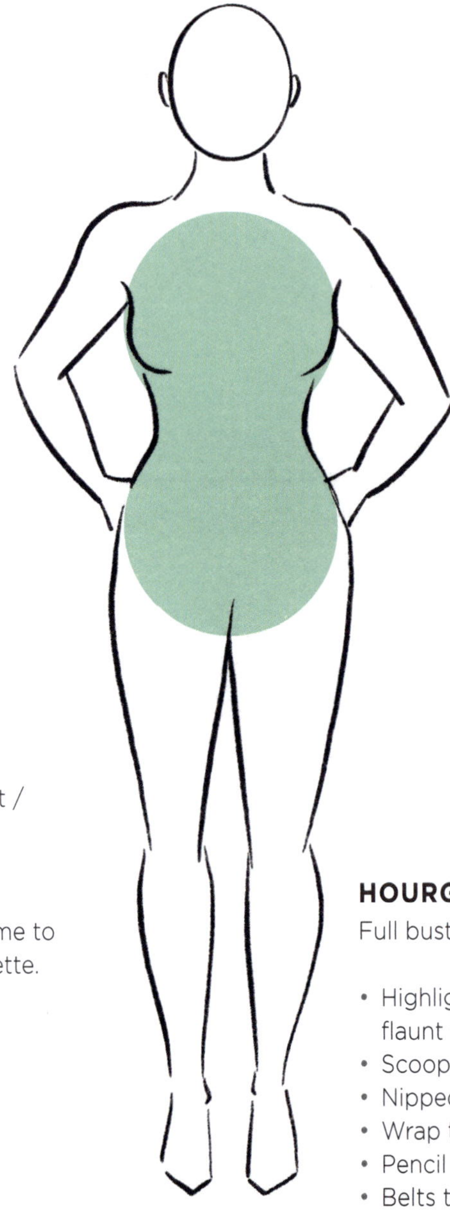

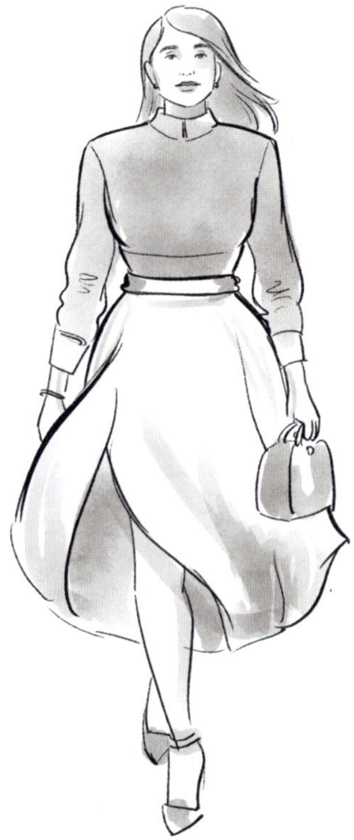

HOURGLASS

Full bust / Narrow waist / Curvy body

- Highlight natural curves and flaunt the well-defined waist.
- Scoop or V-necklines.
- Nipped-in tops and jackets.
- Wrap tops and dresses.
- Pencil skirts, knee-length skirts.
- Belts to accentuate the waist.

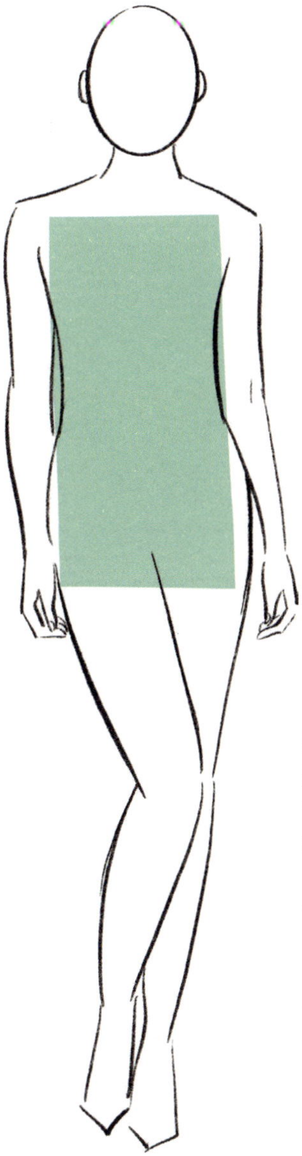

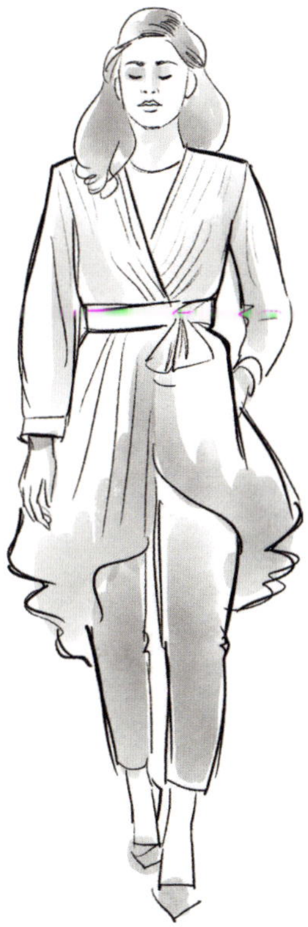

RECTANGLE

Small bust / Undefined waist / Straight hips / Well-aligned shoulders and hips

- Lots of models have this body type.
- Wear off-shoulder or round, open necklines.
- Tops with ruffles.
- Skinny jeans.
- Pencil skirts.
- Cropped pants.
- Belts to define the waist.

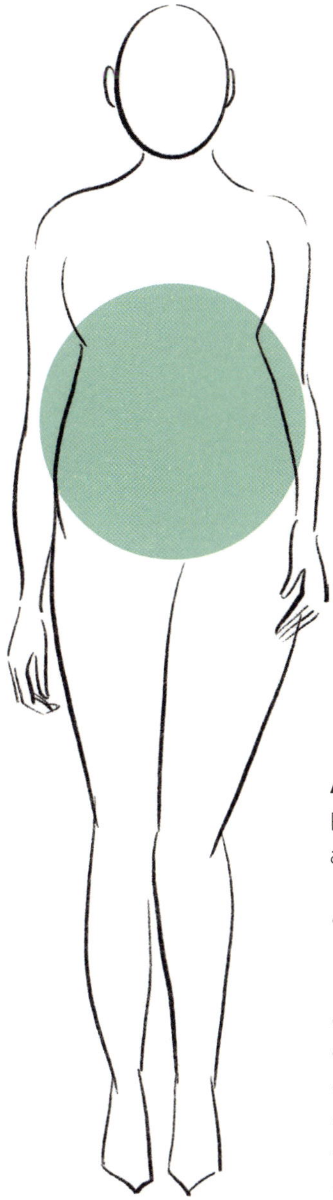

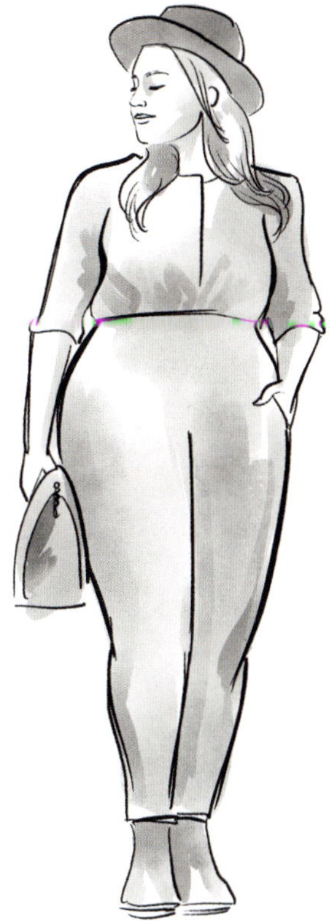

APPLE

Fuller bust / Broad shoulders / Fullness around the waist / Narrow hips

- Draw attention to the legs and create the illusion of a waist with structured pieces that will add definition.
- Wide necklines.
- Empire dresses.
- Wrap dresses.
- Straight-leg jeans.
- Statement necklace.
- Handbags.

Try drawing your own croquis, adapting the shapes on the previous pages to suit you and your vision for your models.

Adding Details to Your Figures

FACE

Bring your fashion figures to life by adding details like facial features and hair!

Here is a rough guide to use when creating a face for your models.

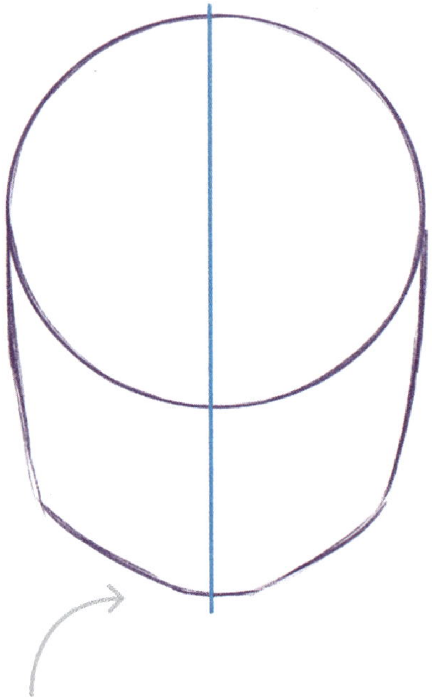

1. Start with a circular shape, then add a U-like shape beneath it to create the lower part of the face. Cross the face vertically with a pencil line.

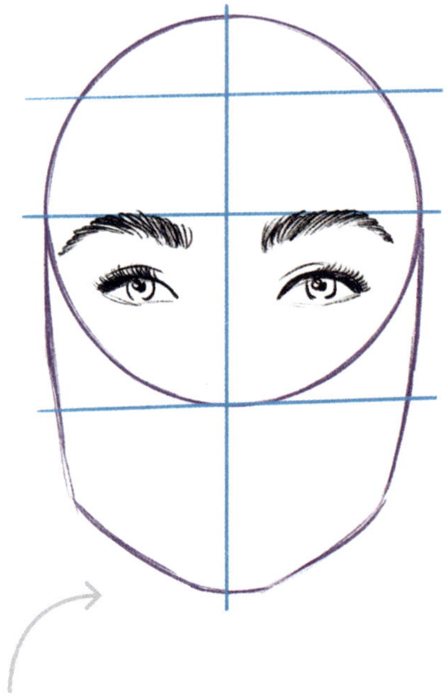

2. Add three horizontal lines to help you place the facial features:

- One in the middle of the circle. This will help you place the model's eyebrows.
- One toward the top of the circle. This will determine the base of the hair.
- One beneath the circle. This is where the base of the nose will start.

Draw in the eyebrows, then the eyes.

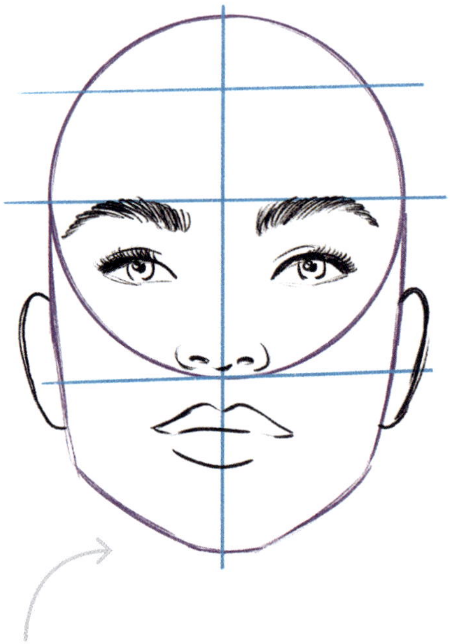

3. Draw the facial features. Place the nose at the base of the circle, then the mouth below it, and the ears on each side of the head.

HAIR

1. The hairline starts around one-third of the way down the forehead. Use the purple line as a guide.

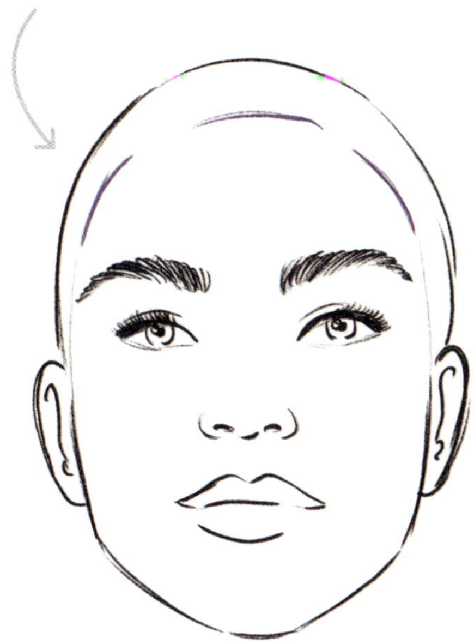

2. Trace a rough outline of the hairline.

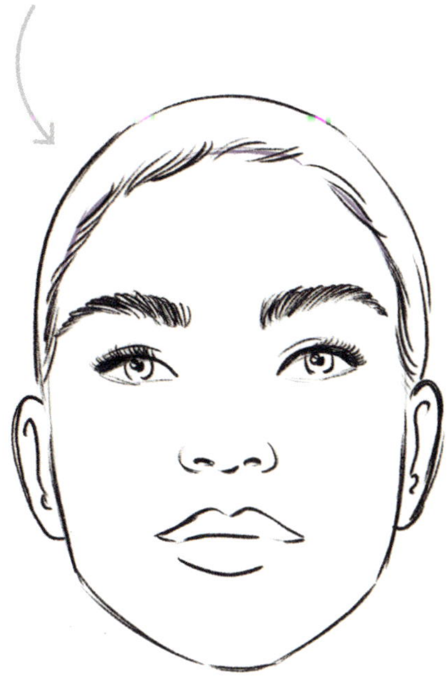

3. Fill in the hair. In this example, the hair is braided, so is traced with a series of curved lines.

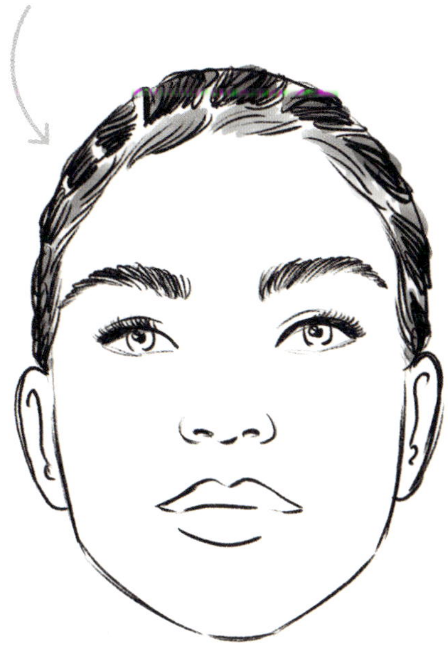

What hair type and style do you want to draw—curly and wild, or straight and sleek? Start at the parting and work downward, thinking about shading to give it life and texture.

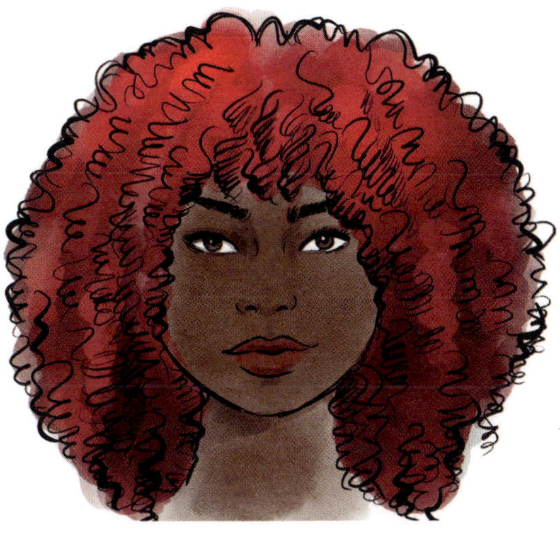

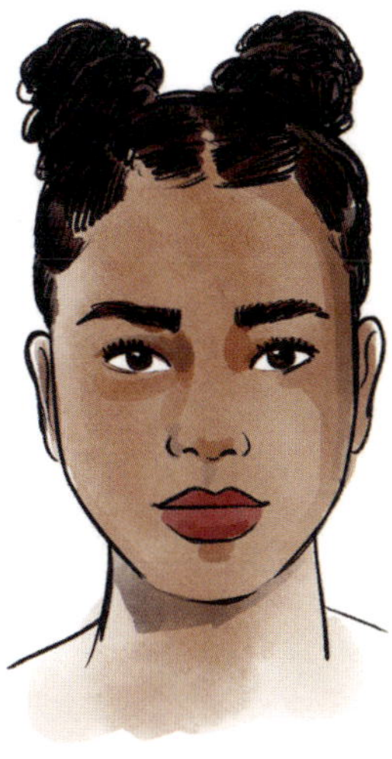

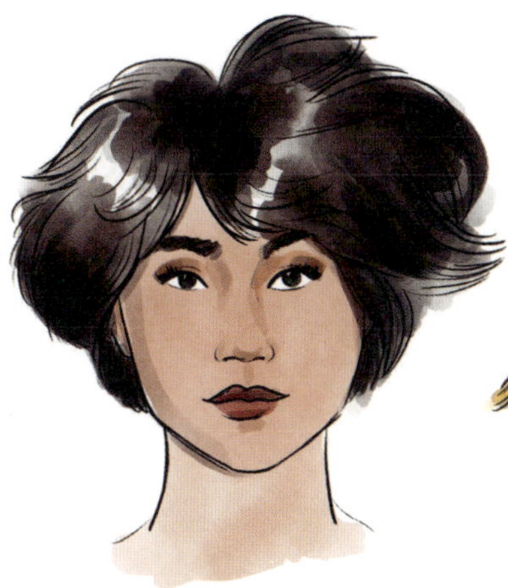

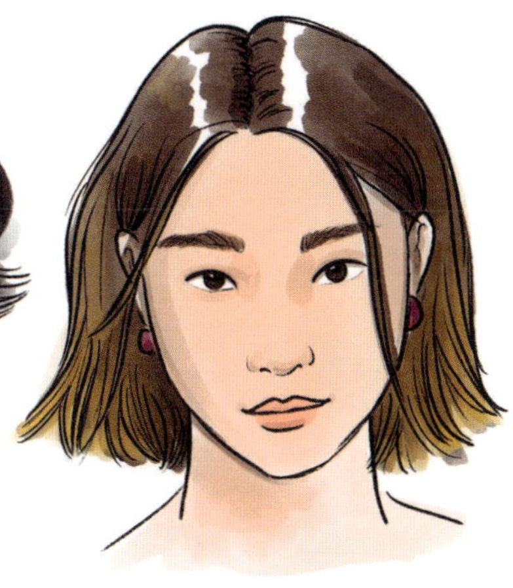

Use these templates to practice drawing faces and hair. See how different you can make your models look using the fundamental principles you've learned and by adding unique features like freckles or blemishes—there's no one single way to be beautiful!

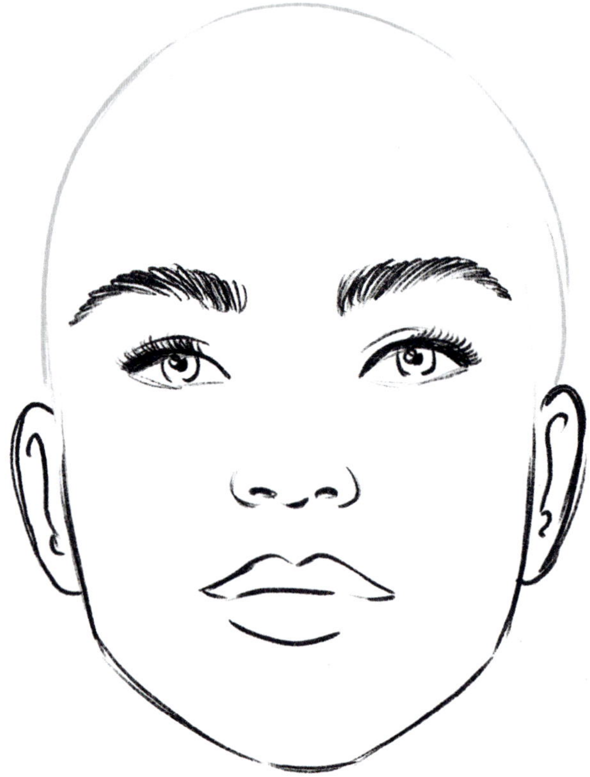

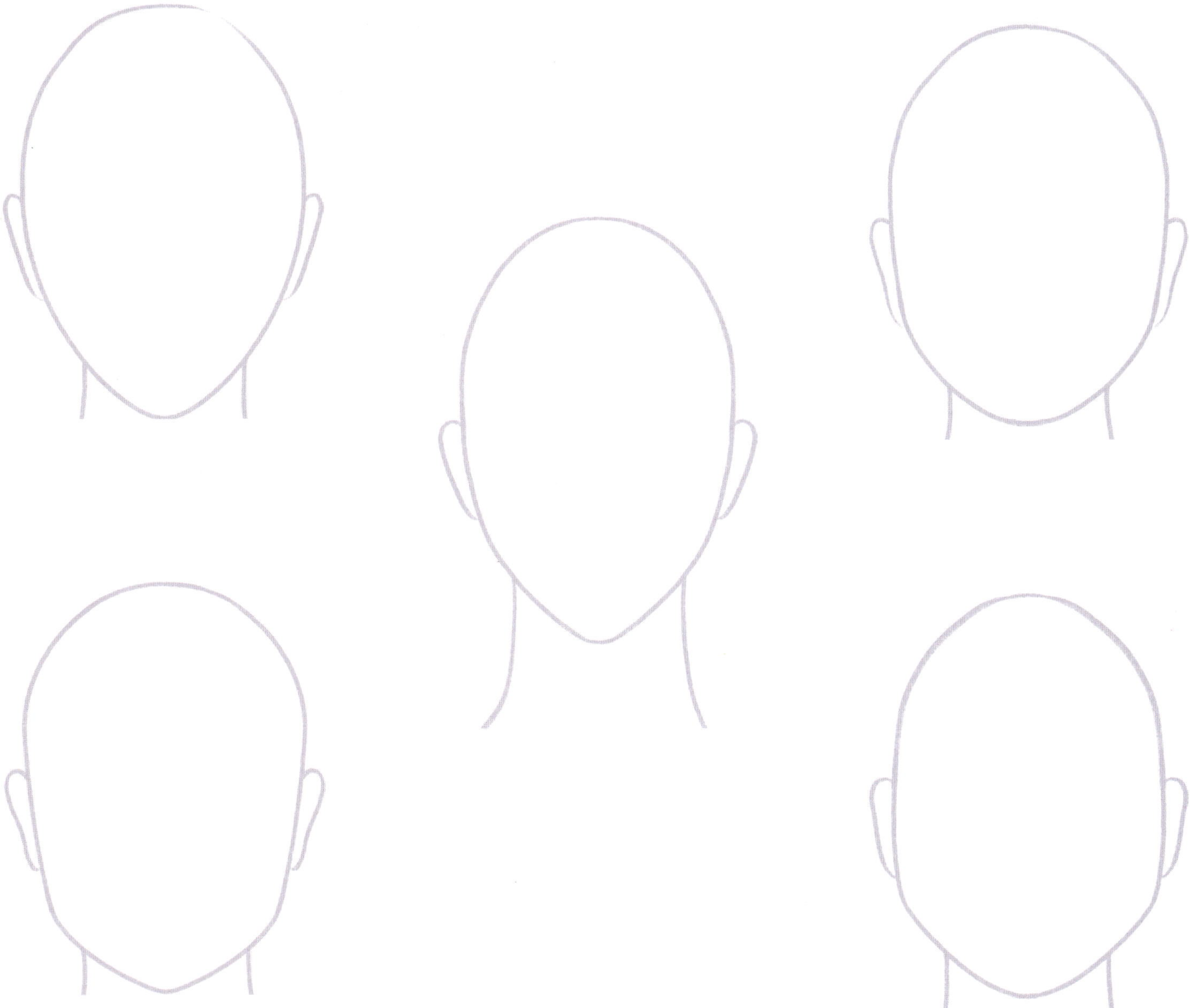

How Fabric Works

When sketching your designs, it's crucial to think about how fabrics will affect the look of a garment and the way it hangs. The feel of soft and flowing fabrics are best captured with free, curving lines of varying thickness, while stiff and crisp fabrics call for sharply defined, jagged lines. These effects can also be achieved or enhanced by using different types of pencil tips or pen brushes.

YOU'LL GET THE HANG OF IT

The same skirt design can look very different depending on what type of fabric it is made of.

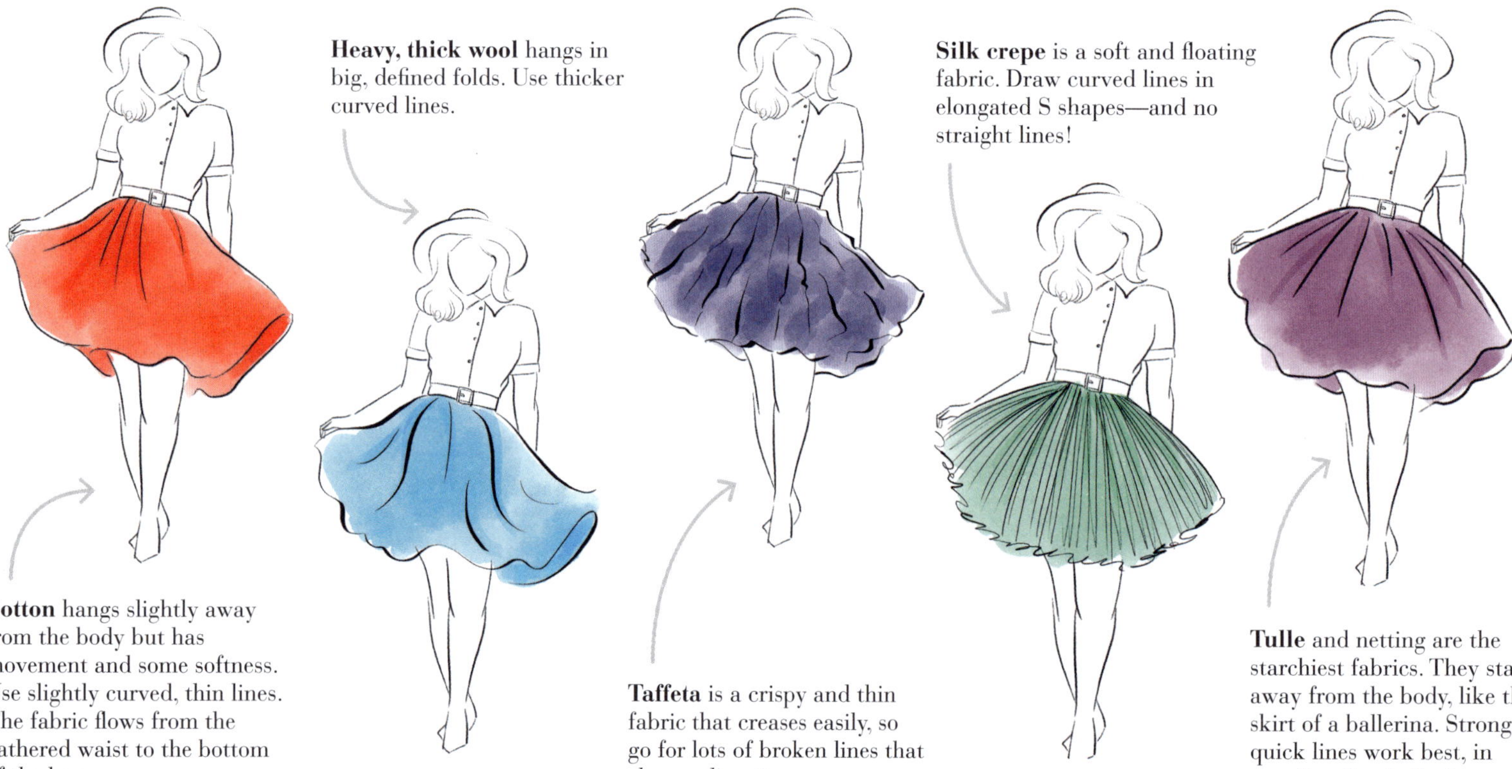

Heavy, thick wool hangs in big, defined folds. Use thicker curved lines.

Silk crepe is a soft and floating fabric. Draw curved lines in elongated S shapes—and no straight lines!

Cotton hangs slightly away from the body but has movement and some softness. Use slightly curved, thin lines. The fabric flows from the gathered waist to the bottom of the hem.

Taffeta is a crispy and thin fabric that creases easily, so go for lots of broken lines that change direction.

Tulle and netting are the starchiest fabrics. They stand away from the body, like the skirt of a ballerina. Strong, quick lines work best, in pencil or fine ballpoint.

BIAS CUT

Some garments have a "bias cut." This means that a garment is cut on the diagonal of the fabric's grain (weave), making the fabric more elastic, so that it clings to the curves of the body.

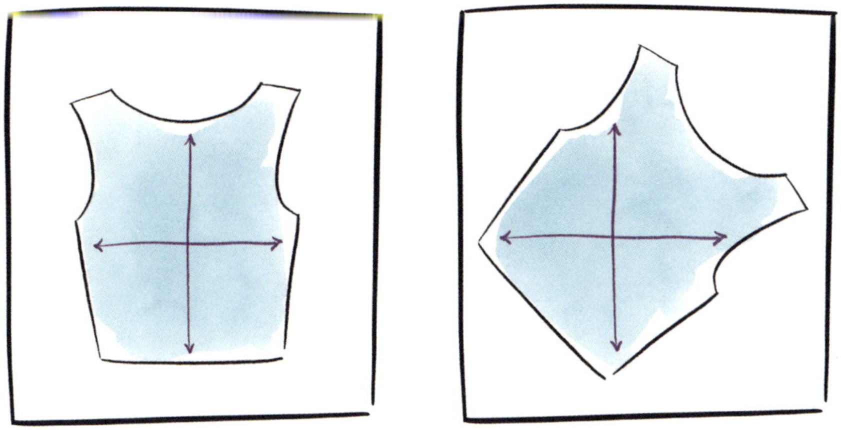

The direction of the grain is indicated by arrows. The garment on the right is cut on the bias.

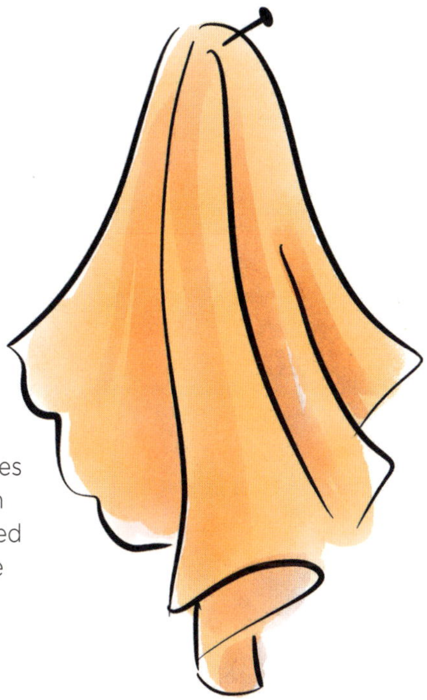

TENSION POINT

This pinned fabric demonstrates the "tension point" from which the fabric falls into cone-shaped folds. This happens on a figure whose knee is bent—the knee becomes the tension point.

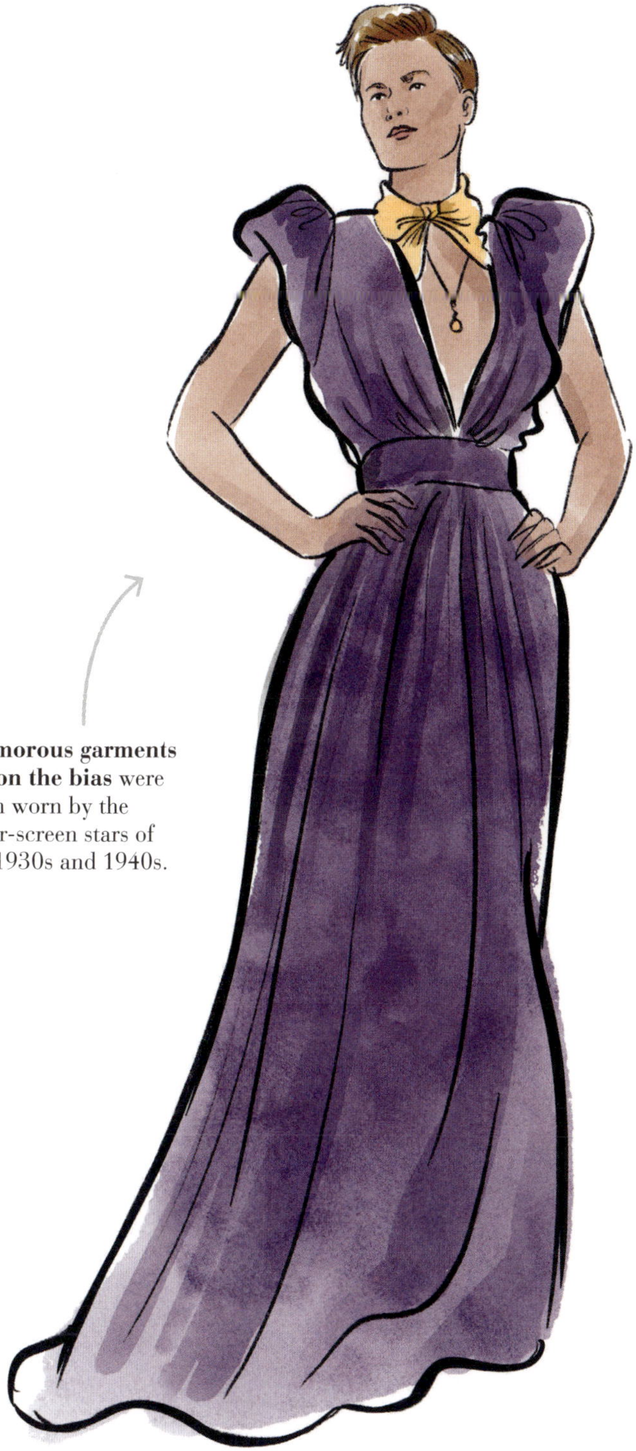

Glamorous garments cut on the bias were often worn by the silver-screen stars of the 1930s and 1940s.

Using Color

Complete your look by adding color to the garments you've designed. Color is one of the most important elements of design and fashion designers create a distinctive color palette for each collection by combining colors that go together (or clash!). Every season welcomes a new color palette onto the catwalks and into the fashion stores.

The color wheel will help you to expand your understanding of color. This wheel has twelve hues—pick out your accent color, then choose complementary colors that either harmonize with it or "pop" next to it.

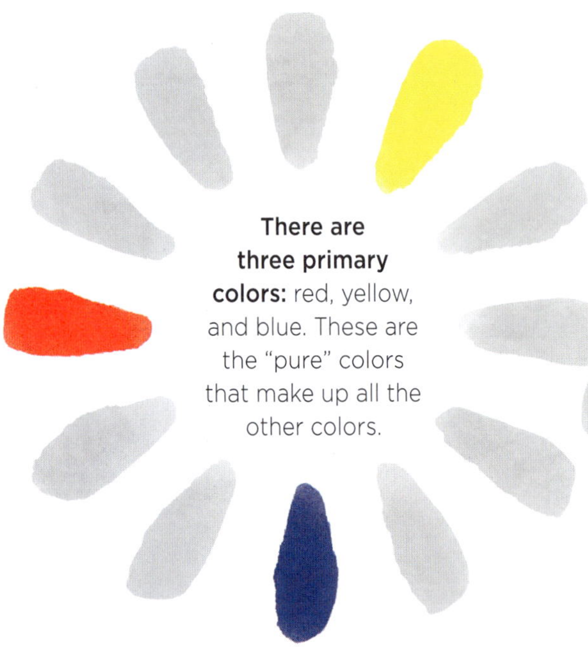

There are **three primary colors:** red, yellow, and blue. These are the "pure" colors that make up all the other colors.

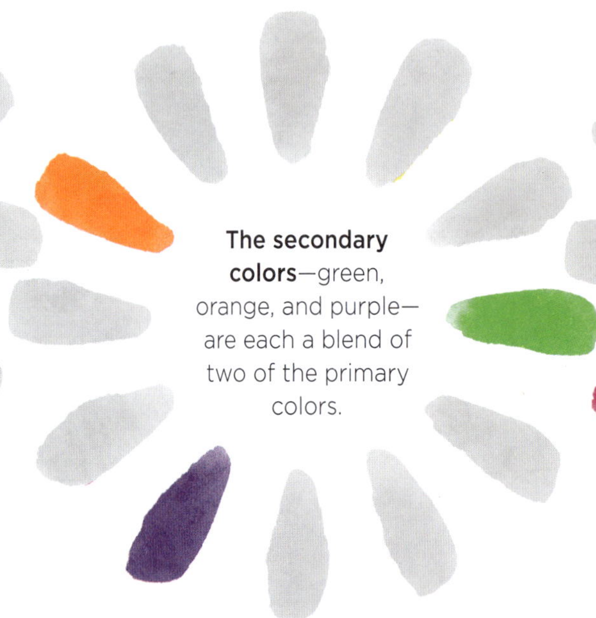

The secondary colors—green, orange, and purple—are each a blend of two of the primary colors.

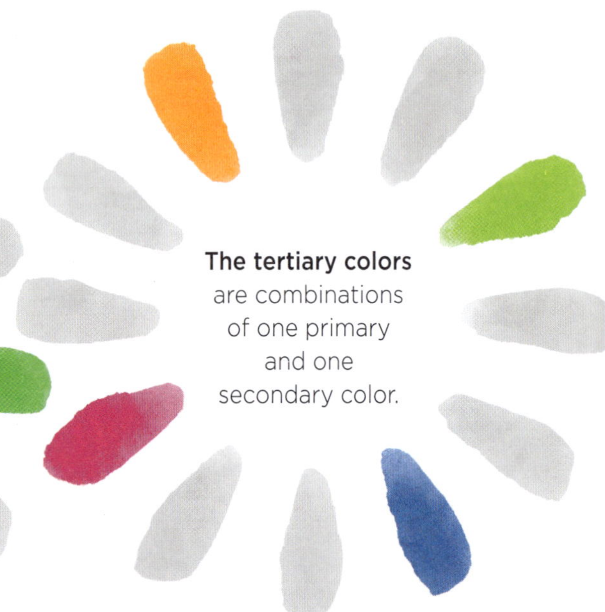

The tertiary colors are combinations of one primary and one secondary color.

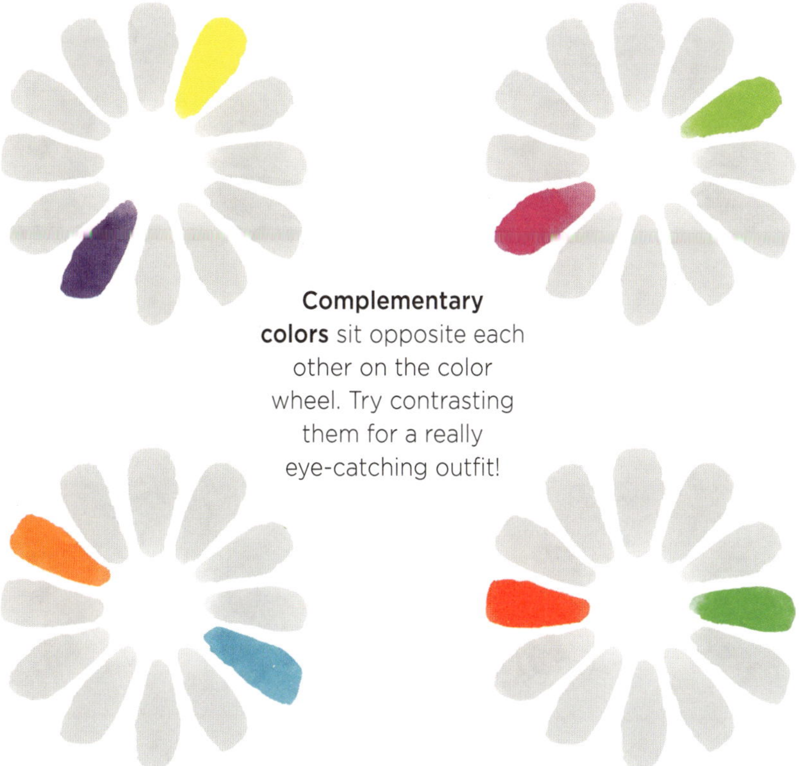

Complementary colors sit opposite each other on the color wheel. Try contrasting them for a really eye-catching outfit!

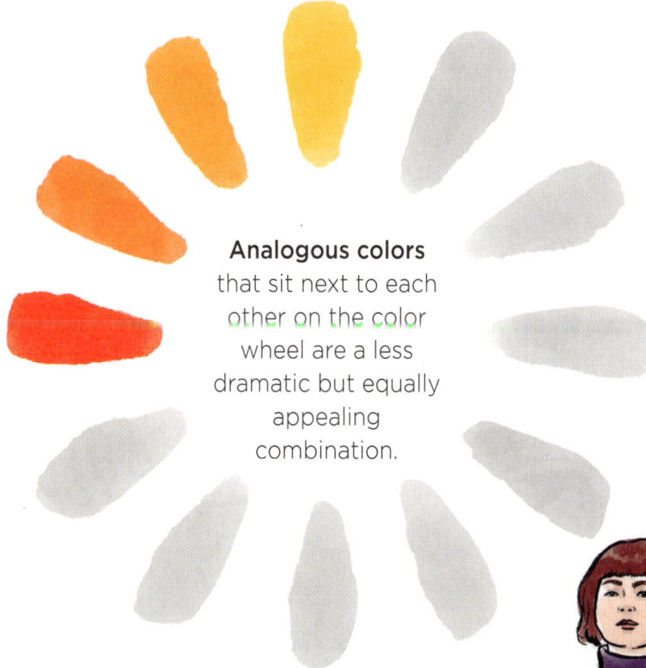

Analogous colors that sit next to each other on the color wheel are a less dramatic but equally appealing combination.

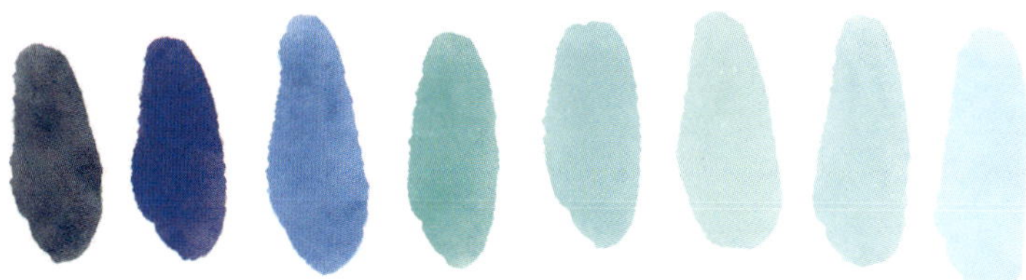

Monochromatic looks feature the same color in varying shades. Blues are cool and serene. They come in lots of tones, from sky blue to navy.

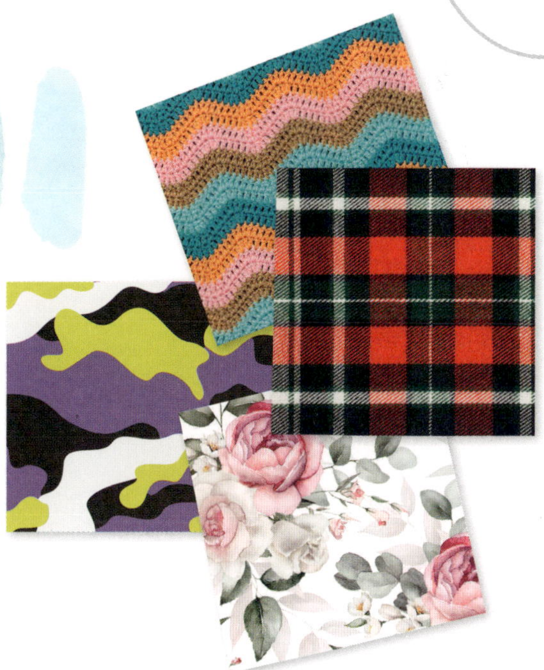

These fabric patterns use complementary colors, creating a striking effect.

Brights are strong, bold colors. They are fun to wear and flashy, especially when you put at least two together!

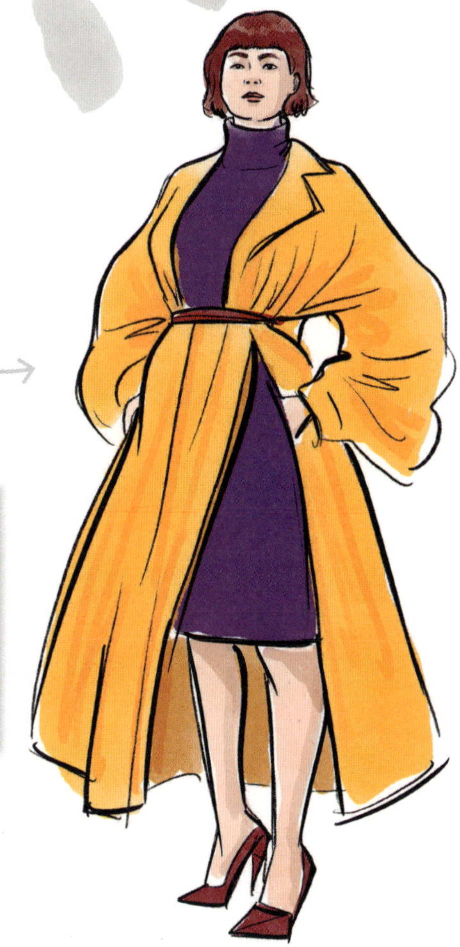

EXPERIMENTING WITH PATTERN AND COLOR

CREATING A TIE-DYE PATTERN

Tie-dye is an ancient dyeing technique, going back 6,000 years, that involves tying off sections of fabric with thread before dipping it in dye. The psychedelic patterns this technique creates were beloved by the hippie subculture in the 1960s and 1970s, trended again in the 1990s, and have recently made another comeback.

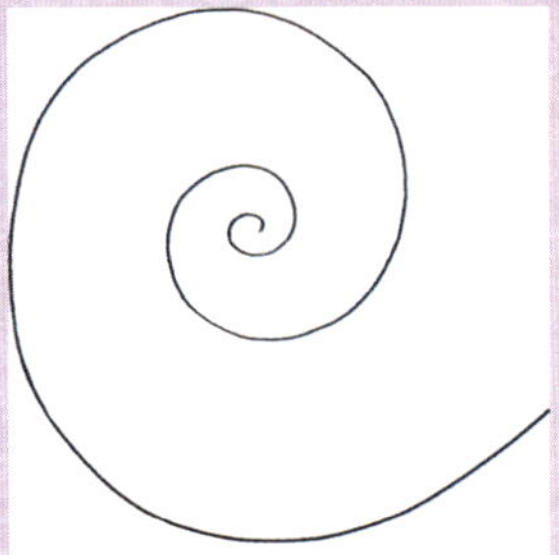

1. Start your tie-dye pattern by tracing a pencil guideline in the shape of a spiral.

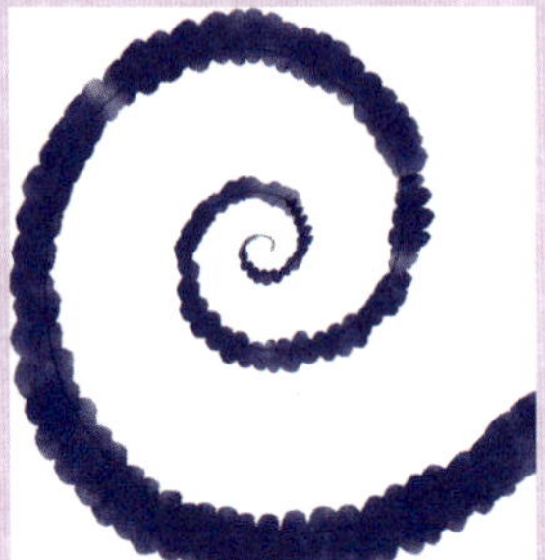

2. Along that pencil curve, add a tight zigzag line in blue.

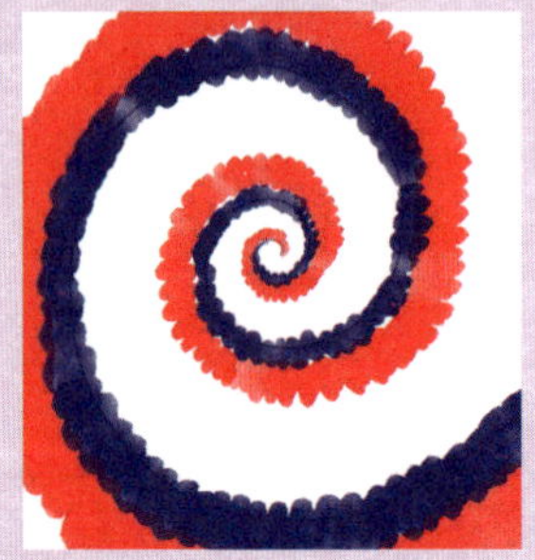

3. Next, trace a red line that hugs the blue line. Have the lines overlap each other a little to create the classic tie-dye effect.

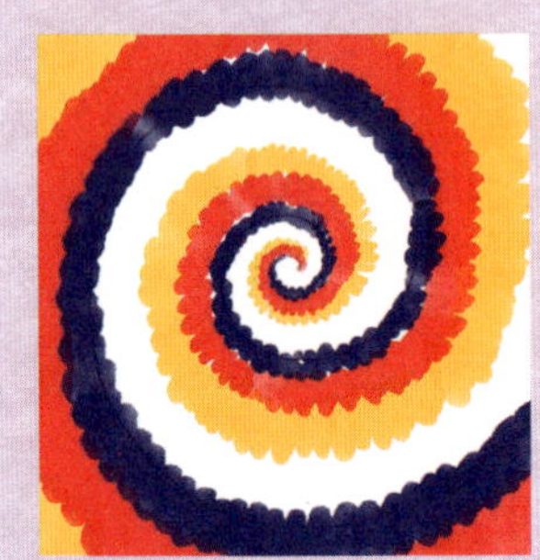

4. Keep going! Add a yellow line next to your red line…

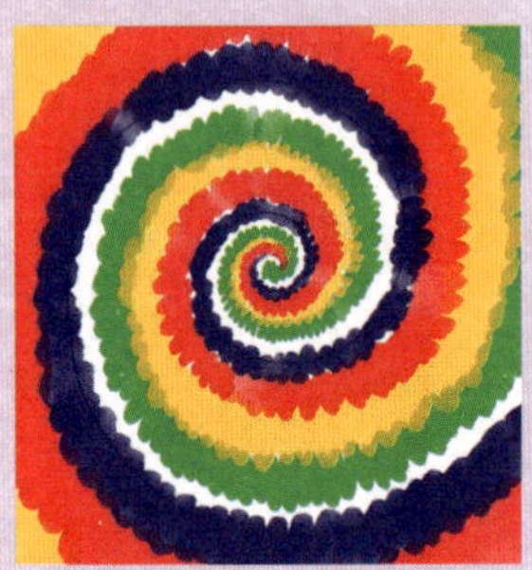

5. Then a green one next to the yellow, again slightly overlapping.

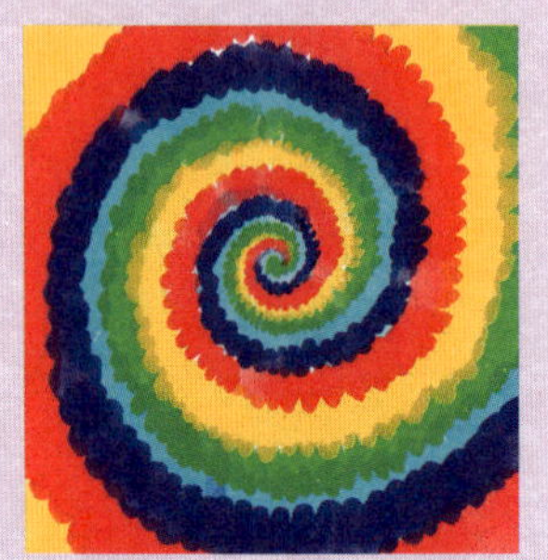

6. Finish the rainbow! Fill in the remaining white space with light blue, and erase your pencil guideline.

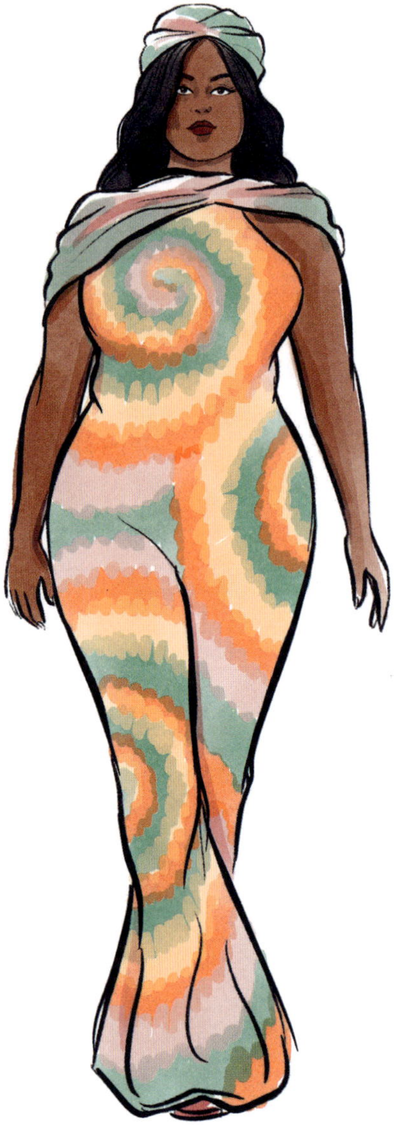

Now come up with your own tie-dye pattern. Will you stick with the pastels the model is wearing in the example, or go for something more vibrant? What shapes can you make?

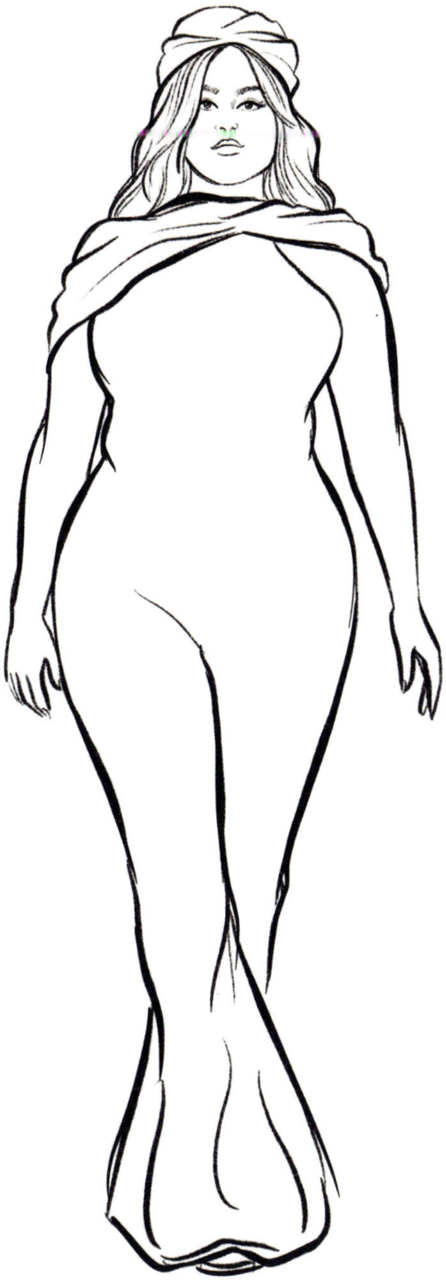

COMPLEMENTARY COLORS

Study the complementary colors that sit opposite each other on the color wheel, such as red and green, blue and orange, or purple and yellow. Using these pairs of colors creates a strong contrast and can make your fashion illustrations really stand out. You can use different shades, tints, and tones of complementary colors to create different effects and moods. Warm and cool colors can be used to create depth and perspective in your illustration, with warm colors advancing and attracting attention, and cool colors receding and creating distance.

The best way to learn about color theory is to practice! Try mixing colors on these models—experiment, and have fun.

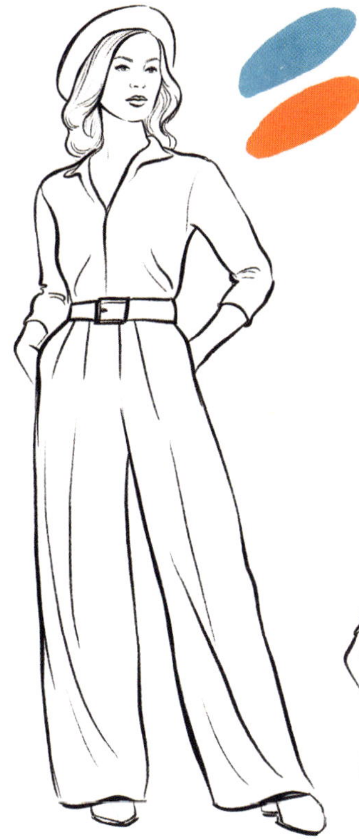

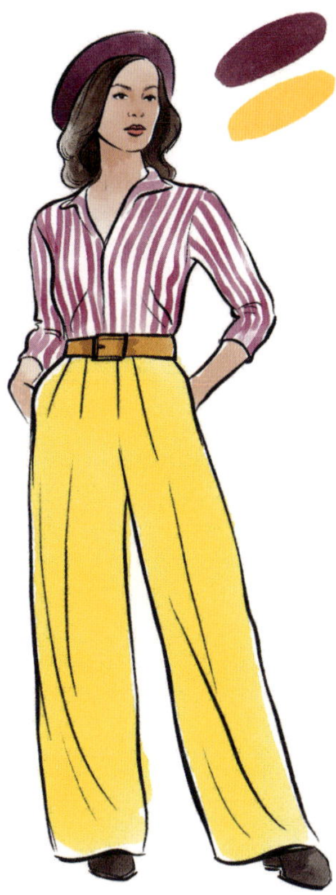

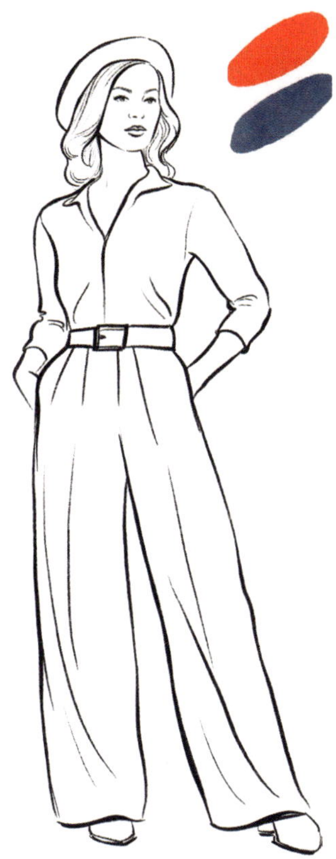

Visual Glossary

This glossary provides a quick guide to the main types of garments and their details. Hopefully it will also be a source of inspiration and a useful tool. It showcases a variety of concepts and styles that may spark ideas for your own work!

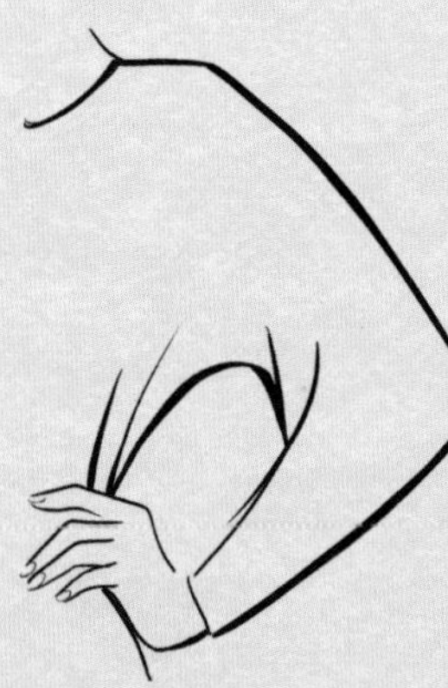
BATWING

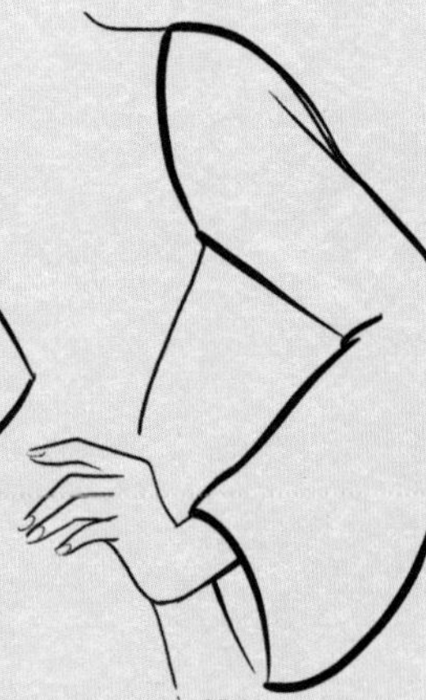
BELL

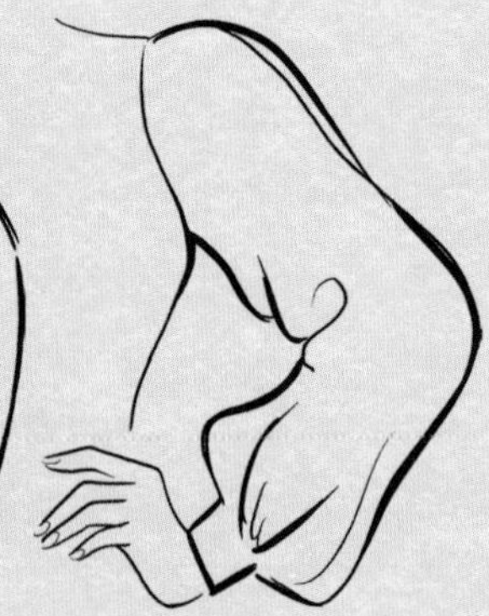
BALLOON

TOPS

SLEEVES

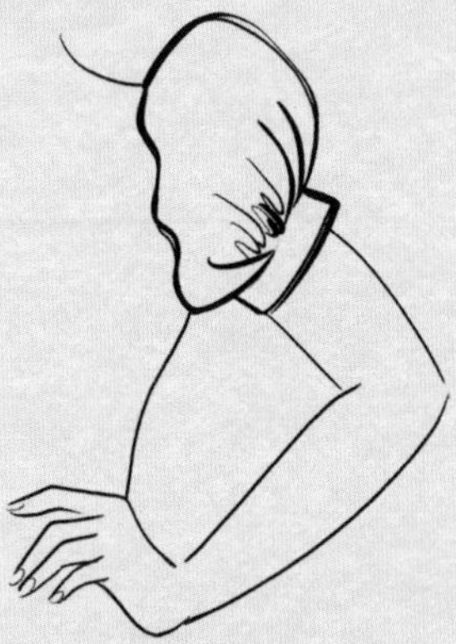
PUFFED

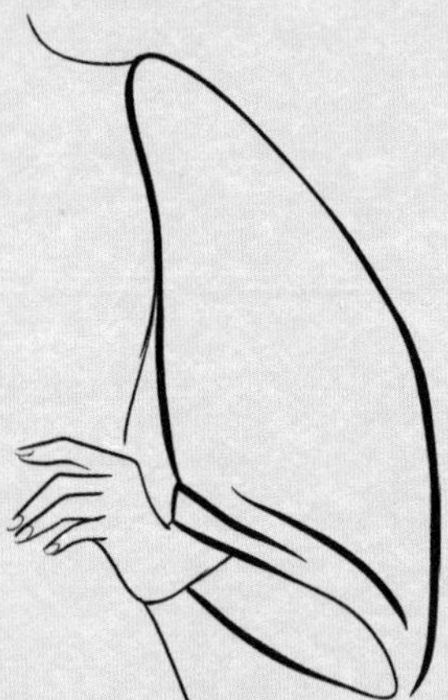
CAPE

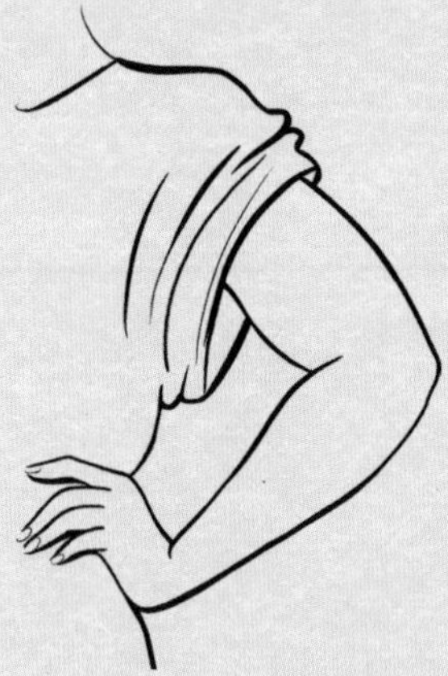
COWL

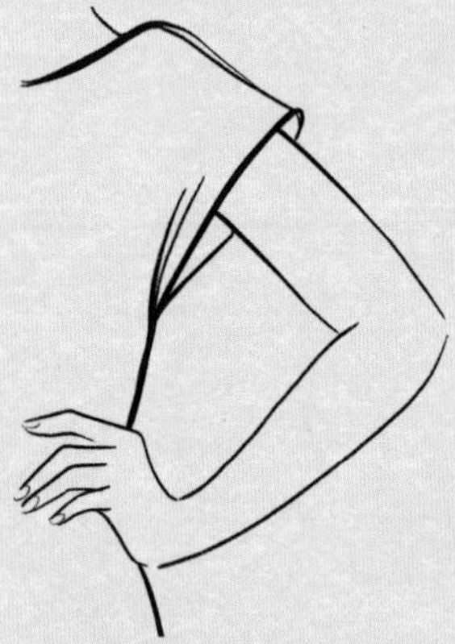
DROP SHOULDER

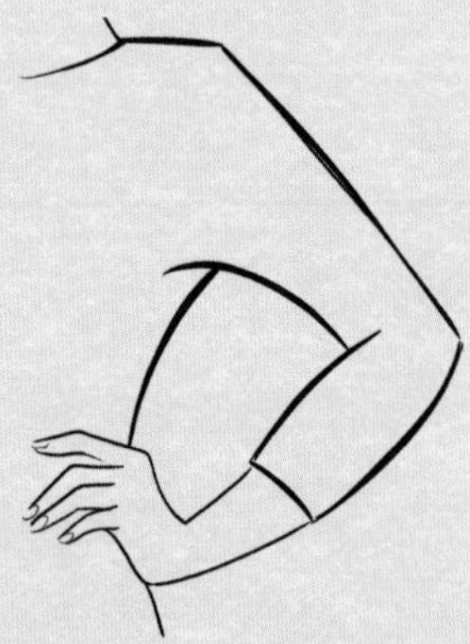
THREE-QUARTER SLEEVE

COLLARS

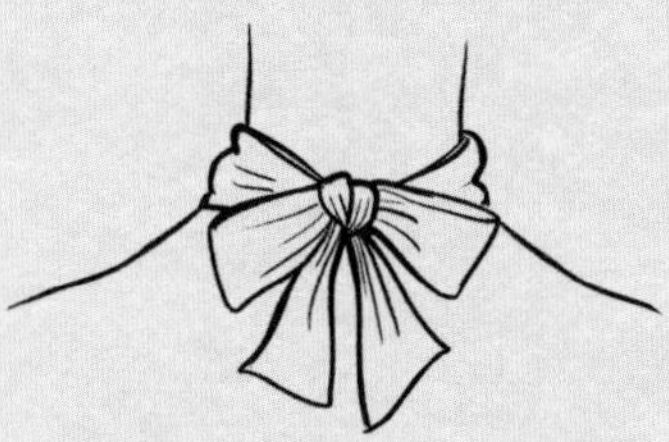
BOW TIE

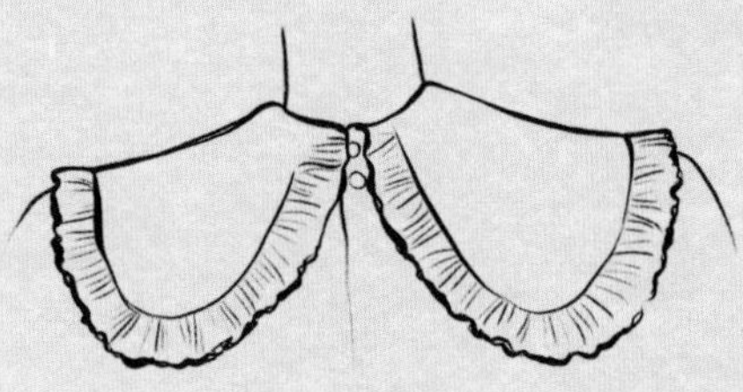
PETER PAN

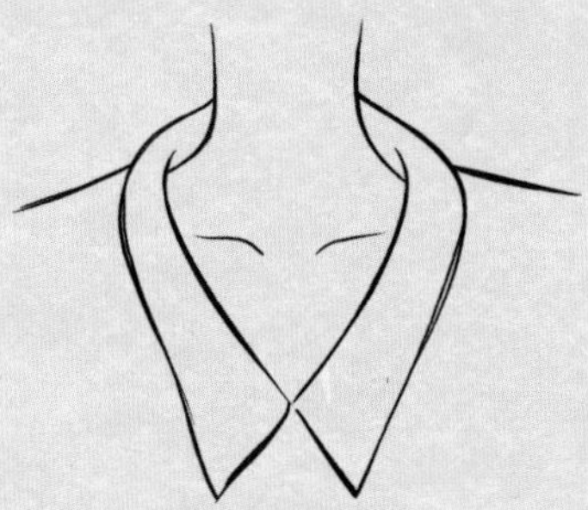
CHELSEA

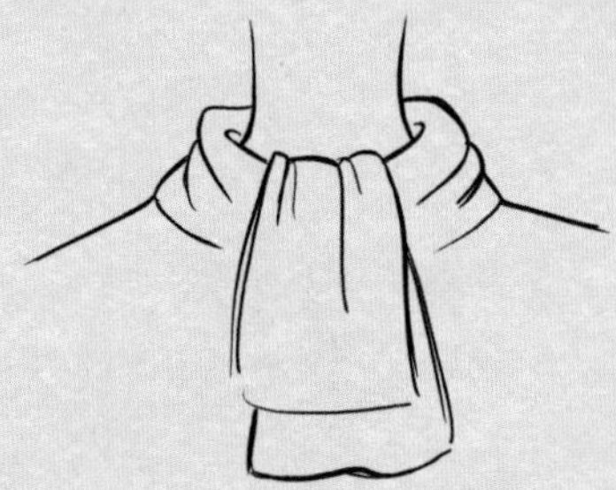
JABOT

NECKLINES

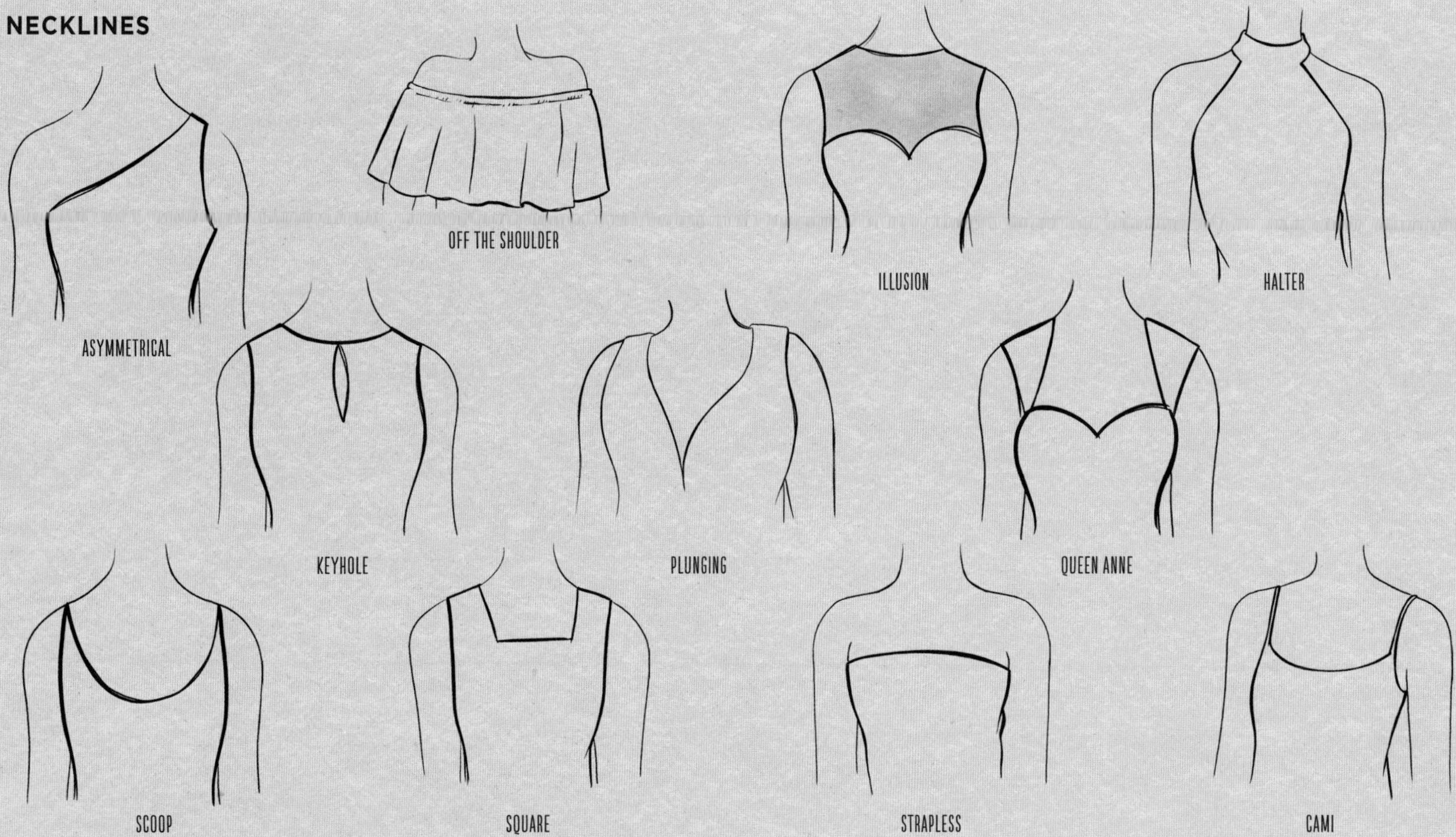

COLLARS

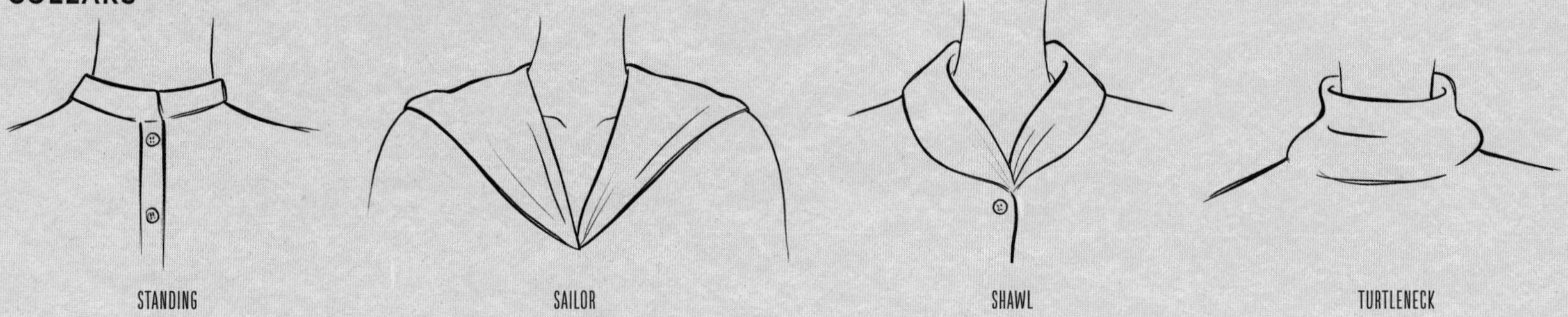

DRAWING A SHIRT

1. Start by drawing your figure's torso. Lightly mark in pencil the neck hole, arm hole, waist, and center line. These marks (shown here in purple) will help when designing the shirt. Work out how high you want the collar to be, and how the garment opens (shown in black).

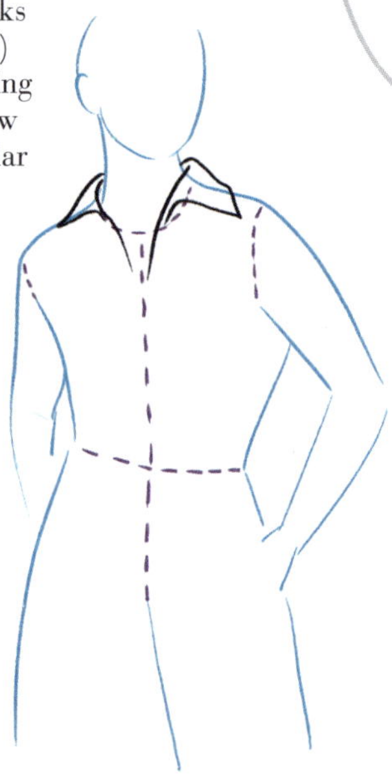

2. Draw the placket (opening), and add detail to the collar.

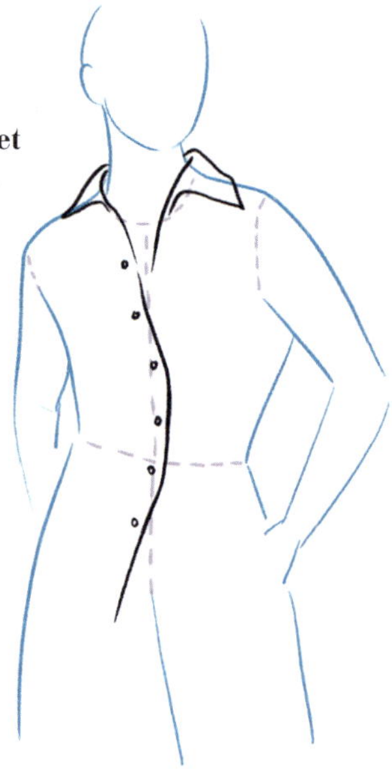

3. Define the shape of the bodice and sleeves. Here they are quite loose and rolled up.

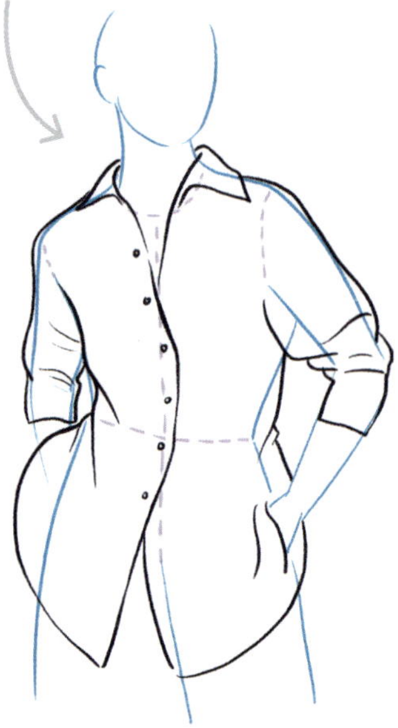

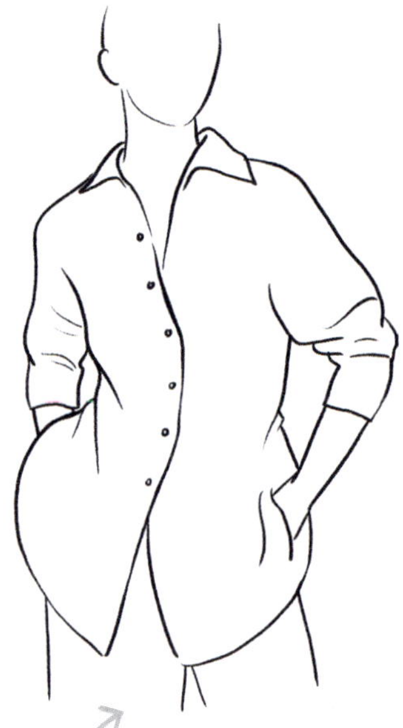

4. Complete the sketch by adding drape and fold lines at the waist and elbows.

COLLARS

1. The dotted lines show the reference points of the center line, neck hole, and shoulder line. They will help you place the collar so that it sits correctly on the figure. In pink you can see the opening for the shirt's collar and the overlap.

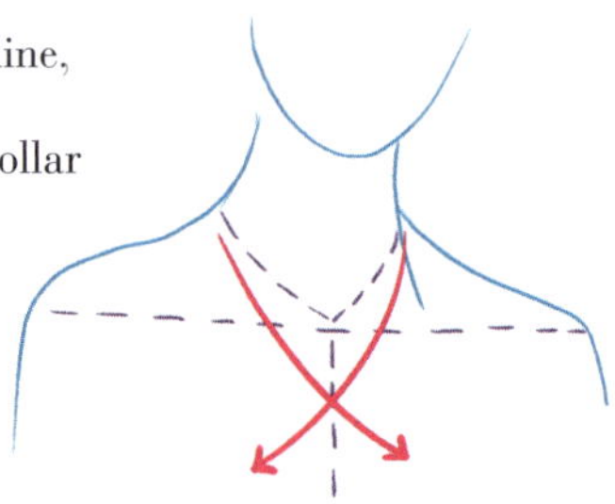

2. Mark the height of the collar on the neck. Make sure it isn't too high: most collars only go about a quarter of the way up the neck. Draw the angle of the collar to the shoulder line.

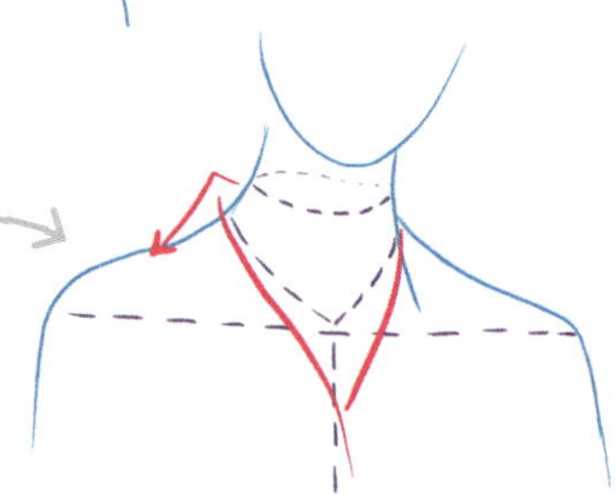

3. Now work out where you want to place the top collar and where the notch will be (where the top and lower collars join). It's usually halfway between the nape of the neck and the bottom of the opening.

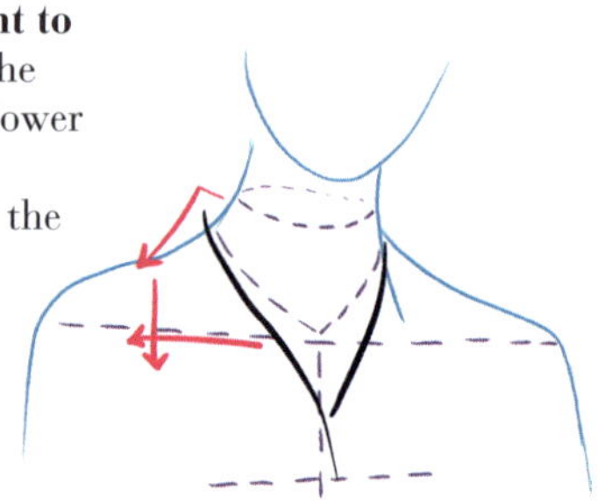

4. Finally, draw in the bottom collar.

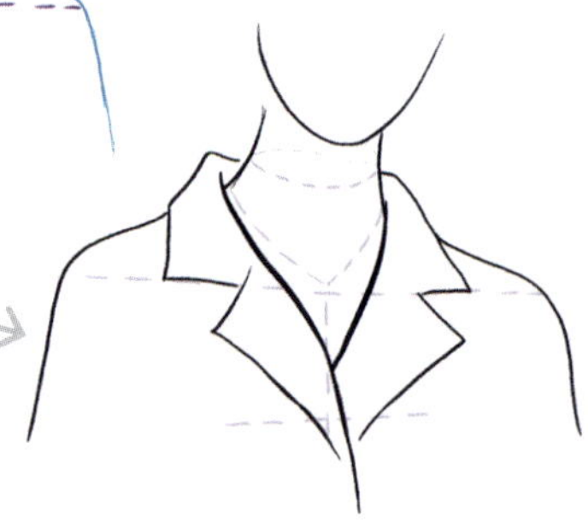

Use this page to practice drawing shirts. Try mixing and matching your favorite styles of tops, collars, and sleeves in the Visual Glossary!

SHORTS

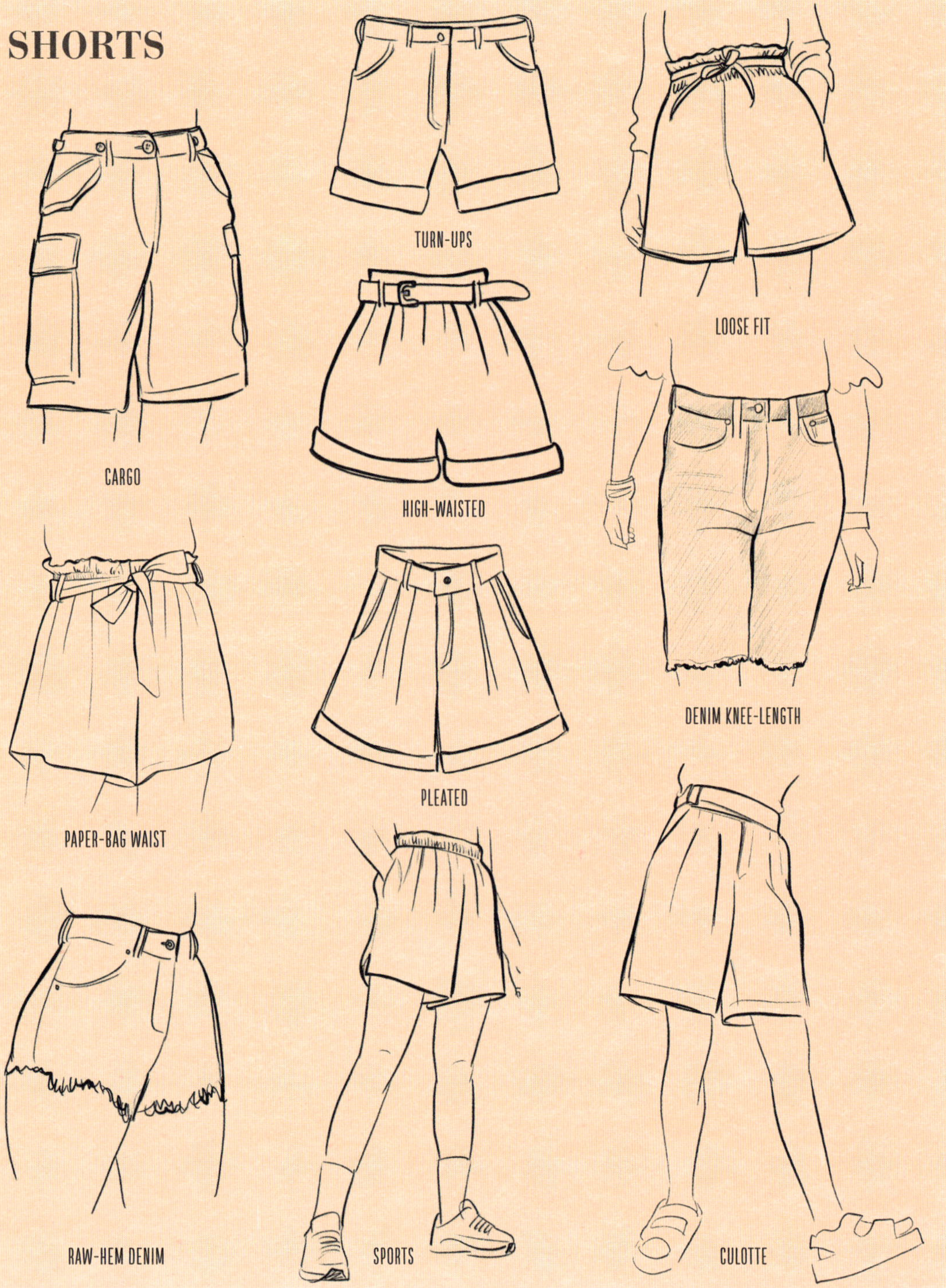

LENGTH AND HEIGHT

The purple lines show the different waist heights shorts and pants can have. The blue lines show the different lengths, from cut-offs to mid-calf shorts.

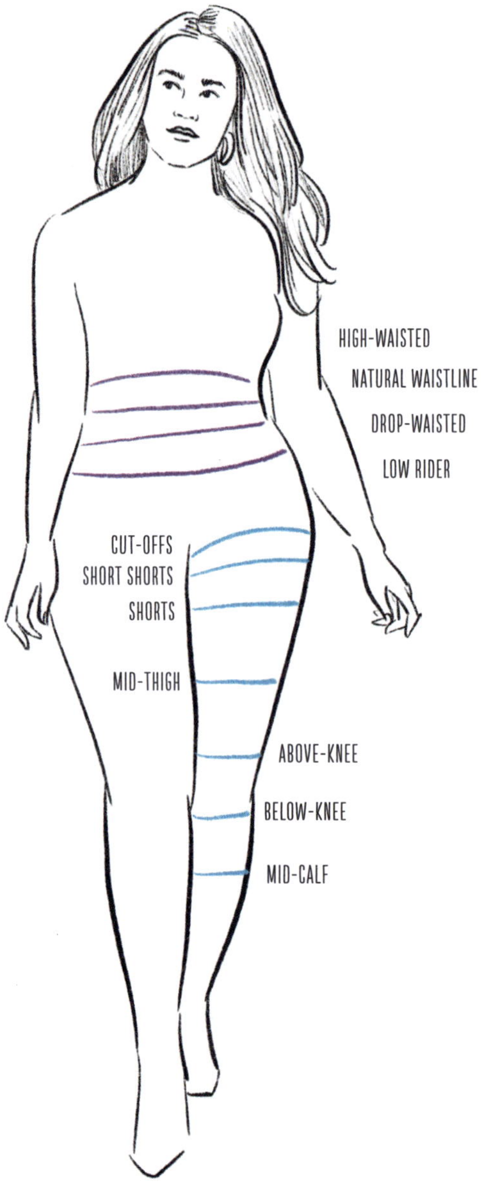

Design a pair of shorts for this model using the top of her outfit and the belt as a starting point. What length will they be? What shape—cargo, loose fit, culotte—would go best with the length you choose?

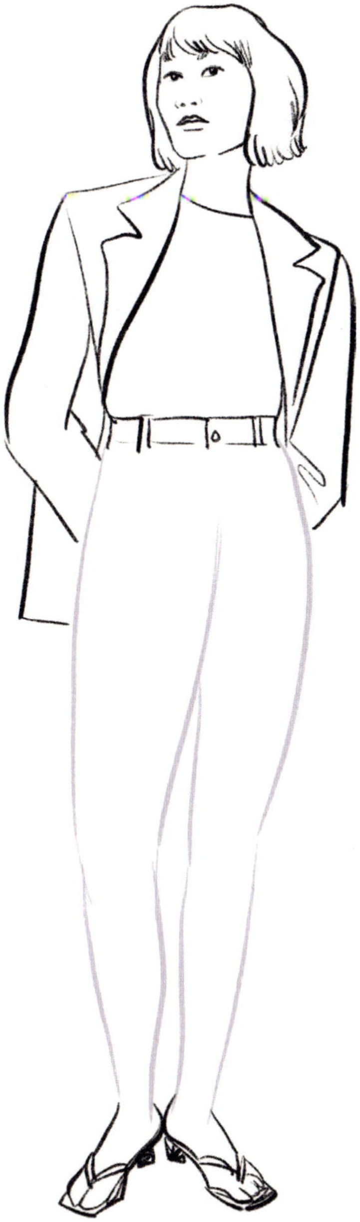

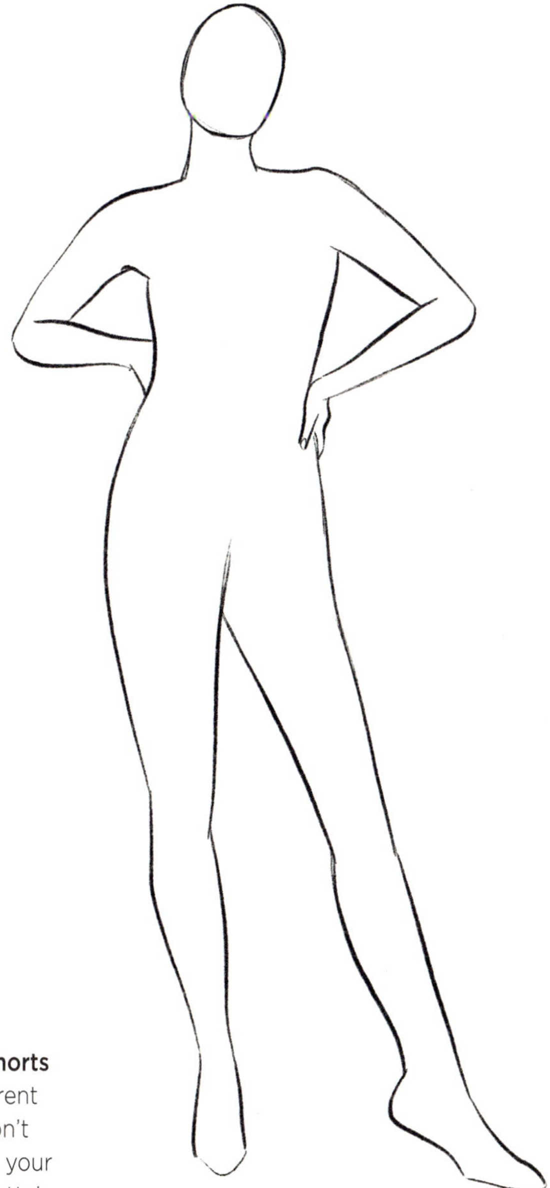

Now try designing shorts of a completely different length and shape. Don't forget to think about your fabrics and color palette!

SKIRTS

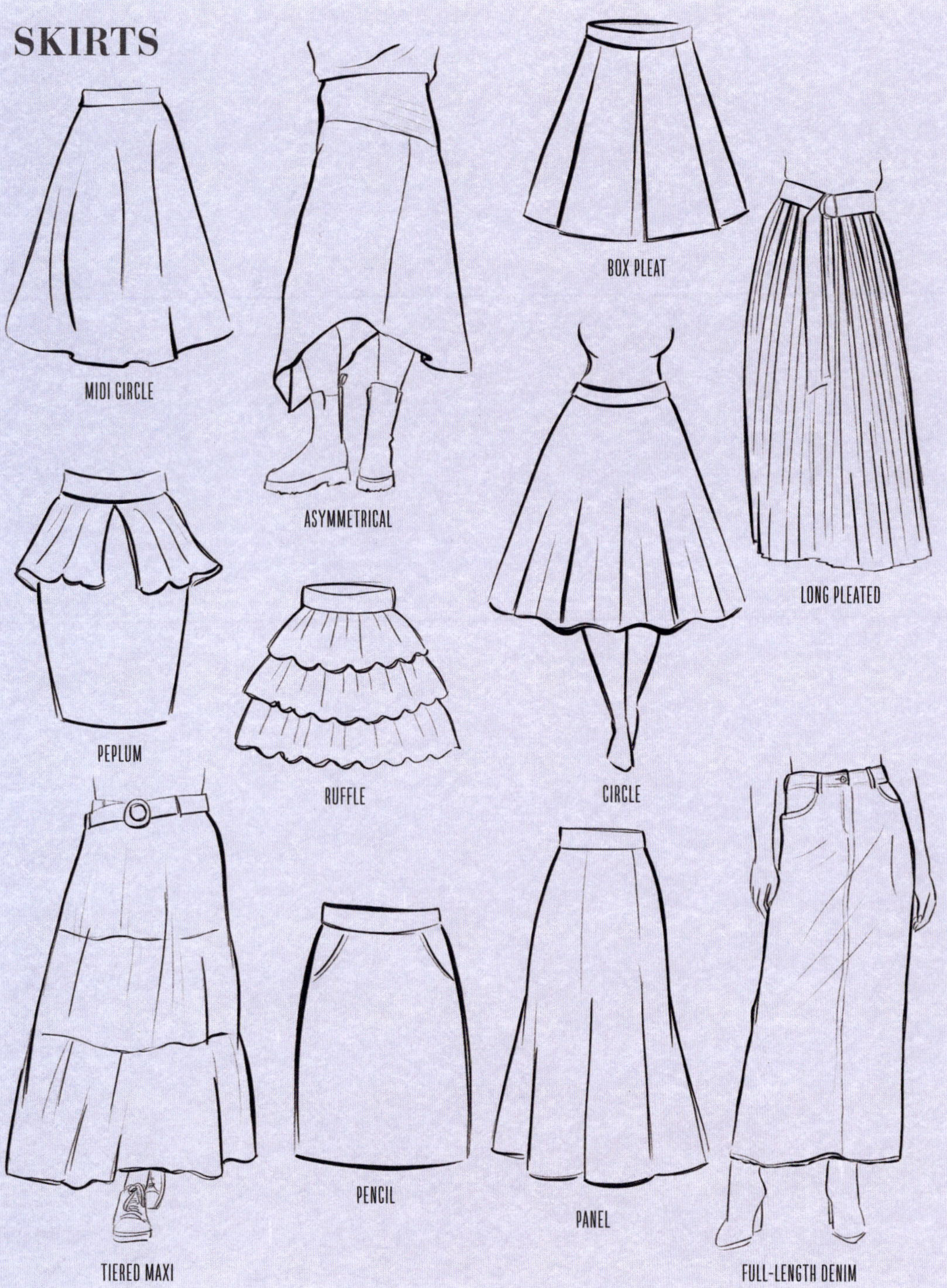

DRAWING A FLARED SKIRT

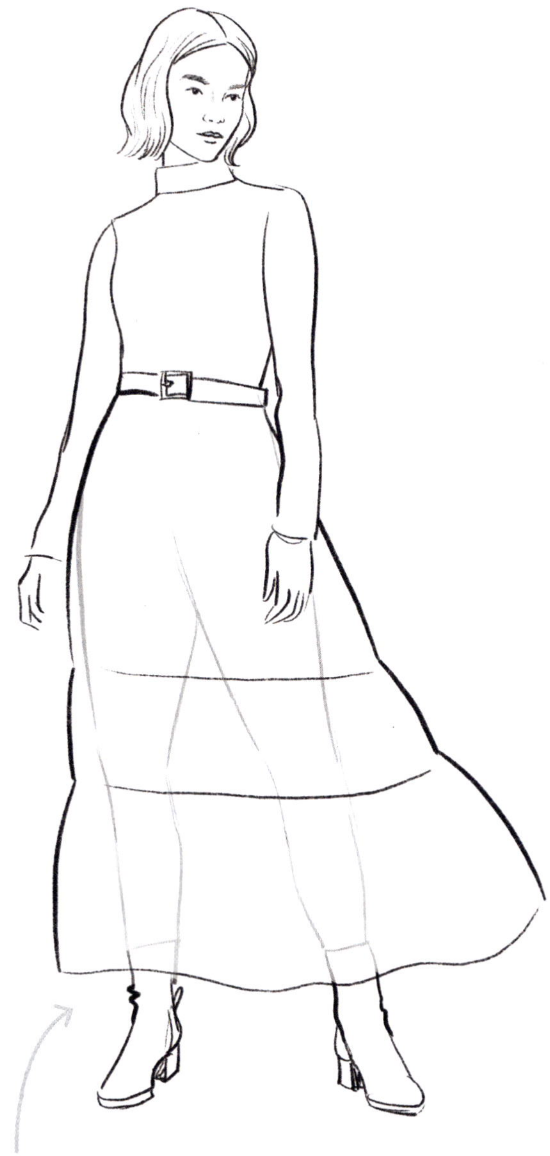

1. Draw the waistband, then add the horizontal tiers of the skirt. Try not to draw them too straight, or too close to the waistband, where they'll give the impression of lots of bulky fabric.

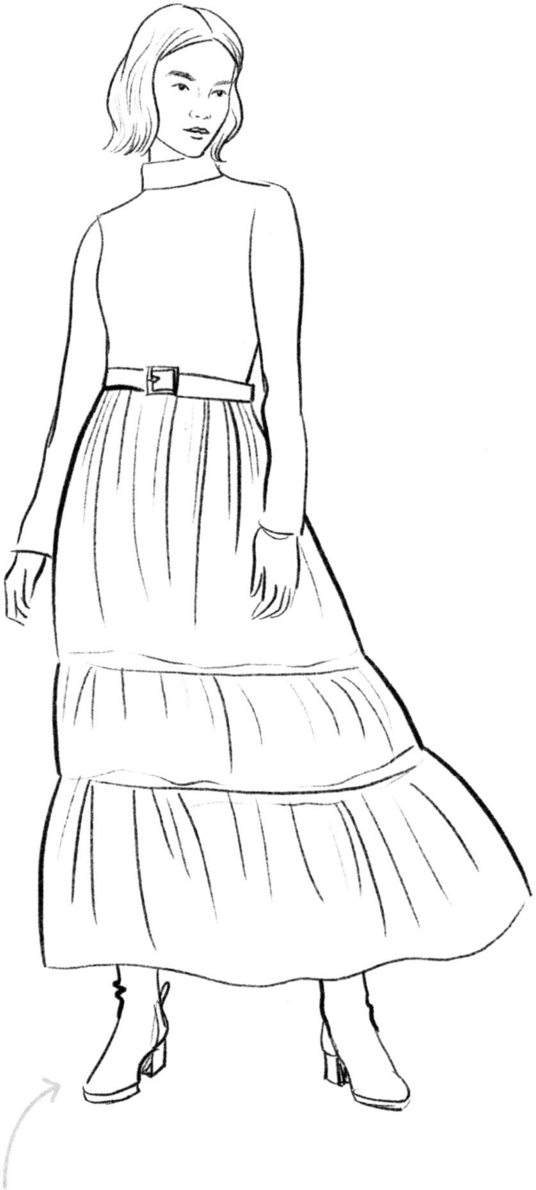

2. Draw in the vertical folds.
Remember that your choice of fabric will affect the size of the folds.

Sketch your own skirt
on this model. What fabric will you use, and how will you adapt your technique to show it off?

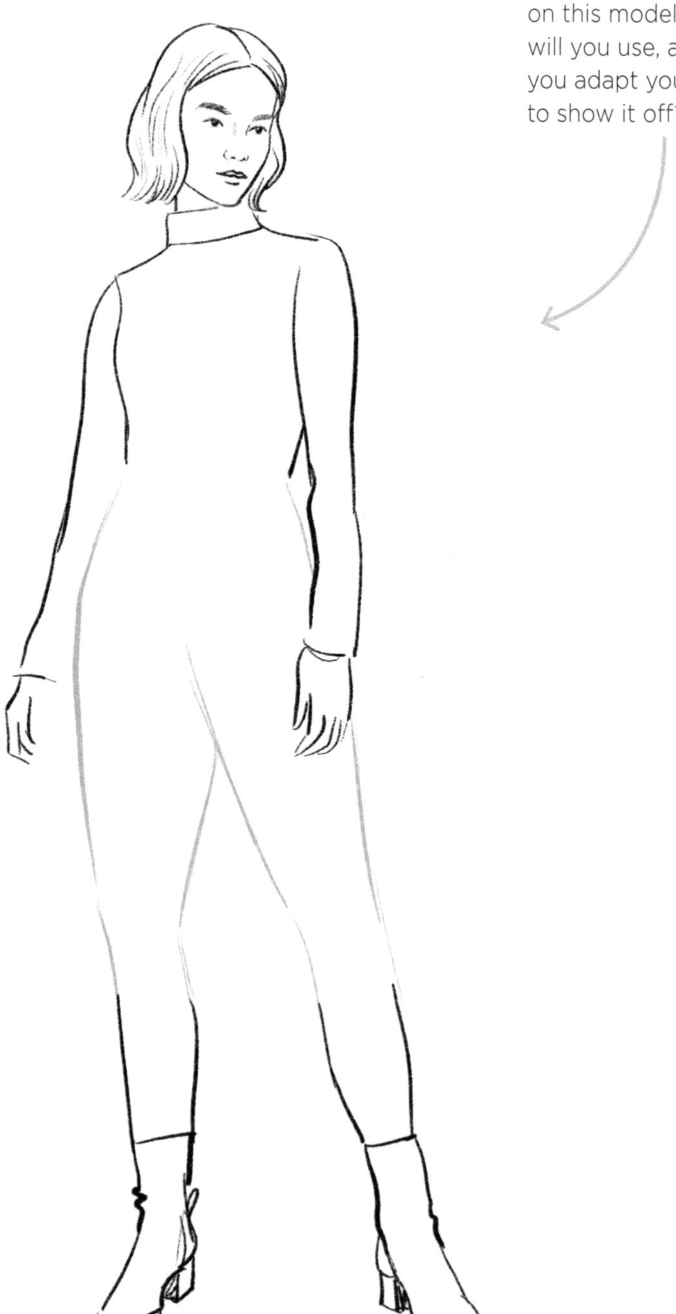

PANTS

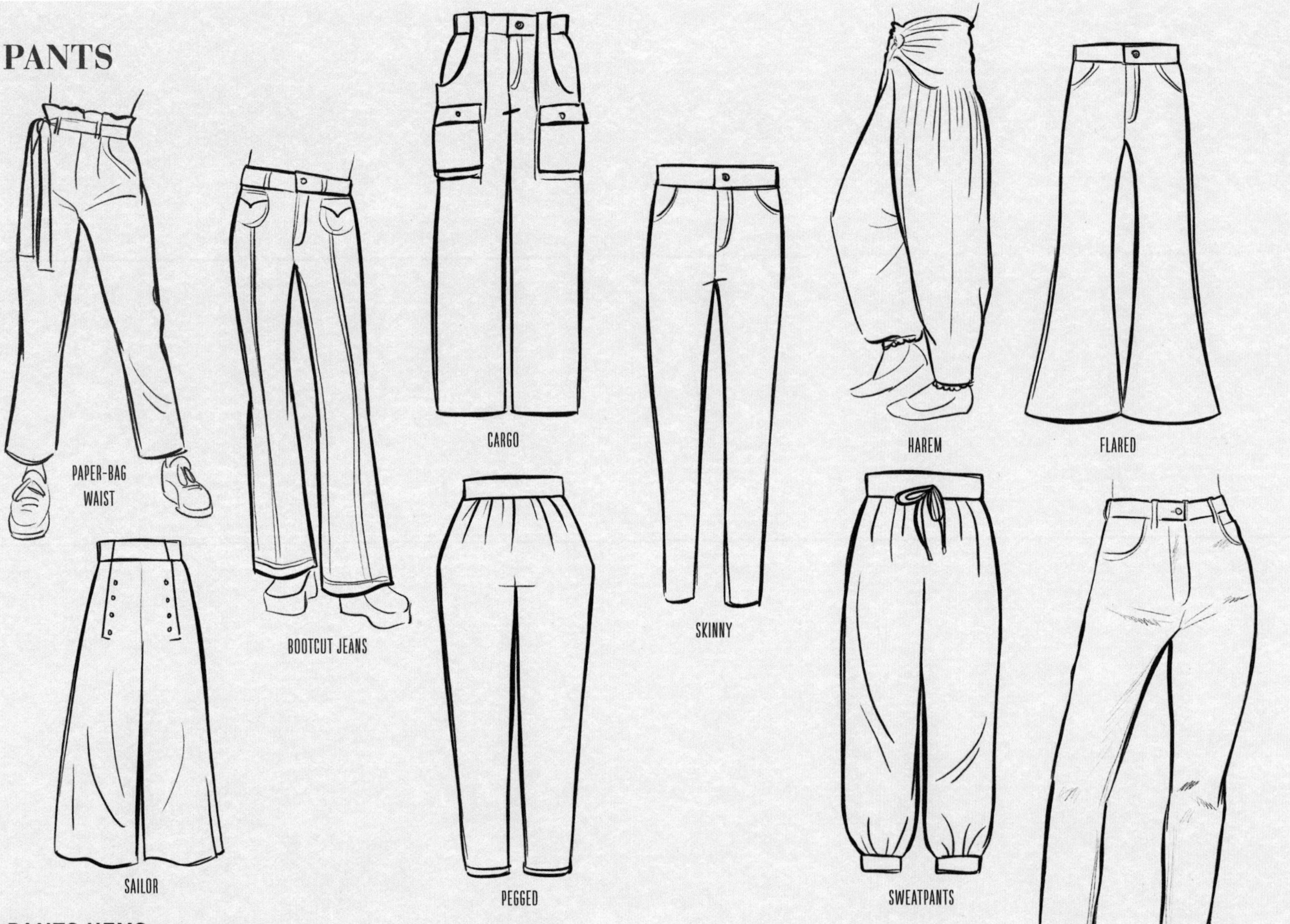

PANTS HEMS

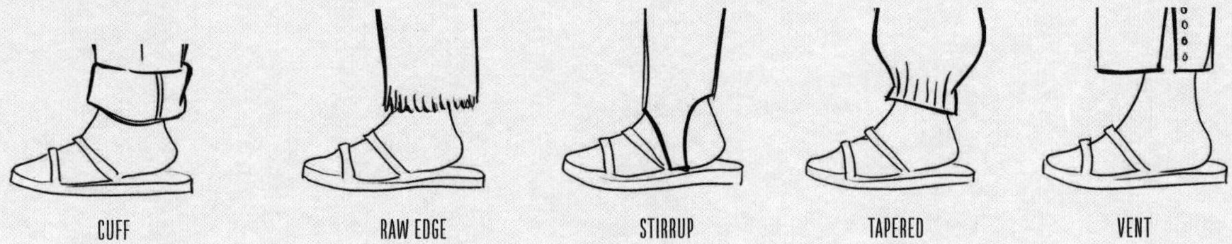

DRAWING PANTS

1. Draw the outline of a figure in a standing pose with the legs traced with a pencil.

1.

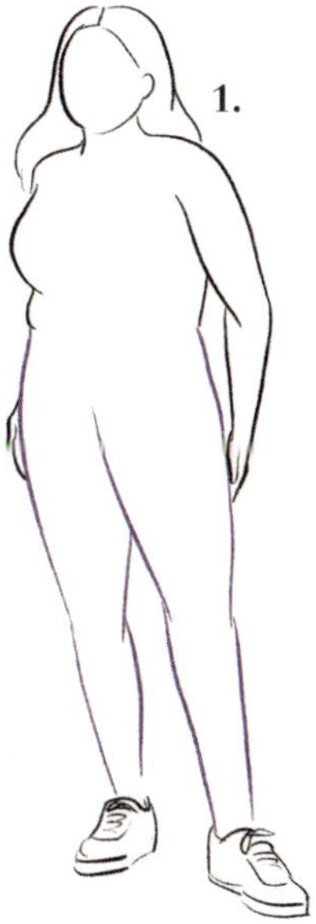

2. Add some markers to help create the general outline of the pants. Draw in the waistband and add the center-front line from the middle of the waistband down to the crotch. Then draw the creases where the legs meet the torso, and the fullness of the pants on the thighs and calves.

2.

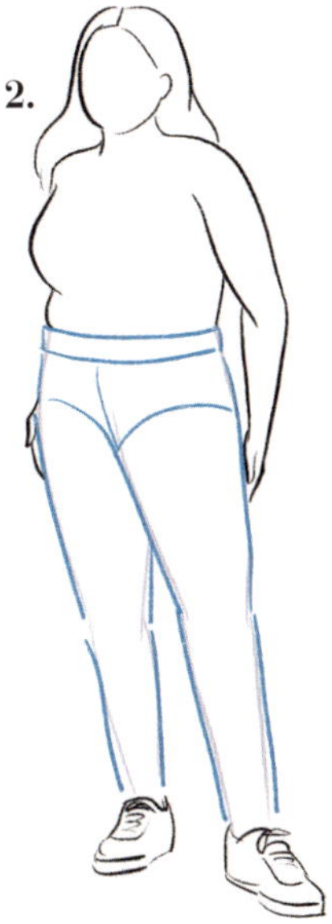

3.

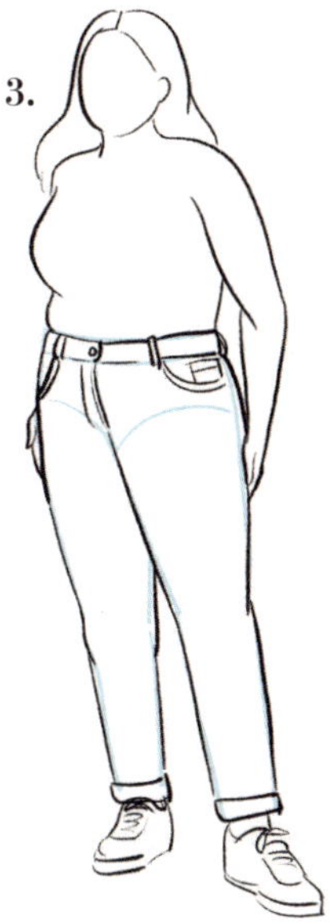

3. Now add more detail to the design, including the opening and buttons or other fastenings. This is a jeans-inspired design, so it needs a fly, pockets, and belt loops on the waistband.

4.

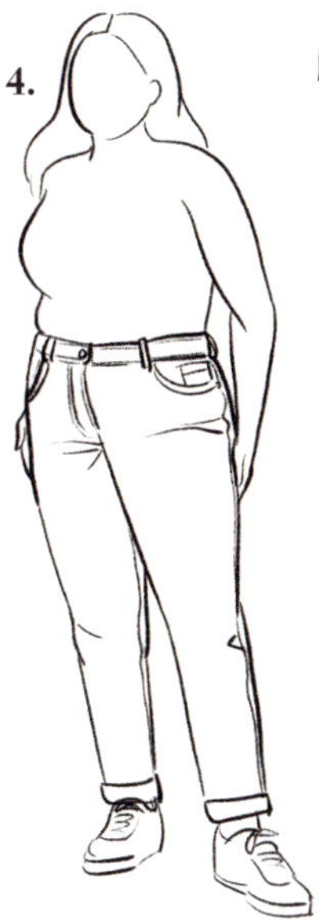

4. To make the drawing realistic, add some lines where the creases occur: around the crotch, at the top of the thighs, and on the knees. Erase the pencil marks to finalize your drawing.

Design your own pants, using the waistband and pocket details as your starting point. What kind of look will complement this model's casual necktie and sneakers?

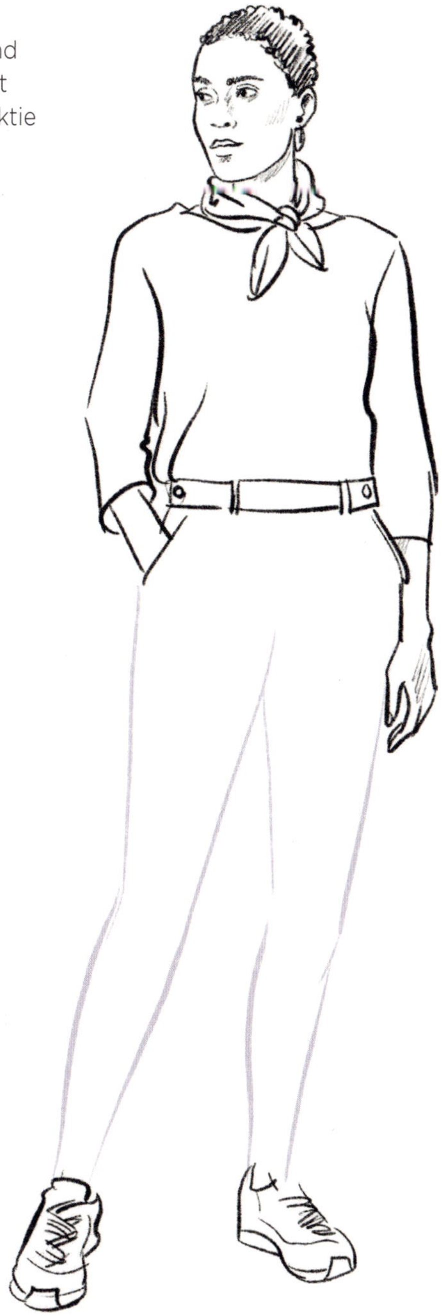

DRESSES

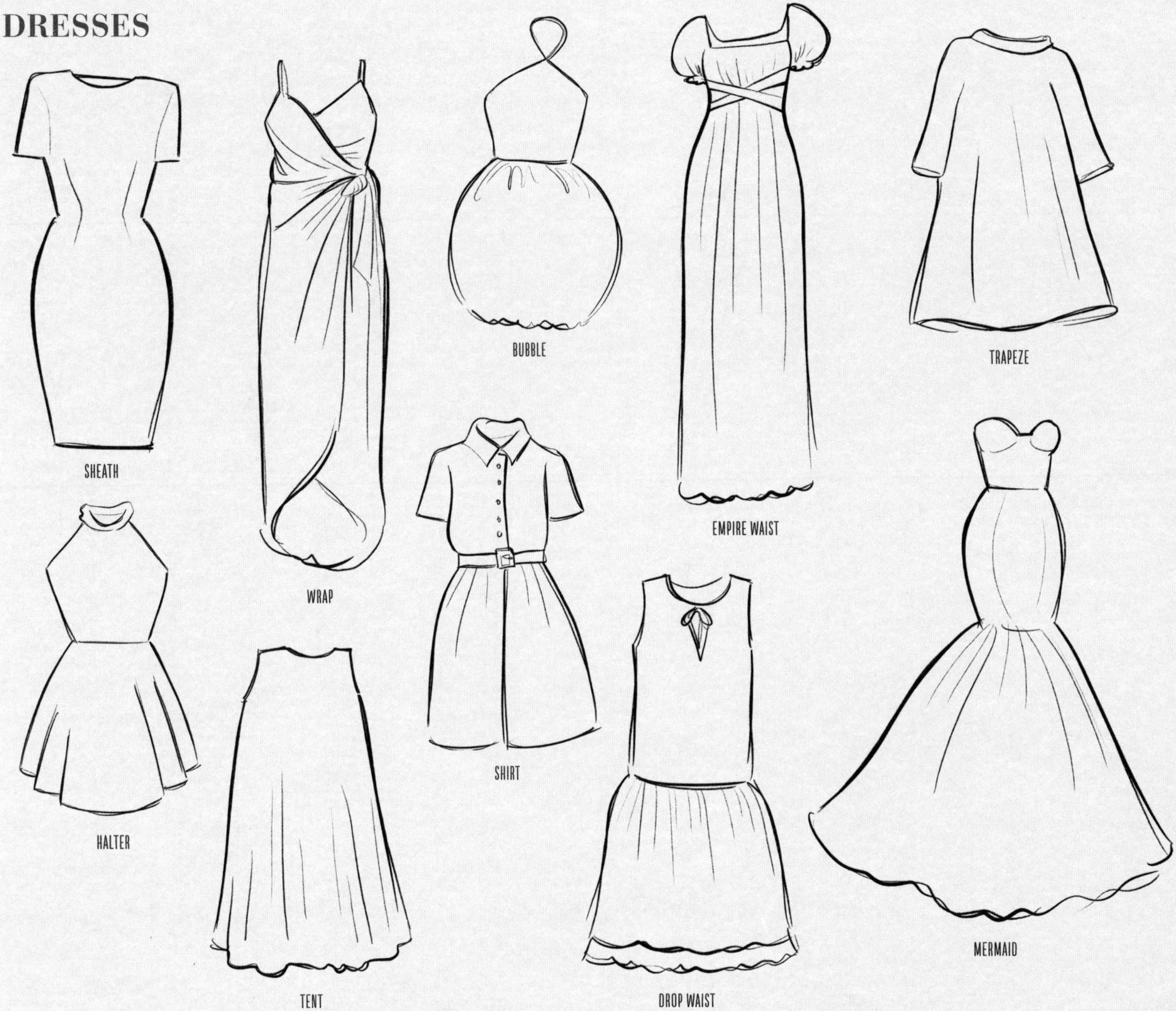
SHEATH
WRAP
BUBBLE
EMPIRE WAIST
TRAPEZE
HALTER
TENT
SHIRT
DROP WAIST
MERMAID

DRAWING DARTS

Darts are essential for a fitted look. They are found in women's tailoring on areas of the body with the greatest curves—the bust, waist, and hips. Notice how the darts and seams on these dresses have helped to shape the designs.

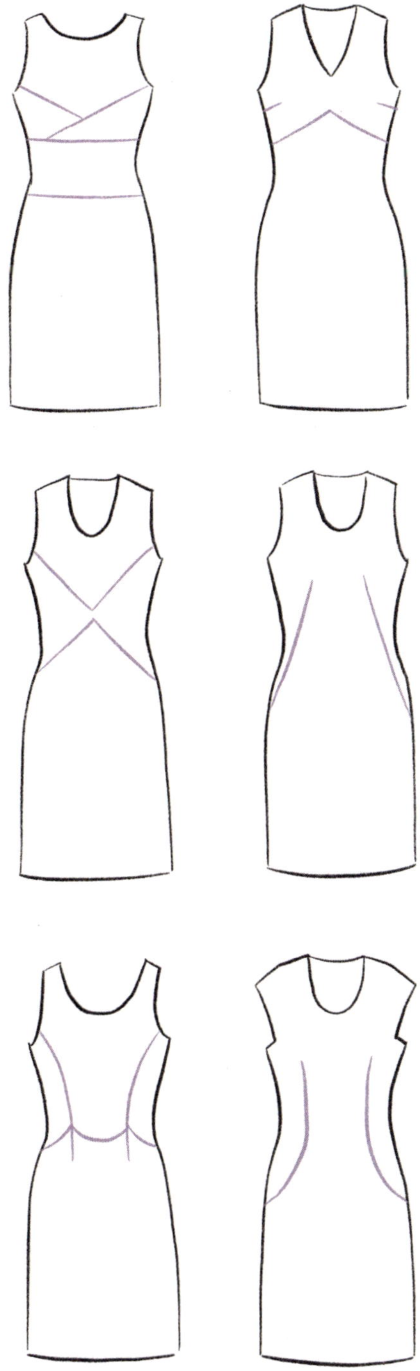

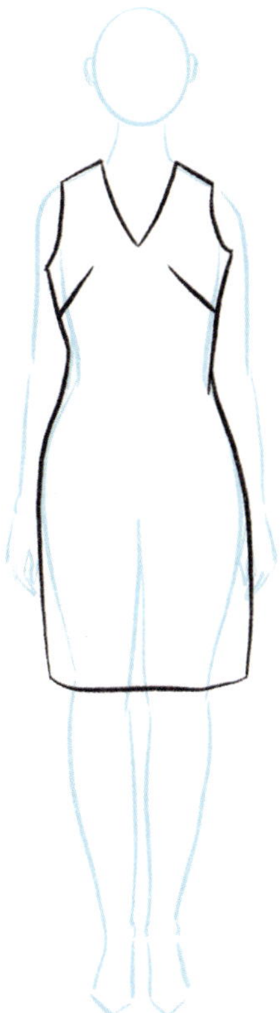

Let's practice drawing darts to shape your dress designs, using a simple shift dress as a template.

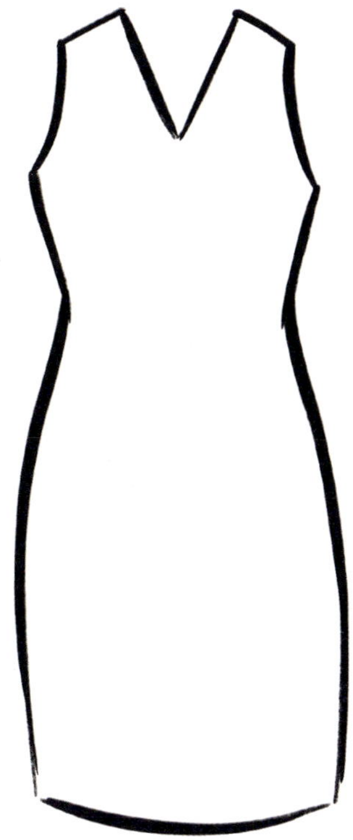

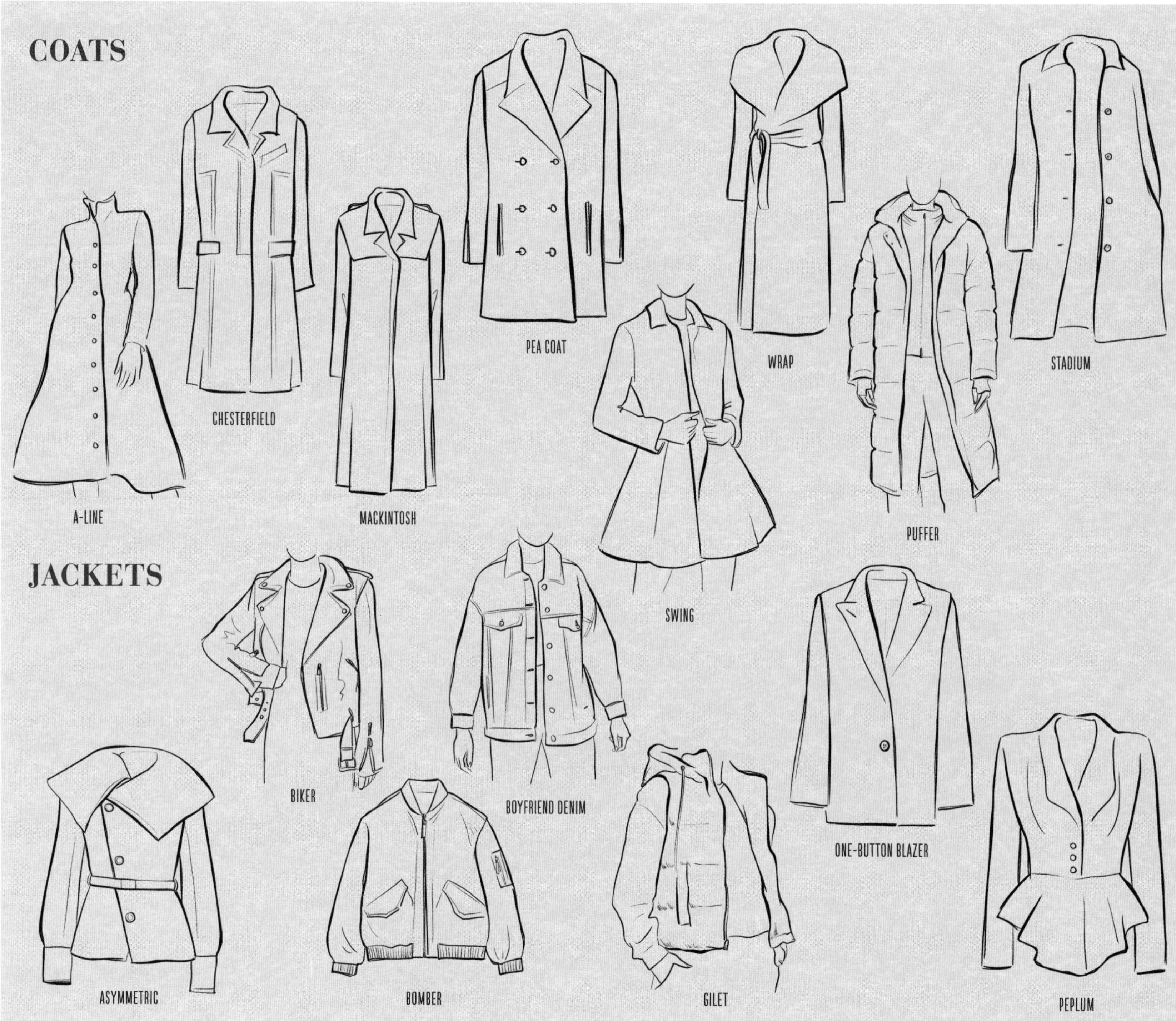
COATS
A-LINE
CHESTERFIELD
MACKINTOSH
PEA COAT
SWING
WRAP
PUFFER
STADIUM
JACKETS
BIKER
BOYFRIEND DENIM
ONE-BUTTON BLAZER
ASYMMETRIC
BOMBER
GILET
PEPLUM

Design your own coat. A coat can either fit or distort your silhouette by using different shapes and fabrics. You can go for something super fitted, or something completely different with an asymmetric design! Look at the shapes opposite for some ideas.

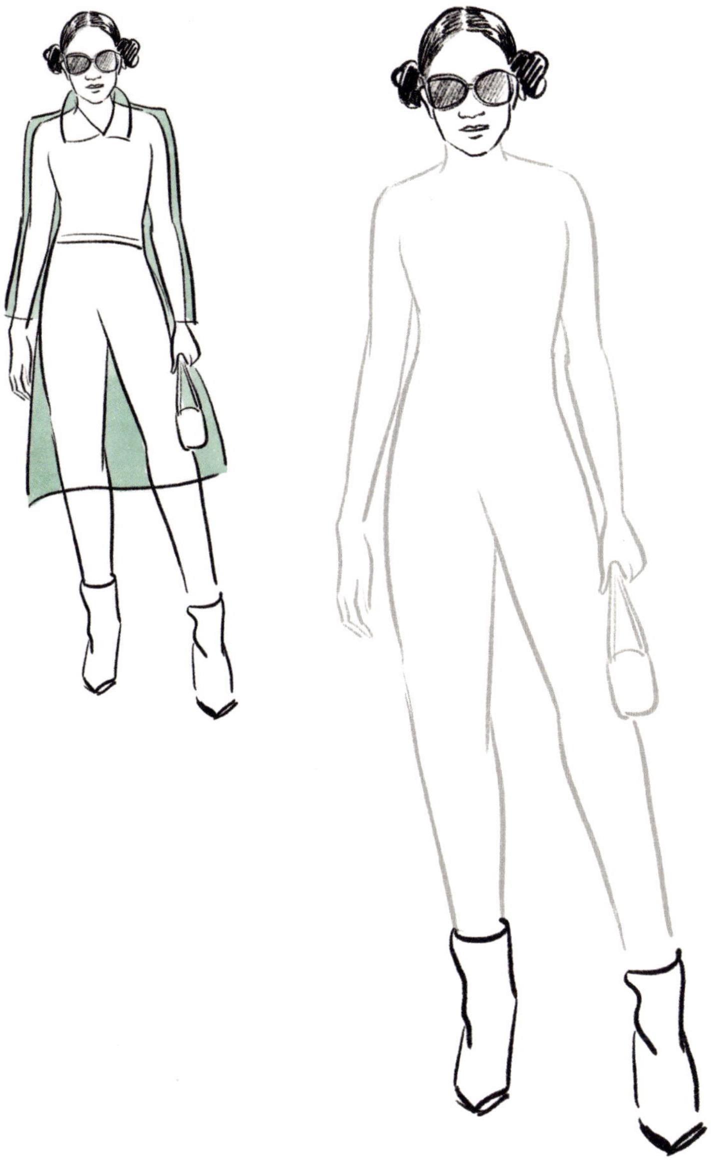

DESIGN A JACKET

1. Draw your figure and mark the neck and arm holes, the center front, the waist and shoulder lines, and the bust (shown here with purple dotted lines).

2. Start by designing the collar and placket (opening). Don't forget to draw the collar curving around the back of the neck—how high do you want it to stand?

3. Draw the jacket's center front and work out what length you want the jacket to be. Here, it is a crop jacket that sits above the waistline.

4. Complete the sleeve design. This jacket has chunky sleeves and cuffs; you can play with different lengths and cuff styles.

5. Tighten up your lines and erase the guidelines. Then add a pattern, like this classic check, or some color to finish off your jacket!

1.

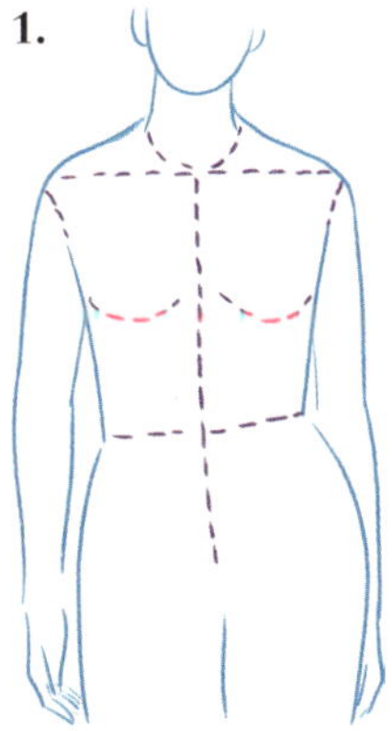

2.

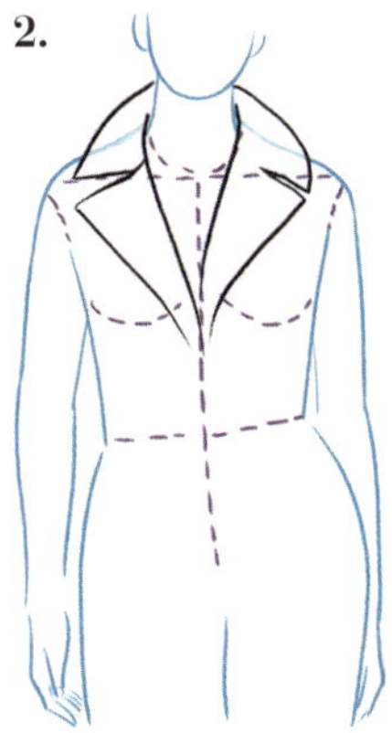

3.

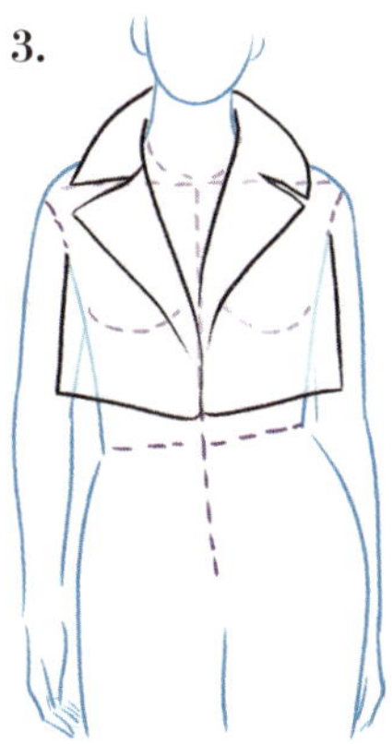

4.

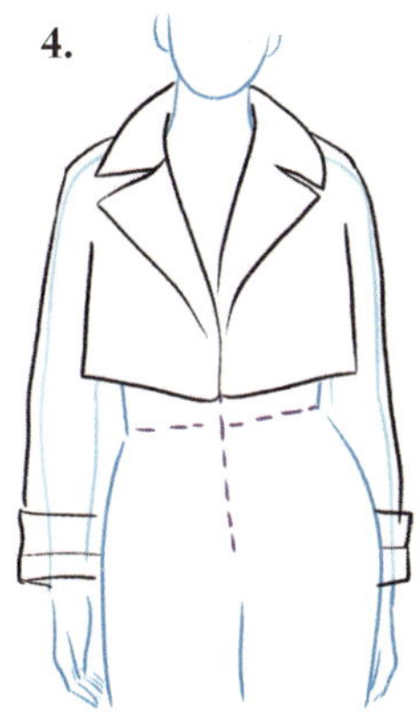

5.

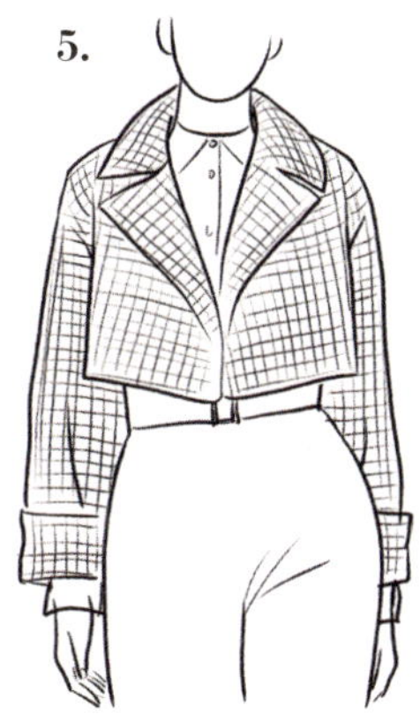

SHOES

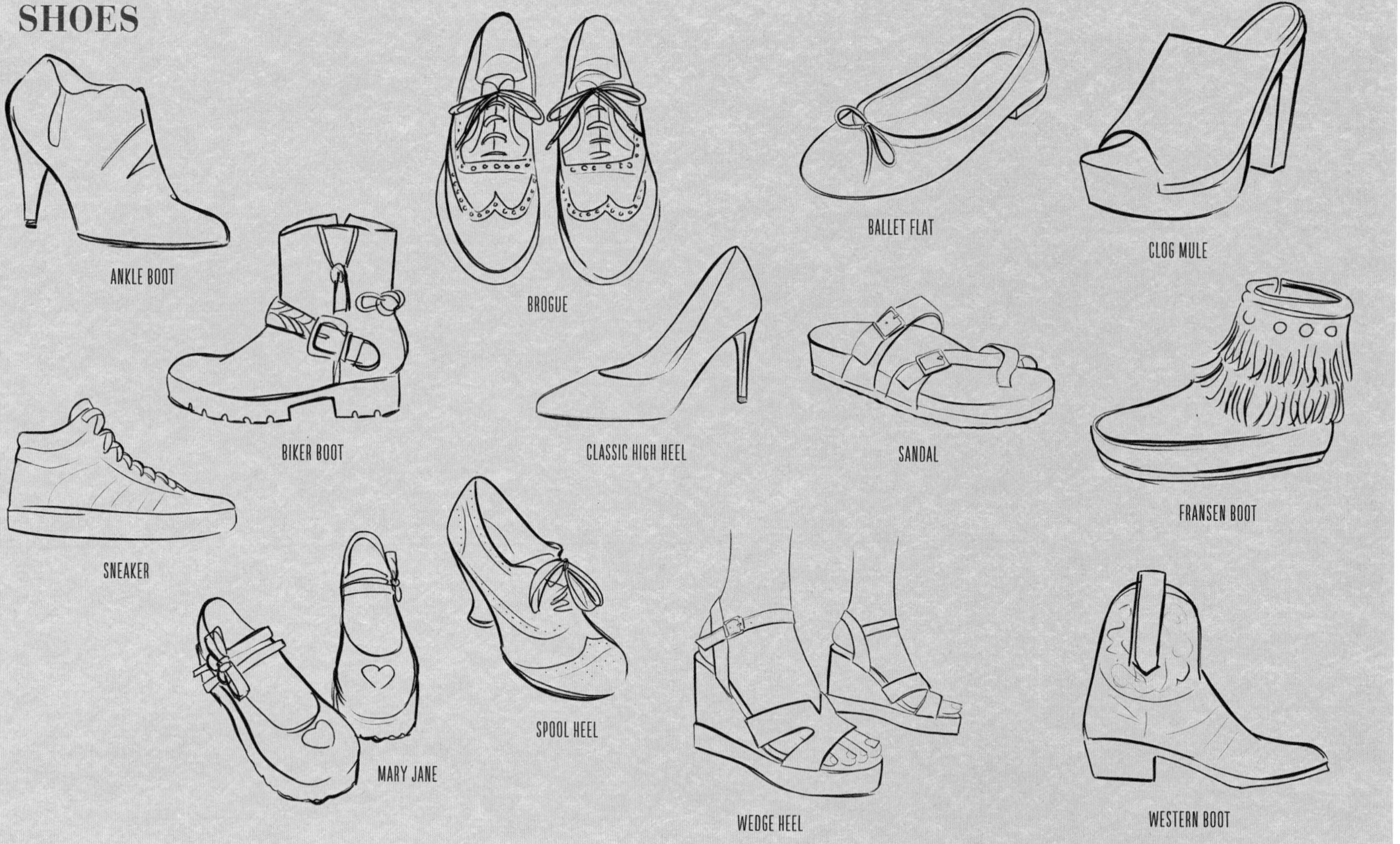

BASIC SHOE SHAPES

The fundamental shape of any shoe is a triangle. The higher the heel, the taller the triangle. When viewing the foot sideways, the sole will rest on the bottom of triangle.

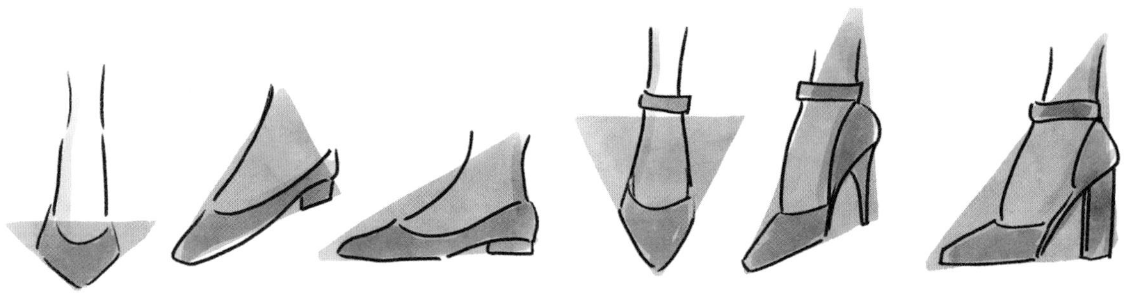

Use the triangle method to draw a flat shoe and two high heels.

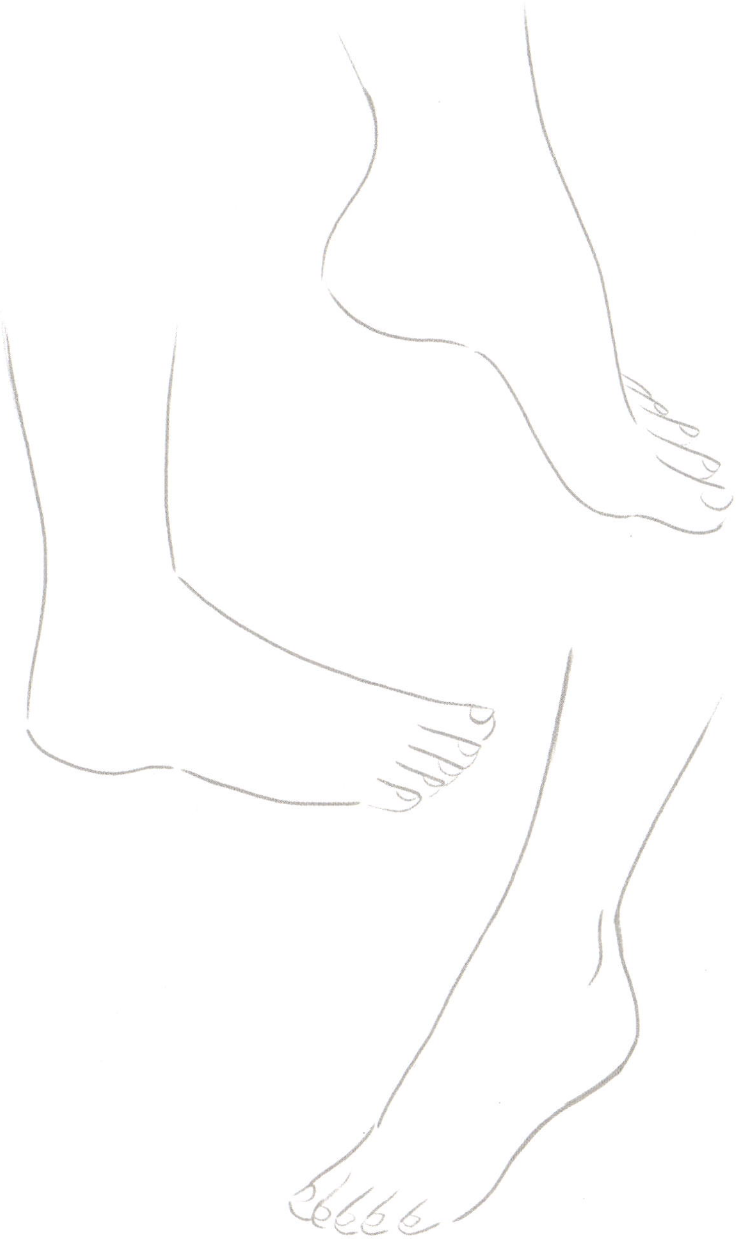

FOOT PROPORTIONS

Here is another way of working out the proportions of the foot and shoe:

1. From the ankle bone, divide the foot into thirds and add a center line (shown in purple). For the upper two-thirds, draw straight lines on each side of the foot. Then draw a flattened O at the tip of the foot. Be careful with the proportions of the base shapes: the feet need to be slightly wider compared to the ankles.

2. Draw a curved line that is pointier than the oval but fits into it to create the tip of the shoe. It helps if you aim for the point to hit the center line.

3. Refine the top of the shoe and start erasing your guidelines.

4. Trace the soles of the shoes and add color and shading to finalize your drawing.

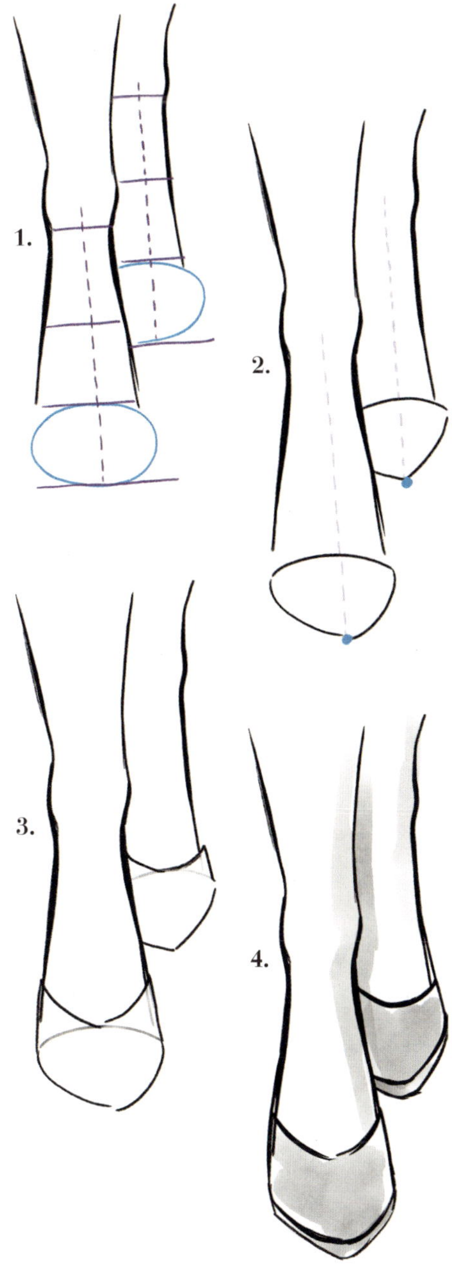

BAGS

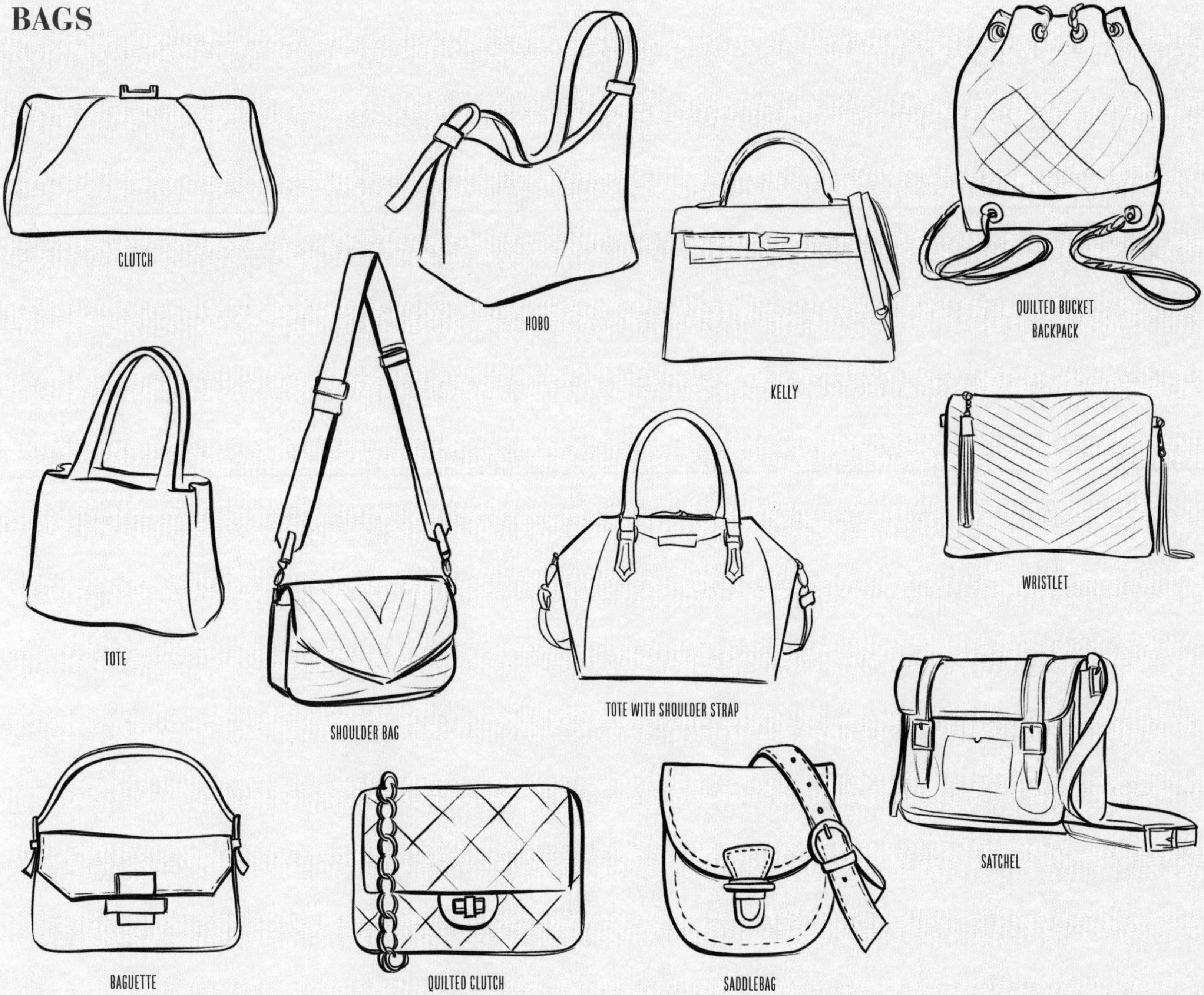
CLUTCH
HOBO
KELLY
QUILTED BUCKET BACKPACK
TOTE
SHOULDER BAG
TOTE WITH SHOULDER STRAP
WRISTLET
SATCHEL
BAGUETTE
QUILTED CLUTCH
SADDLEBAG

DESIGN A BAG

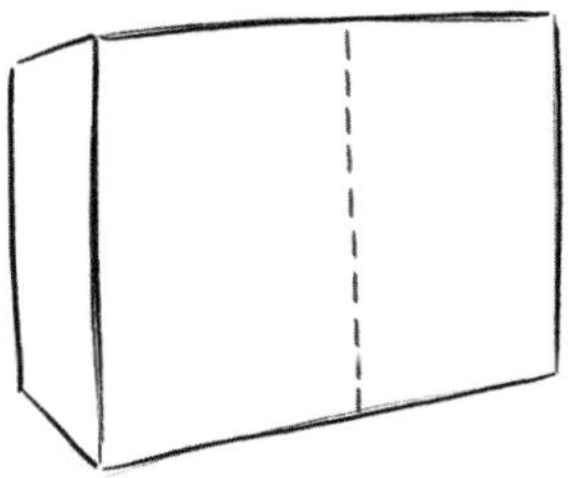

1. Draw the rough shape of your bag and mark the halfway point. It's best to draw the bag from an angle, so you see it in 3D and get a feel for how big it is. The side nearest to you (left side) will appear bigger than the other side (right) because of perspective.

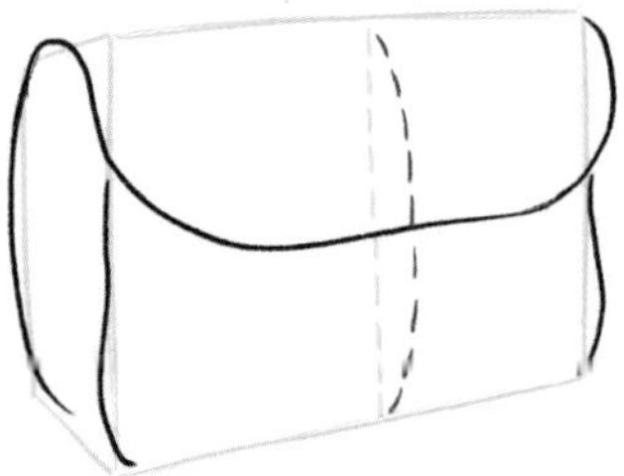

2. Outline the bag's basic shape. How do you want the bag to open—is there a flap? If so, how far down does it reach? Perhaps it is open at the top, and secured in some other way?

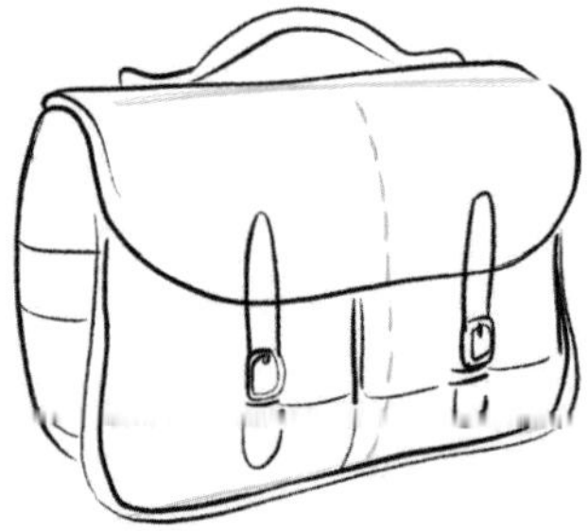

3. It's time for detail! Add pockets, buckles, straps—whatever you like to make your bag unique.

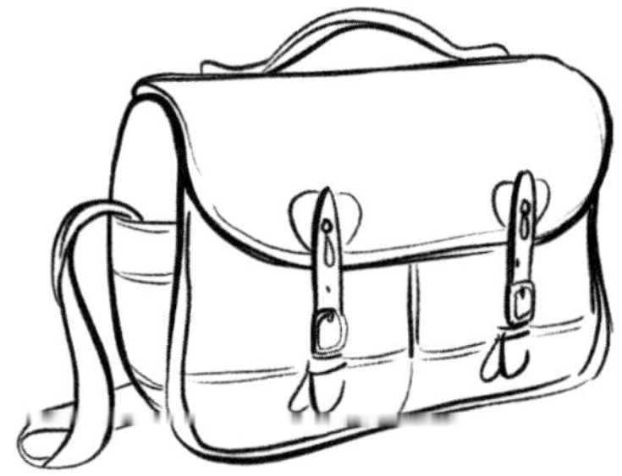

4. Add the finishing touches— perhaps some topstitching or final decorative embellishments.

DRAWING LINKS

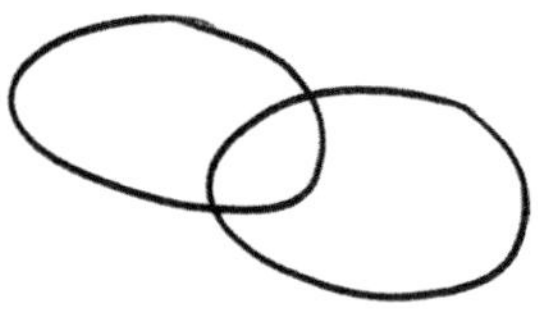

1. Draw two overlapping ovals.

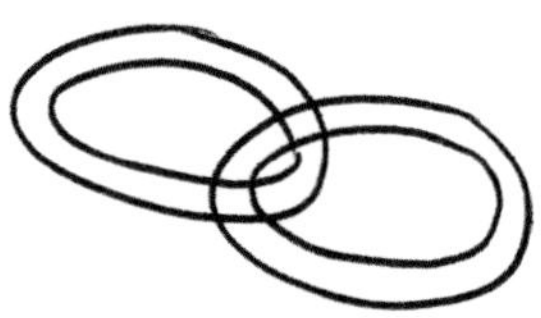

2. Draw a smaller oval inside each oval. There should be a small space where the loops intersect.

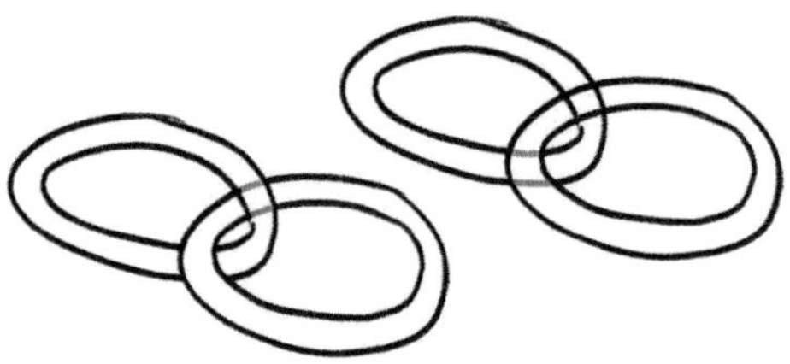

3. Where the links overlap, erase some of the lines (marked blue) to make the links look like they are joined.

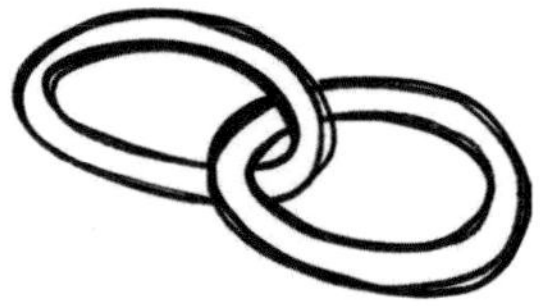

4. Bold up your lines to finish your drawing.

Draw your own dream handbags!

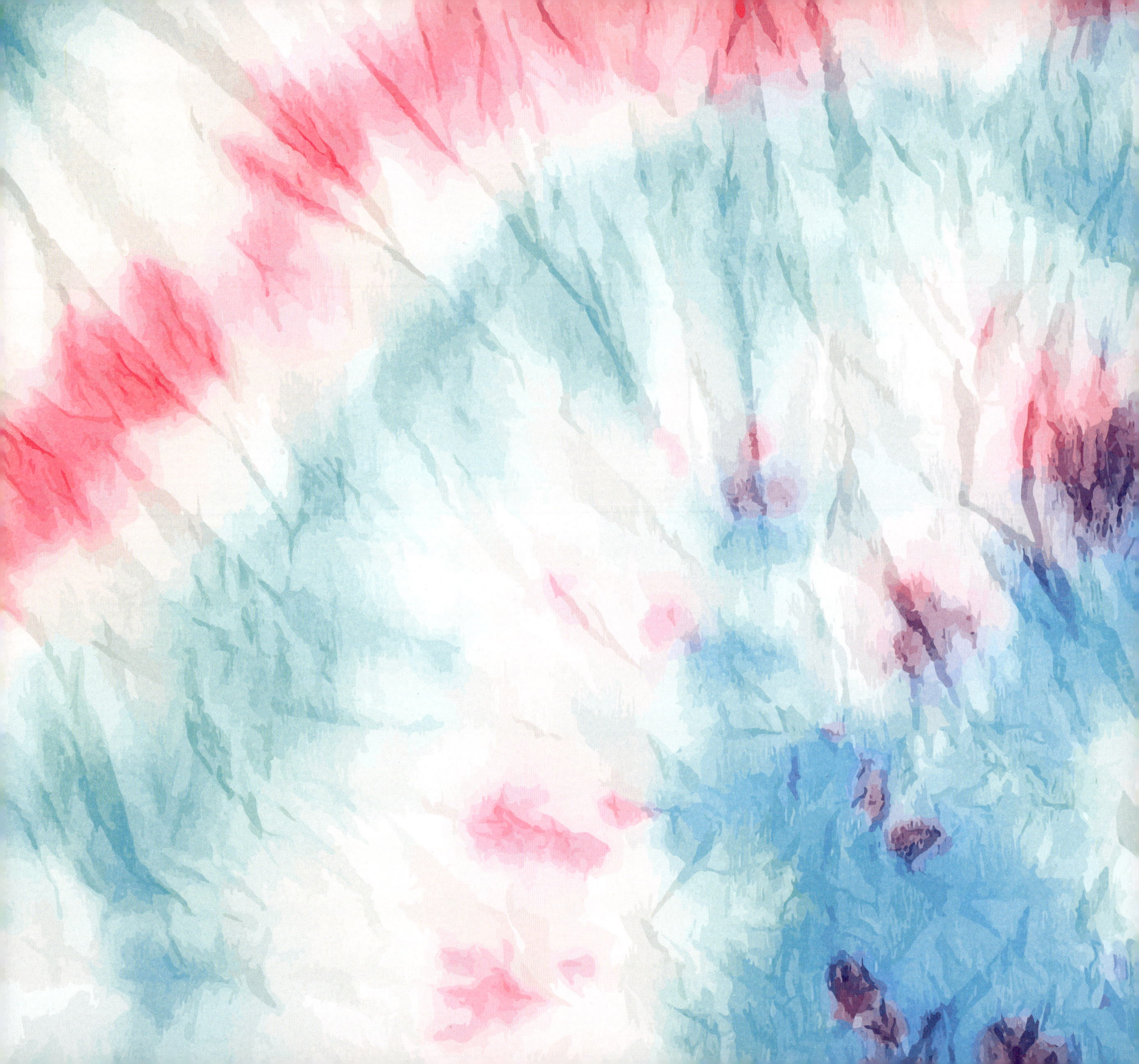

PART TWO

STYLE INSPIRATION

Now that you've learned the basic techniques of fashion sketching, it's time to let your imagination run wild! All fashion designers get their inspiration from somewhere, whether it's the natural world, the creative visions of other designers, photographs and videos on social media, or the style they see every day on the street.

Here we have gathered various looks that might inspire your fashion sketches, and there are also guided exercises to help you incorporate ideas into your own designs.

Style Inspiration Themes

In this chapter you'll find styles and trends from across all different places and periods, showing off fashion's best feature—its diversity!

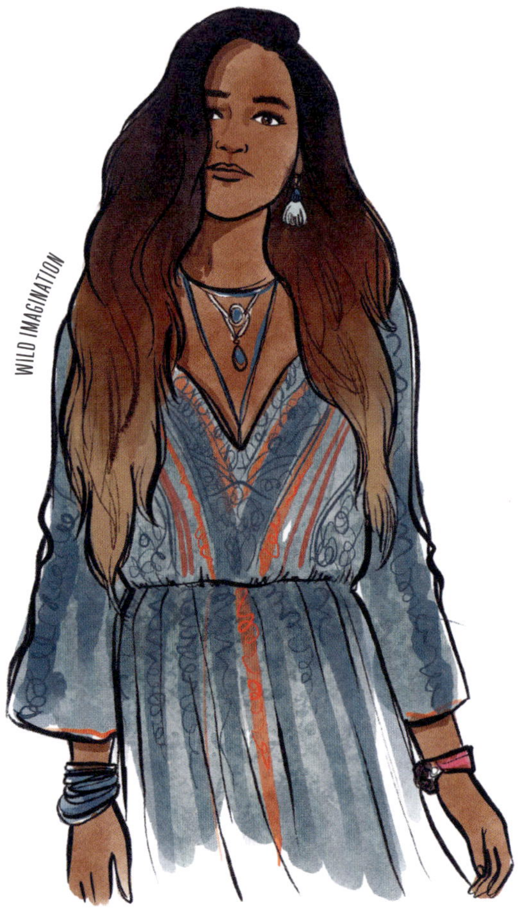

In the first section, we'll look at some **Timeless Classics**. These are styles that have stood the test of time and are immediately recognizable on the runway and in the street, from the precise tailoring of the New Look and French Elegance to the iconic Power Suits of the 1980s and the enduringly popular Preppy look.

The trends in the **Wild Imagination** section stretch aesthetics to their limit, from the bold DIY stylings of Punk to the fabulously flamboyant and fun-filled costumes of Camp. You'll find science-fiction inspired looks by Space Age designers; the dark and edgy ensembles of Goth and Rock Icons; and daring, dramatic Drag looks. All of these styles make a bold statement about the personality of the wearer!

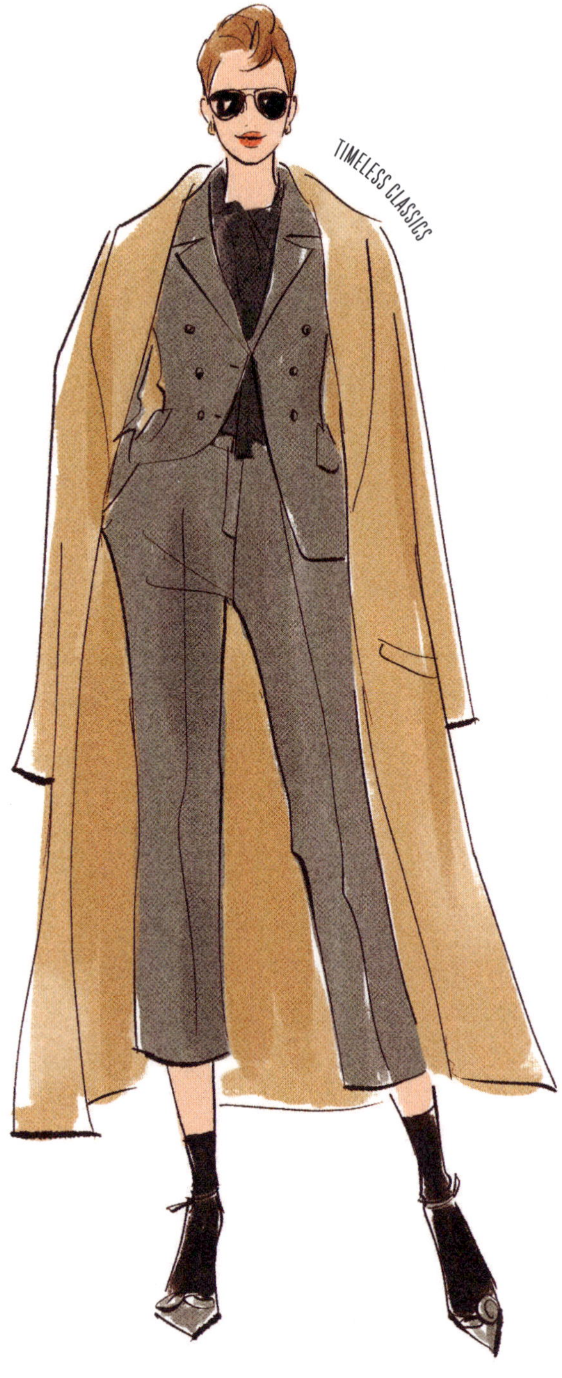

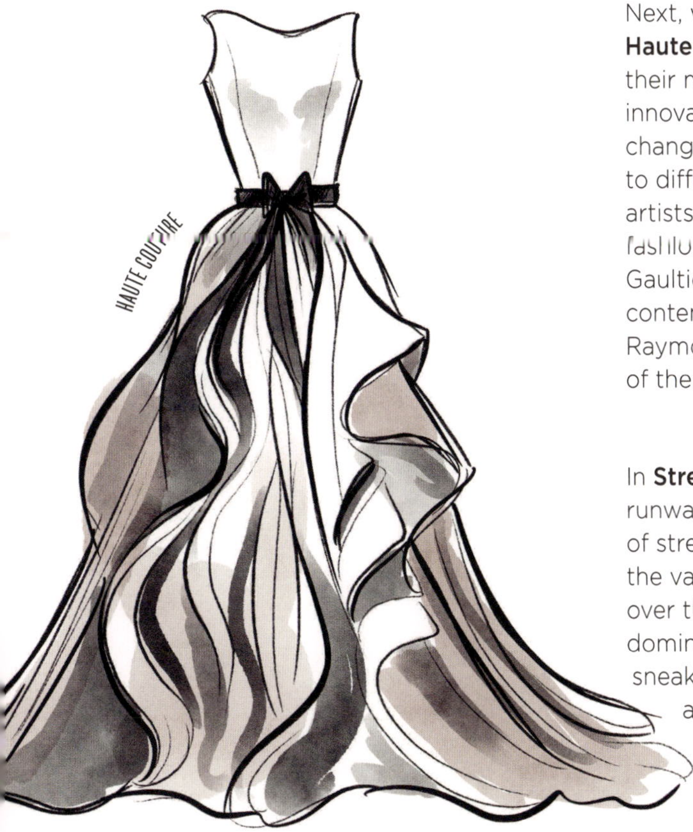

Next, we'll take a look at the work of various **Haute Couture** designers who have left their mark on the world of fashion, the innovators whose forward-thinking designs changed the rules and opened our eyes to different ways of dressing. This includes artists who have lent their name to huge fashion brands like Valentino, Jean Paul Gaultier, and Karl Lagerfeld, alongside contemporary names like Kerby Jean-Raymond and Charles de Vilmorin, all of them with their own unique vision.

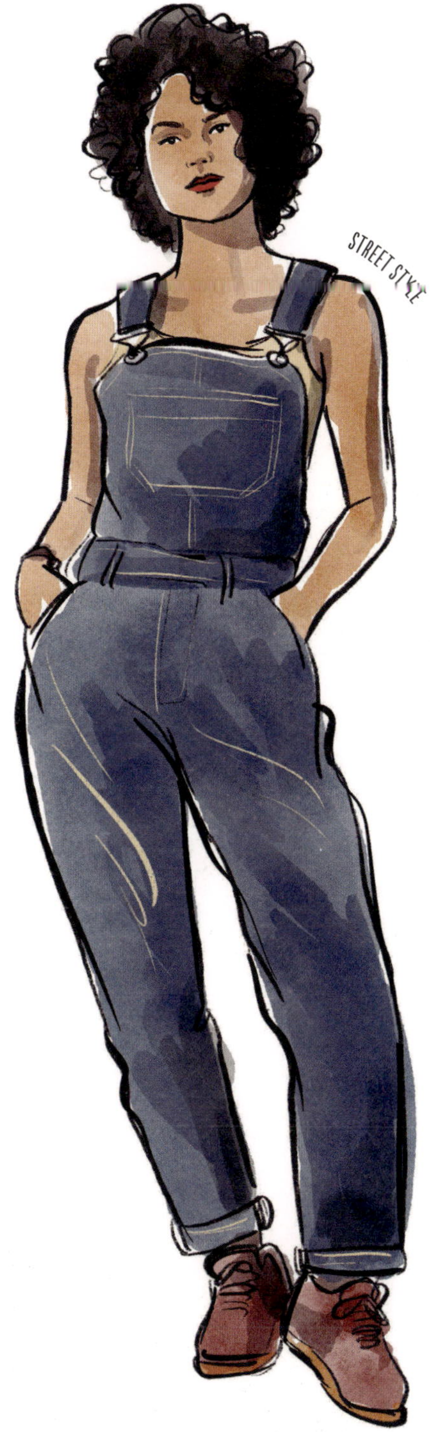

In **Street Style**, we will step away from the runway and study the fascinating impact of street style on the fashion industry, and the various trends that have emerged over the years, from the denim that dominated the 1980s and 1990s to the sneakers and sweats of today's Streetwear and Athleisure. We'll see how people make a statement about their style with Slogan Tees or looks inspired by subcultures like Hip-hop.

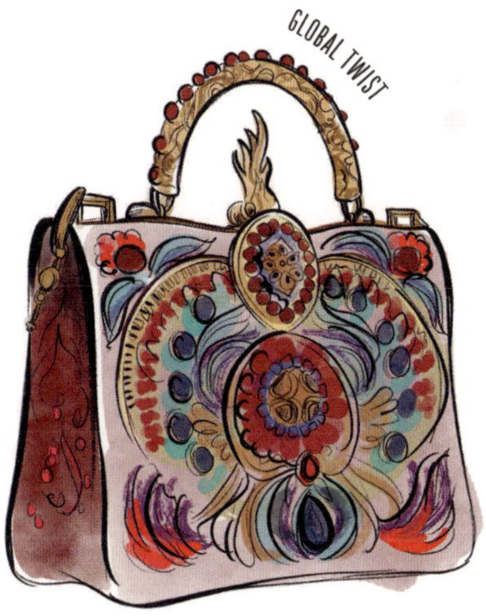

Finally, in our **Global Twist** section, we will explore how diverse and rich cultures have influenced the design and creation of garments. Japanese philosophy inspired the fuss-free, gender-neutral outfits of the modern Minimalist aesthetic, while Bold Prints and Artisan Crafts thrum with vibrancy, celebrating patterns, dyeing and beadwork techniques, and distinctive colorways from all over the world!

Classic Tailoring

A coed, multicolored tweed jacket with a matching waist-marked bodysuit underneath. Logo-printed tights make the outfit unique and fun!

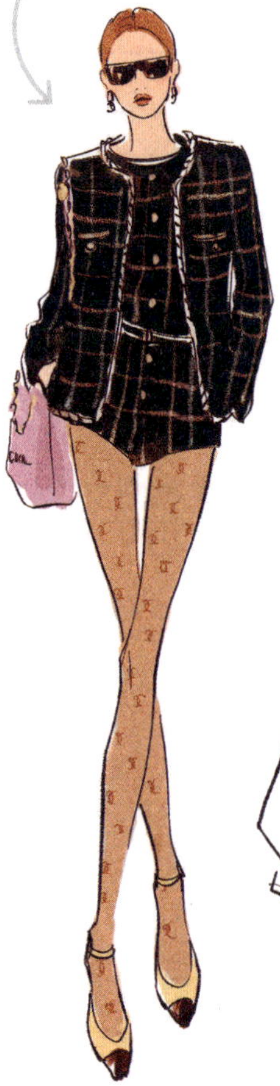

Classic tailoring began with the fashion lover's ultimate dream piece—the Chanel tweed suit. In the early 1900s, women's clothing was highly constructed and constricting. Coco Chanel, who believed that clothes should balance elegance with comfort and practicality, instead offered women freedom of the body that in turn enhanced their lifestyles and led to the rise of more casual and fluid ready-to-wear looks. Chanel's tweed suits, loosely tailored and slightly masculine, debuted in the 1920s and immediately became the house's icon and a timeless classic, continuously reinterpreted by Coco and her successors. Other fashion houses also have their take on classic tailoring, and suit style has been pushed in all directions, incorporating trends in different eras, adding accessories and details like collars, sequins, and weaves, and even surprising us with entirely new silhouettes.

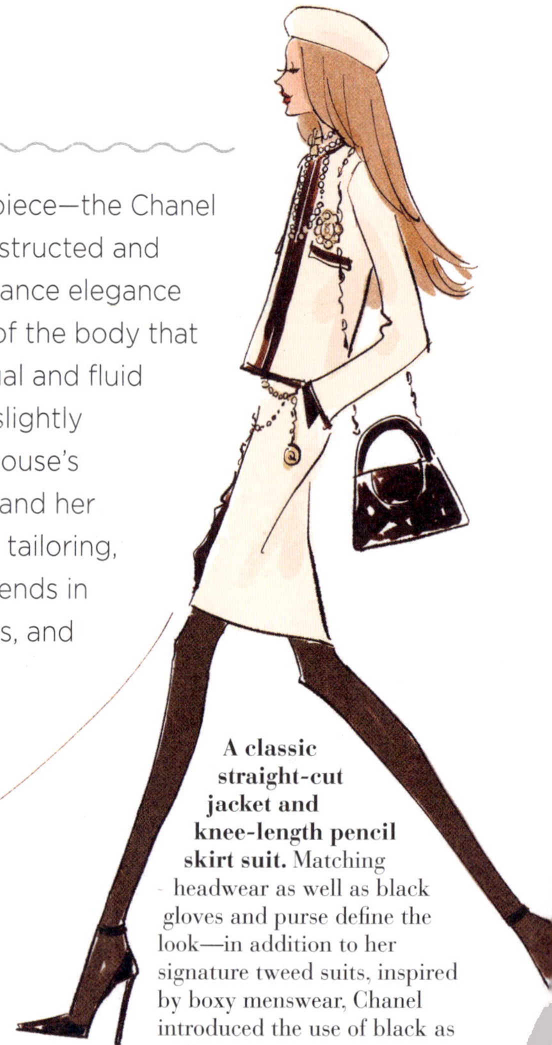

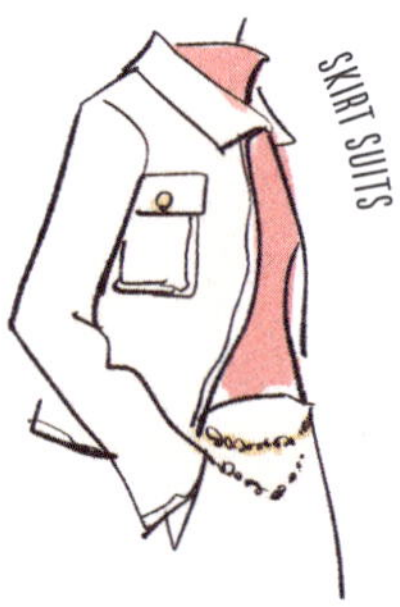

Quality materials like tweed bouclé and wool are the main play here. Also explore delicate houndstooth patterns, contrasting color combinations, and metallic threads for the tweed. Try using chic, fresh colors like red, pink, and purple on a classic monochrome base—black and white or beige would go perfectly with this aesthetic.

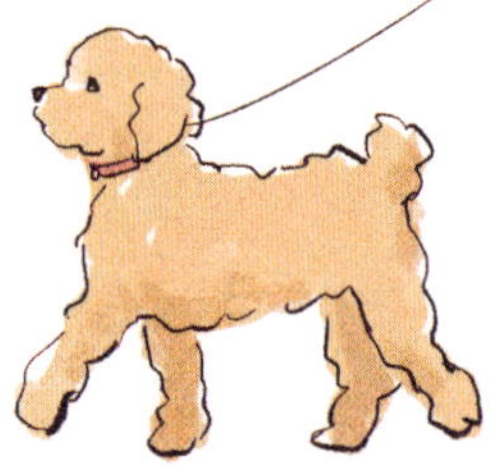

A classic straight-cut jacket and knee-length pencil skirt suit. Matching headwear as well as black gloves and purse define the look—in addition to her signature tweed suits, inspired by boxy menswear, Chanel introduced the use of black as a chic and modern choice of color for both day and night.

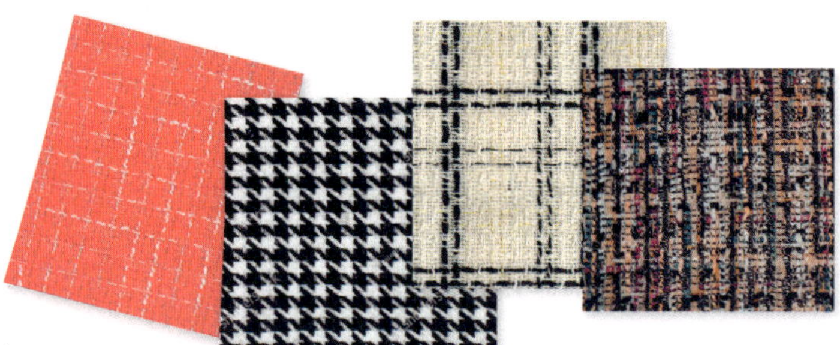

Many of the earlier Chanel suit designs were inspired by men's workwear. They share the beautiful details of motif buttons and trims on the pockets and hems. Pair them with the signature two-tone slingbacks to neutralize and unify the vibrant colors of your choice.

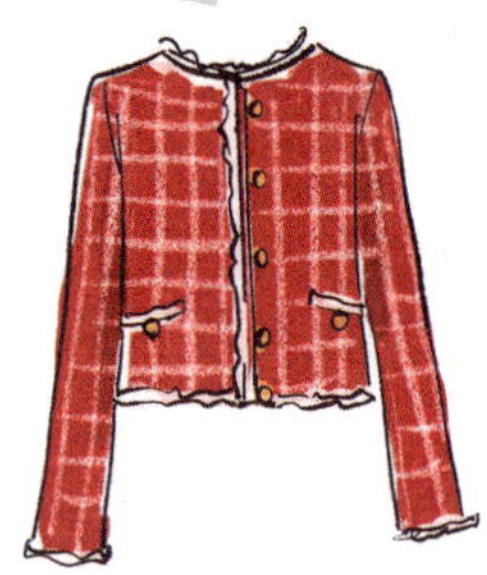

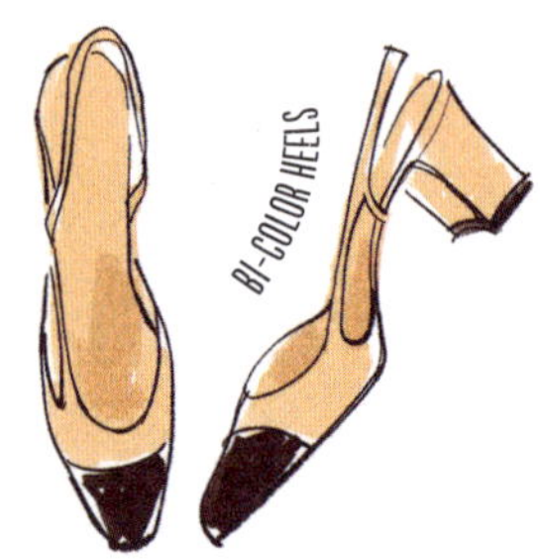

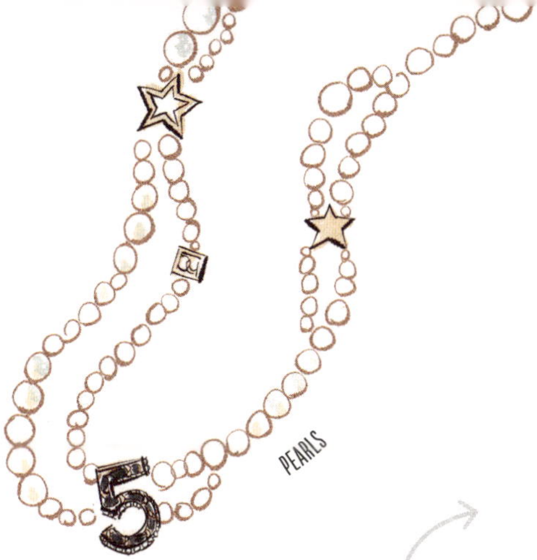

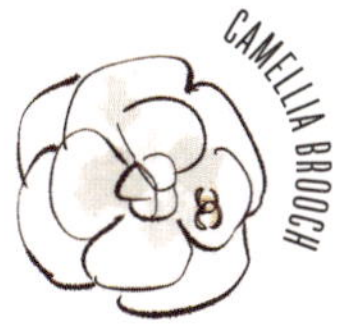

This oversize-fit blazer with big lapels and coordinated micromini bottom gives a modern, cute, androgynous vibe.

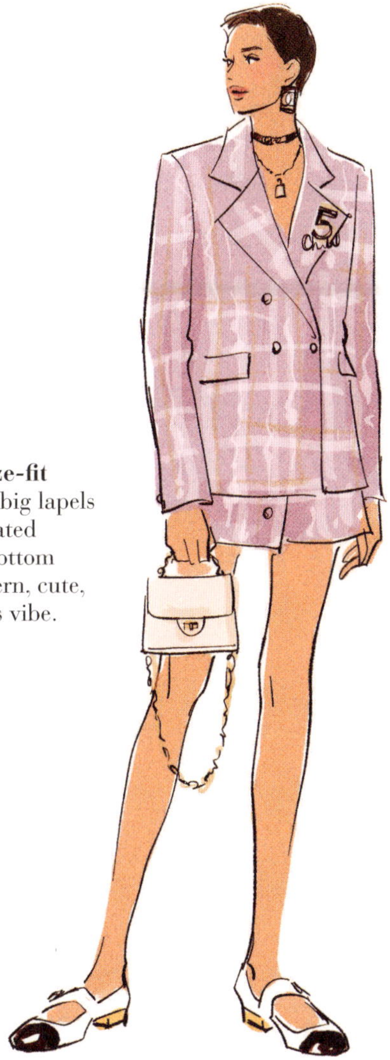

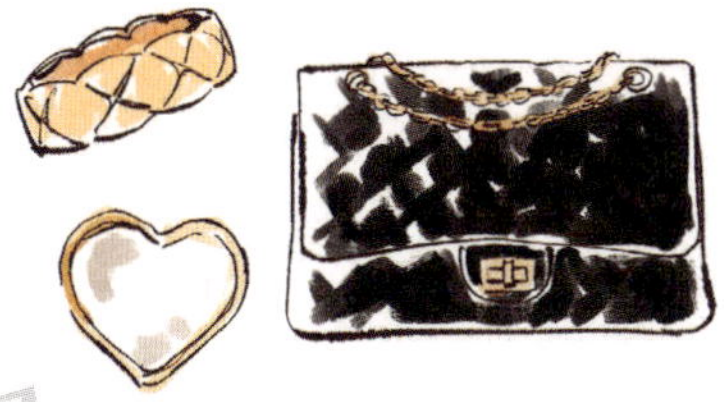

Chanel's philosophy of functionality also applied to accessories, which played a huge role in her classic aesthetic. The famous hands-free quilting chain bag that debuted in the 1950s and costume jewelry are Chanel essentials.

A masculine tuxedo look with plunging neckline, inspired by German-American actress Marlene Dietrich's signature style. The clean, simple lines of the jacket and pants make for a striking, androgynous look.

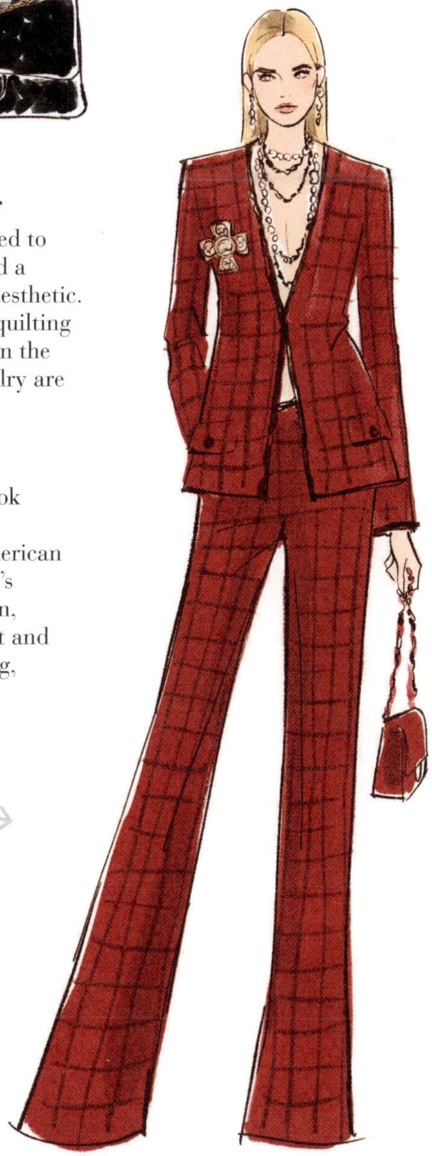

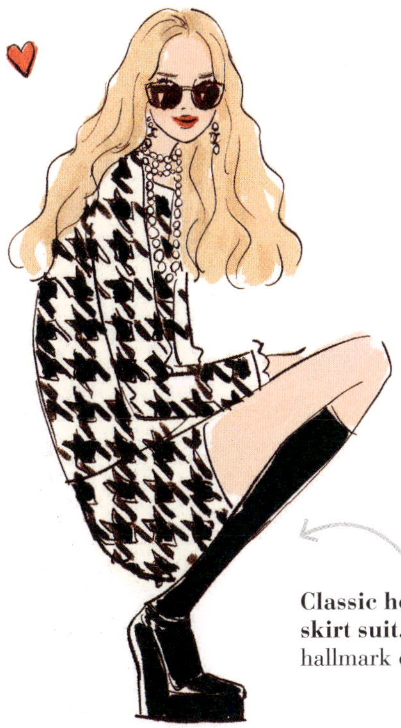

Classic houndstooth-patterned skirt suit. The pearl necklace is a hallmark of the house.

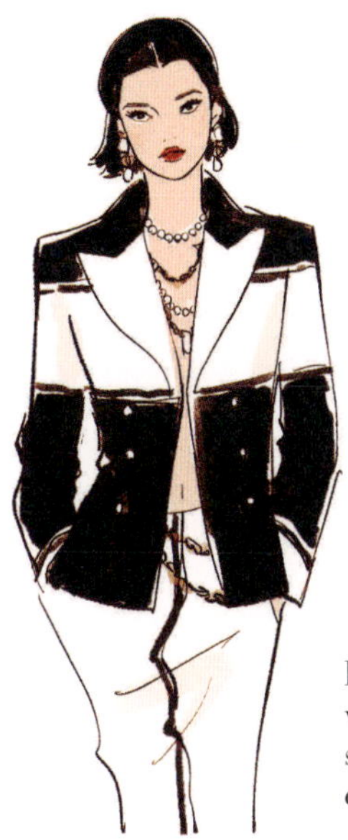

Perfectly tailored jackets can be paired with any bottoms, even jeans. Here, a bi-color structured jacket is paired with a tight-yet-comfortable white skirt.

TIMELESS CLASSICS by *Chloe Takahashi*

Style a classic tweed jacket to make it yours! Pick a jacket in the color of your choice as a starting point, then consider pairing it with items like jeans or a T-shirt to go modern and casual, a miniskirt and thigh-high leather boots to go a bit punk, an elongated jacket worn as a one-piece with a scarf to achieve Parisian chic, or whatever you like! Finally, add character by topping off the look with accessories—a mini bag in a pop of color, a pearl choker, or a matching boater, perhaps.

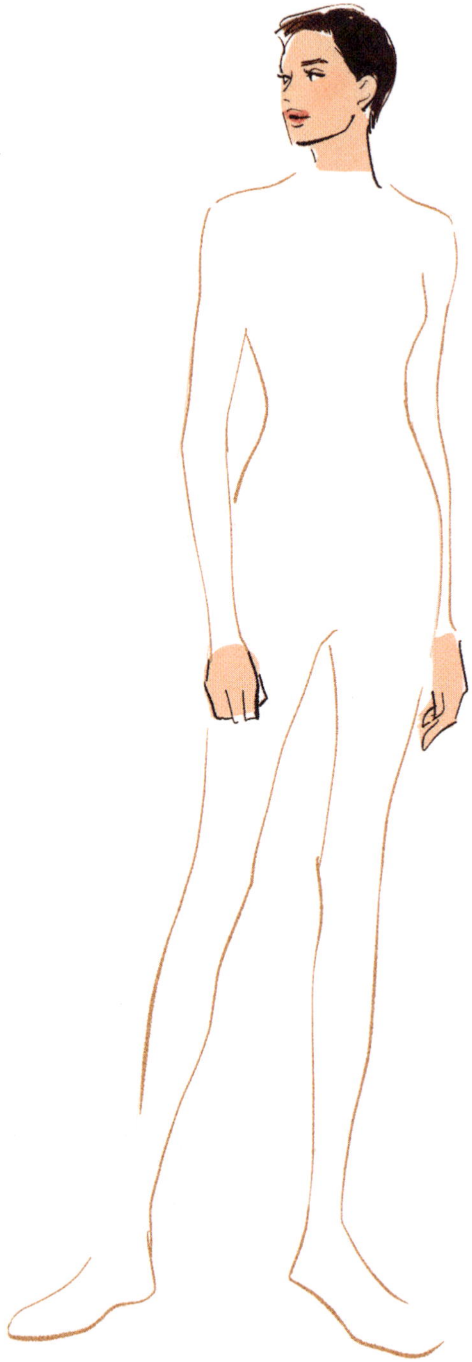

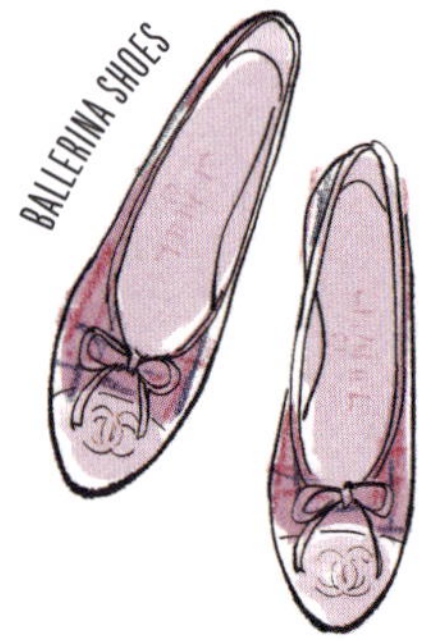

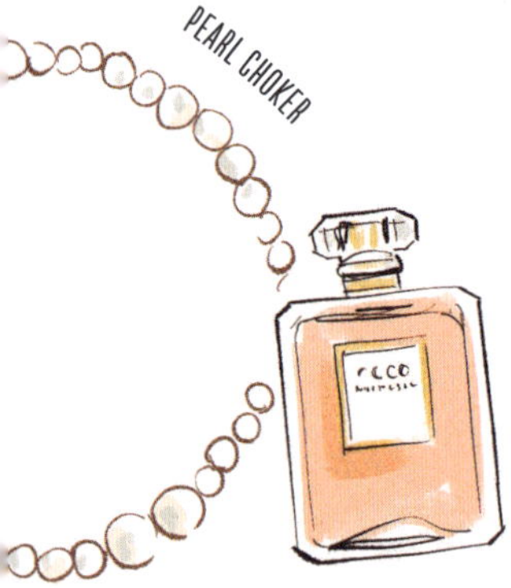

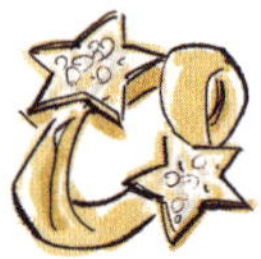

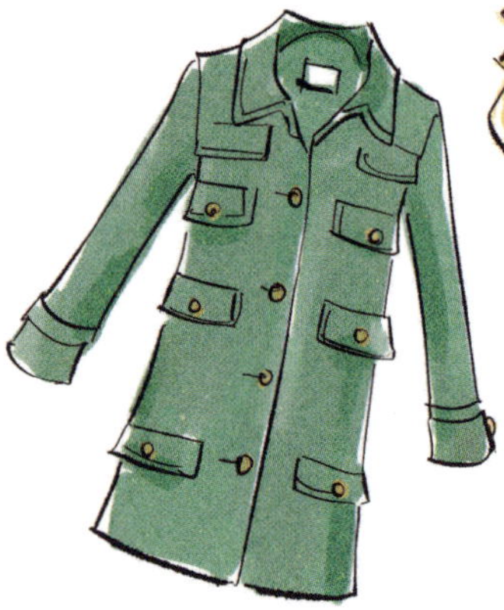

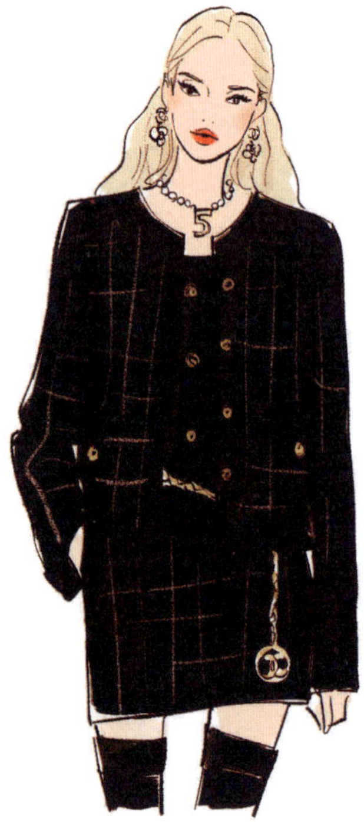

Now make a little tweak with classic tailoring and dress the figure in some different shapes. You can do separates, a large-collared one-piece, a relaxed-fit cardigan, a denim jacket, or go wild with your imagination! Pair with matching footwear, like two-toned boots or even cute rain boots, and add large statement jewelry, like brooches and bangles.

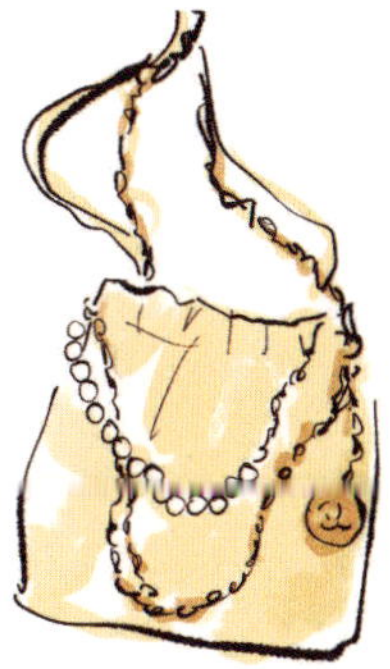

BRACELET WATCH

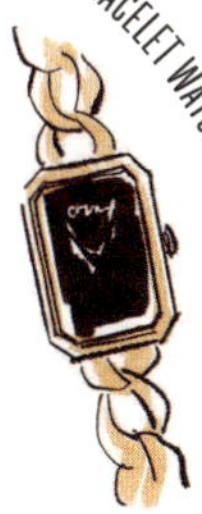

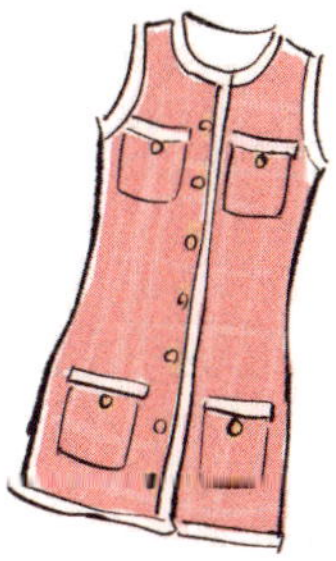

PRINTED DENIM

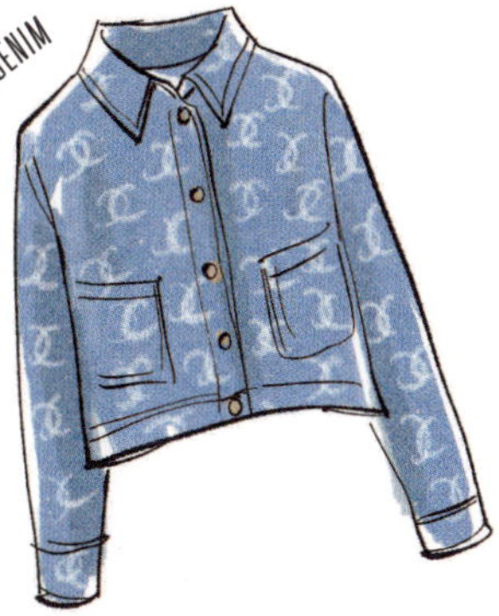

TWO PIECES

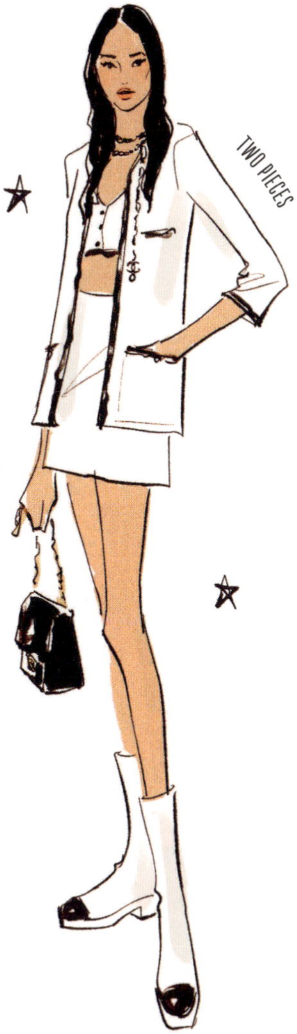

New Look

The "New Look" was a sensational and long-awaited return to ultra-femininity and opulence in women's fashion introduced by Christian Dior in the late 1940s. Dior reimagined the decorative and voluptuous dresses of the 1920s, creating modern, sophisticated pieces that liberated women from wartime restrictions and symbolized the rediscovery of prosperity. This was not merely a revival of the 1920s aesthetic, but an exclusive and glamorous new society. The most iconic ensembles from the New Look's debut were fitted "Bar" suits that celebrated women's curves, with raised bustlines, sloped shoulders, cinched waists, padded hips, and full A-line skirts. Dior's iconic pieces are forever classics still loved by new designers.

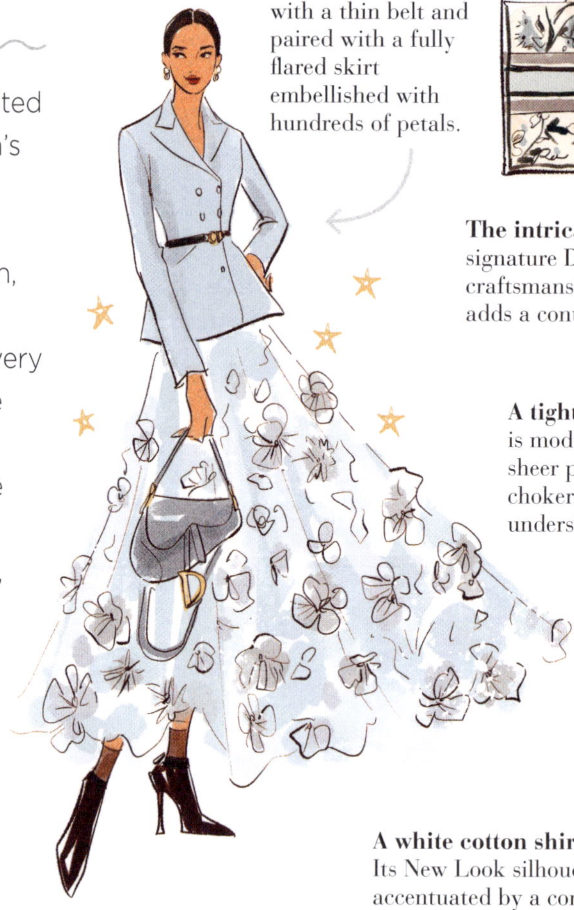

Dior's original notched-collar jacket, cinched in with a thin belt and paired with a fully flared skirt embellished with hundreds of petals.

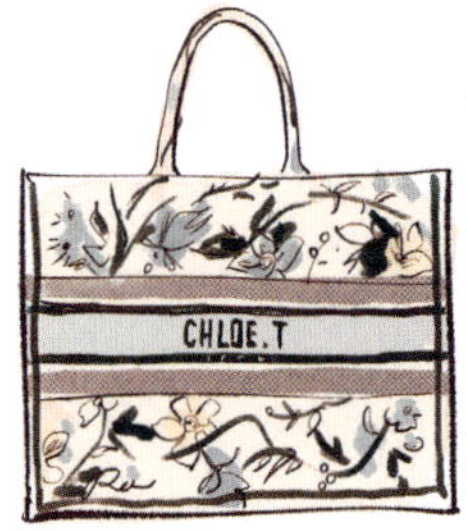

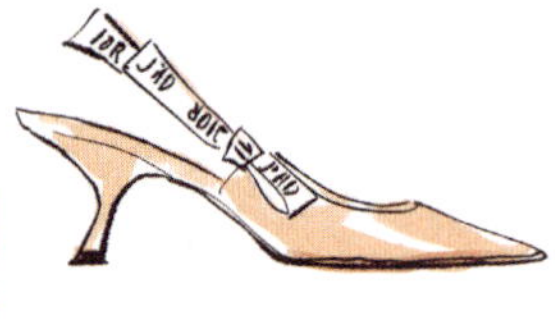

The intricate floral embroideries on the signature Dior Book Tote are true artisan craftsmanship, and its large, square shape adds a contemporary vibe to the classical look.

A tight-fitting bustier is modernized with a sheer polka-dot top, choker, and logo undershorts.

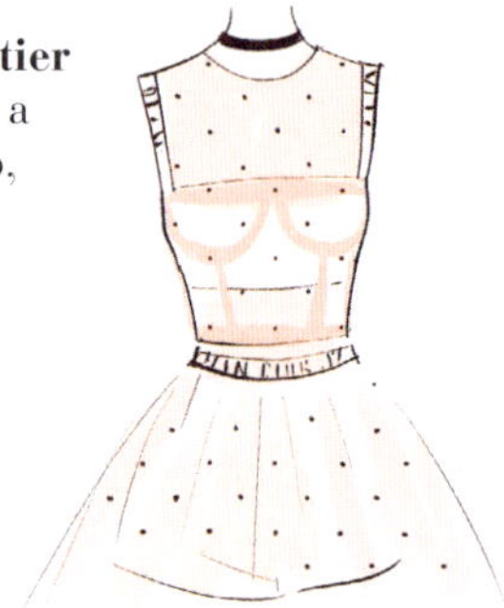

The New Look is all about luxury and abundance: Delicate materials like crepe, chiffon made of quality silk, brocades, laces, and sequins add an elegant touch to rich fabrics like wool and cashmere. Decadent patterns in cool shades, like Dior Gray, blush, beige, and dusty blue, create effortlessly chic garments.

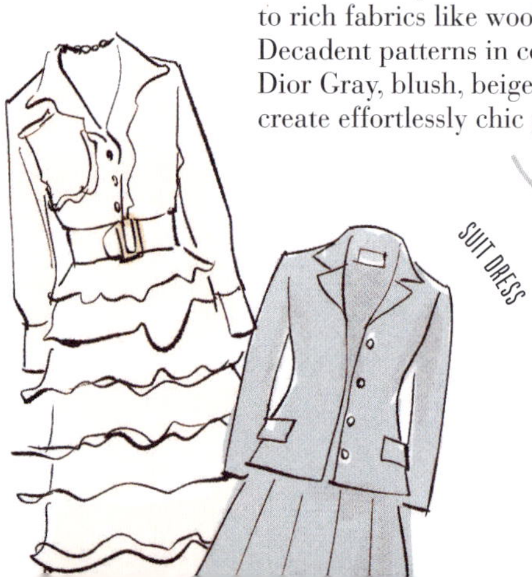

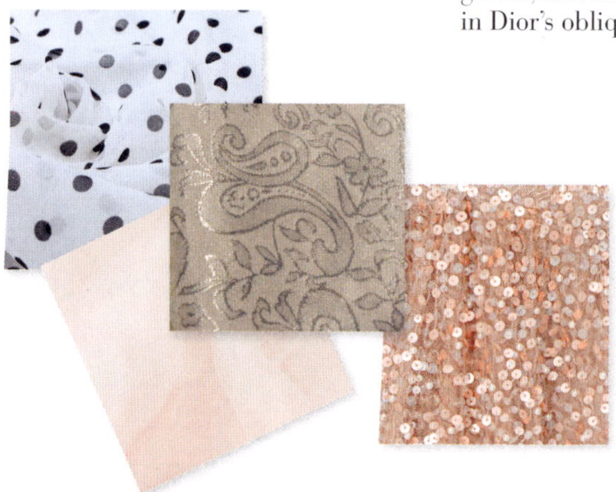

A white cotton shirt dress. Its New Look silhouette is accentuated by a corset, gloves, and a bucket hat in Dior's oblique pattern.

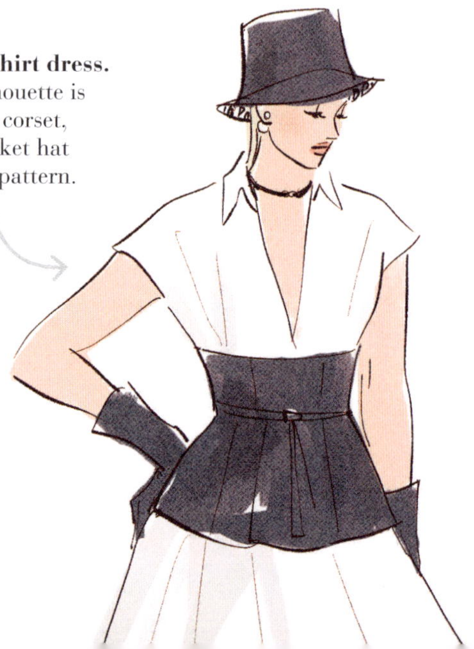

A modern look with an androgynous touch: A big, airy chiffon skirt with a masculine suit jacket and tie. This perfectly balanced yet unbalanced look is heightened by the feminine silhouette of the jacket, with exaggerated hips, and the edgy combat boots.

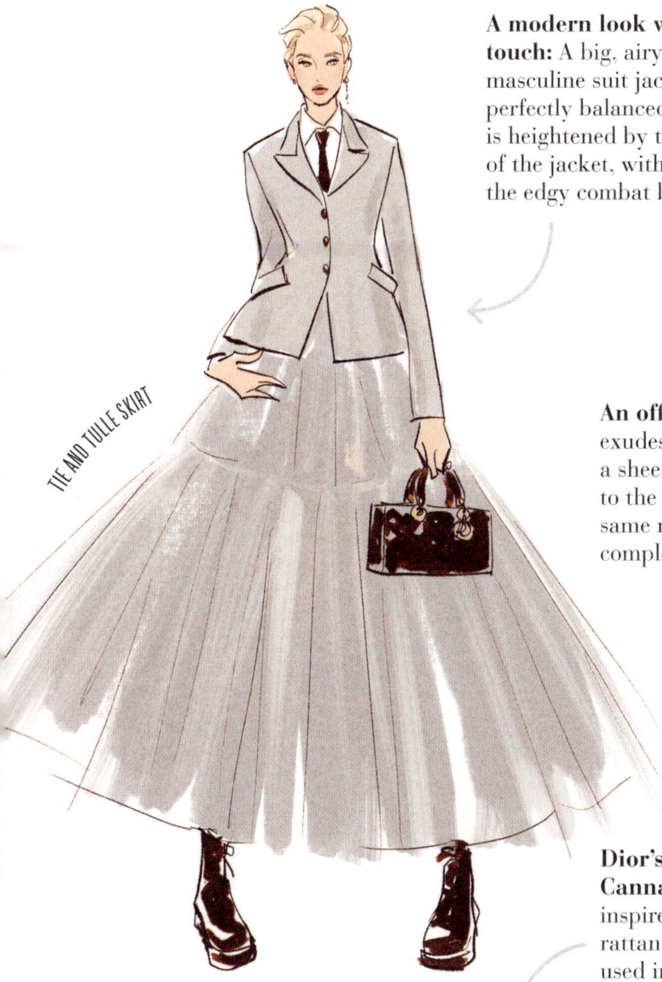

A veiled beret and choker make classic New Look outfits more playful and less conservative.

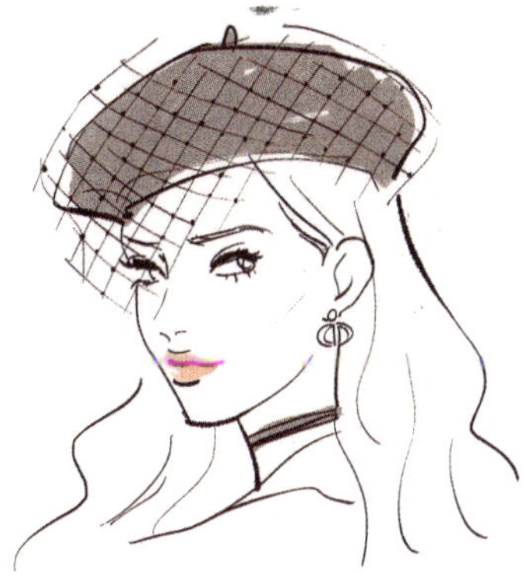

An off-the-shoulder jacket exudes glamour. Pair it with a sheer tulle skirt that falls to the ankles and heels in the same neutral color tones to complete this ladylike look.

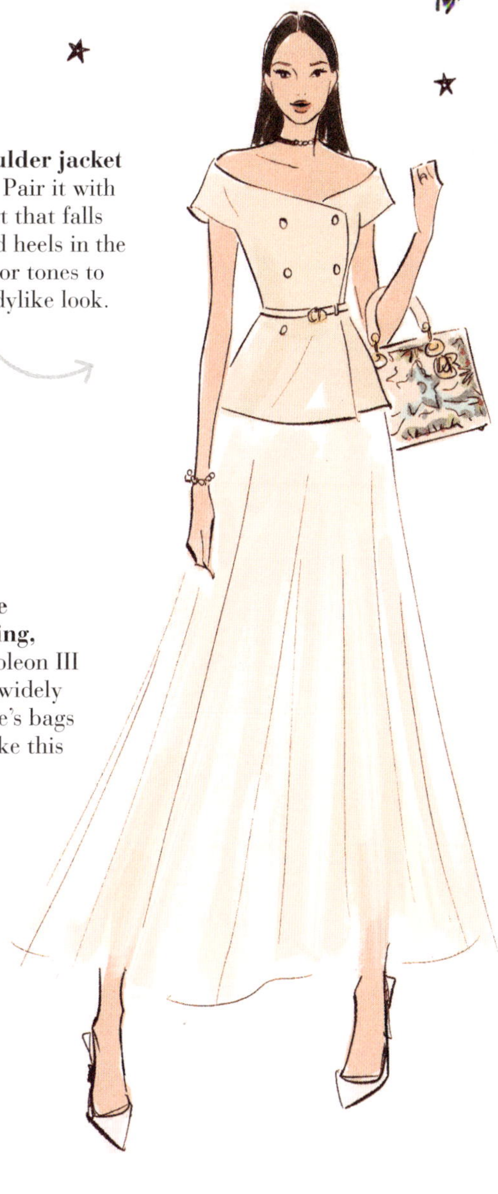

A gingham-print half-sleeve jacket suit offers a different take on the New Look and has a more active and playful feel, but a cropped jacket exaggerates the small waist and maintains elegance.

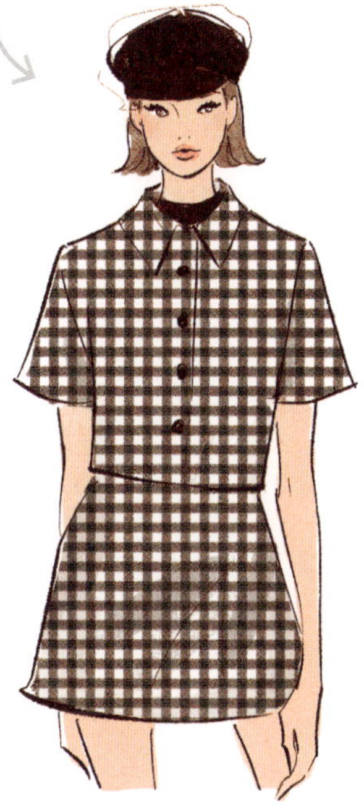

Dior's signature Cannage stitching, inspired by Napoleon III rattan chairs, is widely used in the house's bags and garments, like this Lady Dior bag.

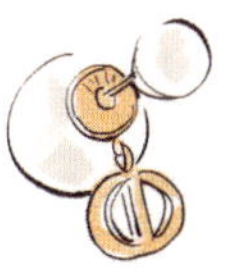

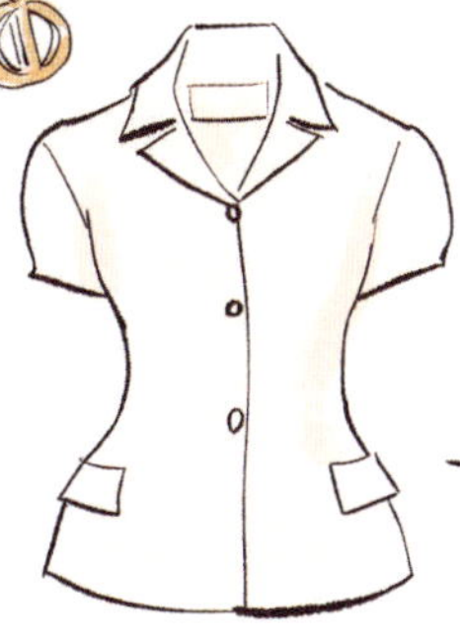

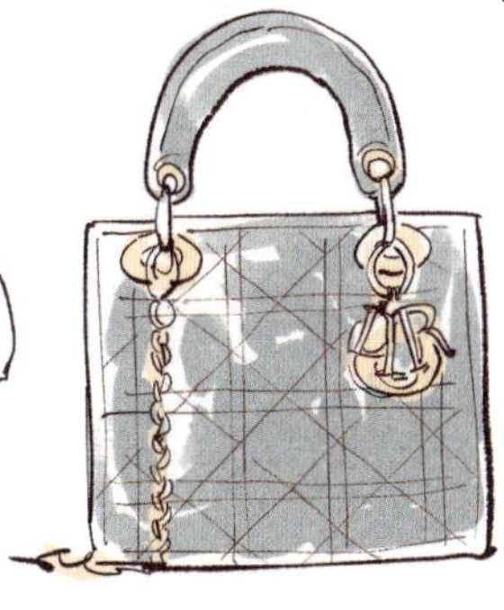

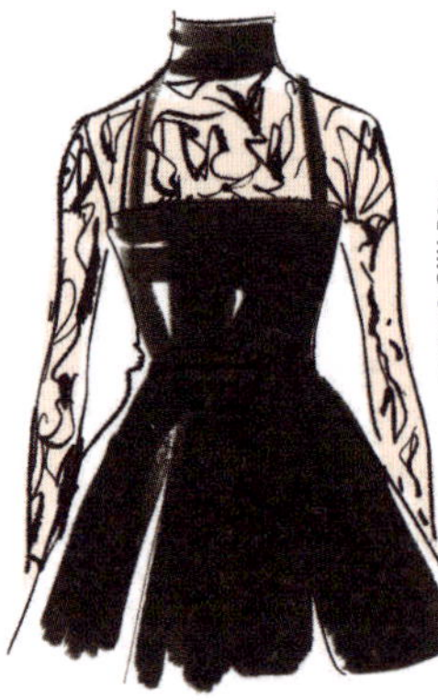

LACE AND ORGANZA

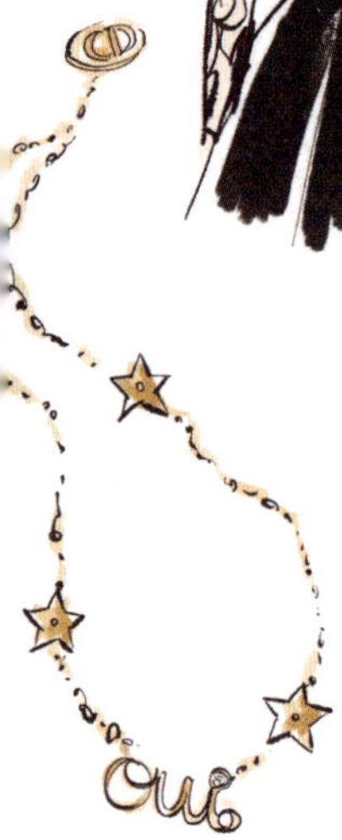

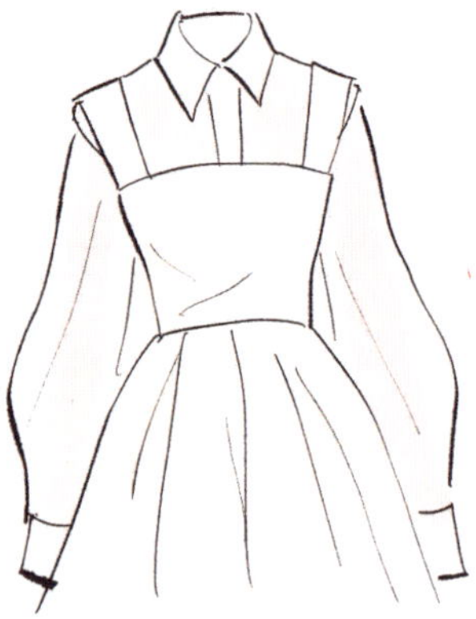

Let your imagination run riot and create your own elegant evening gown to rival Dior's finest pieces. First choose your fabric, then consider adding floral embellishments, rhinestones, sequins, or intricate laces. For the classic New Look silhouette, create a narrowed waist and voluptuous bottom, and finally add your finishing touches—some dainty jewelry, a statement purse, and matching heels.

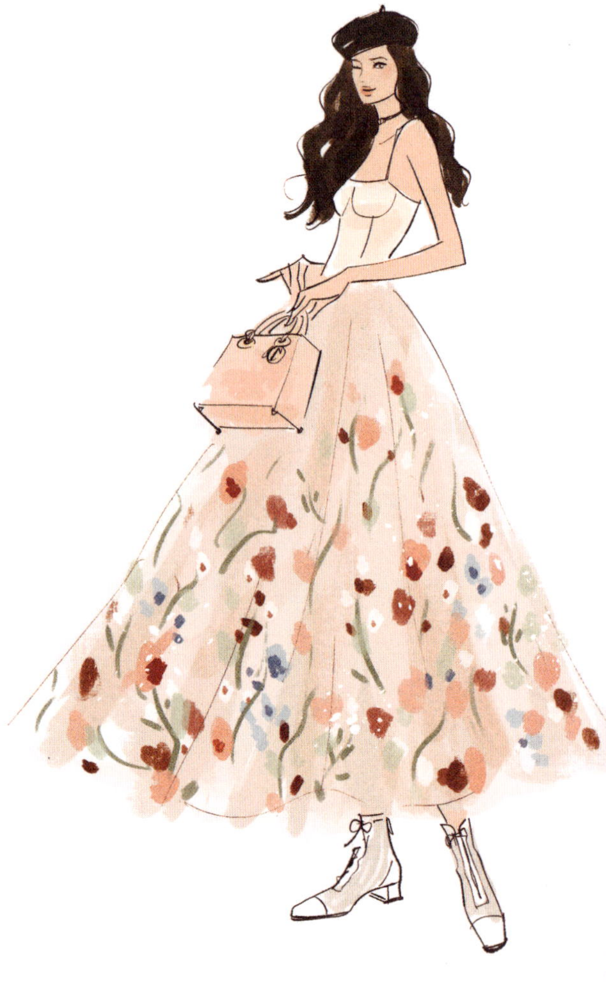

Now try to create a more rigid, androgynous outfit, combining elements of the New Look with masculine fashion. Maybe choose a top in muted colors like khaki, gray, black, or navy, then add items like a skirt with crisp box drapes, a button-down, sneakers, ties, or a wide-brimmed hat to complement it. Do you want to add a military flavor, or a rock-and-roll twist? The choice is yours!

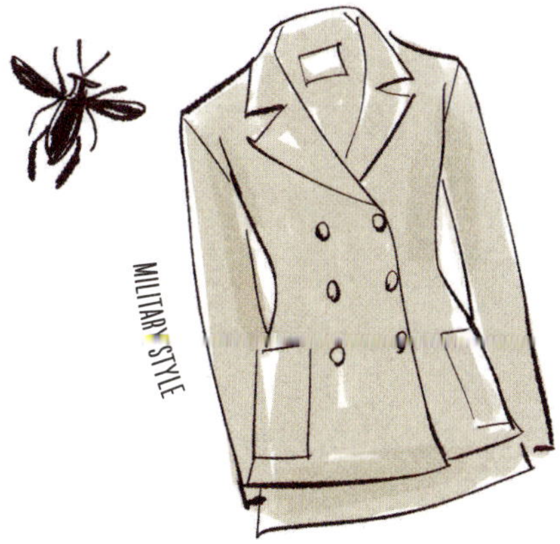

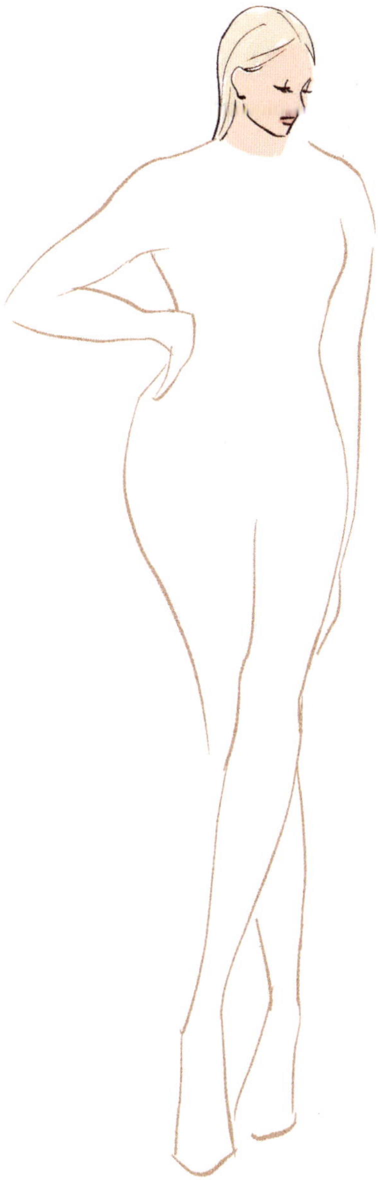

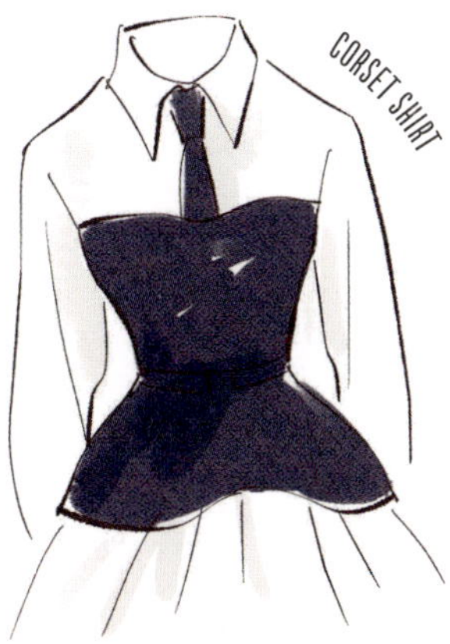

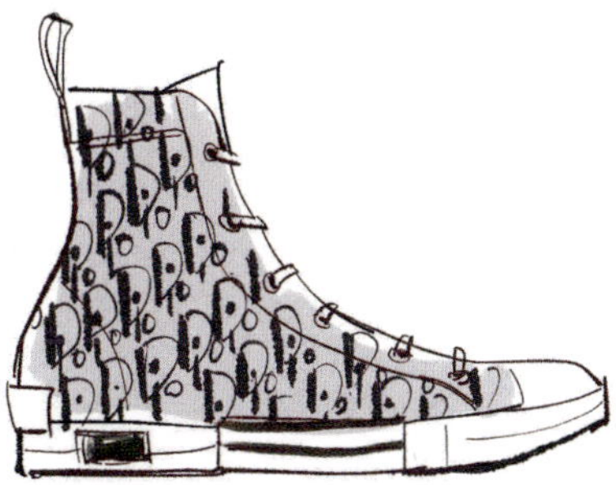

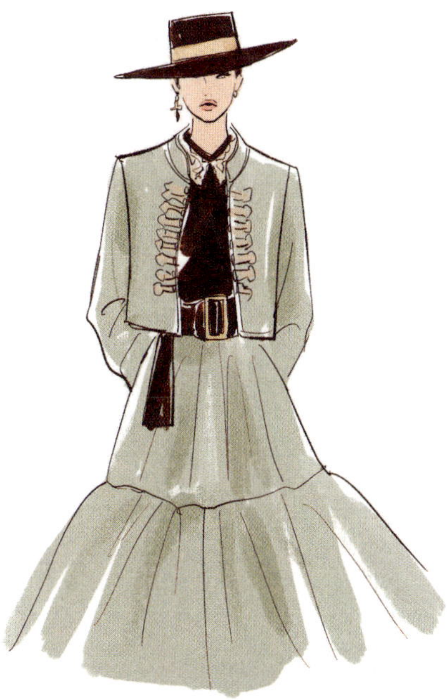

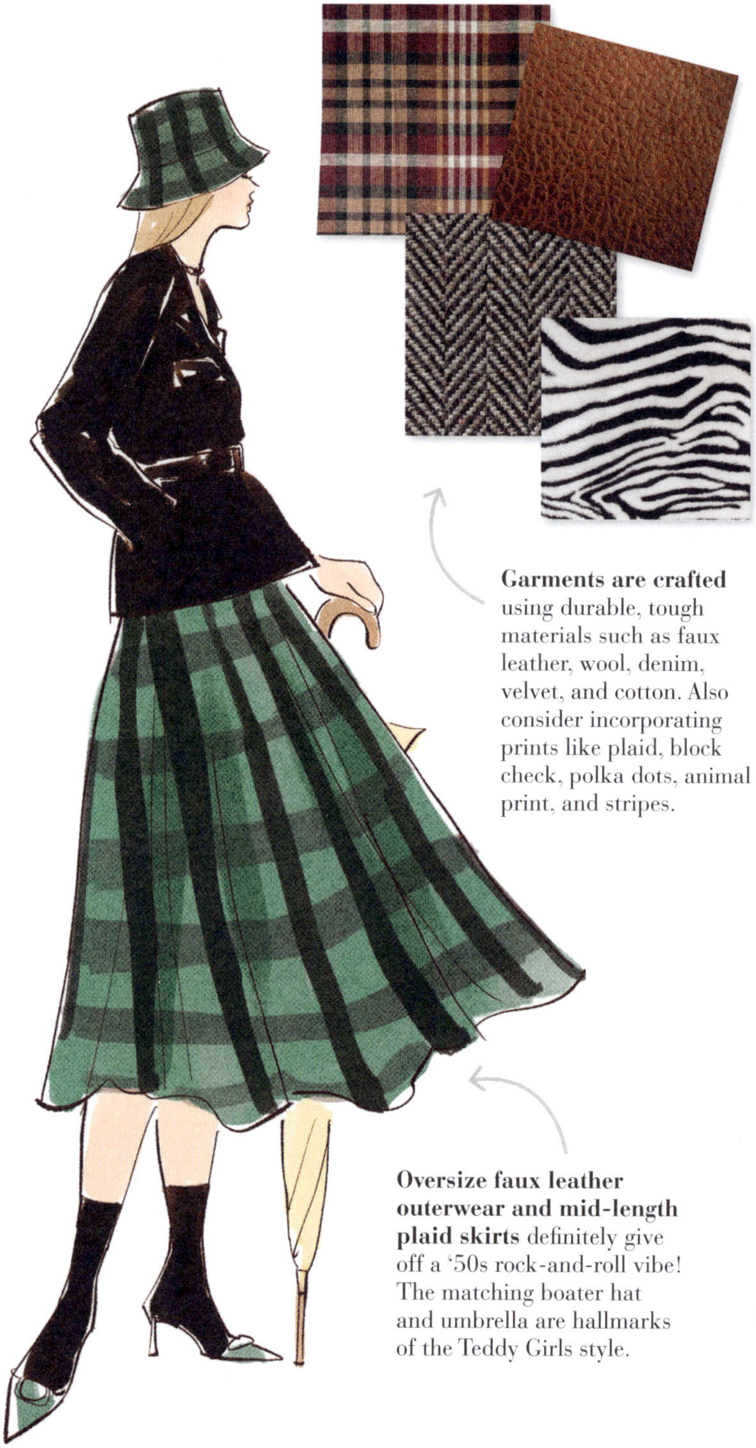

Edwardian Rock and Roll

Edwardian rock and roll emerged in the 1950s as a youthful and playful mash-up of the dandy Edwardian fashions from the early 1900s and the style of emerging American rock-and-roll stars like Elvis Presley. The "Teddy Girls" played an important role in this subculture, from which today's rockers and punks can trace back their origin. Teddy Girls styling was a classic-yet-contemporary mix of preppy and rocker. They dressed tomboy-like and fearlessly, in the spirit of postwar revival. They wore items like tailored jackets with velvet collars, ties, pencil skirts, rolled-up jeans, and pegged pants. In later years, Edwardian rock and roll became more heavily influenced by American 1950s popular fashion, such as full circle skirts and cropped pants, adding more fun variety to the look!

Garments are crafted using durable, tough materials such as faux leather, wool, denim, velvet, and cotton. Also consider incorporating prints like plaid, block check, polka dots, animal print, and stripes.

Oversize faux leather outerwear and mid-length plaid skirts definitely give off a '50s rock-and-roll vibe! The matching boater hat and umbrella are hallmarks of the Teddy Girls style.

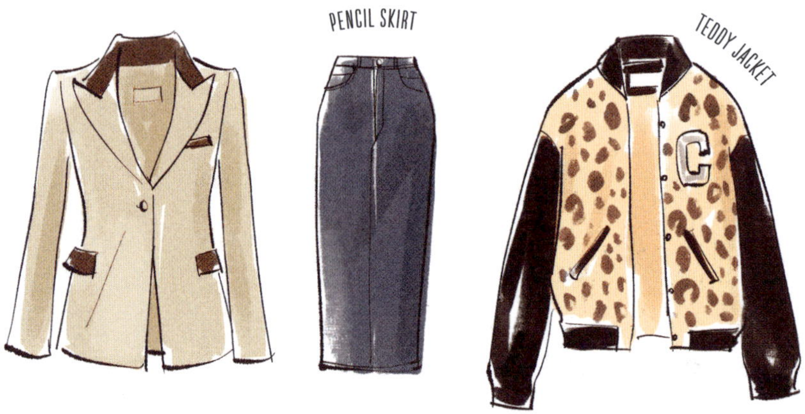

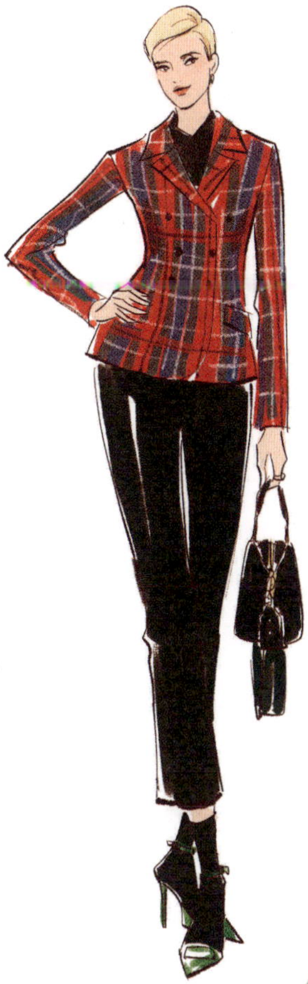

A red-and-green plaid tailored jacket makes the statement. You don't need to add much more—just pair it with simple leather cropped pants, socks, and kitten heels.

CAT-EYE SUNGLASSES

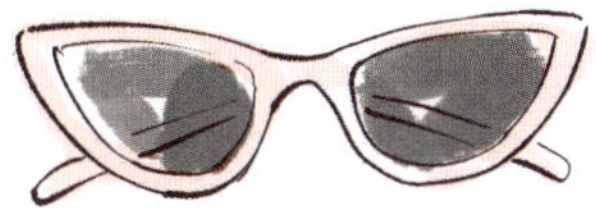

TEDDY BOY

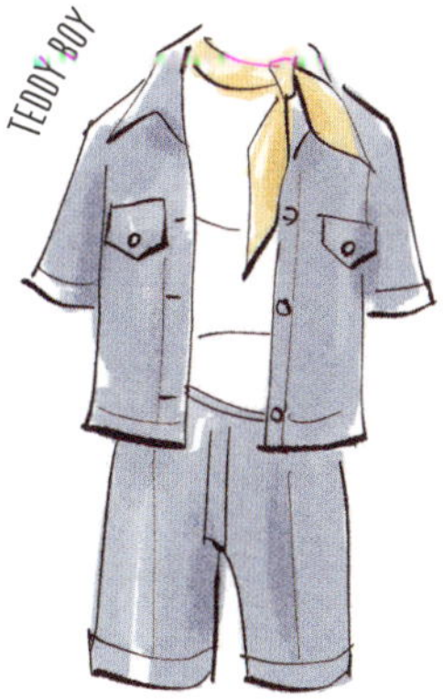

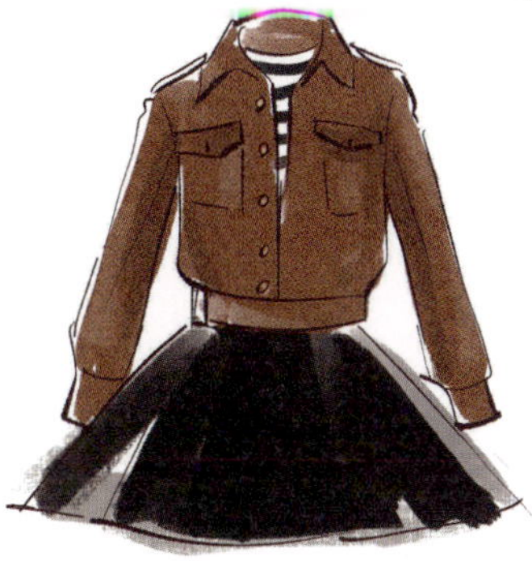

This androgynous suit is pure Edwardian rock and roll! Drape flowy outerwear over shoulders and style hair in a quiff to avoid looking too preppy.

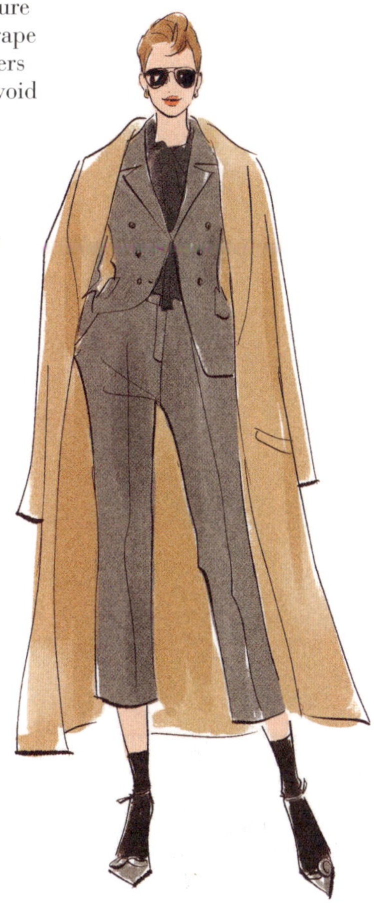

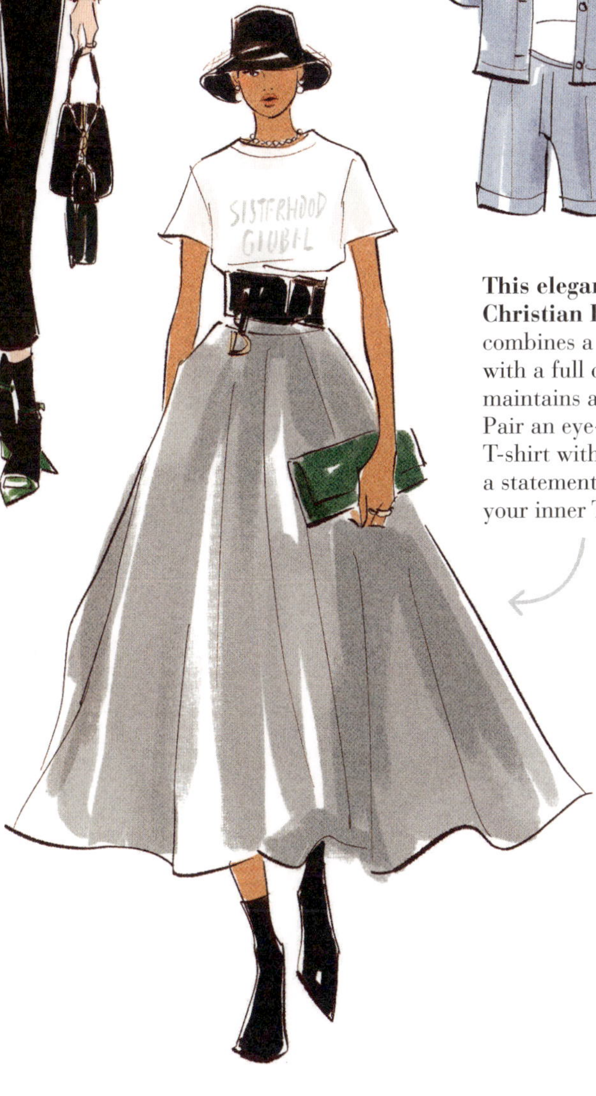

This elegant look by Christian Dior that combines a casual T-shirt with a full circle skirt maintains a tomboy feel. Pair an eye-catching slogan T-shirt with heavy boots and a statement belt to channel your inner Teddy Girl.

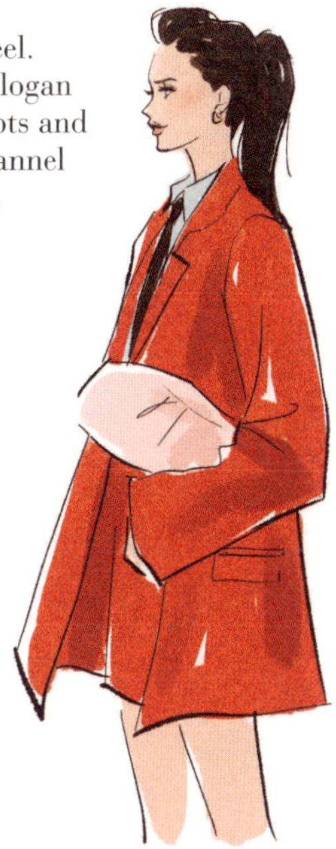

A ponytail and an oversize blazer with a tie is a signature American rock-and-roll style.

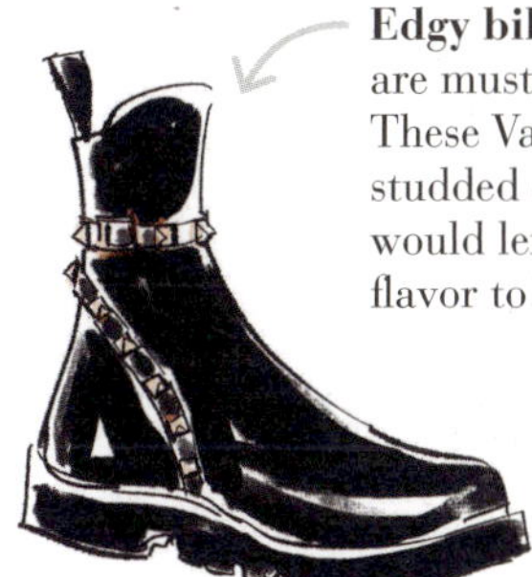

Edgy biker boots are must-haves! These Valentino studded combat boots would lend a rock flavor to any outfit.

Reimagine Edwardian rock and roll for the runway! Draw and dress your own croquis. Start with iconic Teddy Girl items like tailored suits, blouses with ties, pencil skirts, or cropped pants, then throw on some fun additions—a fur coat, sequin jumper, metallic or feather skirt, or studded heels. Don't forget to add a red lip and smudged eyeliner for a fierce look!

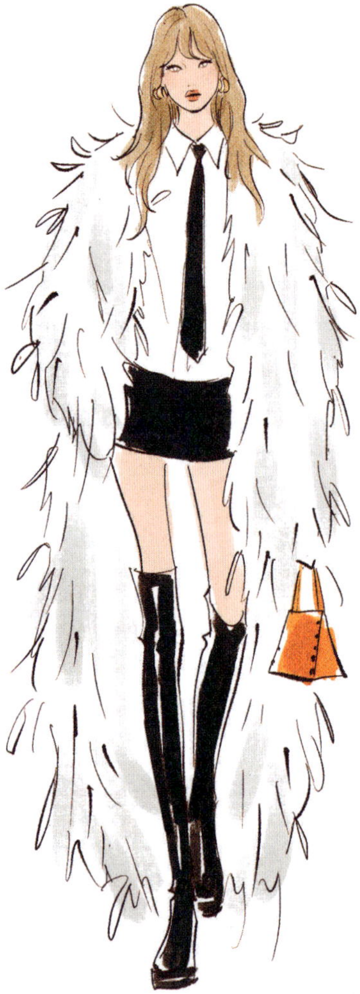

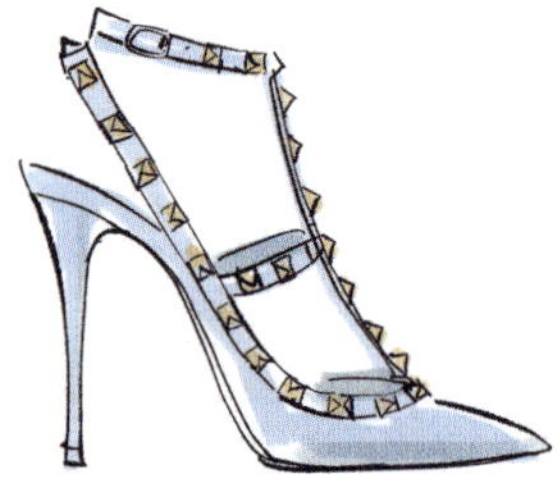

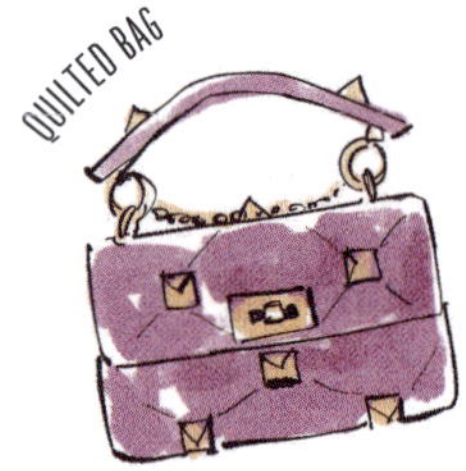

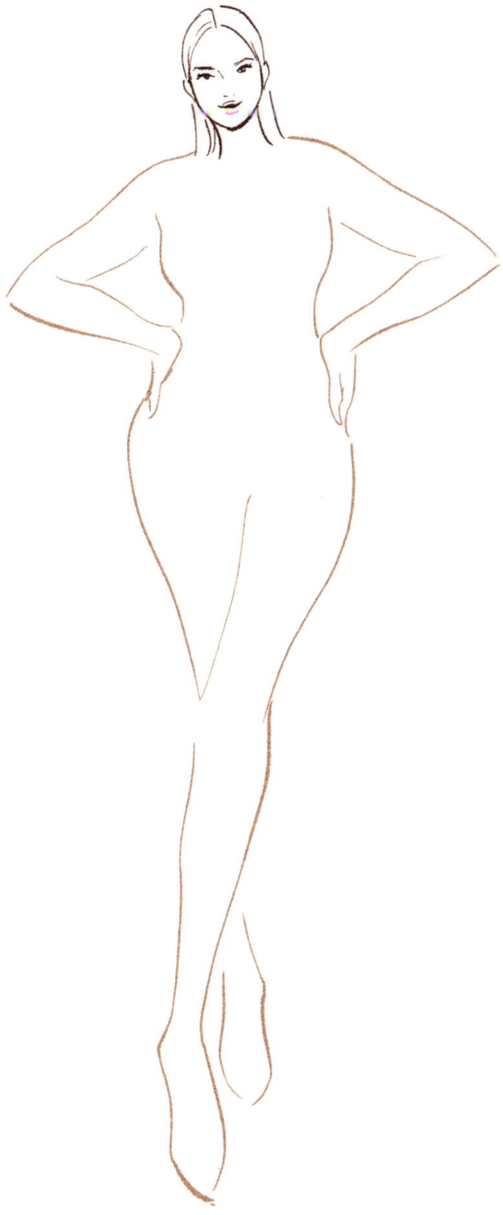

Let's get this model ready to dance the night away! This time take inspiration from '50s American rock-and-roll style. Will you give her a full-skirt dress, leather jeans with a bustier, or a glittery minidress? Play with accessories like a rhinestone choker, brooch, belt, pointy sunglasses, or scarf. For a cute mini-circle dress, like the inspiration below, find a good balance by pairing it with edgy items!

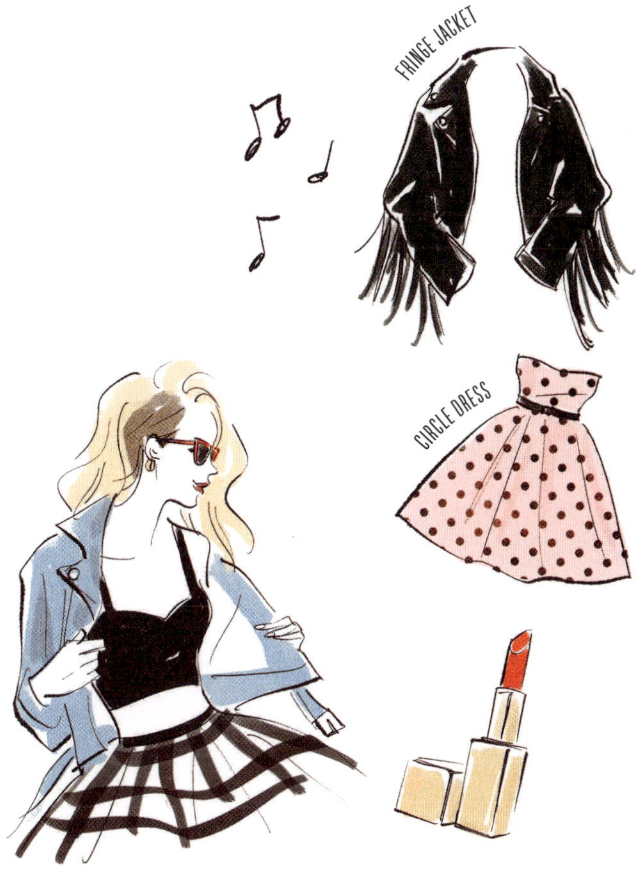

French Elegance

French Elegance is a sleek, sophisticated, and classic style that celebrates simple beauty. Luxury French fashion house Yves Saint Laurent (YSL) has driven this category. Their looks take the best of femininity and masculinity, casual and formal wear, glamour and edge, combining elements of each harmoniously in a single outfit; for example, a menswear-inspired tuxedo or slacks worn with a sheer organza blouse. Understated tones, silky smooth fabrics, and timeless silhouettes define French Elegance.

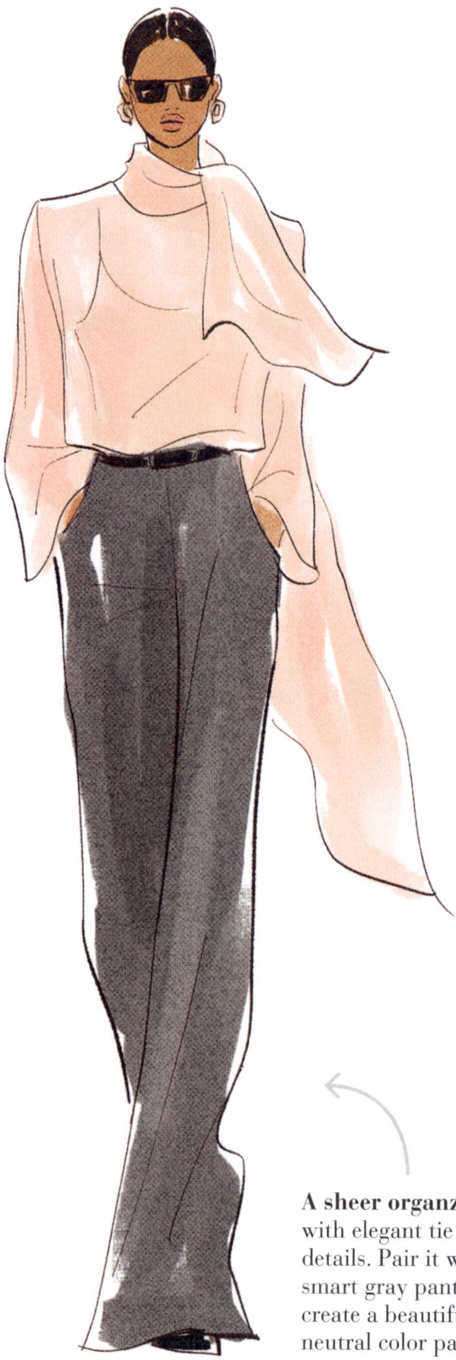

Explore different neutral colors, including black, white, beige, brown, and blush, and maintain tonal harmony while introducing subtle pops of colors like dark dusty blue, bordeaux, and khaki. Create contrasts between heavy and delicate fabrics like silk, leather, and faux fur.

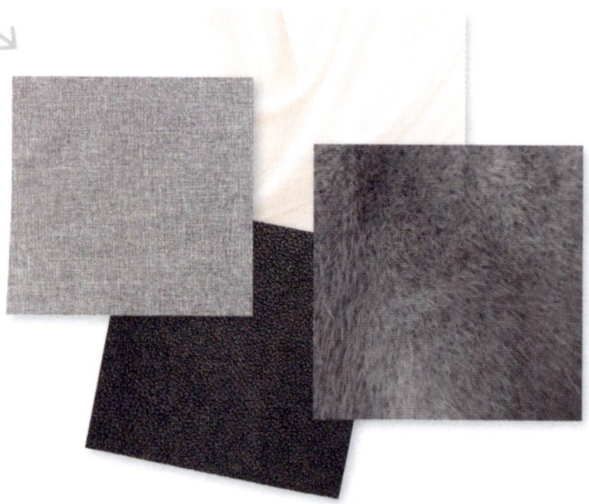

Notice the contrast between a heavy leather jacket and an airy silk maxi dress here, inspired by a classic Yves Saint Laurent look—so refined!

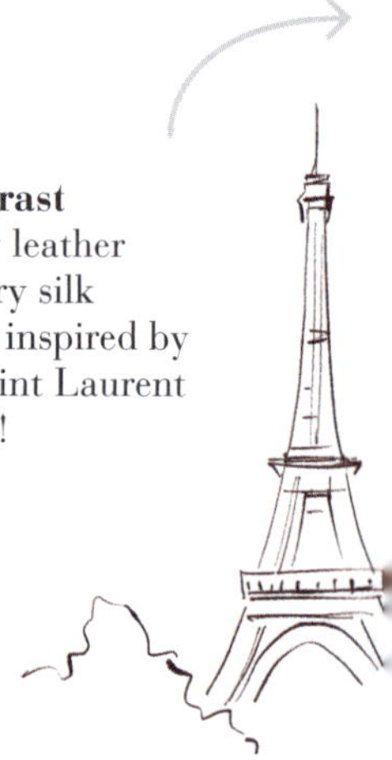

Edgy-yet-elegant accessories, like a chain clutch bag, gloves, or metallic earrings, elevate simple outfits.

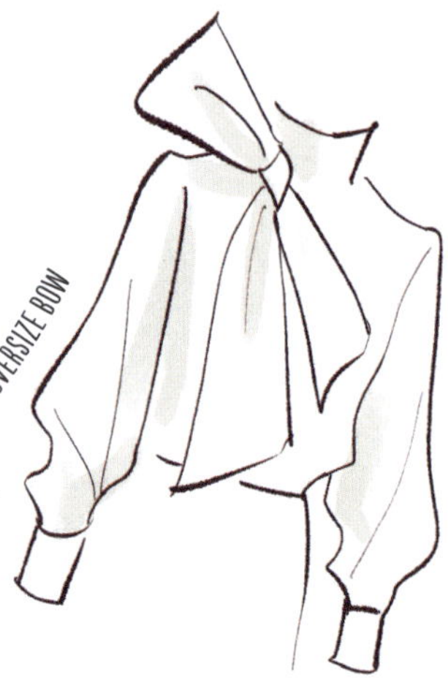

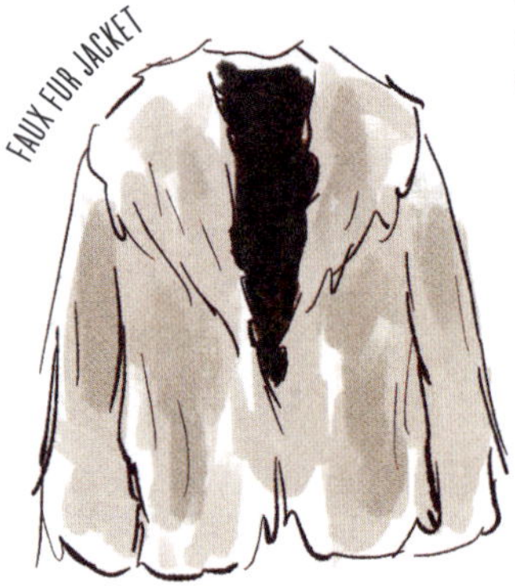

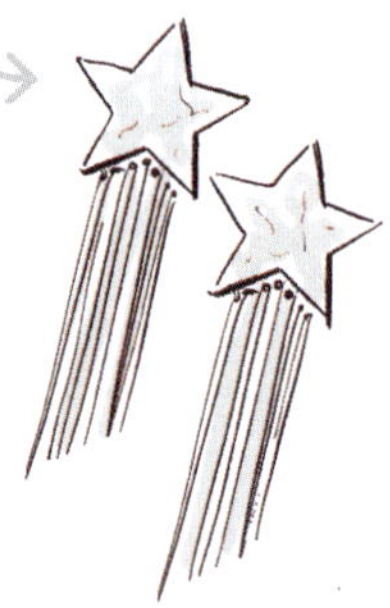

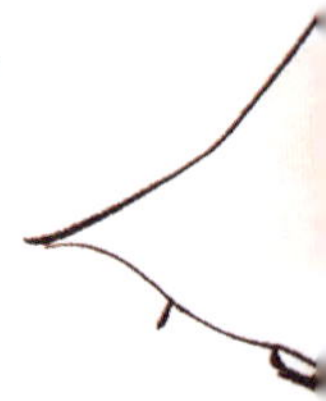

A sheer organza top with elegant tie details. Pair it with smart gray pants to create a beautiful neutral color palette.

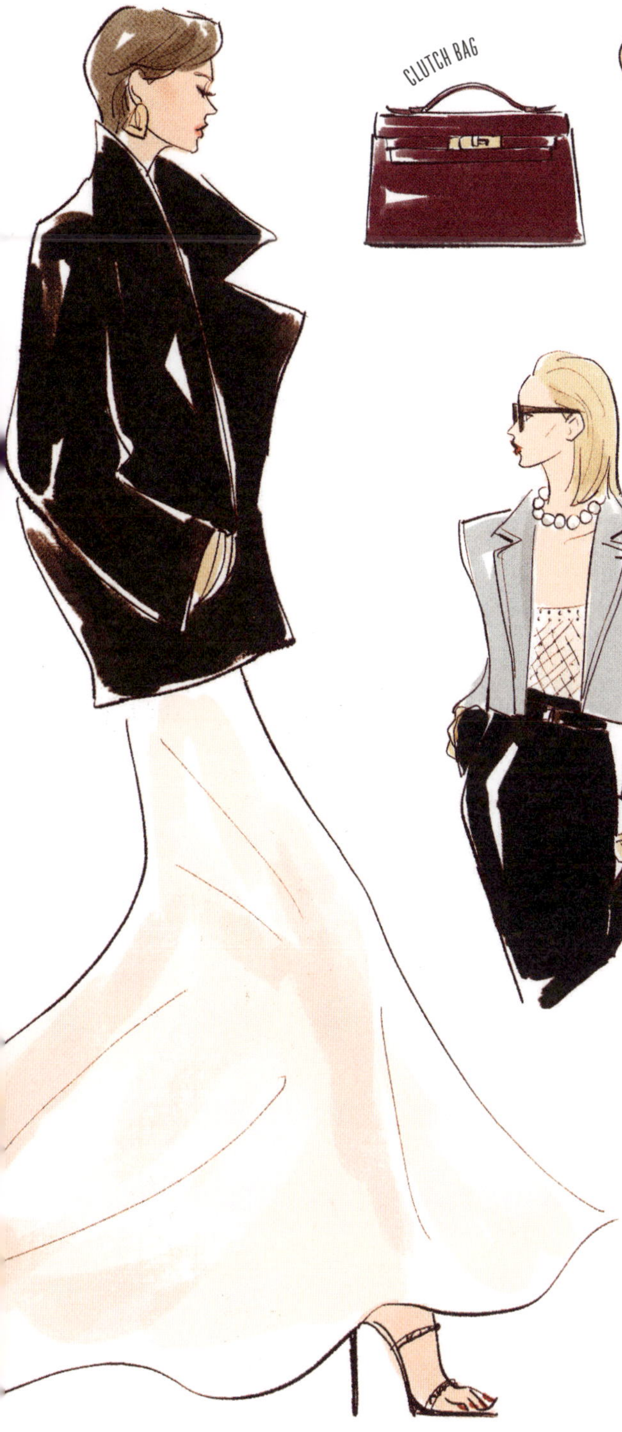

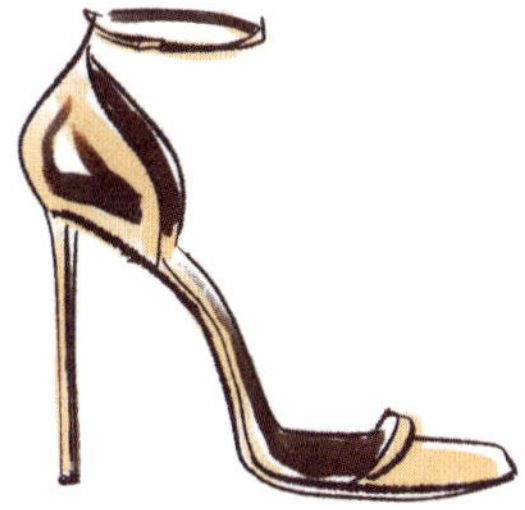

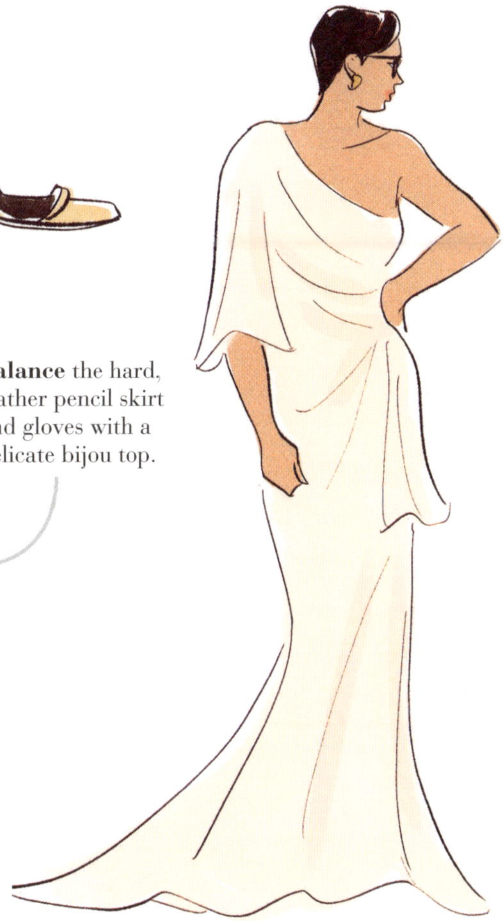

A minimal hairdo and edgy makeup complement this goddess-like gown, with its Grecian drapes and rich fabrics.

Balance the hard, leather pencil skirt and gloves with a delicate bijou top.

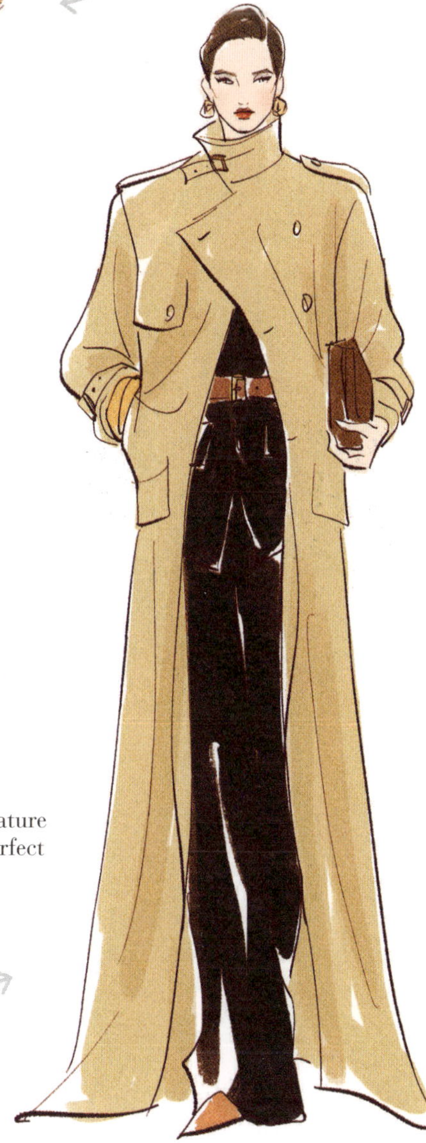

A khaki long coat influenced by YSL's signature safari jacket style is a perfect example of understated, casual elegance.

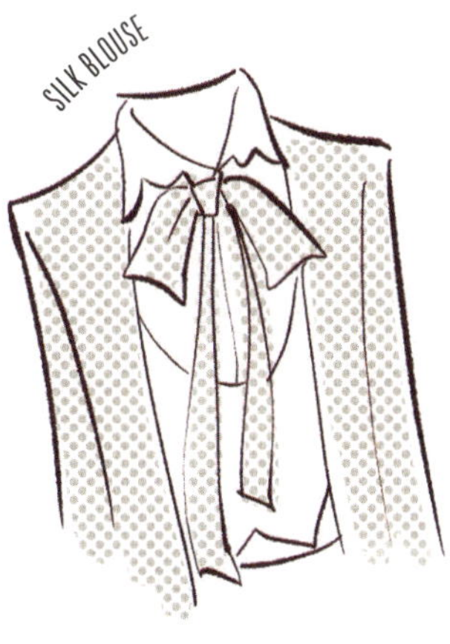

Create your own elegant evening look. What is your dream cocktail dress? Use clean, classic lines and keep it simple. Once you've drawn the dress, add strappy sandals or pumps and some sparkly jewelry. You can go extra edgy with gelled all-back hair or black shades and gloves. Add a dramatic outerwear, like a long wool coat with a big lapel, a leather jacket, or a faux fur coat!

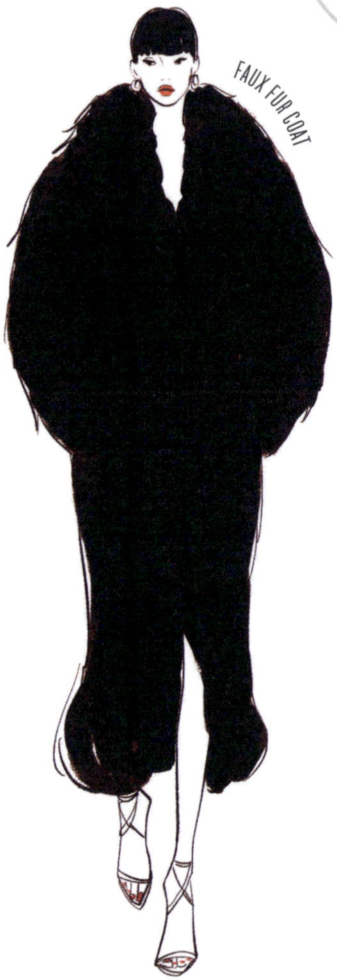

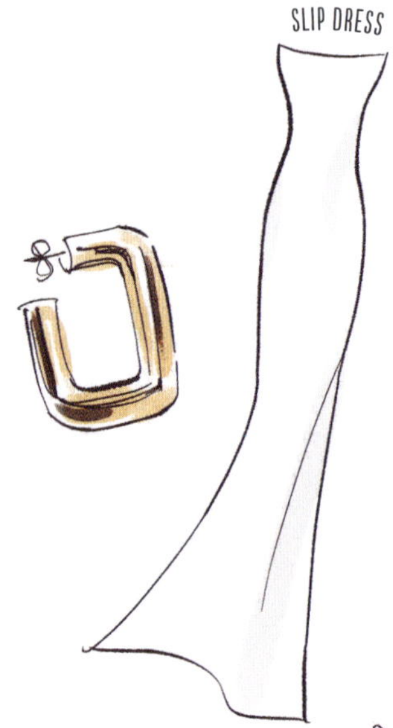

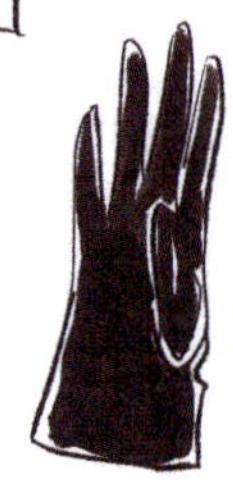

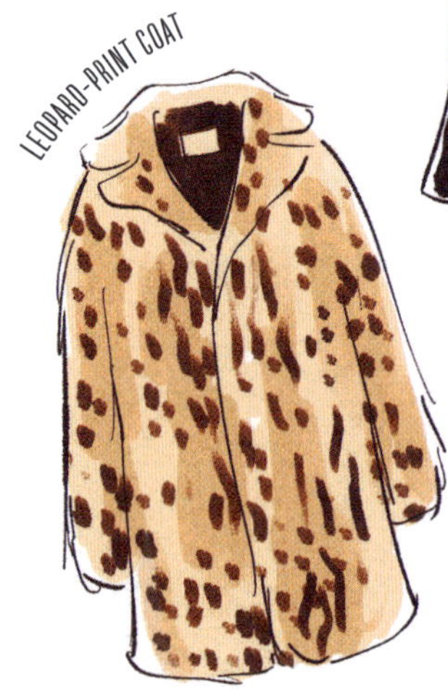

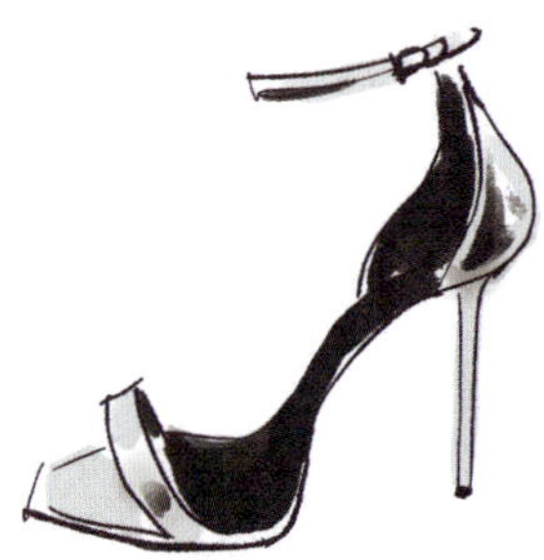

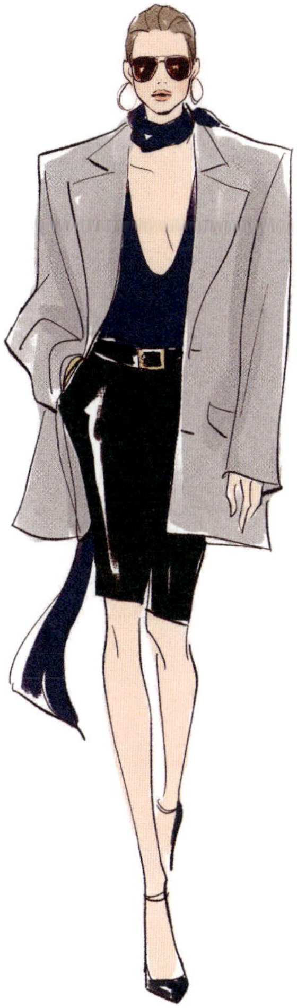

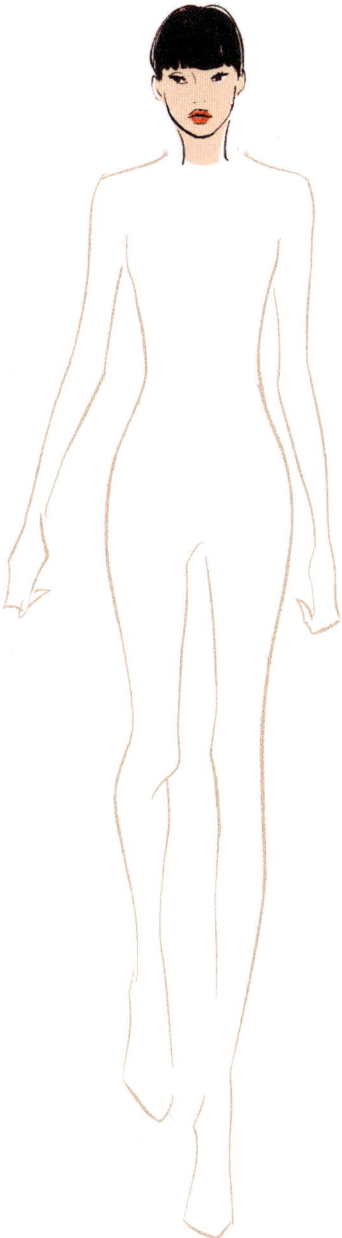

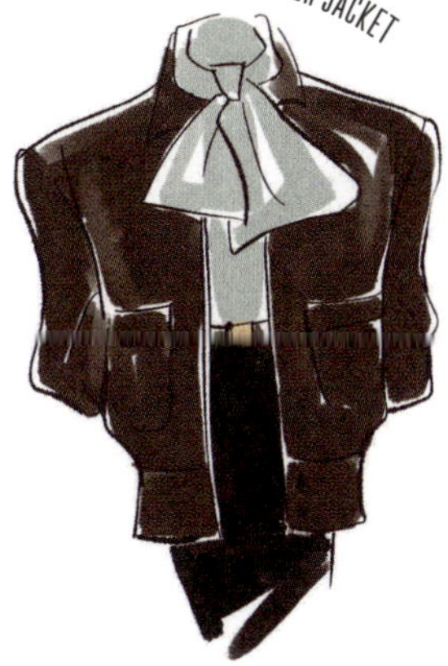

This model is getting ready to go watch a Paris Fashion Week show. The inspiration has an office-inspired look, featuring an oversize blazer, dark-toned draped top, and pencil skirt. How would you like to style her?

Preppy

Preppy fashion arose in America in the early 19th century and swiftly gained popularity as a symbol of affluence among those who frequented private preparatory schools and Ivy League institutions. It was inspired by such school uniforms, as well as upper-class leisure activities like polo, tennis, and rugby. Blazers, crisp button-downs, varsity jackets, polo shirts, and loafers became wardrobe essentials. Characterized by its timeless elegance and a fusion of tradition and casual flair, the fundamental elements of the preppy style have remained unwavering and still exert a strong presence in today's fashion.

A sweater vest, chino shorts, and sports socks make the iconic preppy look that never goes out of style. Definitely play with accessories like a baseball cap in a traditional look like this!

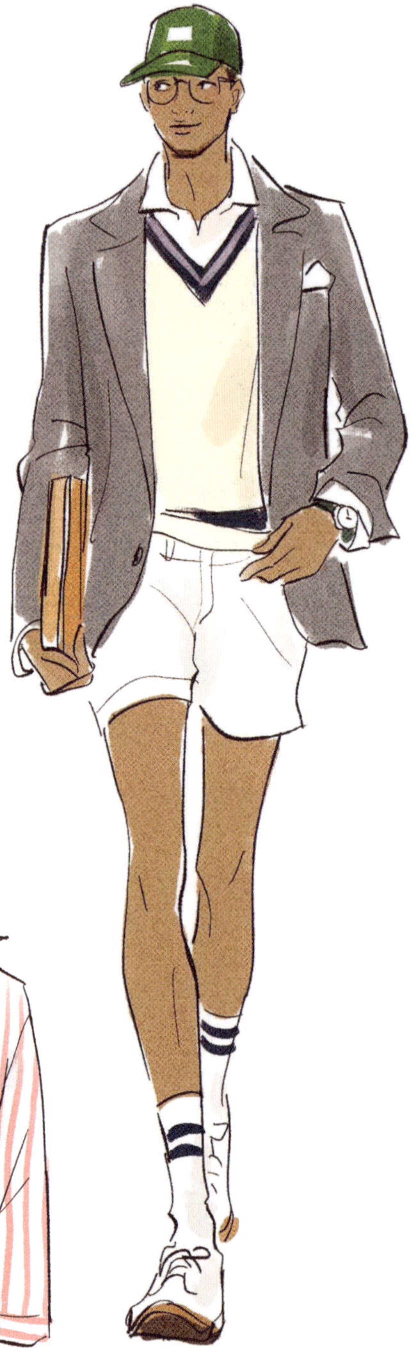

The button-down shirt is a classic, versatile piece that stands the test of time. You can't go wrong pairing it with a cable-knit sweater cardigan and tailored blazer.

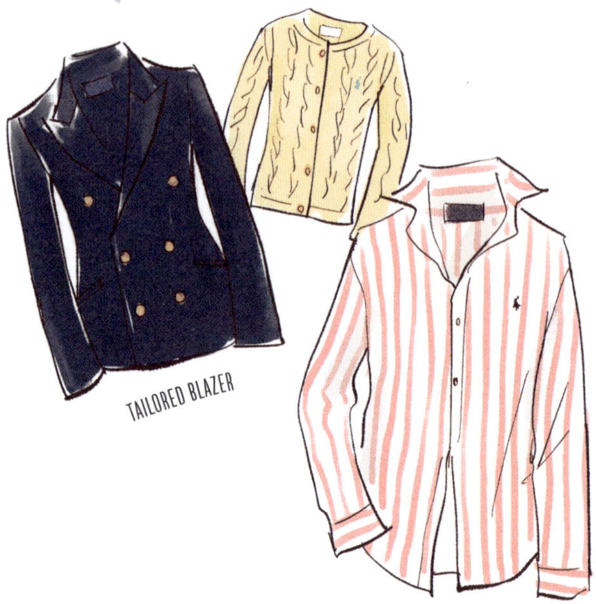

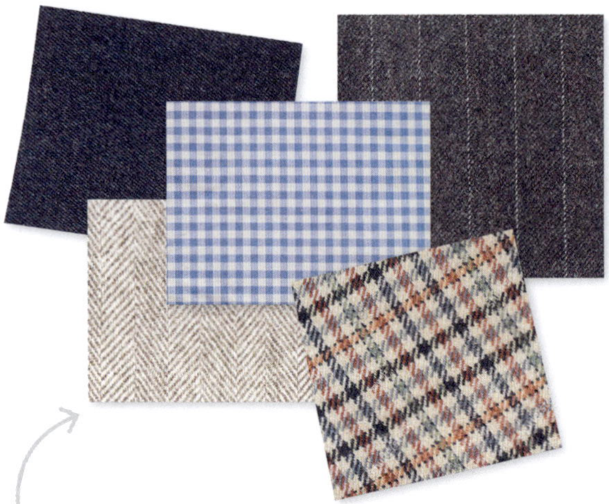

Generally, understated and noble color palettes are perfect here: navy blue, white, crimson, and forest green for base colors with a scholarly feel. Clean and sophisticated patterns, like plaid, stripes, and gingham, in soft pastels contrast with rich materials, like tweed and cashmere, in neutral tones.

Preppy can be feminine, too. Try a fitted silhouette in dresses and bottoms that suit your shape, and pair them with cute shoes like Mary Jane pumps.

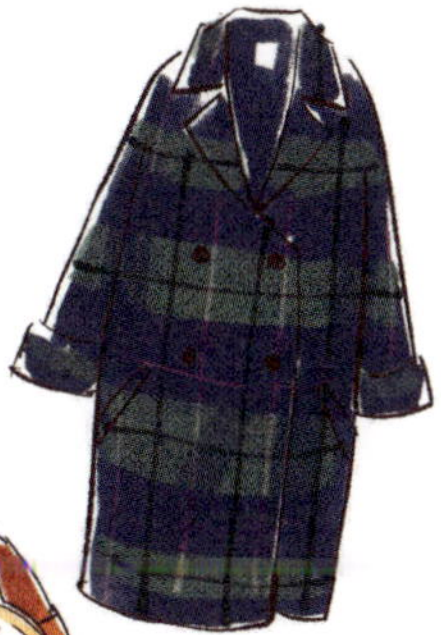

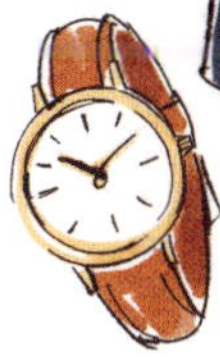

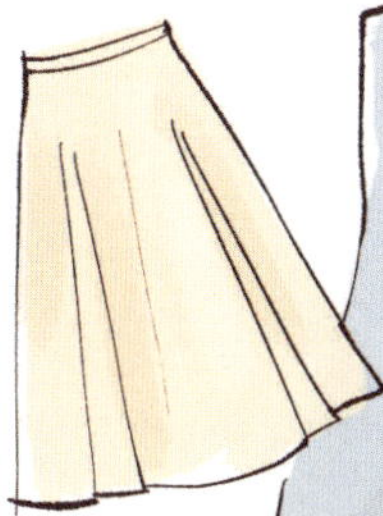

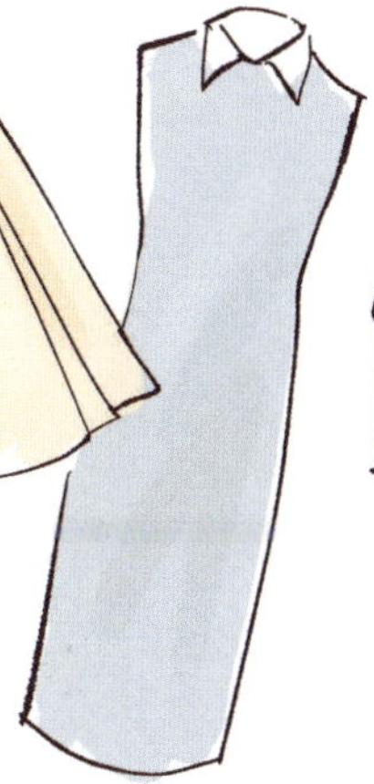

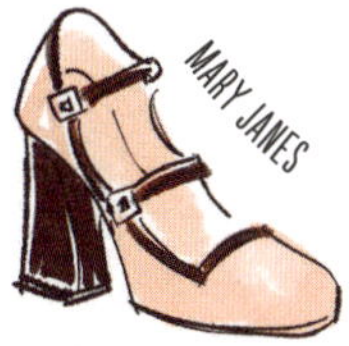

The university sweater has been a staple piece ever since it was introduced. They can be styled in a sporty ensemble, like this outfit, while still giving classic, preppy vibes.

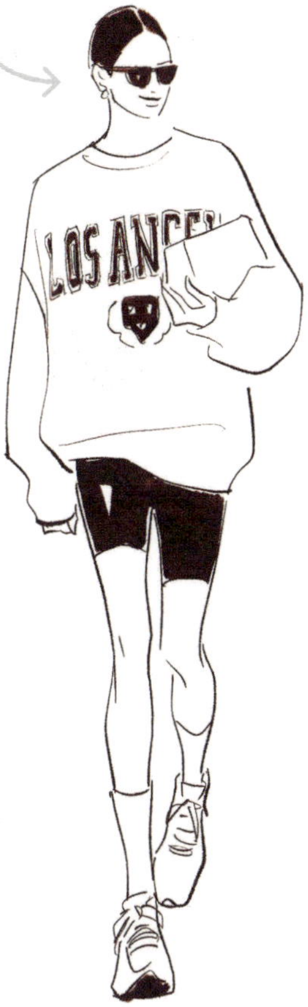

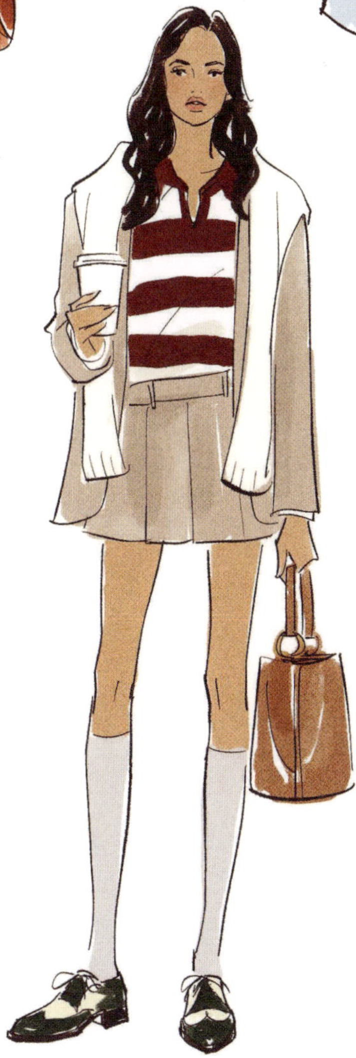

A perfectly fitted navy blazer is the most iconic, must-have item in the preppy style wardrobe. A modern, handsome look can be achieved with wide-legged khakis and an oversize trench coat.

A rugby shirt, paired with a pleated miniskirt and knee-high socks, can be a chic, unisex item. Layering a lighter-toned cashmere sweater adds texture and depth to the overall look.

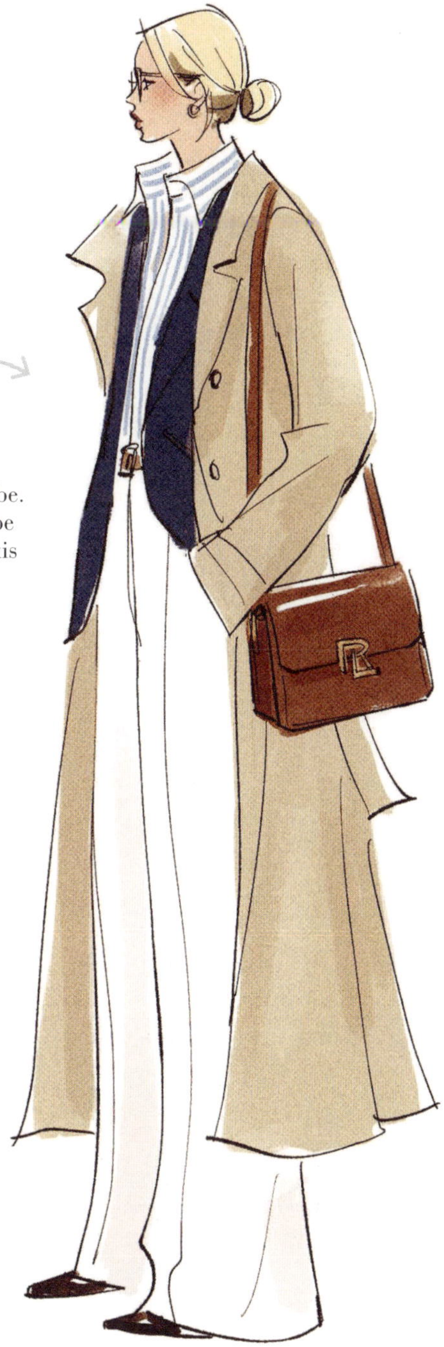

How would you like to dress this student? Do you want to go with a mix of sporty and girly elements, like the logo sweatshirts, pleated skirt, and sports socks she's wearing, or style her more conservatively by throwing a tailored blazer over a fitted dress?

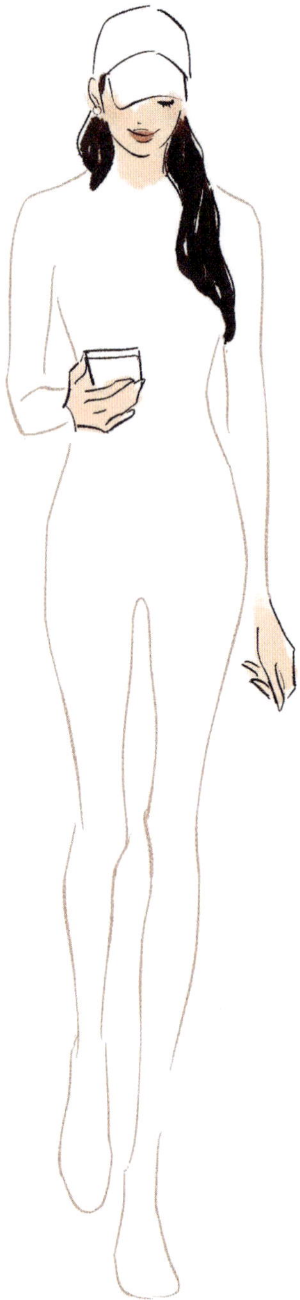

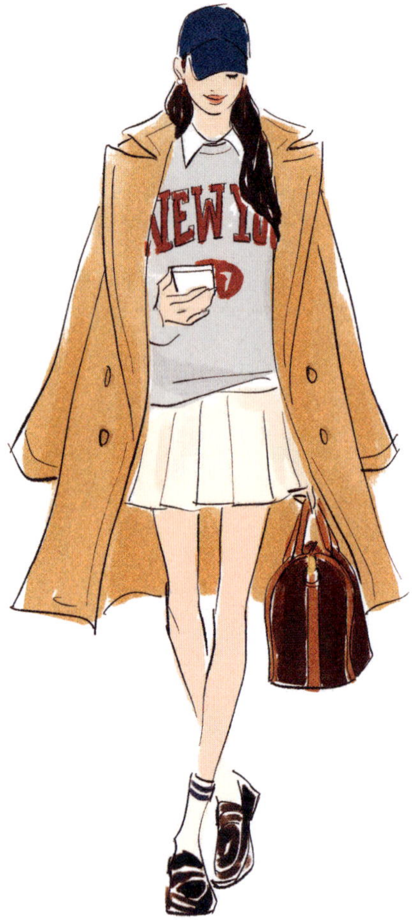

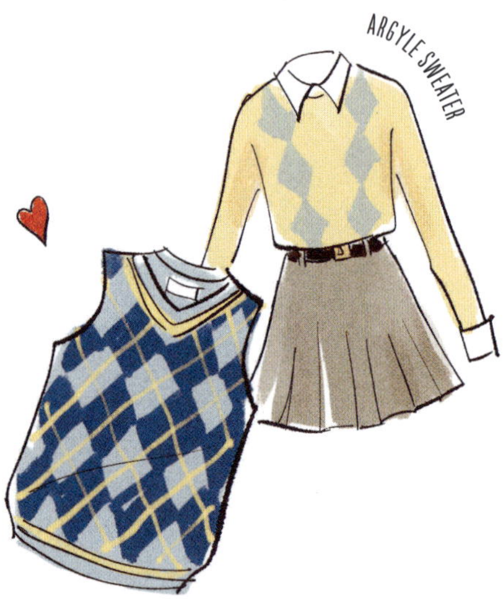

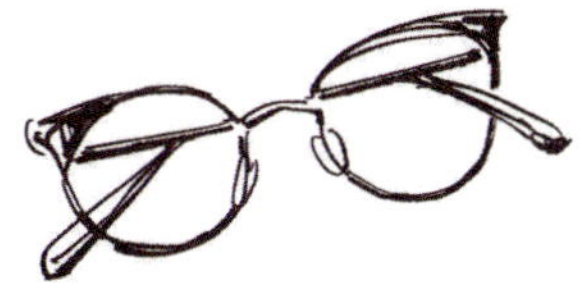

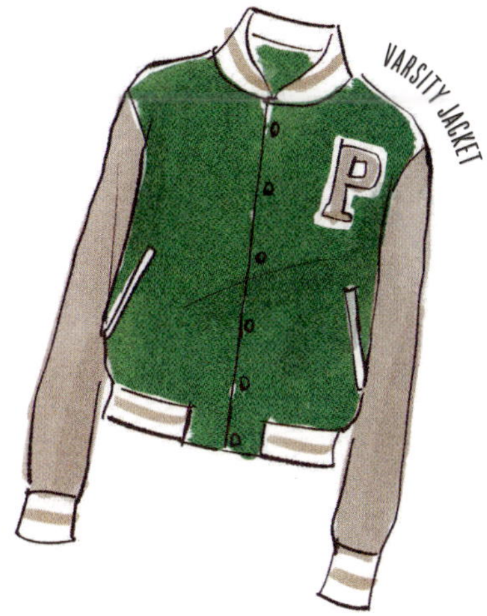

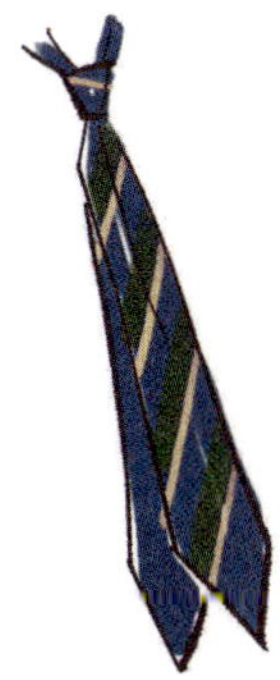

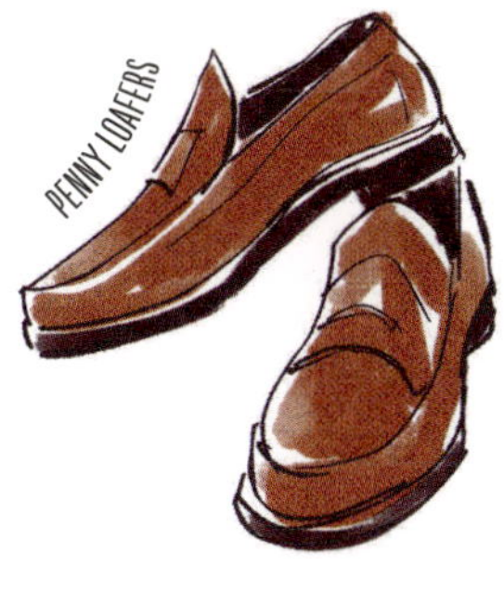

Now it's time to explore on your own! Create your croquis, any shape or size you like, using what you learned in Part One. Start dressing it with a base piece like a button-down shirt, then layer it with blazers, sweaters, cardigans, varsity jackets, and so on. Next, select accessories like penny loafers and ties to best fit your mood—perhaps you'll want to elevate the casual look with elegantly curled hair and pearls, or throw on some preppy glasses to add sophistication to a sporty look? Show us your creation!

Maximalism

Maximalism emerged after the Second World War when people started to use extravagant, loud fashion to uplift their mood. Many elements of maximalist fashion—playful colors, layering patterns, and bold silhouettes—have become fashionistas' all-time favorites: animal prints, chunky heels, exaggerated eyewear, and statement jewelry. This trend in maximal aesthetics was mainstream in the 1970s and was heavily influenced by the hippie culture, which embraced fantasy and escapism.

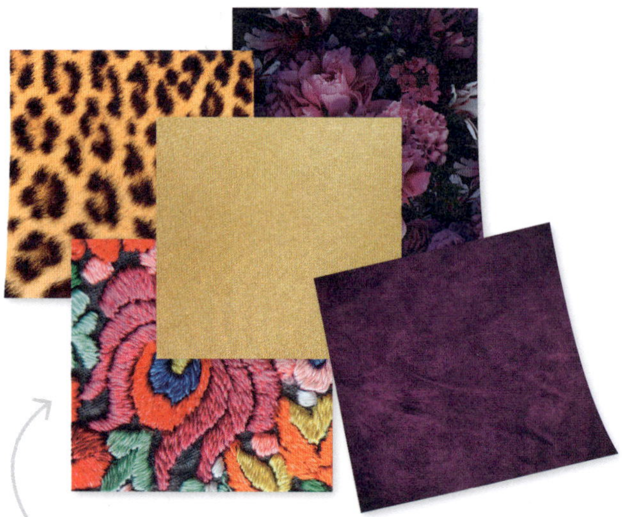

The key is variety! Explore different patterns, bright and contrasting colors, metallic fabrics, and satin. Have fun mixing and matching all kinds of hues and textures.

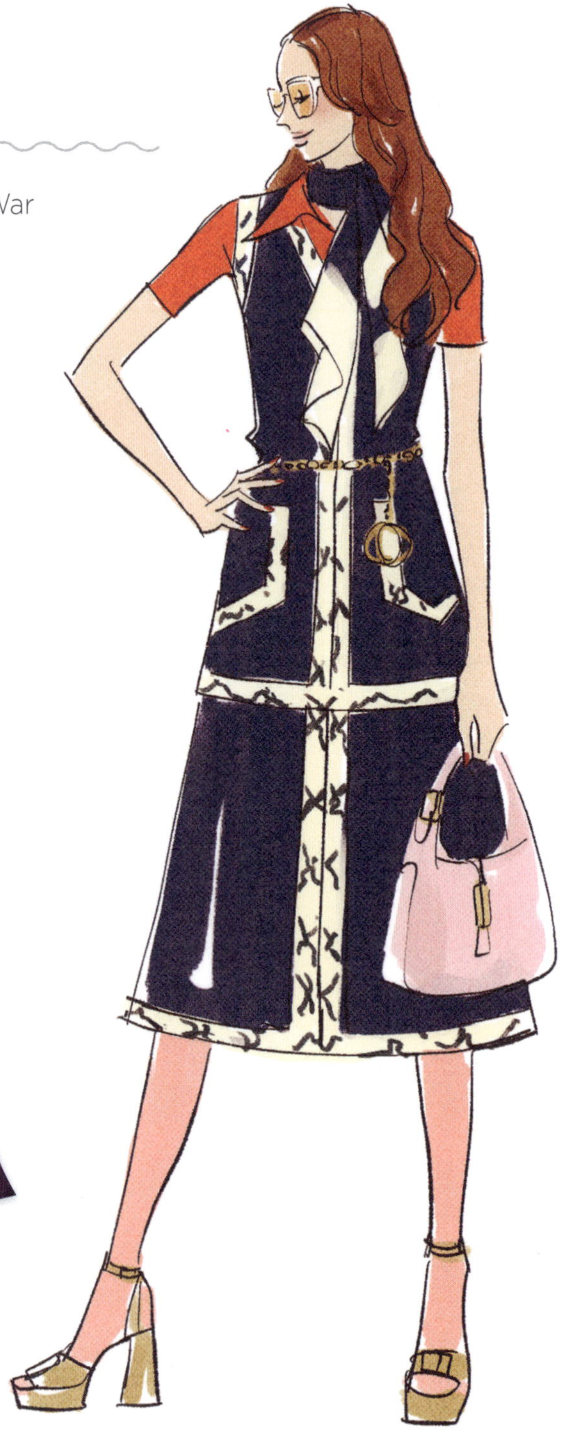

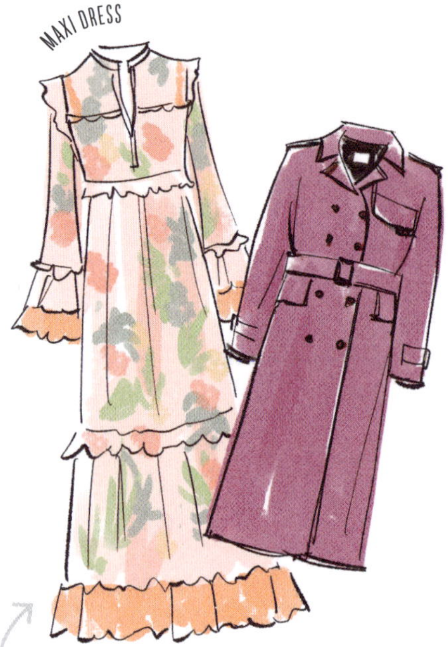

Long-length coats or dresses with extra details like laces and belts evoke a classic 1970s vibe.

A long jacket vest with a decorative gold belt to define the waist, inspired by Gucci. Python-printed piping adds a luxurious touch that elevates the overall look. Chunky heels were everything back in the day!

A maxi dress with bright floral patterns, accompanied by a luxurious faux fur coat. Top it off with a zingy Vitamin-C wide-brim hat to complete the look.

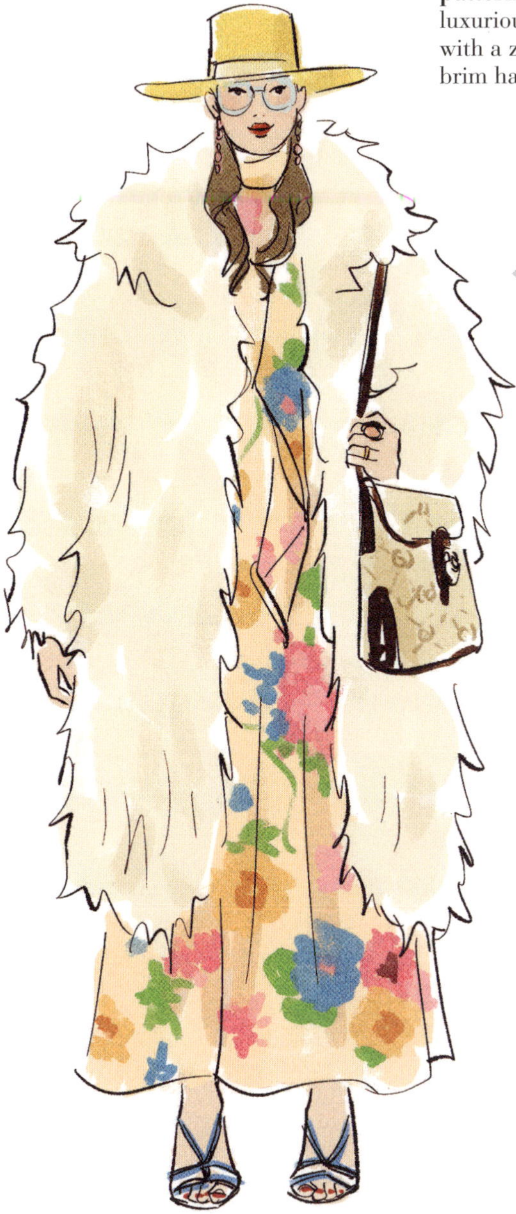

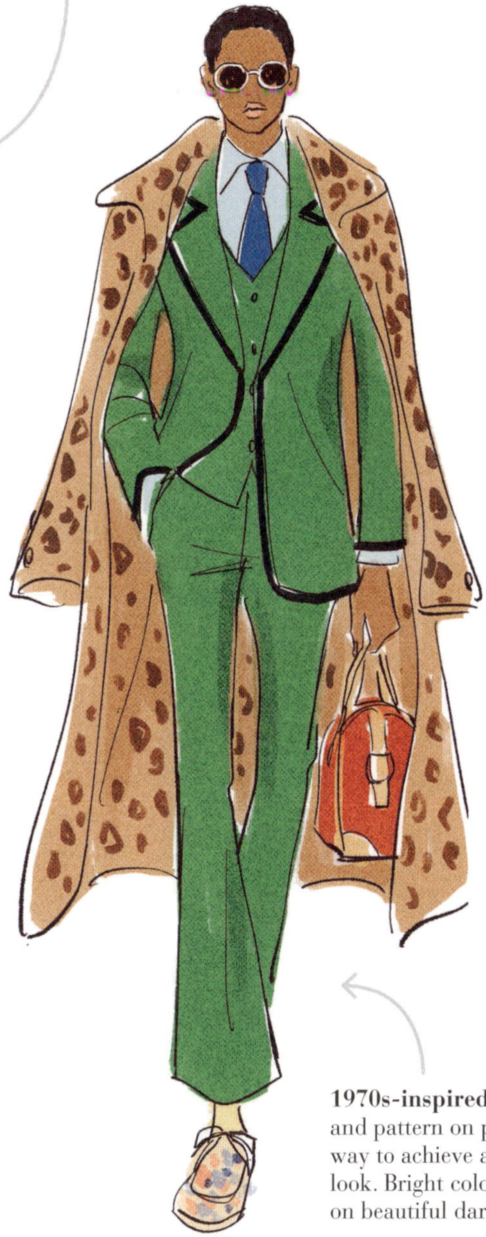

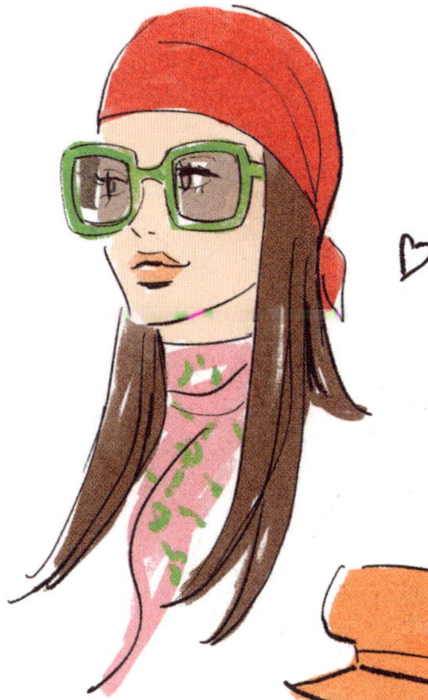

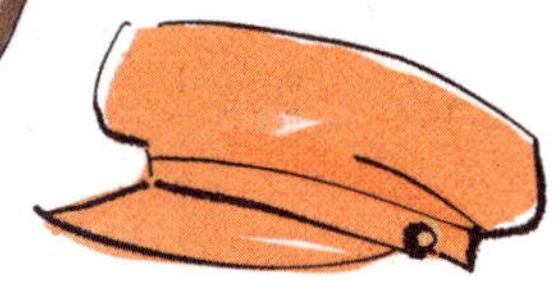

Head accessories and oversize eyewear are fun additions to a maximalist outfit. Go for either a vivid accent color or something more neutral to complement the outfit.

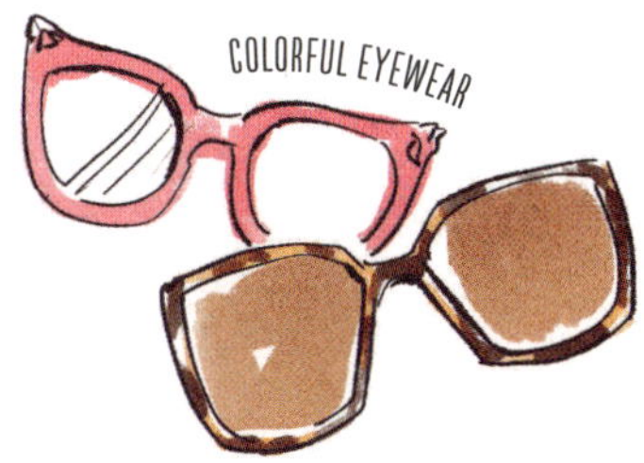

1970s-inspired bell-bottoms and pattern on pattern is a great way to achieve a lavish maximal look. Bright colors look amazing on beautiful dark skin.

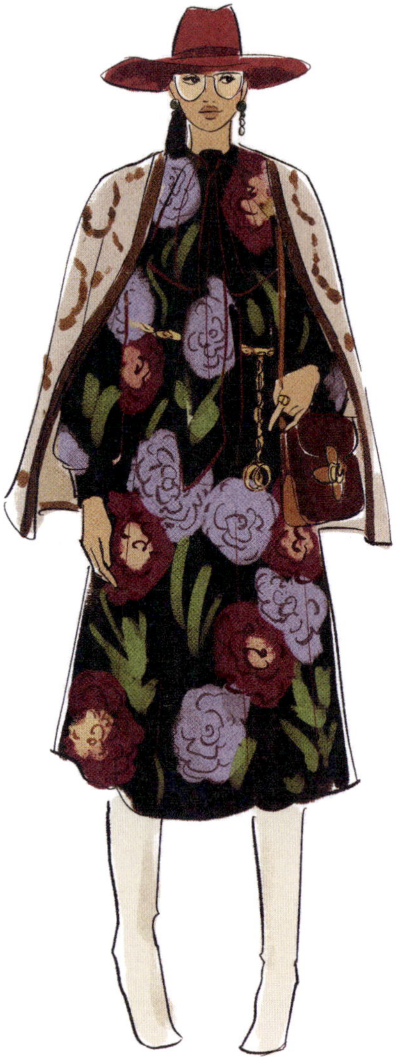

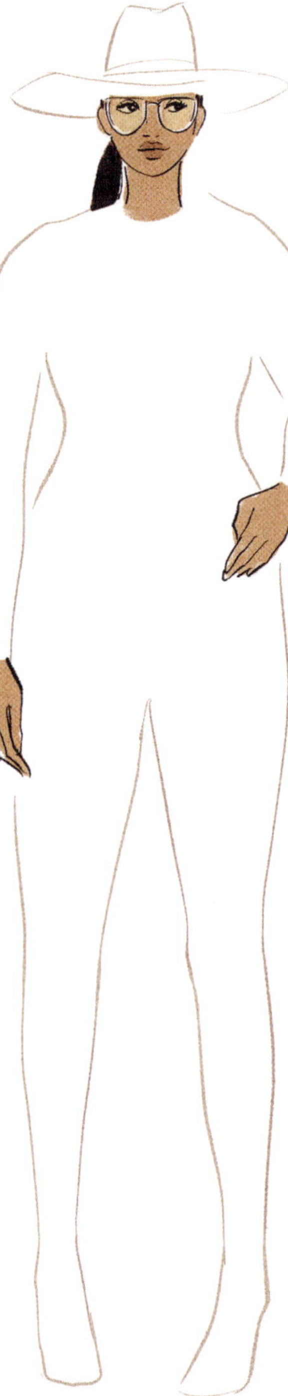

This figure is wearing a chic floral dress with a large bow at the collar. What else would you like her to wear? Experiment with patterns and color combinations!

First, decorate the figure, then draw your own head sketch in the space on the right. Put on a colorful hat, or some stylish eyewear (why not both!). Unleash your creative flair and don't forget to play with fun glam. Choose bold and decorative jewelry featuring large logos or distinctive motifs to personalize the look.

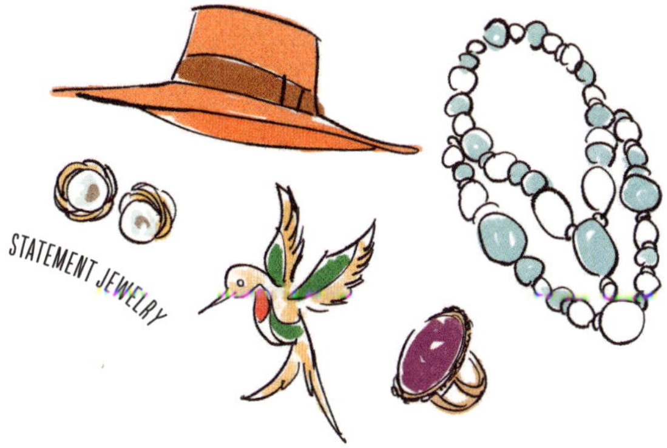

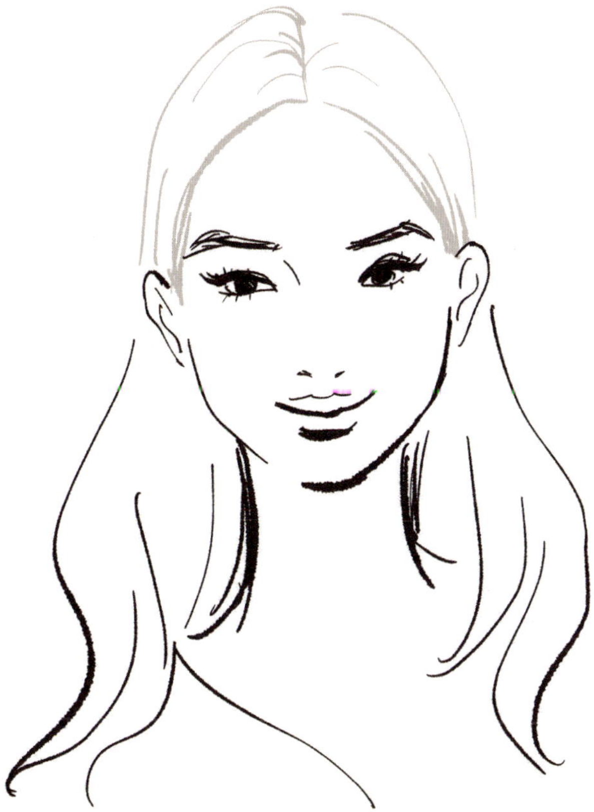

Power Suits

One of the best gifts the '80s gave us? The power suit! Women were starting to take over the workplace, and power suits were not just about fitting in with the men, but expressing their own strength and power. The tastes of the 1980s were excessive, bold, powerful, and vibrant—the bigger, louder, and brighter, the better. That meant shoulder pads, costume jewelry, big hairdos, and heavy makeup. Power suits have continued to inspire gender-free, androgynous looks and mega-proportions that offer a variety of silhouettes.

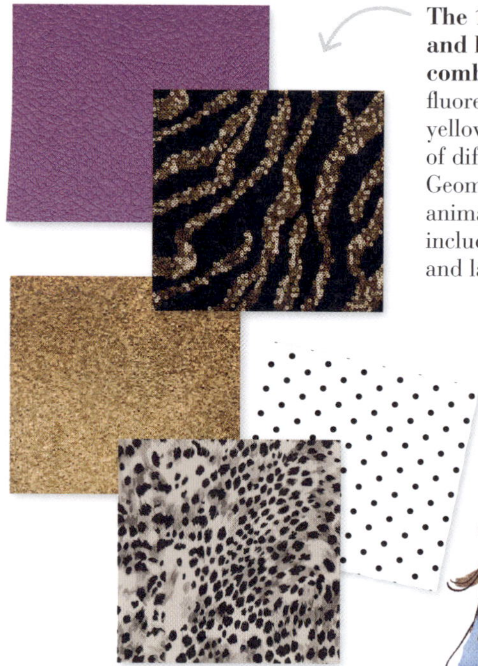

The 1980s were all about bright and high-contrast color combinations. Use neon and fluorescent hues like bright pink, yellow, and orange, in a variety of different prints and textures. Geometric patterns, polka dots, animal prints, logos, and fabrics including vinyl, sequins, metallics, and laces are great options.

Many "street urchin" iconic items were popularized by pop star Madonna in the 1980s, including bustier tops with fine laces, stacking necklaces and bracelets, and bleached hair with dark roots.

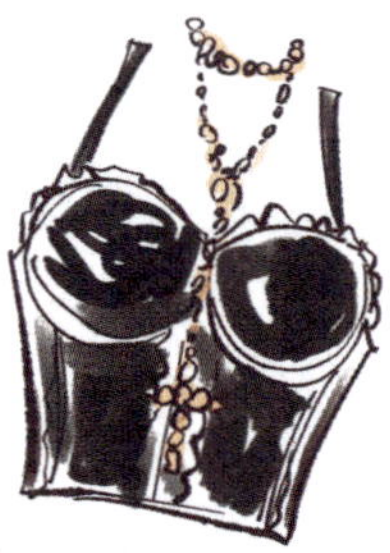

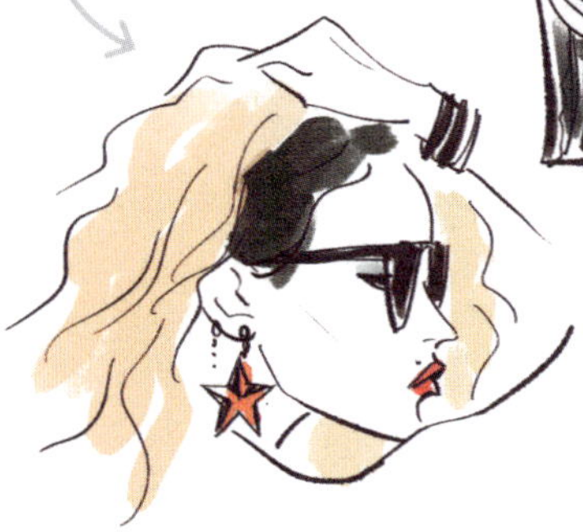

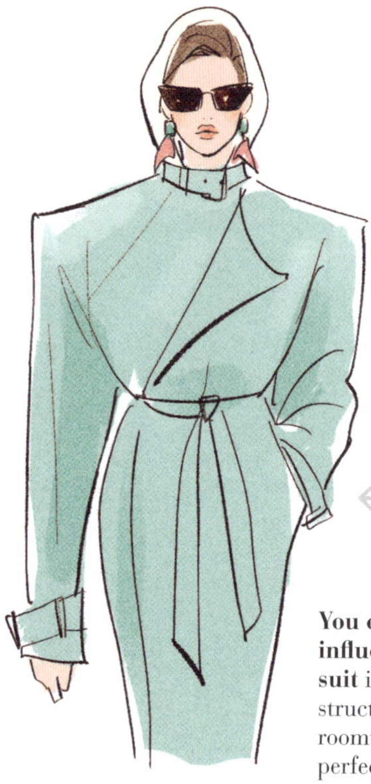

You can see the influence of the power suit in this Balenciaga structured coat—it's very roomy and boxy, yet perfectly elegant.

A classic, oversize power suit look in a vibrant blue styled with playful, messy hair that screams the '80s! Chunky gold jewelry and extra glam, like the bright cheek and lips, will complement it perfectly.

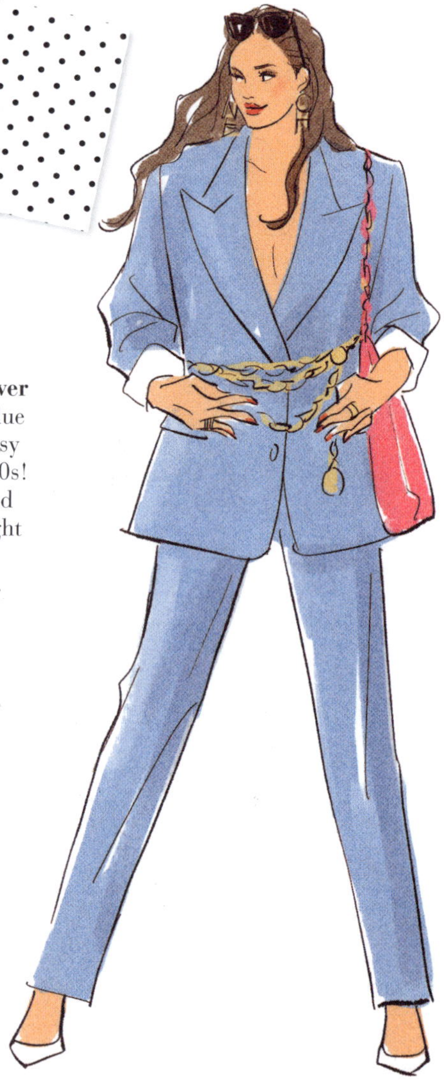

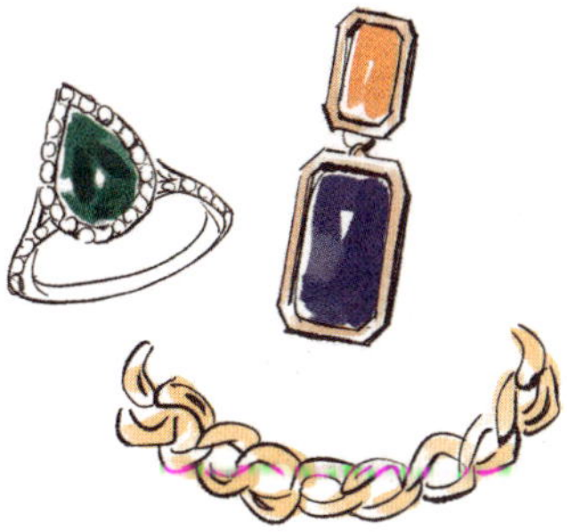

COSTUME JEWELRY

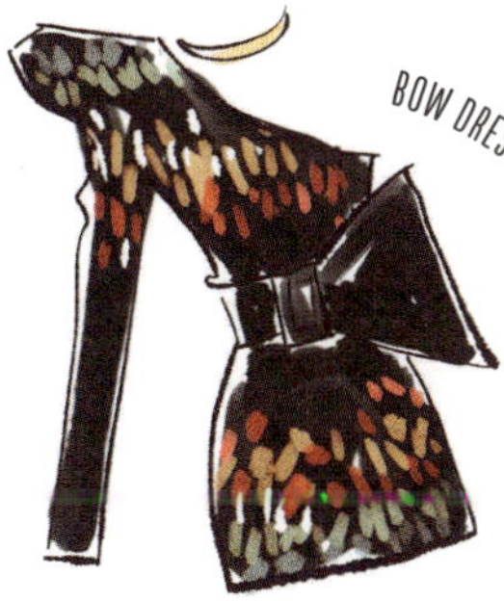

BOW DRESS

Leotards were big in the aerobics years—bodysuits, stretch pants, and leggings give a healthy, athletic vibe. Tailored blazers help to create the iconic androgynous 1980s look.

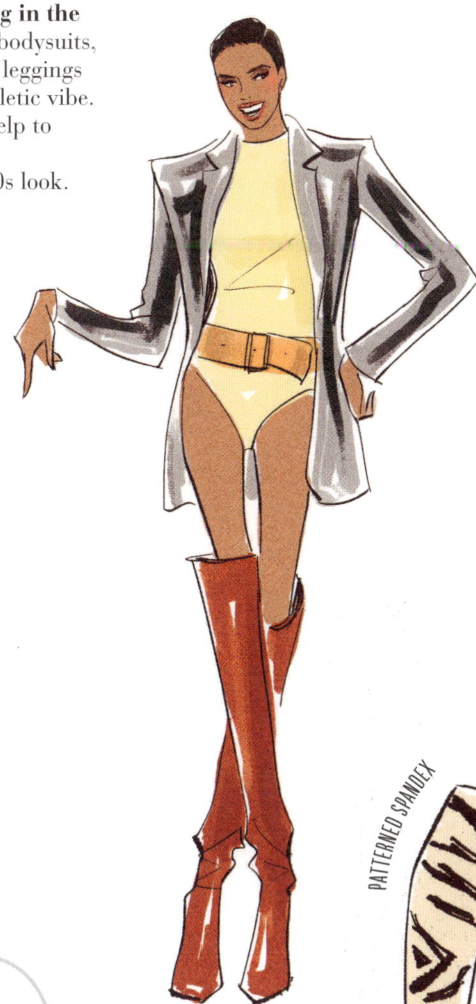

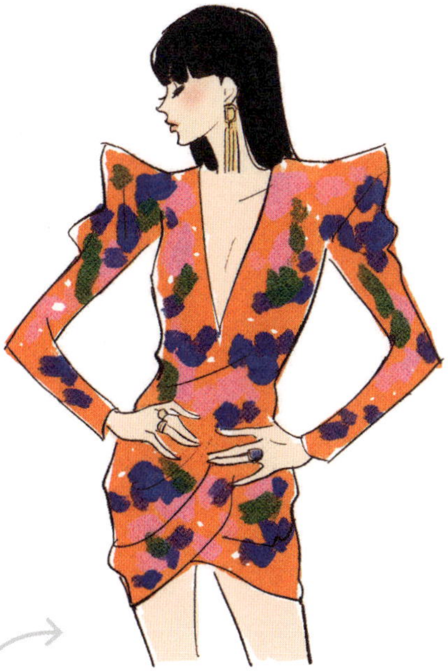

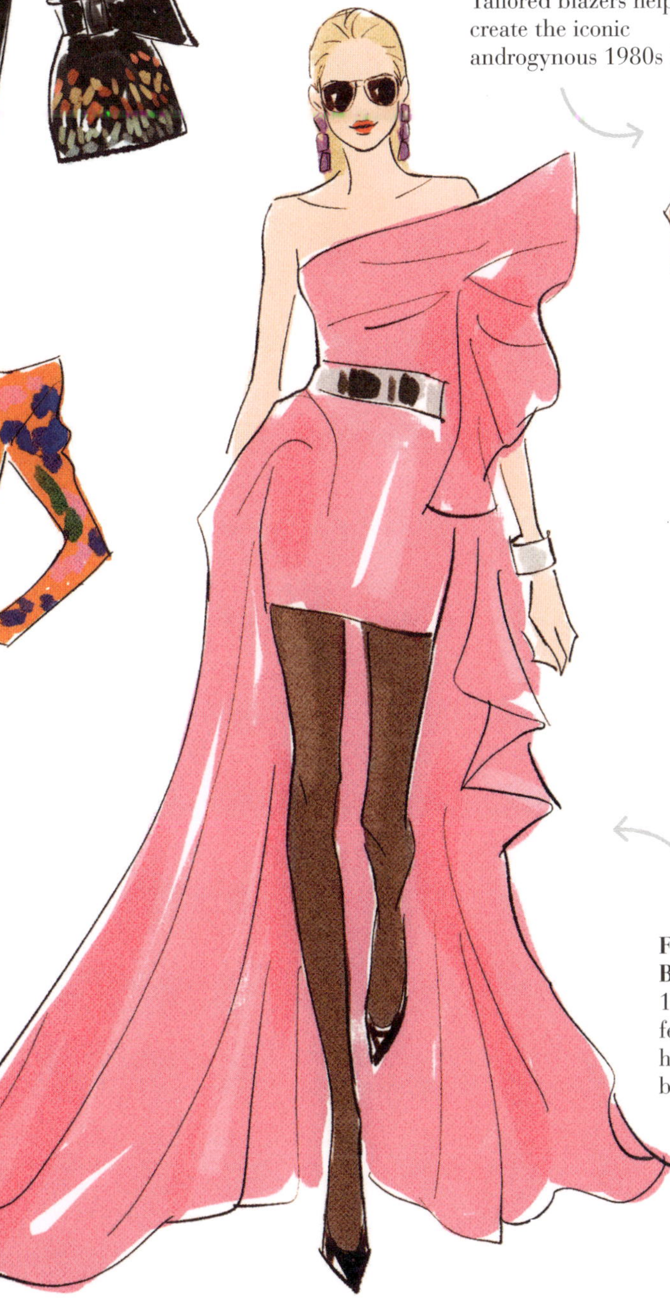

These exaggerated shoulder dresses and big earrings inherited their glamorous elegance from *Dynasty's* Joan Collins. Sequined minidresses, statement jewelry, and chunky gold necklaces capture this look perfectly. Don't hold back with spangles and shine!

French luxury house Balmain's beautiful 1980s-influenced dresses feature bold shoulders, short hemlines, and statement belts that cinch the waist.

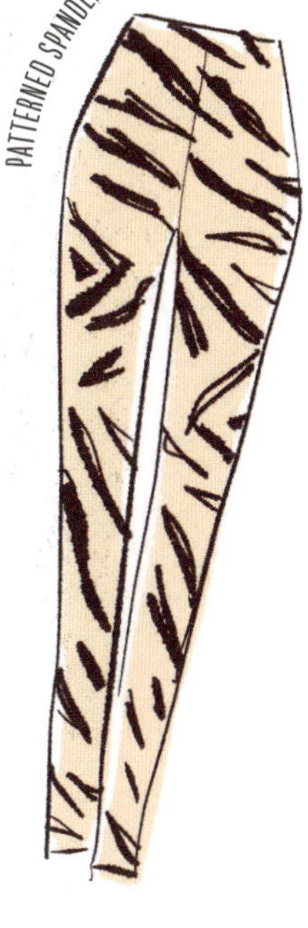

PATTERNED SPANDEX

Time to strike a power pose. Start with your own bold-shoulder outerwear. What's your mood for materials—leather, vinyl, or metallic? Next add bottoms—you can choose from parachute pants, fun and loud patterned spandex, a hooded dress, and so much more! The inspiration below is wearing a pumped-up, vivid faux fur coat and vinyl slouchy pants, with a statement gold belt and earrings, and gelled-up short hair.

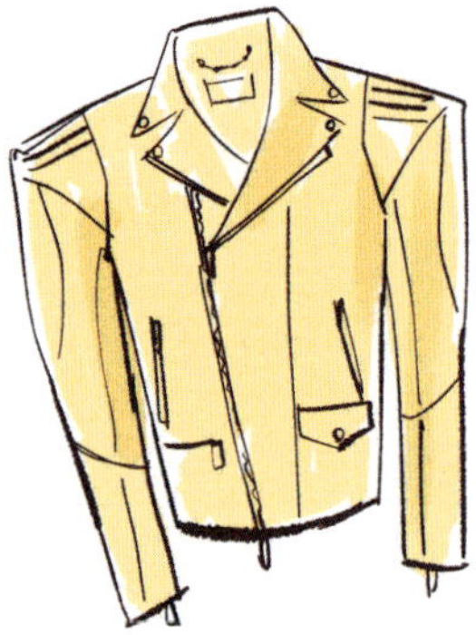

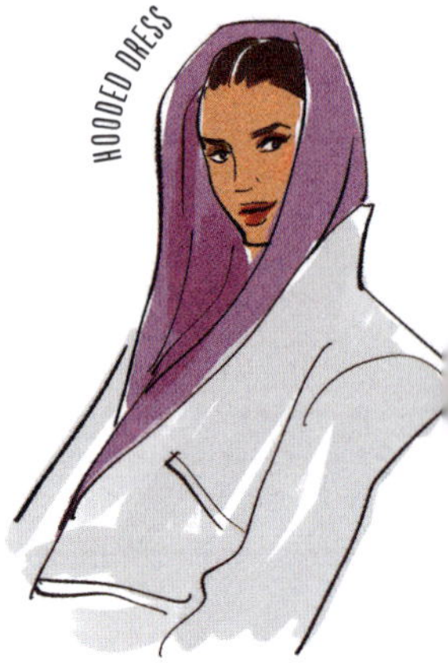

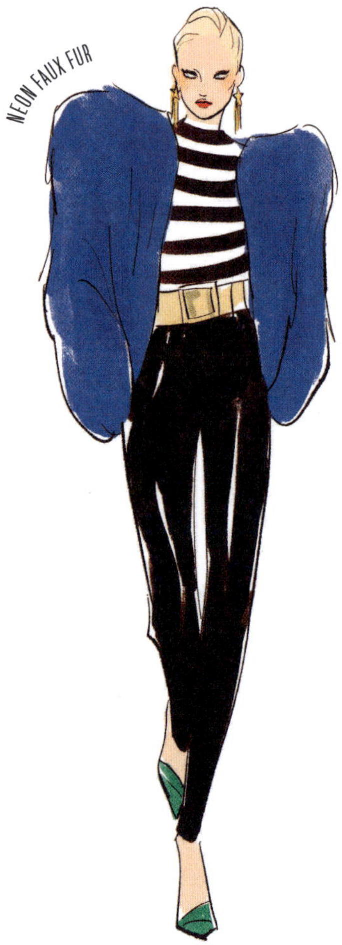

Design a risky, glittering evening dress that stands out in a crowd! Try to include 1980s elements like strong shoulders, a plunging neckline, and ruffles. Let's also play with after-hours glam—bright eyeshadows, heavy cheeks, and striking red lips!

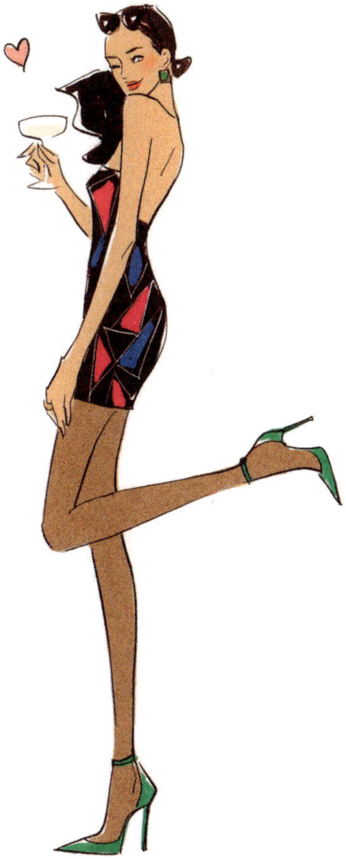

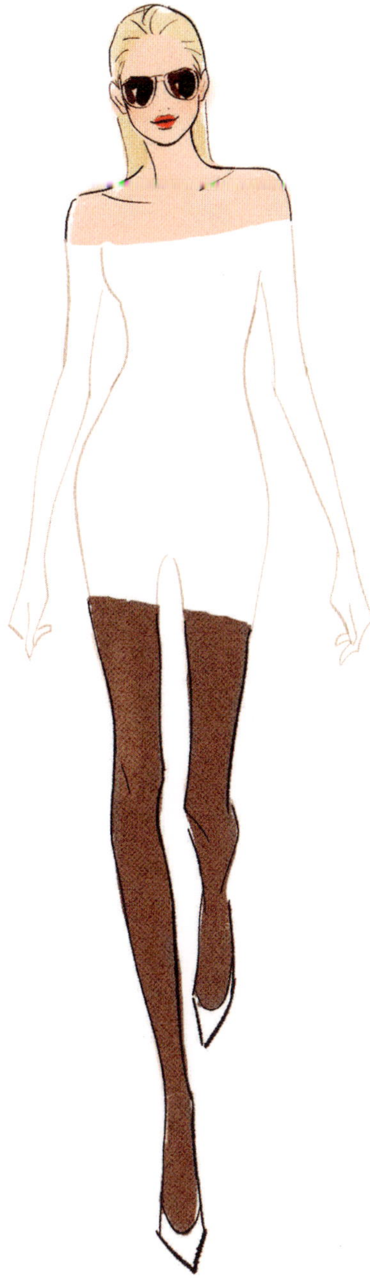

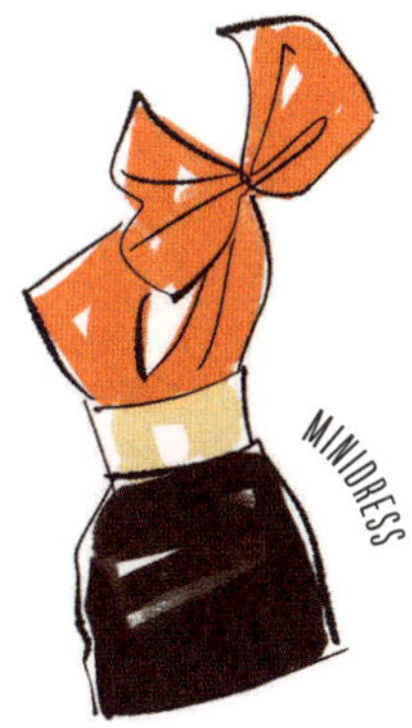

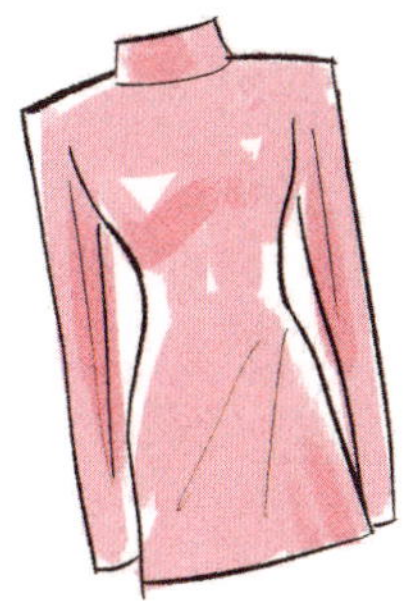

Space Age

"Space Age" fashion emerged in the mid-1960s, inspired by the global space race and a futuristic vision of the 21st century. It expressed optimism, empowerment, and readiness for a new era, and was pioneered by designers like André Courrèges and Pierre Cardin, who created outfits that looked like they belonged to astronauts, aliens, or intergalactic travelers. They pushed the boundaries of fashion further than ever before, experimenting with new materials and silhouettes.

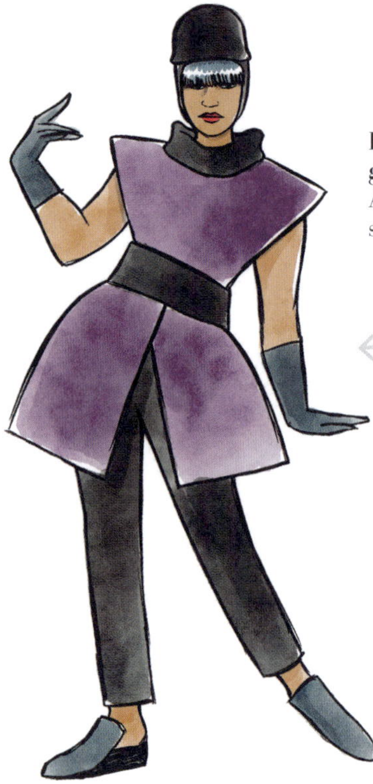

Futuristic and geometric shapes, A-line skirts, and spherical helmets.

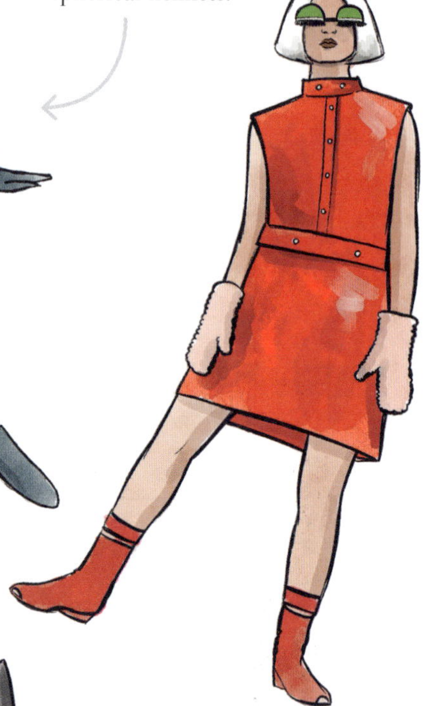

Space Age fashion was a visual means of declaring a new age where women were empowered in society.

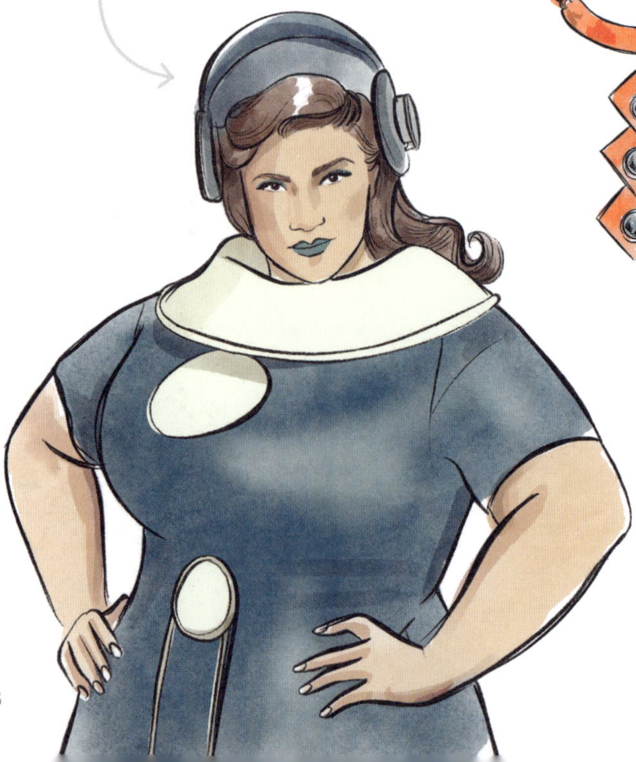

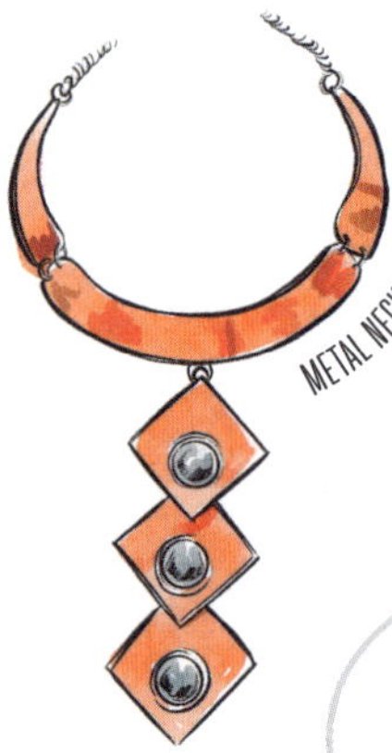

Space Age accessories like goggles, gloves, or metallic boots wouldn't look out of place on the Space Shuttle!

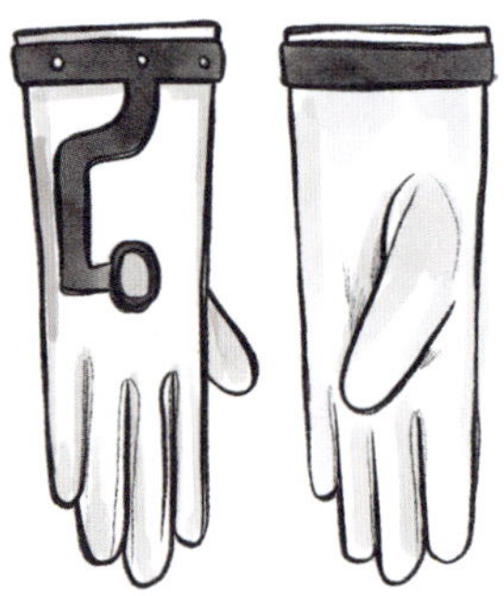

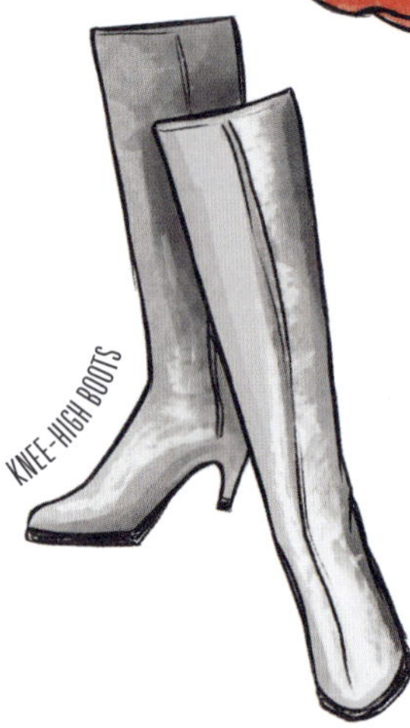

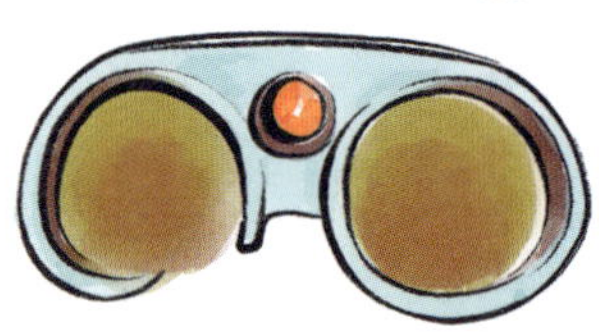

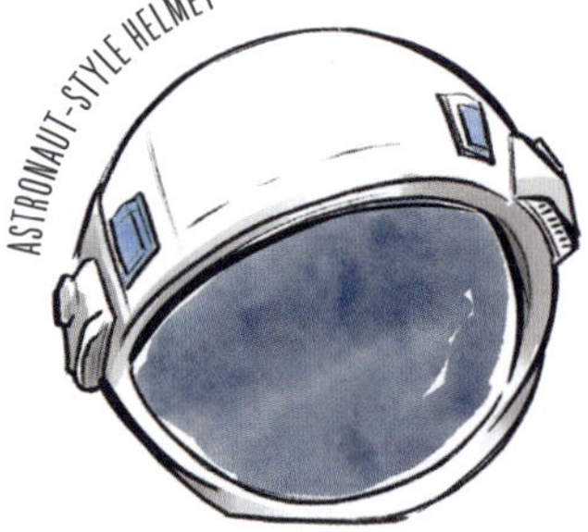

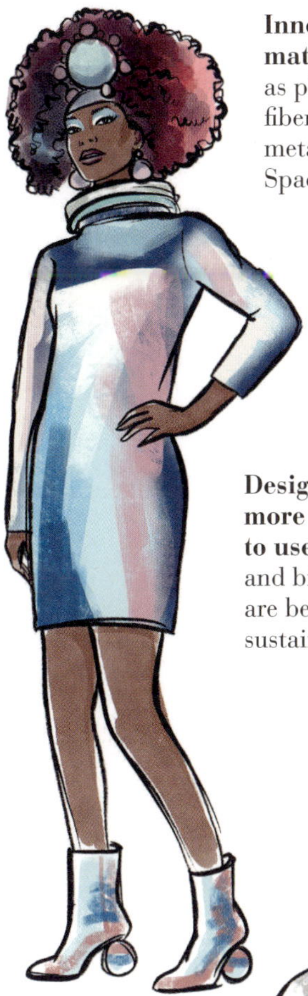

Innovative materials, such as plastic, fiberglass, and metal, define Space Age design.

Bright, contrasting colors give a classic shape a modern, playful feel.

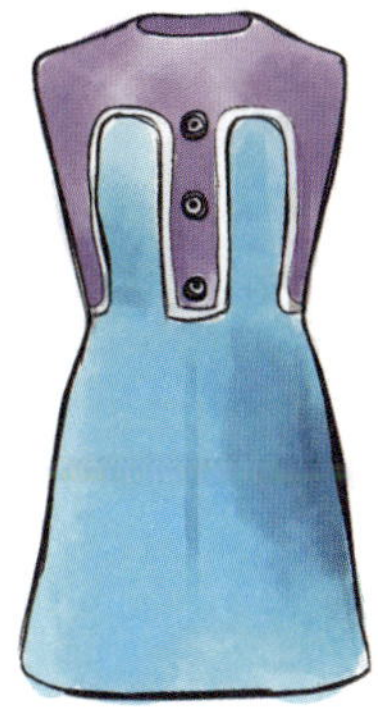

Bold shapes are made even more striking with the use of metallic fabrics, such as silver lamé, vinyl, or PVC.

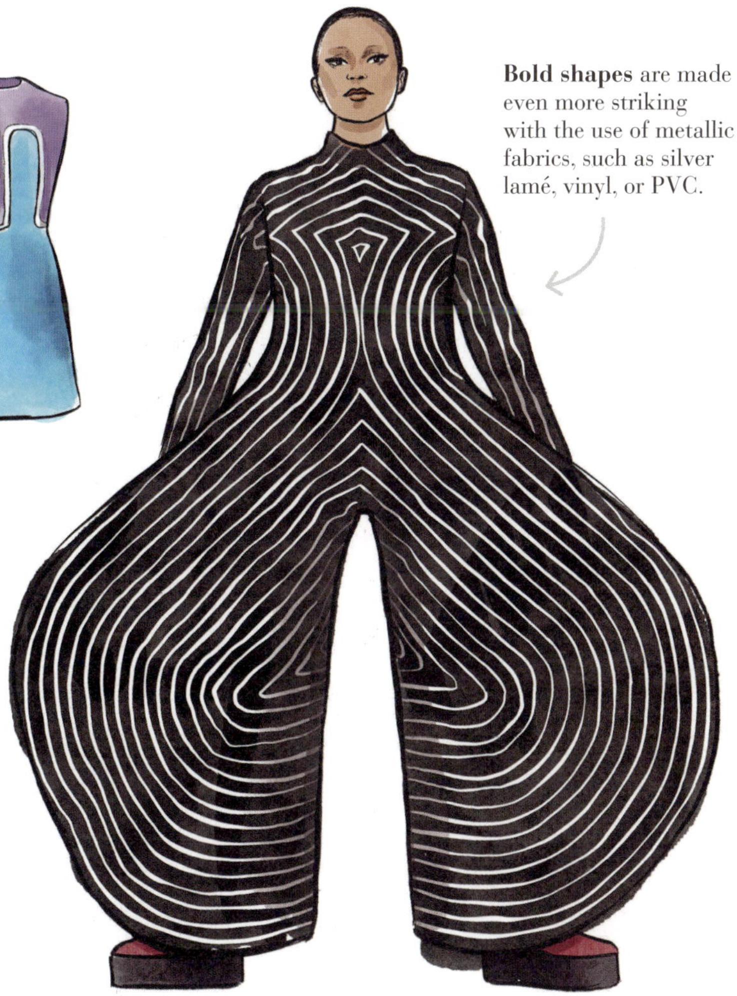

Designers are exploring more responsible ways to use plastic. Recycled and biodegradable plastics are being used as more sustainable alternatives.

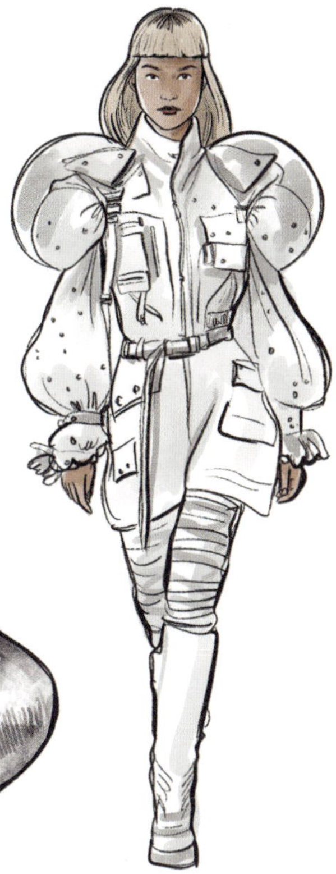

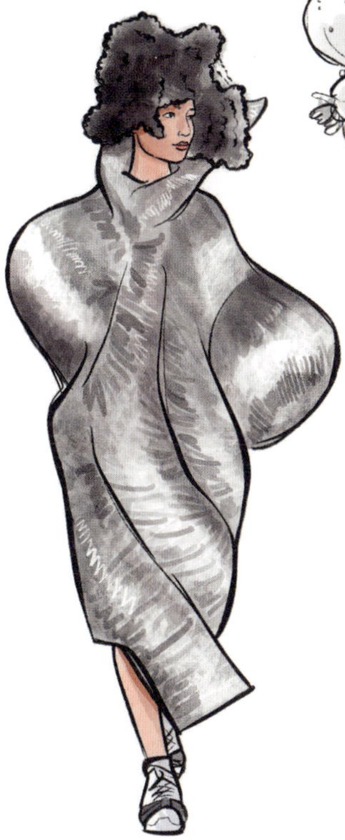

Rei Kawakubo's collection for Comme des Garçons was inspired by Space Age fashion, only more abstract. The inflated garments worn by Kawakubo's models were made from silver insulation material and looked like floating pieces of space debris.

Shiny fabrics, vinyl, wool-acrylic, sequins, glass, and PVC help to create futuristic, otherworldly looks.

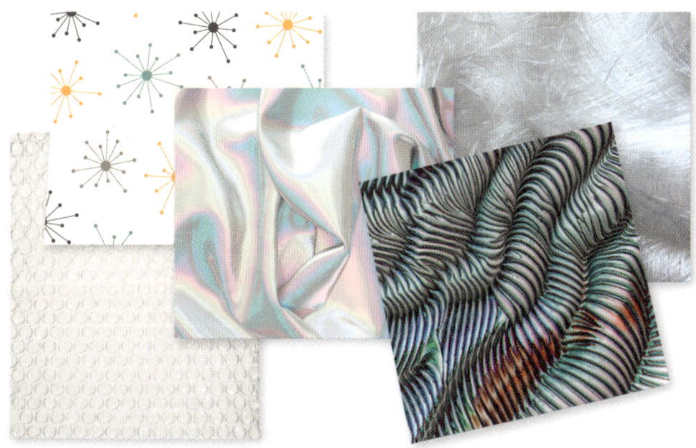

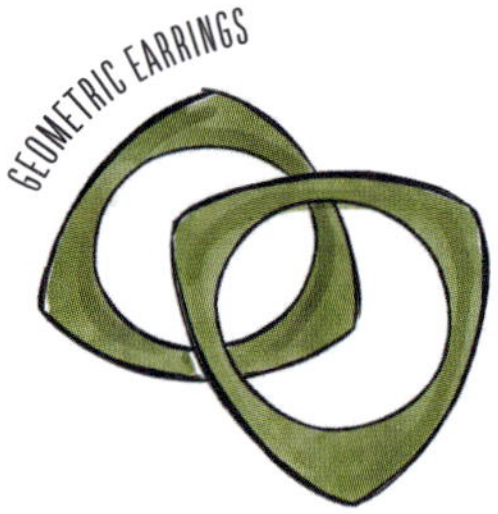

Design the rest of this model's look, using the astronaut-inspired helmet as a starting point.

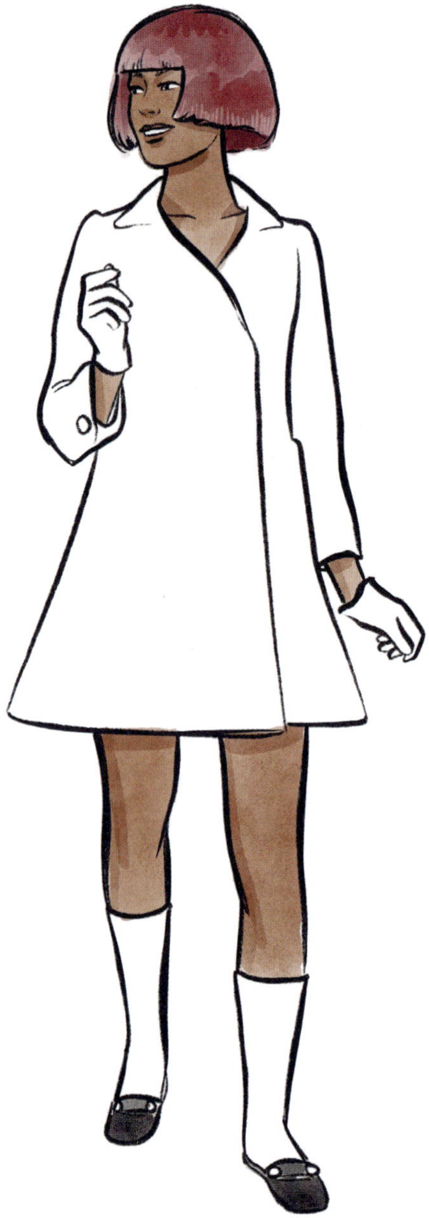

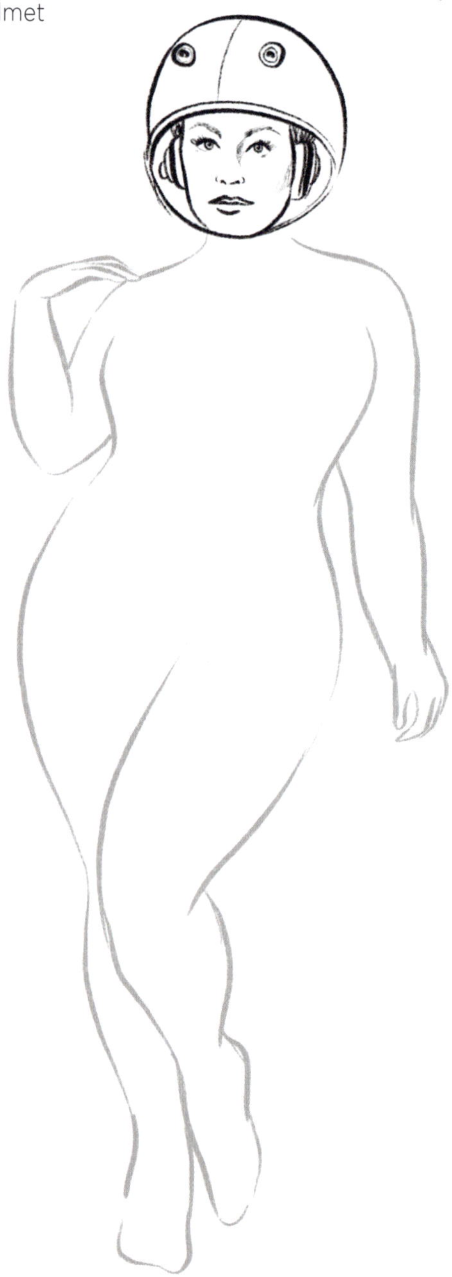

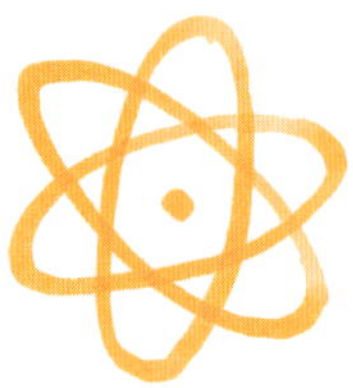

Add details to finish off this Space Age look. Think about using bold colors and patterns for the dress, boots, and gloves.

Your turn! Design two Space Age outfits. You could draw inspiration from modern sci-fi movies, or classic cartoons. Boldy go where no fashion designer has gone before!

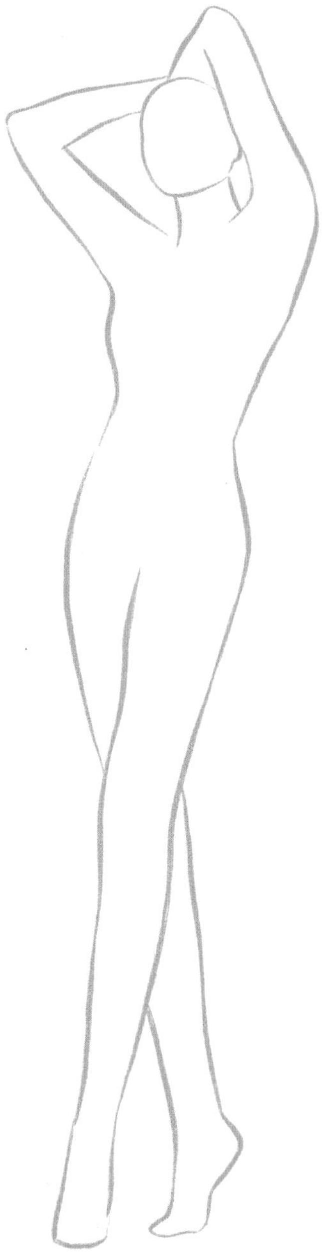

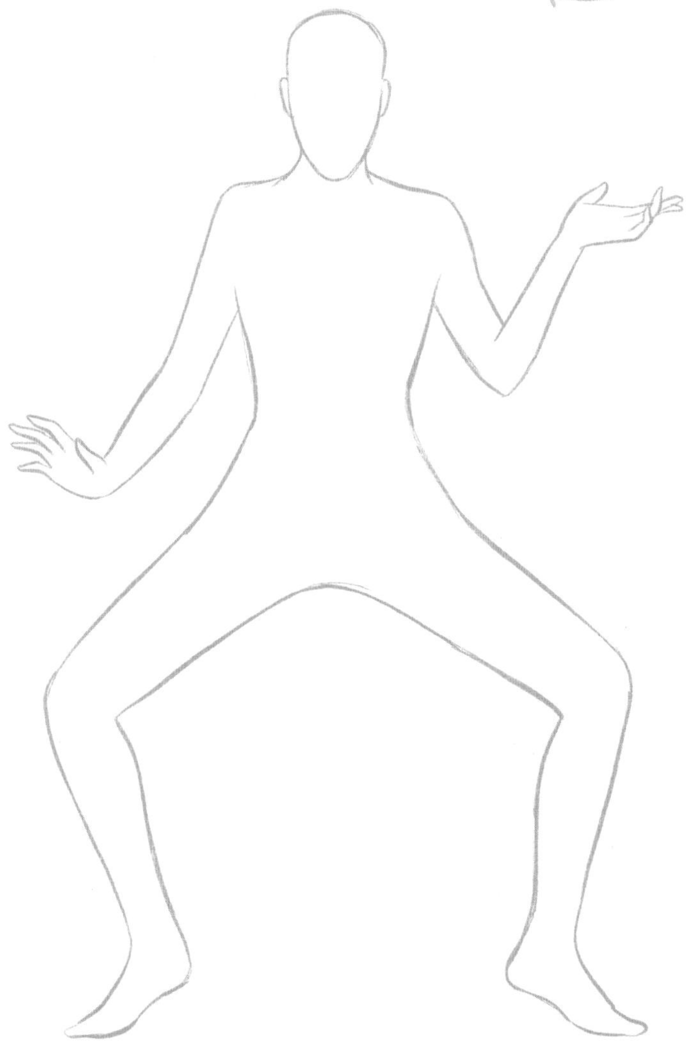

Free Spirit

This casual, romantic style embraces creativity and freedom. It is inspired by many different cultures, as well as the hippie subculture of the 1960s and 1970s. It mixes elements of vintage and ethnic fashion, with an emphasis on natural fabrics and accessories—think frills, fringes, feathers, and beads. Kate Moss, Sienna Miller, Vanessa Hudgens, and Alessandra Ambrosio have all rocked the style at fashion shows, festivals, and movie premieres.

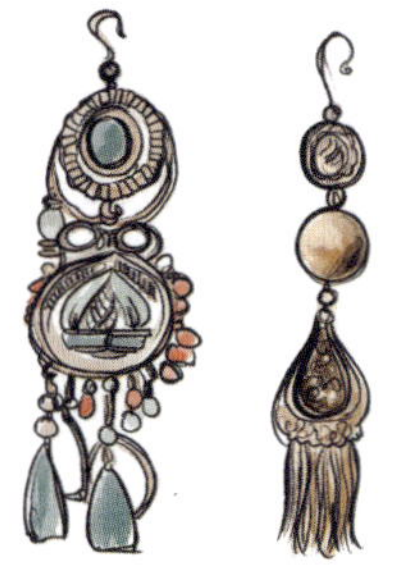

Long, dangly earrings are staples and are usually composed of beads, feathers, leather, and metal.

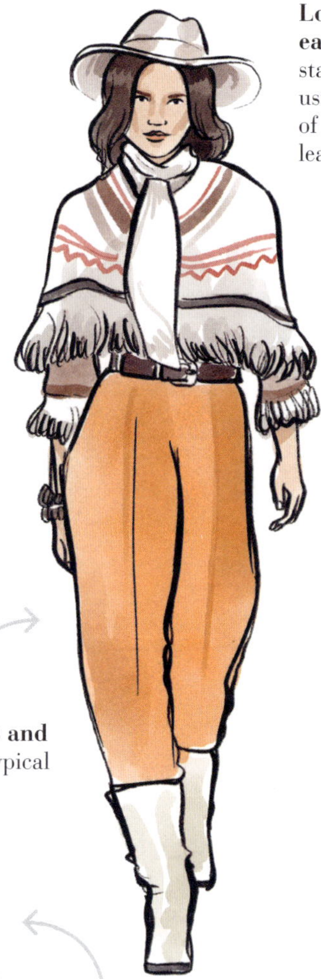

Earthy tones and fringes are typical elements.

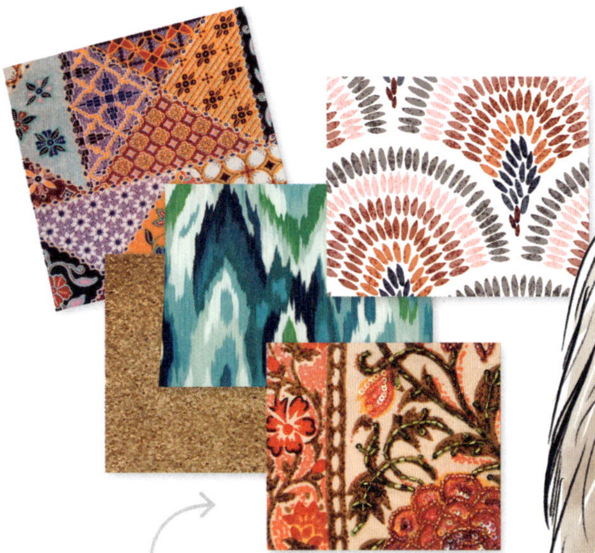

This look is grounded in natural fabrics: silks, linens, and cottons. Mix and match textures, floral and paisley patterns, and rich, earthy colors.

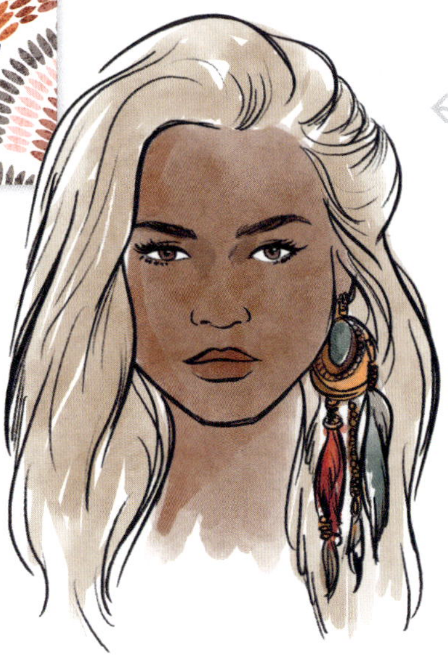

Vibrant, contrasting colors and chunky jewelry make for a modern take on the style.

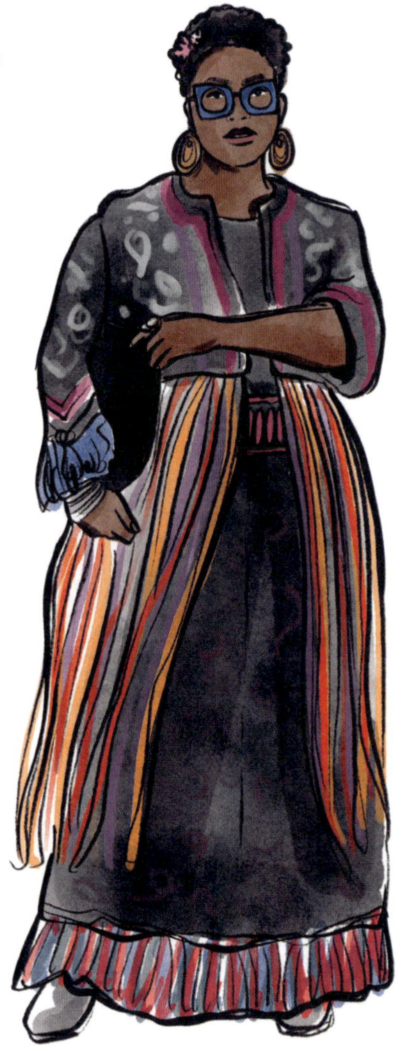

There are many ways to mix textures and materials to create a unique outfit.

Long, loose-fitting dresses create a soft, flowing silhouette.

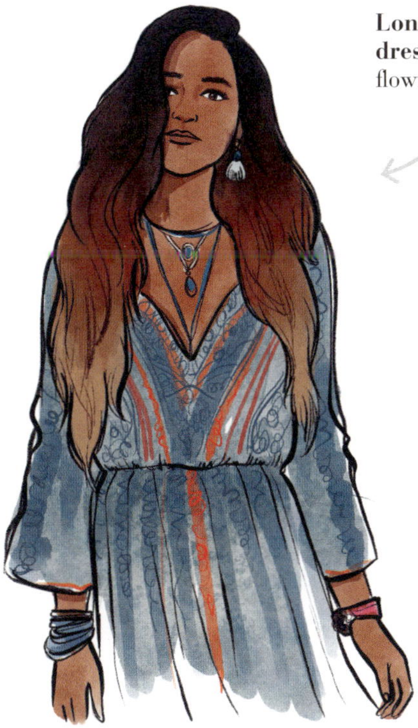

This pink, floral dress is paired with beaded bracelets and necklaces and a wide hat for a chic and comfortable outfit.

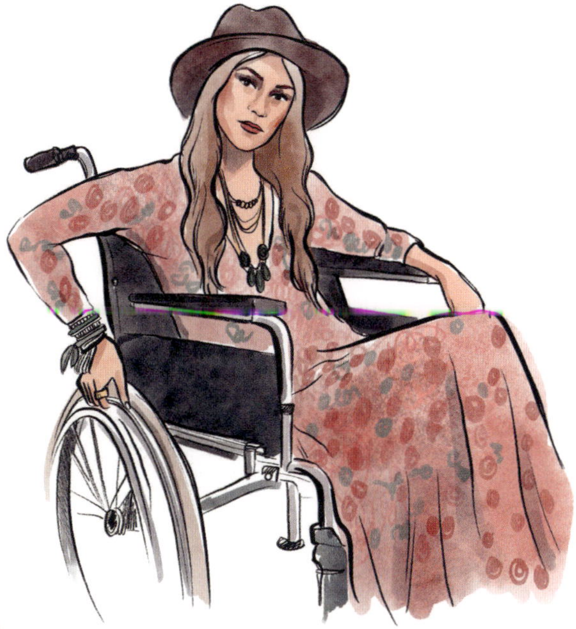

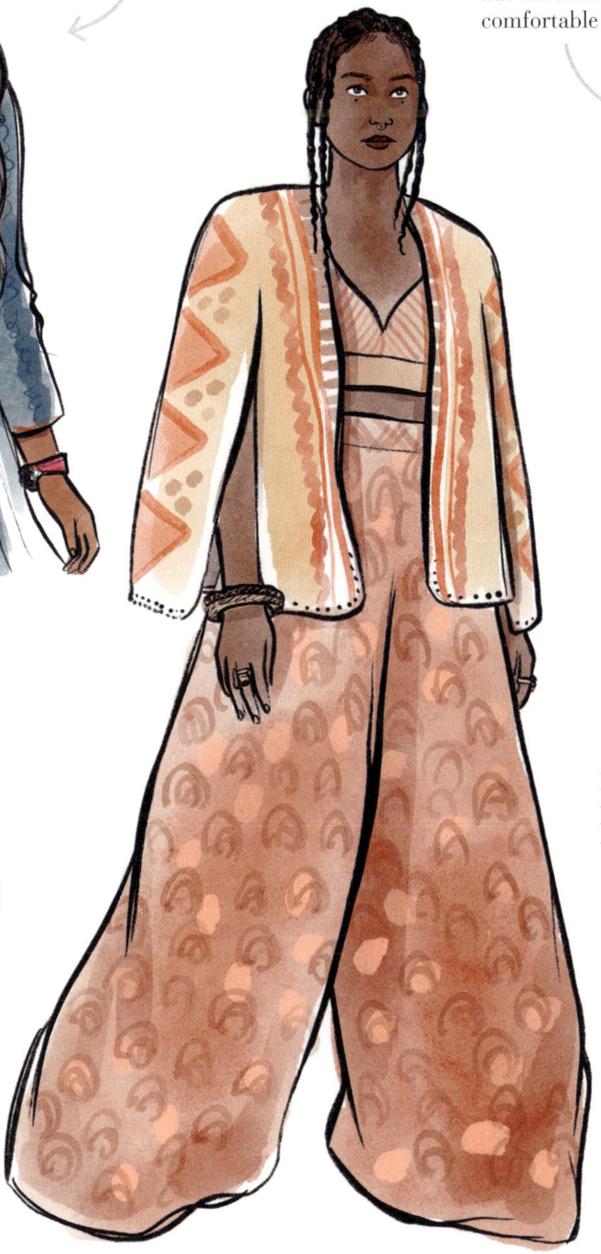

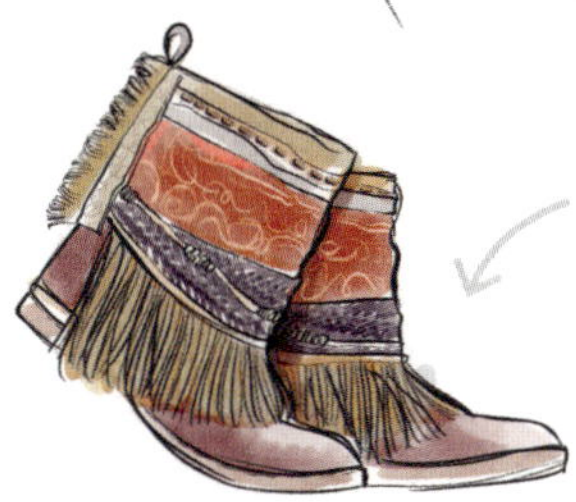

Fringed boots go perfectly with a long, floaty dress.

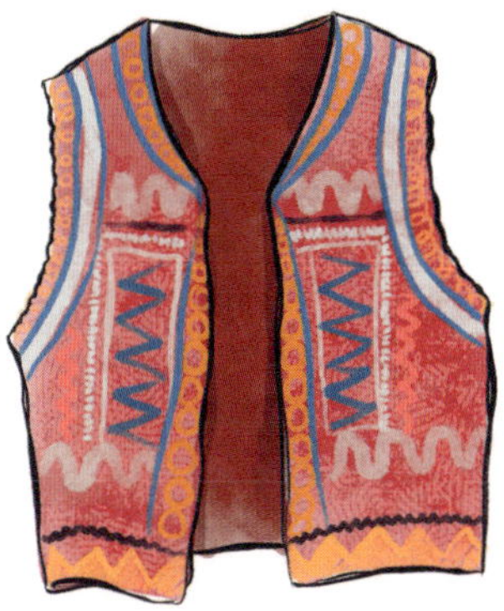

Motifs inspired by Indigenous cultures adorn this colorful vest.

Loose, relaxed pieces are comfortable and flattering.

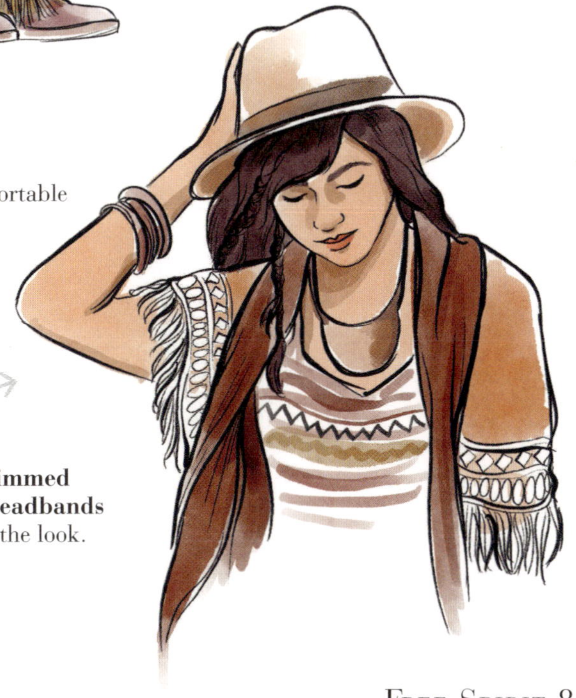

Wide-brimmed hats or headbands complete the look.

Design a dress that this model can wear under her oversize cardigan. Experiment with different patterns and decorative details.

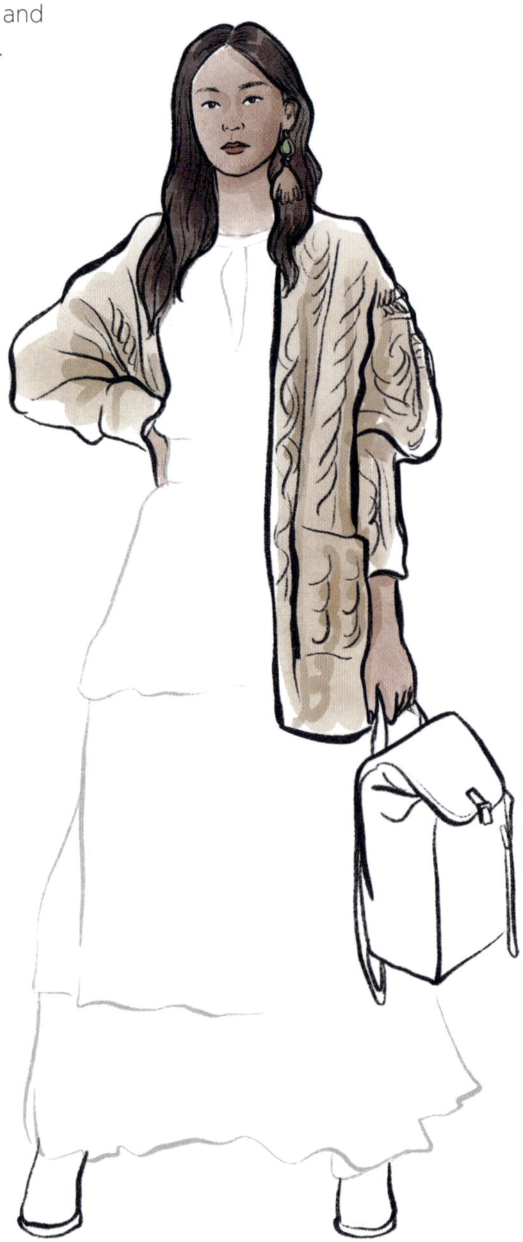

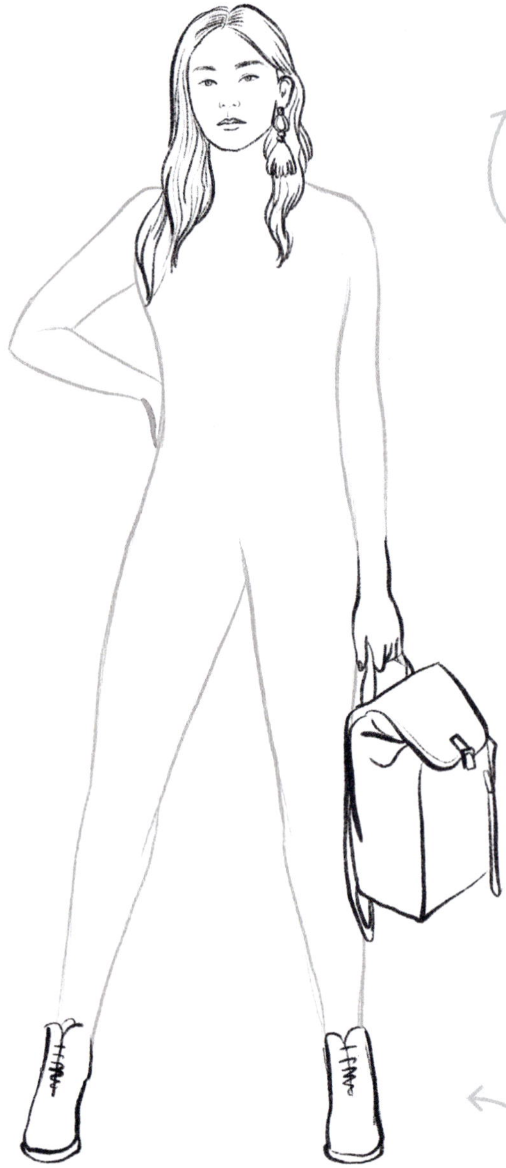

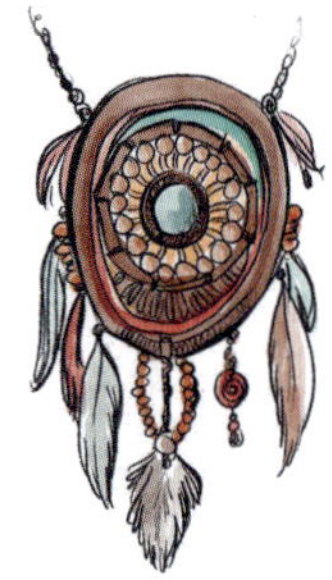

A necklace inspired by the Native American dreamcatcher.

Now see if you can make one that's completely different, but still goes with her leather bag.

Now try a look for you! Think about what materials you might combine to create a relaxed, natural look that's still complex and stylish.

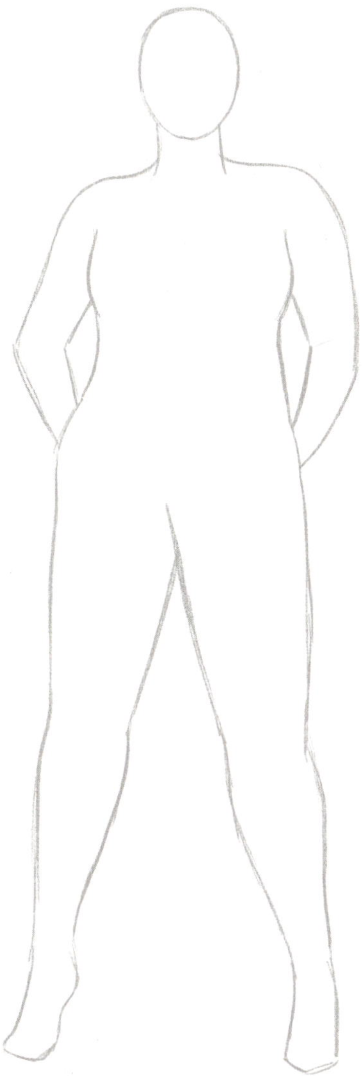

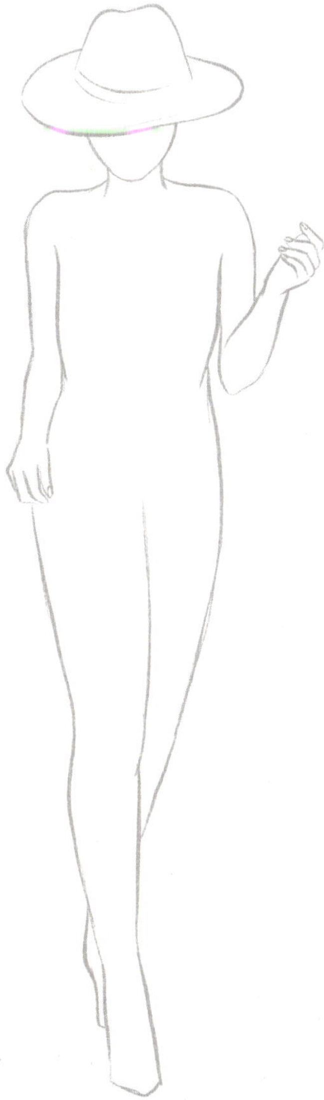

Design a modern free spirited look, complete with shoes and accessories.

Soft leather handbag decorated with eclectic embroidered designs, beads, and fringe.

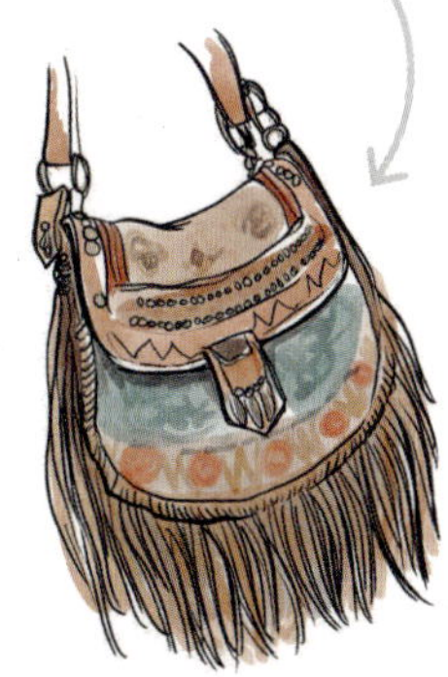

Punk

Punk fashion reflects the rebellious spirit of the punk subculture of the 1970s, drawing inspiration from various music genres—like rock, metal, ska, reggae, and glam—while embracing individuality and creativity. A DIY attitude is essential: ripped jeans might be held together by safety pins and leather jackets decorated with studs, spikes, chains, or political slogans. Because of its core antiestablishment values, punk fashion has evolved over time, and has influenced many other styles and subcultures, such as steampunk and cyberpunk.

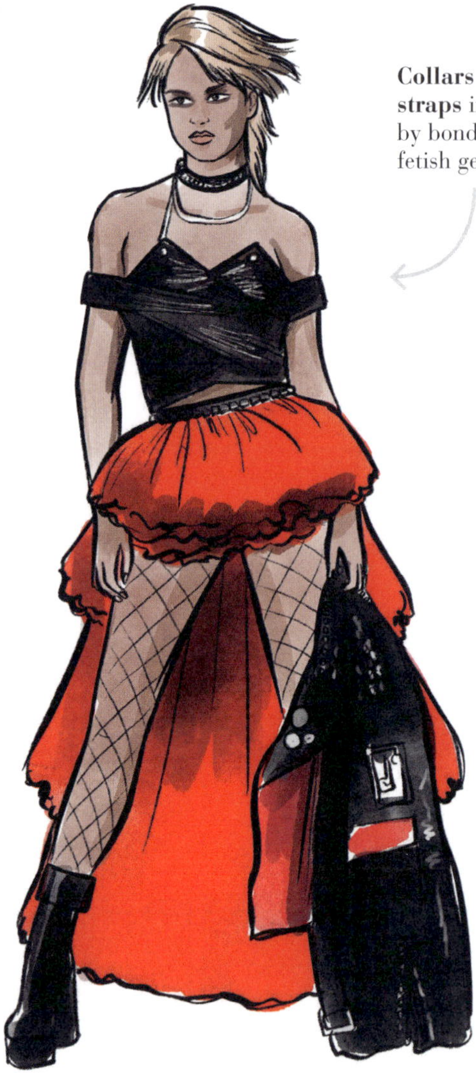

Collars and straps inspired by bondage and fetish gear.

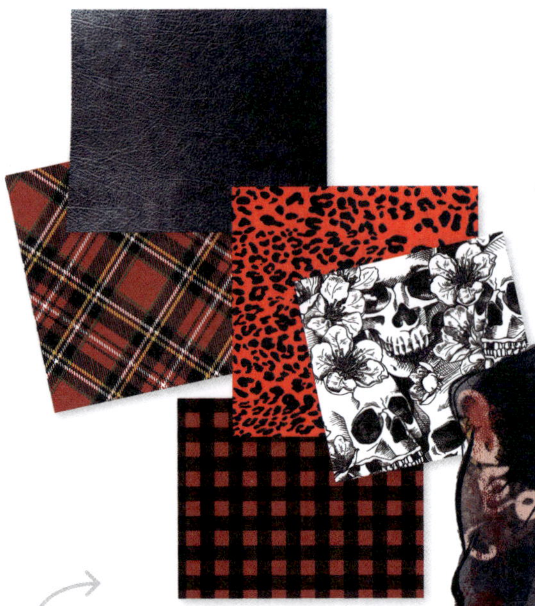

Combine materials like plaid (in strong colors like black and red), leather, and denim with metal spikes, studs, and chains.

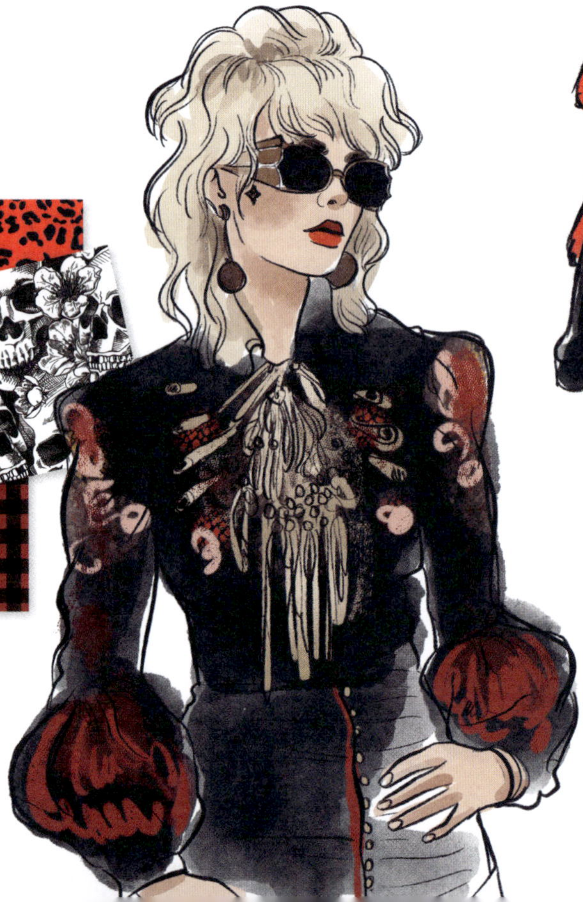

An ornamental punk look.

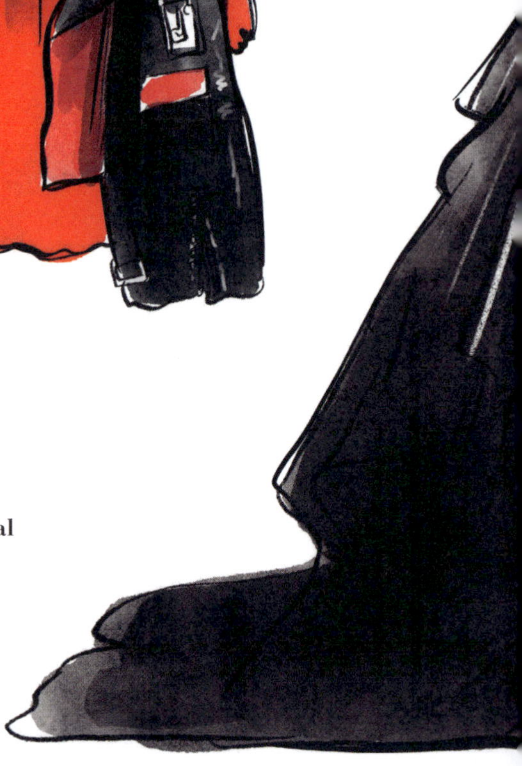

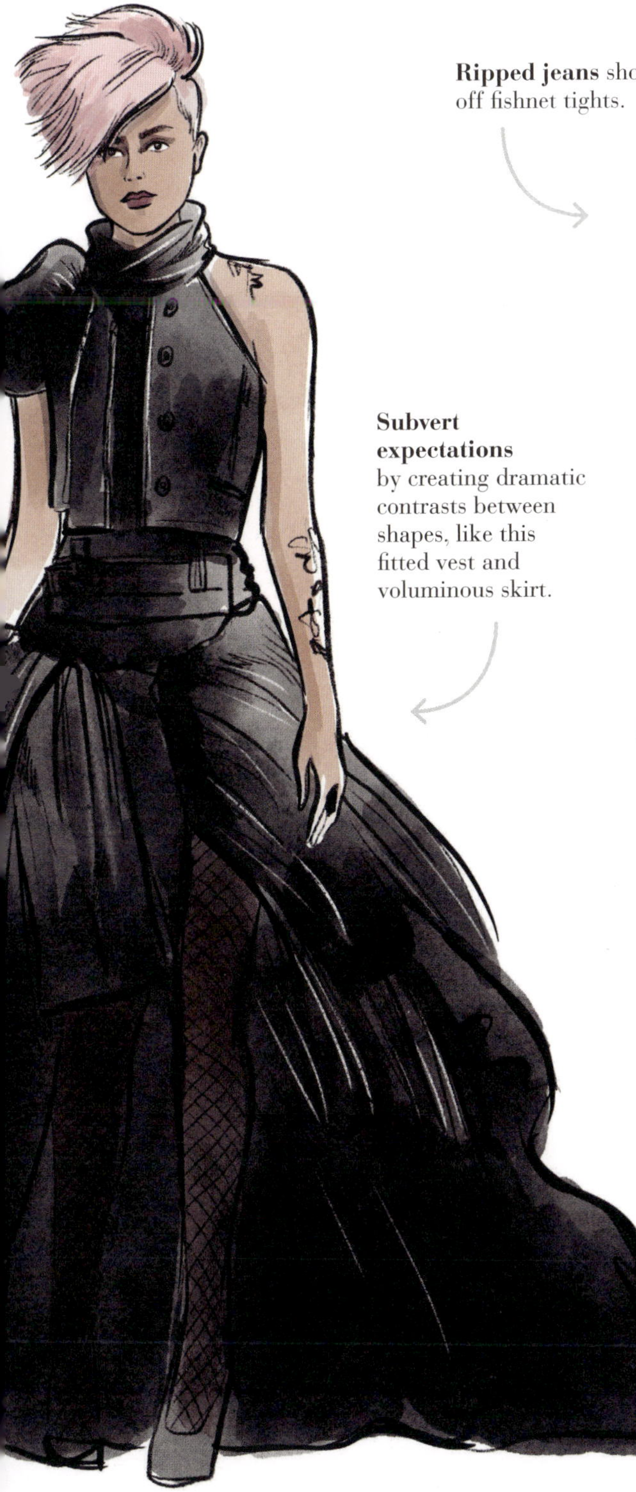

Subvert expectations by creating dramatic contrasts between shapes, like this fitted vest and voluminous skirt.

Ripped jeans show off fishnet tights.

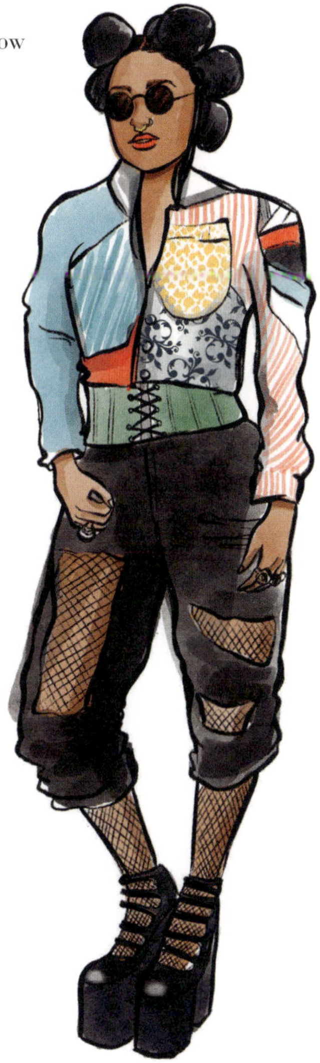

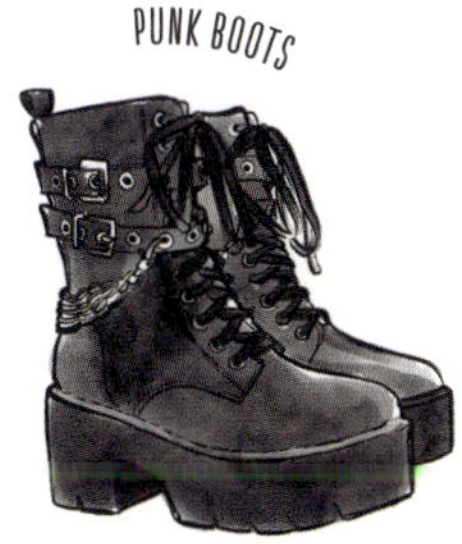

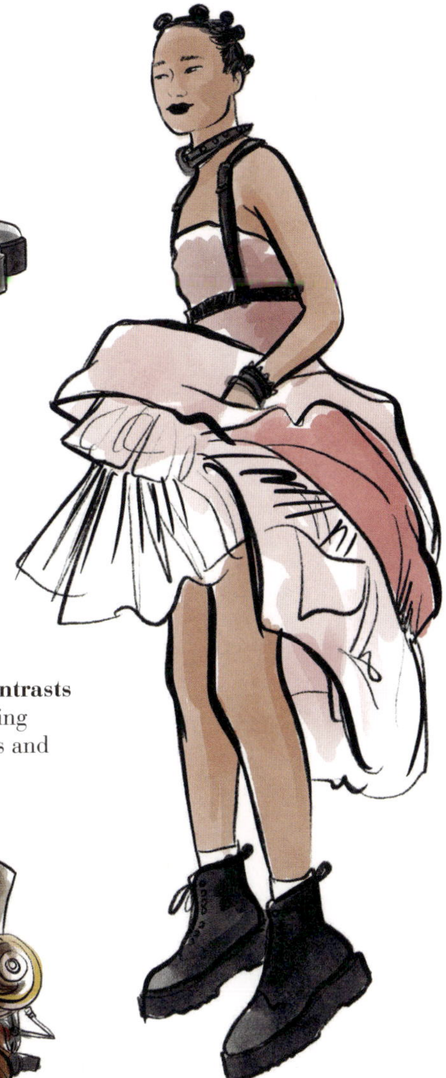

Create surprising contrasts by pairing a soft, flowing dress with heavy boots and leather accessories.

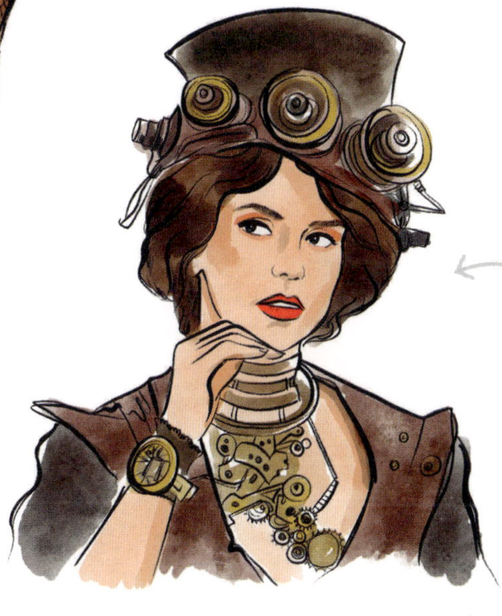

Steampunk is a retro futuristic genre that explores the wonders and dangers of a steam-driven alternative reality. It mixes typical punk elements with Victorian accessories, bringing together the elegant and the rugged.

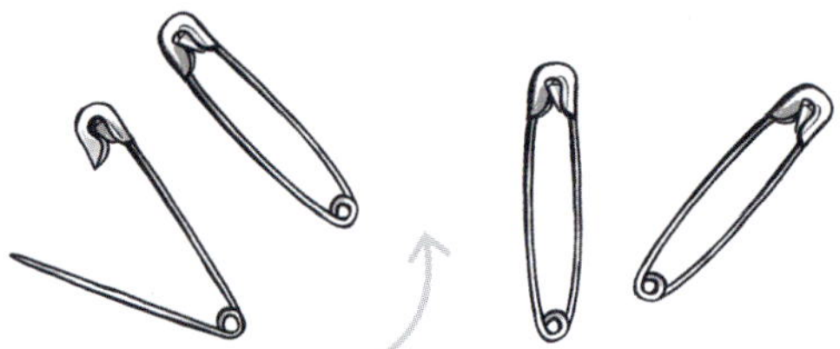

Safety pins encapsulate the DIY punk ethos: great for holding together ripped clothes, piercing ears or noses, or creating patterns on fabrics.

Hair might be shaped into mohawks or liberty spikes, or shaved off entirely. Tartan or plaid fabrics, especially kilts or skirts, contrast with solid black.

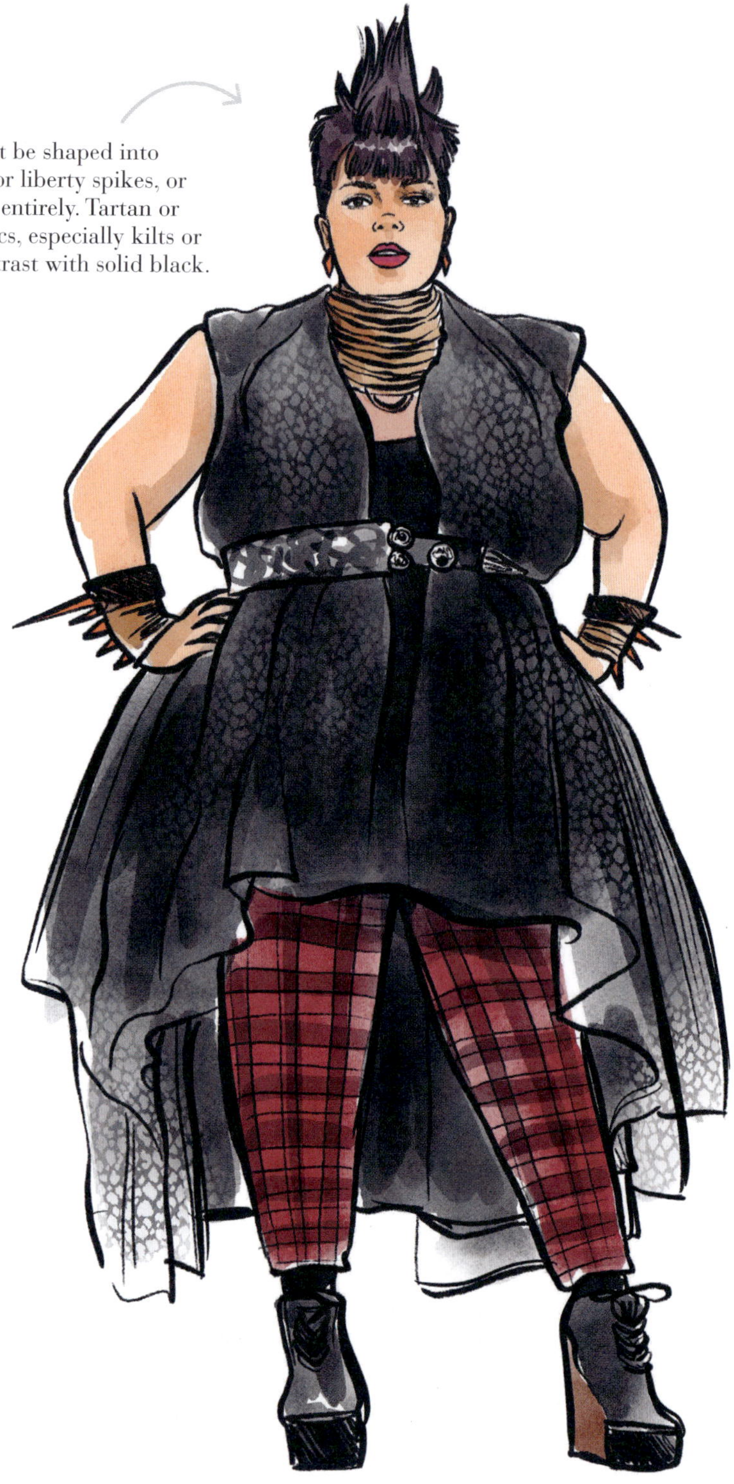

Brightly colored hair, as well as red eyeshadow and lipstick, contrast with this black choker and its silver spikes and chains. A studded leather jacket completes the look.

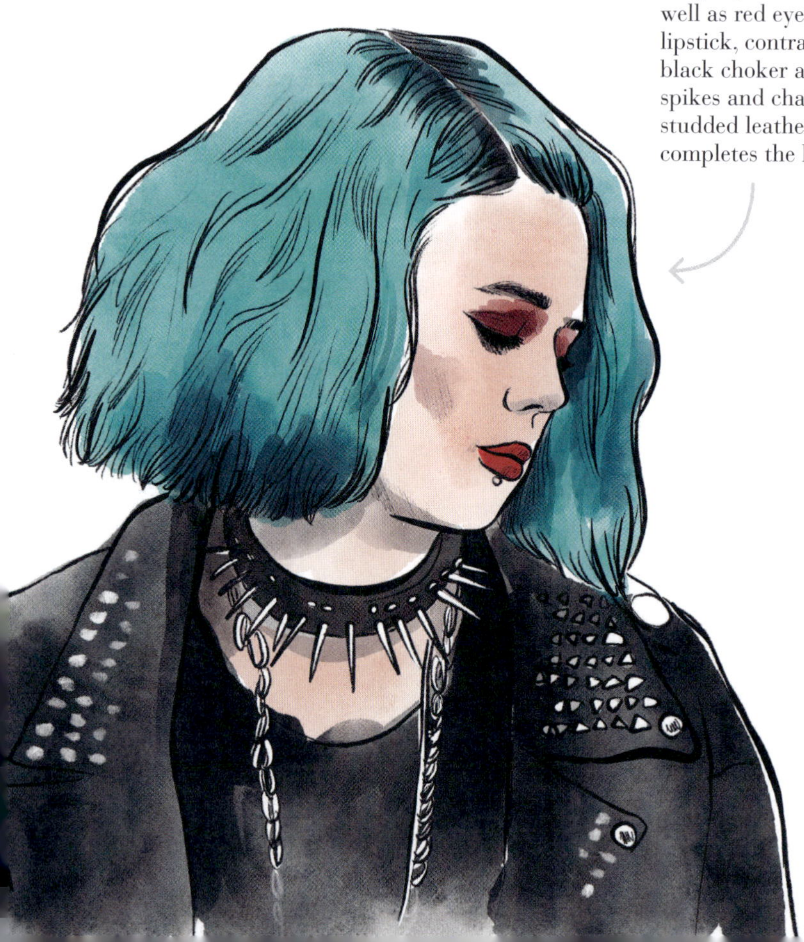

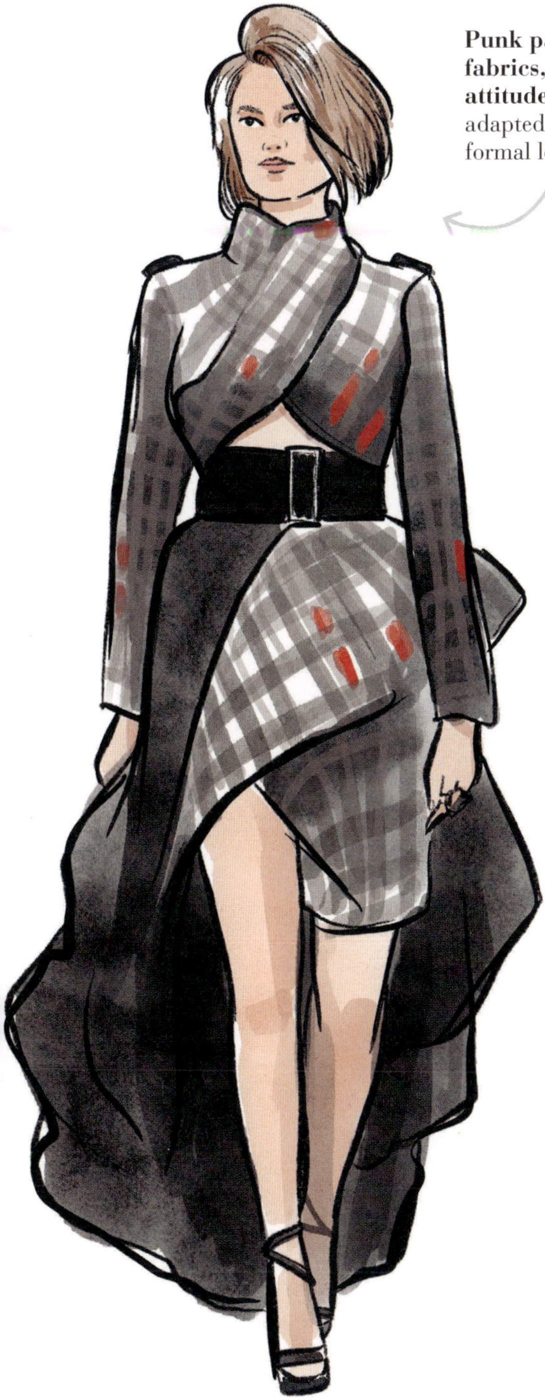

Punk patterns, fabrics, and attitude can be adapted to more formal looks, too.

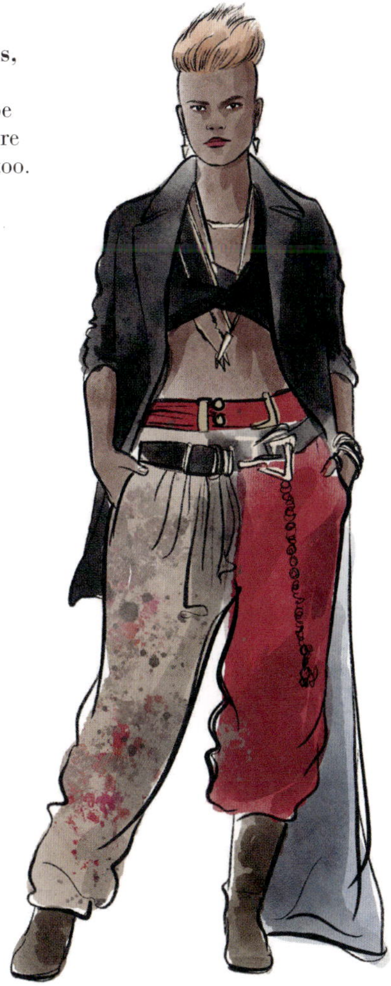

Leather bracelets decorated with metal spikes, stars, and skulls.

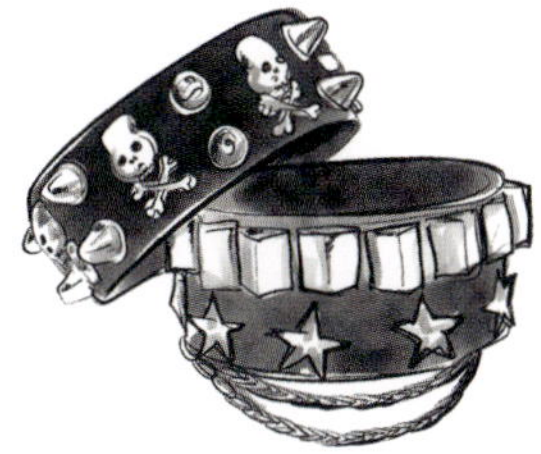

Punk designers like Vivienne Westwood often play with asymmetry in their creations—breaking the line, surprising the audience, and creating the unexpected, while maintaining a look that's balanced overall and oozes punk spirit.

Cyberpunk fashion imagines how punks might respond to a dystopian society dominated by technology and corporations.

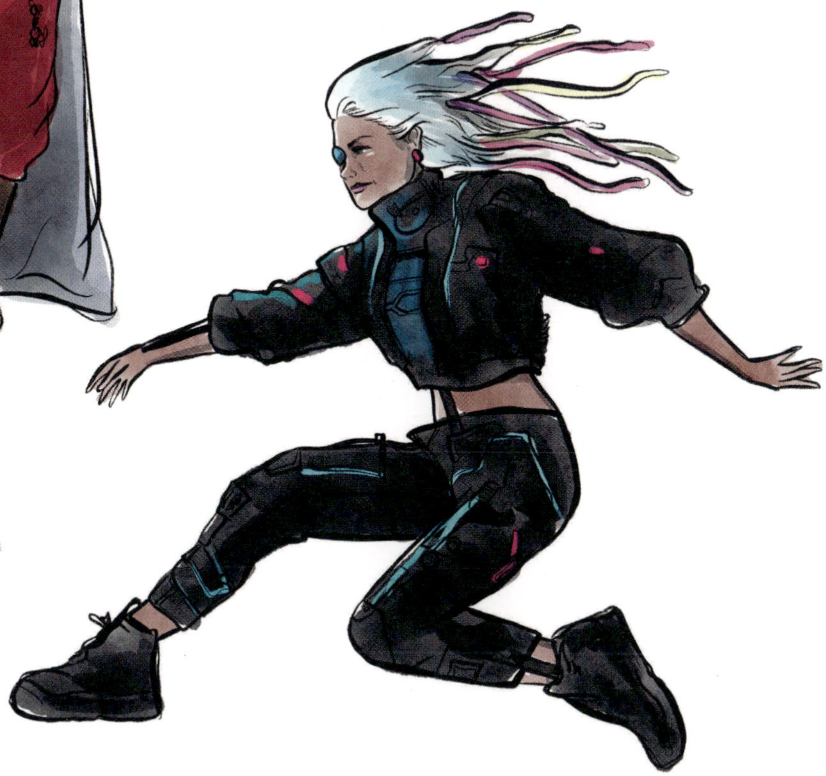

Now draw your own punk dress. Think about what fabrics might complement the leather choker, gloves, and boots.

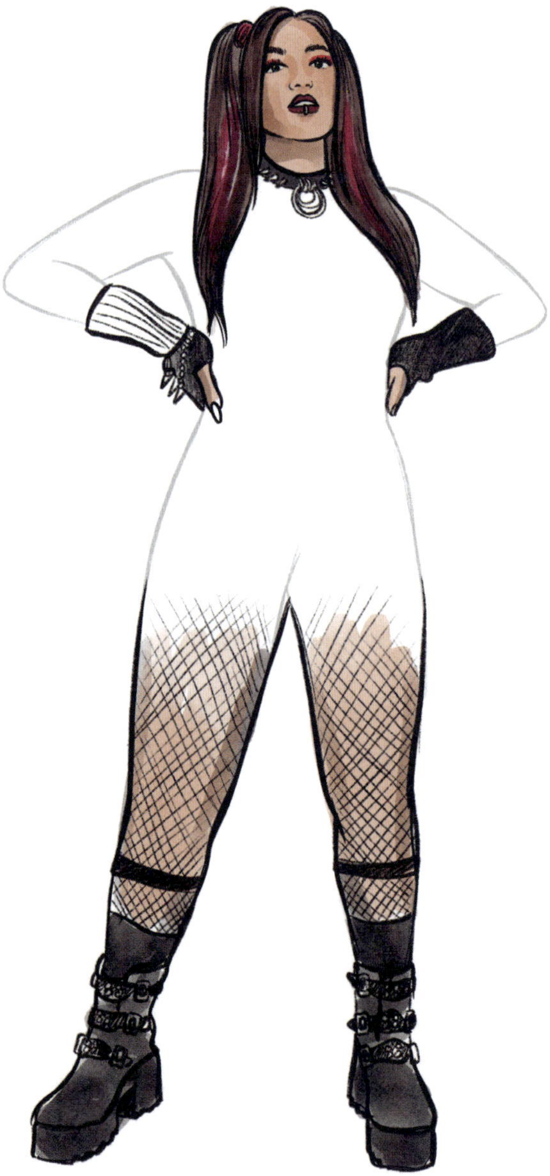

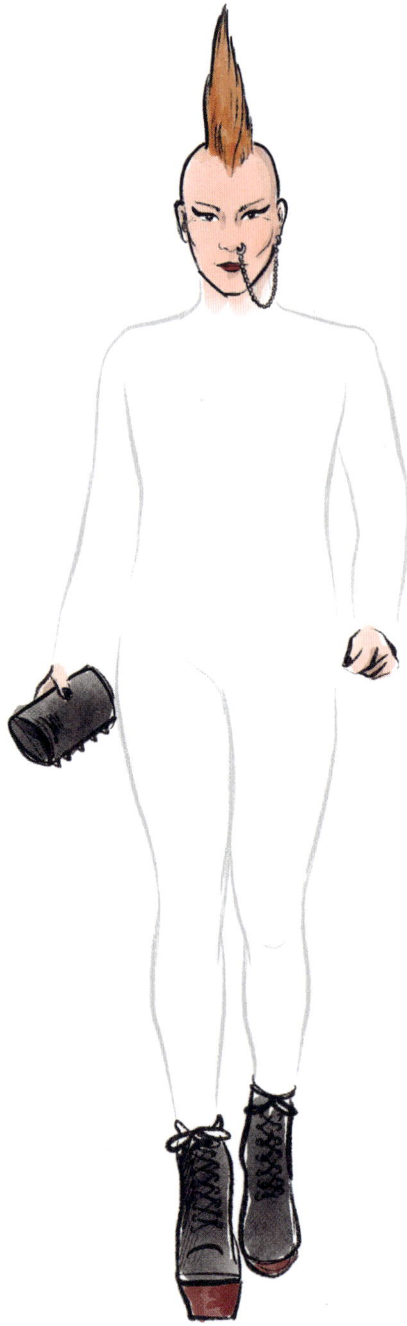

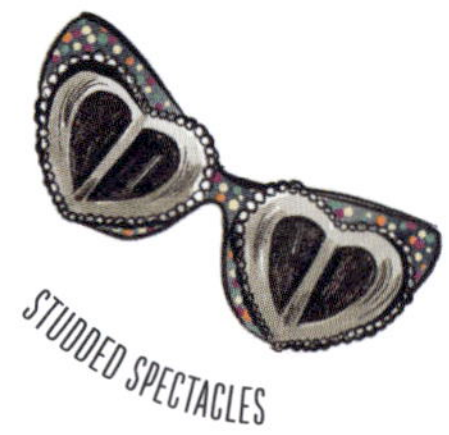

This model's mohawk demands a daring outfit to match. Do you imagine ripped jeans, or a vinyl dress? Add a touch of plaid to complete the punk look.

Now design a punk-inspired outfit for this figure. What kind of slogan might she scrawl onto her clothes to express her rebellious spirit? How might she have modified her clothes to make them her own?

Create a strong silhouette with punk colors, patterns, and accessories.

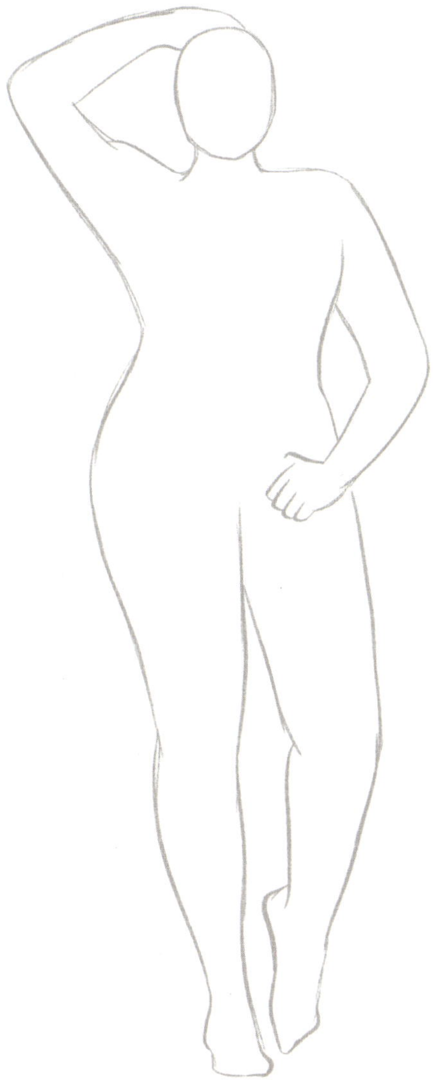

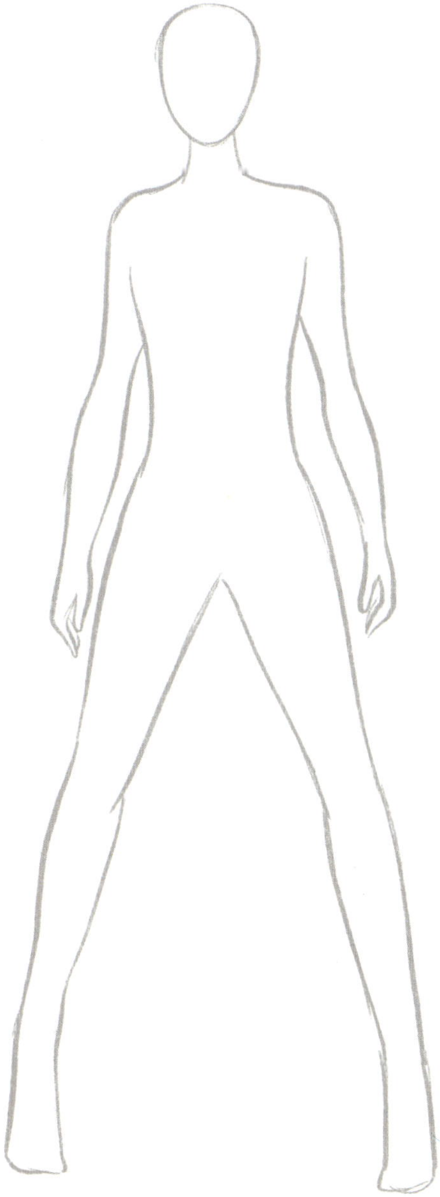

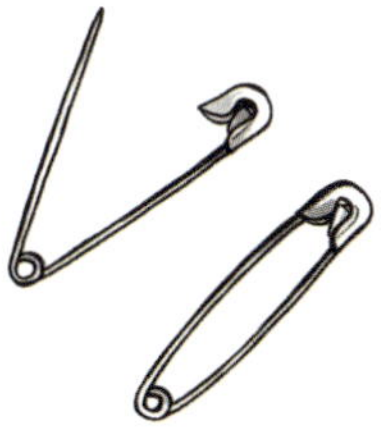

Goth

The Goth counterculture emerged in the late 1970s and early 1980s as a branch of the post-punk music scene. Goth fashion is characterized by its bold and dark aesthetic that borrows from the musical, literary, and cinematic influences of the Goth subculture. Solid black—symbolizing death, darkness, and mystery—dominates, complemented by romantic or morbid elements such as lace, velvet, leather, fishnets, corsets, buckles, chains, or spikes, lending the look an eerie quality.

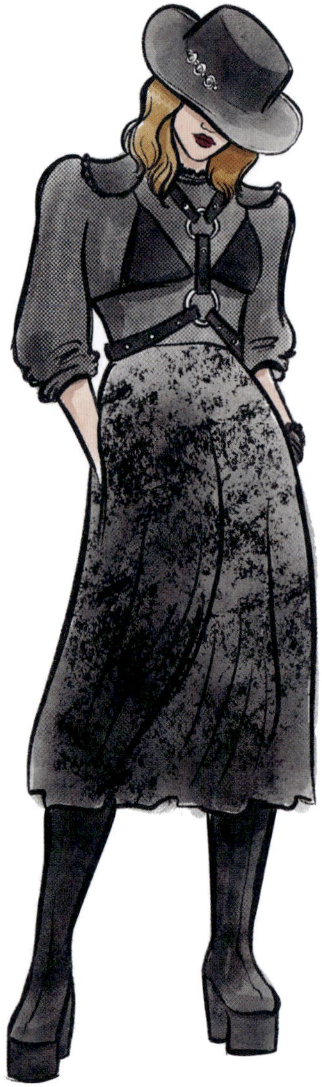

Leather belts, chains, heeled boots, and fedora hats are core elements of Goth fashion.

Lace, velvet, and satin are popular in the Goth sphere, in dark colors like black, red, purple, or gray. Patterns featuring skulls, bats, roses, or crosses add visual interest.

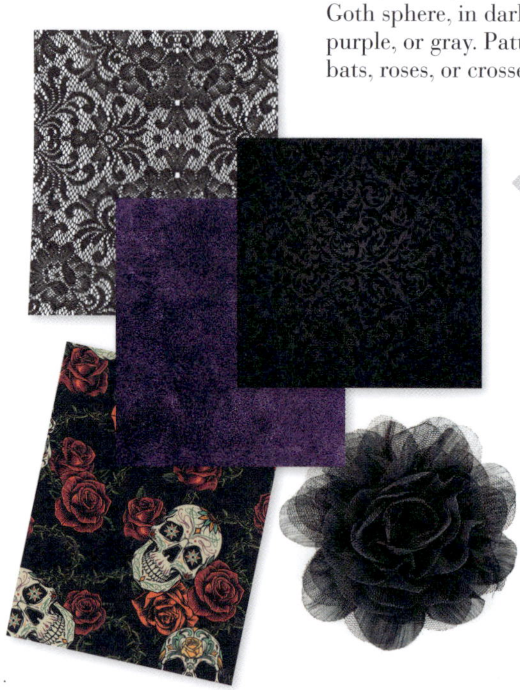

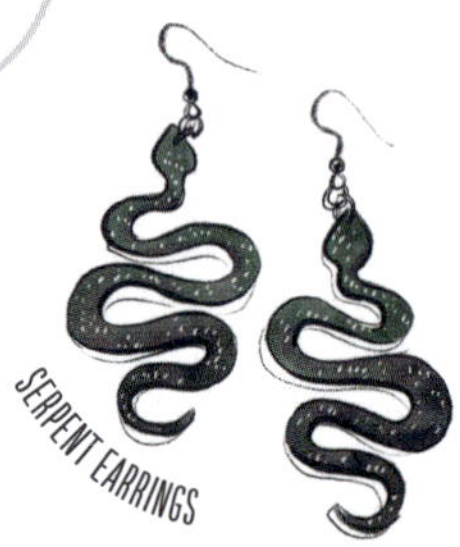

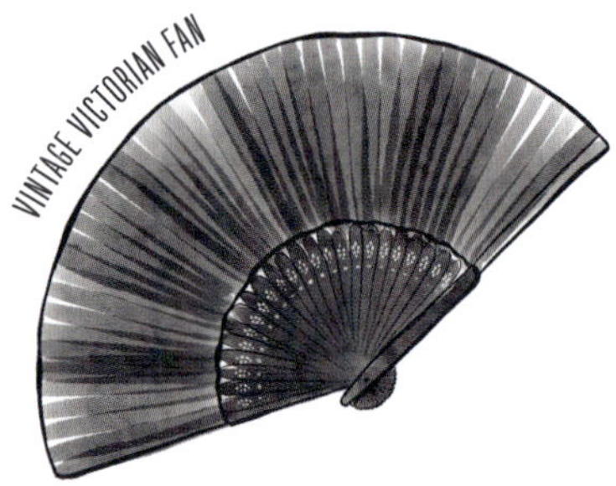

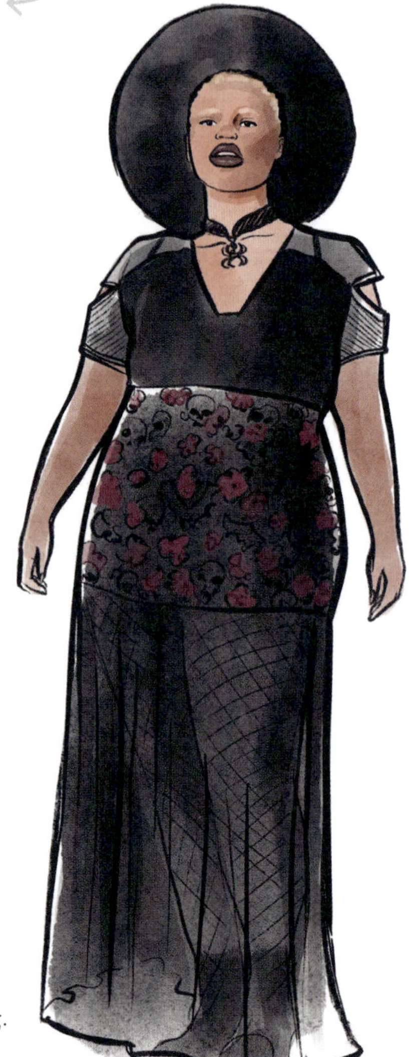

Goth fashion can be beautiful and elegant, as well as severe and striking.

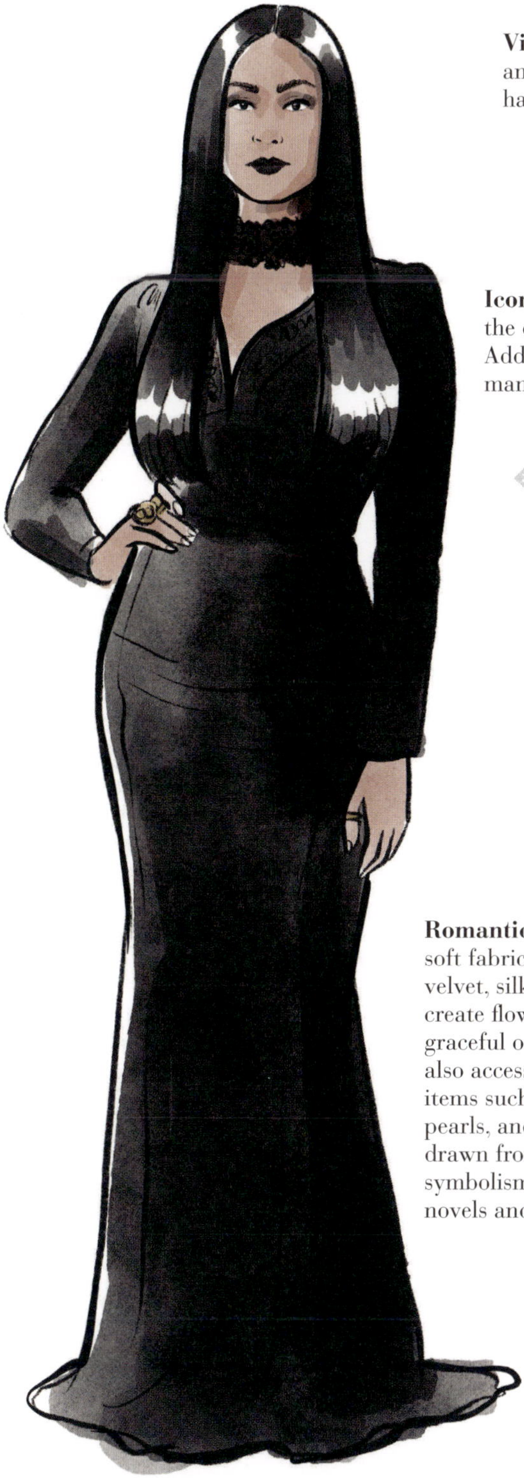

Vintage lace and Goth go hand in hand.

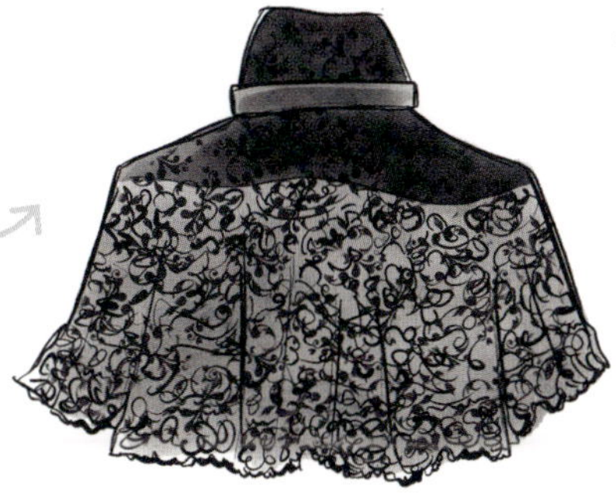

Iconic Goth: the diabolical Morticia Addams inspires many Goth looks.

High-fashion Goth. Structured lines and exaggerated shoulders update the Gothic look for the runway.

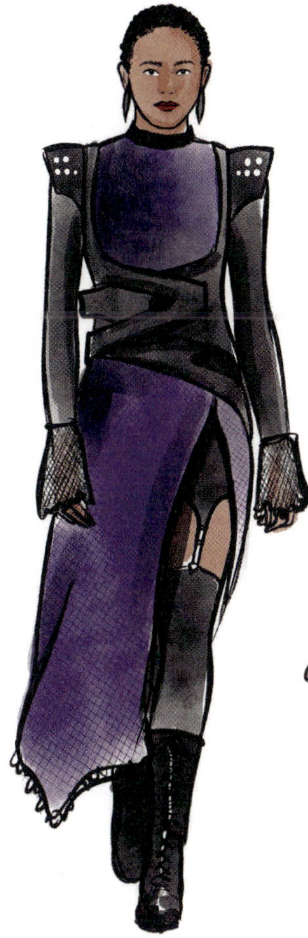

Platform boots with distinctive embellishments are a staple.

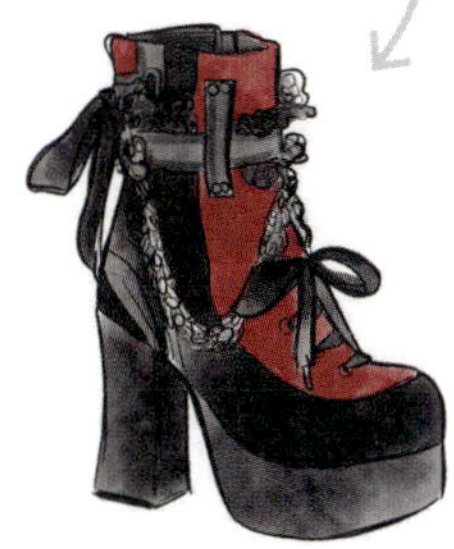

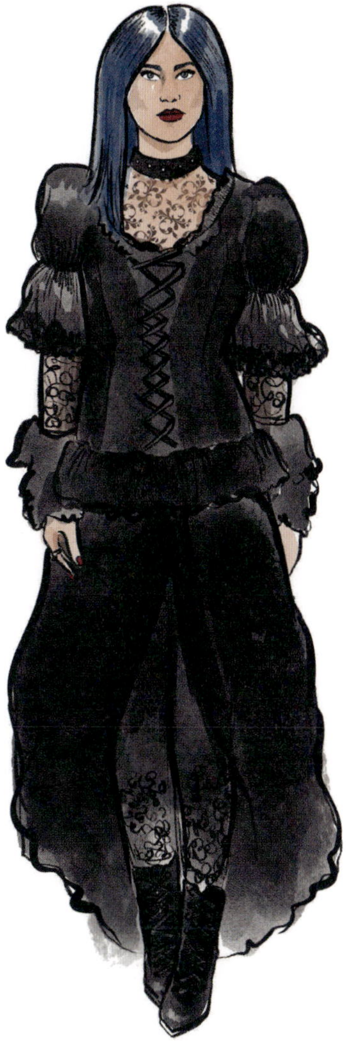

Romantic Goths use soft fabrics, such as lace, velvet, silk, or satin, to create flowing and graceful outfits. They also accessorize with items such as roses, pearls, and ribbons, drawn from the symbolism of Gothic novels and movies.

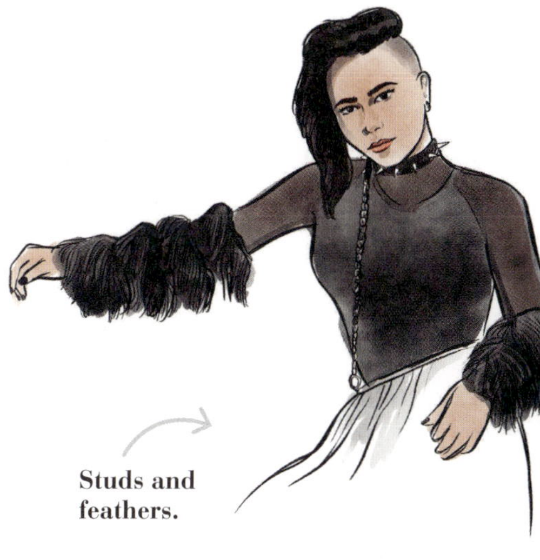

Studs and feathers.

Draw your own Goth-inspired look. Don't be afraid to add spooky touches!

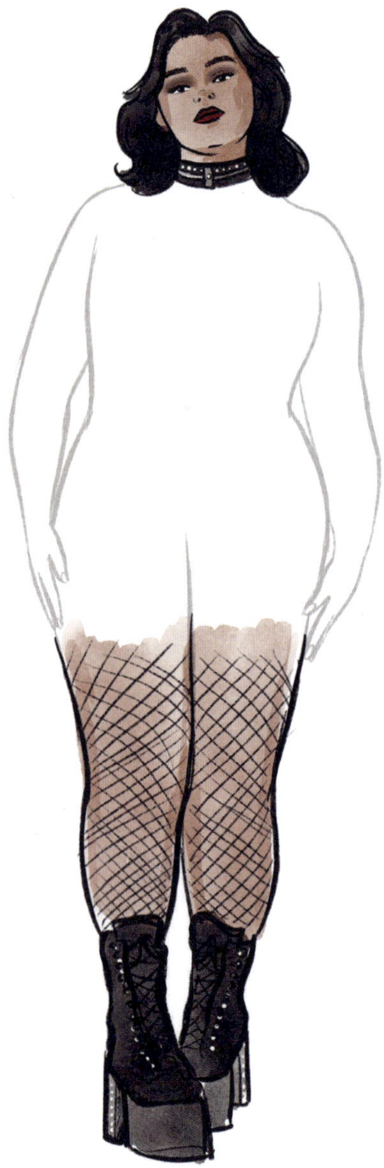

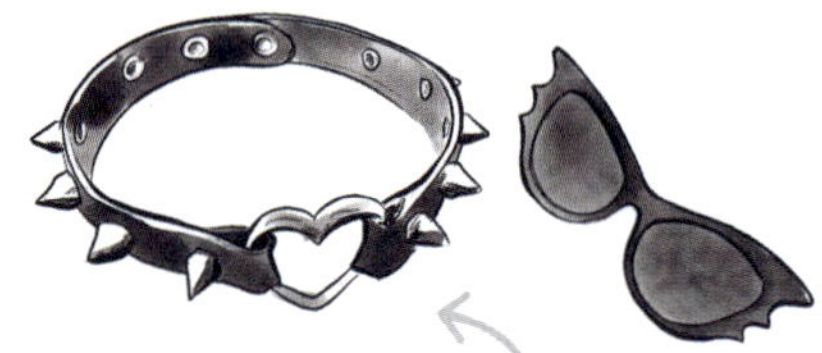

Studded choker with silver heart and statement spectacles.

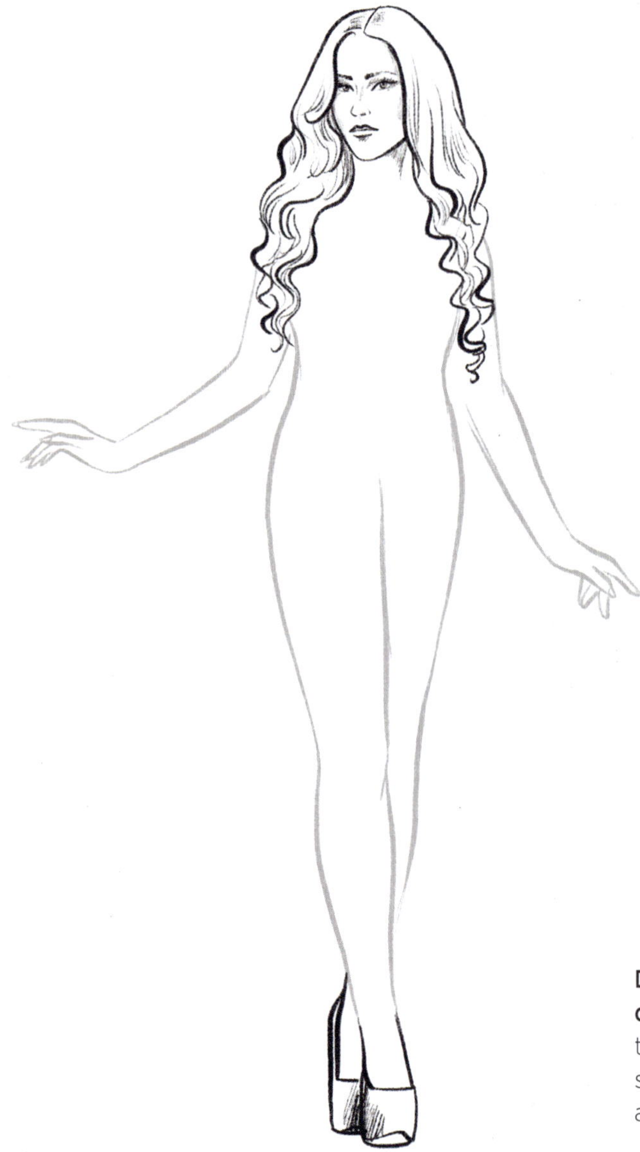

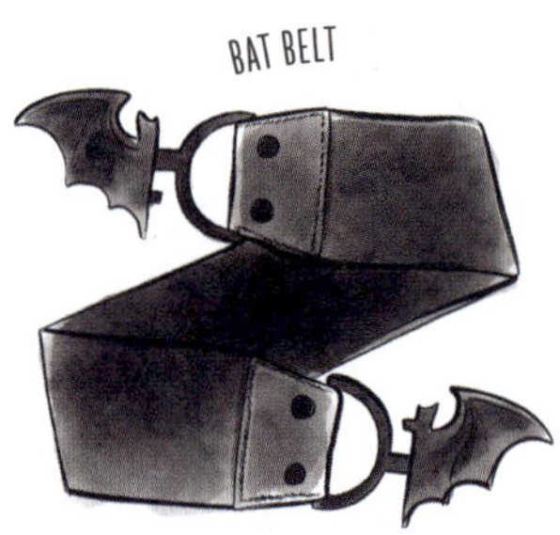

Design this Goth's dream dress. You could try contrasting a structured corset with a full, flowing skirt.

Now try a look for you! Will you opt for studs and spikes, or romantic lace—or a combination of the two?

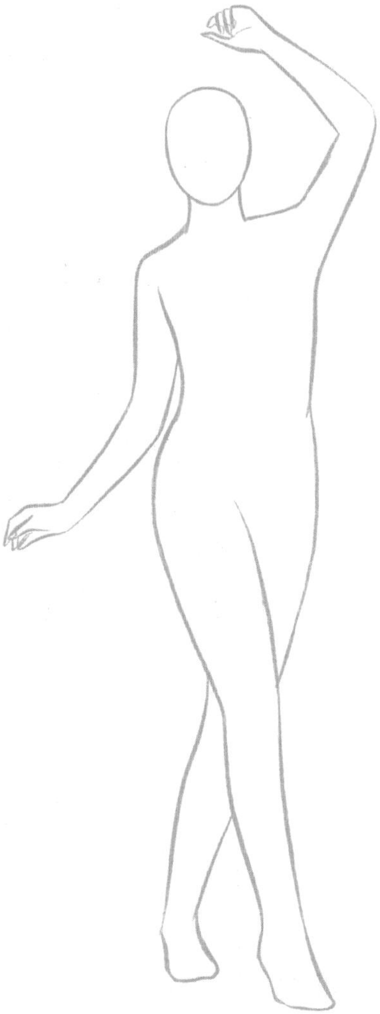

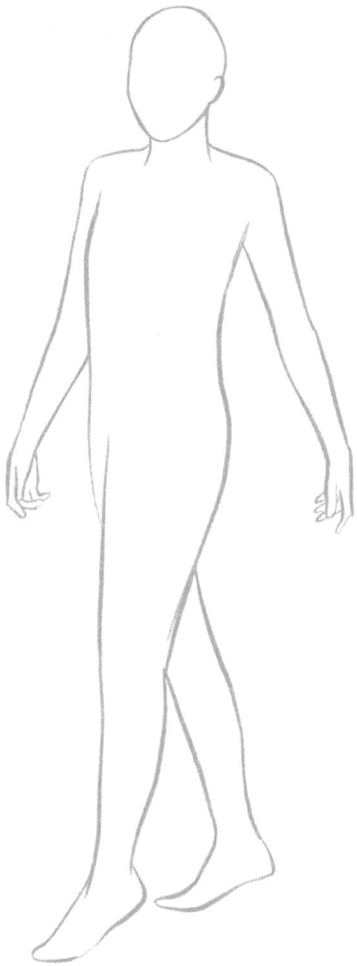

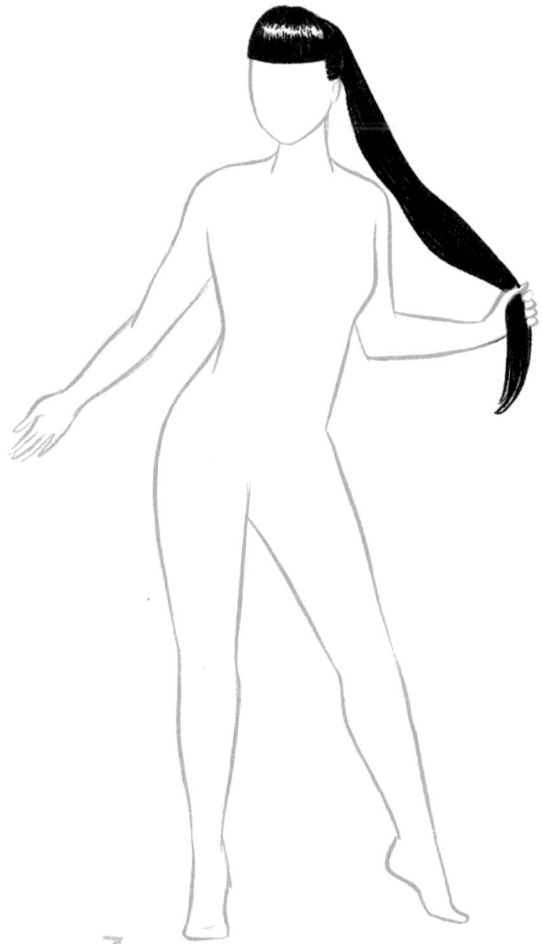

Give this model a wide black hat—the witchier the better.

Experiment with different textures, lines, and patterns to create a Goth-inspired runway look. Which elements of Gothic fashion will you use or adapt for the catwalk?

Inspired by Nature

Many designers use the colors, textures, shapes, and patterns of things they find in nature to create stunning and original pieces. Alexander McQueen was known for his dramatic, spectacular creations that incorporated flowers, feathers, antlers, and shells. Nature-inspired fashion can be elegant, whimsical, edgy, or romantic, depending on the mood and message of the designer, who might use organic, recycled, or biodegradable materials to make a statement about the importance of protecting our environment.

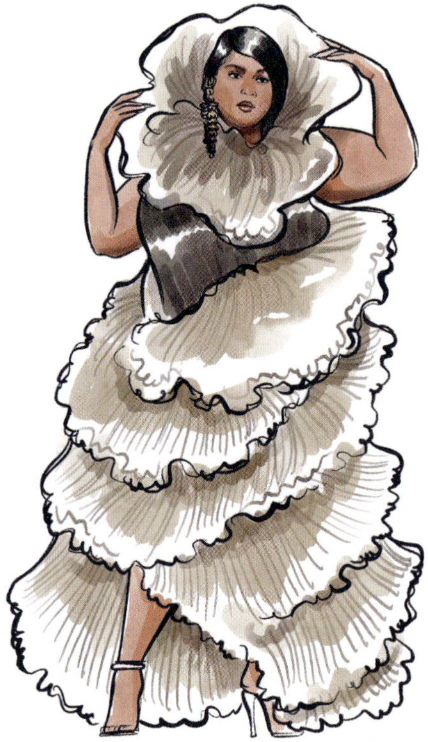

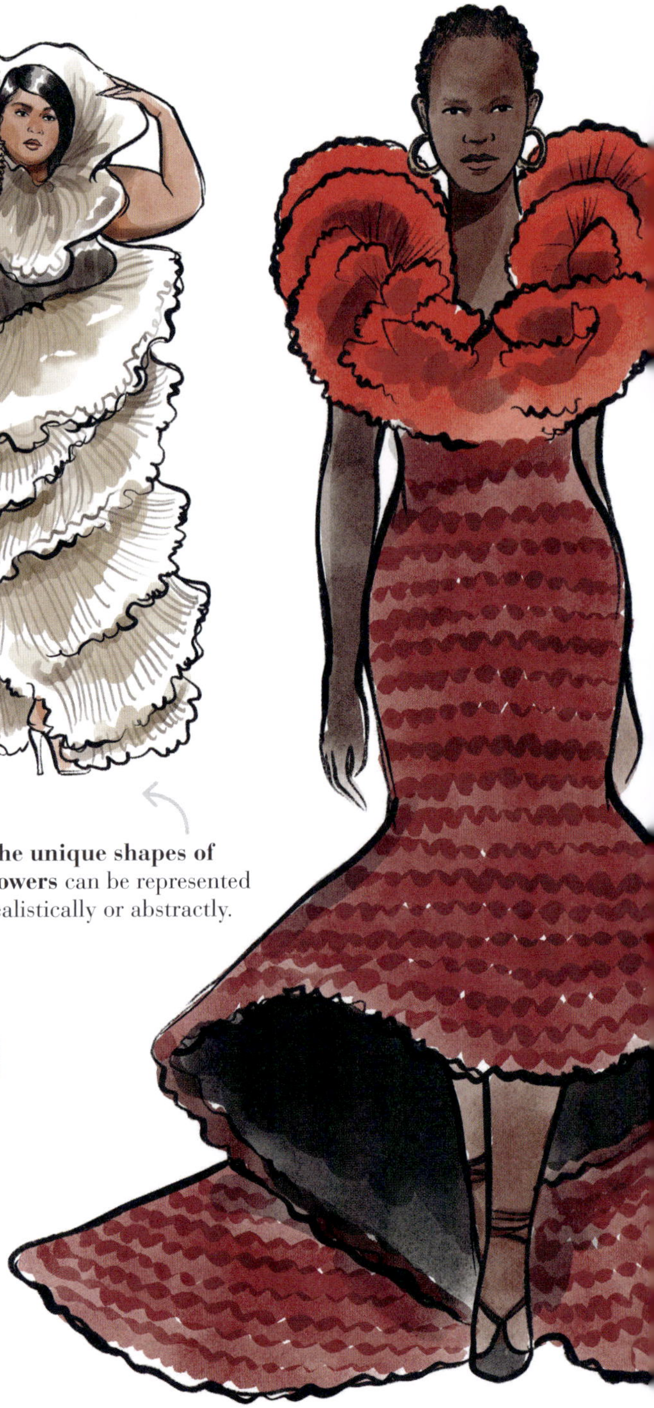

The unique shapes of flowers can be represented realistically or abstractly.

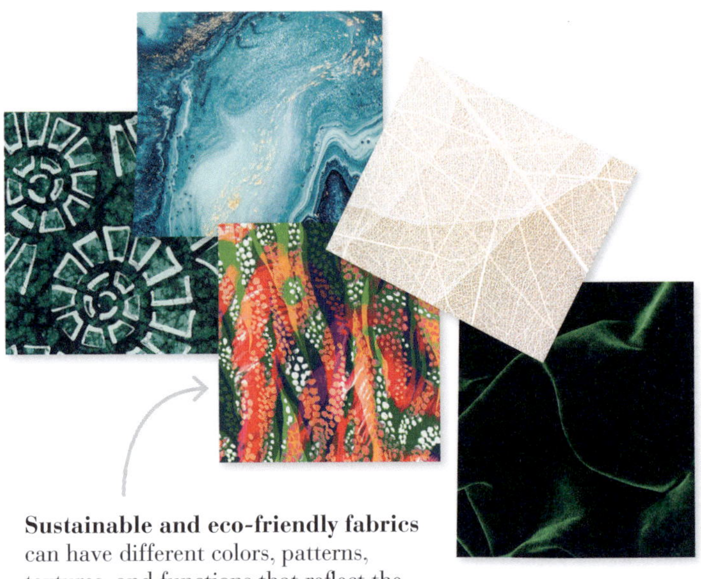

Sustainable and eco-friendly fabrics can have different colors, patterns, textures, and functions that reflect the beauty and diversity of nature.

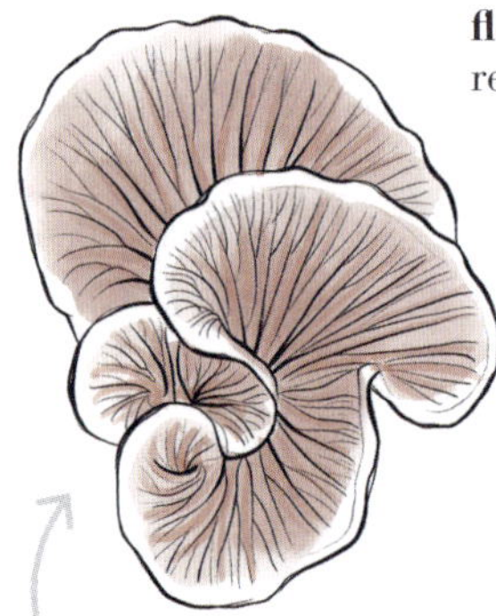

The structure of this garment takes inspiration from seashells.

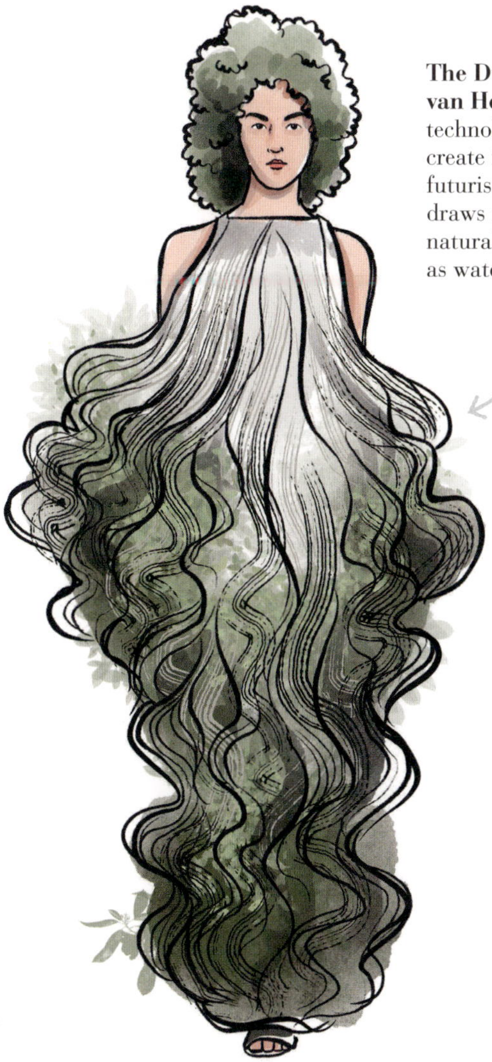

The Dutch designer Iris van Herpen combines technology and artistry to create innovative and futuristic designs. She often draws inspiration from natural phenomena, such as water, fire, air, and light.

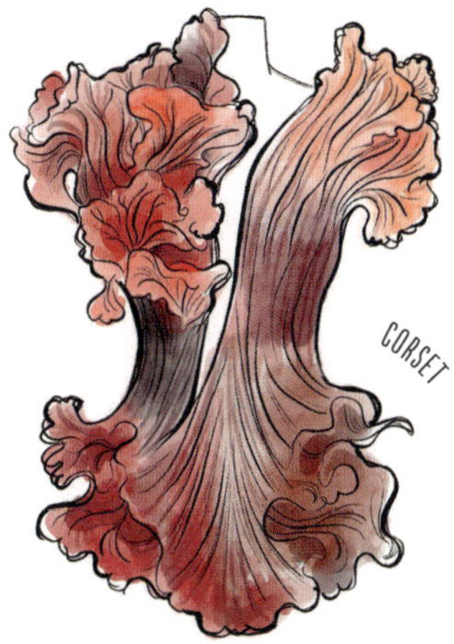

The delicate patterns of a butterfly's wings inspired this print.

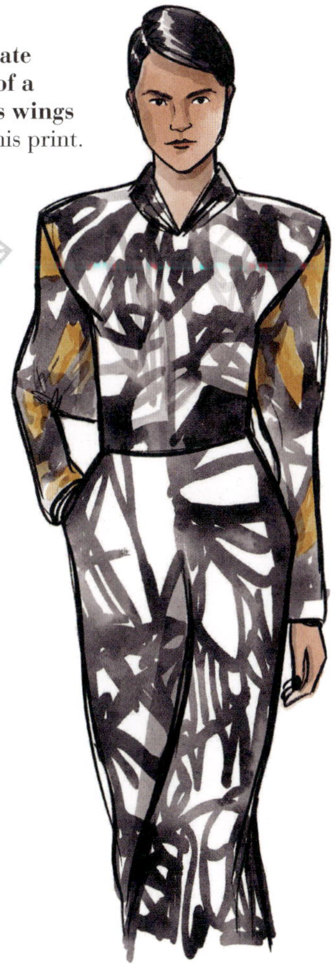

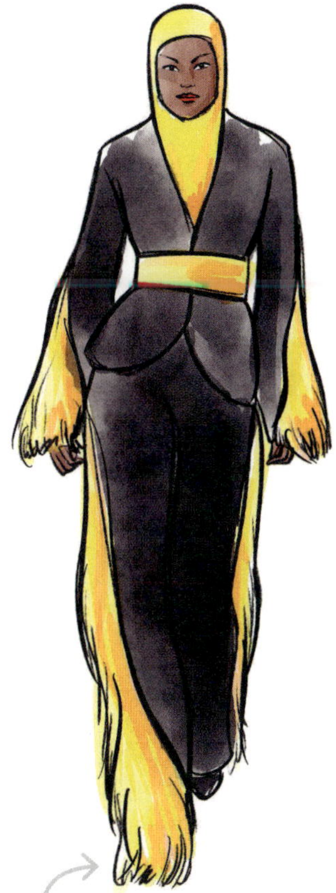

Fabulous feathers: a bird-inspired design.

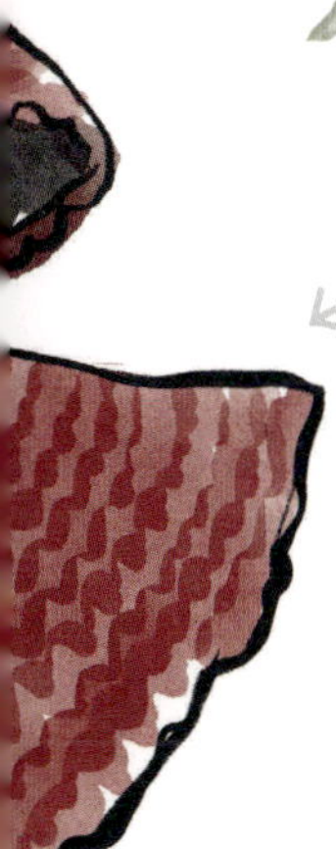

A striking red dress made of organic material.

The beauty of nature is recreated with gentle strokes of luxurious fabrics and natural colors.

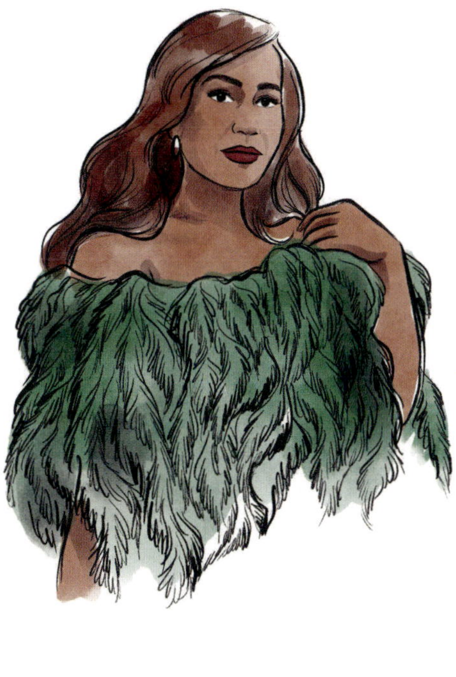

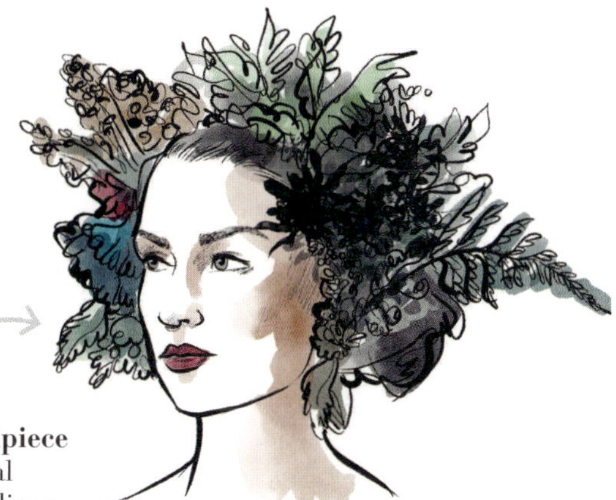

A forest headpiece made from real flowers and foliage.

Try continuing this feathery dress design. What kind of bird does it make you think of? You can make it as big and puffy as you like!

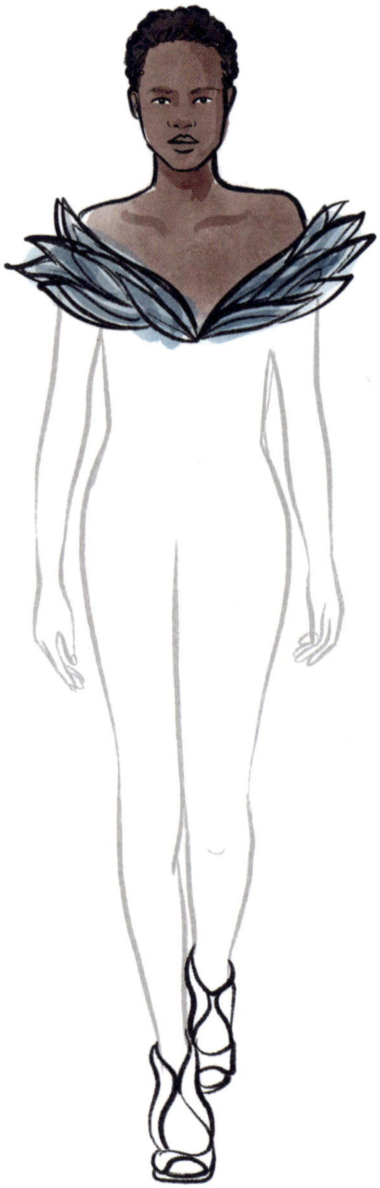

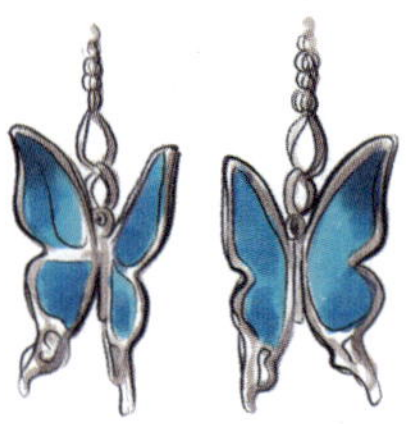

BLUE BUTTERFLY EARRINGS

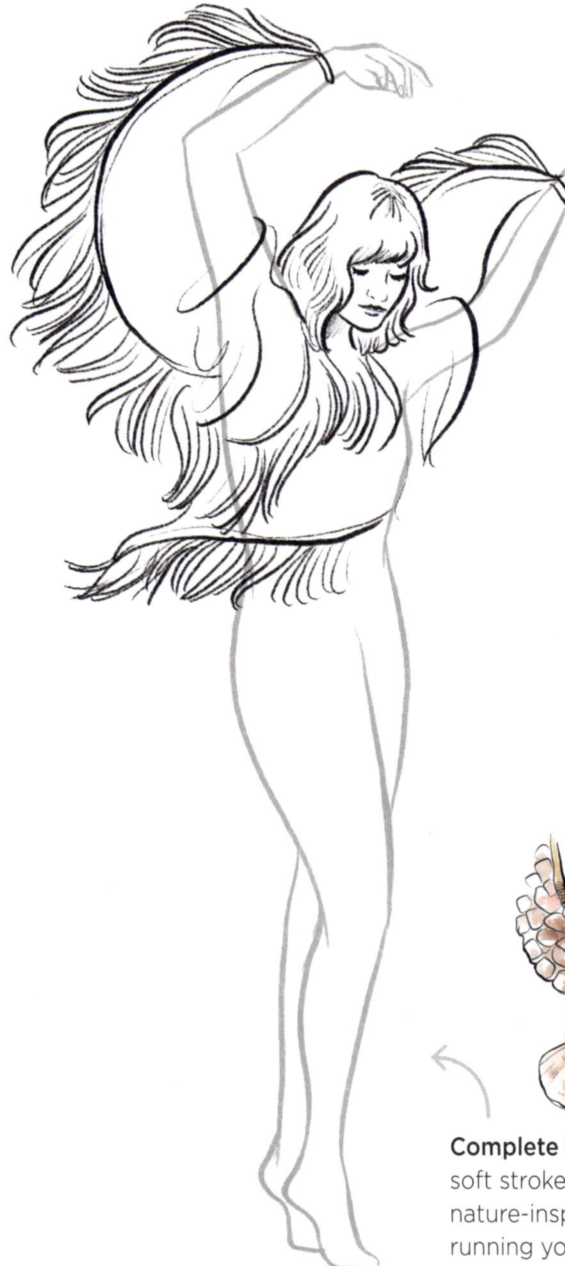

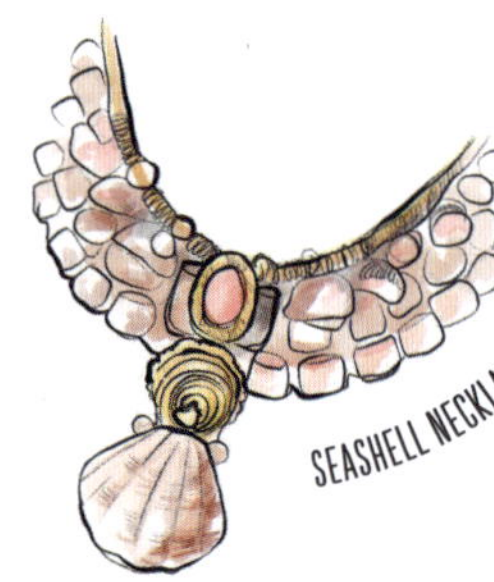

SEASHELL NECKLACE

Complete this look with soft strokes to create a nature-inspired outfit. Try running your pencil freely around the model, to see where it takes you and what shapes you create.

Pick a simple silhouette for your outfit, and then add patterns and details to make a truly unique creation.

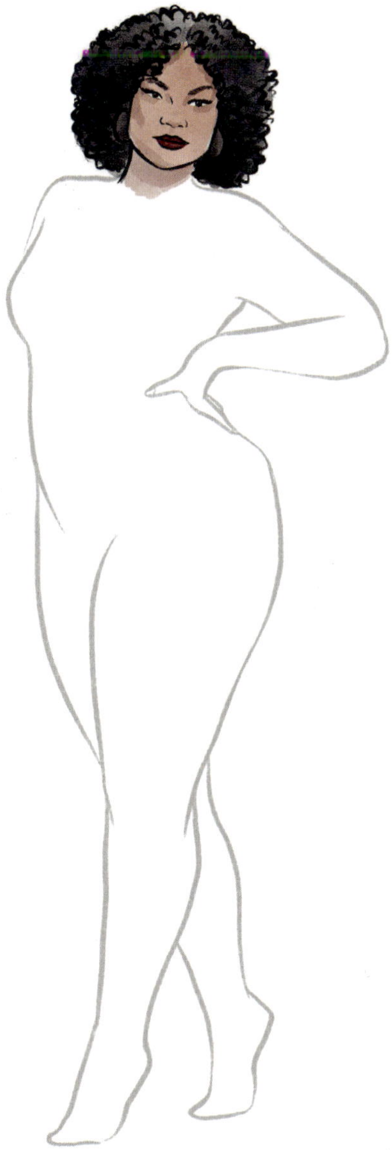

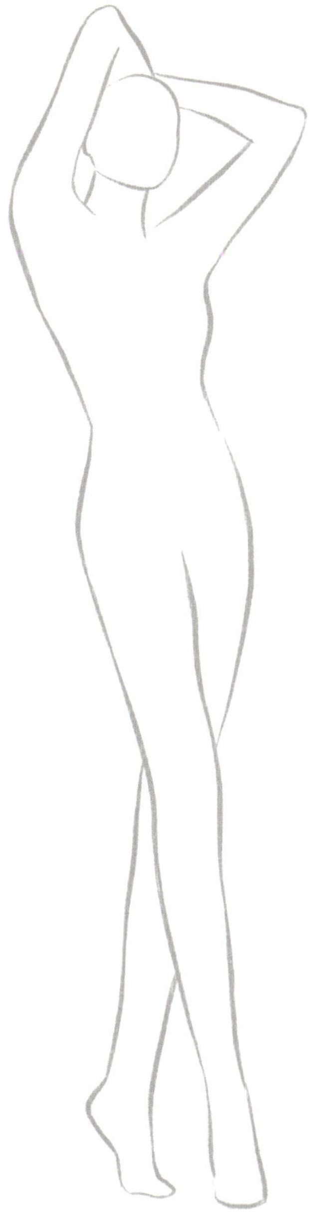

Create your own nature-inspired dress, using only materials that you could find in the natural world. Will your model look like they've just stepped out of the rainforest, or off a beach?

Think about the way the fabric gathers and falls to create wave-like shapes.

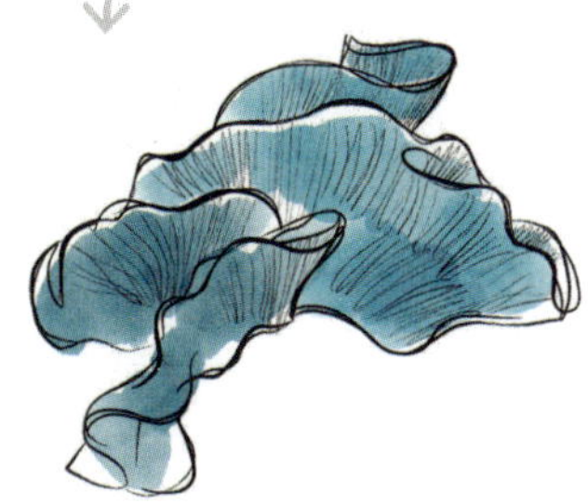

Camp

Camp fashion playfully embraces irony, exaggeration, and bad taste. A sense of humor is key for camp! It aims to subvert the accepted rules of "good taste," combining high and low culture seamlessly and conferring the same weight to each. It's a theatrical and dramatic aesthetic, where performers deliberately craft attention-grabbing looks that surprise and delight the audience.

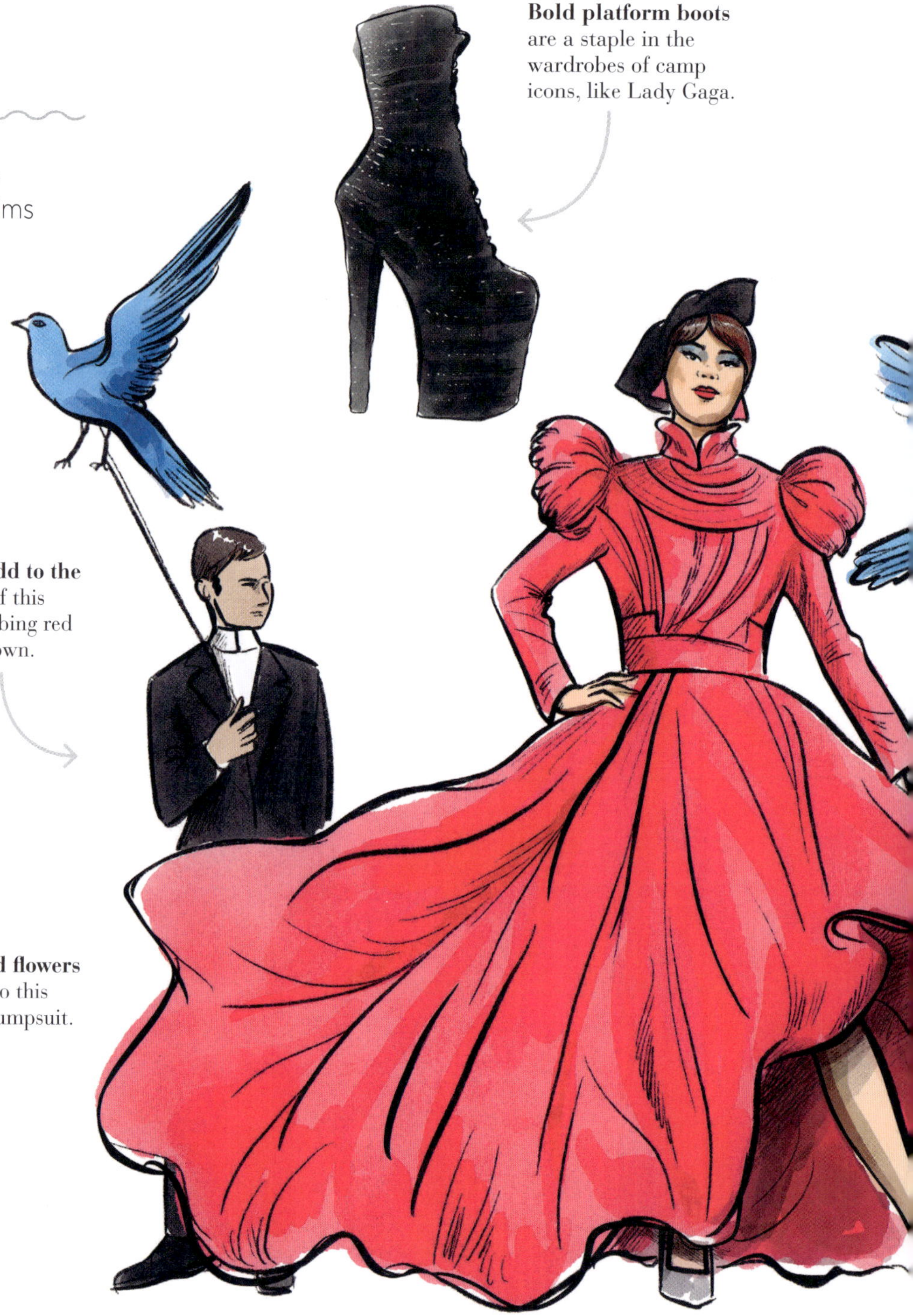

Bold platform boots are a staple in the wardrobes of camp icons, like Lady Gaga.

Props add to the drama of this eye-grabbing red carpet gown.

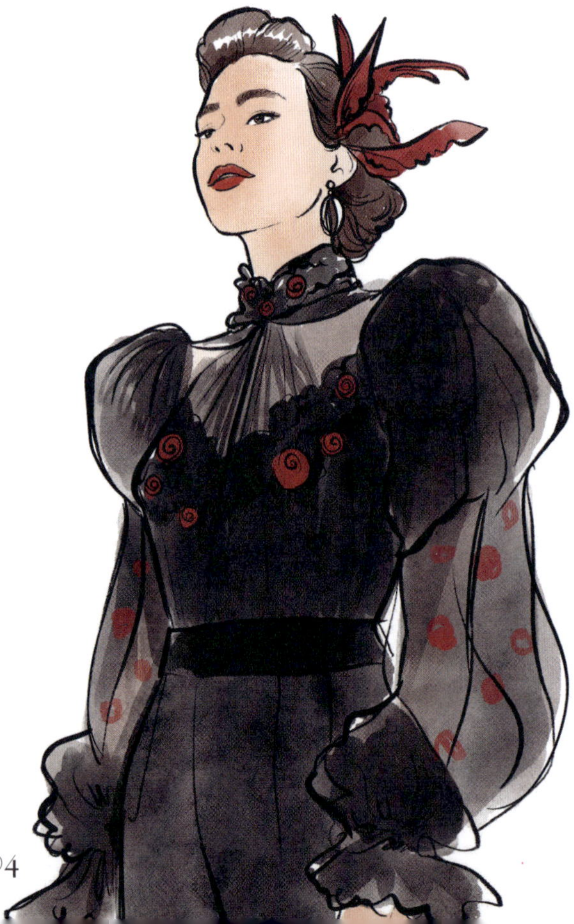

Feathers and flowers add pizzazz to this sheer black jumpsuit.

A feathery fan is a great accessory to a camp outfit.

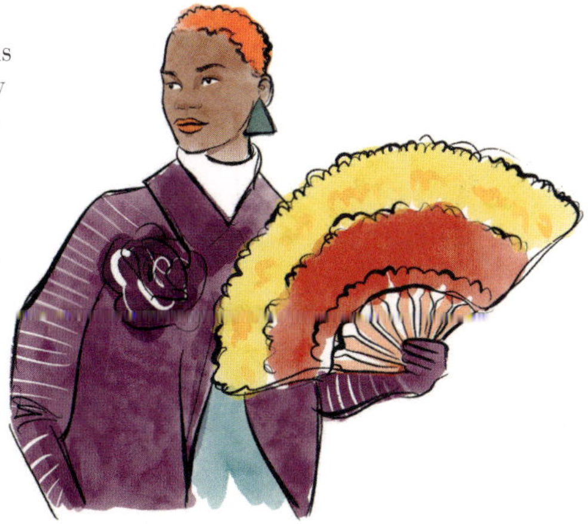

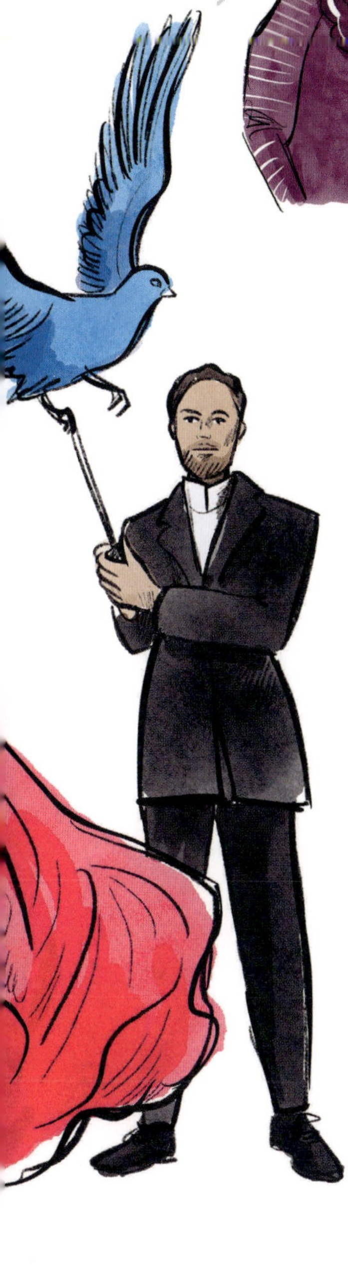

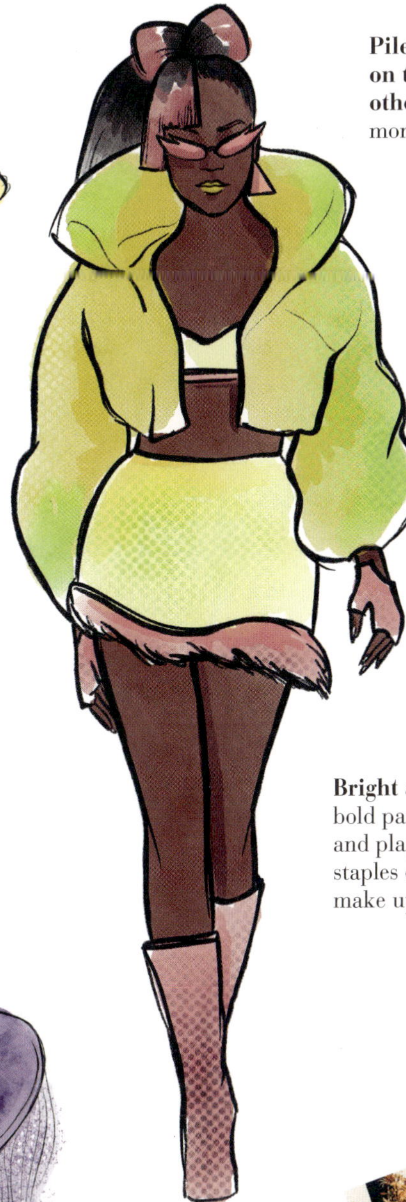

Pile accessories on top of each other—more is more!

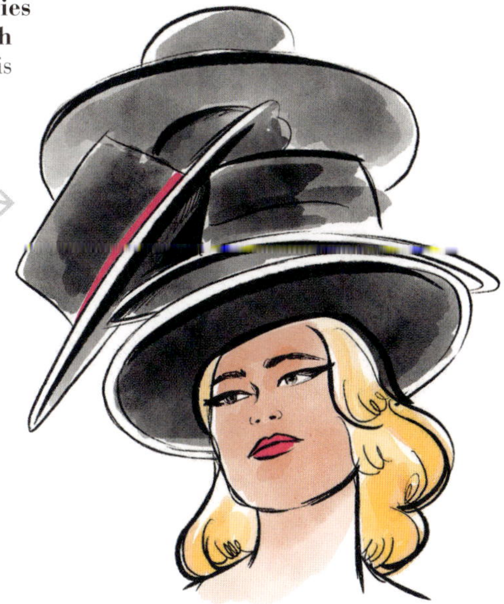

High-fashion brands such as Gucci embrace retro influences, gender fluidity, flashy colors, and whimsical details.

Bright and clashing colors, bold patterns, shiny textures, and playful motifs are all staples of the fabrics that make up the camp wardrobe.

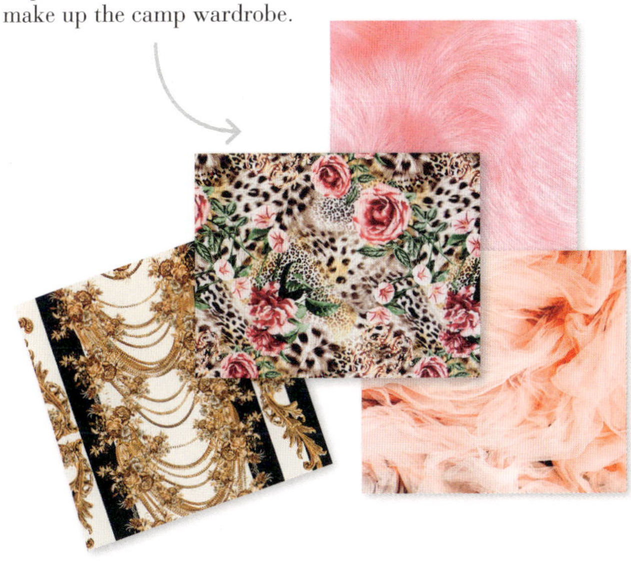

Fringe, pearls, velvet—pile on the glamour!

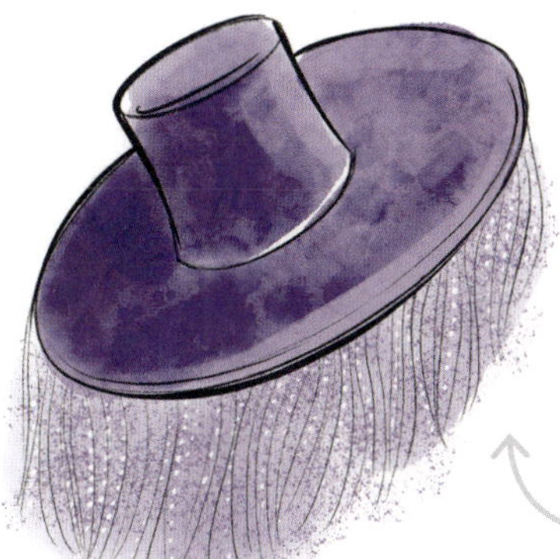

This model needs a hat—the more over-the-top the better! Try making it asymmetric, and adding fun details like frills or feathers. How will you style the hair? Will it be as big as the hat?

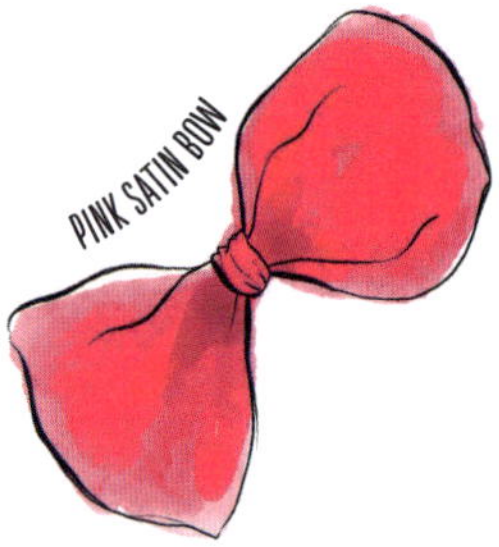

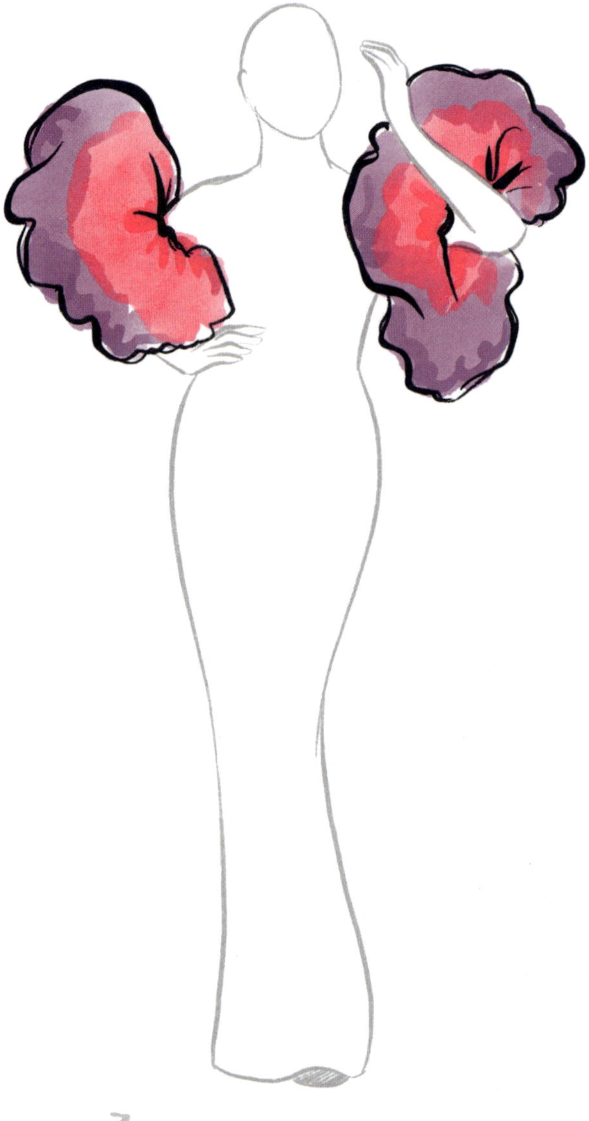

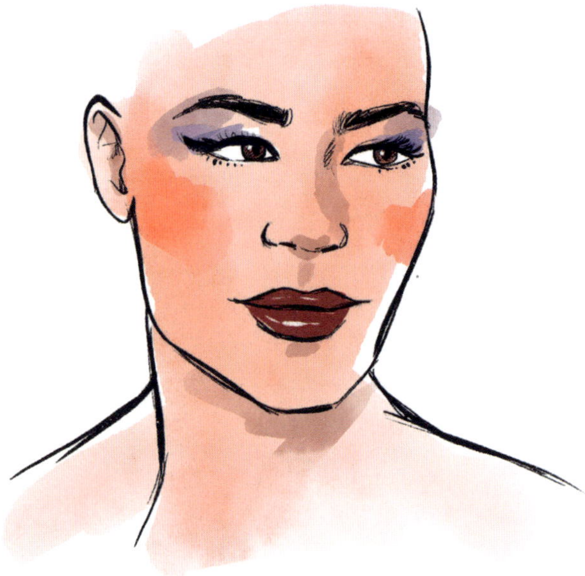

Finish the design for this model's outfit. It could fit tightly around the waist, then billow out to echo the puffy sleeves. Will you stick with the pink palette, or throw in some contrasting colors?

Camp it up! Think about how to put a spin on traditional high-fashion designs to add a touch of humor and the unexpected.

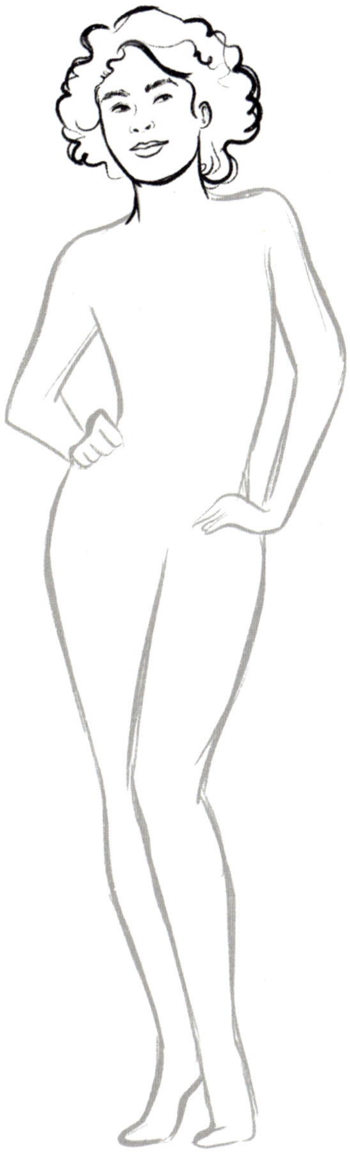

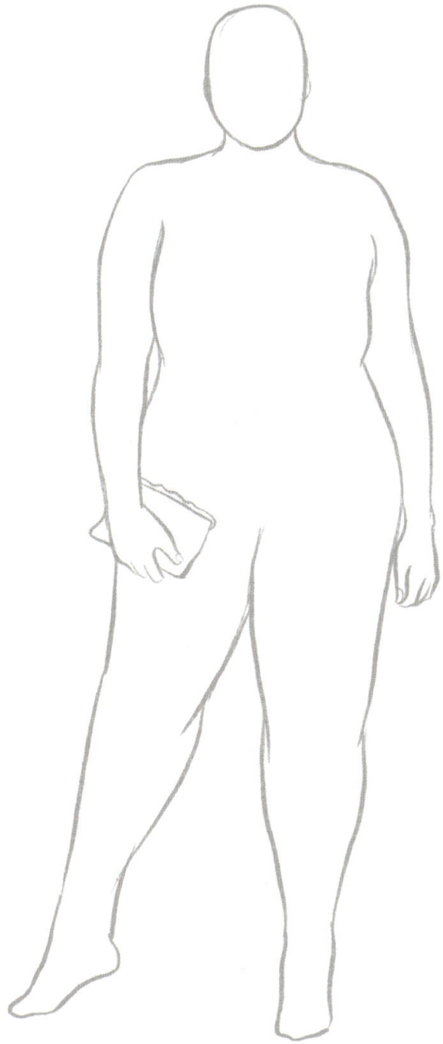

Give this model some dramatic accessories—maybe an oversize headpiece, a gaudily embellished clutch bag, or extra-high platform shoes.

Drag

Drag fashion is all about breaking out of the binary categories of "male" and "female" and showing off your unique personality and artistic vision. Drag queens and kings transform themselves into larger-than-life characters, often inspired by celebrities or pop culture. Drag celebrates the diversity and fluidity of gender expression, and can also be a form of social commentary, challenging the norms and stereotypes of mainstream society. Drag fashion draws heavily on costume, but it's more than just dressing up: it is a performance art that showcases the talent and charisma of drag artists.

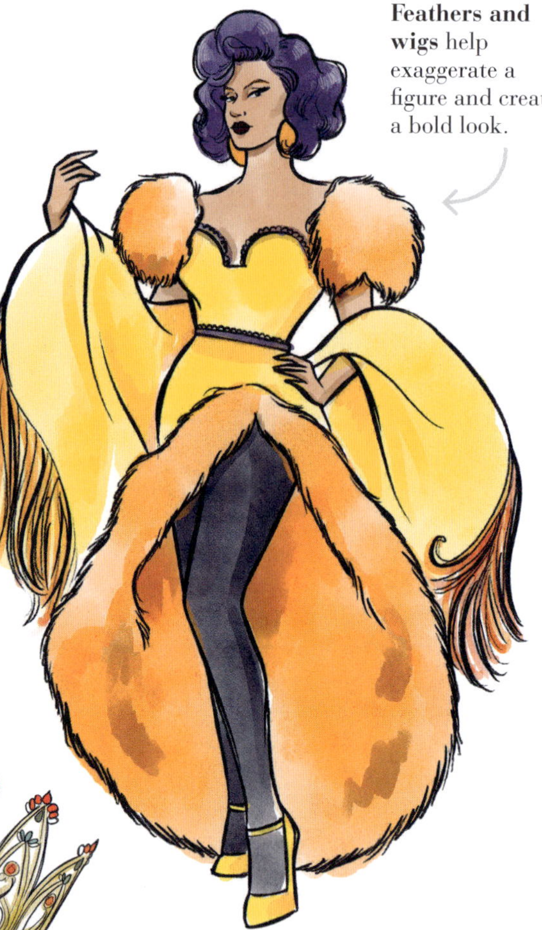

Feathers and wigs help exaggerate a figure and create a bold look.

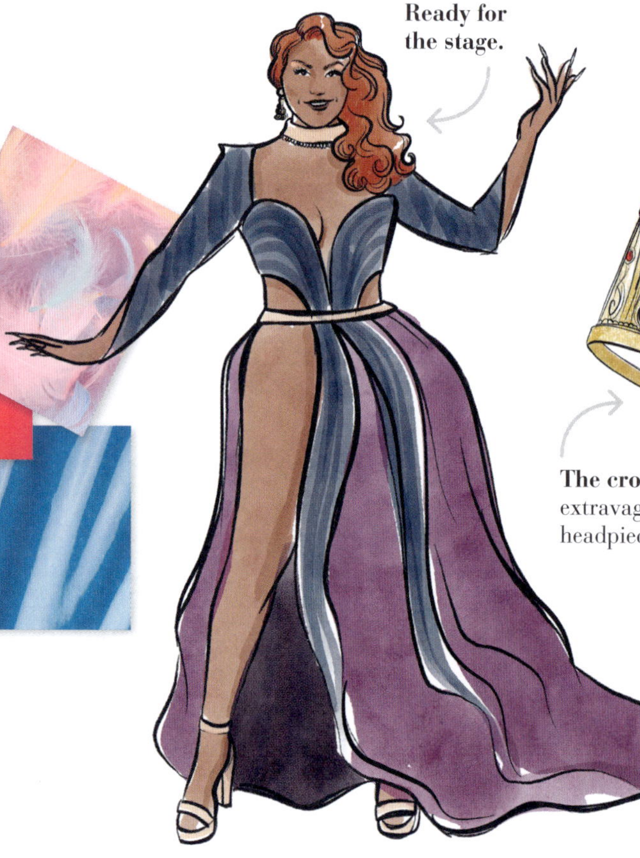

Ready for the stage.

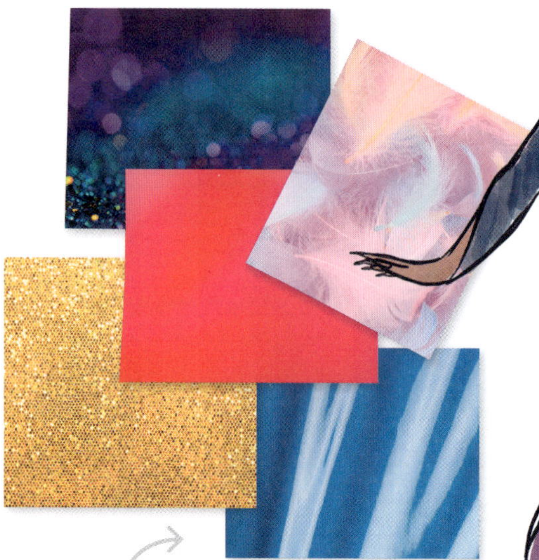

Faux fur, sequined, and vinyl fabrics are very popular in drag, as they create dazzle and glamour.

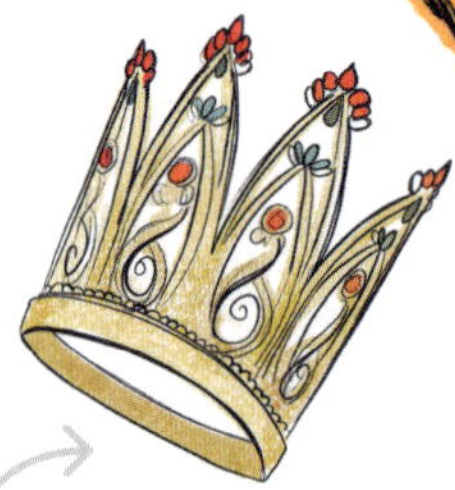

The crown or extravagant headpiece is a staple.

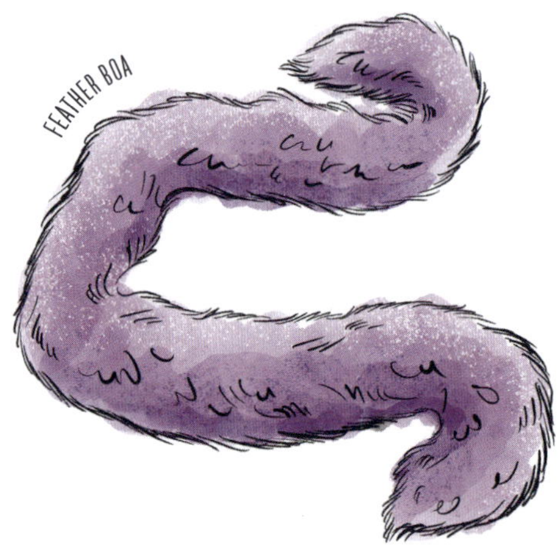

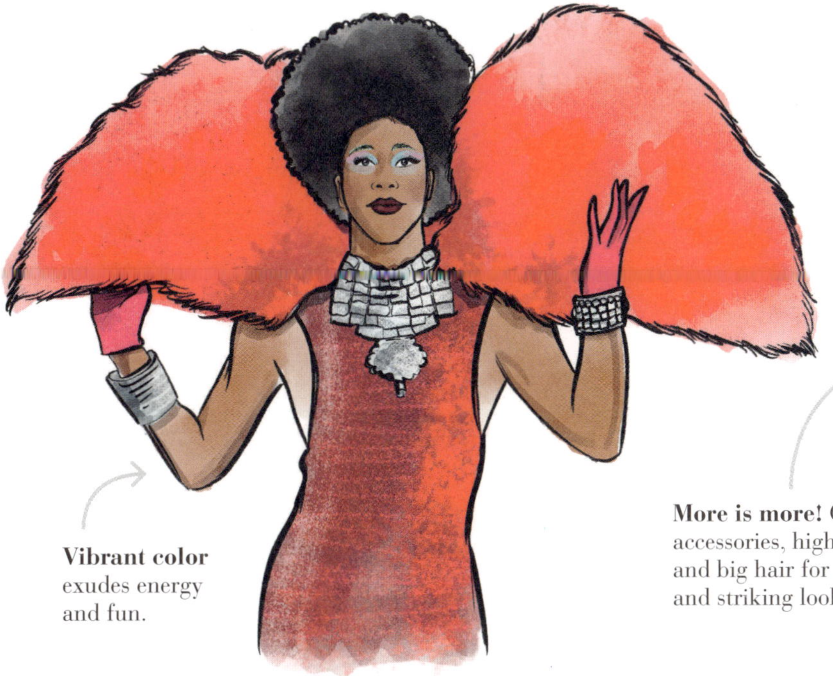

Vibrant color exudes energy and fun.

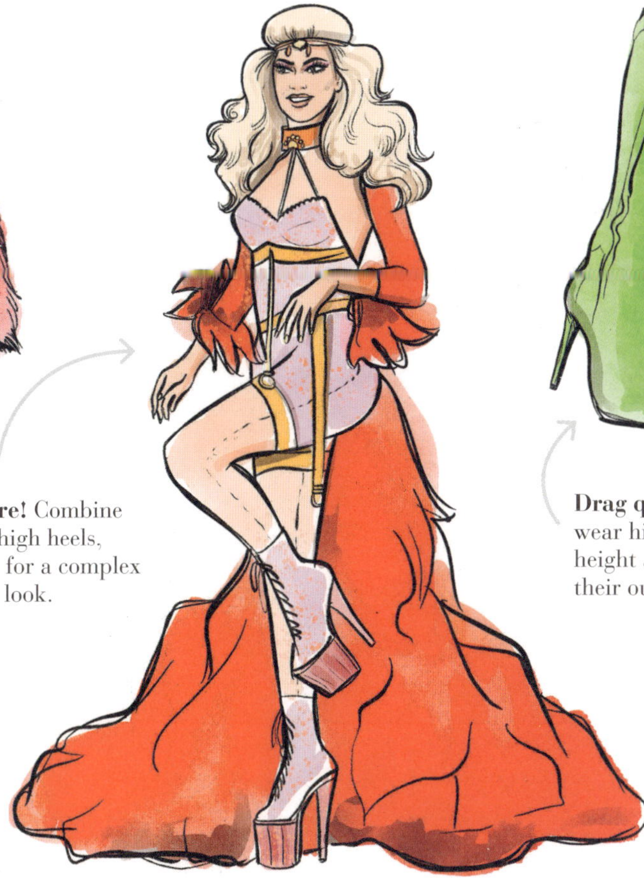

More is more! Combine accessories, high heels, and big hair for a complex and striking look.

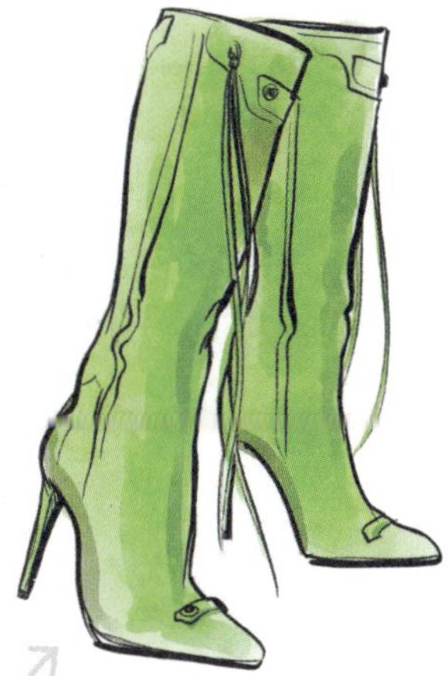

Drag queens often wear high heels to add height and elegance to their outfits.

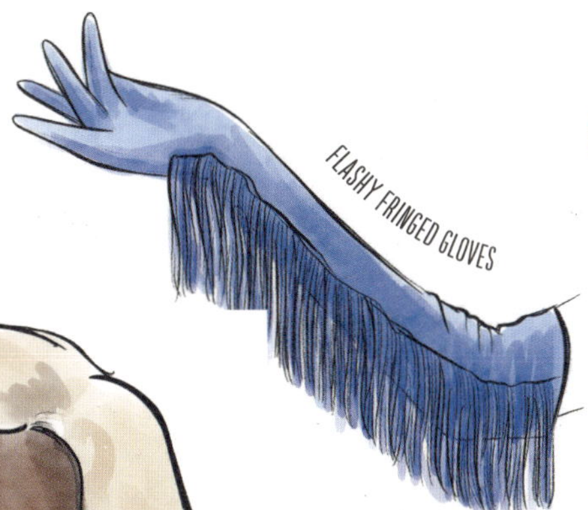

Glamorous makeup creates a dramatic look.

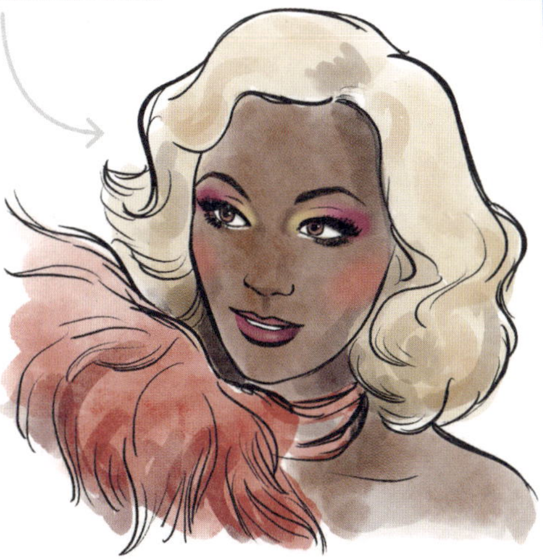

Embrace burlesque with a feather fan.

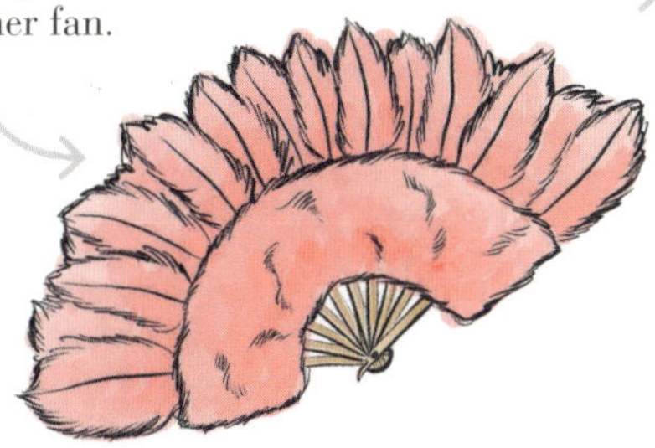

Flamboyant makeup can transform a person into a performer.

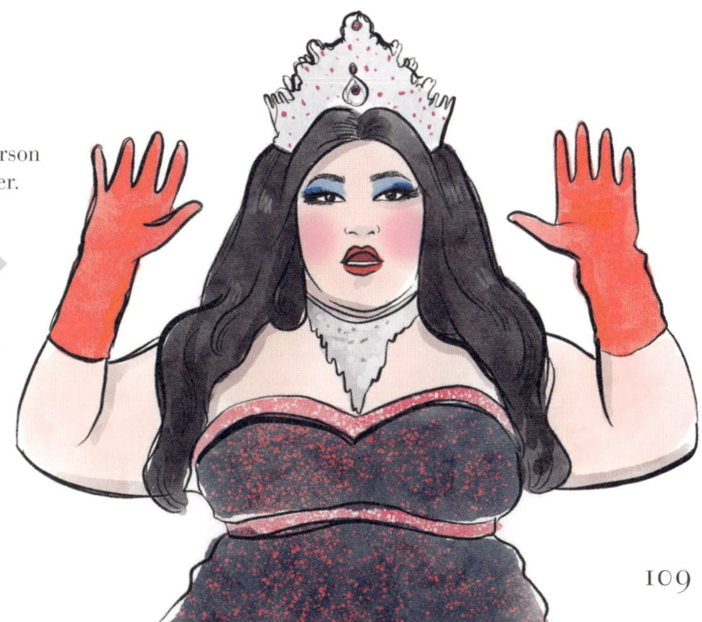

Complete this look using the bow and boa as a starting point. Pick colors that will complement the pink accessories, and go wild with textures and volume.

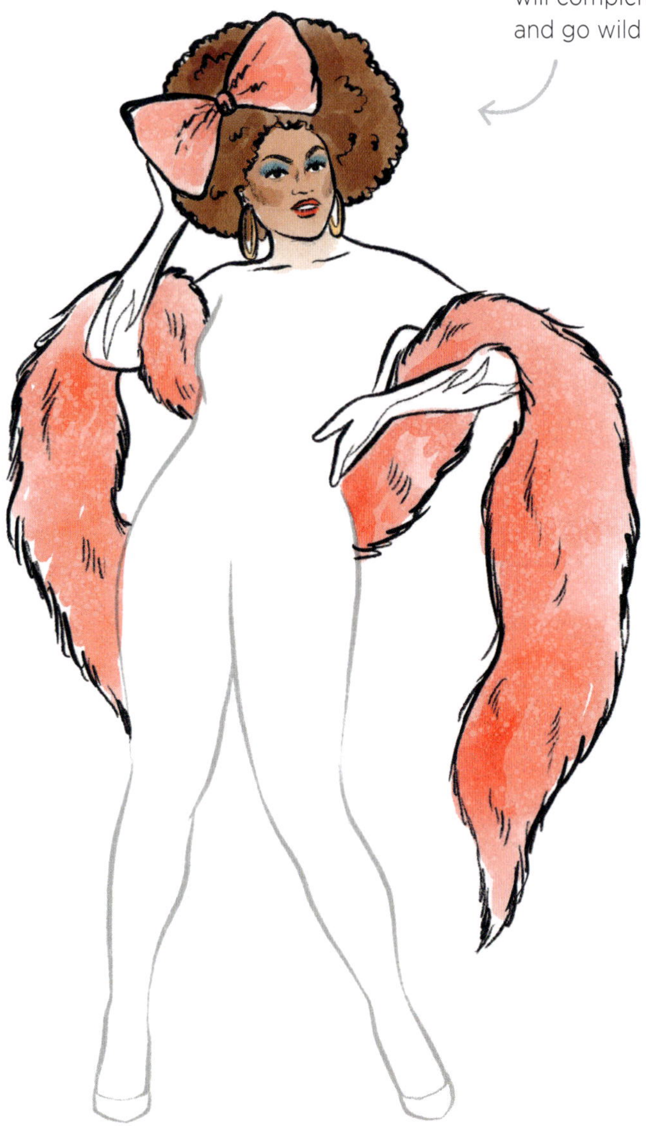

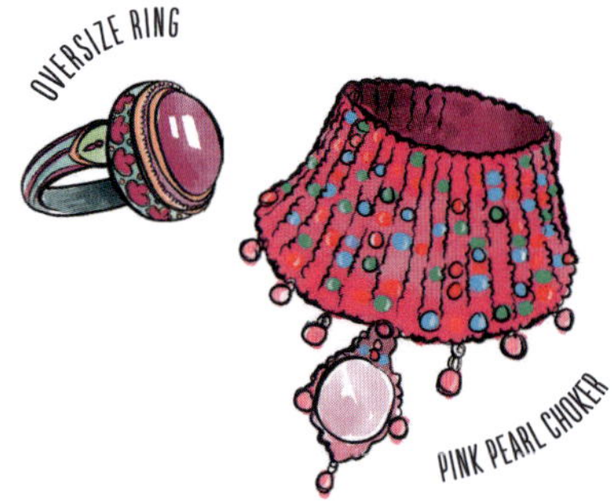

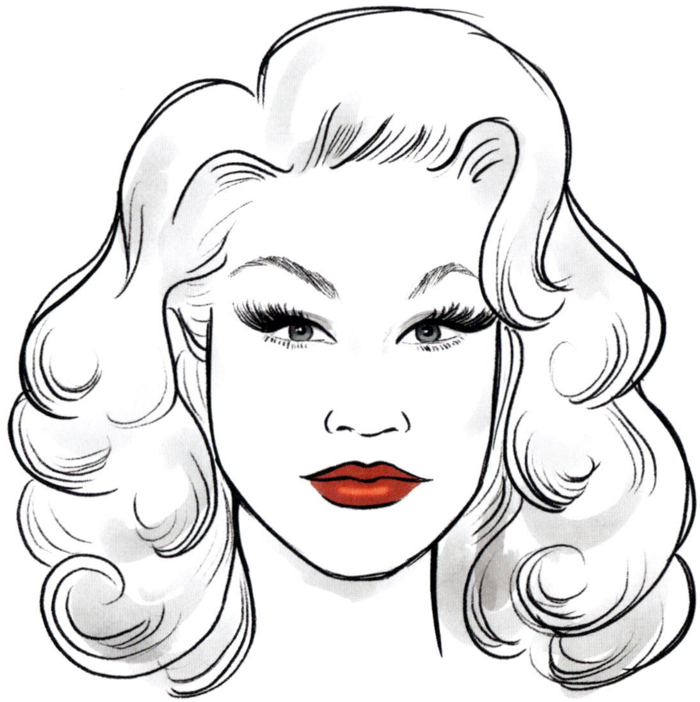

Style your model's makeup. Don't forget that drag is all about drama!

Design an outrageously over-the-top outfit for this model.

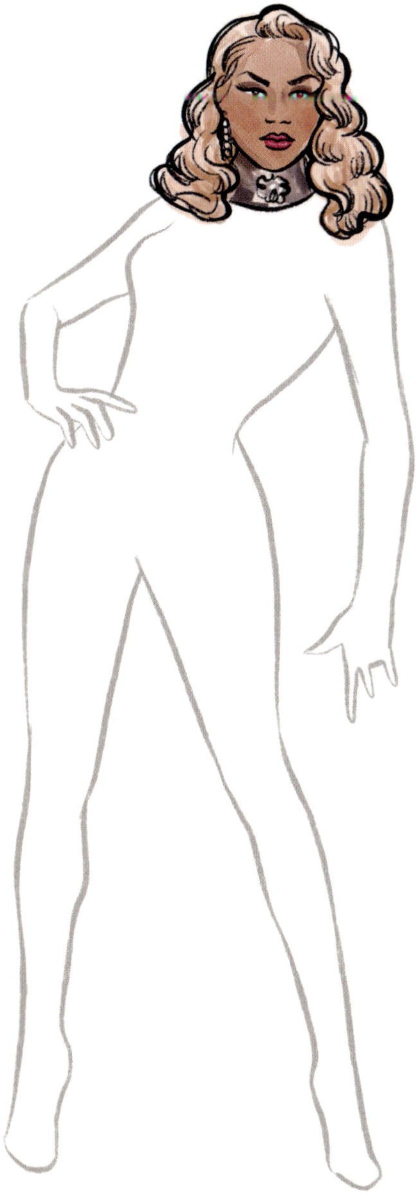

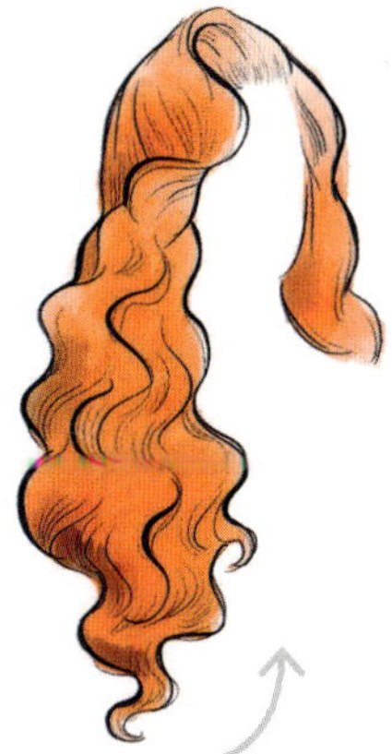

Drag performers often wear wigs to change their hair color, style, or length.

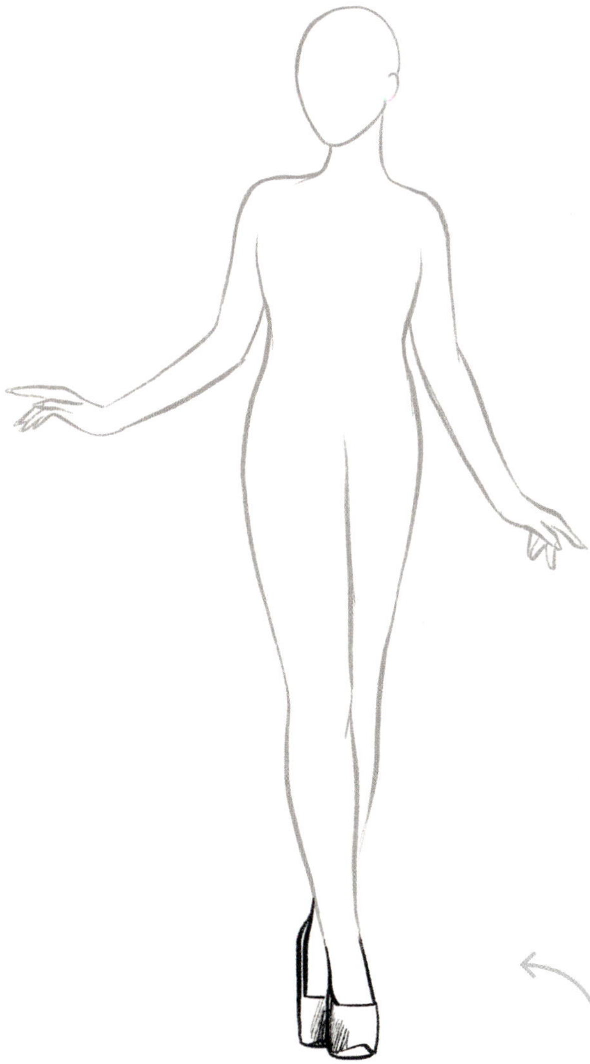

Create your own drag outfit! What would you call yourself? How will your style express your character's personality?

Rock Icon

Rock stars are the world's style influencers. The daring outfits donned by performers from Elvis to the Beatles and David Bowie have been a constant inspiration to the fashion world. You'll see their influence in the work of Yves Saint Laurent, Alexander McQueen, and Andreas Kronthaler for Vivienne Westwood. British model Kate Moss always gives her outfits a chic, rock twist. Beyond the catwalk, who doesn't want to be a rock star? Elvis's iconic flared pants, biker jackets, and tight shirts remain popular to this day.

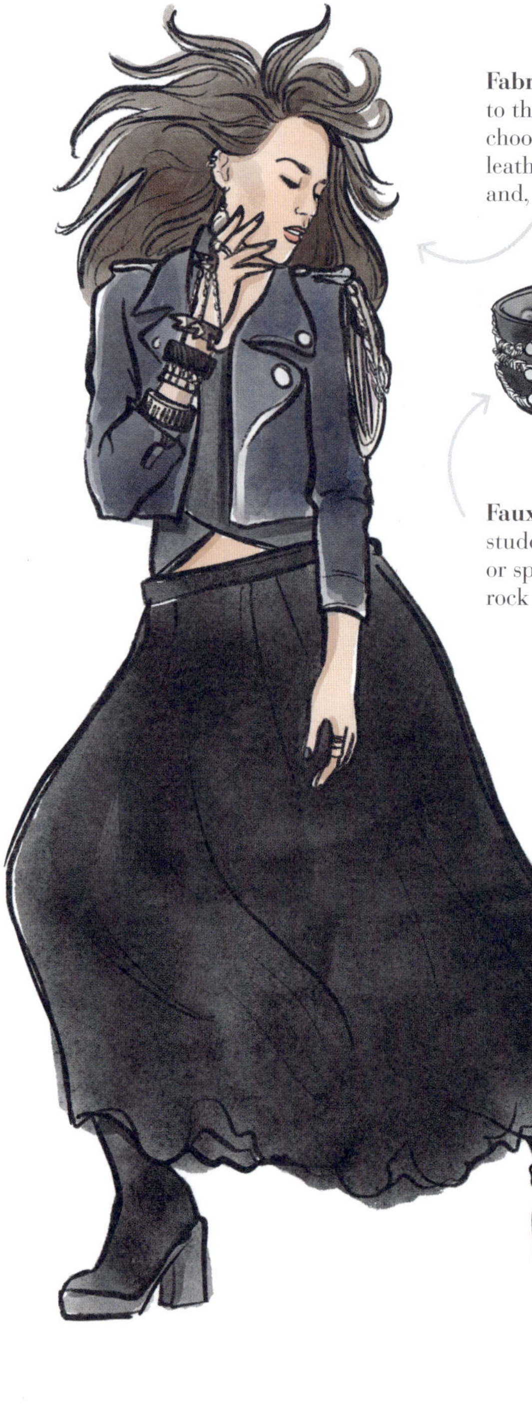

Fabrics are fundamental to the rock aesthetic: choose tight-fitting faux leather, patent leather, and, of course, denim.

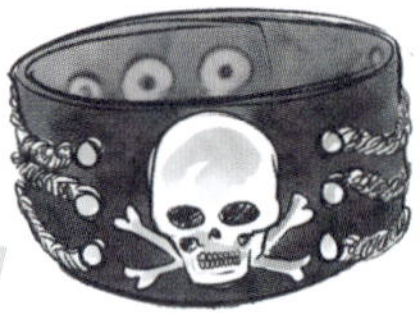

Faux leather cuffs, studded with skulls or spikes, are a great rock accessory.

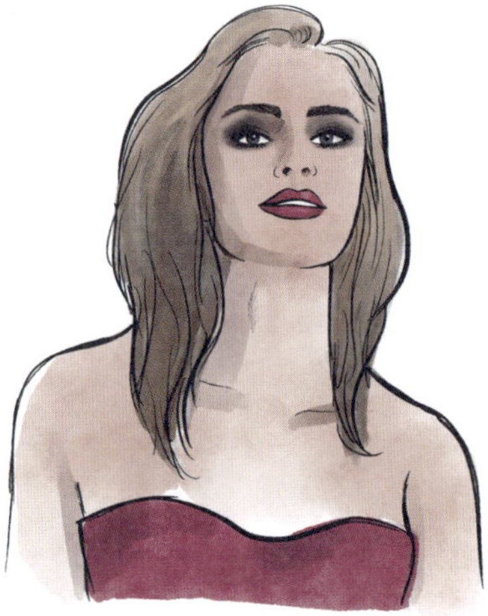

Bold and dramatic eye makeup.

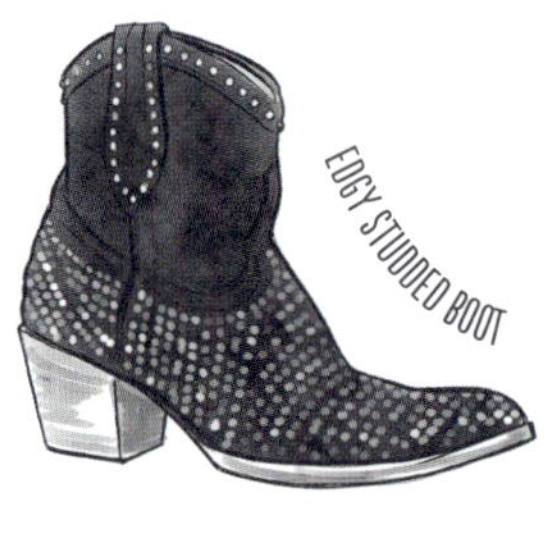

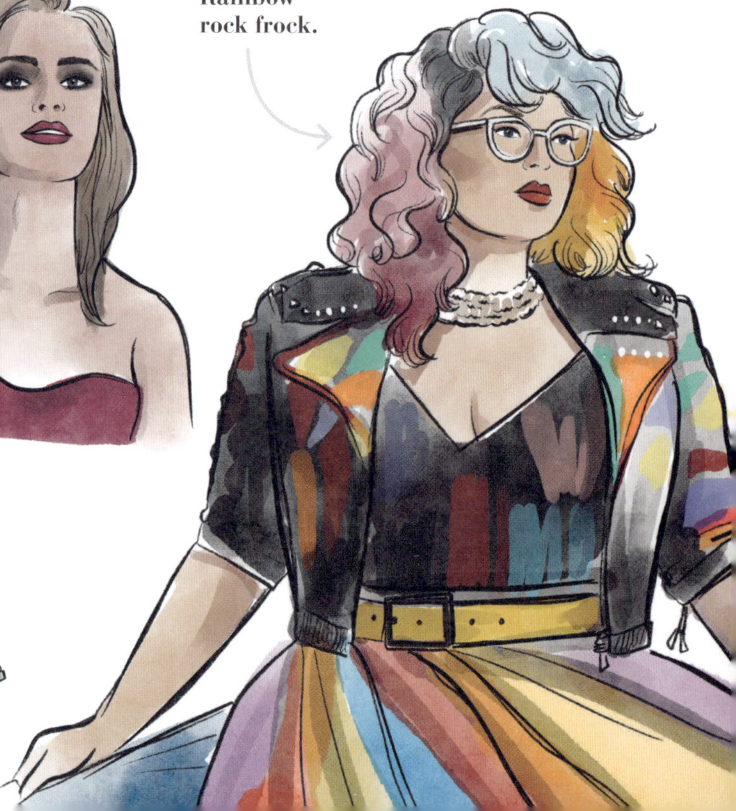

Rainbow rock frock.

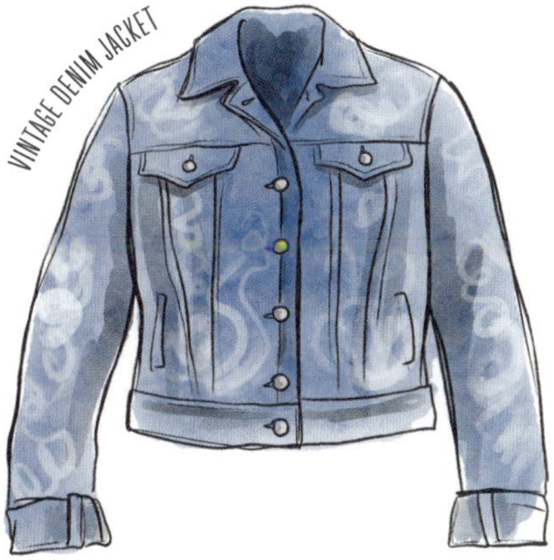

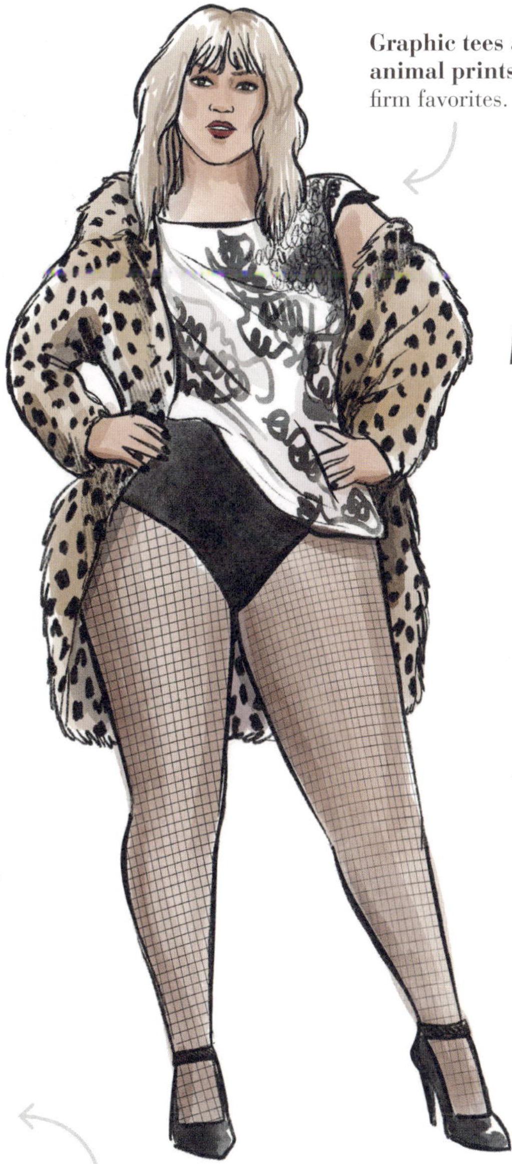

Graphic tees and animal prints are firm favorites.

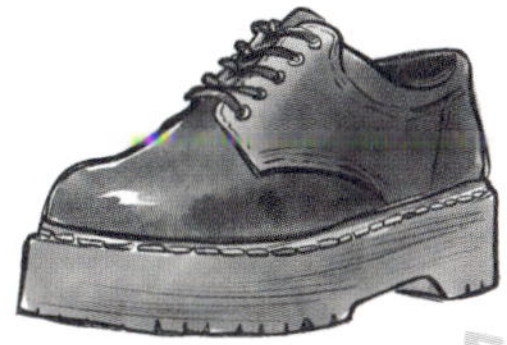

Low-cut platform boots or shoes complete the rock look.

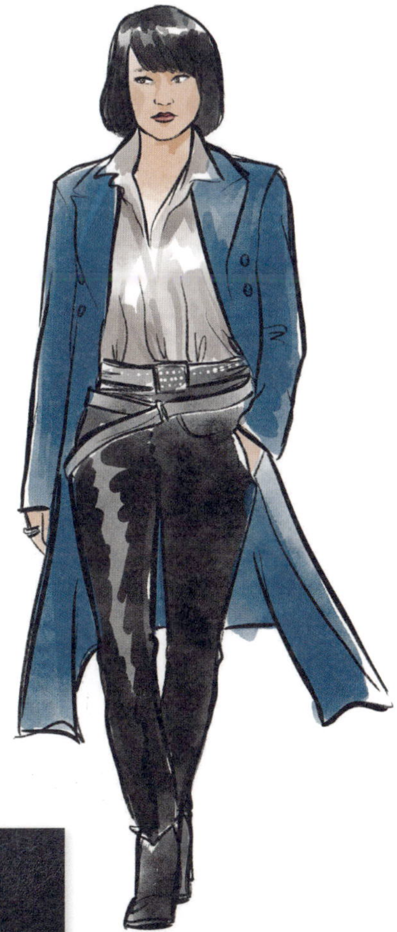

Leather pants and studded belts give a rock-and-roll twist to a more casual outfit.

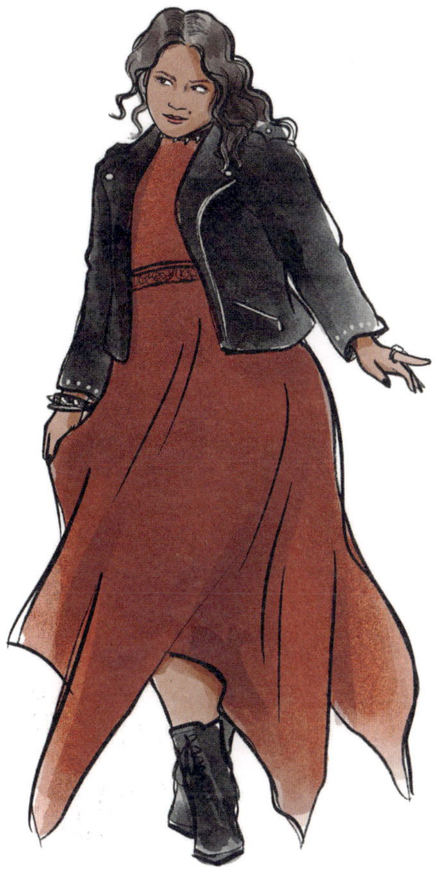

Own the night in a satin slip dress, combined with a biker jacket and some shiny accessories.

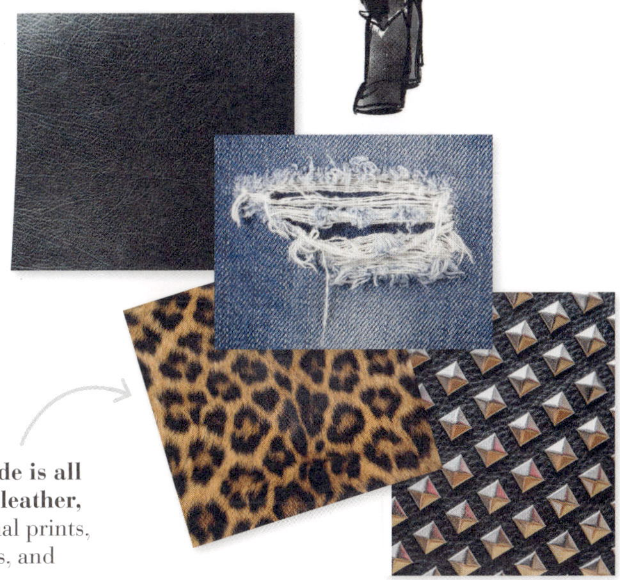

Rock attitude is all about faux leather, denim, animal prints, studs, stripes, and metallics.

Bring some stage presence to this look with PVC pants and studded platform boots.

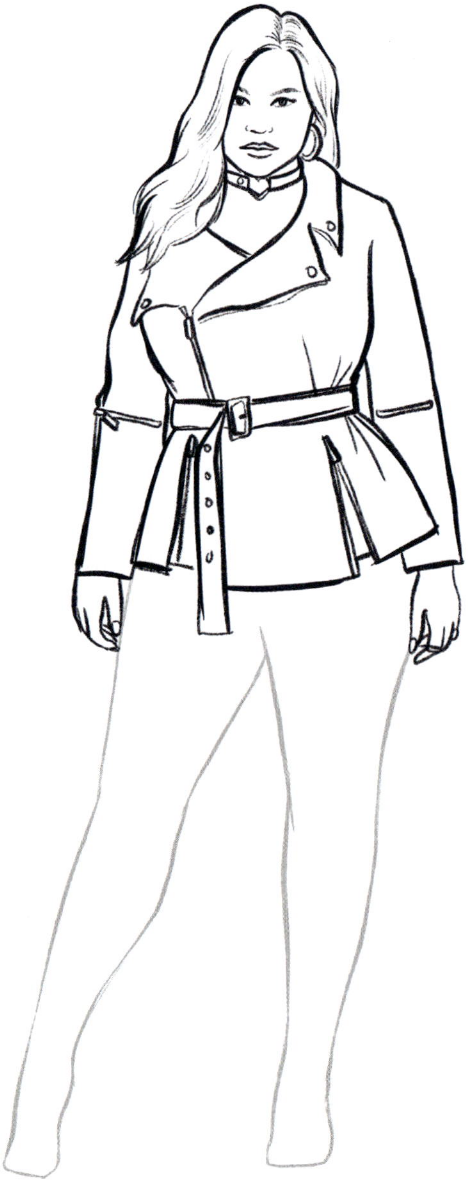

Straight and simple. Finish the design for this model's outfit.

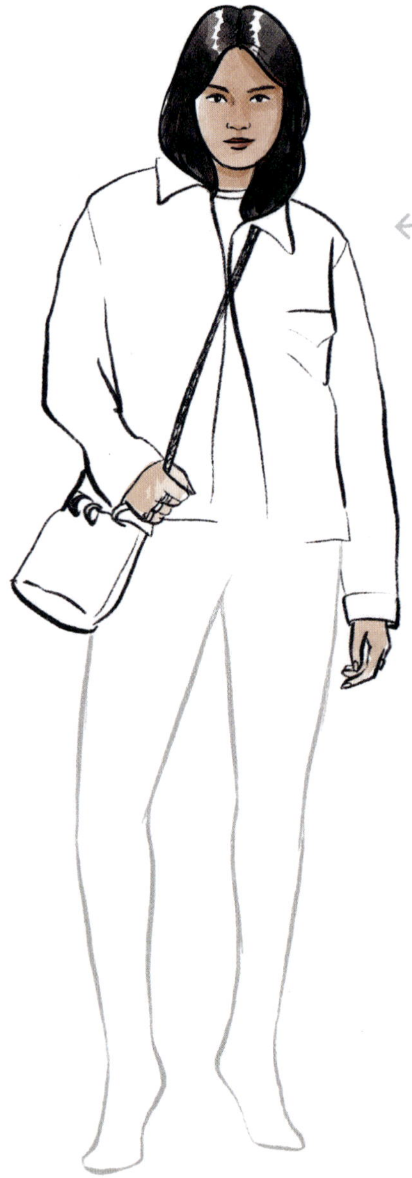

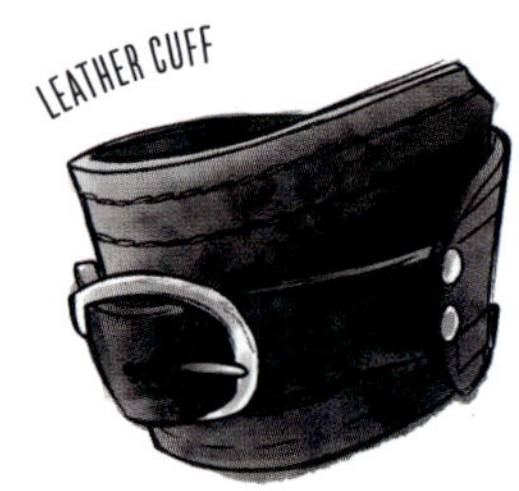

Design a daytime rock look for this model. Could you incorporate some references to your favorite bands?

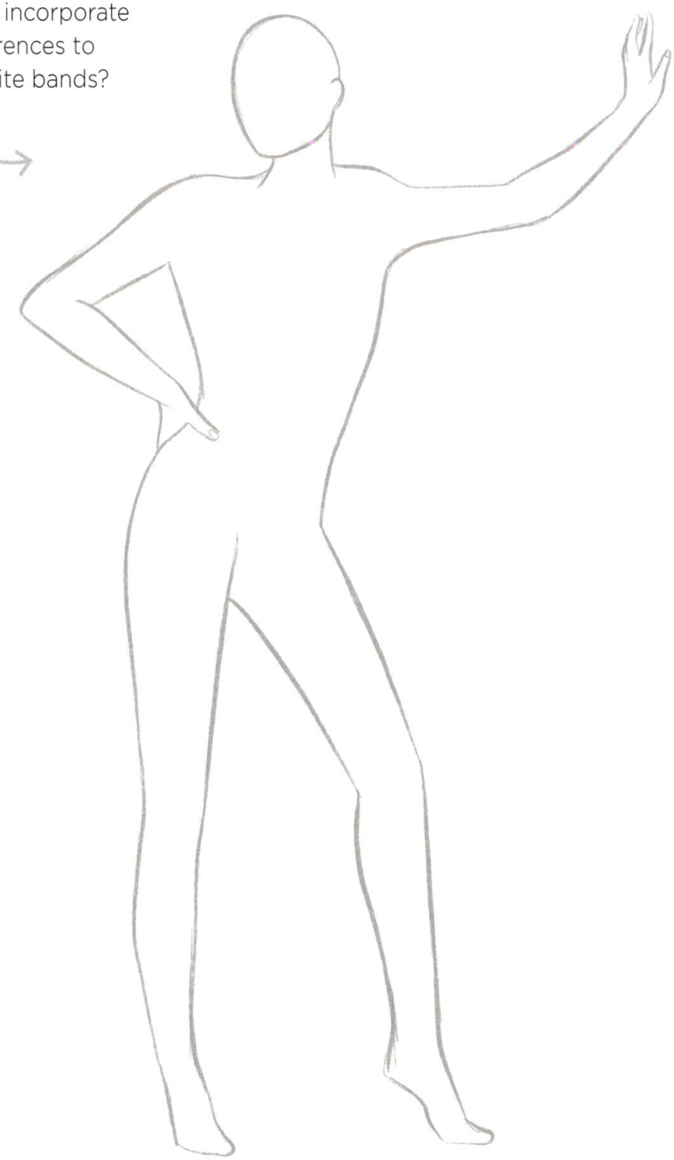

Now adapt her outfit into a bold evening look. Throw on some heavy eyeliner and style her hair. Maybe she'll swap out platform boots for spiked stilettos?

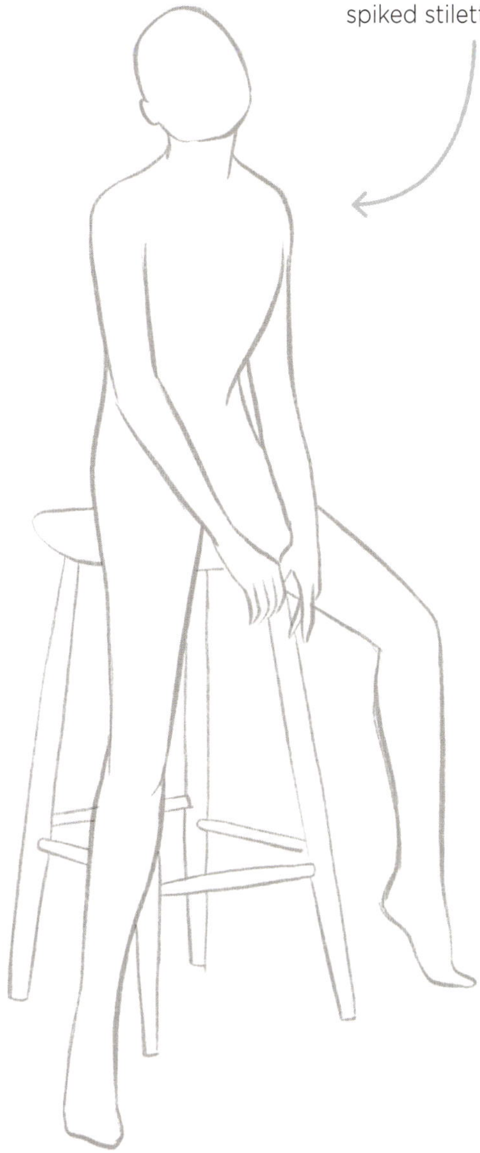

Valentino

Valentino Garavani moved to Paris at the age of 17 to pursue his interest in fashion, studying at the prestigious École des Beaux-Arts and at the Chambre Syndicale de la Couture Parisienne. He quickly became the darling of socialites and aristocrats from around the world, and a star of the Italian fashion scene. His signature red, known as "Valentino Rosso," is the symbol of timeless elegance "Made in Italy." Couture gowns are Valentino's forte, and are easily recognizable for their delicate swing around the body. Valentino understood the way a material moves, and whether he worked with tiered lace or ornate brocade, used the evening dress as his seductive medium of choice.

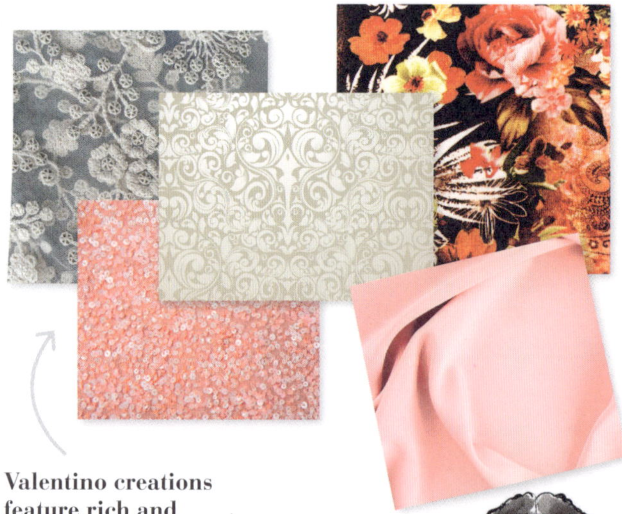

Valentino creations feature rich and luxurious materials, such as silk, wool, lace, or leather.

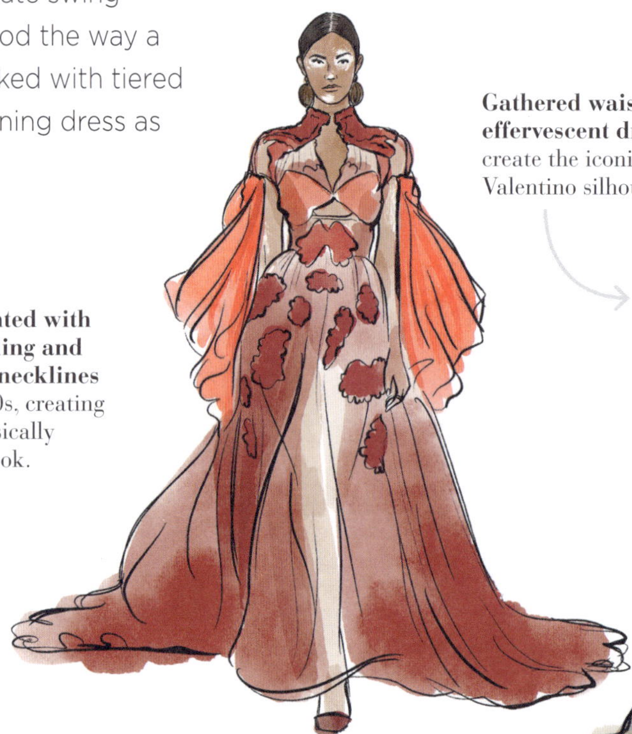

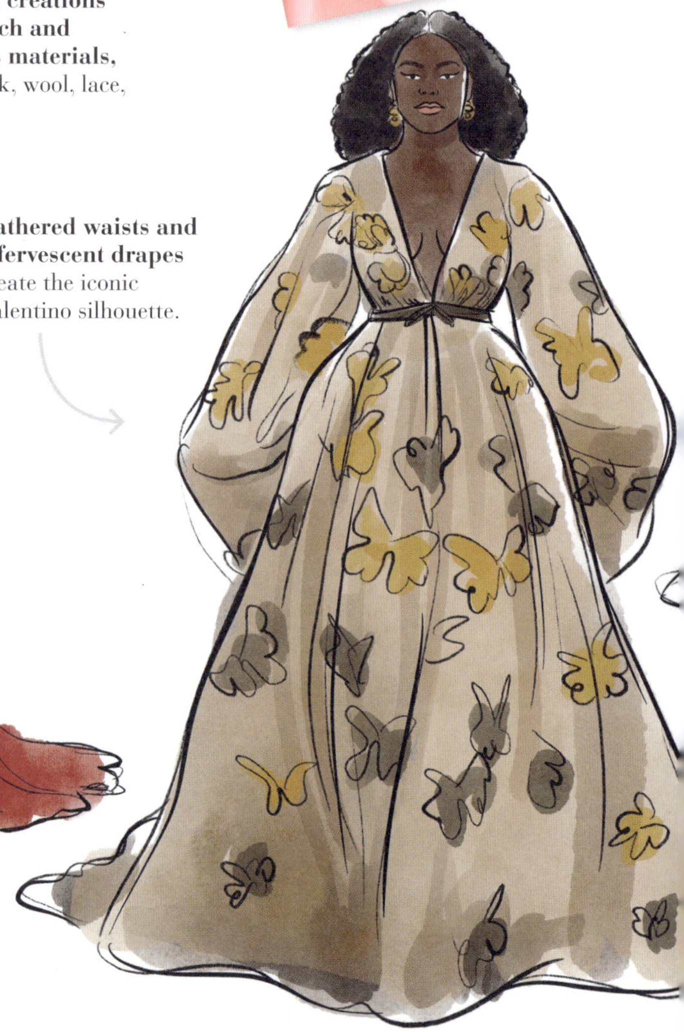

Gathered waists and effervescent drapes create the iconic Valentino silhouette.

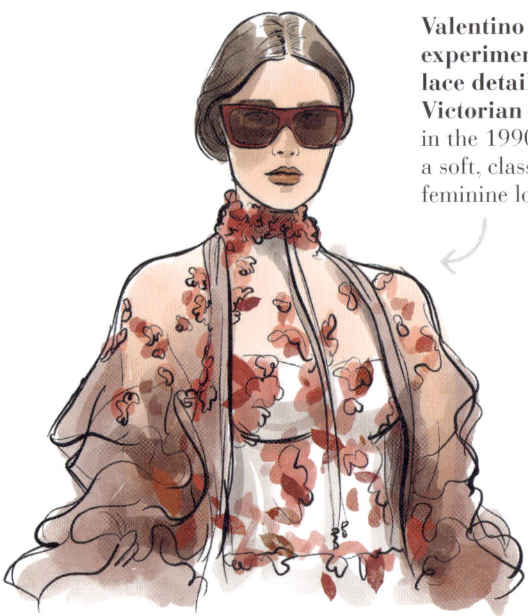

Valentino experimented with lace detailing and Victorian necklines in the 1990s, creating a soft, classically feminine look.

Clean, futuristic lines and billowing material combine to create a unique look.

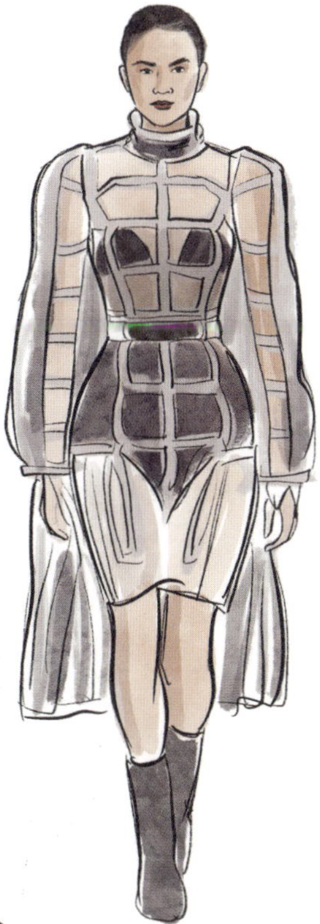

Wool coat with all-over crystal, sequin, and bead embroidery.

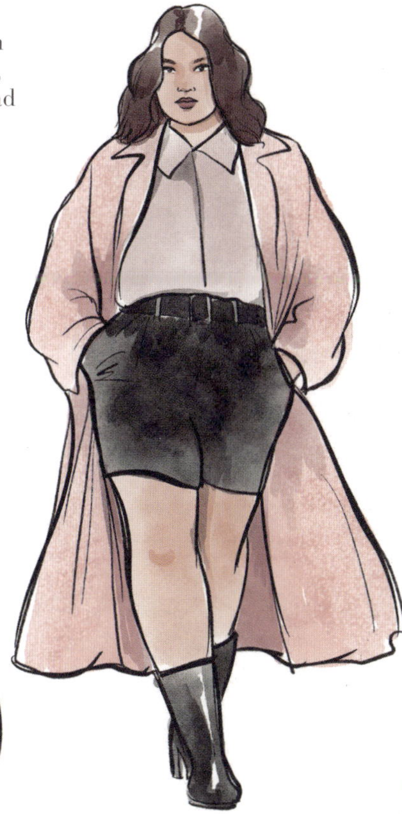

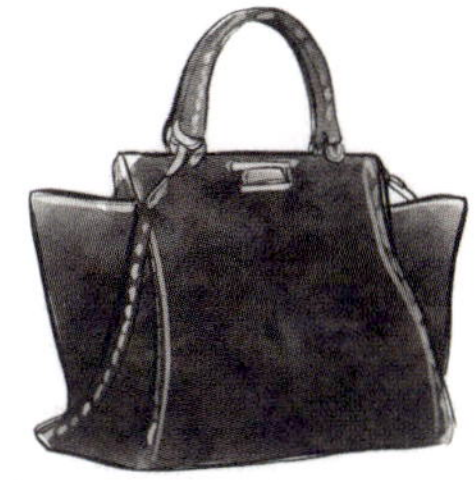

Classic leather handbag with studded detailing.

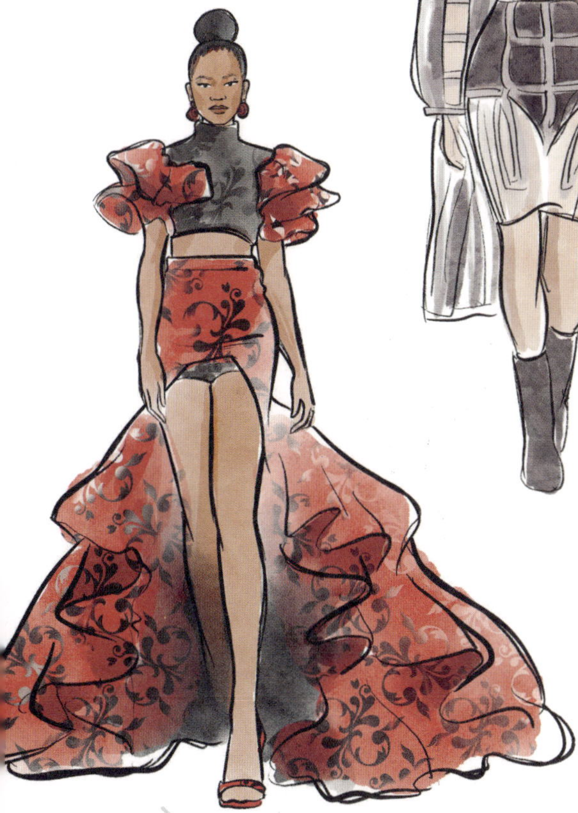

A dramatic, voluminous gown with Valentino's signature red accents.

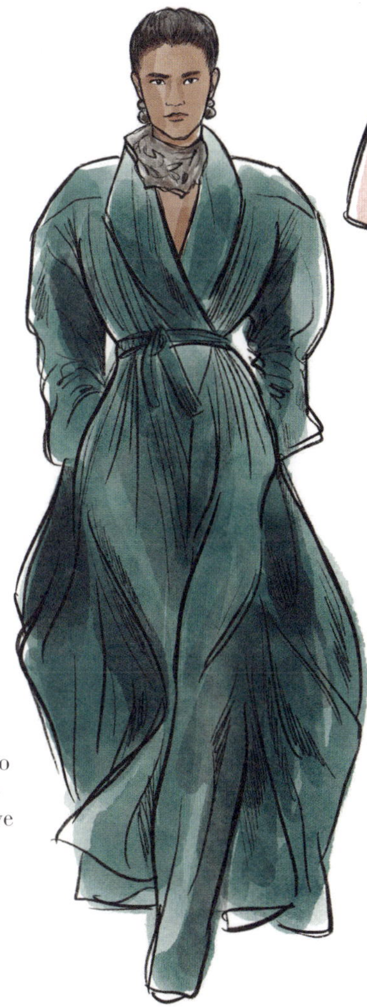

A gender-neutral silhouette. Valentino offers a vision of the world that is sensitive and nuanced, all-embracing and consciously diverse.

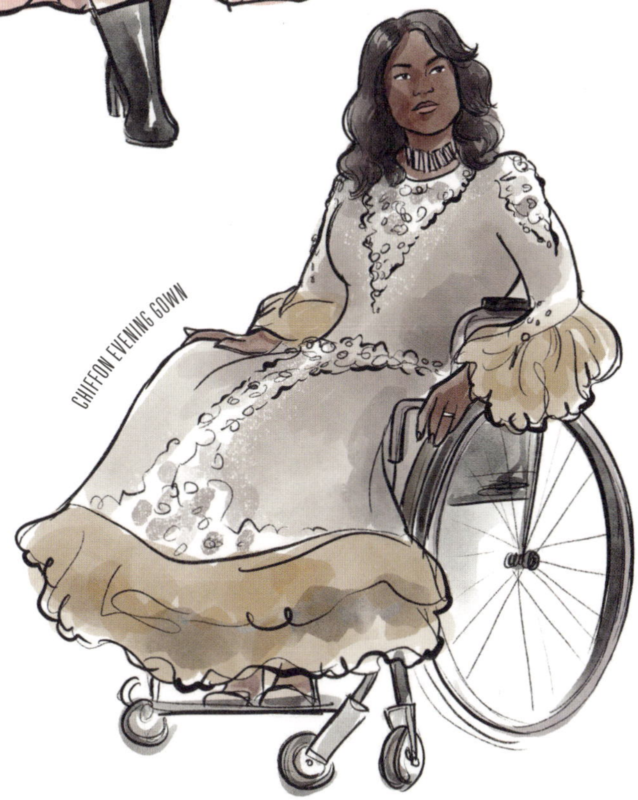

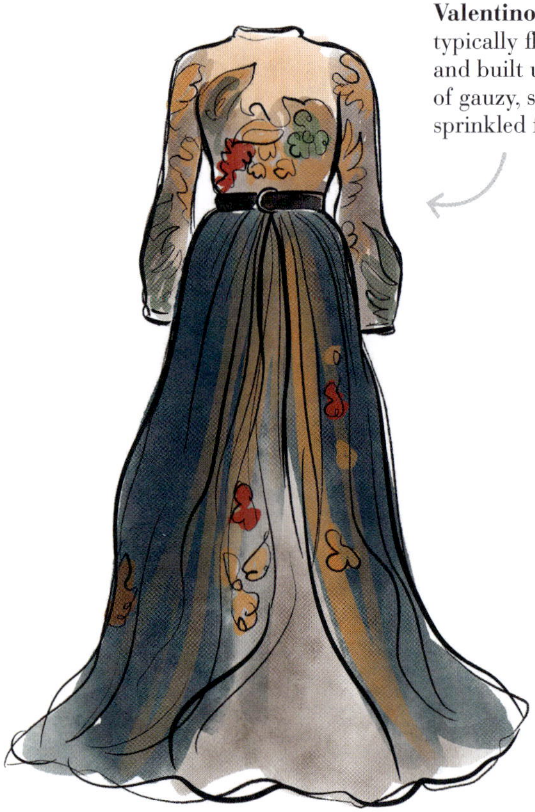

Valentino's dresses are typically floor-length and built up with layers of gauzy, sparkle-sprinkled fabrics.

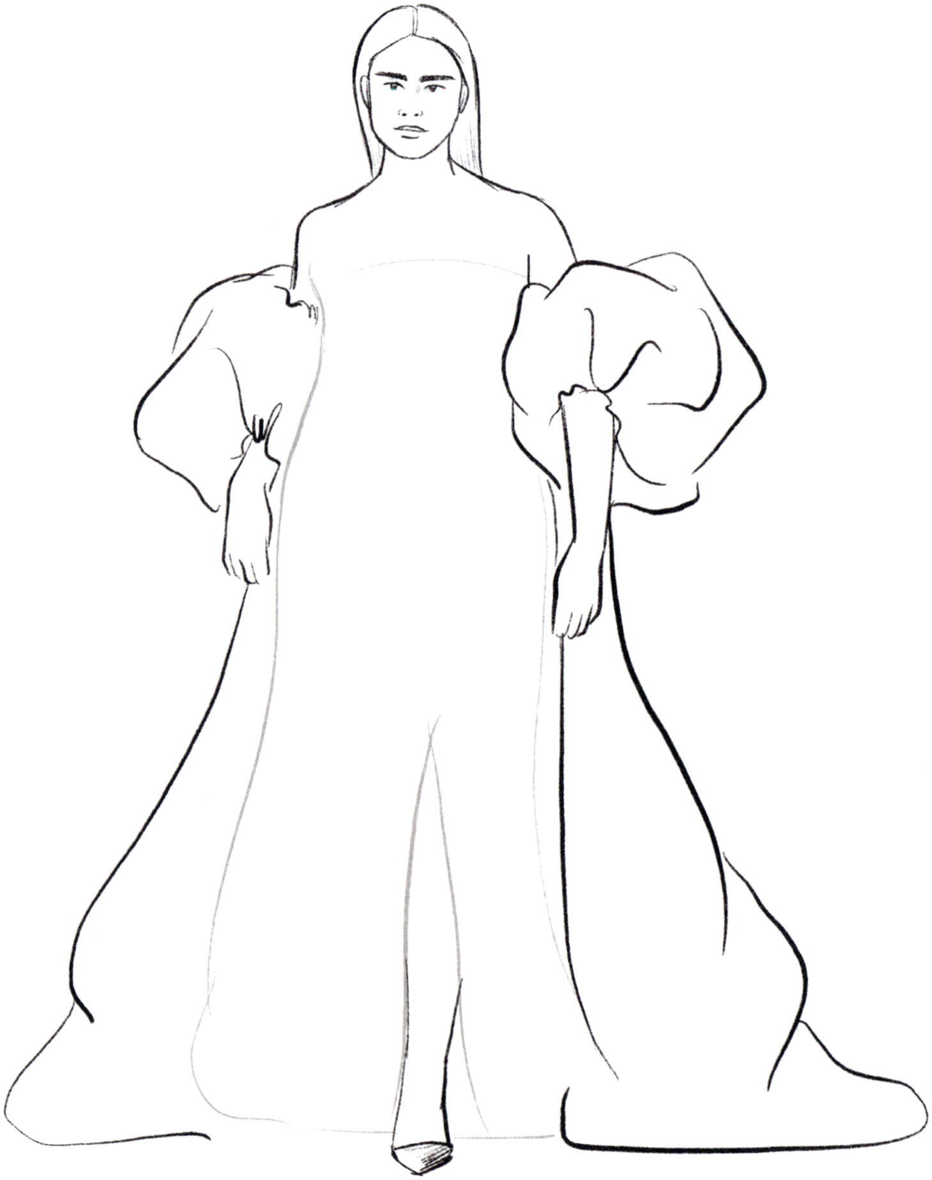

Finish this cocktail dress, featuring Valentino's luxuriously full sleeves and flowing fabrics.

Now design your own Valentino from scratch!

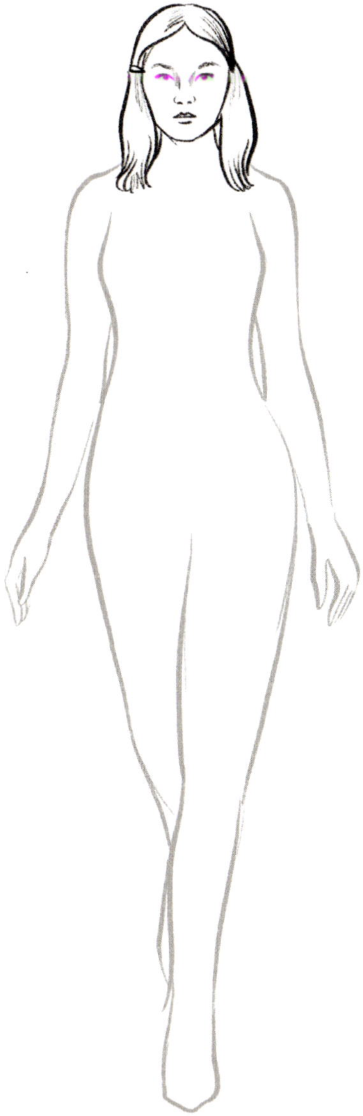

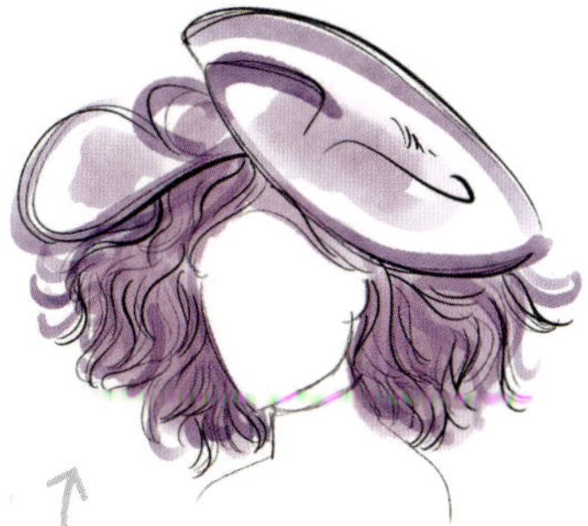

Purple headpiece made of soft, organic shapes.

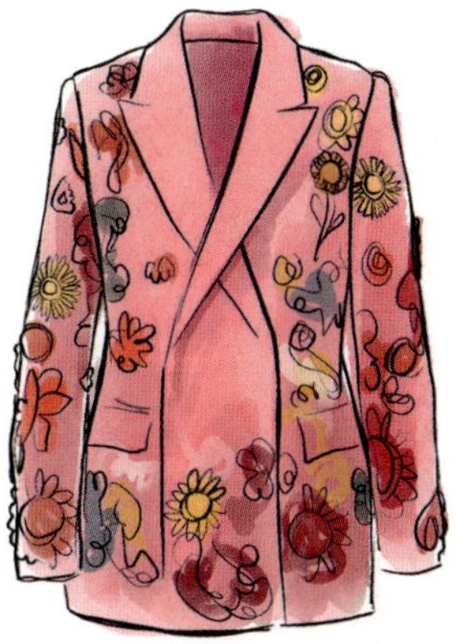

A double-breasted, embroidered jacket, drawing patterns from nature.

Jean Paul Gaultier

Glamour, drama, and camp. Jean Paul Gaultier is an iconoclast who breaks all the rules, mixing trash bags with haute couture, corsets with kilts, and marinières (striped tops) with tin cans. He is the "enfant terrible" of French fashion. In the 1980s, infatuated with all things punk, he was drawn to London's nightlife scene, frequenting Soho and taking inspiration from the figures that came out after dark. To this day, his looks challenge normative views of fashion and gender.

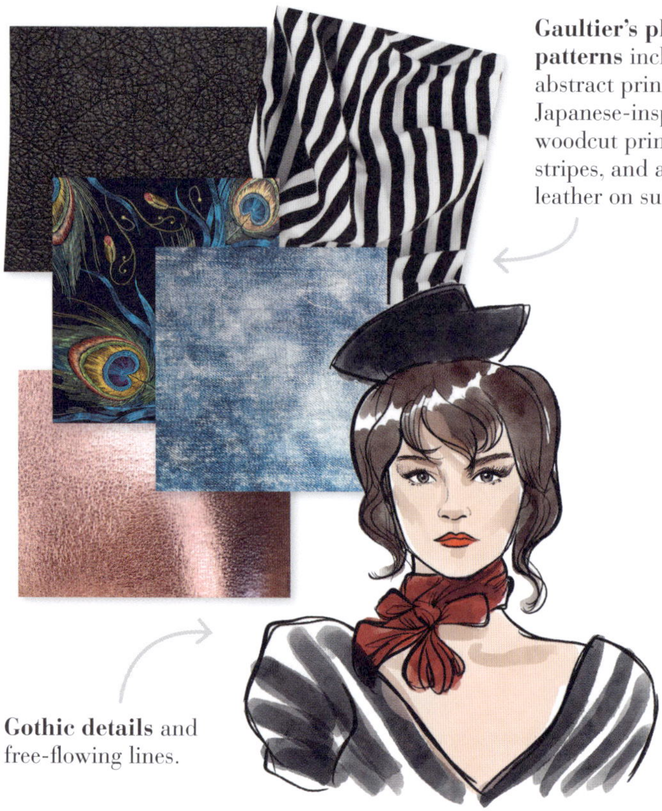

Gaultier's playful patterns include abstract prints on denim, Japanese-inspired woodcut prints, sailor stripes, and appliqué leather on suede.

Gothic details and free-flowing lines.

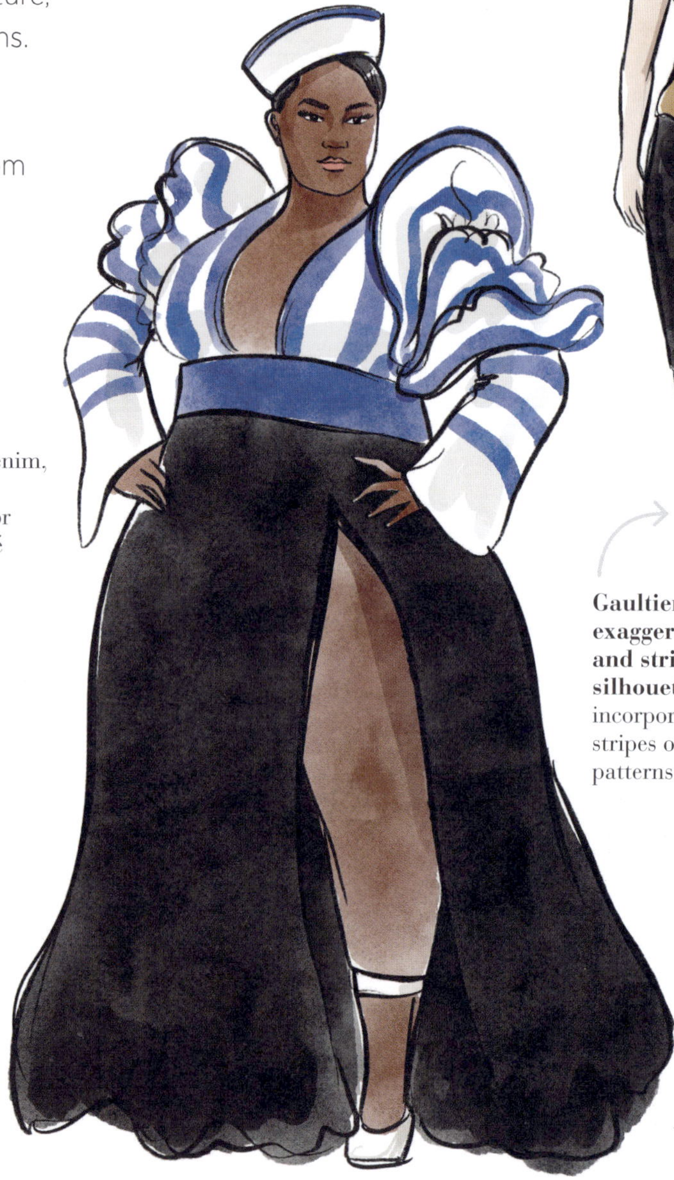

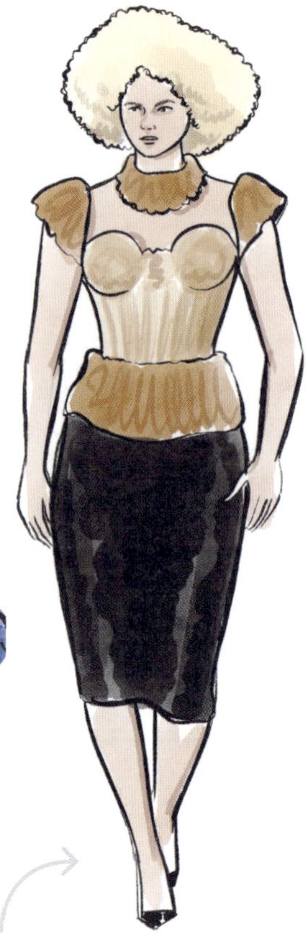

Gaultier favors exaggerated tailoring and striking silhouettes. He often incorporates nautical stripes or experimental patterns.

Sculpted layers and leather.

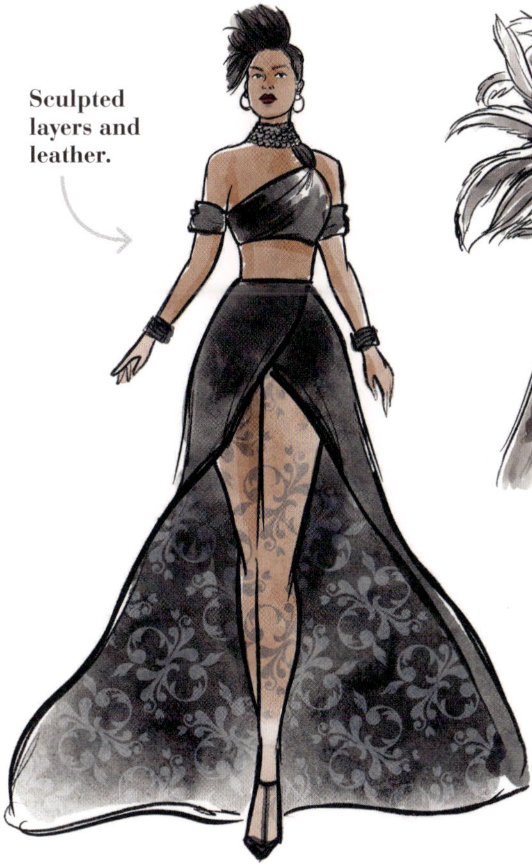

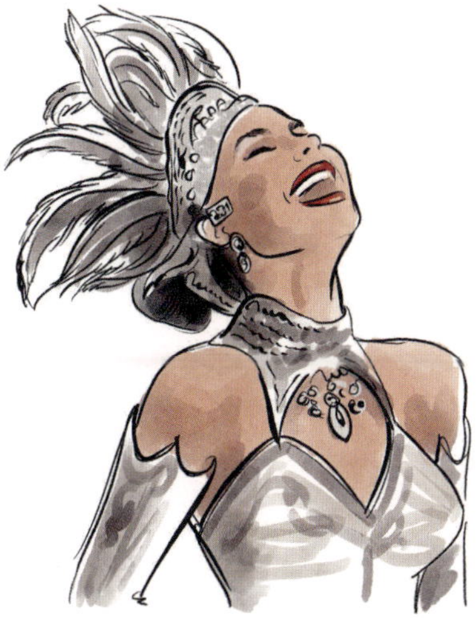

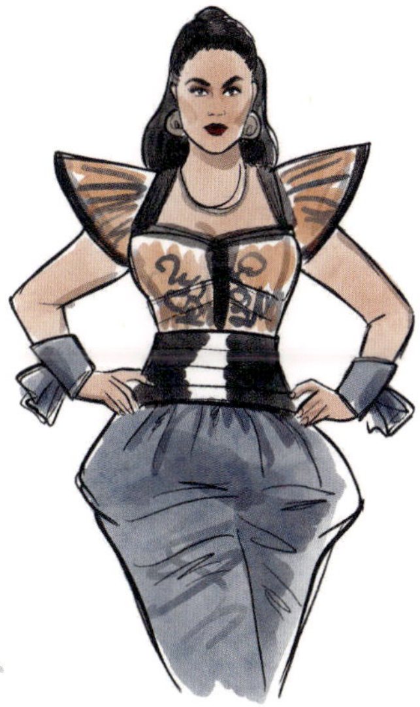

Many of Gaultier's creations draw inspiration from the colorful, camp world of cabaret.

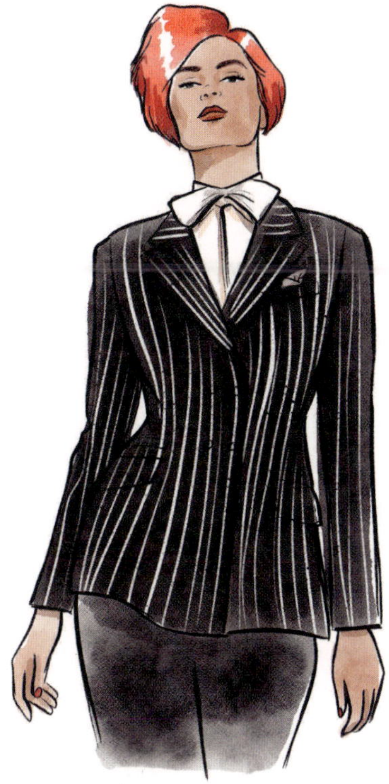

Gaultier's signature aesthetic often blurs the lines between masculine and feminine styles.

Tiny pleats create an origami effect.

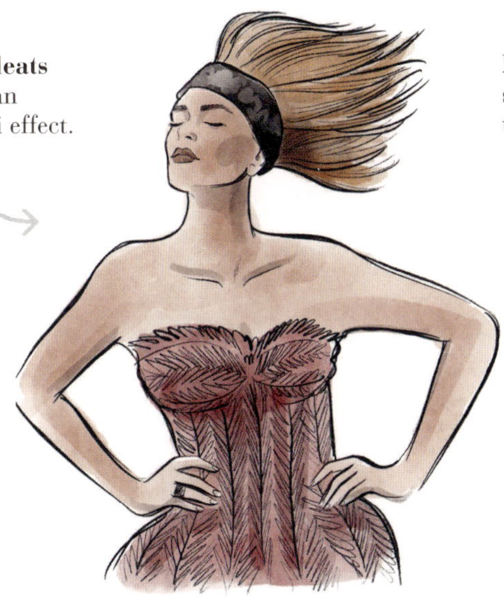

Molded rococo swirls hug the figure.

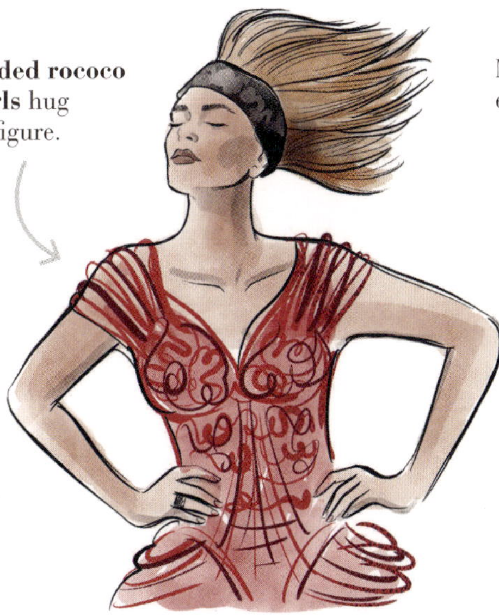

Metal ribbons encase the body.

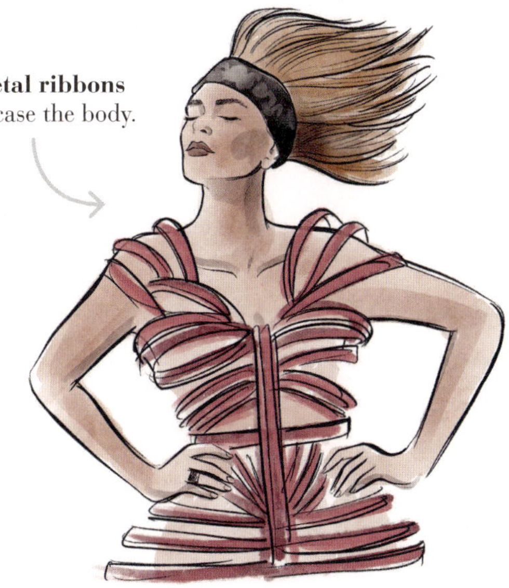

Create your own Gaultier-inspired outfit, using this birdcage headpiece as a starting point.

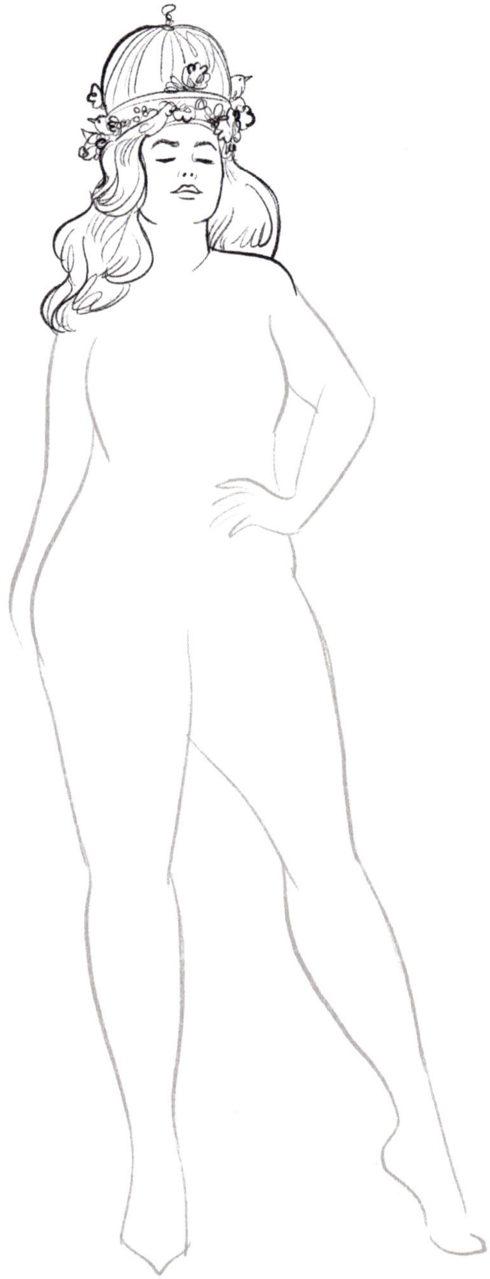

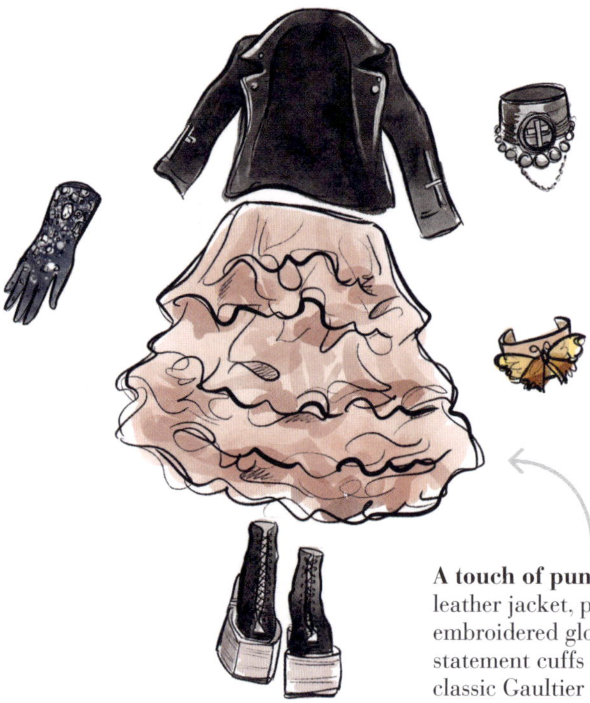

A touch of punk: A tutu, leather jacket, platform boots, embroidered gloves, and statement cuffs create a classic Gaultier outfit.

Now draw your own!

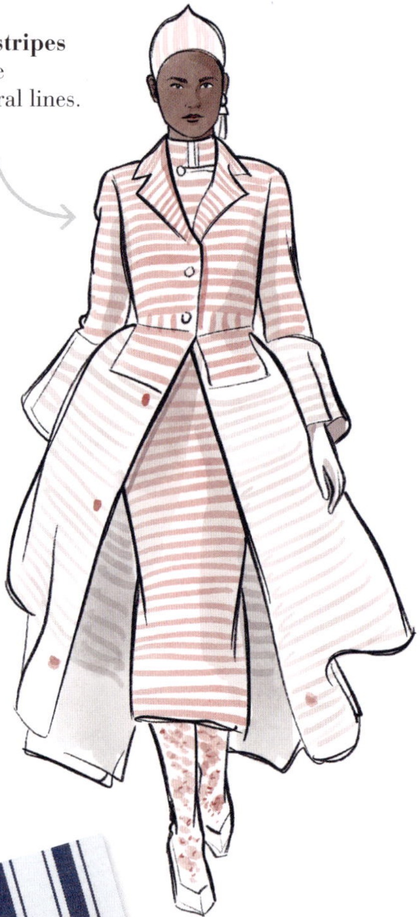

Pastel stripes enhance sculptural lines.

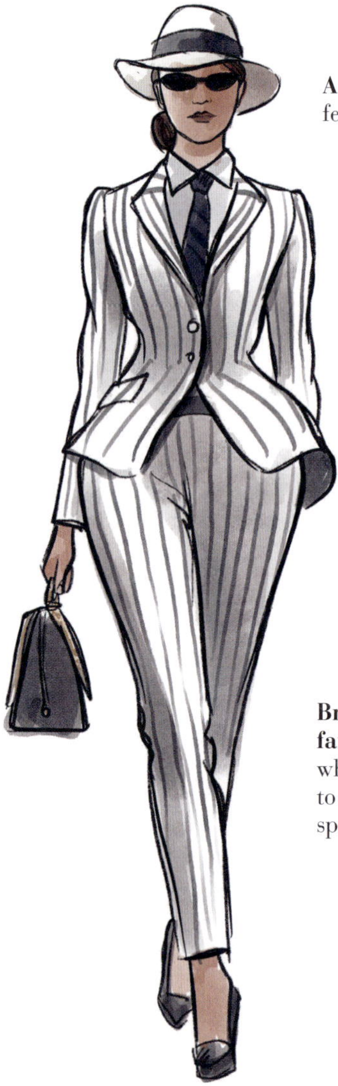

A sharp, suited female silhouette.

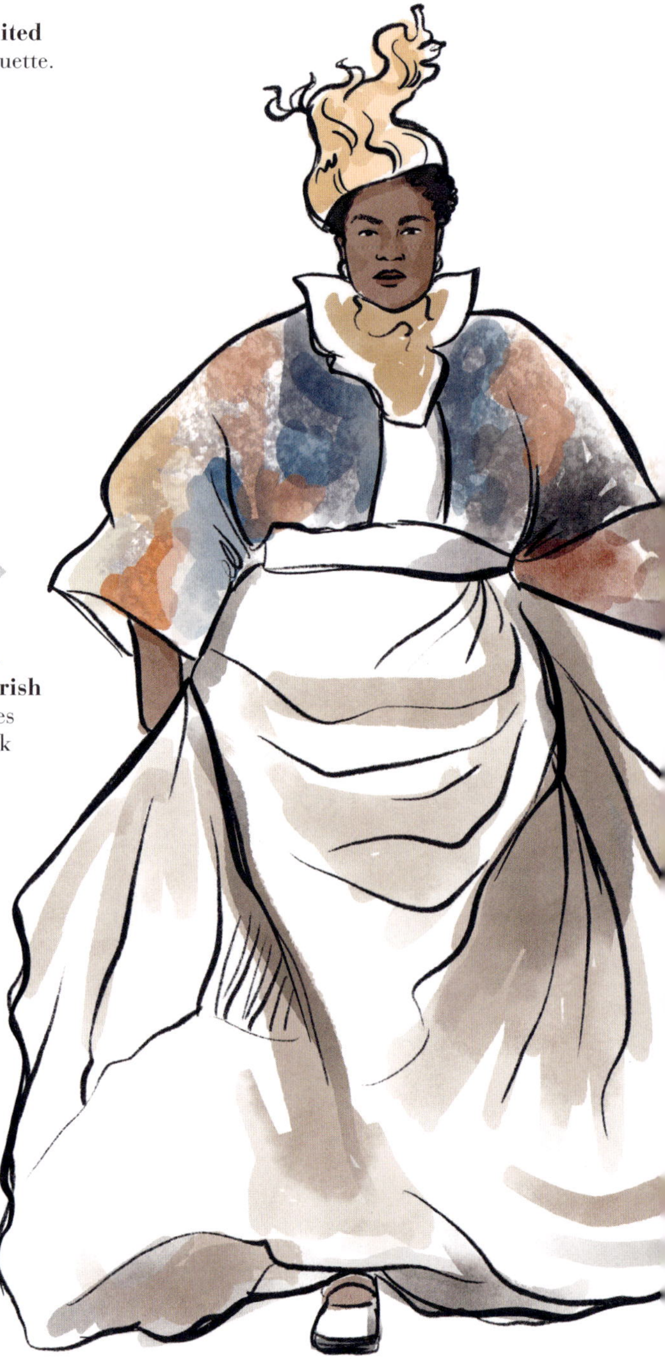

Browne lets fantasy flourish when it comes to his catwalk spectacles.

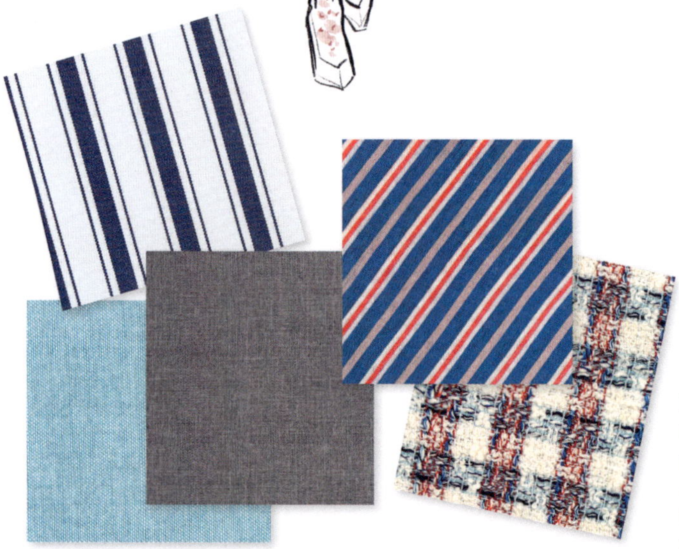

Browne uses high-quality materials and innovative techniques, often combining different patterns, colors, and fabrics, such as stripes, checks, tweed, and wool.

Thom Browne

If Thom Browne's shrunken suit jackets and pants were once seen as provocative, they are now part of the fashion dictionary. Inspired by his father, who wore a gray suit to work every day, Browne leans heavily on just two colors—gray and navy—to put together his masterful formalwear collections. He is renowned for his superbly crafted and imaginative take on tailoring: First Lady Michelle Obama tapped Browne to dress her for President Barack Obama's 2013 inaugural ceremony. The look was an expertly tailored pleated coat, accented with a J.Crew waist belt.

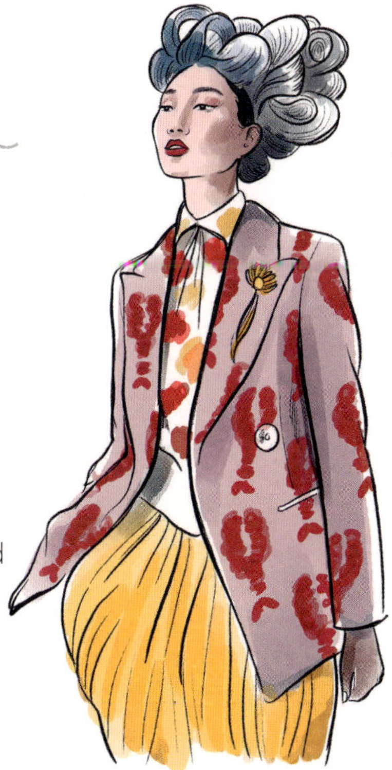

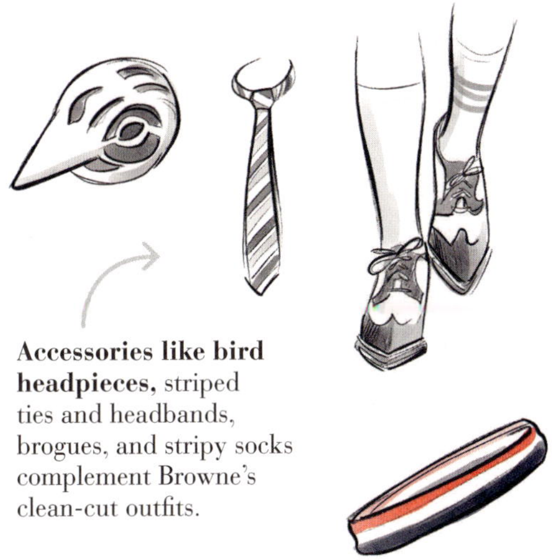

Accessories like bird headpieces, striped ties and headbands, brogues, and stripy socks complement Browne's clean-cut outfits.

Chiffon tweed frocks, sequin jackets, and pinstripe suiting appear in Thom Browne's show regularly.

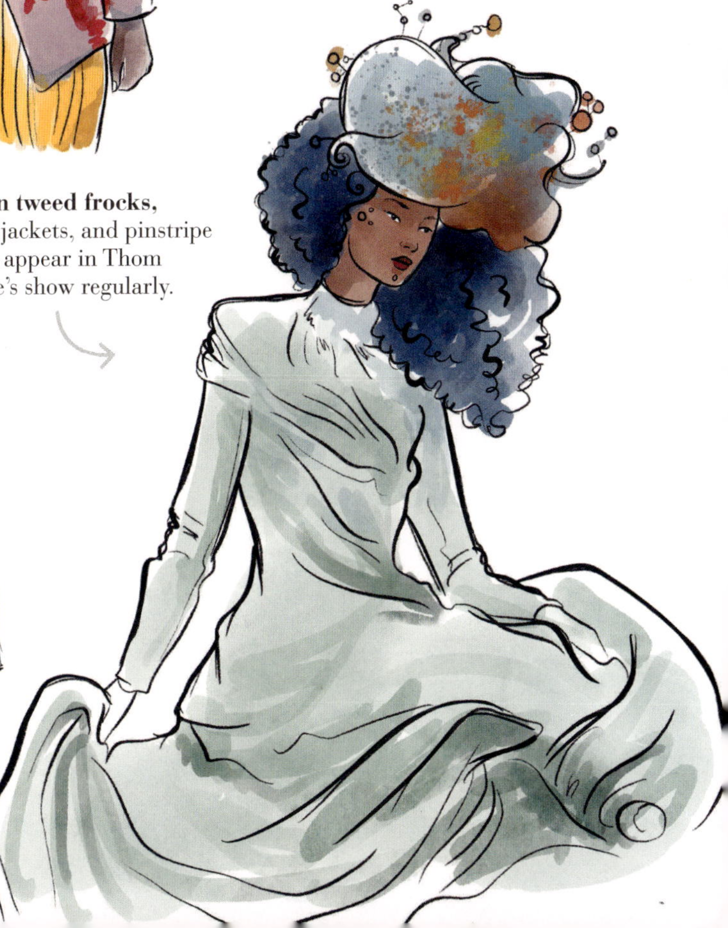

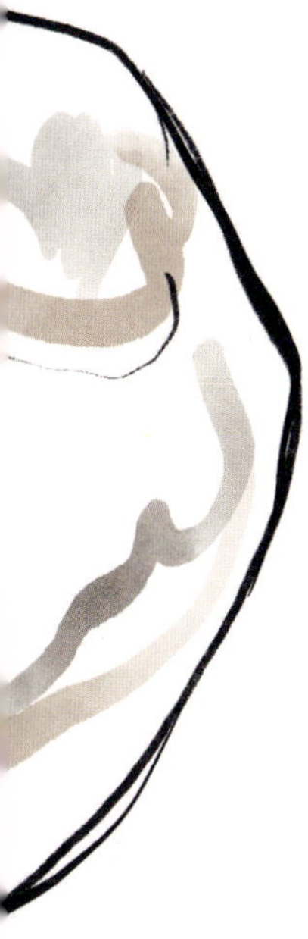

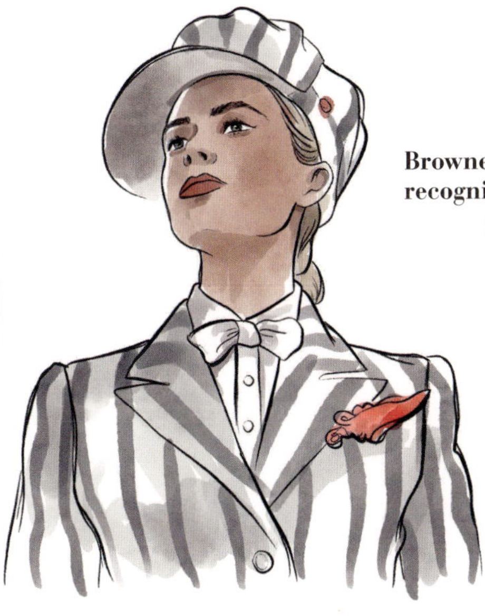

Browne's instantly recognizable gray flannel.

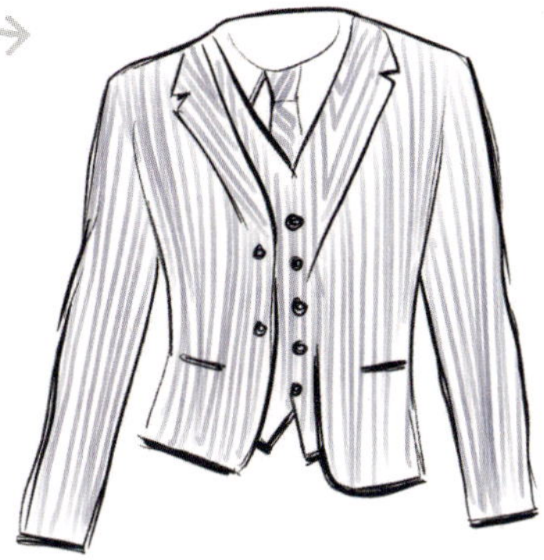

Stripes conjure up the classic, patriotic American look that is at the heart of every Browne collection.

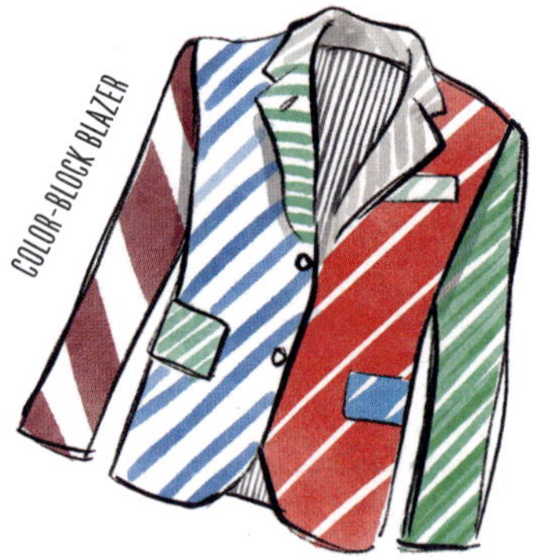

Complete this model's outfit in the Thom Browne style.

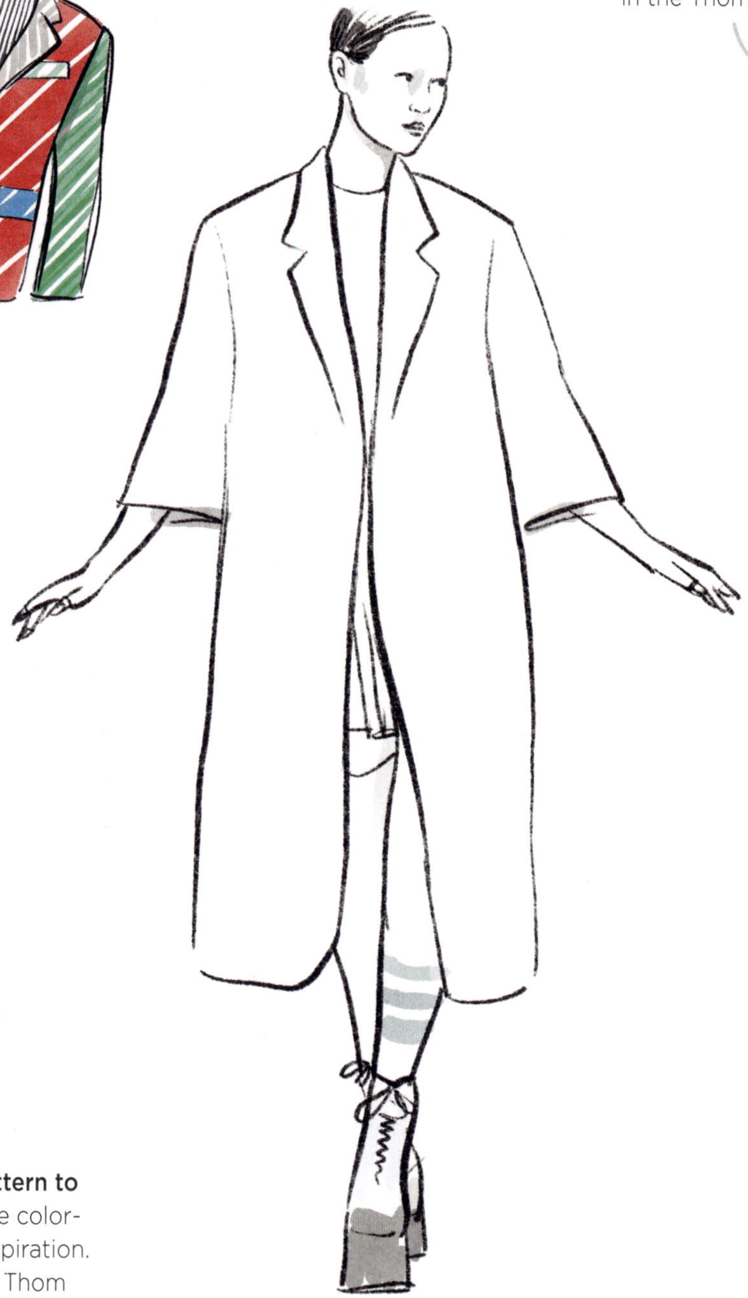

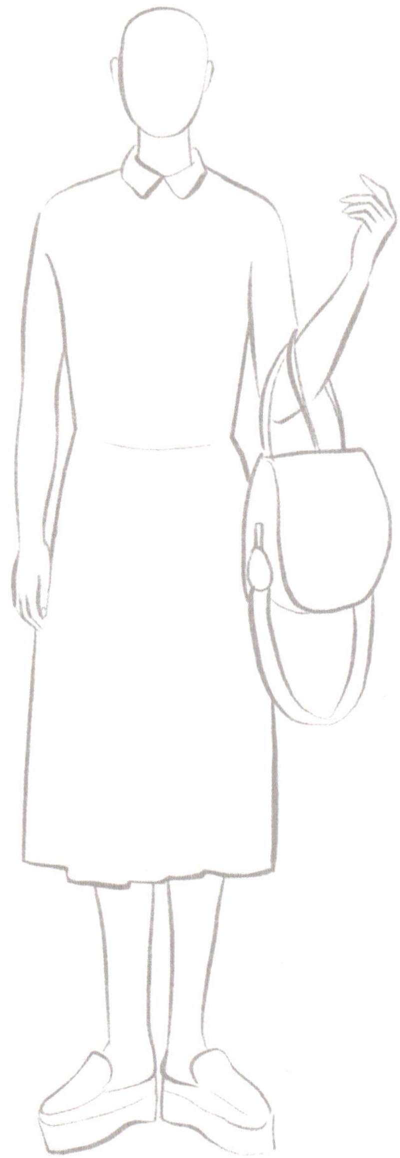

Add color and pattern to this coat, using the color-block blazer as inspiration. Giver her a classic Thom Browne headpiece, too!

Draw your own Thom Browne outfit. Will you design a sophisticated suit, or a more daring catwalk look?

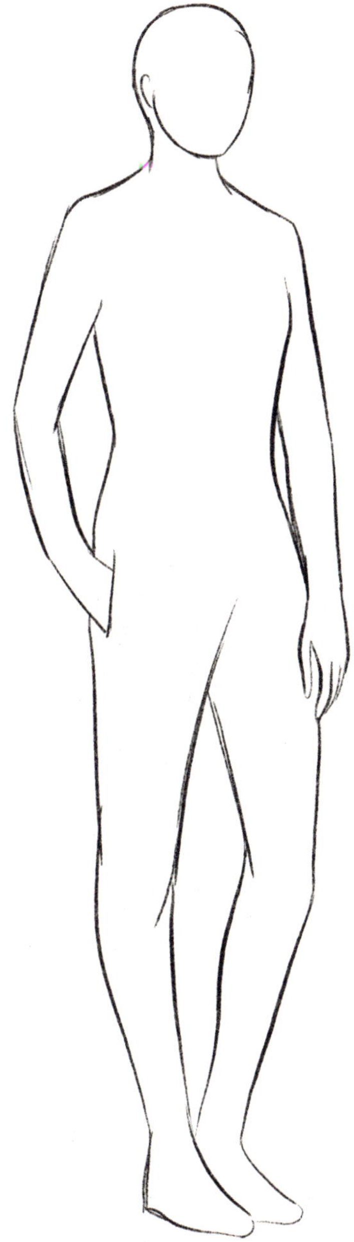

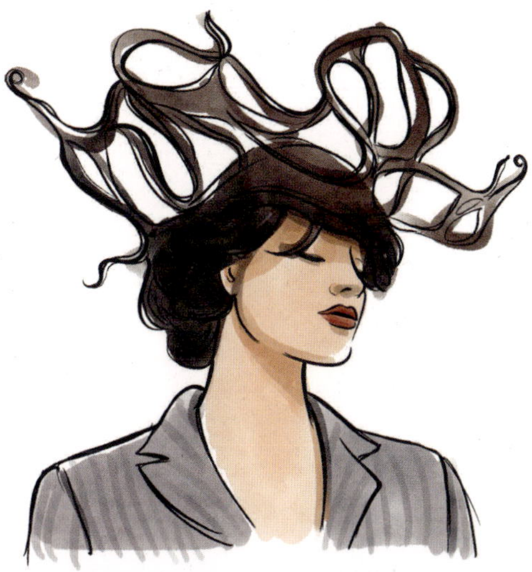

Karl Lagerfeld

German fashion designer and photographer Karl Lagerfeld was the creative power behind the modern revival of Chanel. He reinvigorated the iconic French fashion house with his interpretations of their signature styles, blending Parisian classics with a rock-chic attitude and using jewelry, shoes, and handbags to add glamour and sophistication to his designs. Lagerfeld also had his own eponymous fashion label, founded in 1984. The brand is particularly popular with young, fashion-forward consumers, who are drawn to its edgy, modern aesthetic.

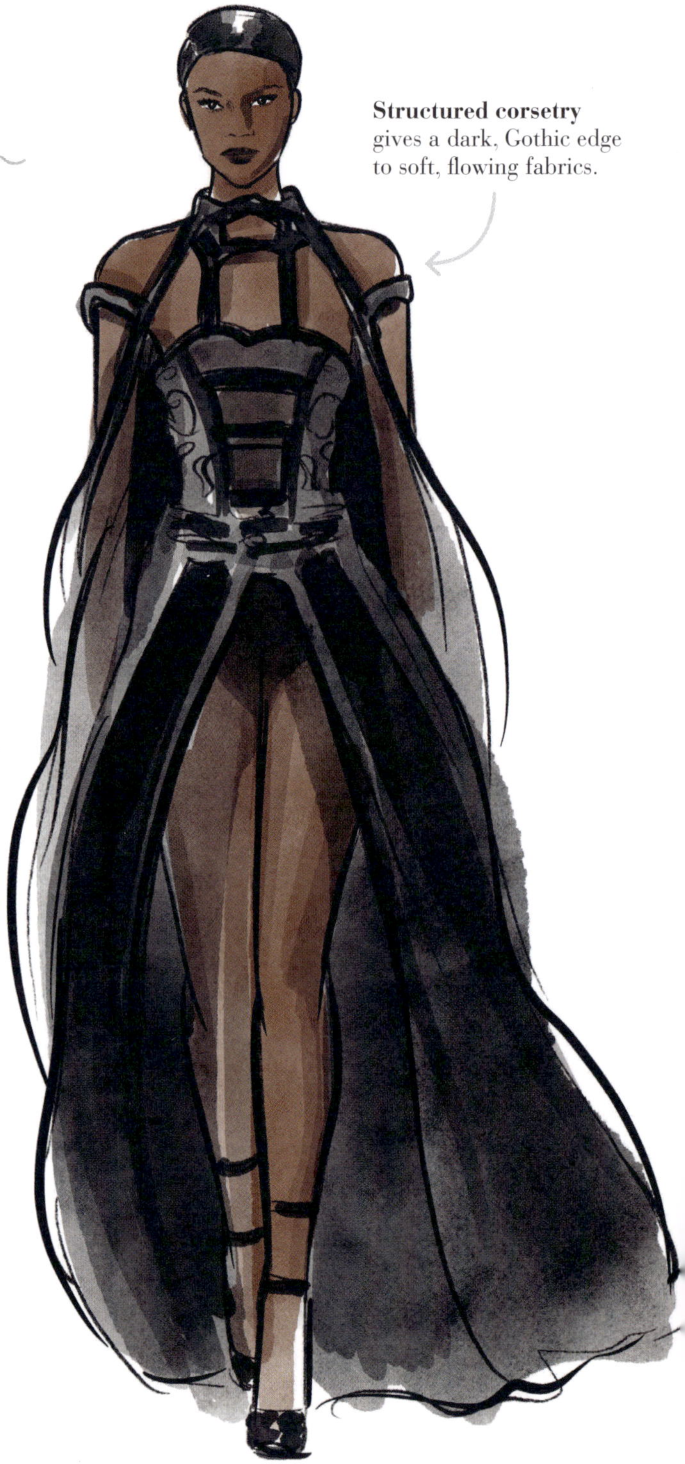

Structured corsetry gives a dark, Gothic edge to soft, flowing fabrics.

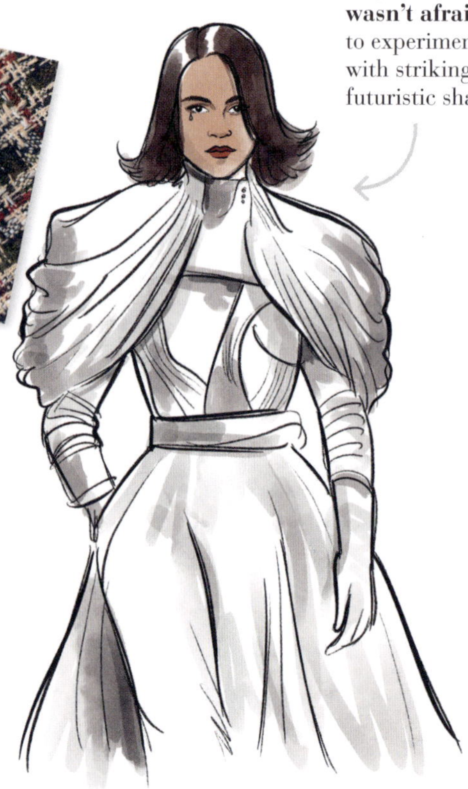

Lagerfeld wasn't afraid to experiment with striking, futuristic shapes.

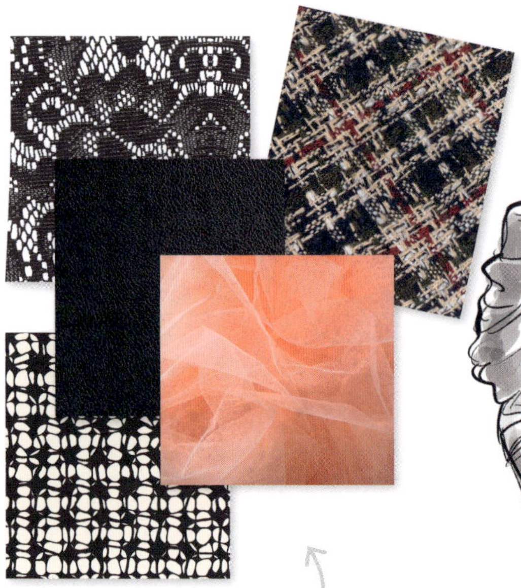

Lagerfeld fabrics include tweed, lace, leather, and silk—fabrics known for their quality, elegance, and sophistication.

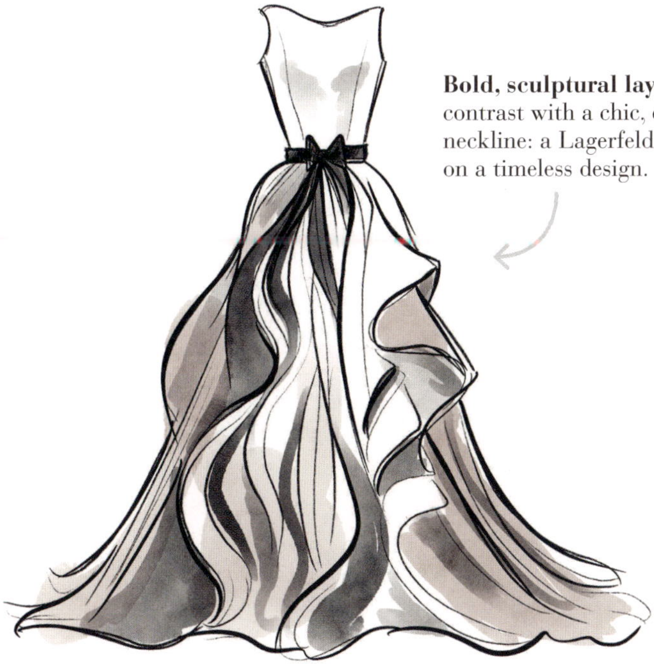

Bold, sculptural layers contrast with a chic, elegant neckline: a Lagerfeld twist on a timeless design.

This dramatic ensemble shows off Lagerfeld's love of street style.

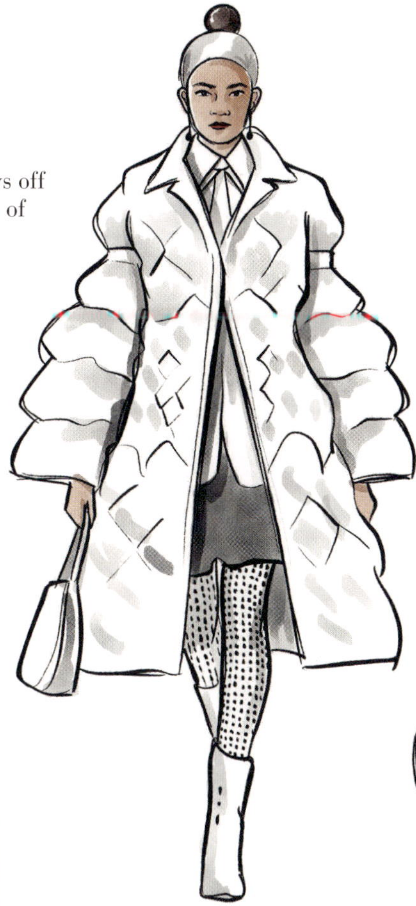

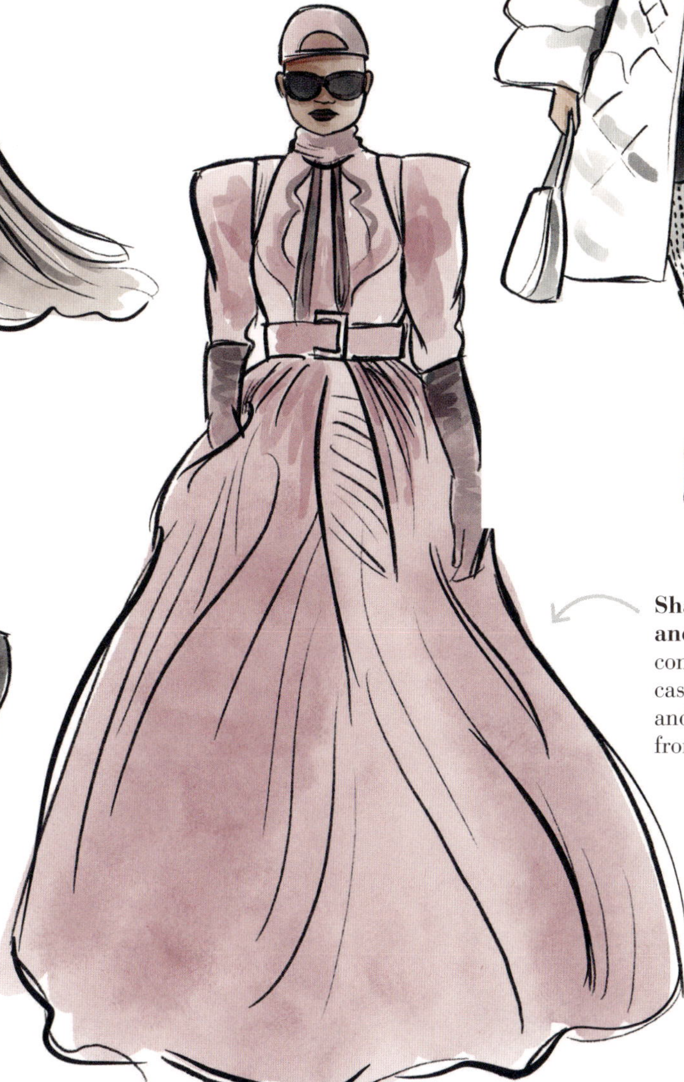

Sharp shoulders and tailoring contrast with casual sunglasses and a cap straight from the street.

Bulbous sleeves add interest to a corset, accessorized, of course!

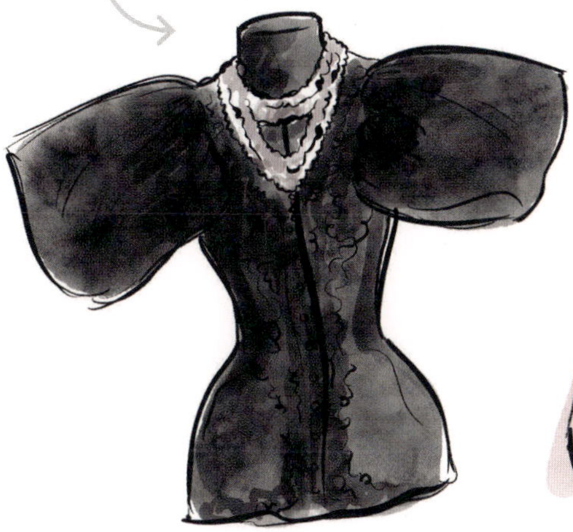

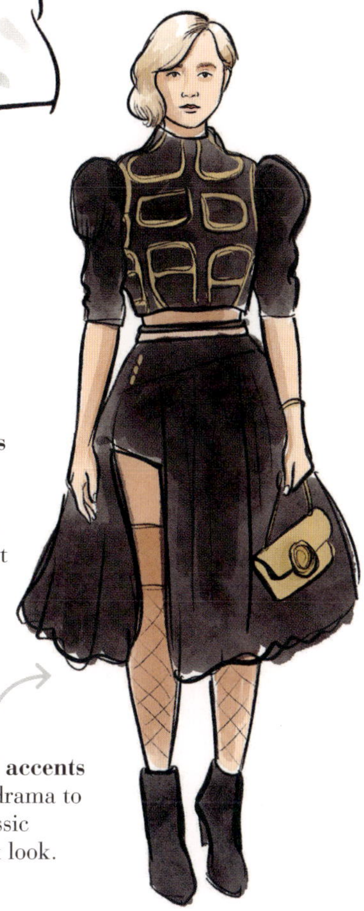

Gold accents add drama to a classic black look.

Give this model a gown that won't be overshadowed by her long veil. You could add bold sleeves, or contrast black and white to play up the drama.

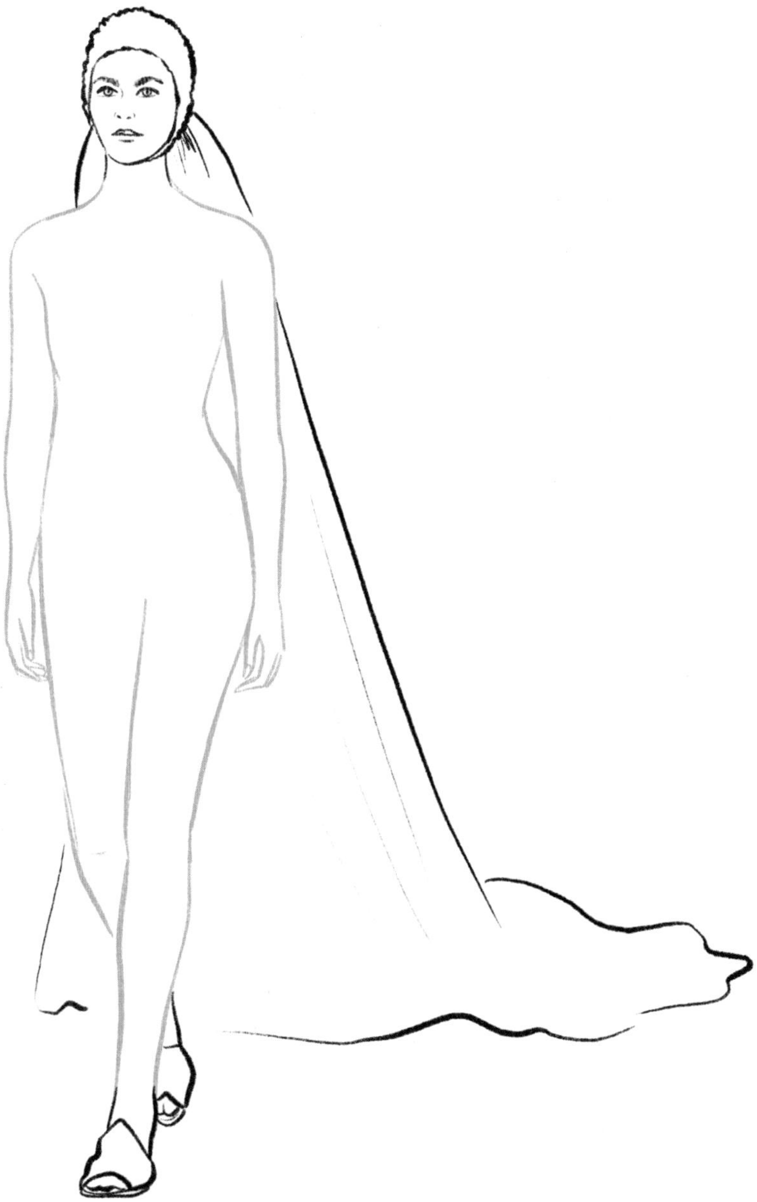

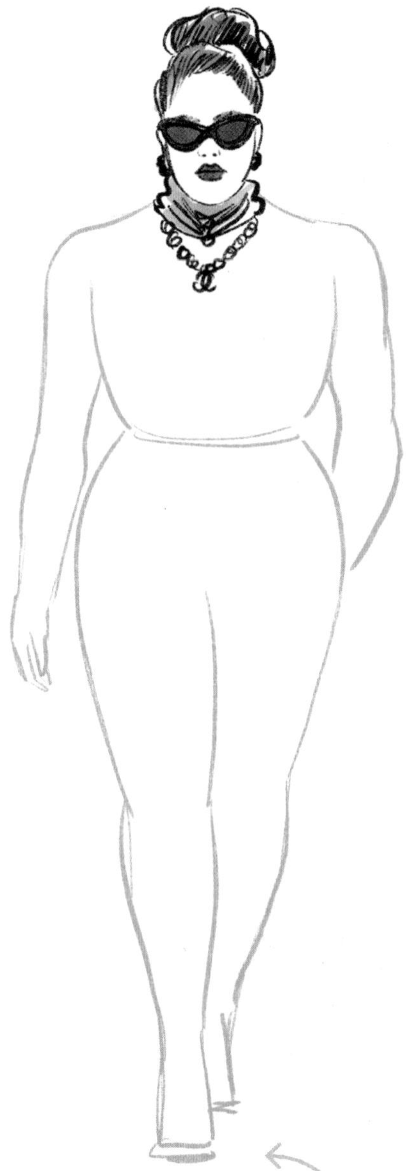

This model is already rocking some Lagerfeld bling! Design an outfit that matches her attitude.

Keep experimenting with elements of Lagerfeld's style to create two brand-new outfits. You could try one for the catwalk, and one for the street—how would you design them differently? Don't forget the accessories!

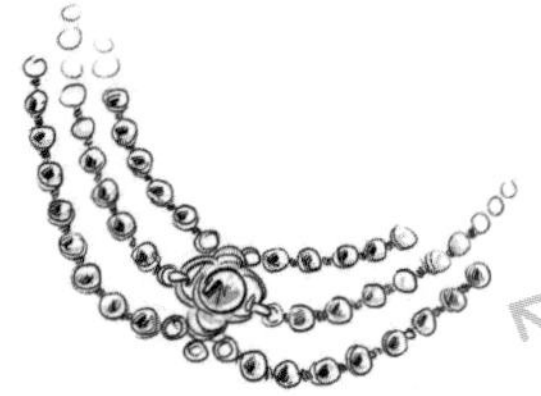

Très chic: pearl necklace inspired by the iconic Chanel.

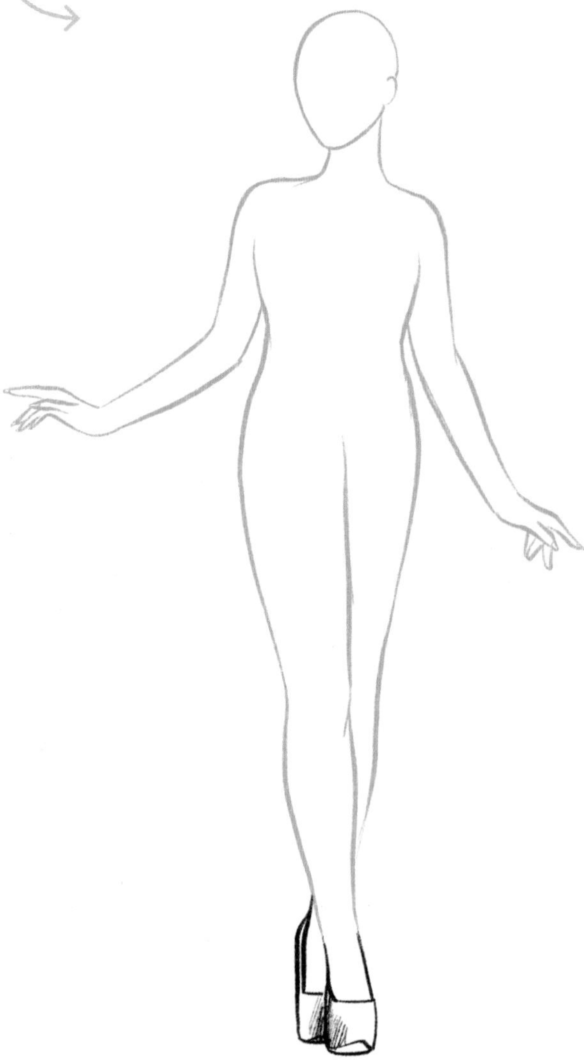

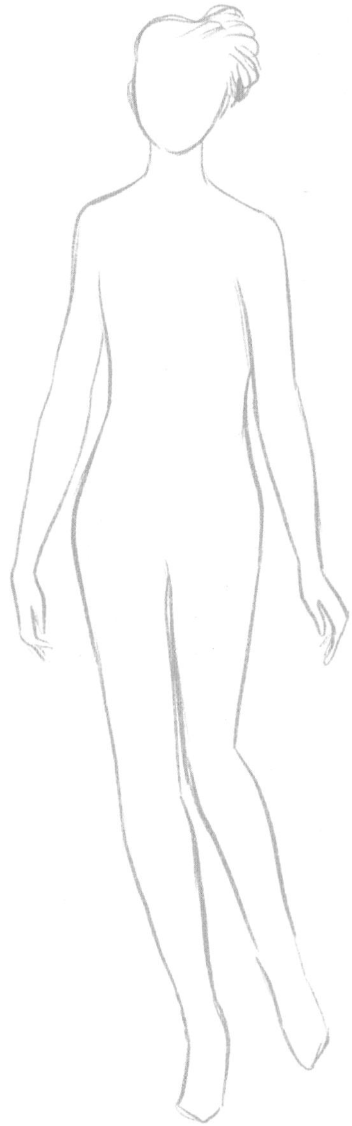

Kerby Jean-Raymond

Fashion trailblazer Kerby Jean-Raymond is the founder and creative director of Pyer Moss, a label that celebrates Black American experience through personal storytelling and provocative showmanship. In 2021, Jean-Raymond became the first Black American designer to show haute couture during Paris Couture Week. His work has a political conscience, and is characterized by rebellion and risk-taking. He abandons the usual catwalk silhouettes, opting instead for bulbous and quirky forms in block colors, often incorporating elements of modern technology or consumer culture.

Bold colors and forms inspired by material culture.

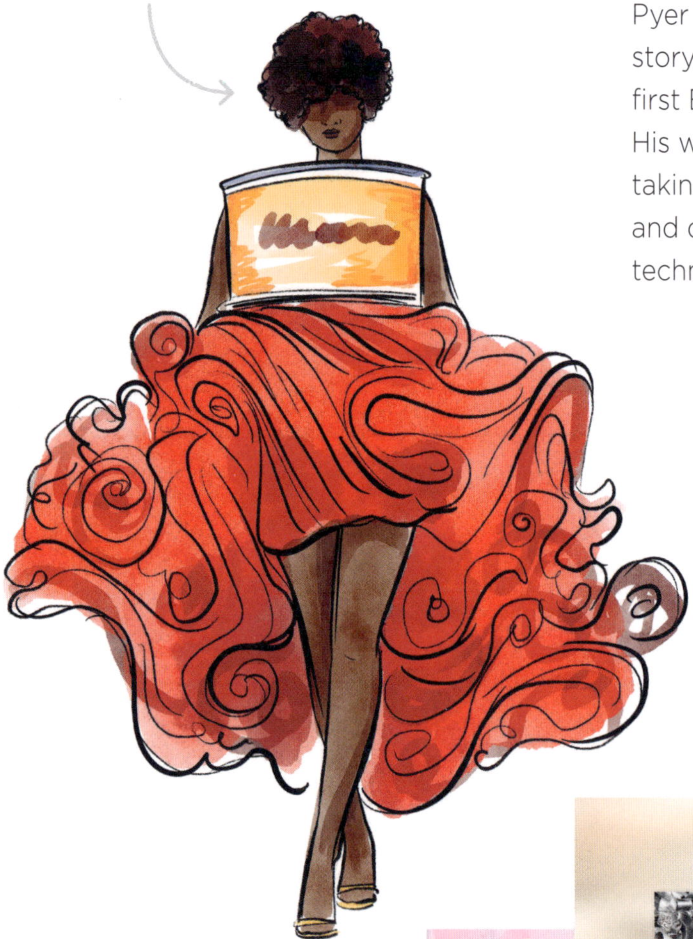

Bright primary colors paint knee-high boots.

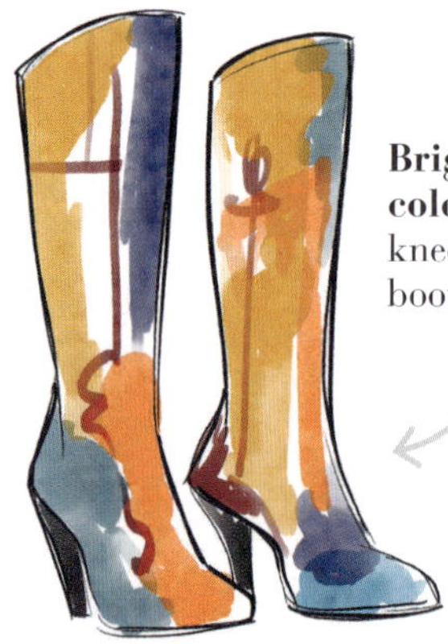

Futuristic, monochromatic pantsuit.

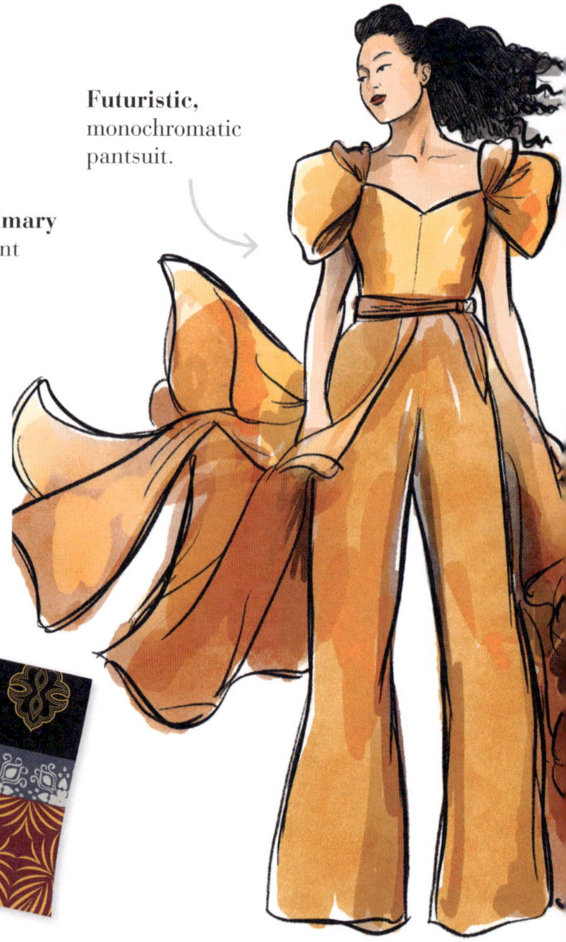

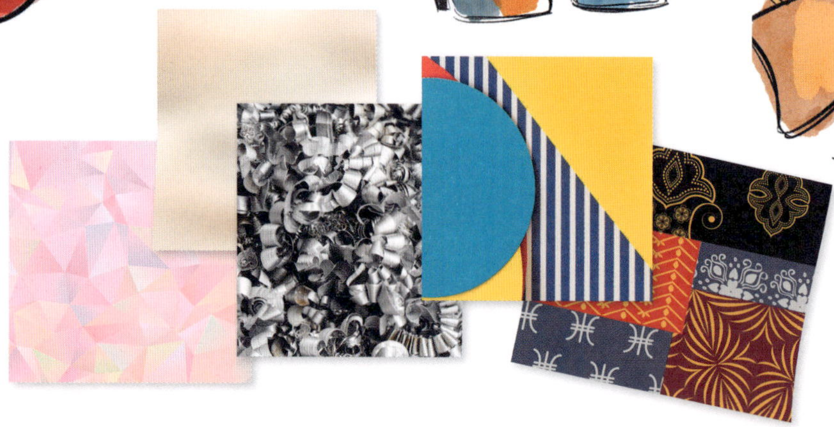

Contrasting colors and patterns, unusual materials, and fun textures are at the heart of Jean-Raymond's work.

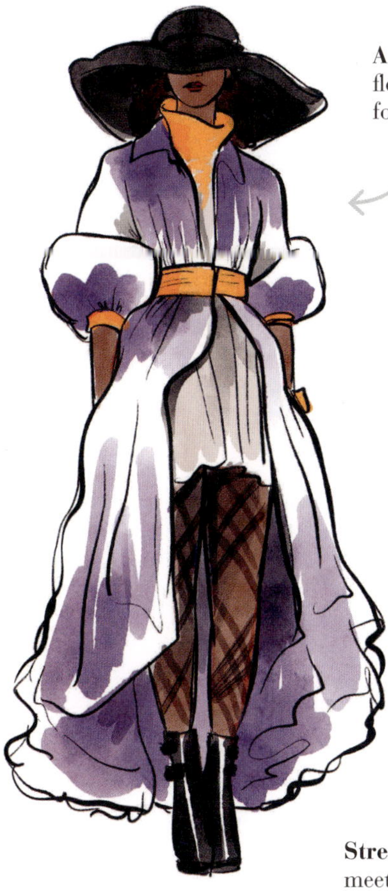

A statement hat and flowing fabrics make for a bold silhouette.

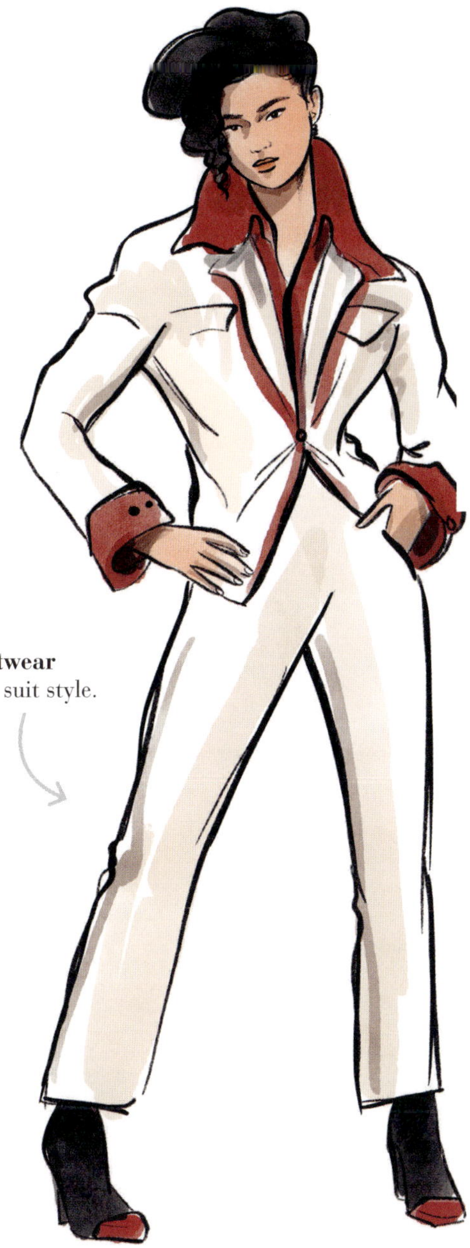

Streetwear meets suit style.

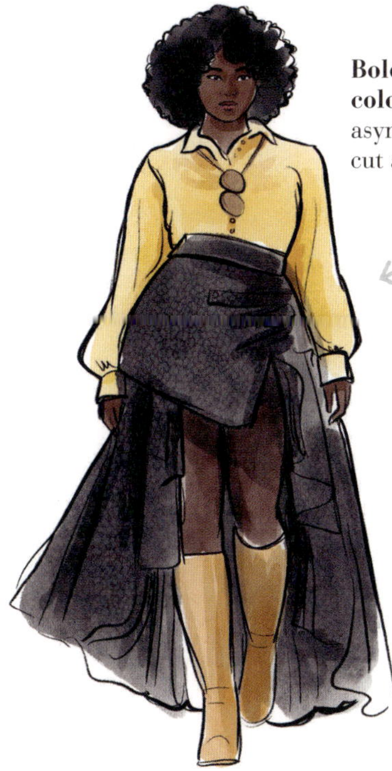

Bold, contrasting colors and an asymmetric hem cut a striking figure.

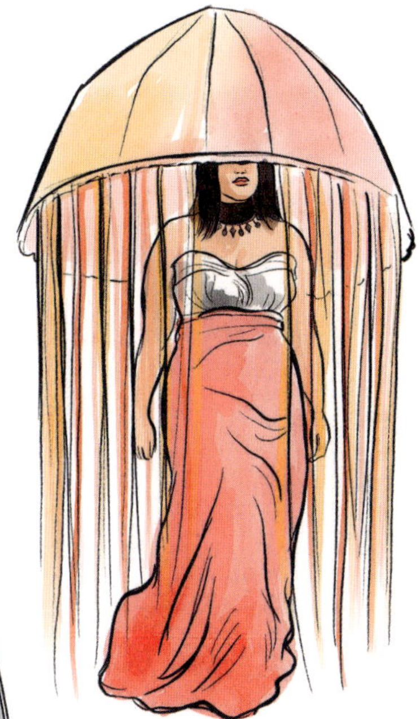

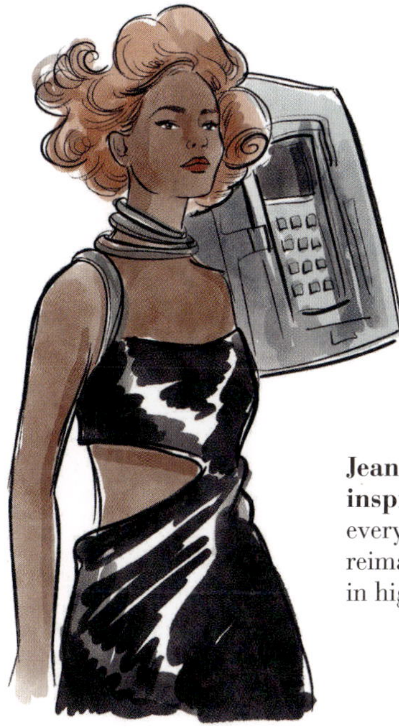

Jean-Raymond draws inspiration from everyday objects, reimagining them in high fashion.

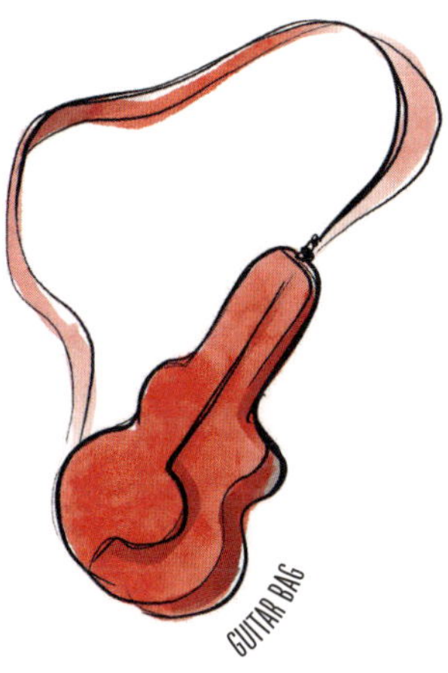

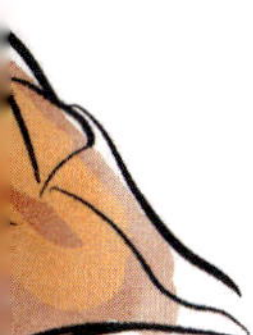

Finish this model's dress. Think about using bold shapes and colors to complement the geometric, metallic shapes they are holding.

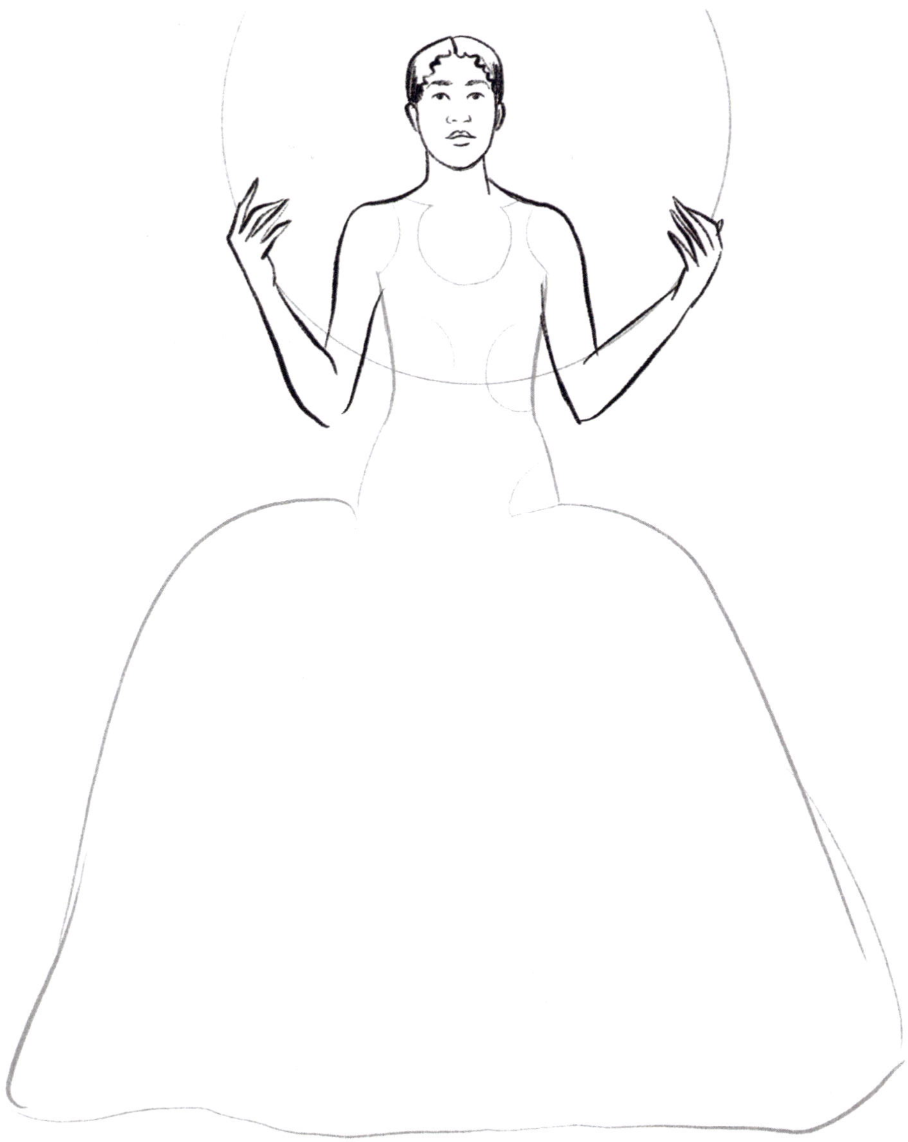

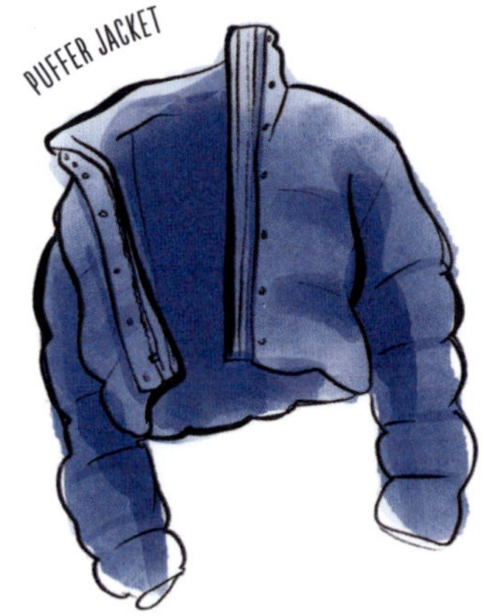

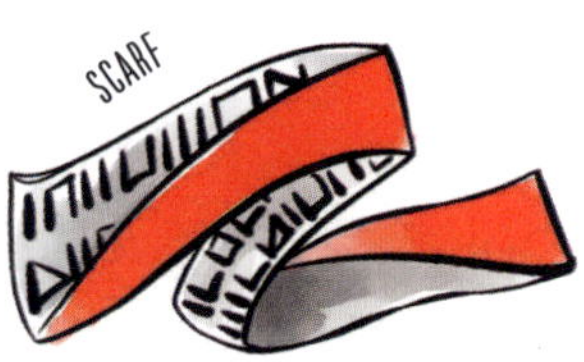

Now have a go at creating your own Jean-Raymond outfits.
You could put a fun twist on a haute-couture staple by designing it around an object you can see while you sketch!

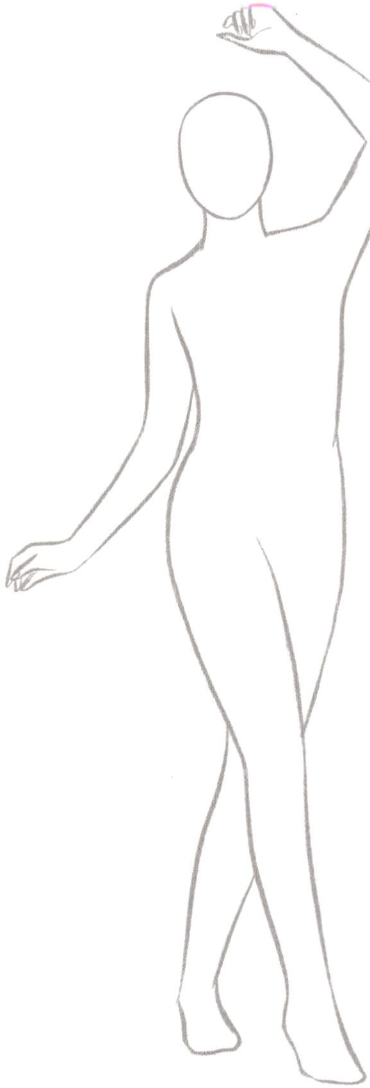

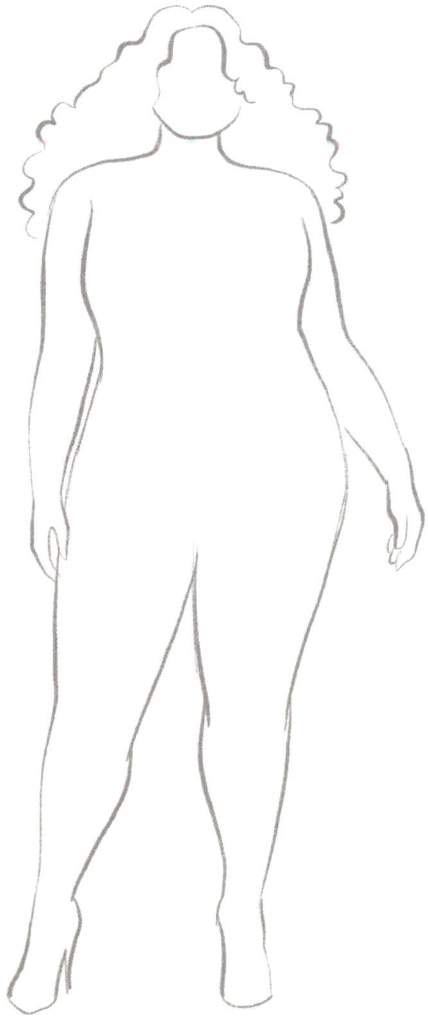

Charles de Vilmorin

Charles de Vilmorin is a French designer and couturier who launched his eponymous label on Instagram during the COVID-19 pandemic, when he was just 23 years old. His colorful and abstract creations, inspired by his family of botanists and artists, quickly gained a following. His favorite techniques are painting on fabric, patchwork, and printing, drawing from contemporary influences. His debut collection of quilted jackets was inspired by Niki de Saint Phalle's famous Nana sculptures, and more recently he created a world that is part Tim Burton-esque science fiction, part commedia dell'arte.

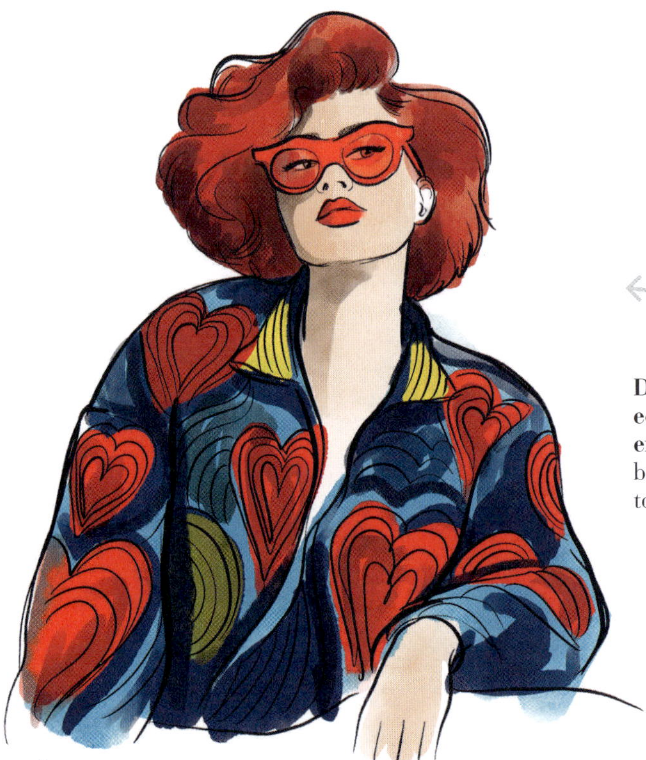

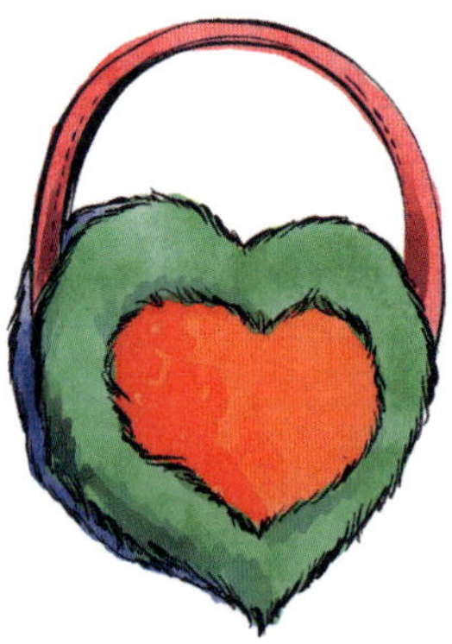

De Vilmorin's colorful, eccentric, and experimental fabrics bring a youthful energy to haute couture.

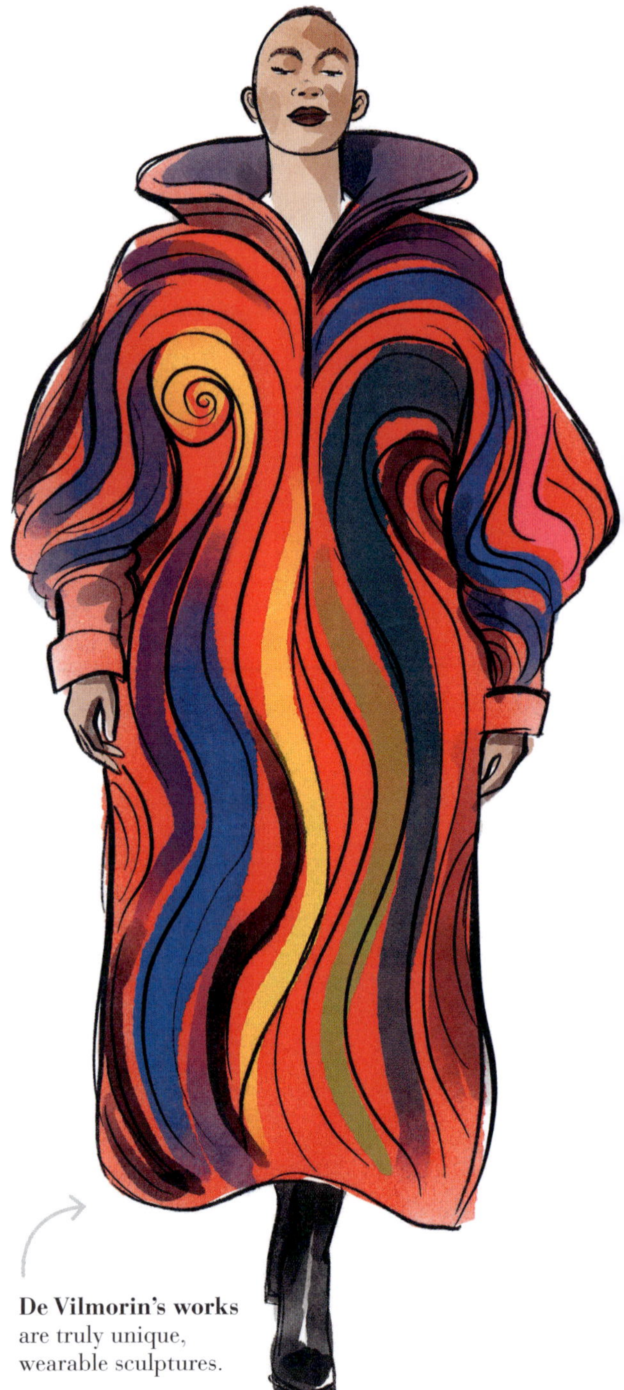

De Vilmorin's works are truly unique, wearable sculptures.

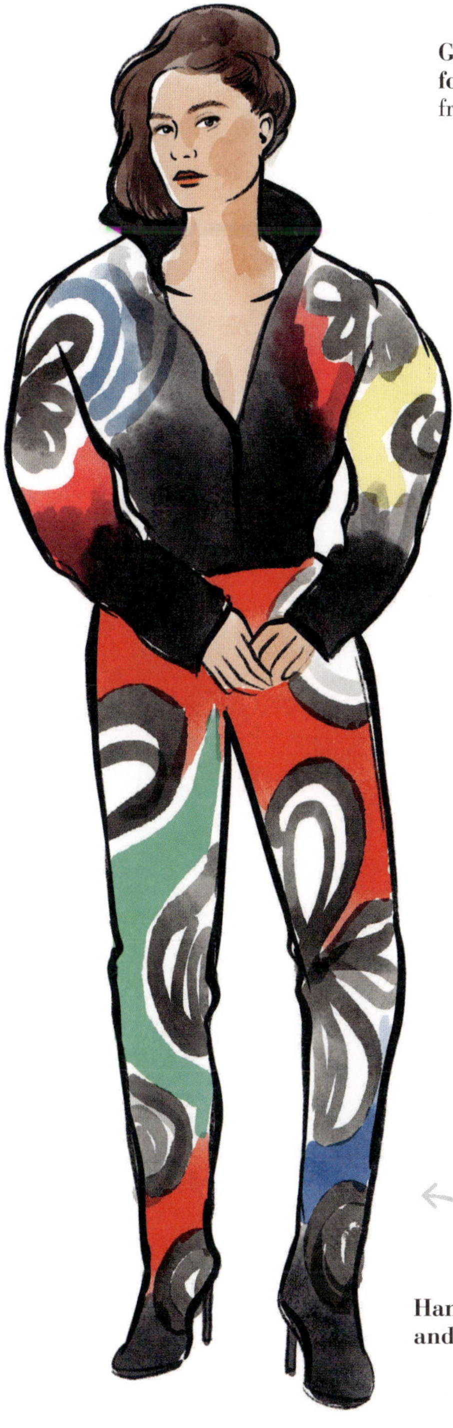

Gender-neutral forms celebrate freedom.

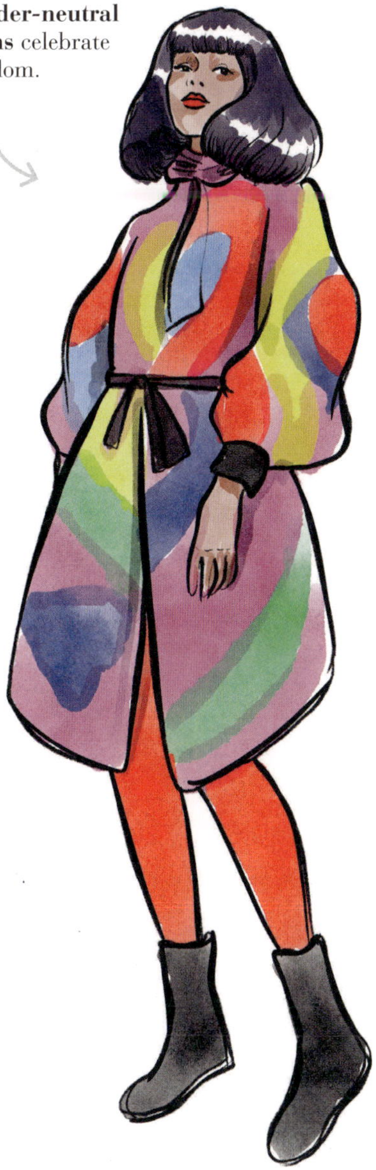

Hand-painted coat and jumpsuit.

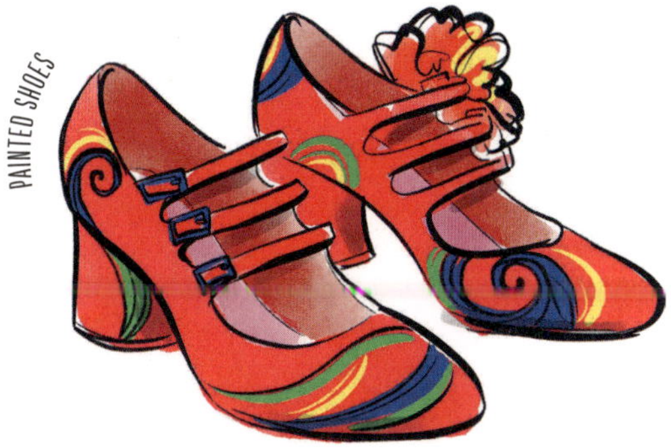

De Vilmorin's Spring 2022 collection was inspired by Tim Burton's dark, Gothic aesthetic.

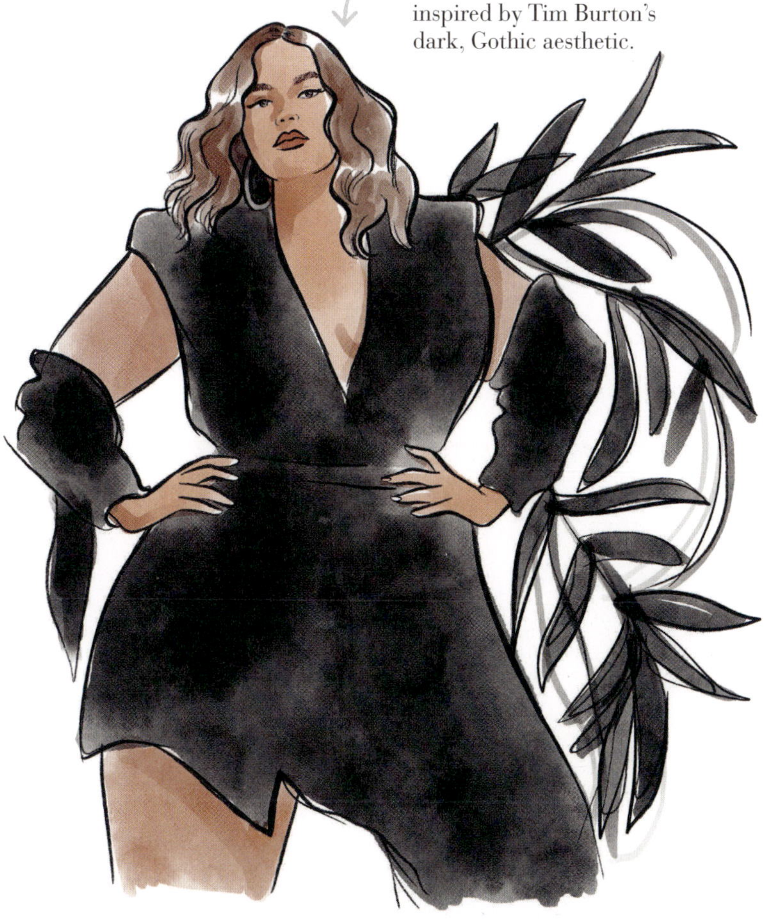

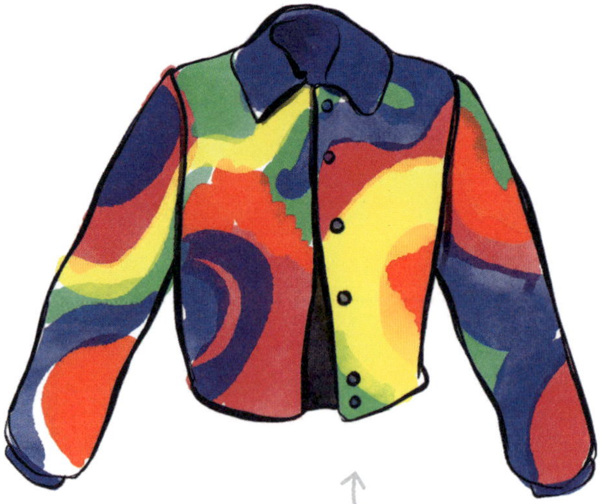

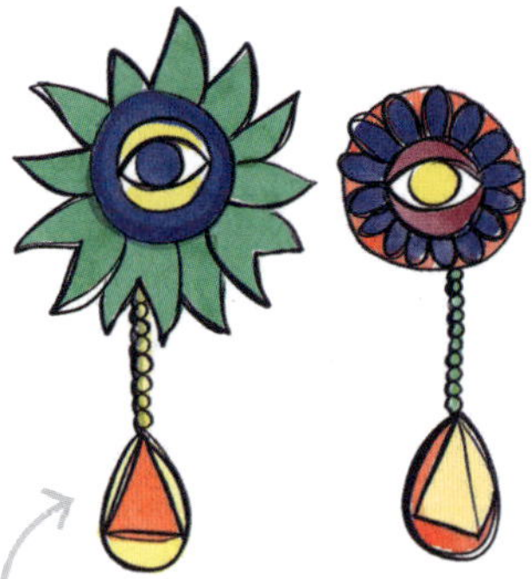

De Vilmorin's work often reflects his whimsical artistic sensibility.

Eye-catching and unconventional color combinations contribute to a playful aesthetic.

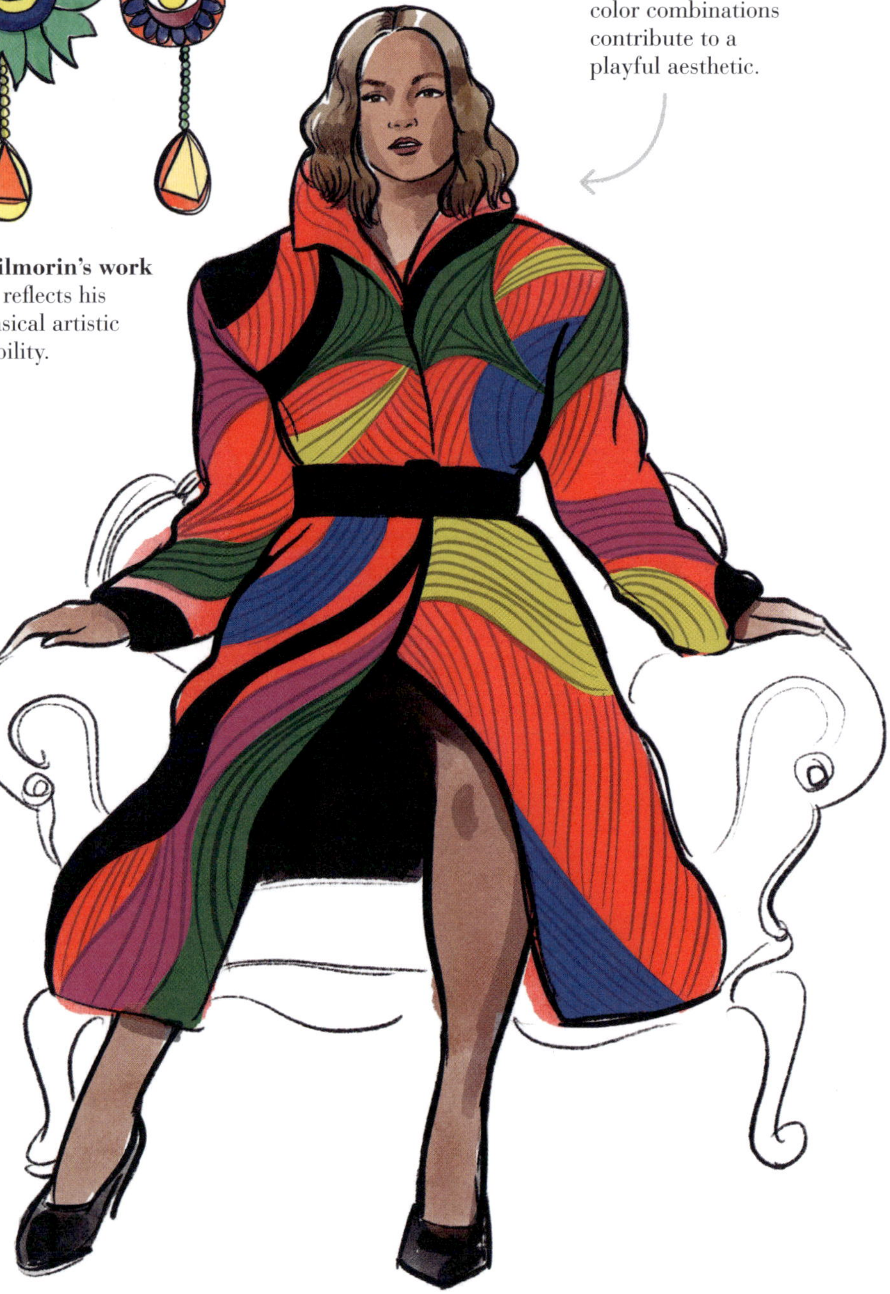

The combination of different textures creates visually interesting and dynamic pieces.

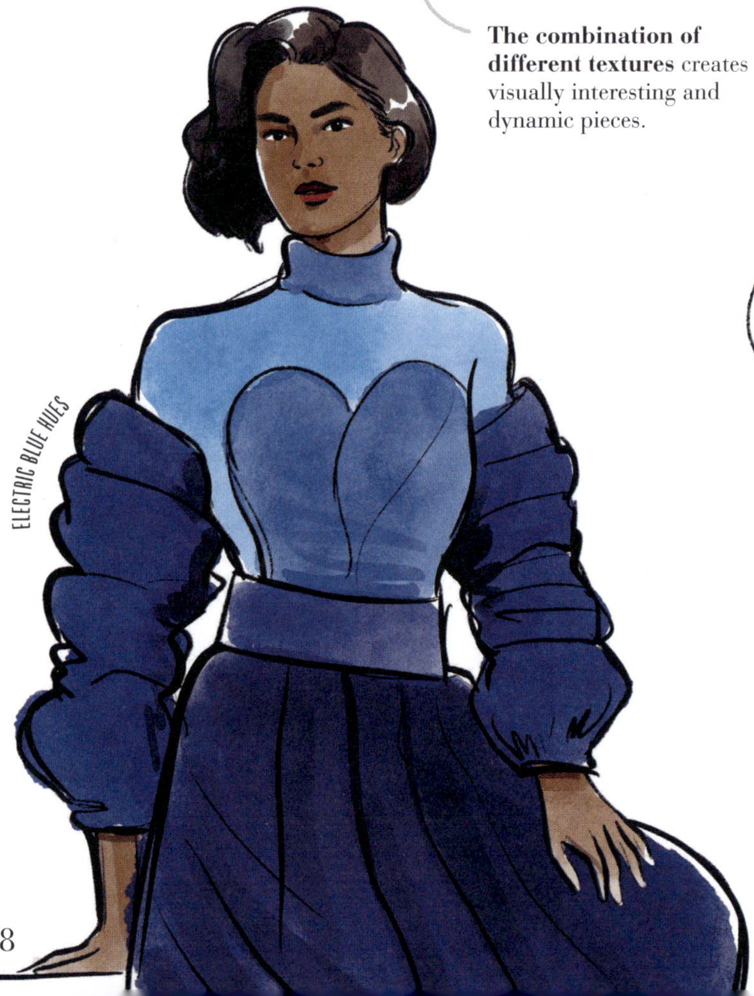

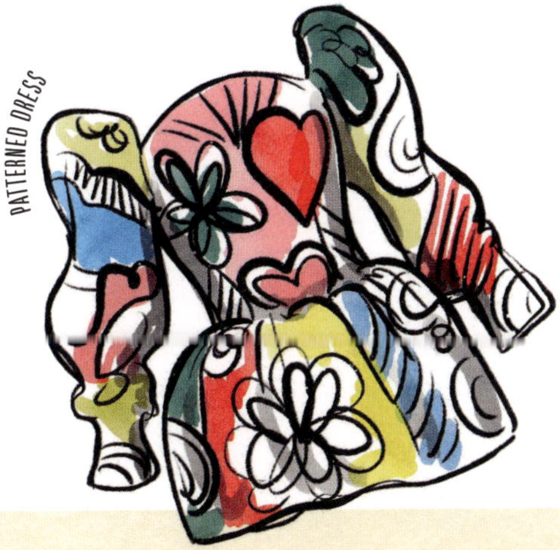

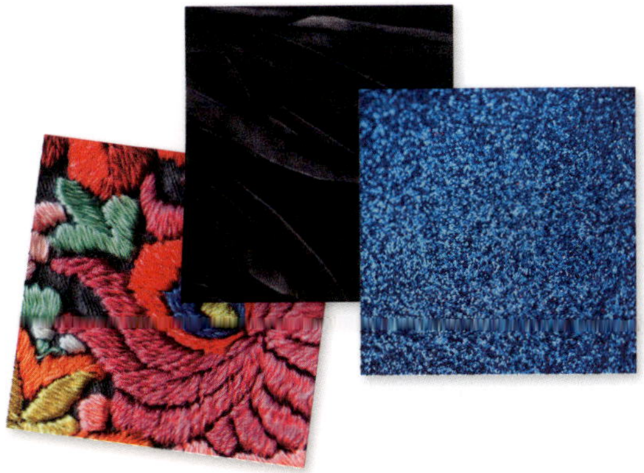

De Vilmorin's favorite techniques are painting on fabric, patchwork, and printing. His designs are made of hand-printed waterproof polyester and include four layers of padding. Meticulous stitchwork gives relief to the garment.

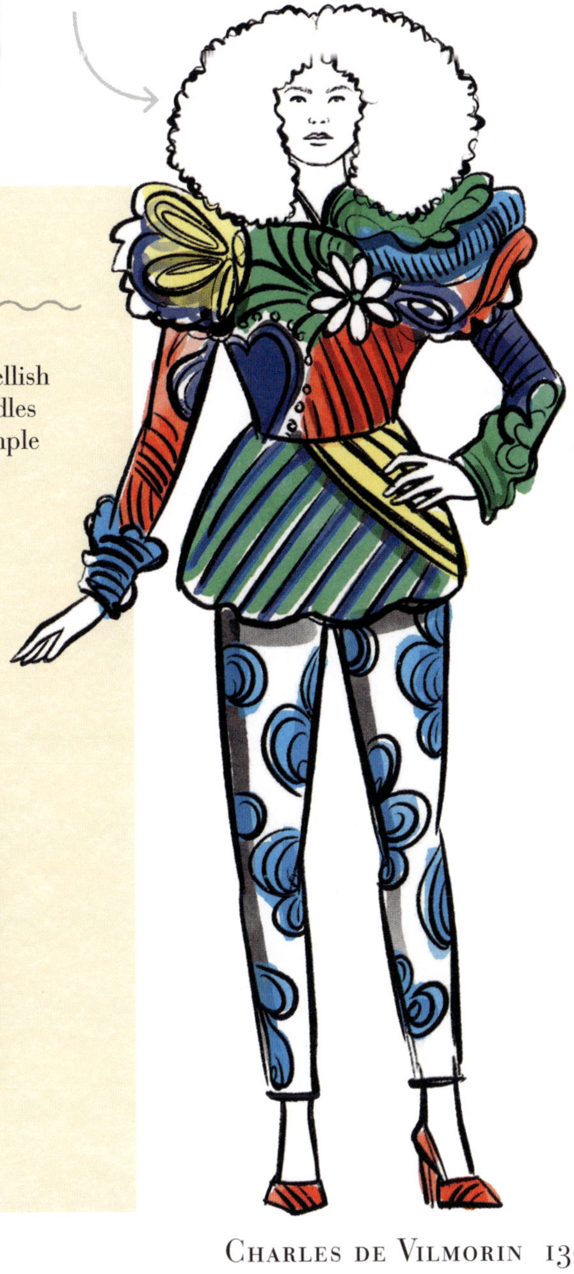

CREATE YOUR OWN DE VILMORIN-INSPIRED PATTERN

1. Start with a simple outline drawing.

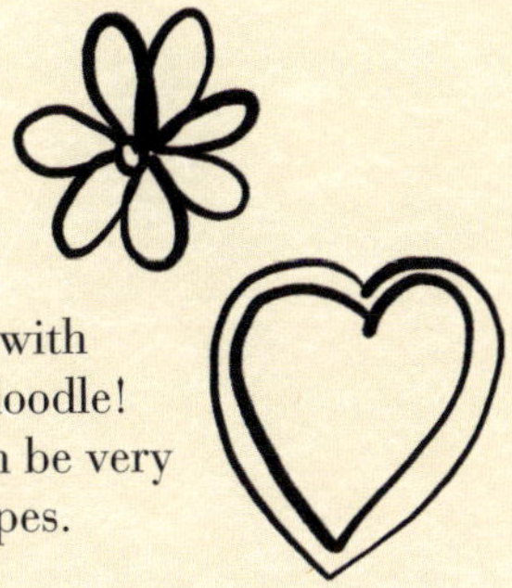

2. Pair it with another doodle! These can be very basic shapes.

3. Embellish the doodles with simple designs.

4. Join your shapes together by adding lines all around them, some curved, some straight, heading off in different directions.

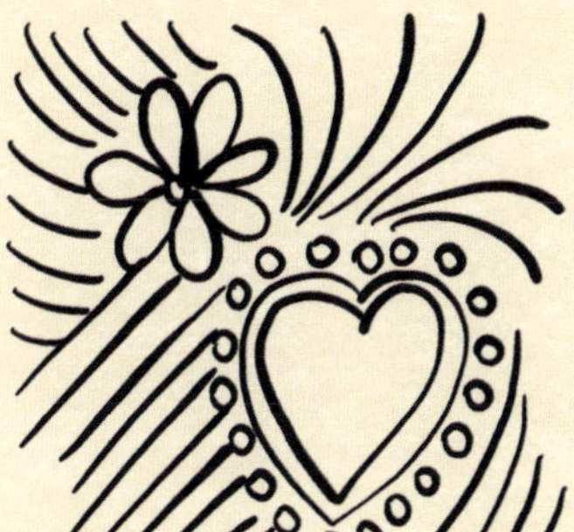

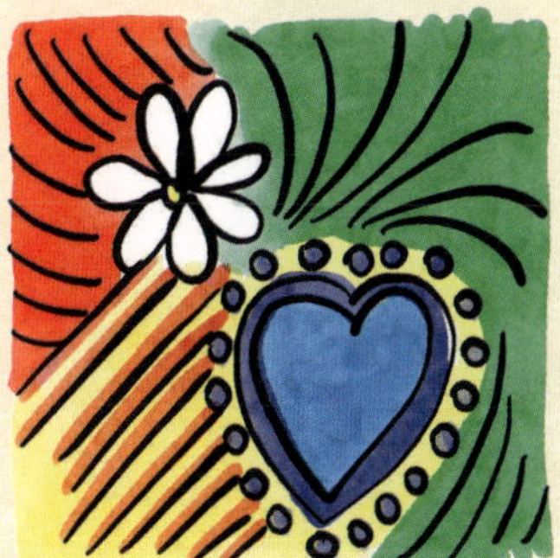

5. Bring in some bright, bold colors.

Finish this silhouette's puffy look by adding some painted motifs. Will you draw flower designs, or take inspiration from abstract art?

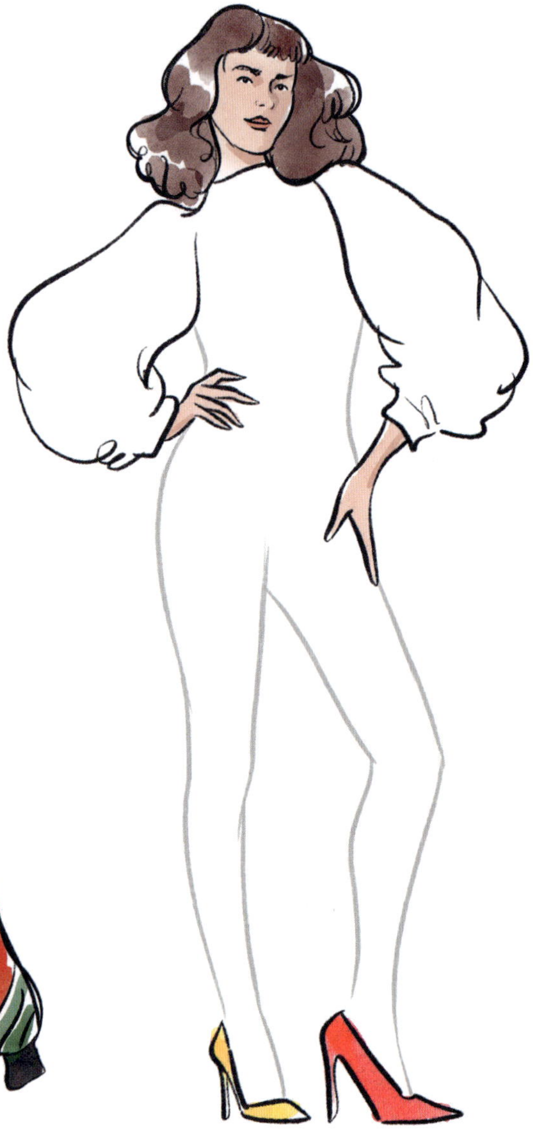

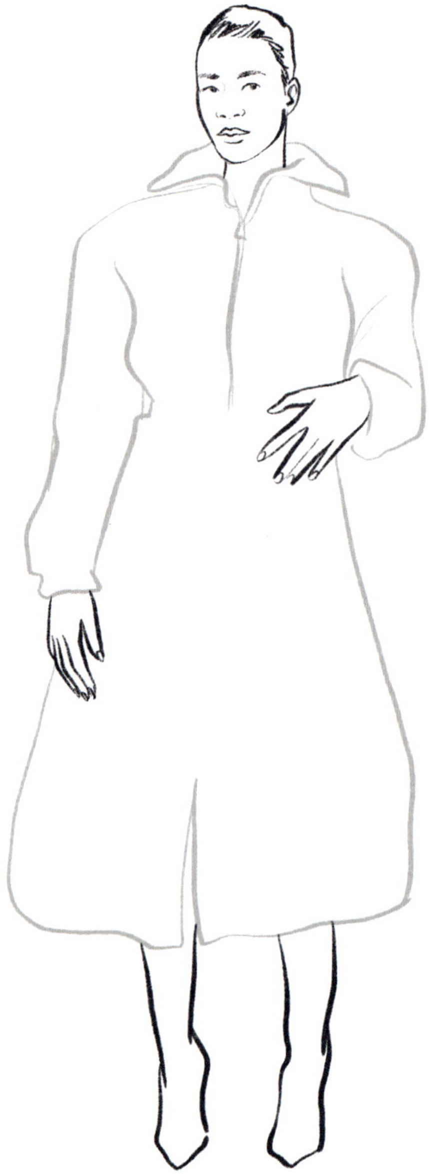

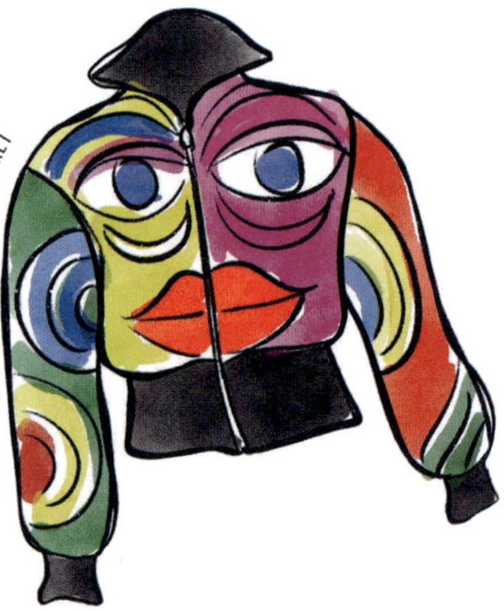

PATTERNED JACKET

Complete this model's coat with some colorful embroidery.

Now design your own De Vilmorin looks!
How will you style the models' hair and makeup to complement your bright and busy outfits?

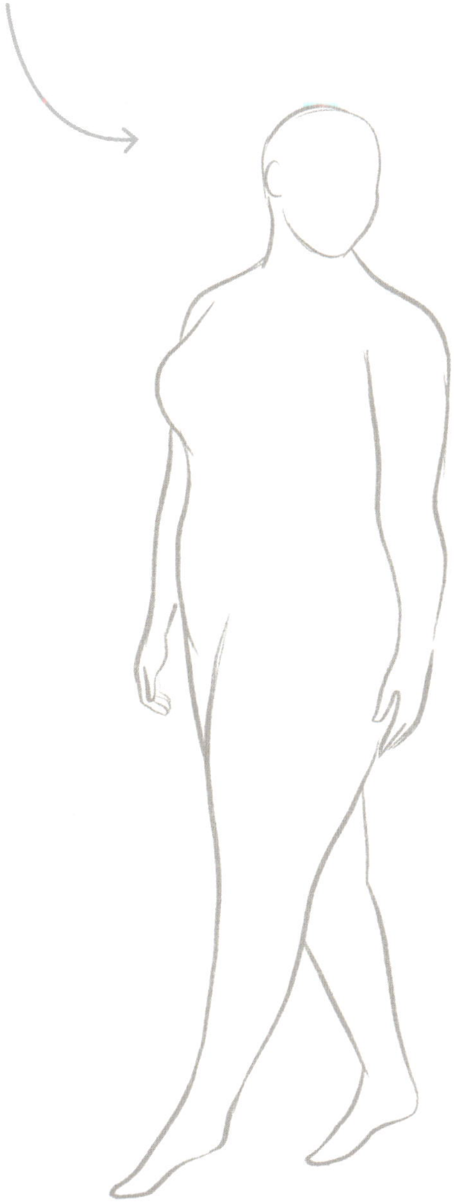

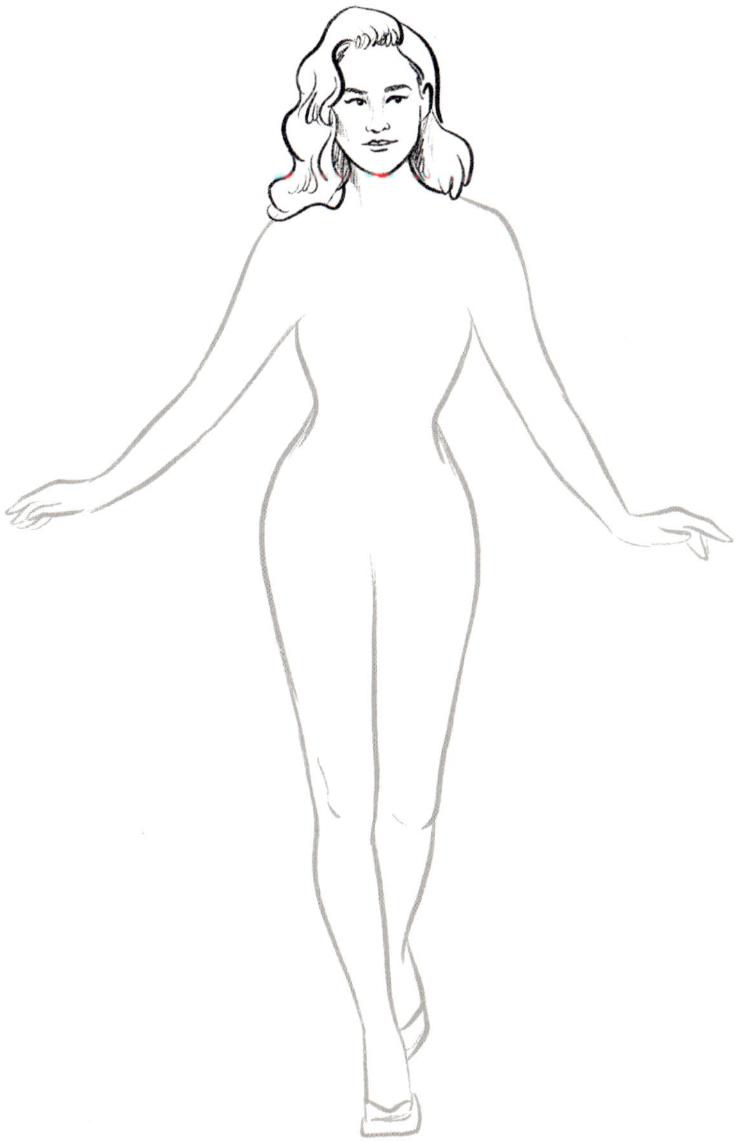

80s Casual

The '80s Casual look is all about being cool and comfortable, with a flash of neon zing! Whether you were going to the mall or hitting the arcade, you wanted to look stylish and relaxed. Sneakers became everyday wear, and denim reigned supreme, paired with branded track tops, patterned sweaters, or sporty polo shirts. Bombers, leather jackets, and windbreakers added some edge to the look. To this day, fashion brands channel the '80s vibe, celebrating its youthful, carefree energy.

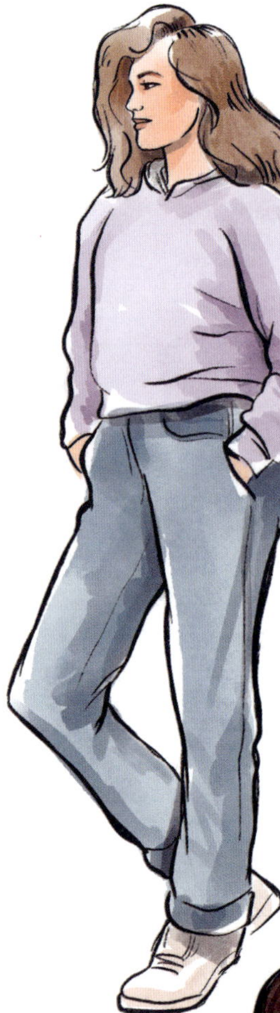

Vibrant '80s colors on a contemporary outfit.

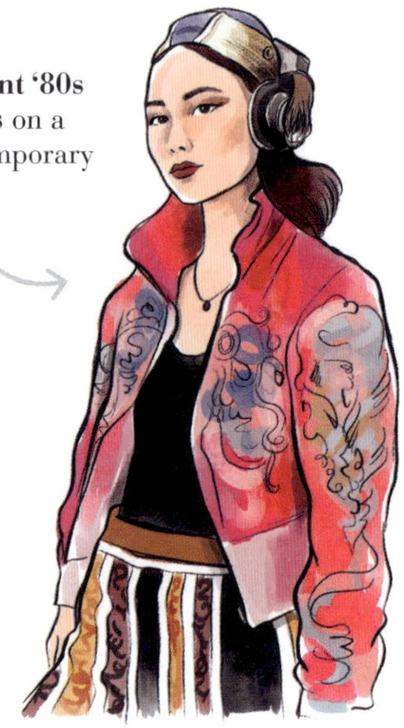

Denim was everywhere in the '80s, from jeans to jackets to skirts. Denim was often worn in matching sets or mixed with other fabrics and colors.

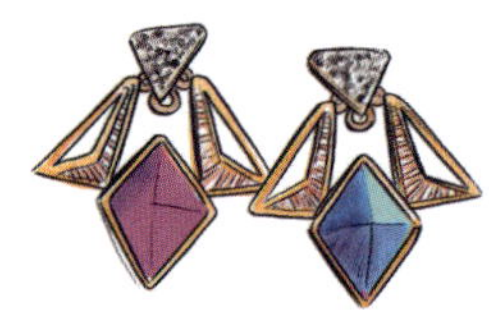

Bright earrings in bold, geometric shapes—the more glitter, the better!

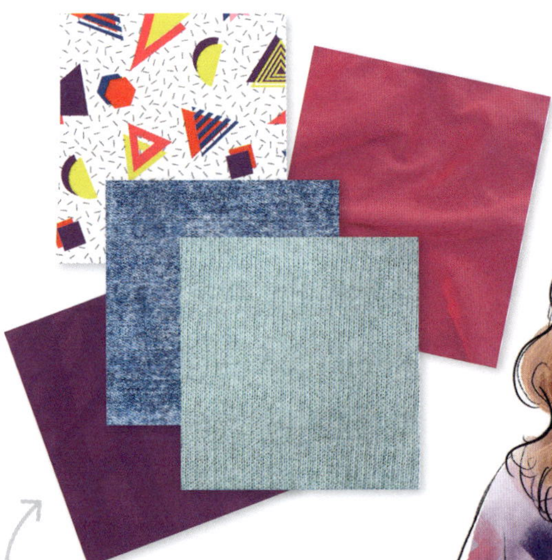

Velour, spandex, and Lycra ruled the '80s, especially in jazzy, busy, and brightly colored prints. Comfortable cotton and natural silk were also popular choices.

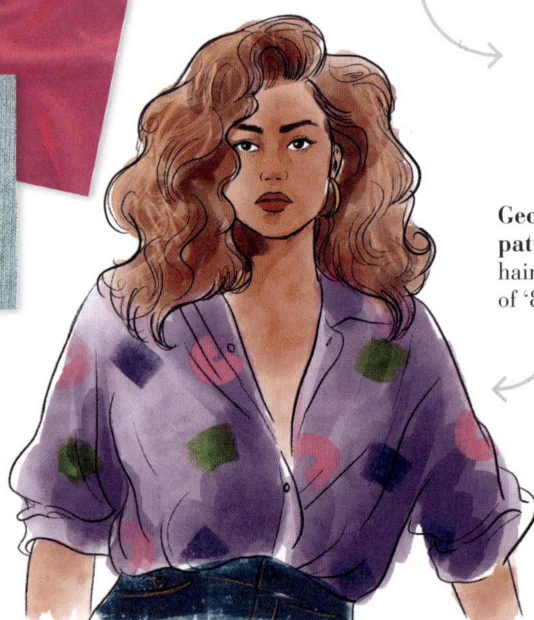

Geometric patterns and big hair were a staple of '80s fashion.

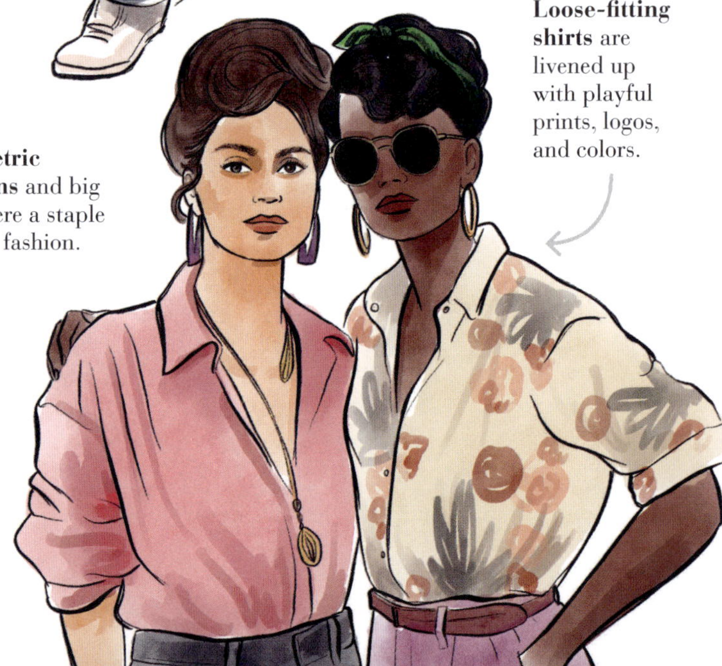

Loose-fitting shirts are livened up with playful prints, logos, and colors.

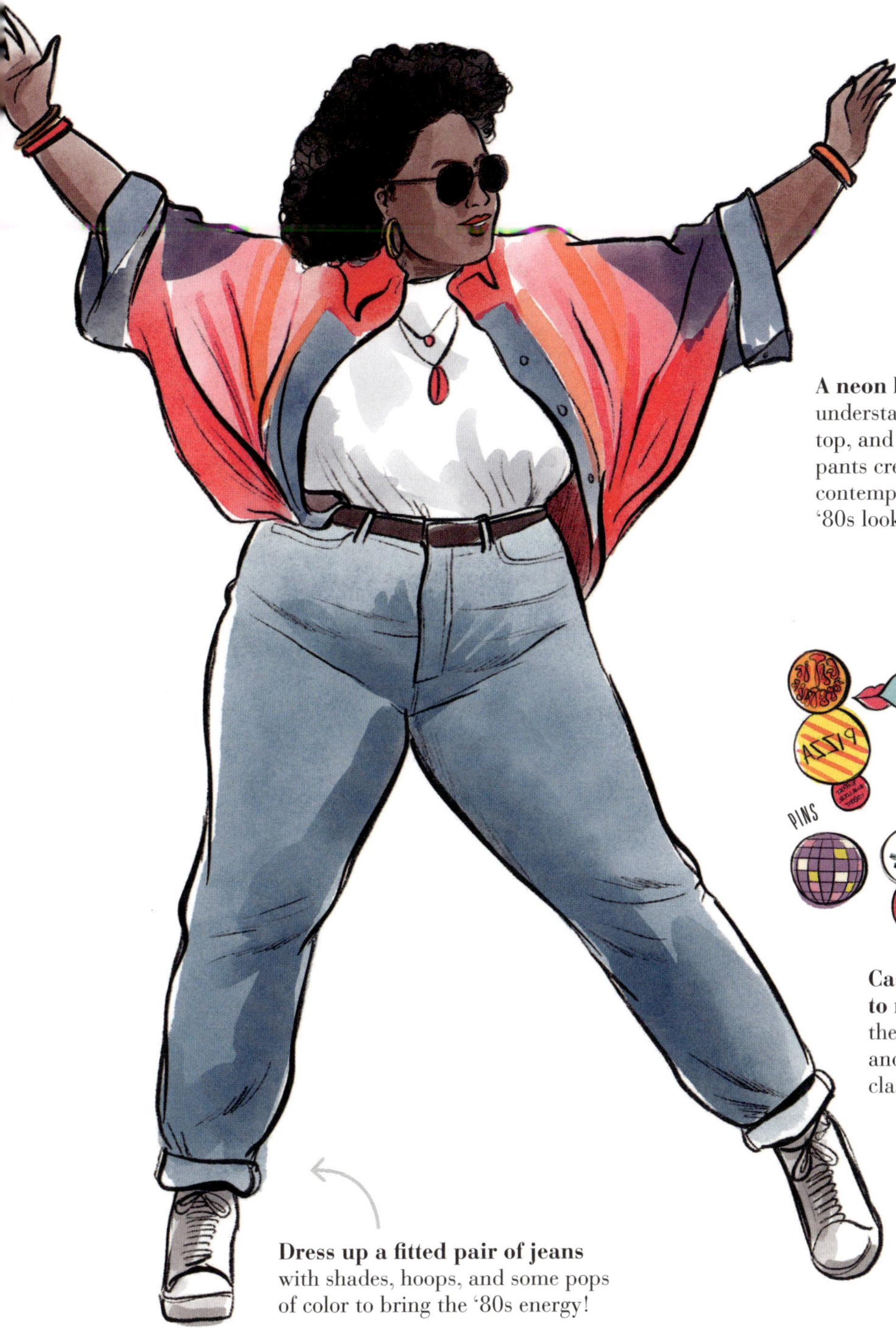

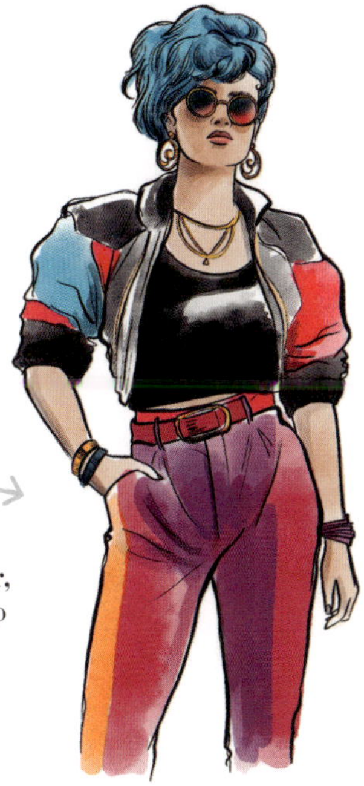

A neon bomber, understated crop top, and bright pants create a contemporary ‘80s look.

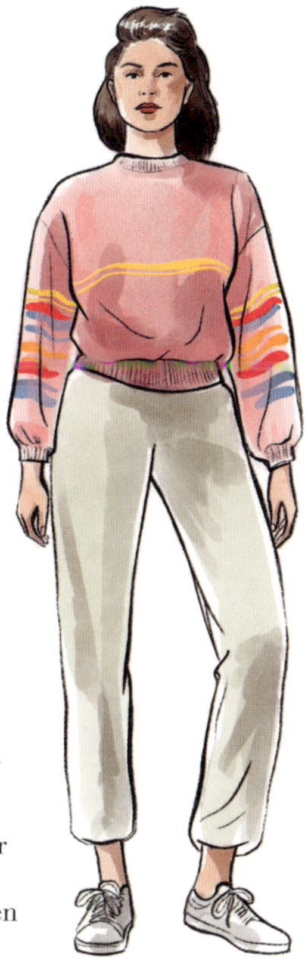

Pastels were hugely popular in the ‘80s. This cropped sweater in coral pink is taken to the next level with its stripes in primary colors.

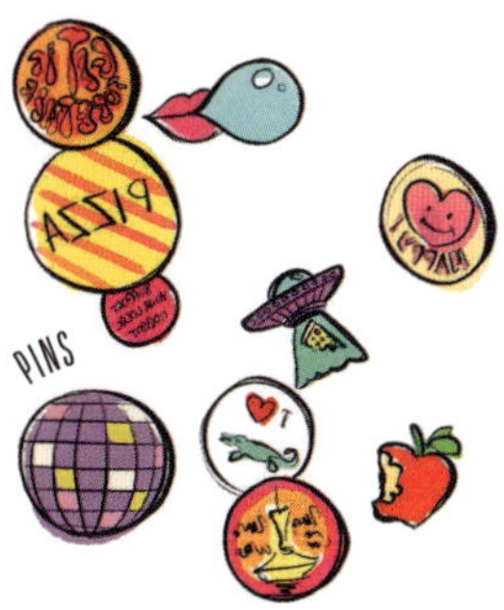

Casual doesn’t have to mean plain—over-the-top jewelry, pins, and hair elevate a classic denim jacket.

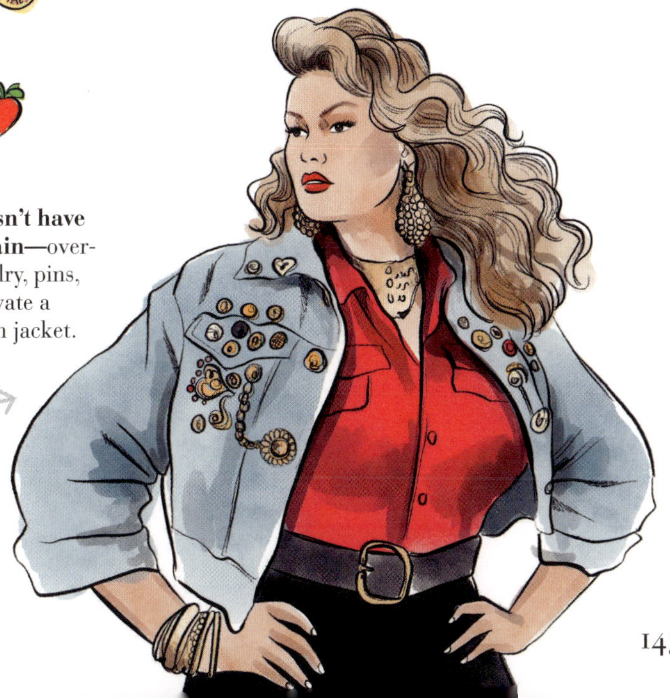

Dress up a fitted pair of jeans with shades, hoops, and some pops of color to bring the ‘80s energy!

Finish this model's '80s Casual look by adding a wild pattern to her sweater, and designing a pair of acid-wash denim jeans.

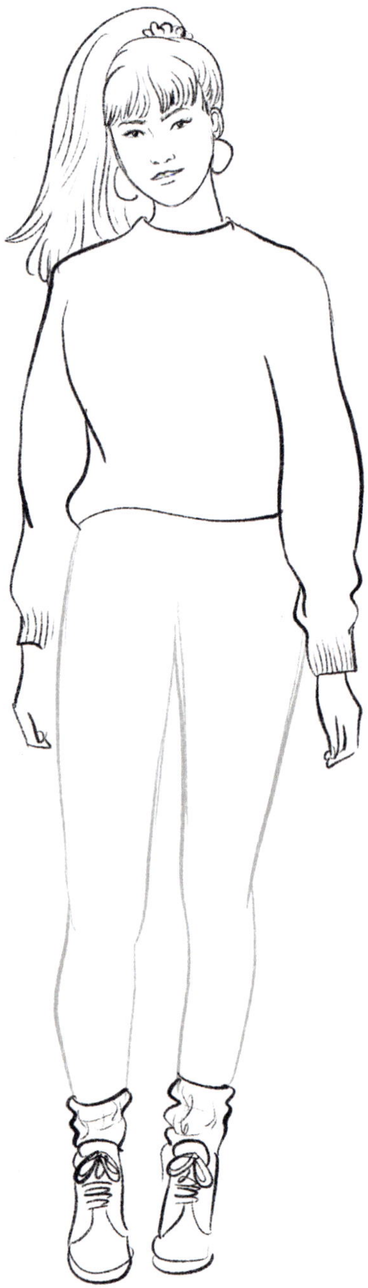

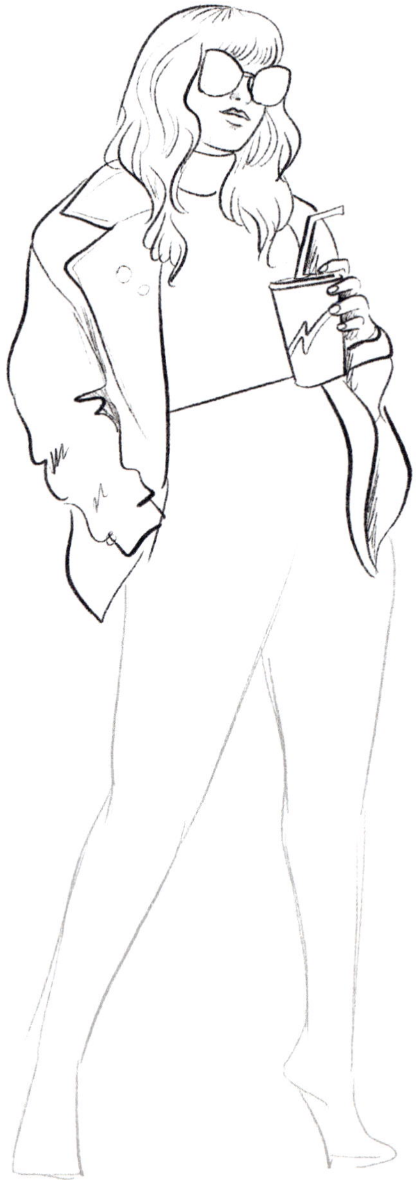

Oversize jackets add some edge and structure to any outfit. Layer them over jeans, skirts, dresses, or shorts, and go large with shoulder pads and sequins!

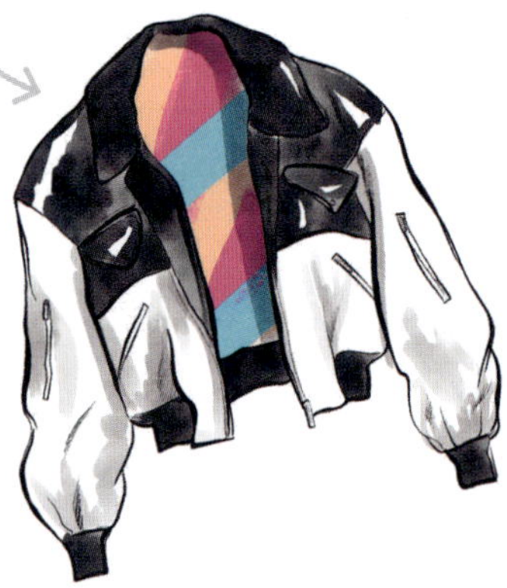

This girl is ready to hit the mall! Give her some platform heels and leather pants, or perhaps a full tulle skirt.

Time to create your own '80s throwback! Will you pile on fluorescent accessories and patterns, or use more understated pastels? How will you style your model's hair and makeup? Embrace the spirit of the decade and experiment!

The high ponytail is back, but the '80s did it first! Keep it in place with a rhinestone-studded scrunchie.

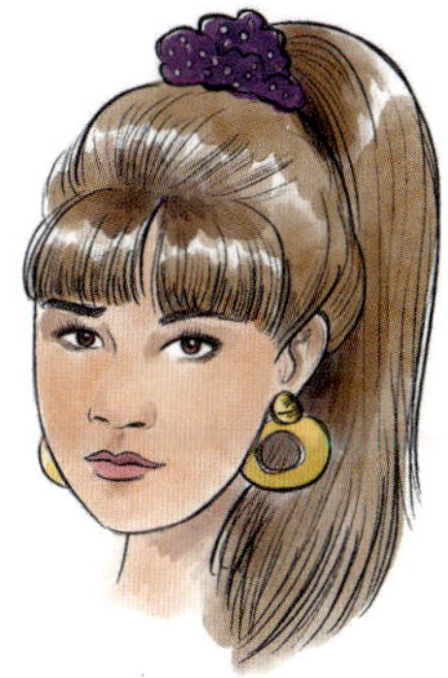

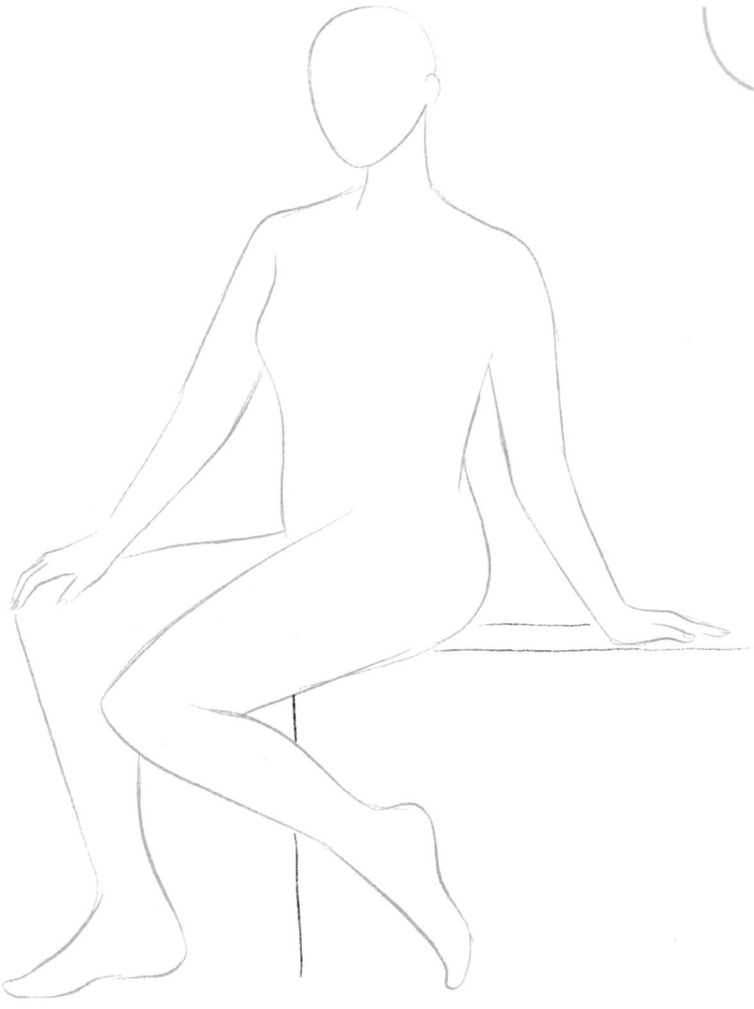

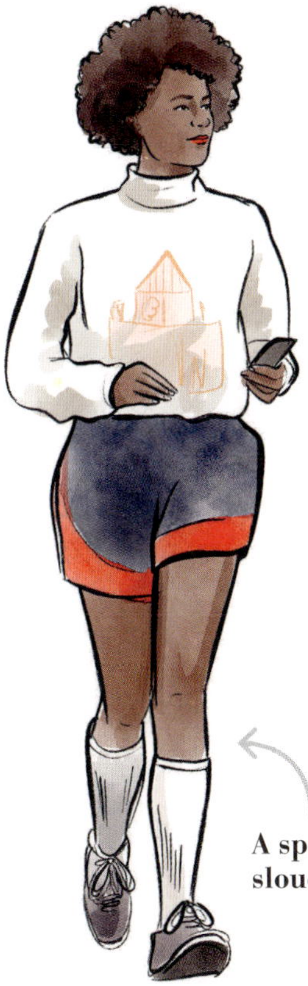

A sporty-yet-slouchy look.

Sneakers became a daily staple, customized with bright laces or worn with patterned socks or legwarmers.

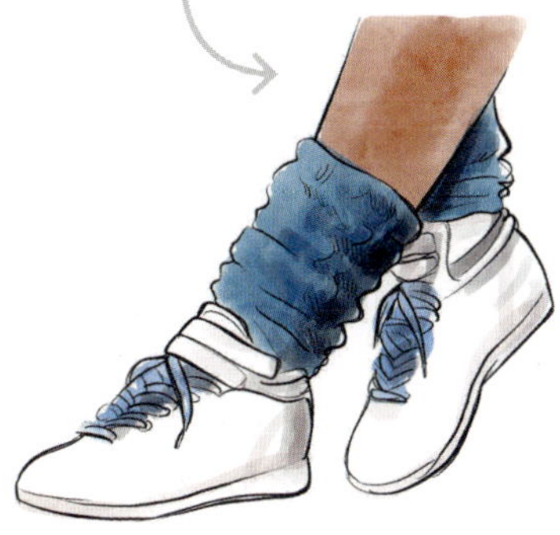

Slogan Tee

There is something audacious about wearing a subversive slogan T-shirt with a smart blazer and a pair of jeans. Hailey Bieber styles her designer tees with distressed denim and crops any oversize fits by tying them in a knot. Slogan tees can be political, humorous, ironic, or graphic. As well as being a way of expressing yourself through fashion, they can make a statement or show support for a cause, like the iconic "We Should All Be Feminists" tee from Dior's 2017 spring collection.

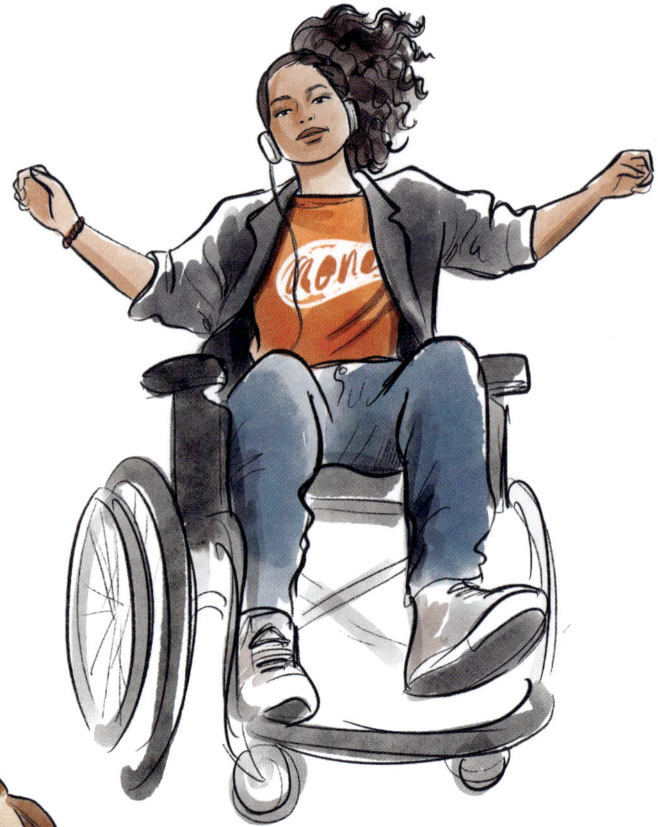

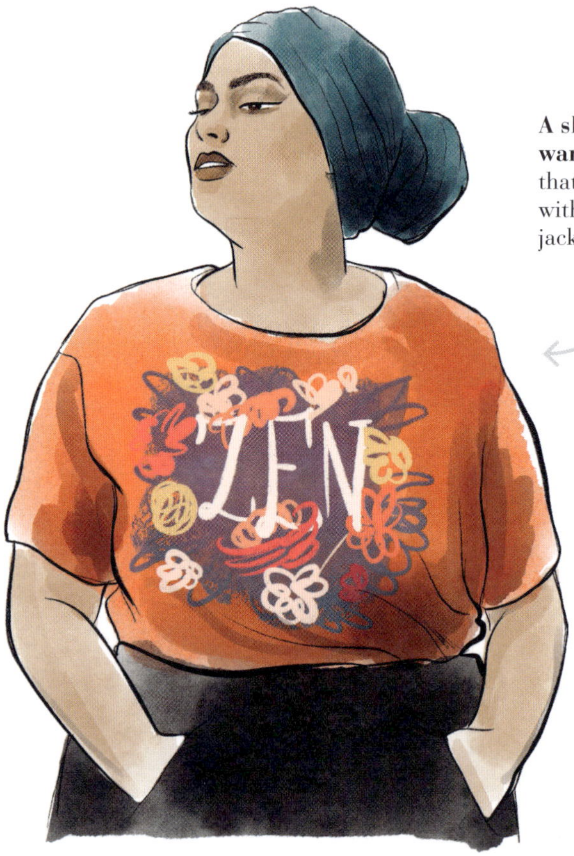

A slogan tee is a wardrobe essential that can be paired with jeans, skirts, jackets, or sneakers.

Slogan tees might include a brand name, or a graphic motif.

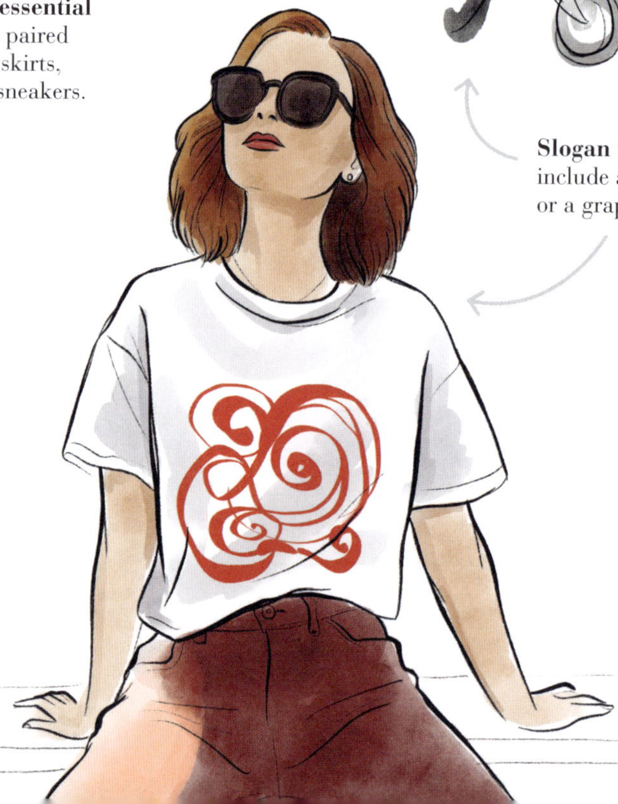

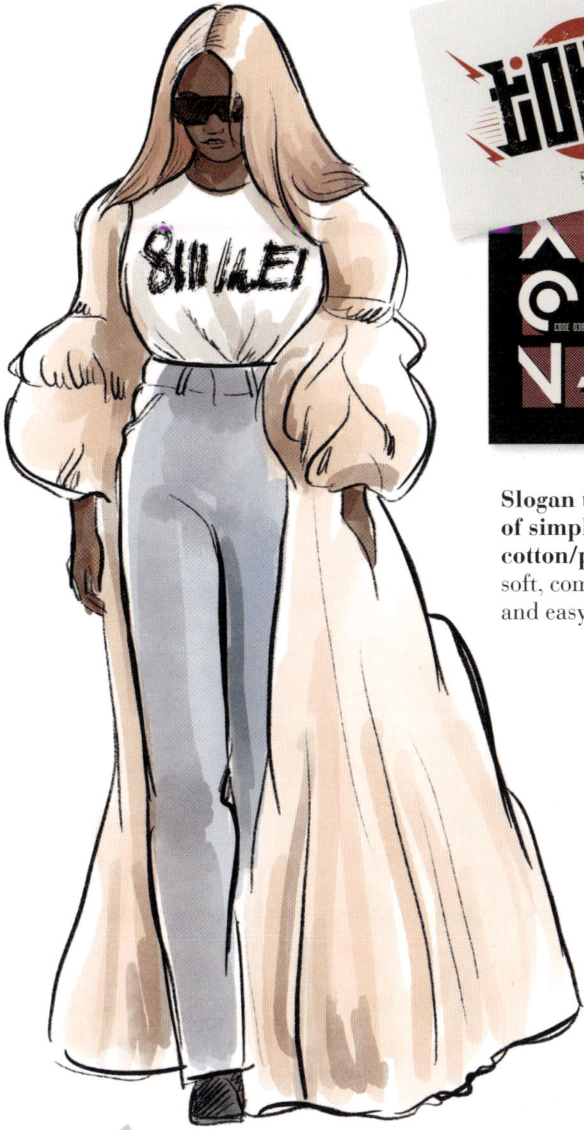

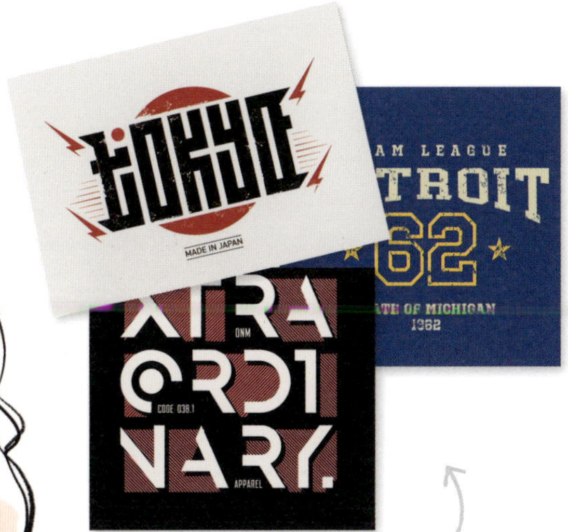

Slogan tees are usually made of simple cotton, polyester, and cotton/polyester blends, which are soft, comfortable, biodegradable, and easy to print on.

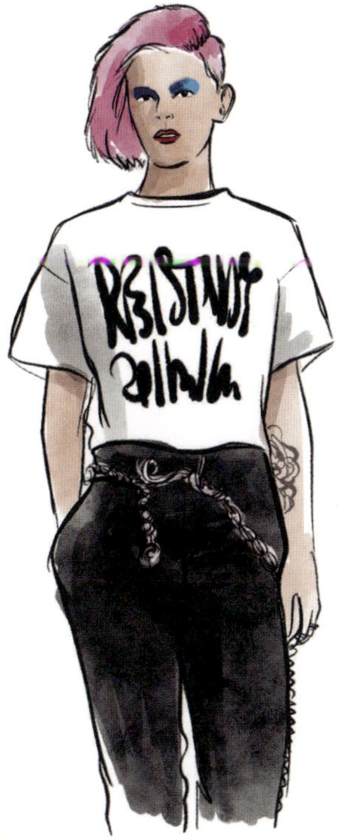

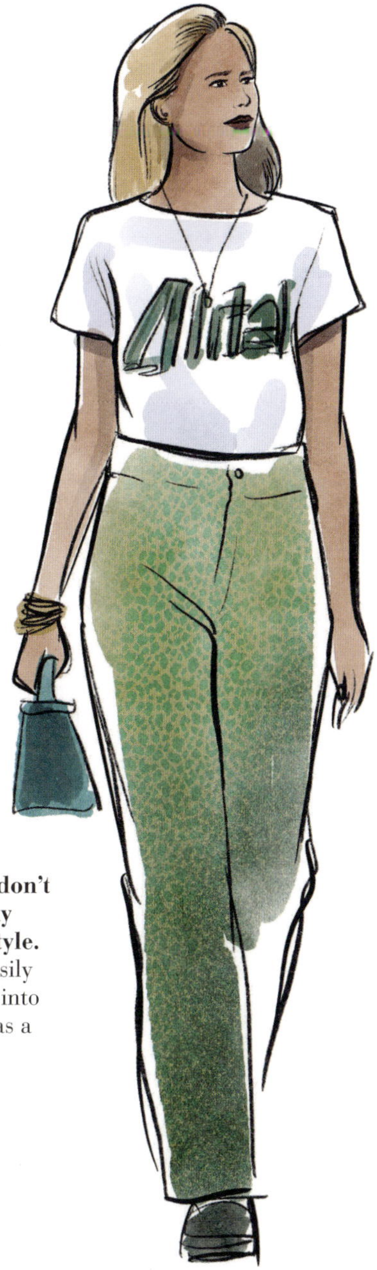

Slogan tees don't belong to any particular style. They're as easily incorporated into a punk look as a casual one.

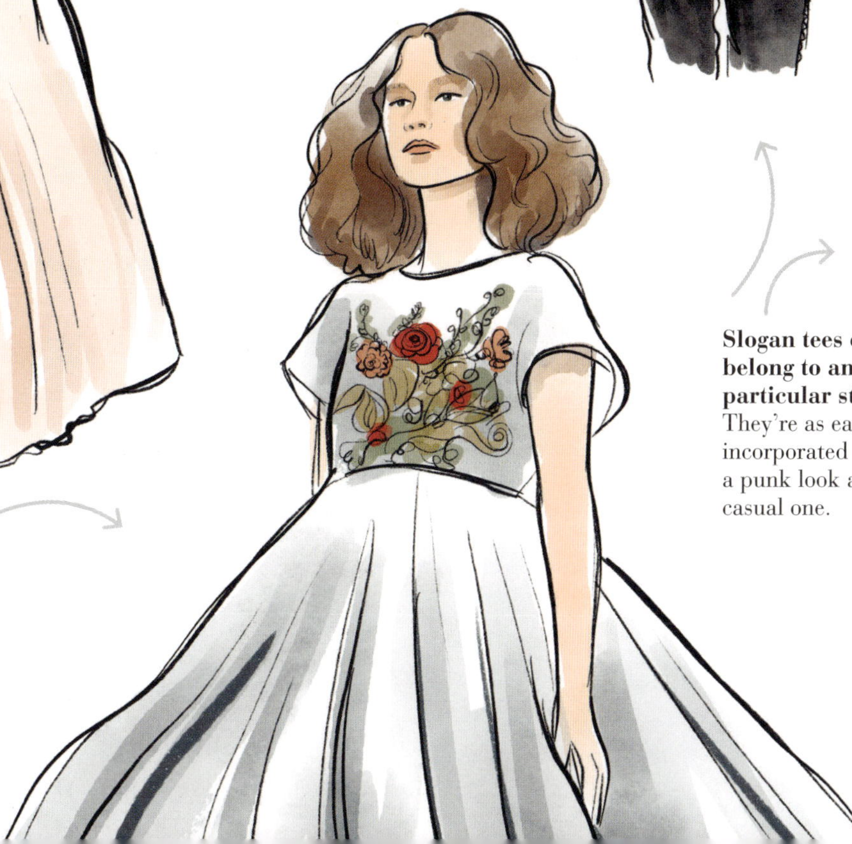

High fashion taking inspiration from the streets.

Design your own slogan tee for this model. What message will you choose?

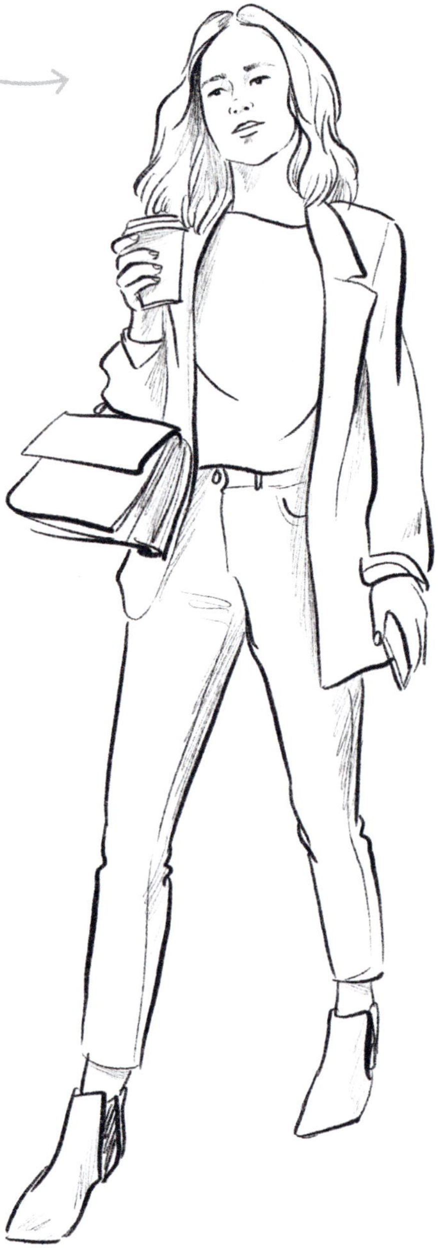

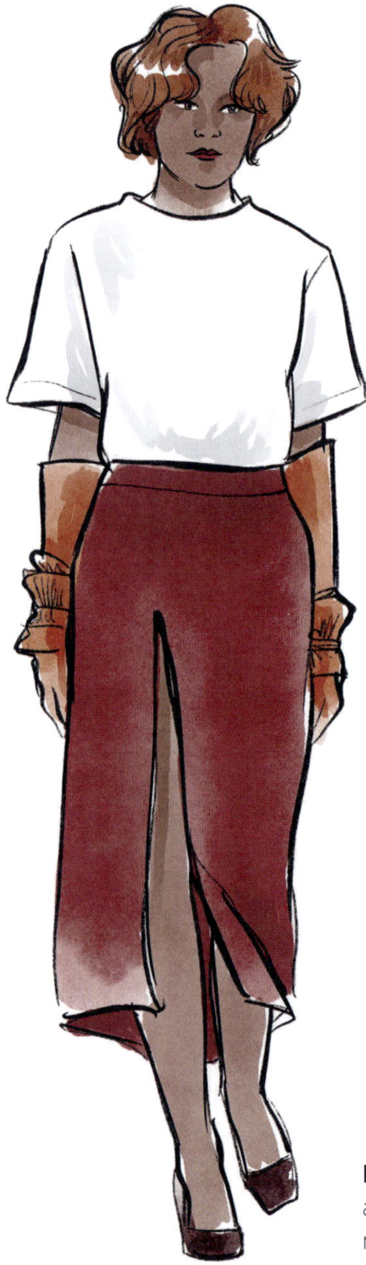

Finish this strong look by adding a bold logo to the model's tee—a blank canvas waiting to be drawn all over! How will you design the logo's color and shape to complement her outfit?

Now come up with a brand-new outfit inspired by the classic slogan tee. You could slap slogans on the skirt, the jacket, even the shoes—wherever you want, with whatever you want to say!

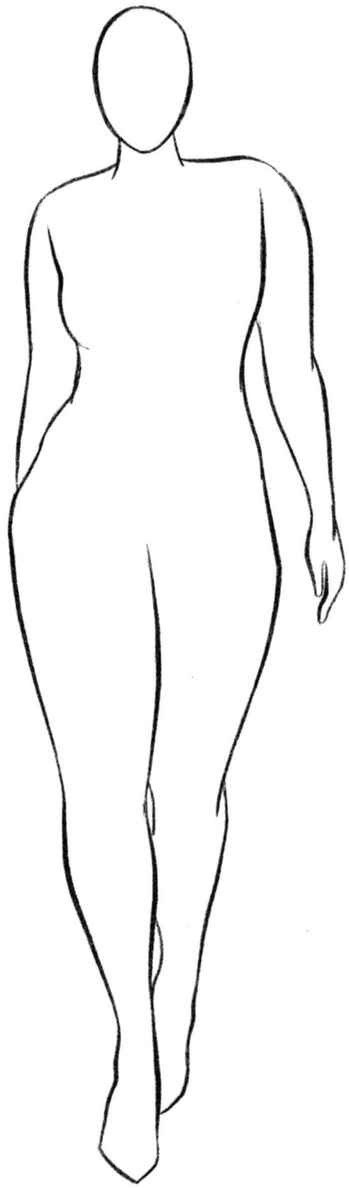

90s Denim

After the elaborate, flashy trends of the '80s, the '90s saw a return to minimalist fashion. More unisex, casual-chic looks gained cachet. But the popularity of denim, a favorite of the '80s, was at an all-time high; people wore it high-waisted, oversize, hip-hugging, however they wanted! The denim jacket was a wardrobe staple, and the '90s take on denim is making a comeback, bringing a nostalgic, retro vibe to modern looks.

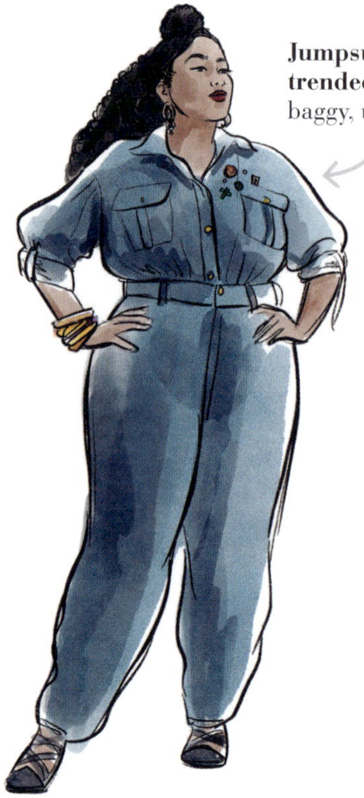

Jumpsuits trended toward baggy, unisex cuts.

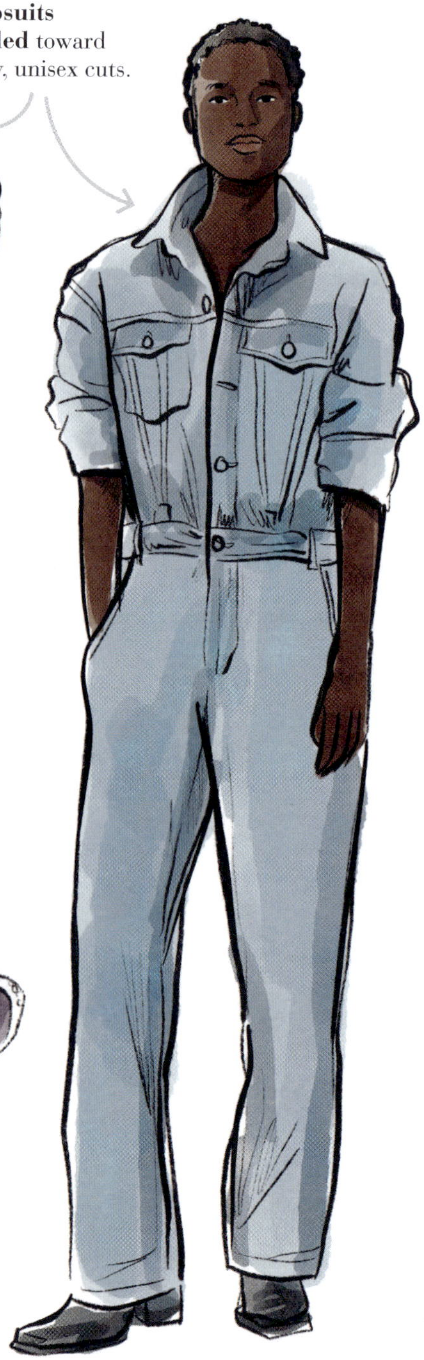

High-waisted denim jeans look great with an oversize jacket.

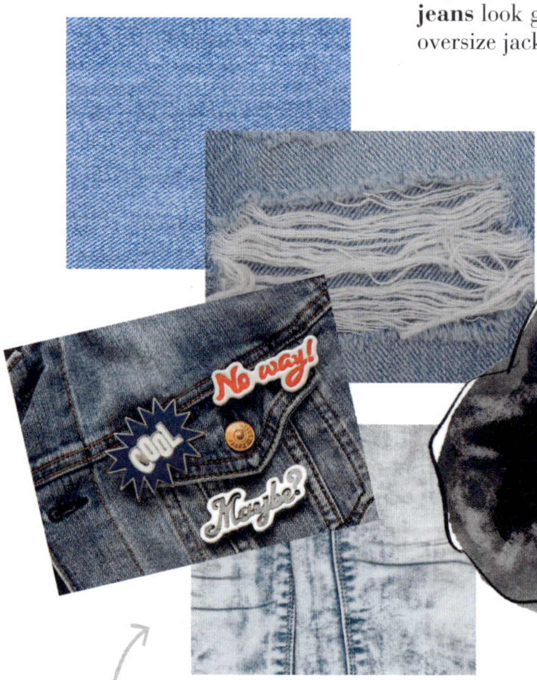

Distressed denim, acid denim, raw denim... there are so many different types of denim to have fun with! Denim works well with plaid, bandana prints, and knitwear.

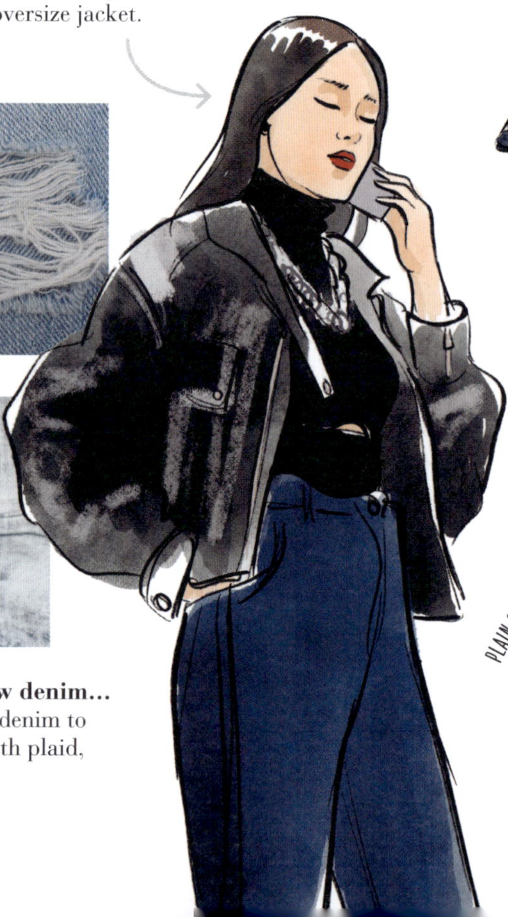

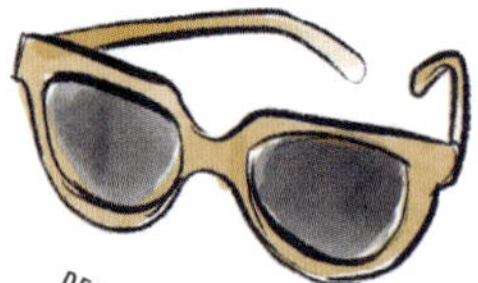

DESIGNER SHADES

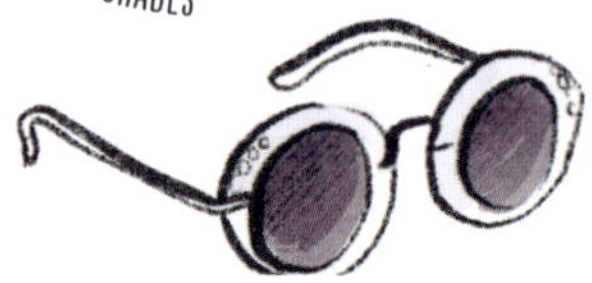

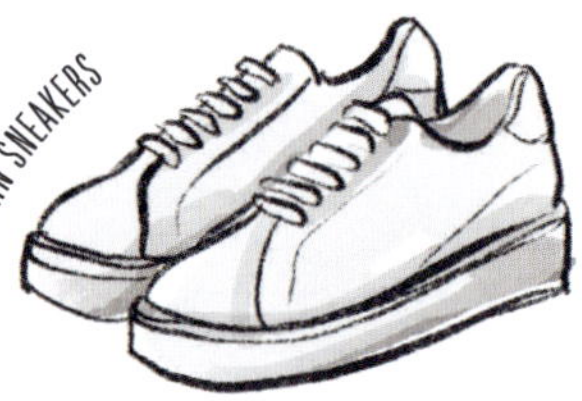

PLAIN SNEAKERS

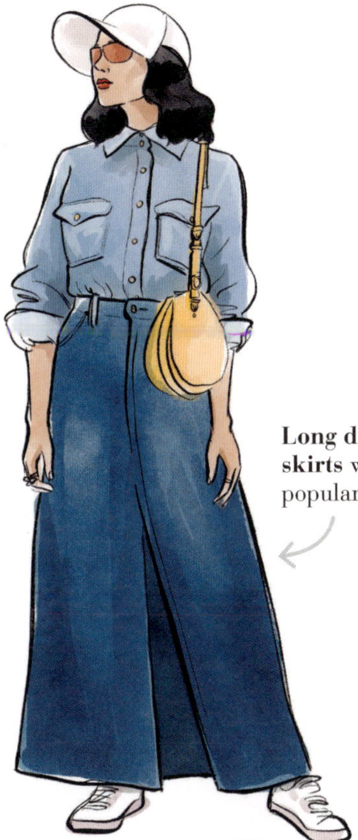

Long denim skirts were popular.

DISTRESSED JEANS

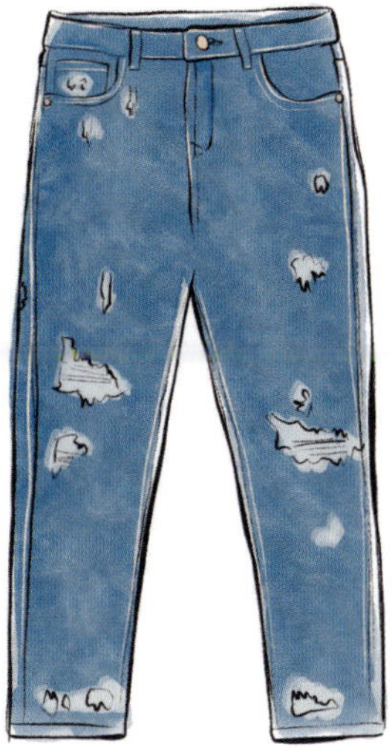

Loose-fit pleated denim pants were everywhere in the '90s.

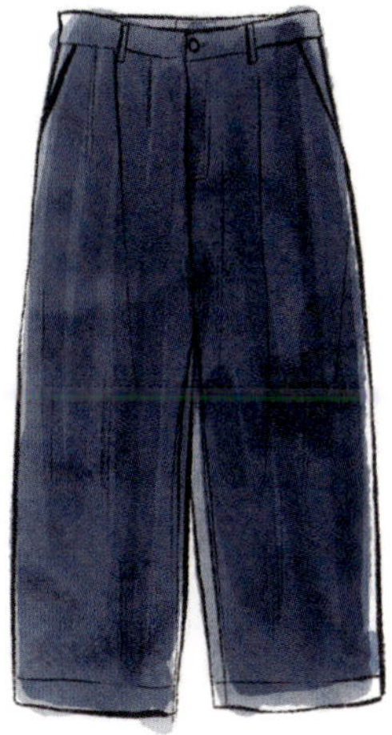

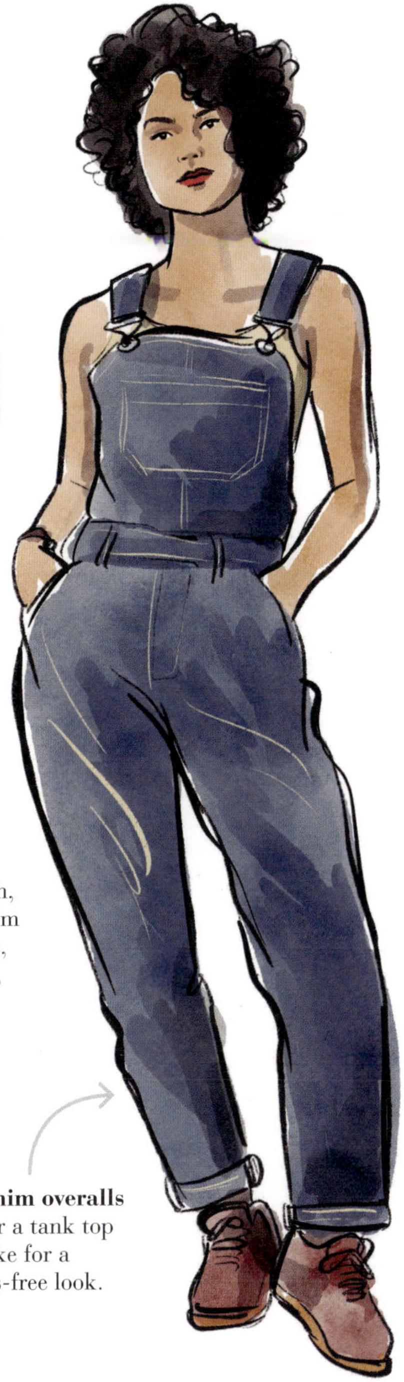

Does anything go better with denim than denim? Maybe some sneakers!

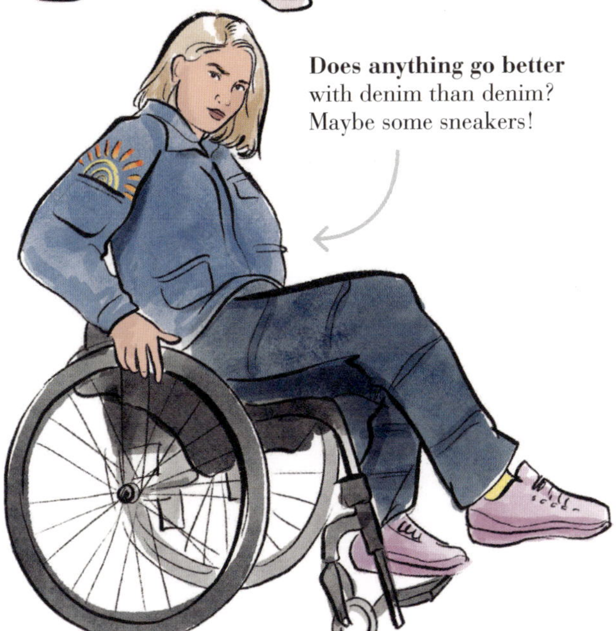

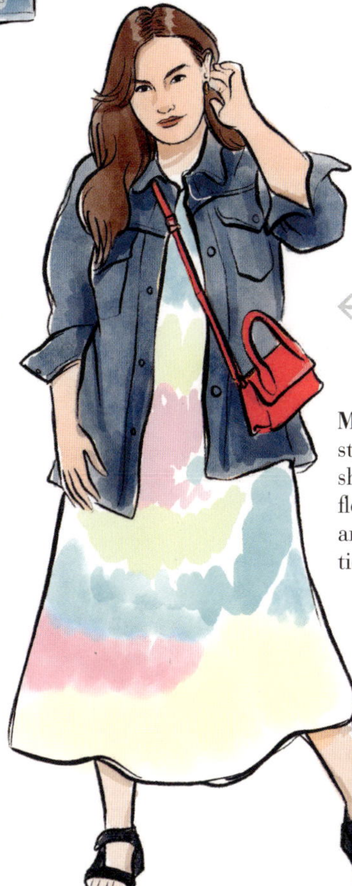

Mix up a rough, structured denim shirt with loose, flowing fabrics, and throw in a tie-dye print!

Denim overalls over a tank top make for a fuss-free look.

This model is looking slouchy-chic in her denim overalls. Will you add any details to the denim—embroidery, rhinestones, studs? What colors will you use?

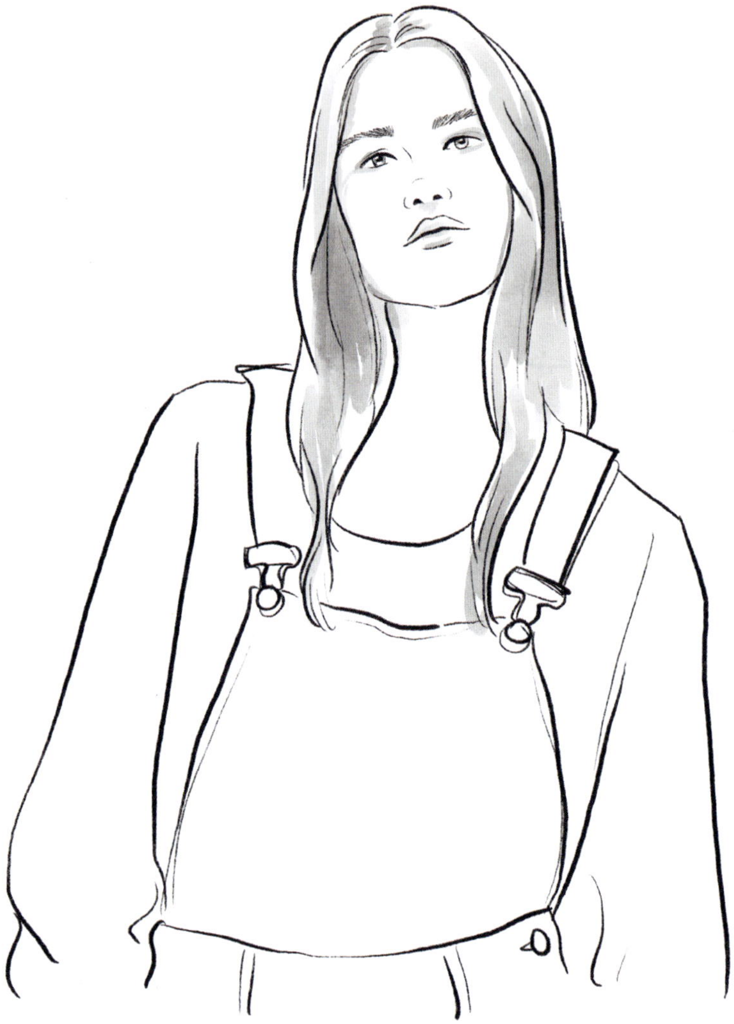

A small, round handbag with long shoulder straps.

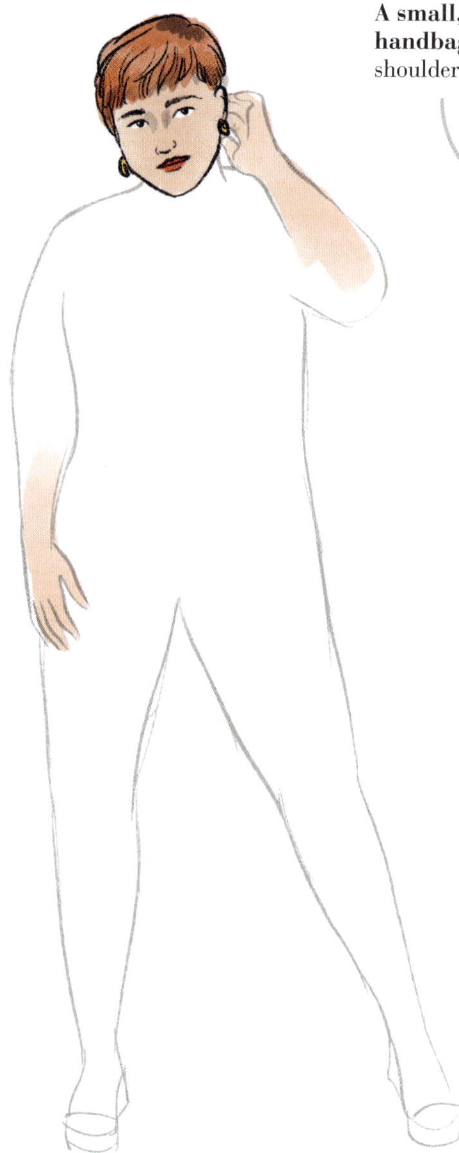

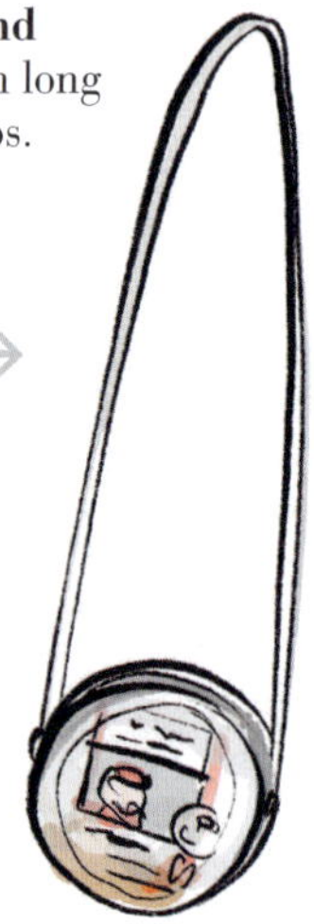

Give this model a relaxed and minimalist denim look with an oversize, unisex feel.

Give this model a slogan tee with a denim jacket. Throw on a print bandana or a bucket hat to complete the look.

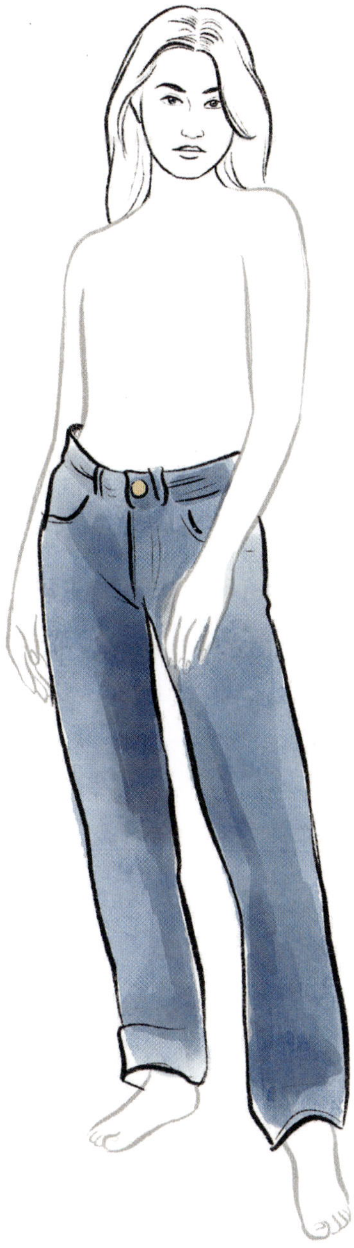

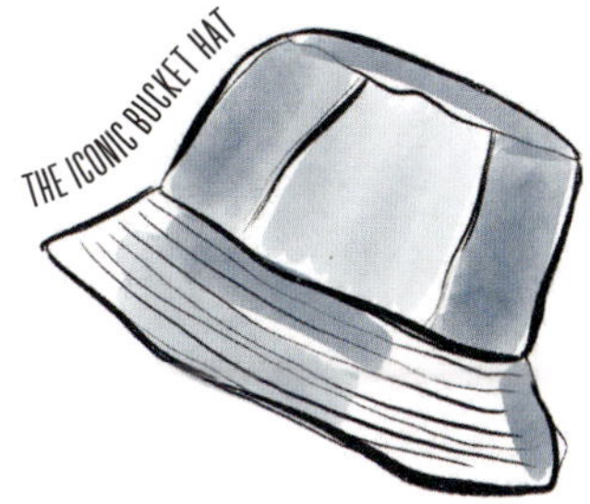

A square-cut jacket looks great with acid-wash jeans.

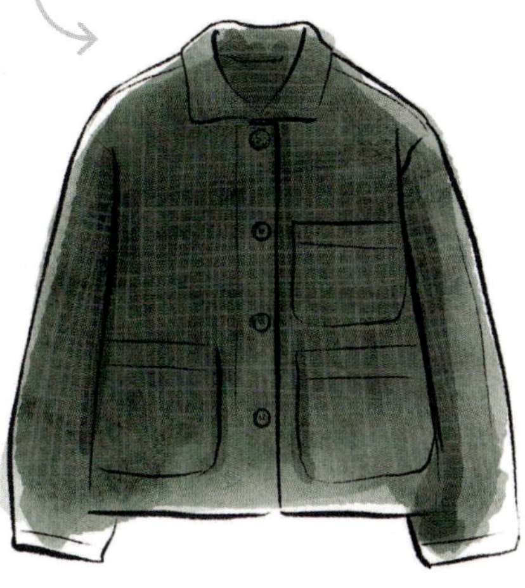

A bandana is a must-have addition to the '90s Denim look.

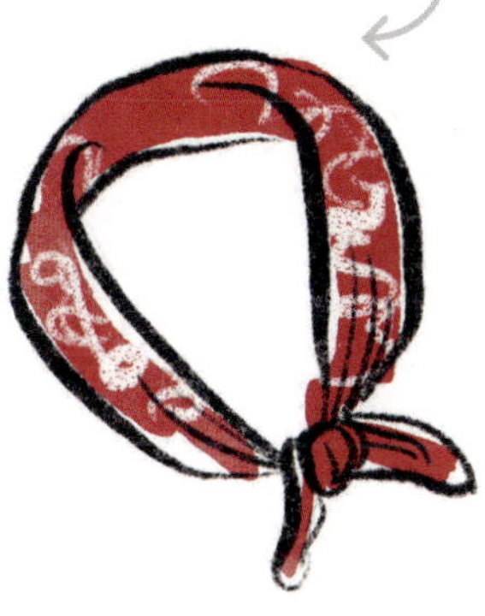

Hip-hop

Hip-hop fashion emerged with the music and culture in the 1970s. Sportswear and fashion brands such as Le Coq Sportif, Adidas, and Pro-Keds attached themselves to the emerging hip-hop scene. In the 1990s, hip-hop fashion underwent a gradual evolution as the community began to draw inspiration from traditional African American dress. Artists like Public Enemy, Queen Latifah, and Salt-N-Pepa started celebrating African heritage by wearing nationalist symbols, as well as the traditional Pan-African colors yellow, red, black, and green. Hip-hop fashion also influenced the high fashion world: In one of Chanel's 1990s shows, models wore black leather jackets and piles of gold chains.

A classic '90s hip-hop look: bright colors, oversize pants, and headwear.

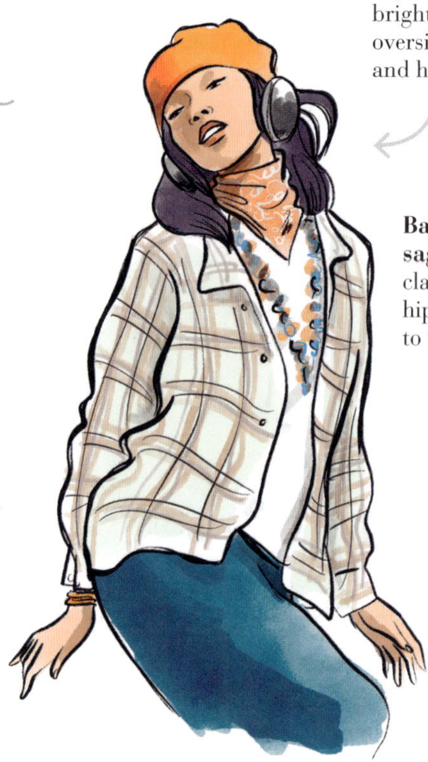

Baggy and saggy is the classic hip-hop way to wear denim.

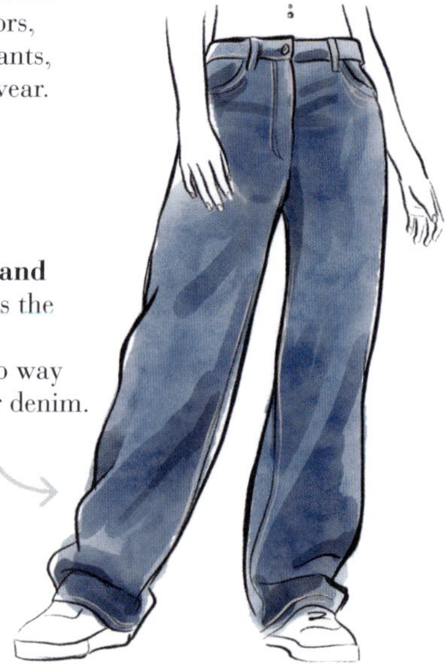

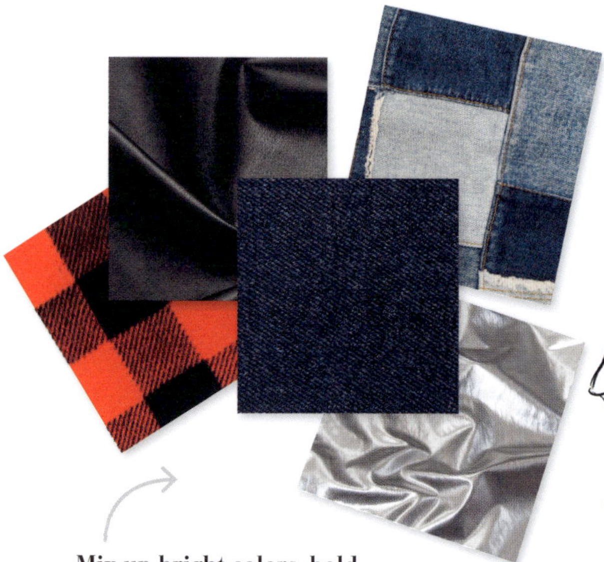

Mix up bright colors, bold patterns, and urban motifs in your hip-hop outfits.

No matter the occasion, a graphic tee is a wardrobe essential.

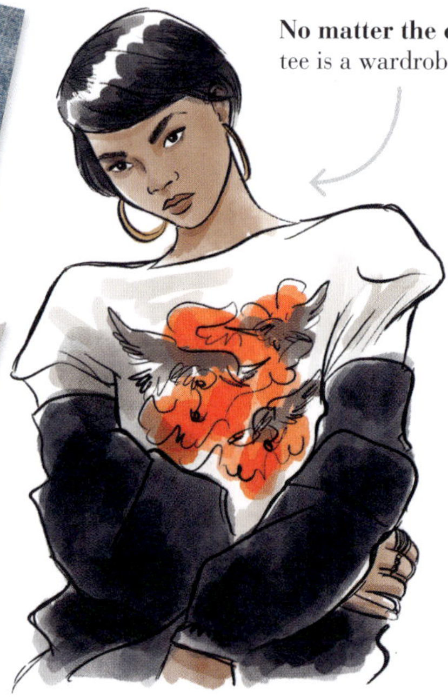

A bright yellow tracksuit with gold earrings and necklace. The bold baseball cap is a hip-hop essential!

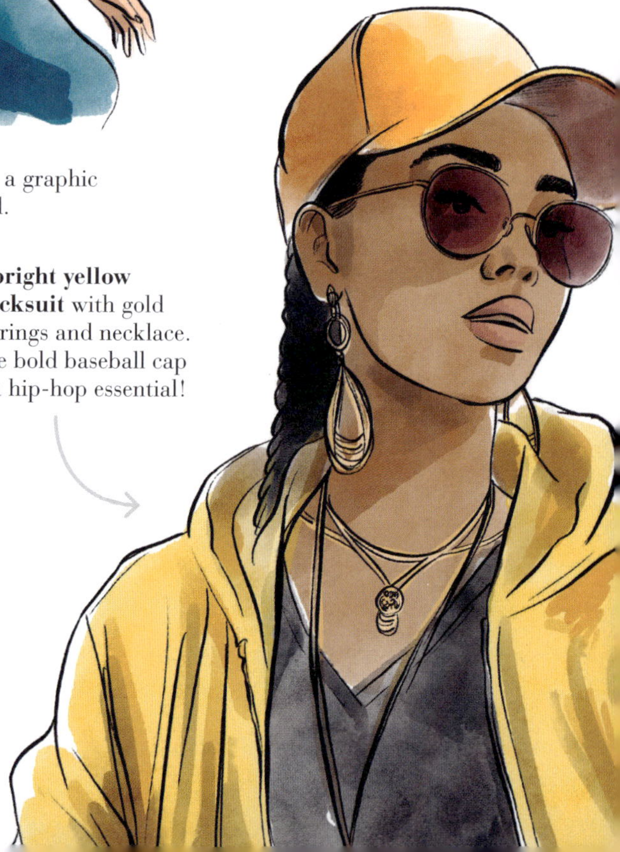

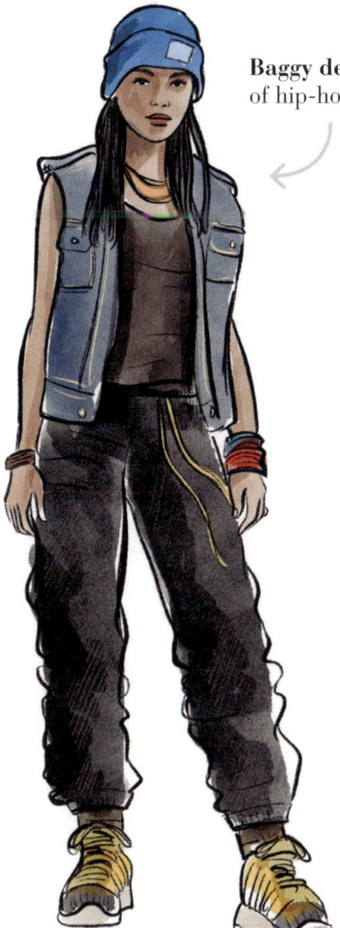

Baggy denim is a staple of hip-hop fashion.

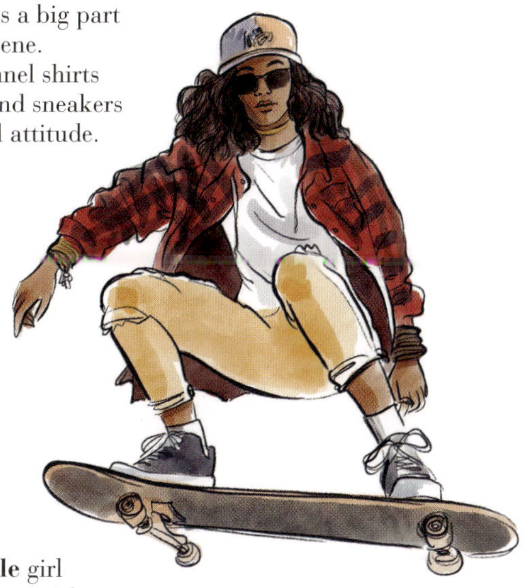

Skater culture is a big part of the hip-hop scene. Loose-fitting flannel shirts over white tees and sneakers show off a casual attitude.

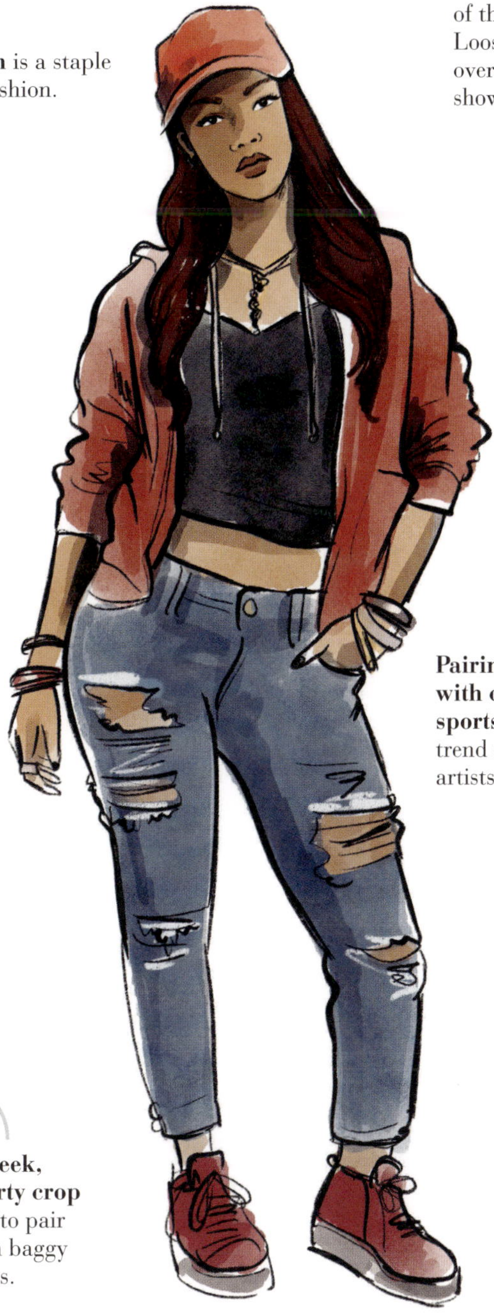

Rapper-style girl in ripped jeans with matching hoodie, cap, and sneakers.

Pairing baggy pants with crop tops or sports bras was a trend started by R&B artists like Aaliyah.

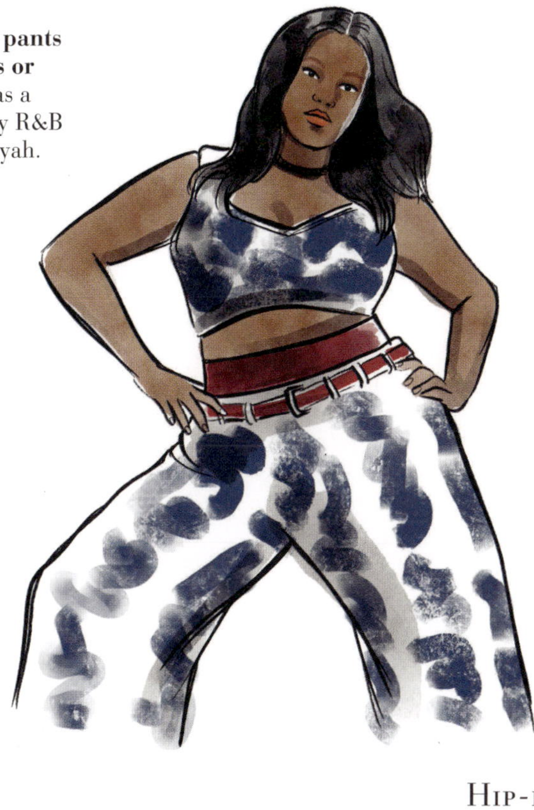

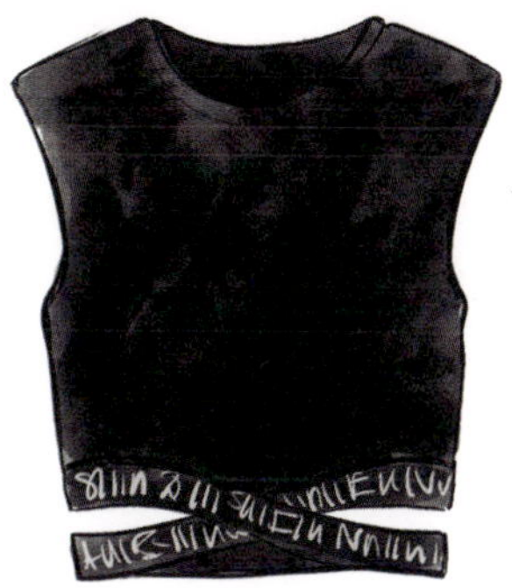

A sleek, sporty crop top to pair with baggy jeans.

Add the details to this model's jacket and crop top to complete her hip-hop outfit. Trace a cap or a bucket hat on her head. What colors or patterns will you use on her blazer and shoes?

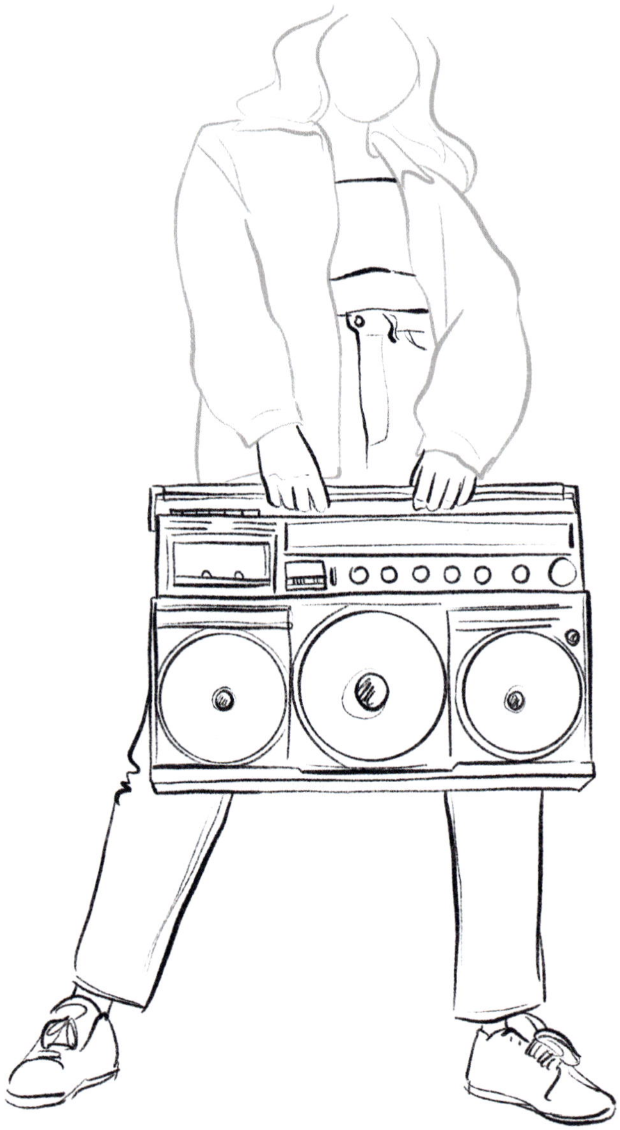

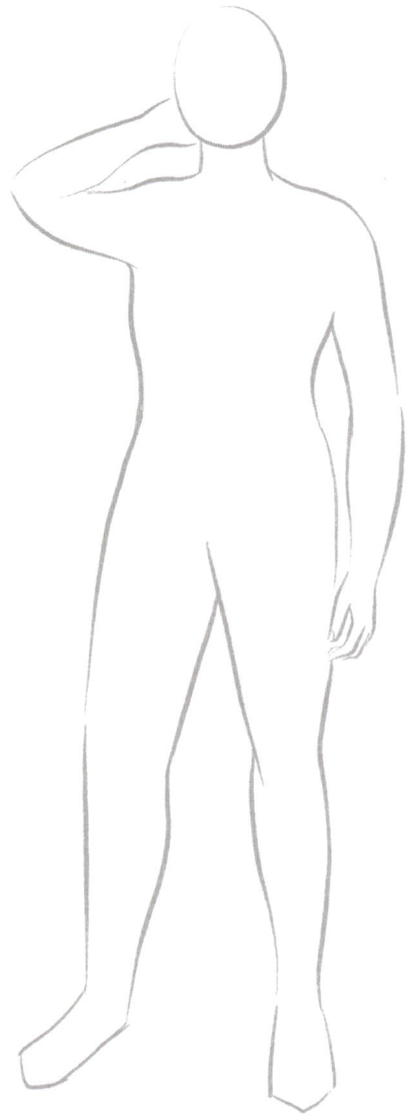

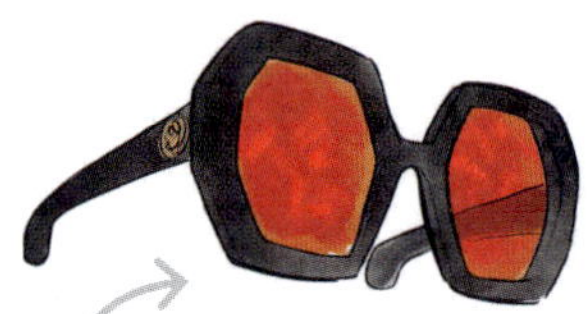

Oversize, tinted sunglasses, bucket hats, nameplates, name belts, stacked rings, and heavy gold jewelry add the finishing touches to a hip-hop look.

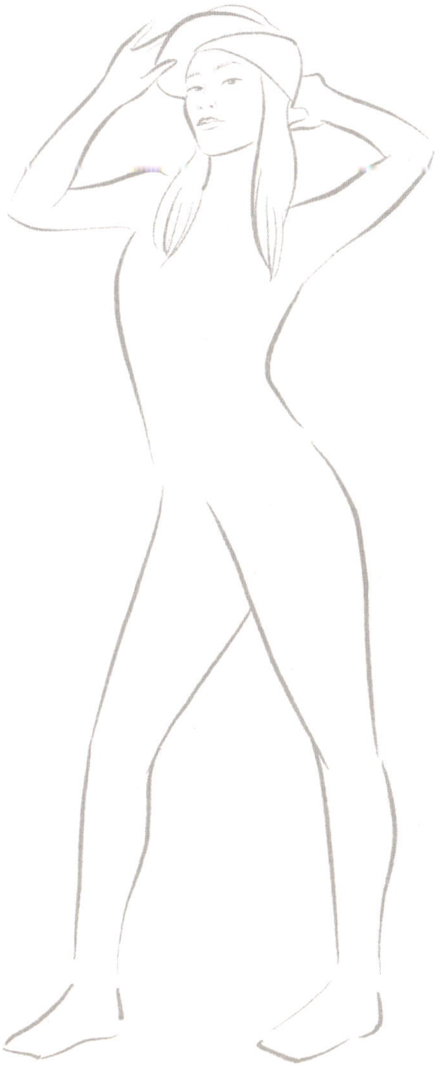

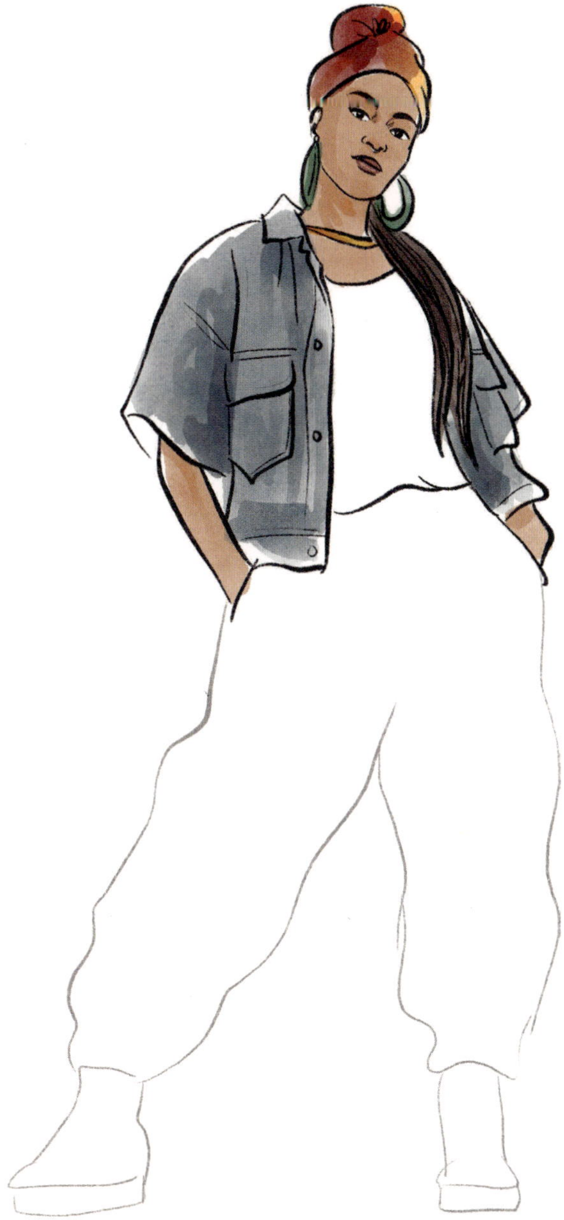

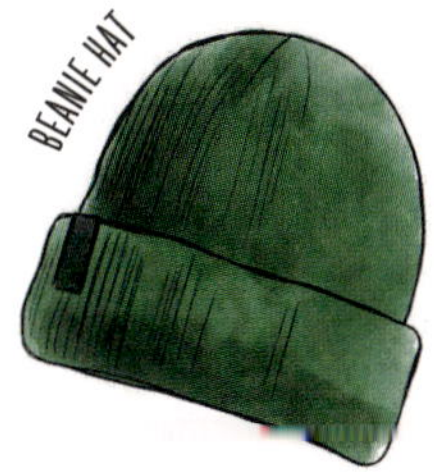

Sneakers are the ultimate hip-hop footwear.

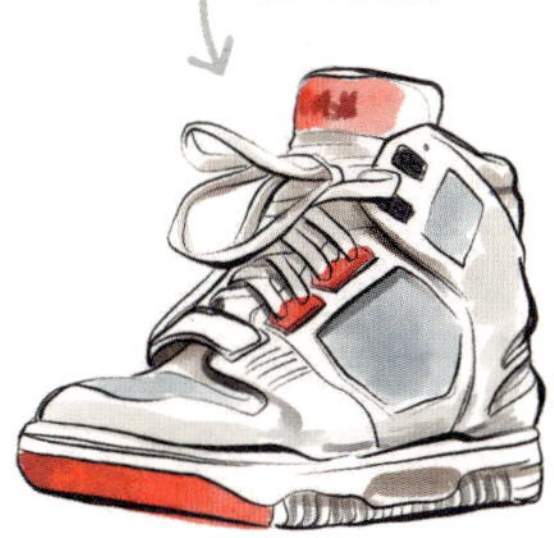

Complete this look by adding a pair of baggy jeans and some sneakers. You can style your look with a graphic tee as well!

Matchy Matchy

The art of matching fashion is in combining different patterns or prints in a harmonious way. It can create a dynamic, unique look that showcases your personality and makes you stand out. There are some basic rules to think about if you want to avoid clashes in your outfits—but sometimes clashing is part of the fun!

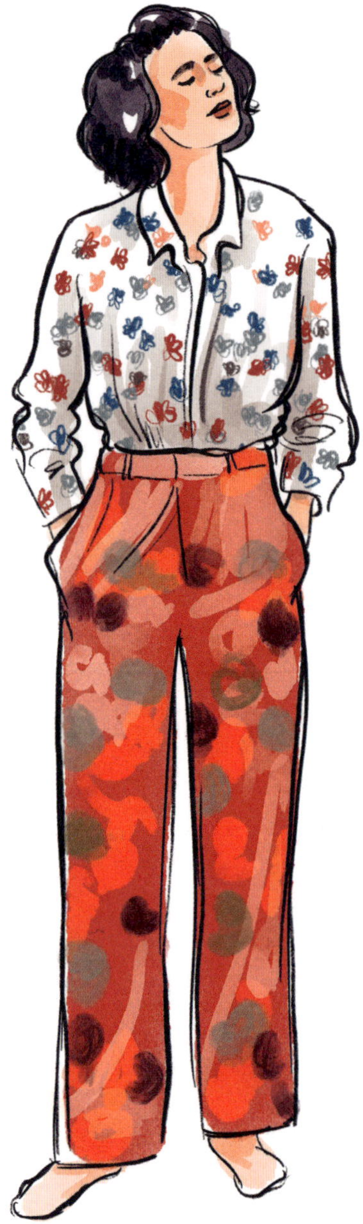

Experiment with varying the size and scale of the patterns in a single outfit.

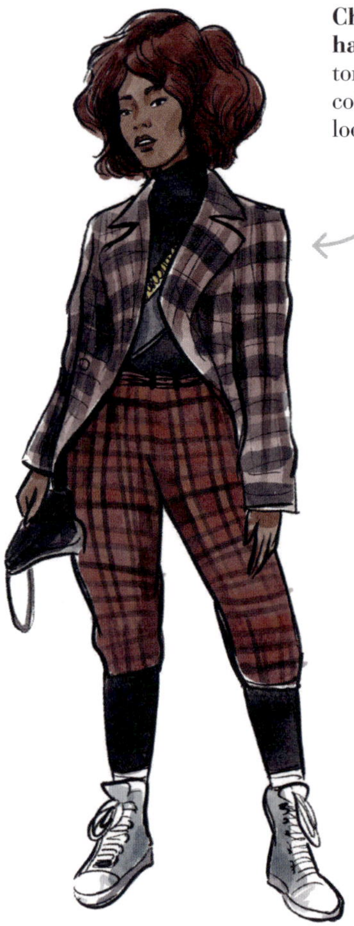

Choosing patterns that have similar colors or tones will create a cohesive and balanced look that does not clash.

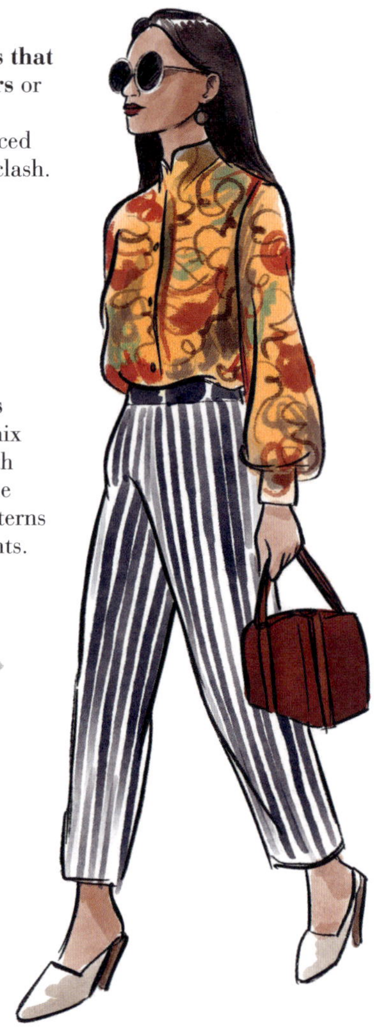

Certain types of patterns mix really well with each other, like geometric patterns and floral prints.

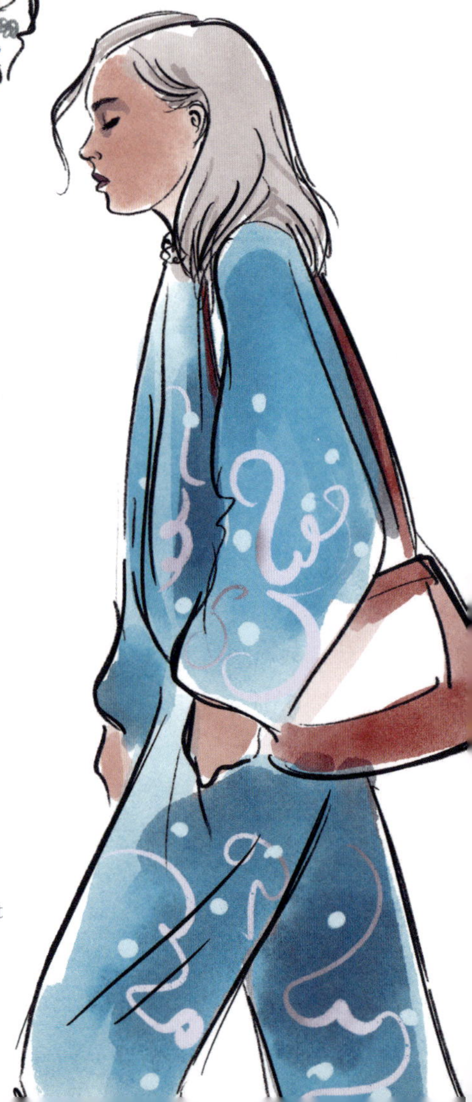

You can also repeat a pattern on different garments for a maximalist look!

In this fun, matching outfit, a similar pattern appears in reversed colorways on top and bottom.

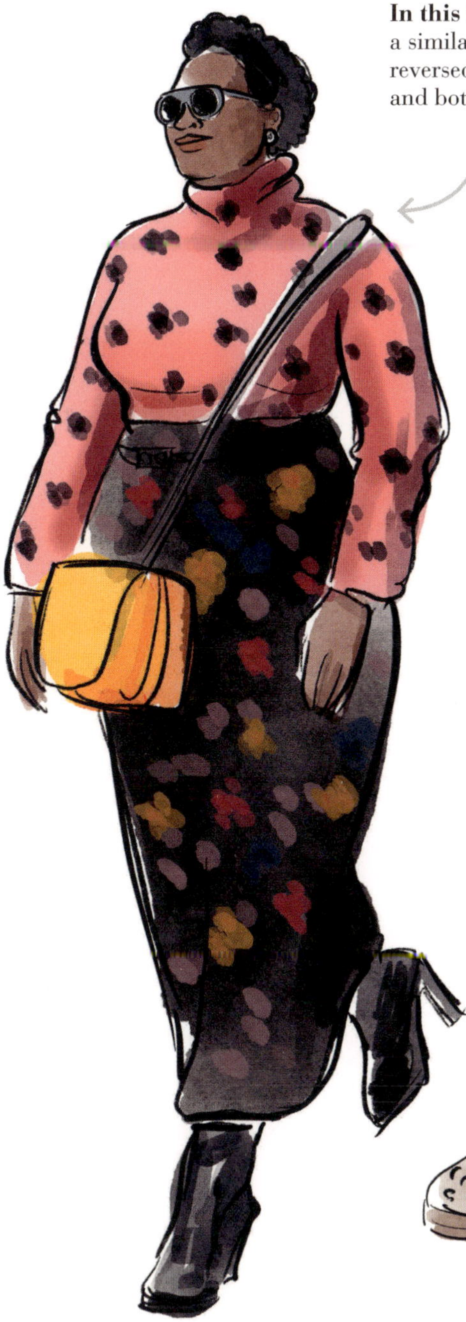

The dots on these garments and bag create a visual link between clashing items of clothing.

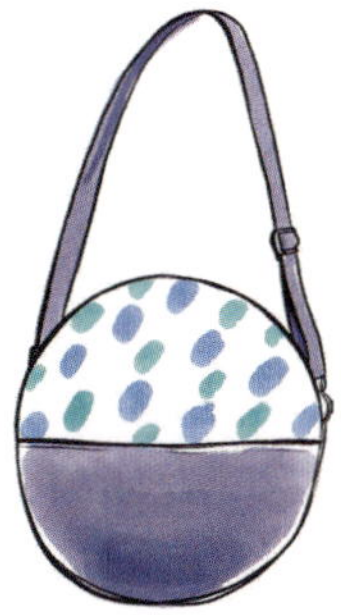

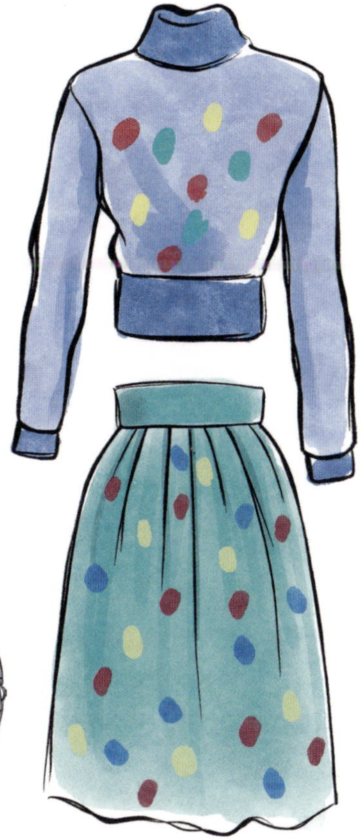

Use colors that complement each other for a distinctive, cohesive look.

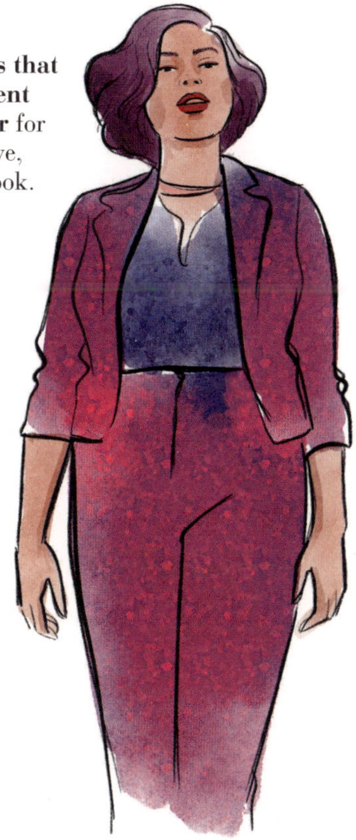

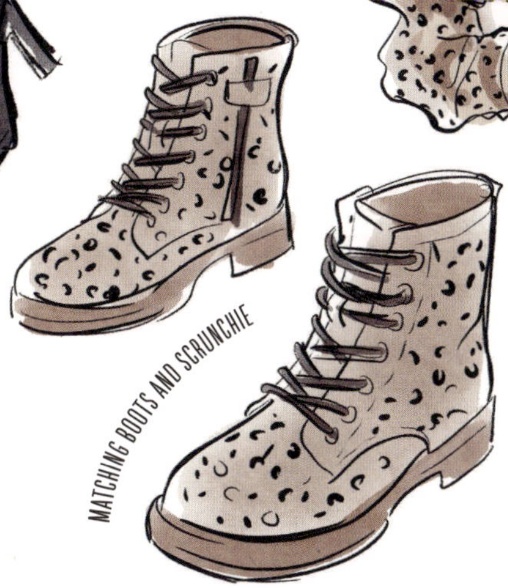

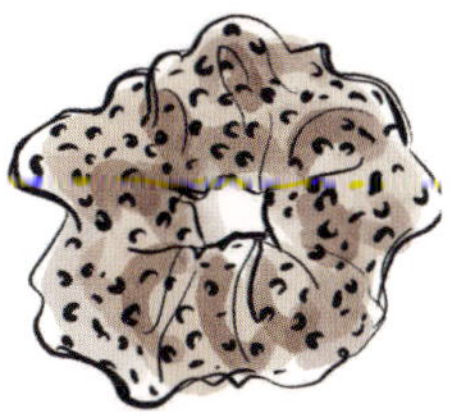

All kinds of patterns and fabrics can go into a matching outfit—the only limit is your imagination!

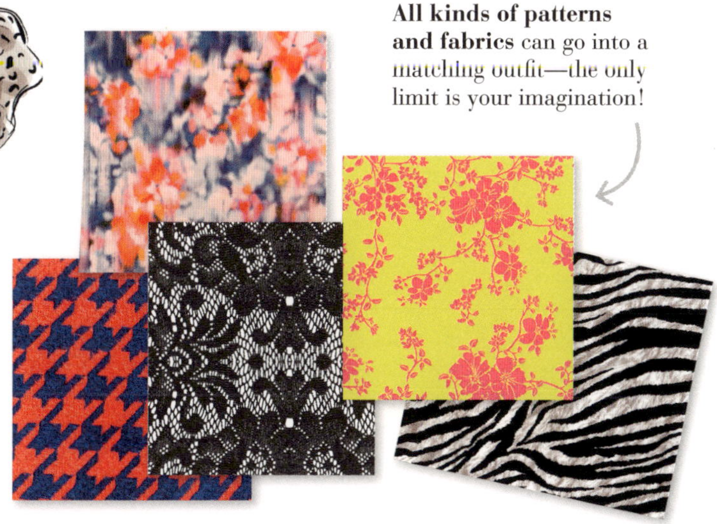

Go wild with patterns and colors for this model's look. Try mixing up different styles and prints—how far can you push them?

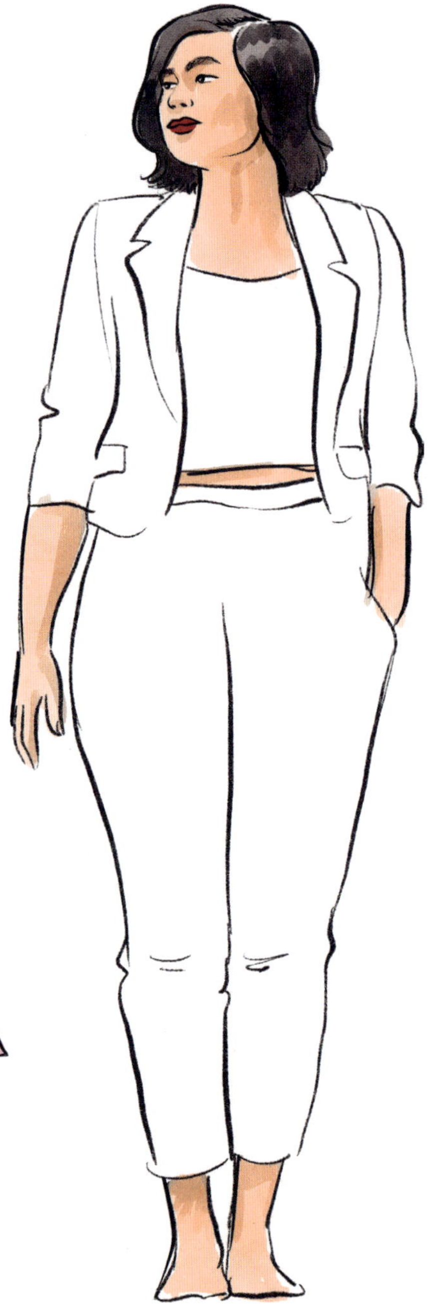

Try designing a heeled shoe to match her outfit!

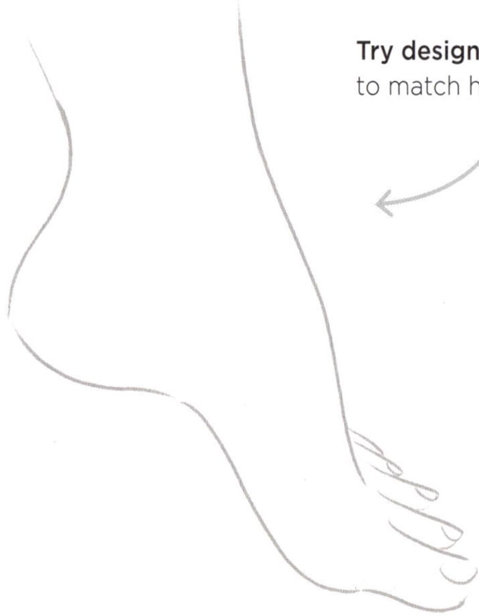

Blocks of color help match a shirt and bandana.

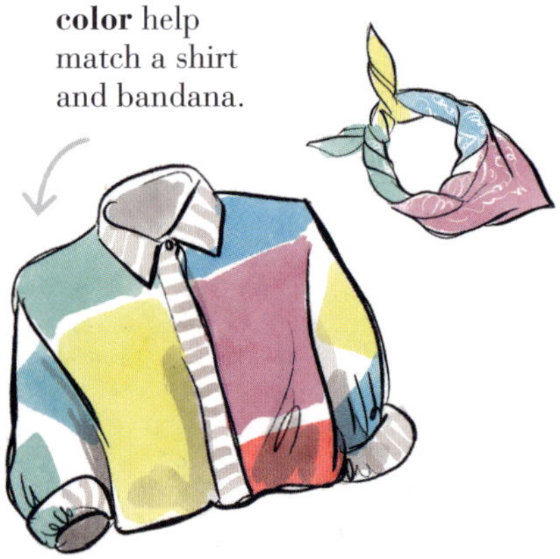

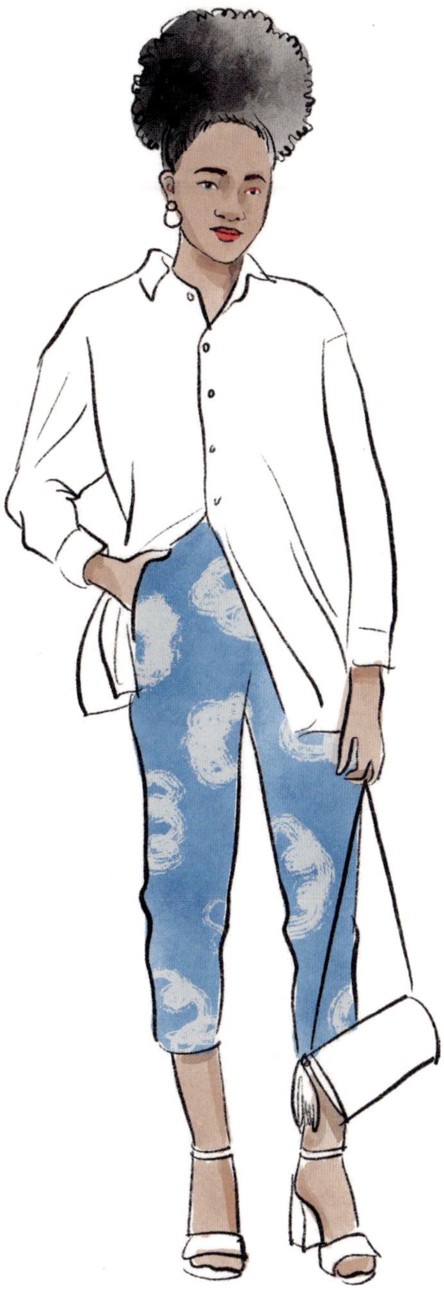

Design a print for this model's shirt that fits in with their loose-fitting, patterned pants. Don't forget about the bag and shoes! How does adding color and pattern change her overall look?

Streetwear

The essence of streetwear is hard to pin down. It combines urban fashions with haute couture, transcending notions of social class. Streetwear is a relaxed style, involving oversize and comfortable clothing. One important element of it always remains: the sneakers. Sneaker culture is undeniable, and entire outfits revolve around it. A lot of haute couture brands, which until the 2010s had ignored the potential of streetwear, now create hybrid collections that take urban pieces and turn them into luxury items.

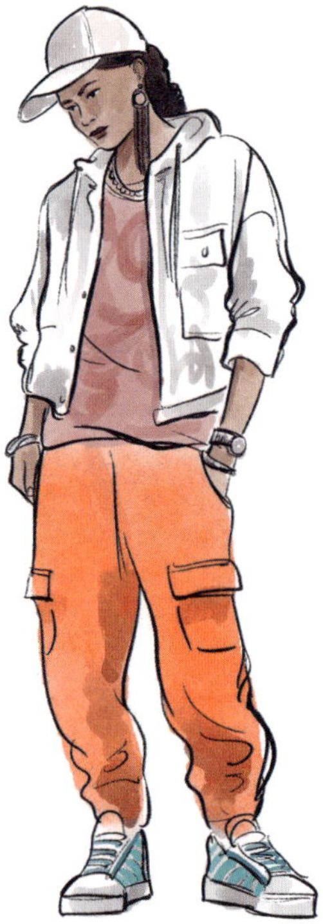

A baseball cap and sneakers complete a classic streetwear look.

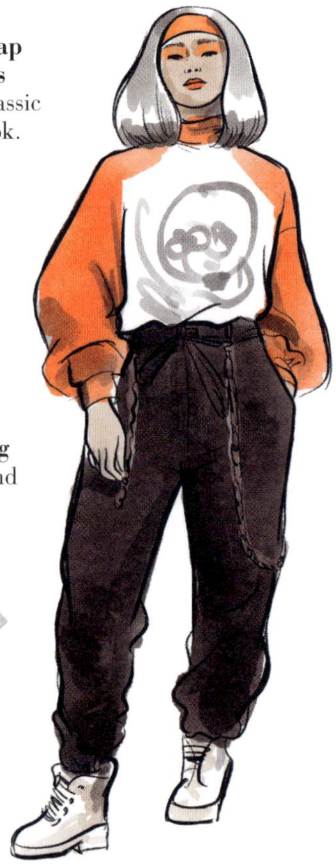

Loose-fitting sweatshirt and cargo pants.

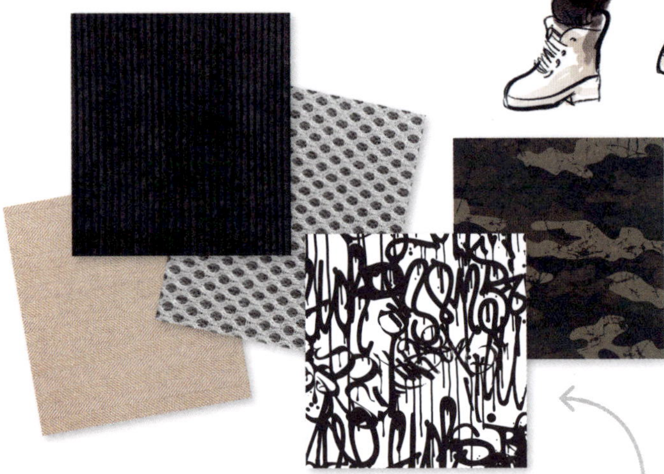

Streetwear is all about durability and affordability. Fabrics like polyester, one of the most widely known synthetic fabrics, and corduroy, with its unique twill weave texture that results in a thick and hardy fabric, are both popular in streetwear.

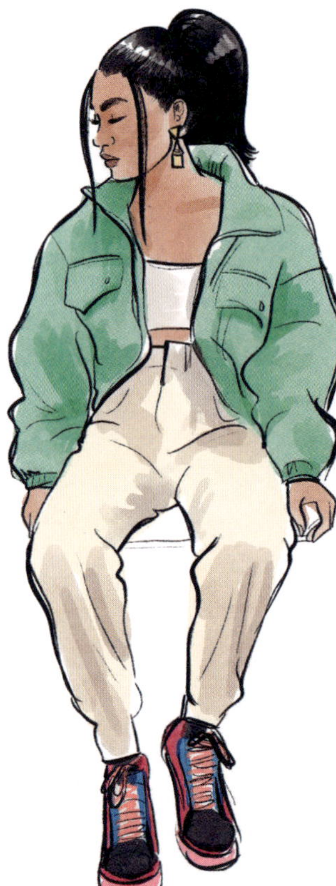

The bold bomber jacket is doing all the work in this simple and casual streetwear outfit.

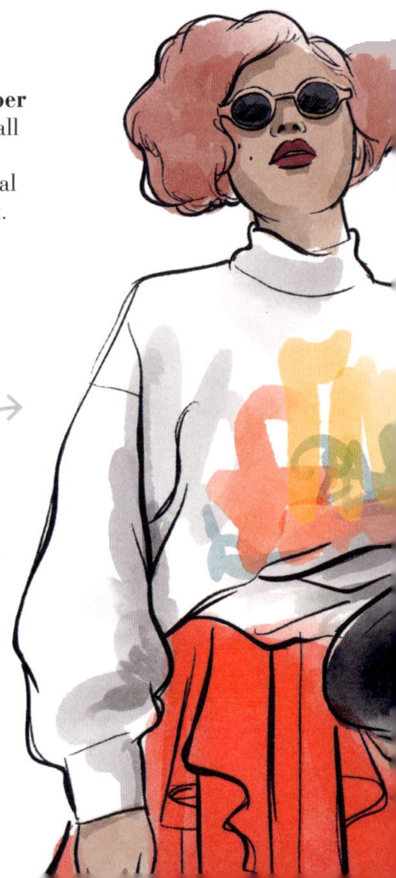

Oversizing is in streetwear's DNA.

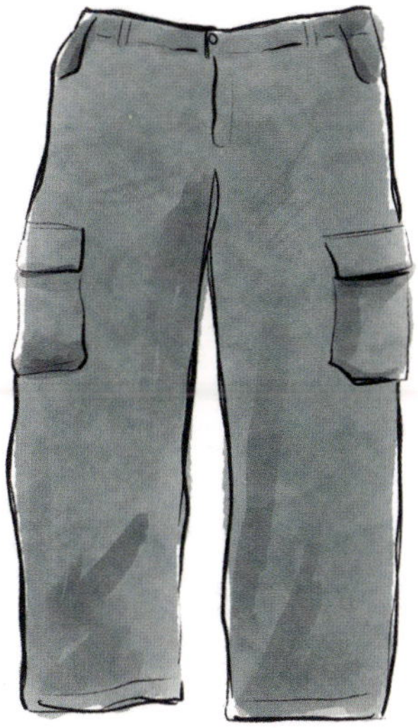

Cargo pants, originally part of workwear and military style, naturally fit into the rugged, utility sub-style of streetwear.

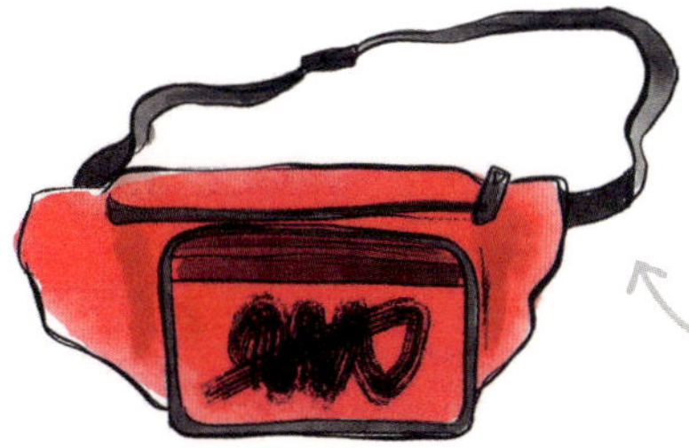

Belt bags, also known as bum bags, waist bags, or fanny packs, make waves as functional and trendy additions to workwear and everyday attire.

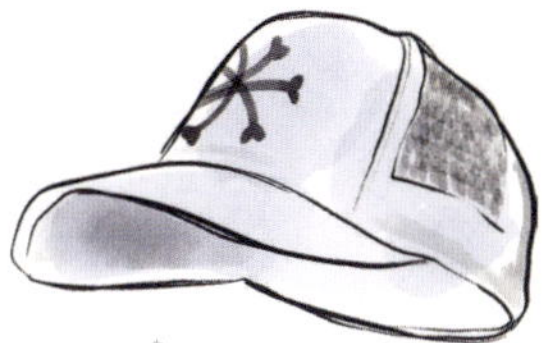

The baseball cap is a simple accessory that gives a streetwear edge to any outfit.

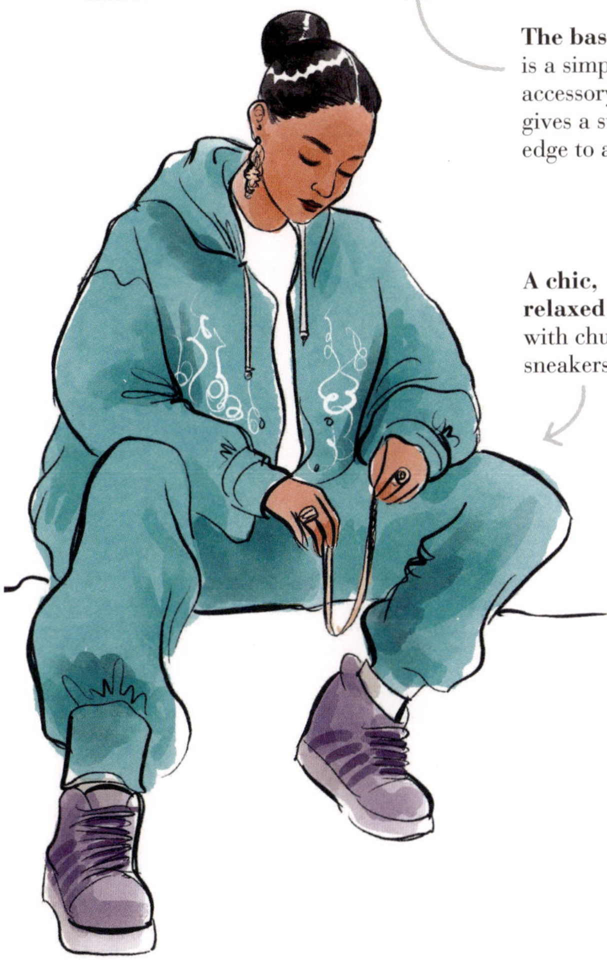

A chic, relaxed outfit with chunky sneakers.

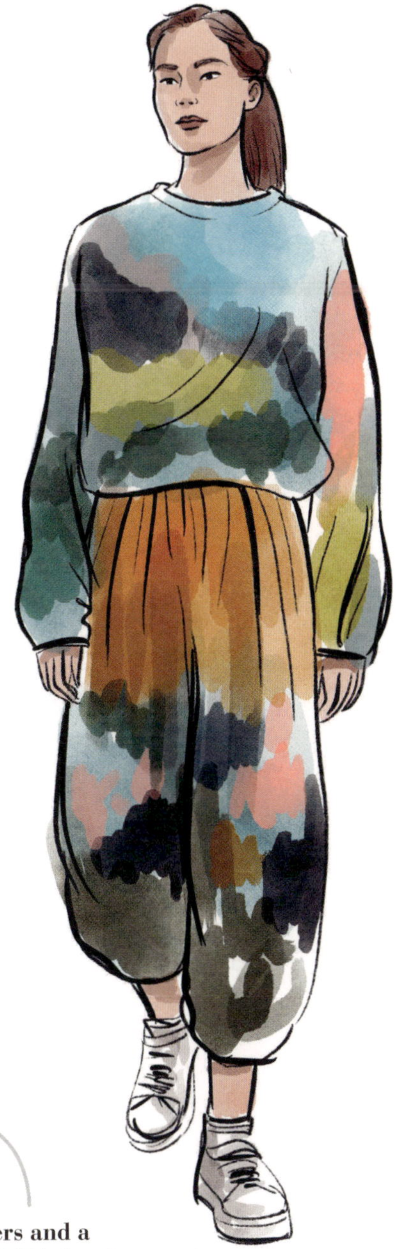

A tie-dye twist on streetwear shapes.

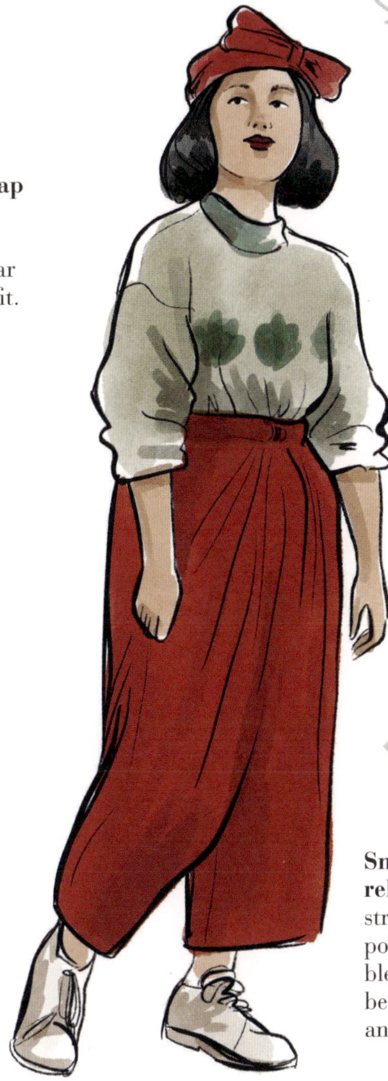

Sneakers and a relaxed fit bring the streetwear vibe to a polished outfit, blending the lines between streetwear and couture.

Design and color this model's streetwear look. Give her an oversize shirt or bomber jacket.

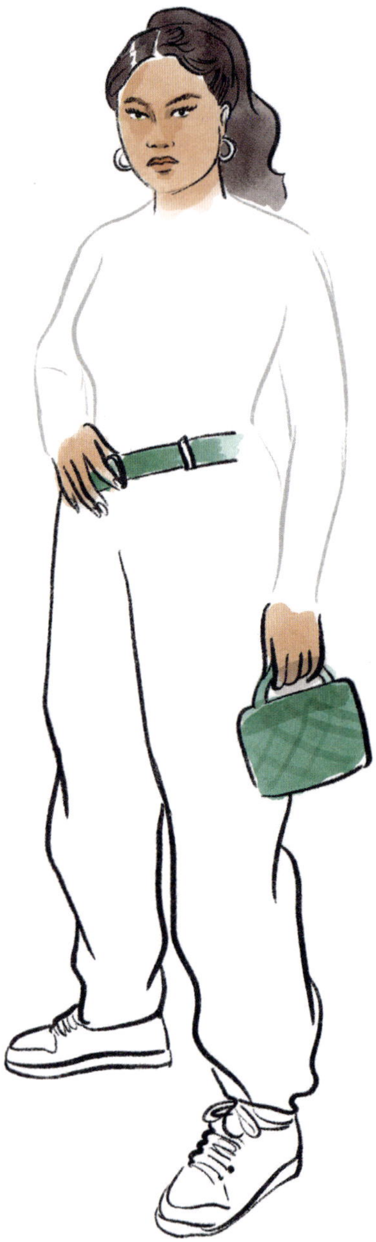

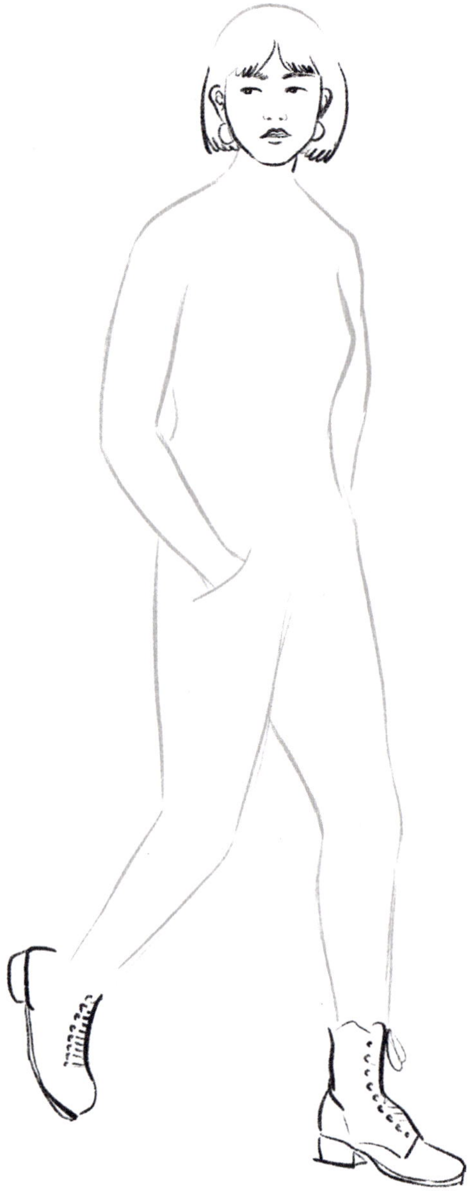

This model is breaking the streetwear mold with her boots. How will you style the rest of her outfit to give her a modern, urban look?

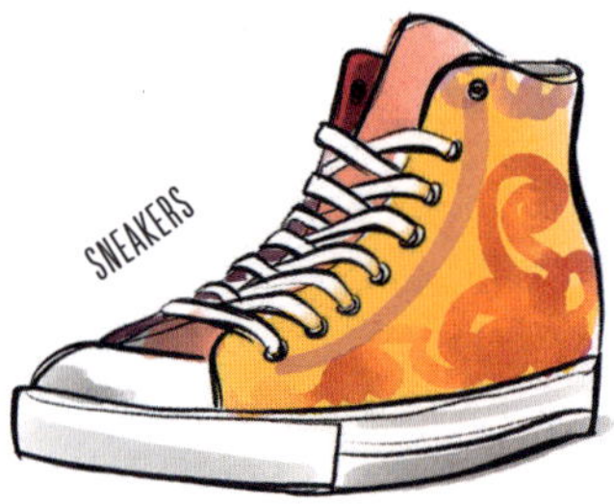

Now design a look for you! Will you go for a baggy, relaxed look or something more contemporary for the catwalk?

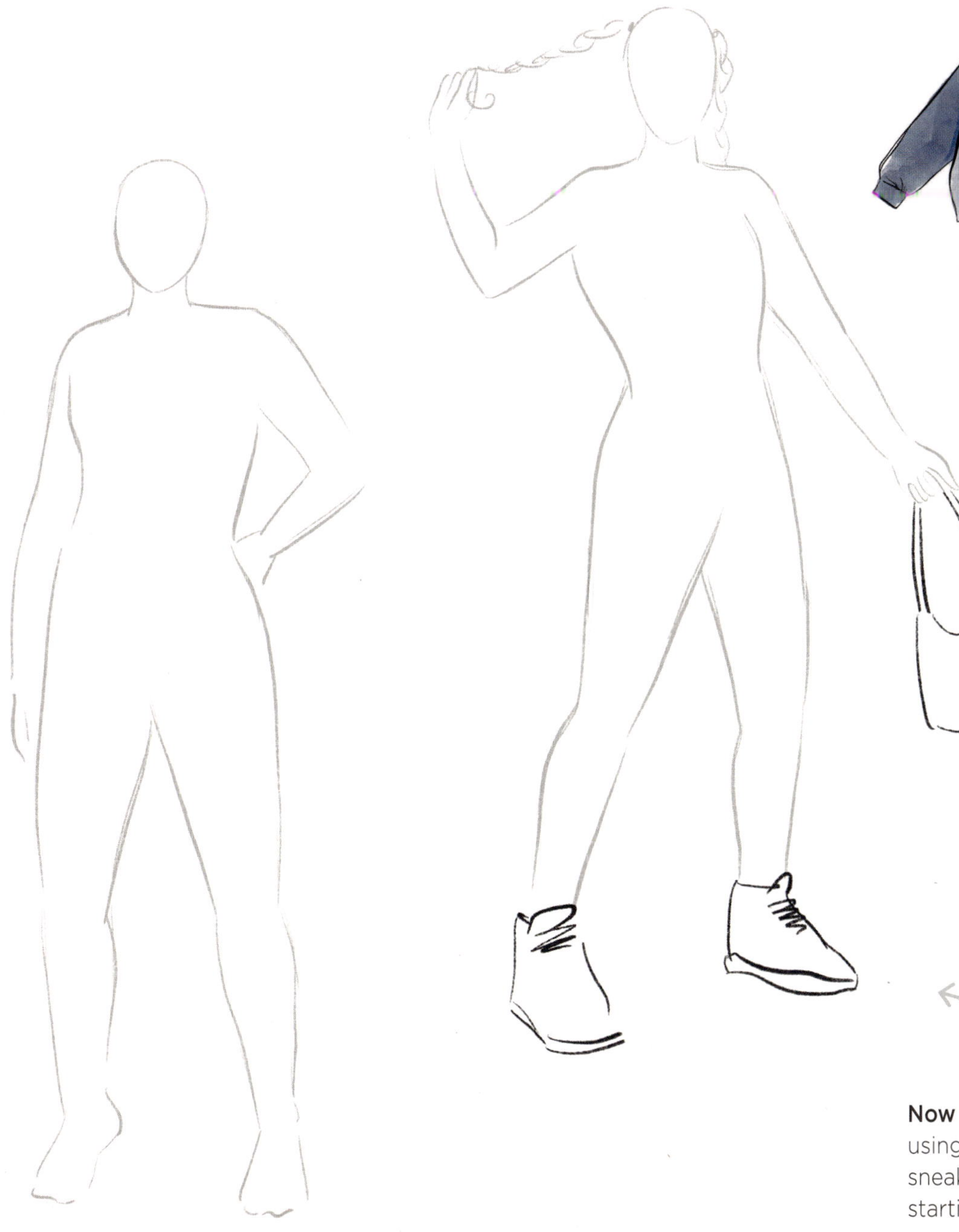

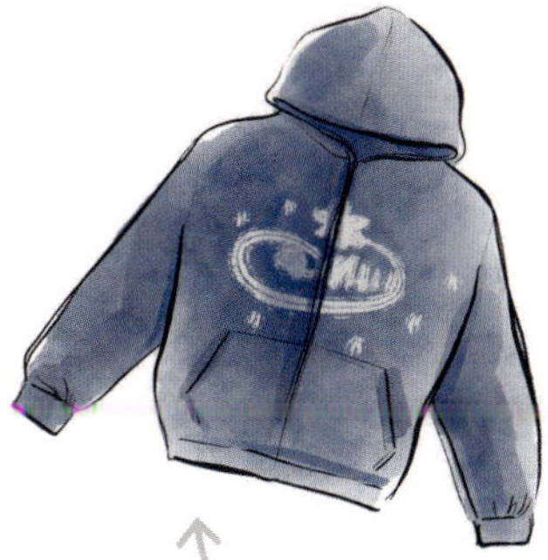

A branded hoodie is a great shortcut to streetwear style.

Now try out another look, using this model's sneakers and bag as a starting point.

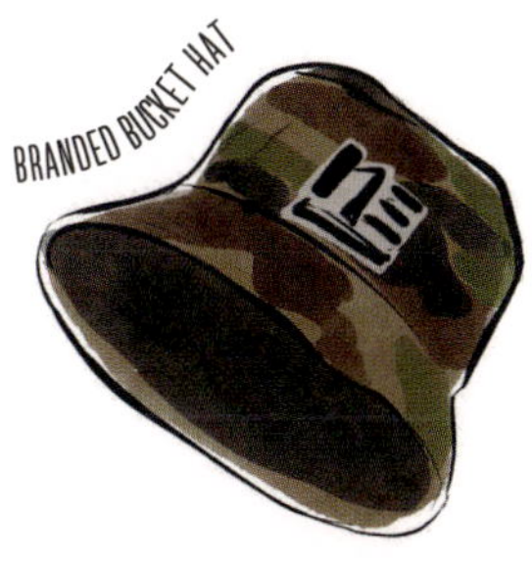

Athleisure

We're not just wearing sports clothes when we're doing sports anymore; they have become a fashion choice in and of themselves. Vivienne Westwood was one of the first high-fashion designers to introduce the sneaker on the catwalk. Athleisure originates from professional sports, especially tennis and golf. It also takes influences from modern pop culture, such as movies, music, and celebrities. To create the perfect athleisure outfit, keep it simple: Combine a colorful sweatshirt or hoodie with tracksuits or yoga leggings and, of course, a pair of sneakers.

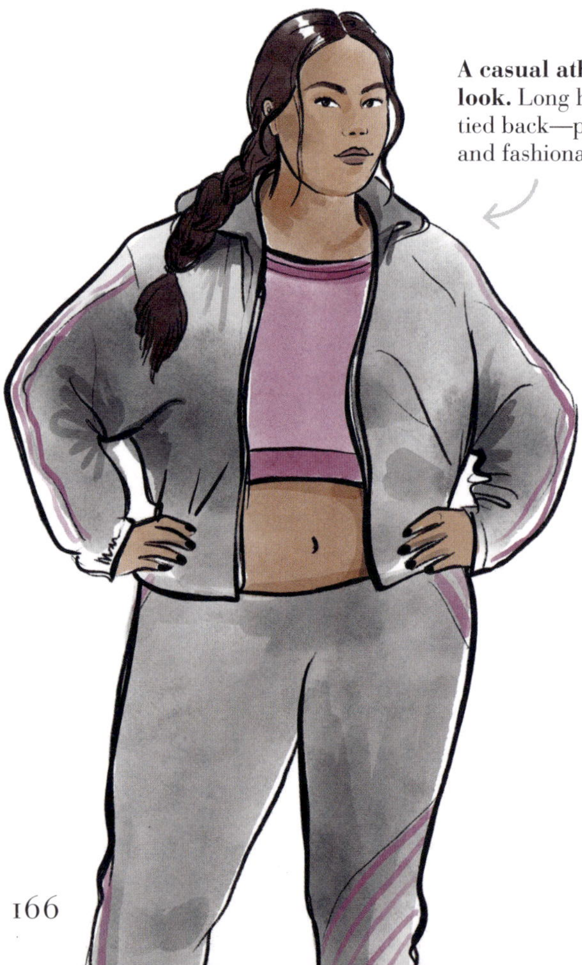

A casual athleisure look. Long hair is tied back—practical and fashionable.

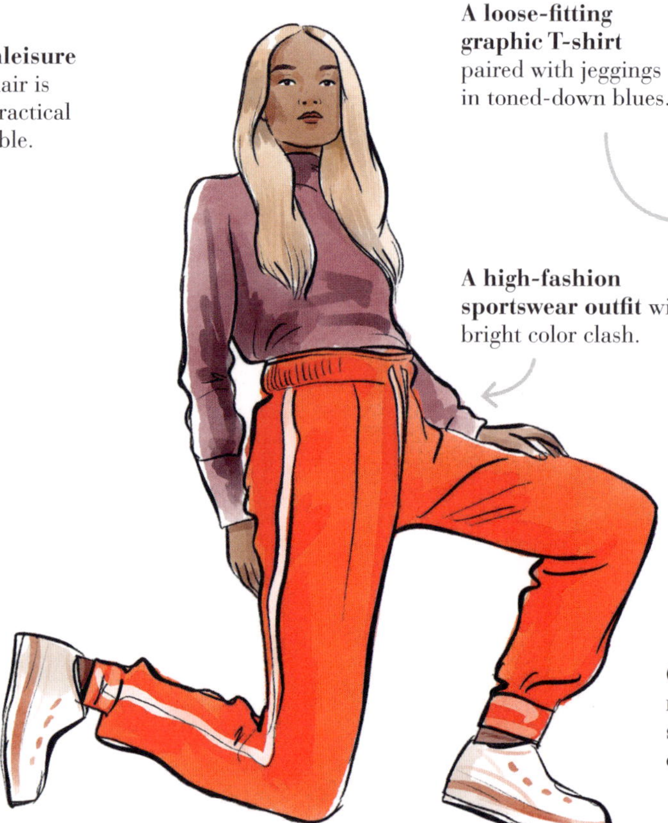

A high-fashion sportswear outfit with bright color clash.

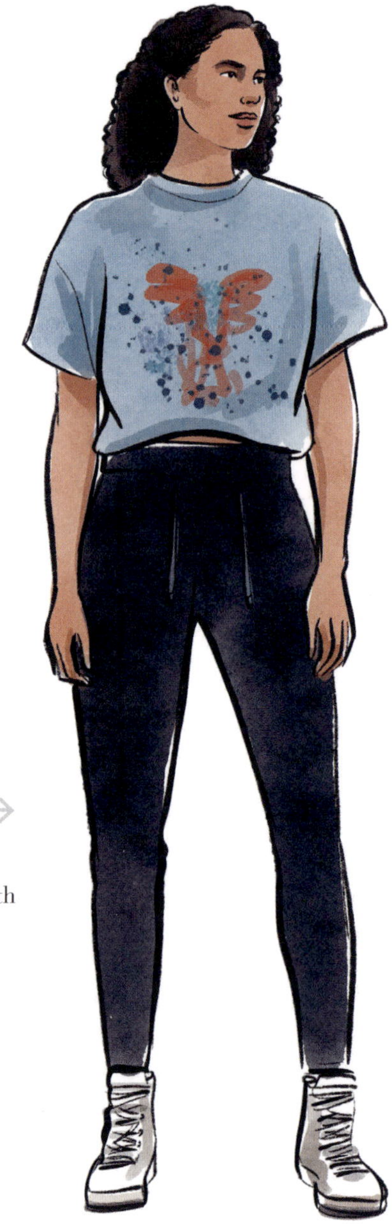

A loose-fitting graphic T-shirt paired with jeggings in toned-down blues.

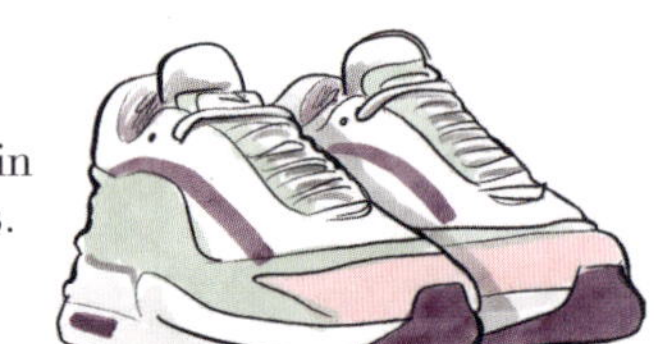

Chunky, modern sneakers in cute colors.

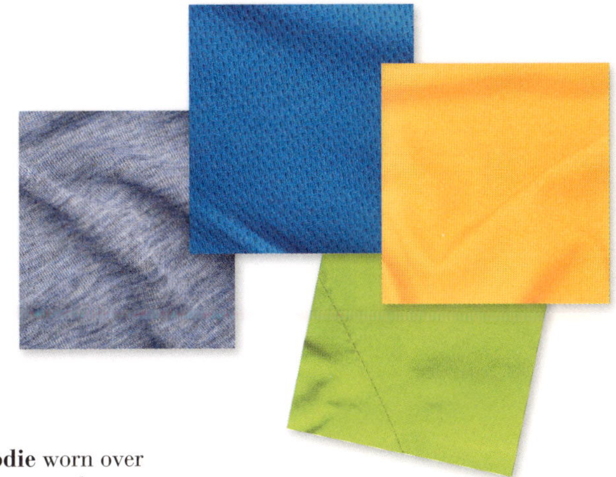

Polyester, often blended with spandex to create a fabric with good stretch, is often used in leggings, yoga pants, compression garments, and swimwear. Nylon fabric is durable and lightweight. Because it's very gentle, merino wool is often used in base layers and other garments worn next to the skin.

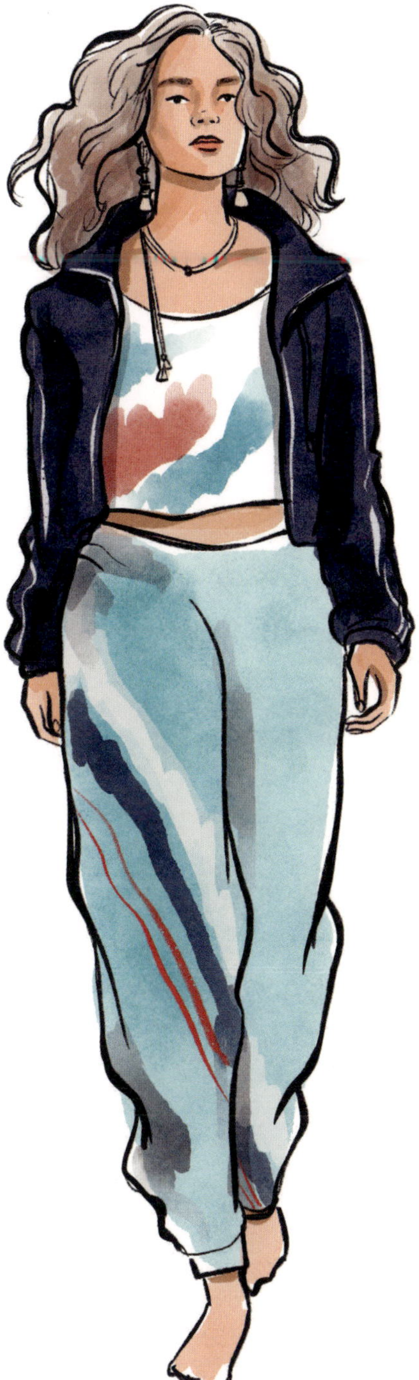

A casual look can be hyped up with striking patterns.

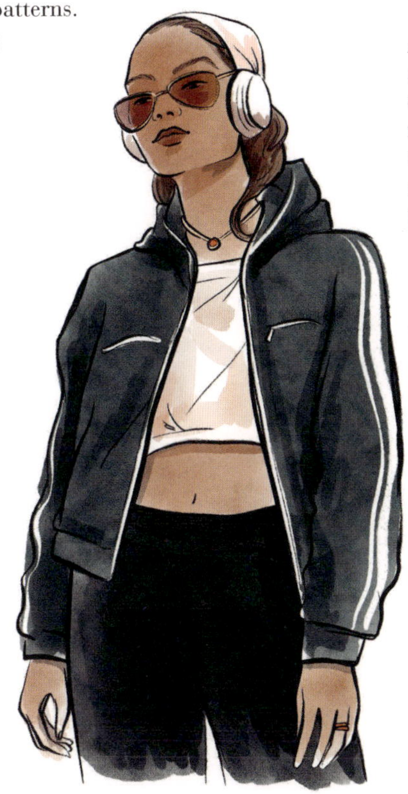

A hoodie worn over a crop top with over-ear headphones makes for a chic athleisure look that's still relaxed and practical.

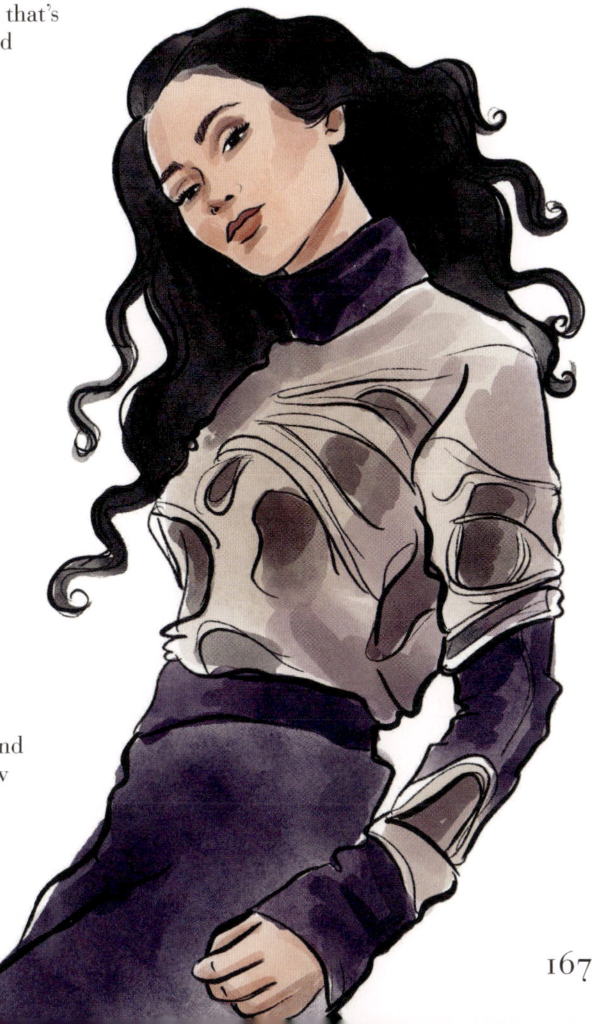

High fashion and sportswear have a long and rich history of collaboration and inspiration. Activewear uses a lot of new material and shapes (like mesh and silicone), while what we now call "athletic couture" makes utilitarian pieces also look elegant.

Give this model a matching yoga set in a fun pattern.

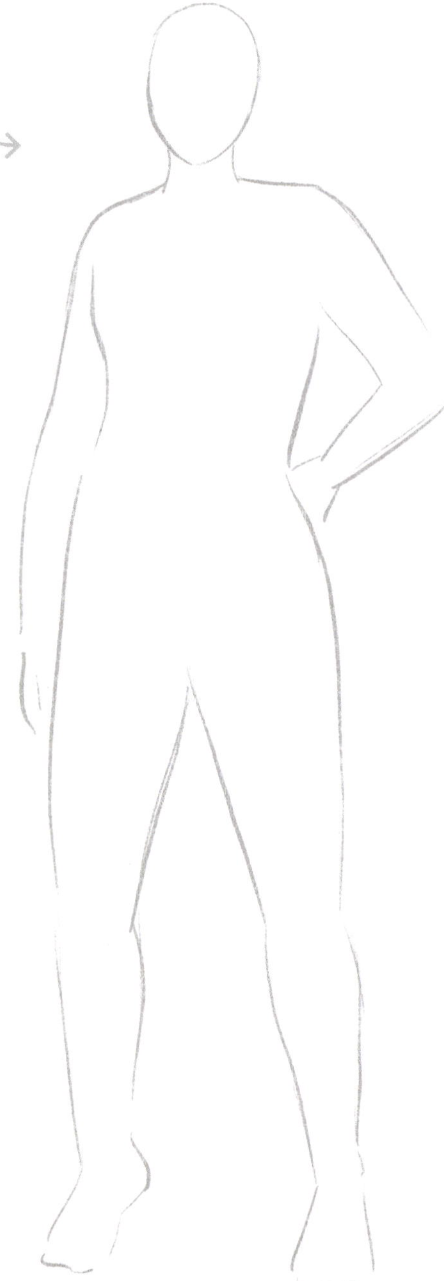

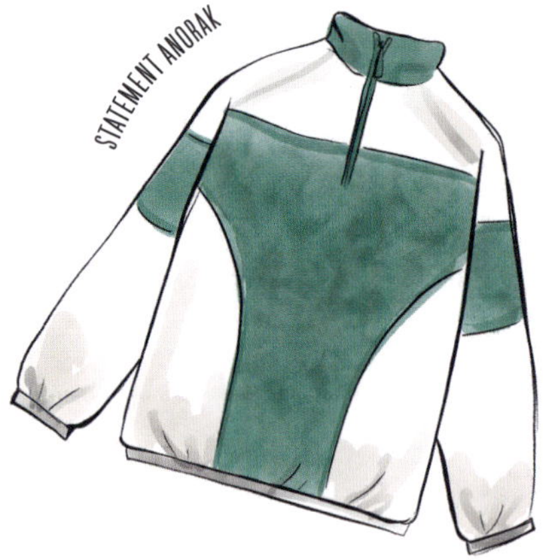

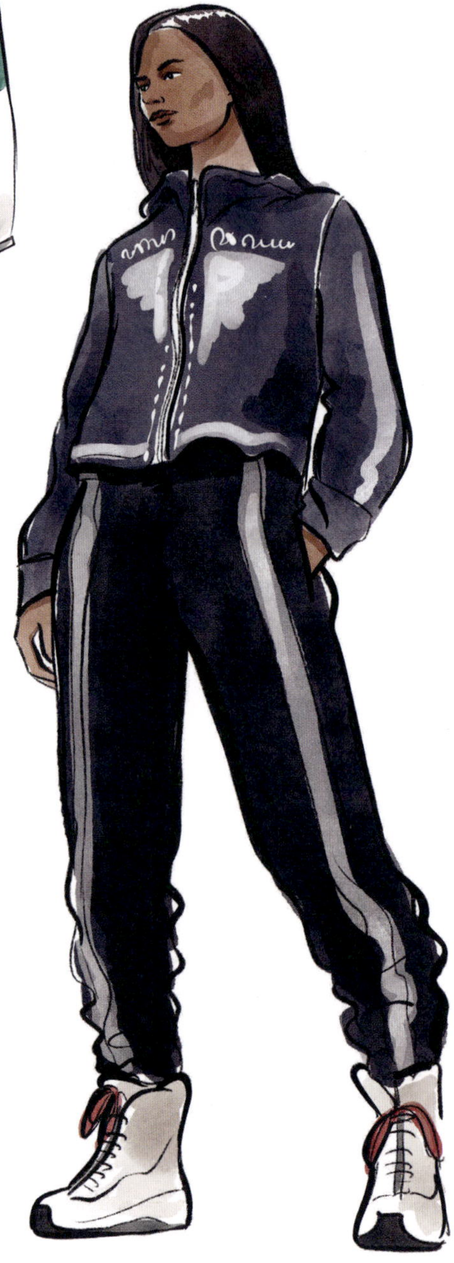

Sportswear is one of the most popular and versatile fashions. It can be comfy and edgy at the same time.

Create an athleisure look for this model, adding some sneakers, sweatpants, and a crop top.

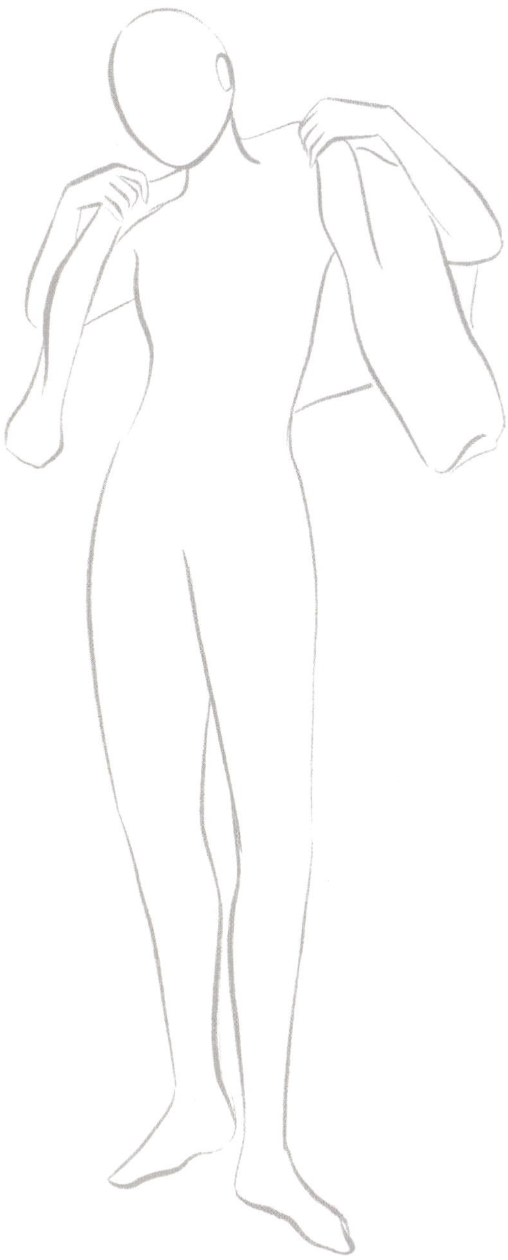

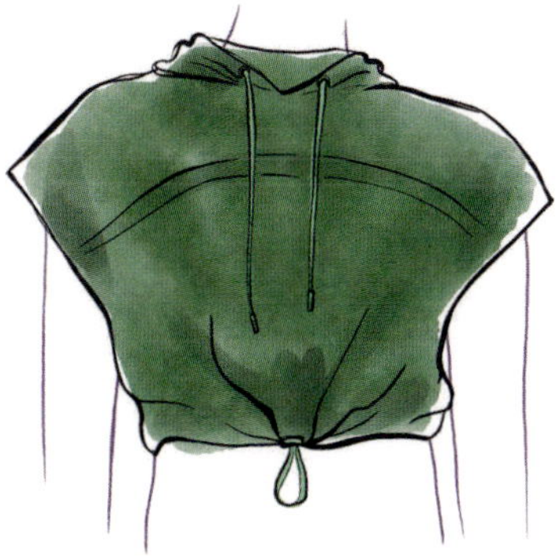

Create a simple and relaxed athleisure look for this model, using bold patterns and colors, and matching their sweater with their pants.

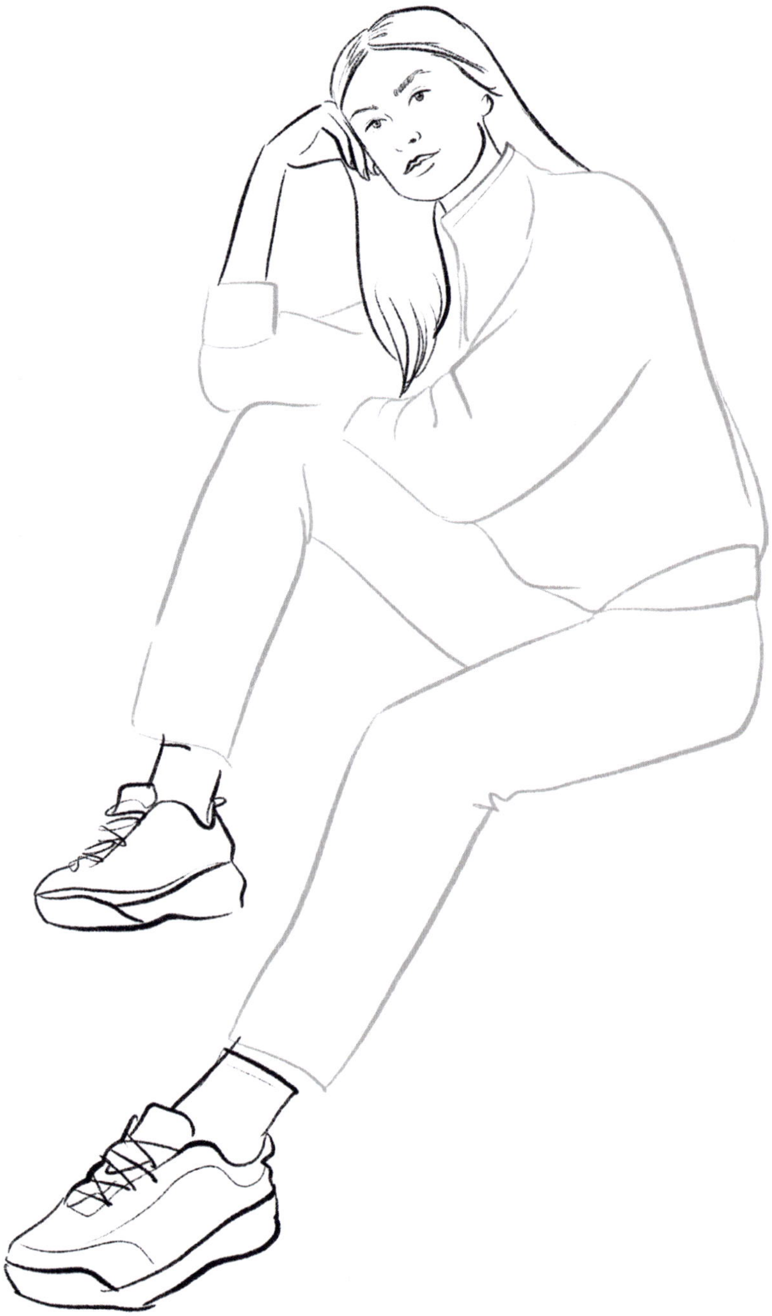

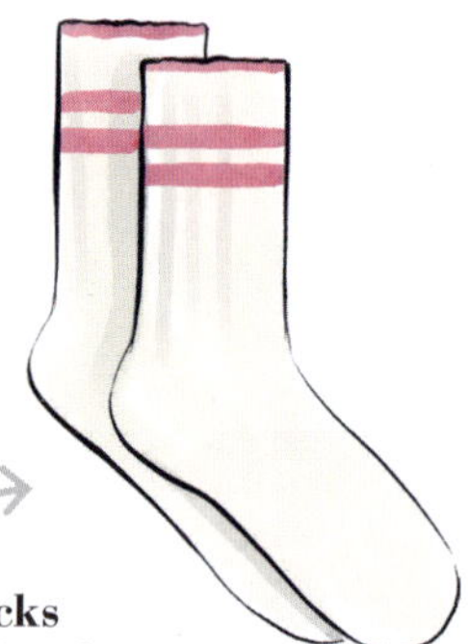

Sporty socks with an '80s vibe.

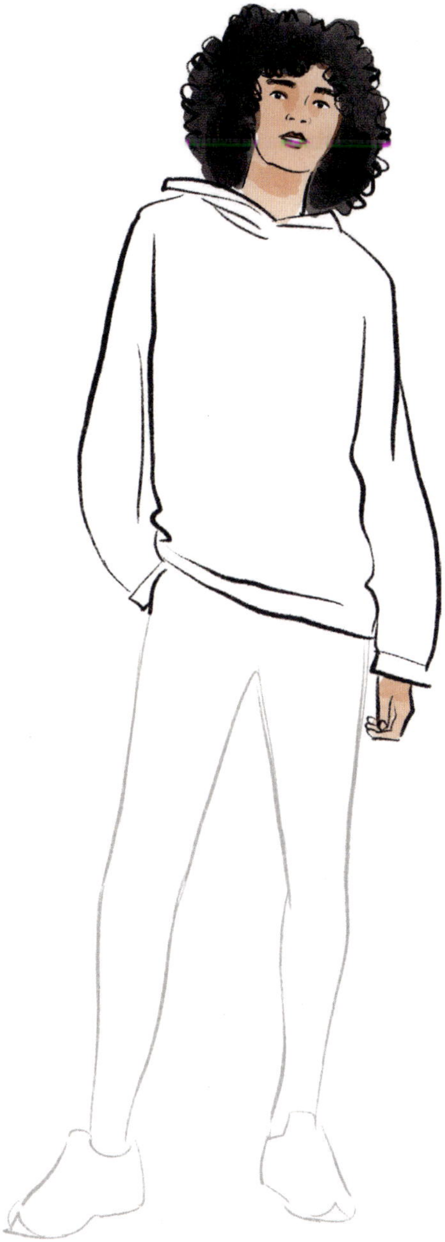

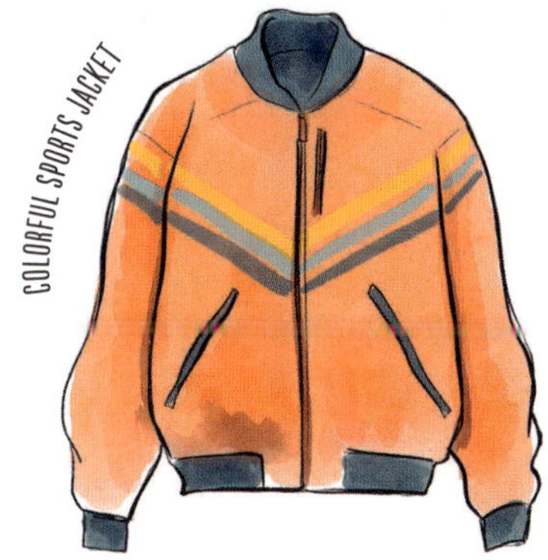

What outfit will you design for this model? Use their hoodie as a starting point and trace some leggings or pants to complete the look. Are they going for a run, or hitting the runway?

Minimalism

Minimalism is all about simplicity, quality, and functionality, calling for timeless pieces that are made to last, as opposed to the short-lived, trend-led clothes that make up fast fashion. The aesthetic of minimalism embraces a neutral color palette, simple shapes, and clean lines, often resulting in an inclusive, androgynous look that is still sophisticated and elegant. Modern Japanese fashion in particular promotes the freedom to choose how to dress, for not only gender but also age and body shape.

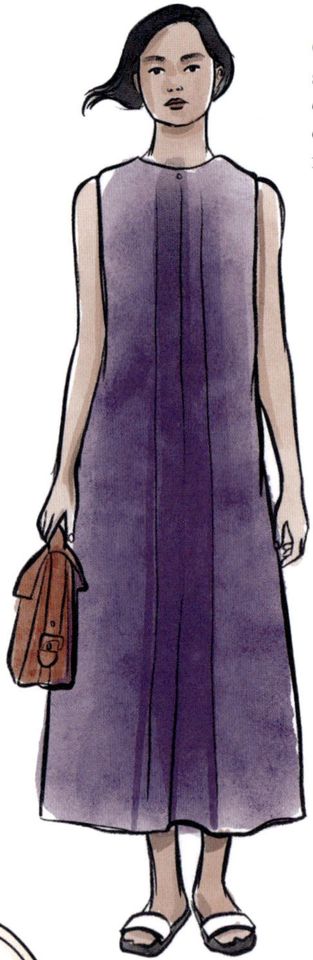

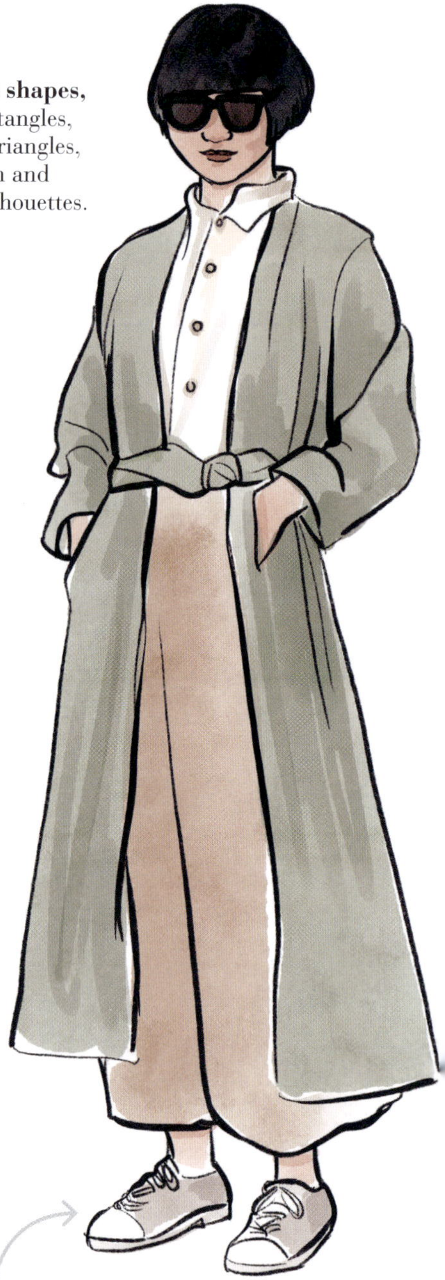

Geometric shapes, such as rectangles, circles, or triangles, create clean and minimal silhouettes.

High-quality wool, linens, and heavy cottons go well with minimalist design as they are practical, drape well, and are made to last.

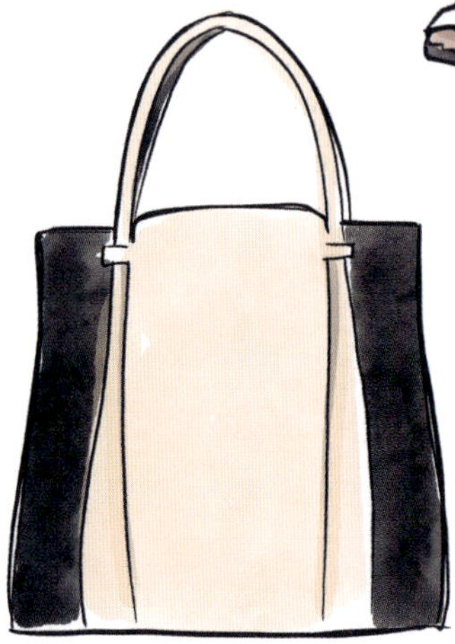

A simple leather handbag won't overwhelm a minimalist look.

Layering complementary, neutral shades over one another diversifies an outfit, adding another focal point to draw the eye and keeping it from looking boring.

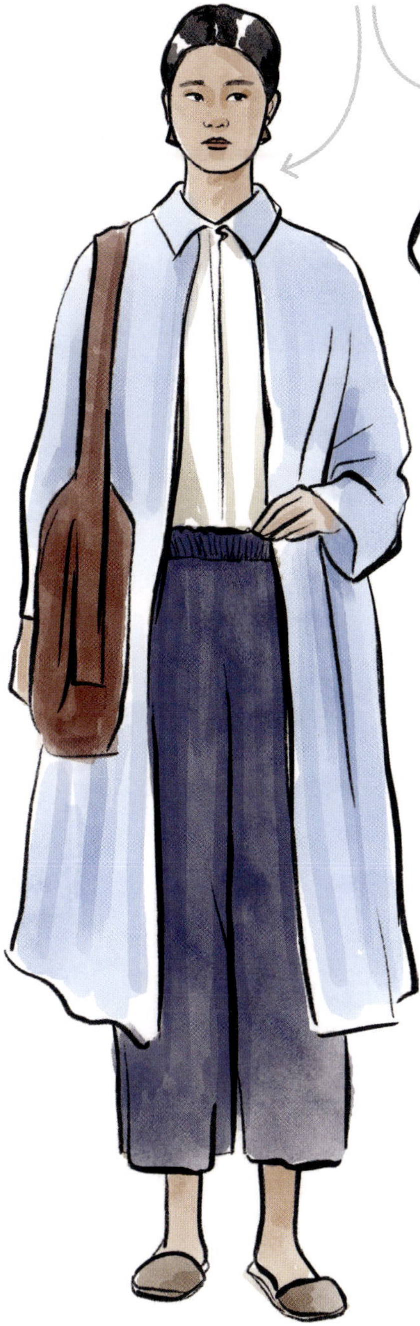

Muted tones and a simple silhouette.

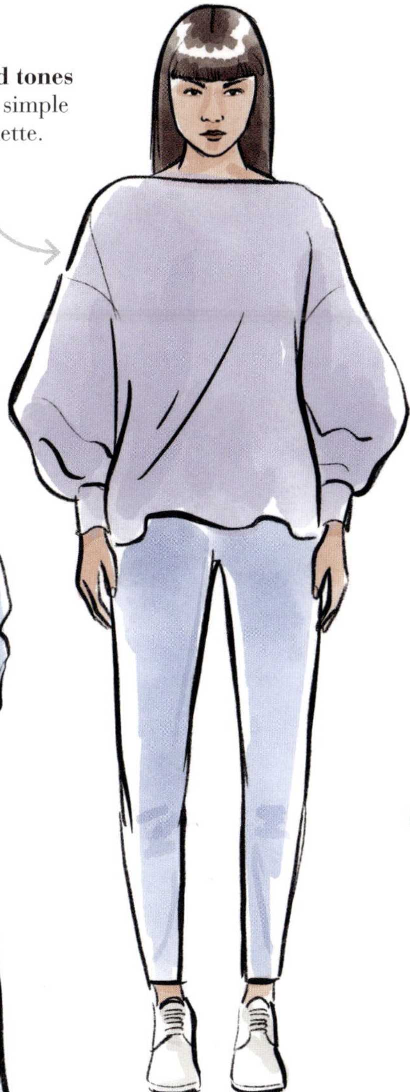

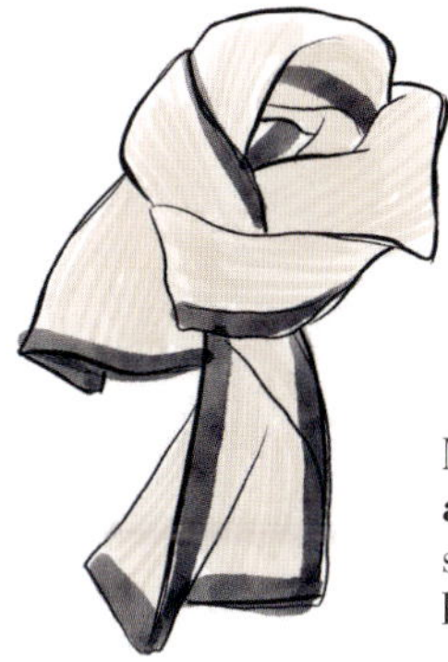

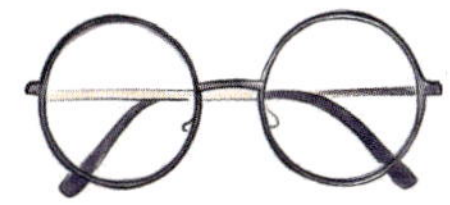

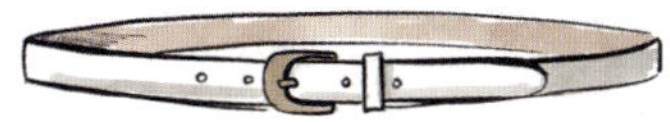

Minimalist accessories keep a simple design and block colors.

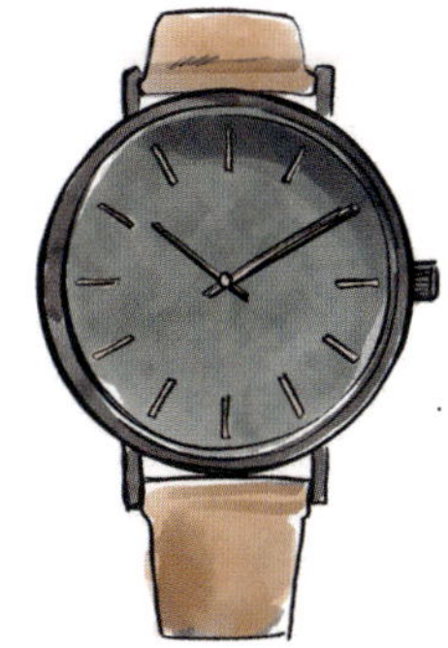

Match muted tones with a strong accent color for a statement look.

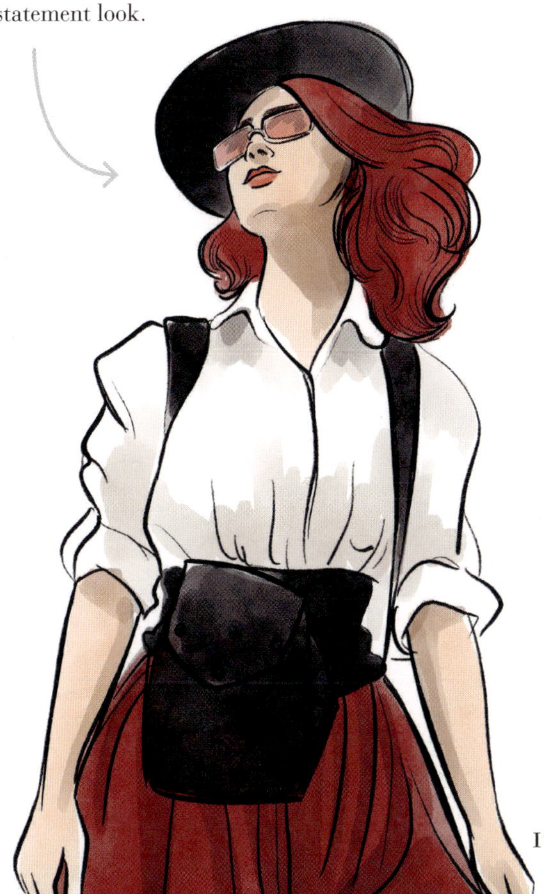

Stick with an all-white or all-beige color palette to look neat and put together.

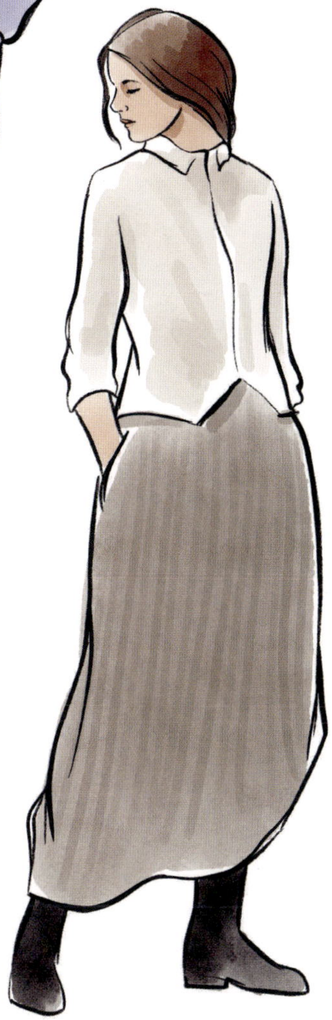

Finalize this model's outfit, using neutral colors like black, white, gray, beige, or navy. Think about clean design lines for her bag and her shoes.

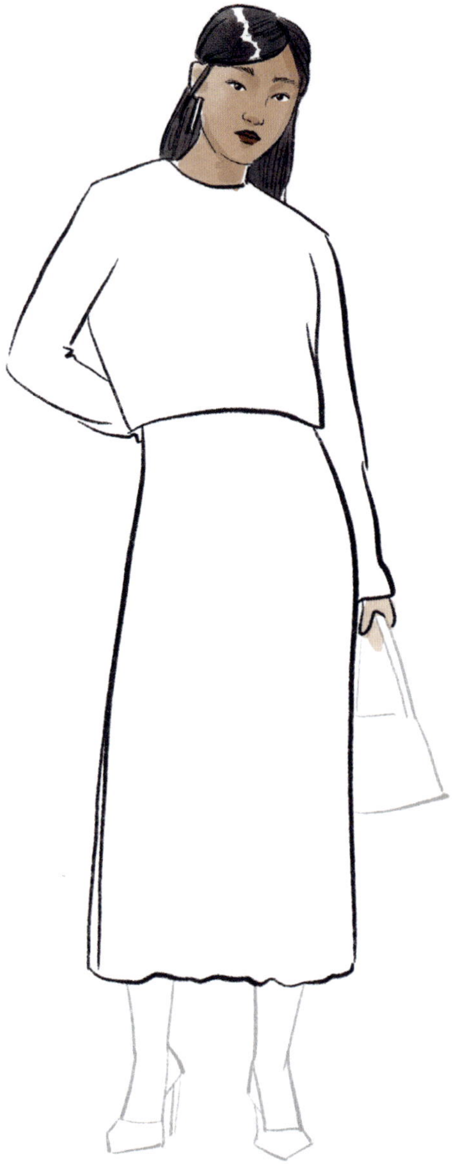

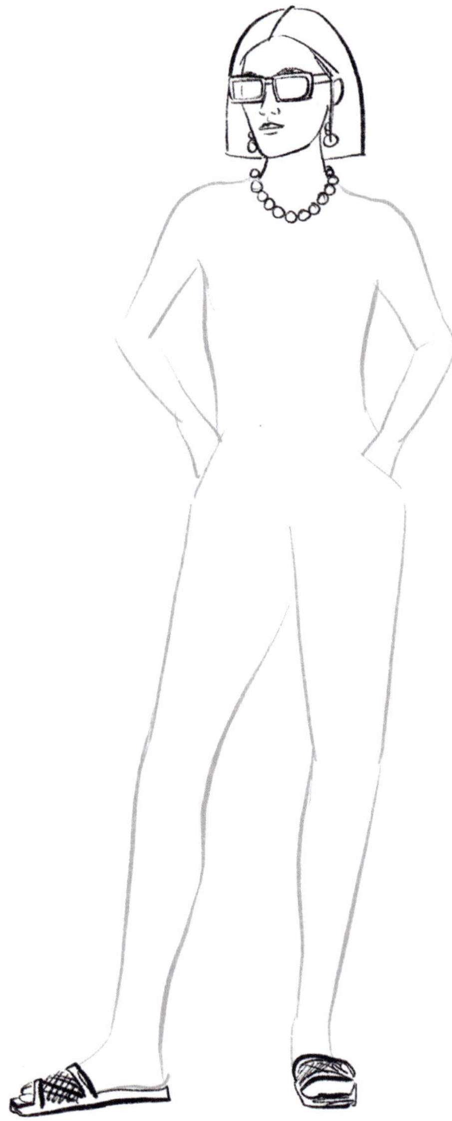

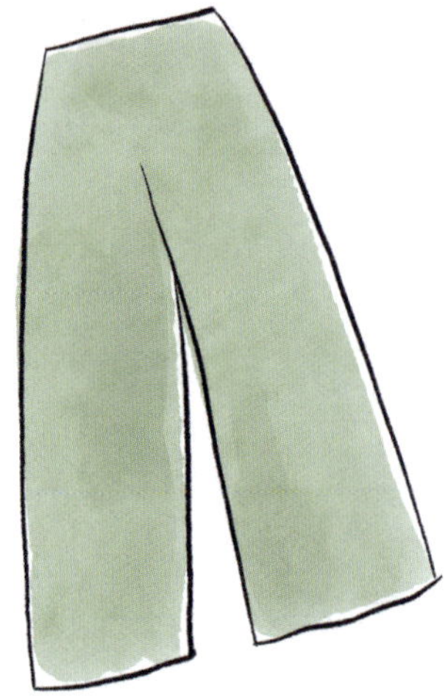

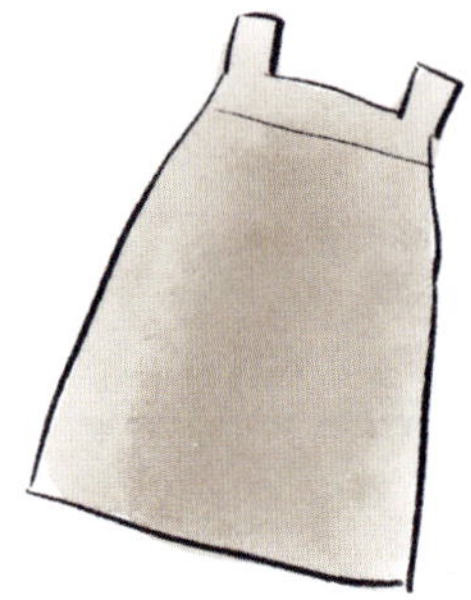

Dress this model to match her accessories. Feel free to use inspiration from the garments drawn here!

Create your own minimalism-inspired look. What kind of fabrics will you use? Corduroy, leather, linen, and silk are popular among minimalist designers, since they each present a unique finish at just a glance.

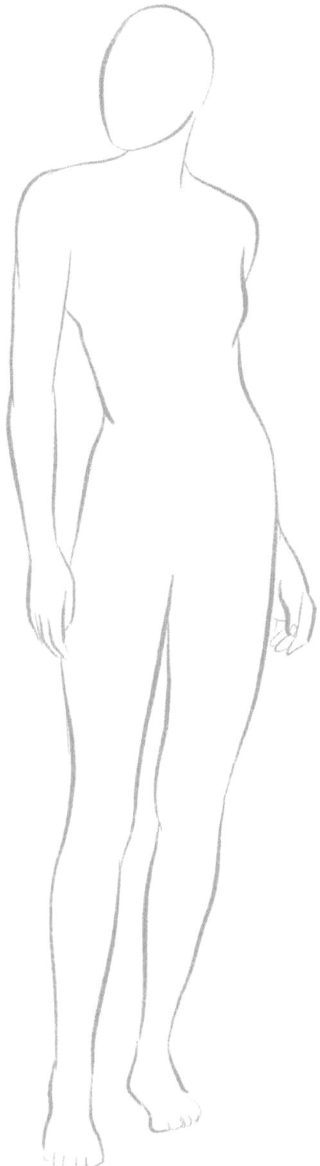

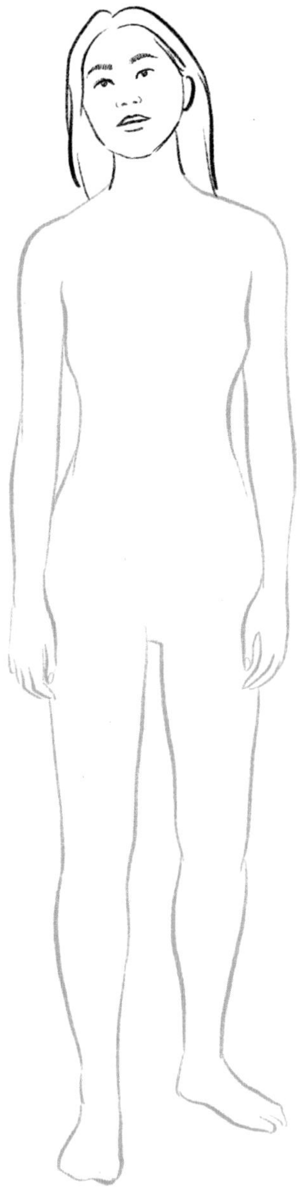

Design another outfit for this model. Remember that less is more!

Bold Prints

Many designers are inspired by the beauty and diversity of traditional textiles, using loud and eye-catching patterns that reflect the culture, identity, and creativity of different regions and communities to celebrate both the past and the present. For instance, contemporary designer Oscar de la Renta is often credited with launching the trend of incorporating ikat designs in Euro-American fashion. Originating from Asia, ikat is a technique of resist-dyeing yarns prior to weaving fabric. It creates a distinct style of textile patterns with blurred or multicolored designs.

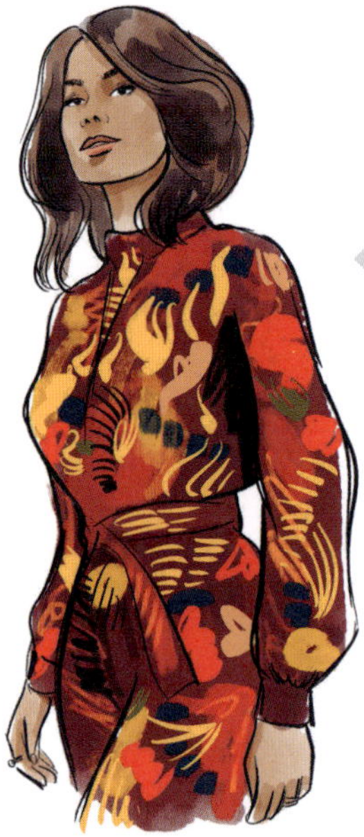

A bold print on a modern cut.

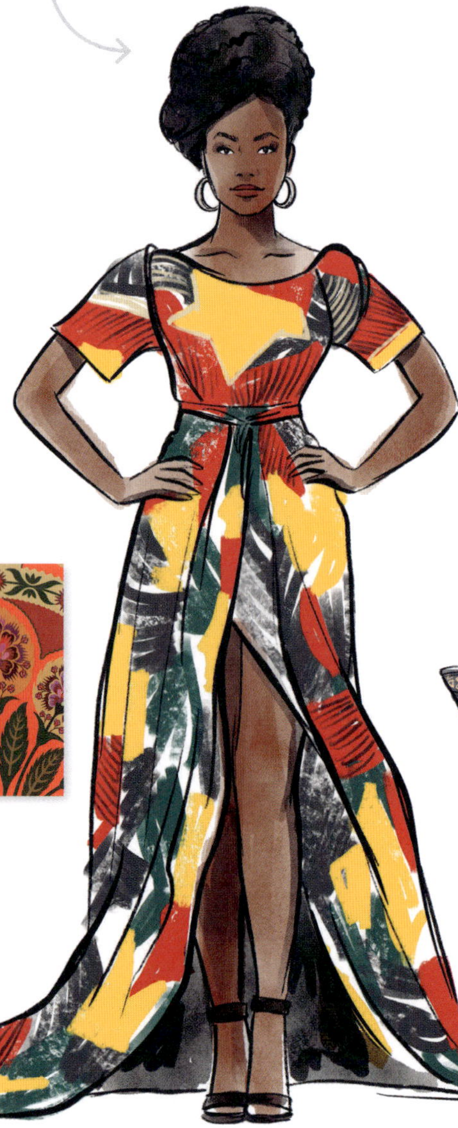

Reclaiming heritage fabrics is sparking a boom in African fashion.

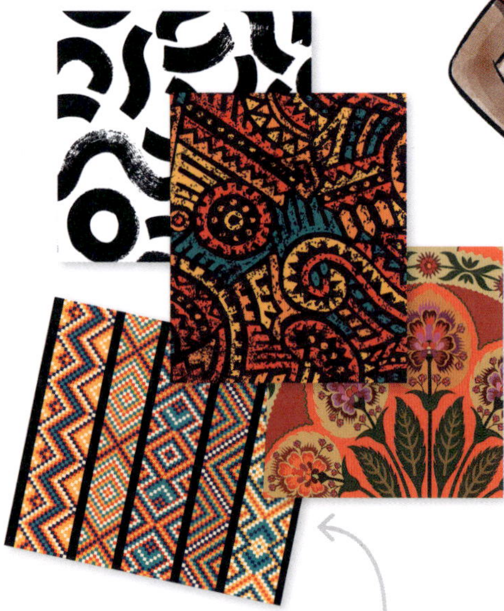

Bold graphics and patterns might be woven into fabrics, or embellished with bead and embroidery work.

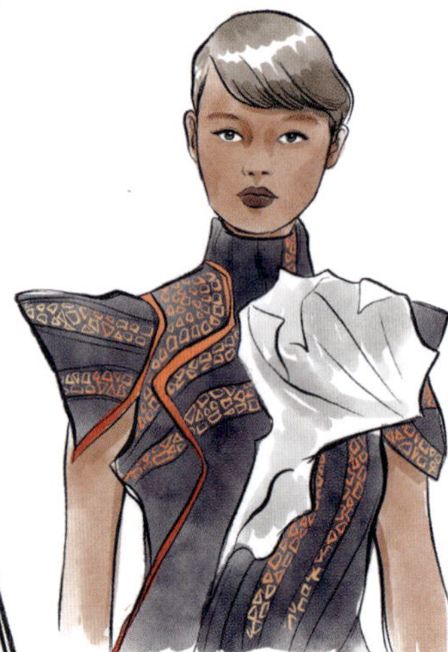

3D-printed fabric drawing influence from traditional Japanese techniques and ikat weaving—some fashion designers use 100% recycled filament and fabric made from ocean waste yarn production in their outfits.

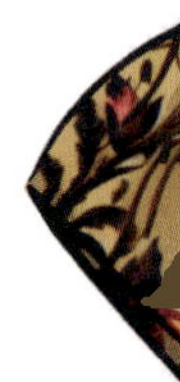

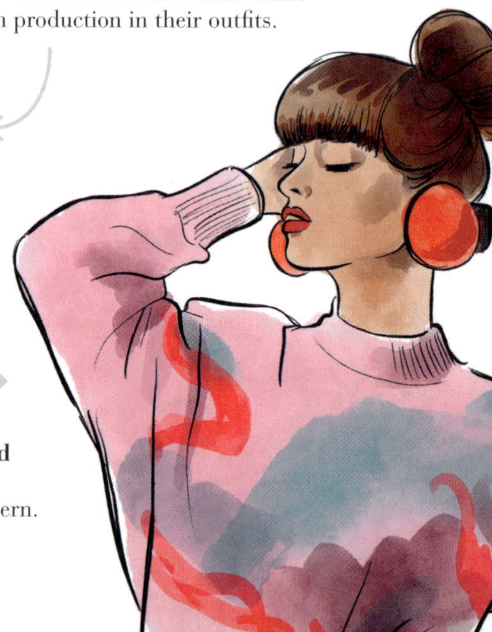

A fun and loud '80s Euro pattern.

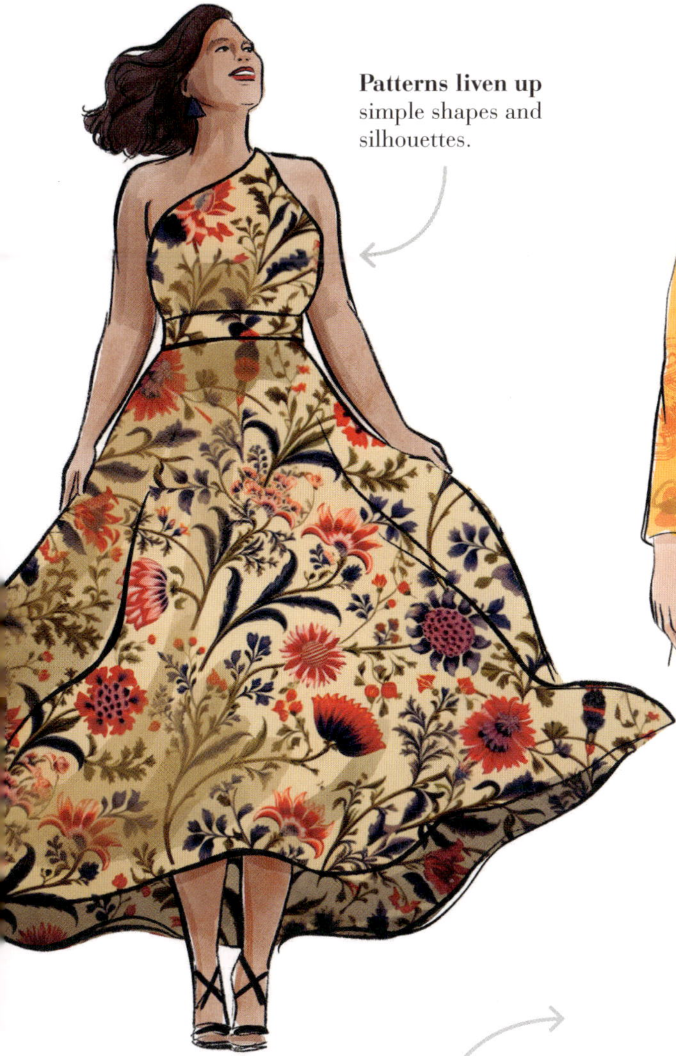

Patterns liven up simple shapes and silhouettes.

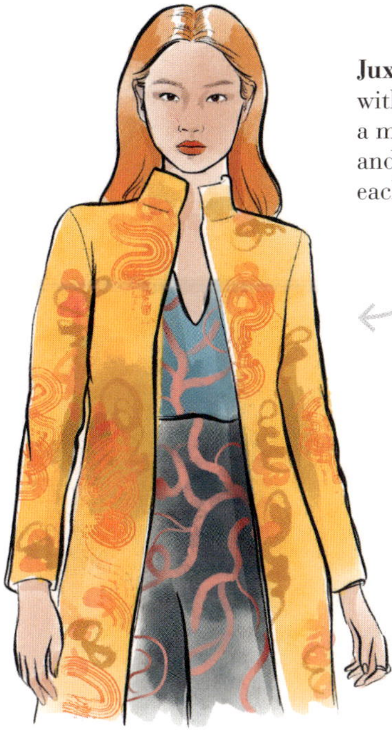

Juxtaposition of patterns and styles, embroidered with Chinese motifs. Translating traditional motifs into a modern aesthetic requires a great amount of research and deep consideration. The key is to truly understand each motif's historical and cultural origins.

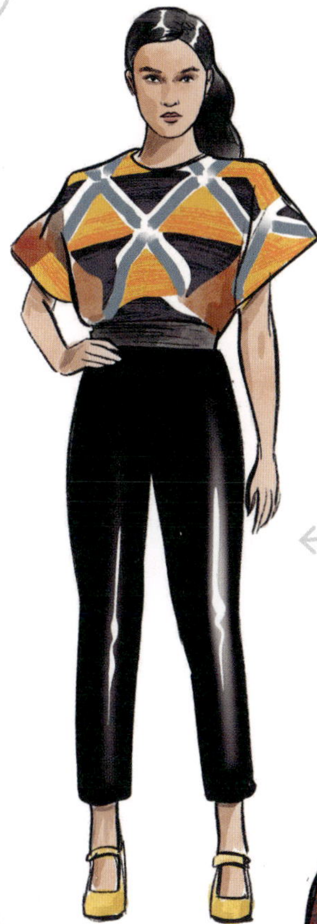

Black leather pants let these chic Asian patterns take the spotlight.

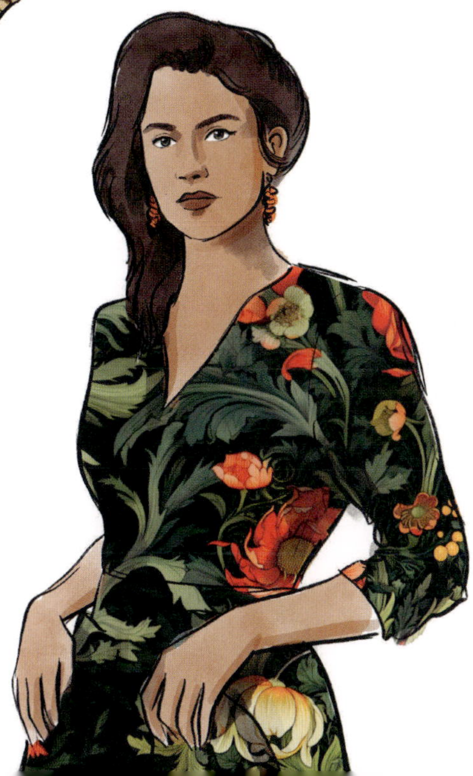

Floral prints are a classic and versatile option for bold prints. Wax Hollandais is a type of print that originated from the Netherlands and became popular in West and Central Africa. It features colorful and elaborate designs that are created by applying wax to the fabric before dyeing it. The designs often include floral motifs, such as lotus blossoms, sunflowers, or hibiscus.

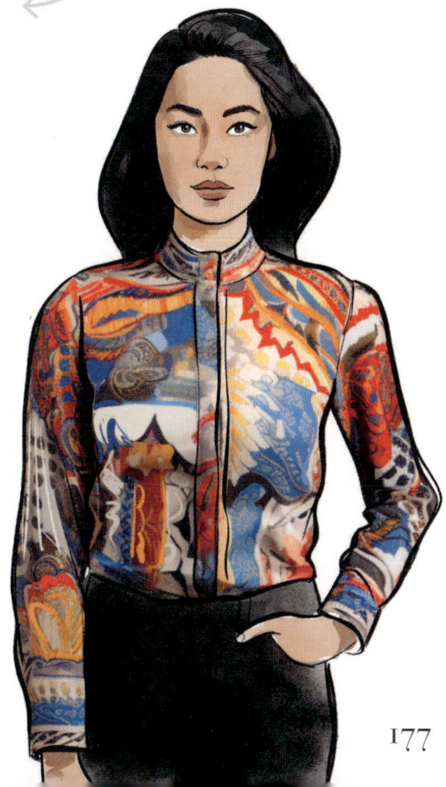

Add a beautiful print to this model's dress. Will you pattern the shoes, too, or choose a block color to complement or contrast with the dress?

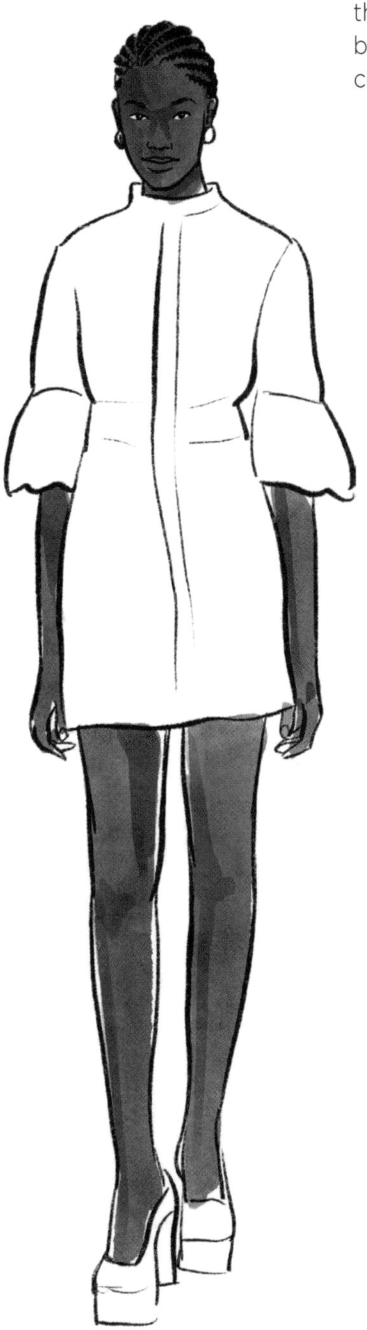

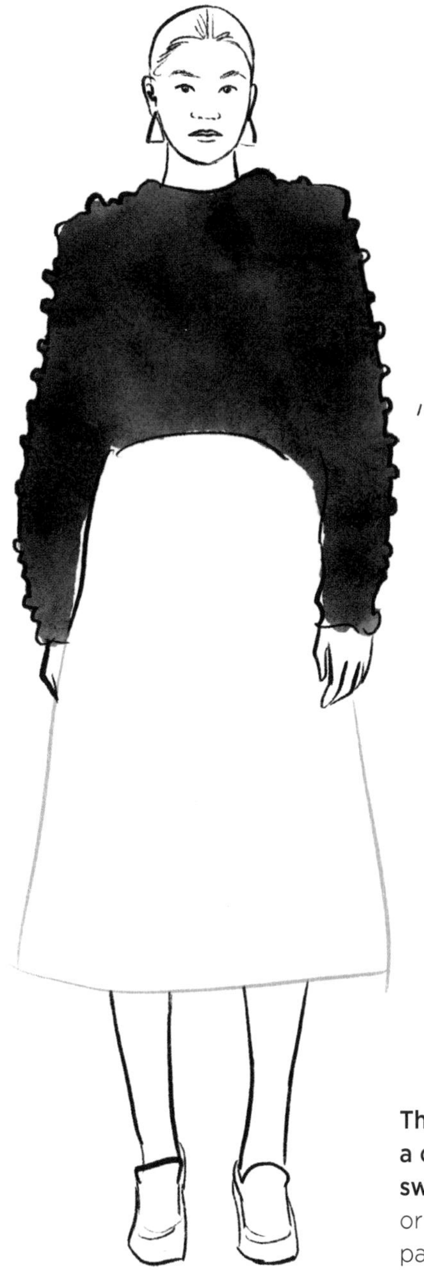

This model is wearing a chic and textured sweater over a skirt or dress. What kind of pattern will you give the skirt—something bold and geometric, delicate and floral, or something entirely different?

Now try drawing a bold print outfit for yourself! Will you use traditional draping techniques, or change things up with a more contemporary take on a traditional fabric? You could accessorize the look with a big, bold bag or hat. How will you style your hair and makeup for maximum impact?

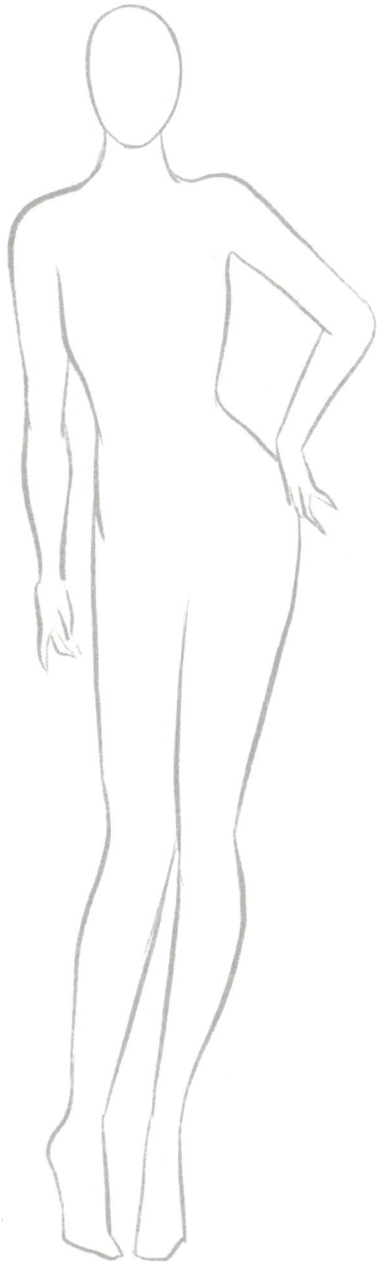

Geometric prints in high-contrast colors are a modern, edgy option.

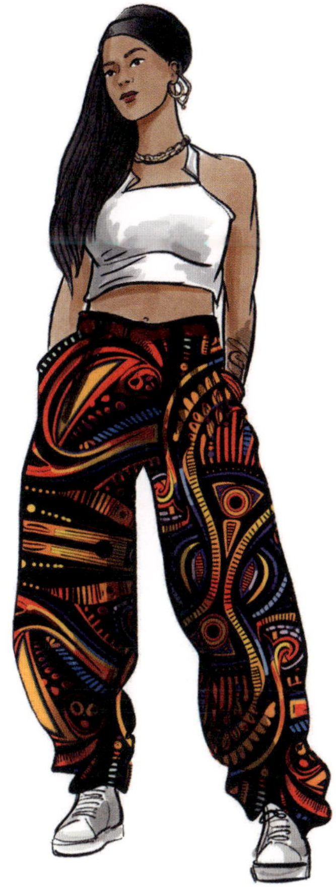

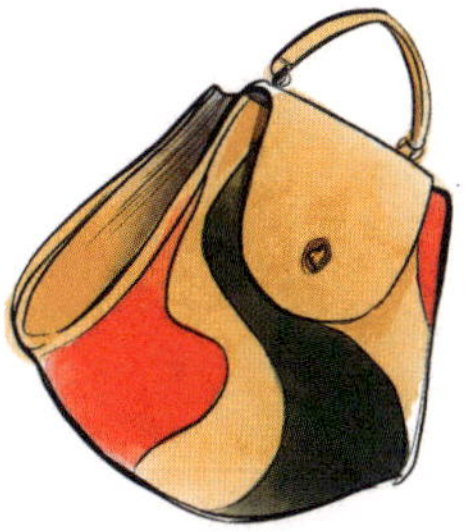

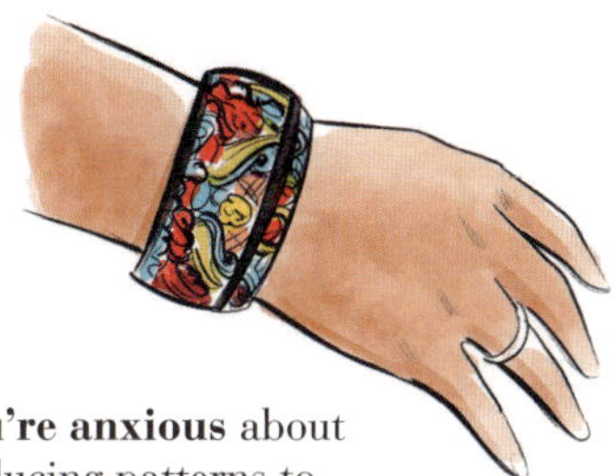

If you're anxious about introducing patterns to your wardrobe, start small by adding pops of color with accessories!

These patterned shoes would look amazing paired with black leather pants or dark denim jeans.

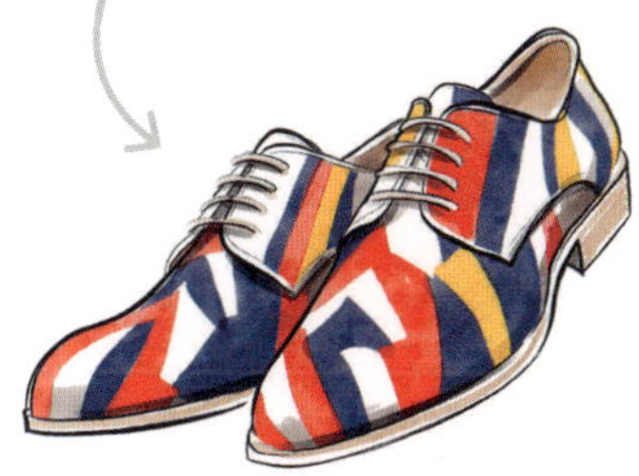

Layered Look

Layered fashion can be chic and sophisticated as well as warm! Layering allows you to change up your look by shedding or adding pieces as you see fit, which can give tired outfits a new lease of life. You need to be willing to throw disparate elements together, while keeping an eye on color and textures to create a visually cohesive ensemble. Accessories like scarves, hats, belts, and statement jewelry play a crucial role in completing a layered look, as well as adding a personal touch to layered outfits.

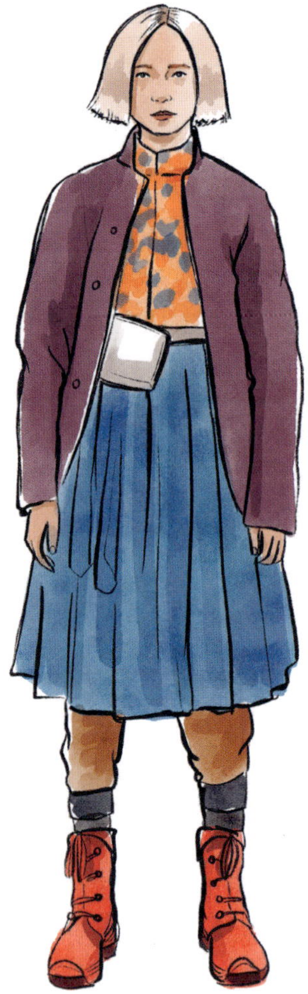

Layer both top and bottom—cardigan over shirt, skirt over pants.

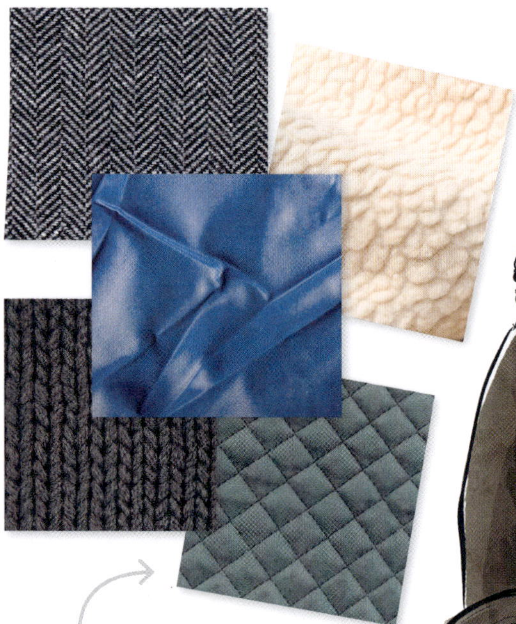

Cotton, polyester, merino wool, and down are versatile, breathable fabrics that make them suitable for layering.

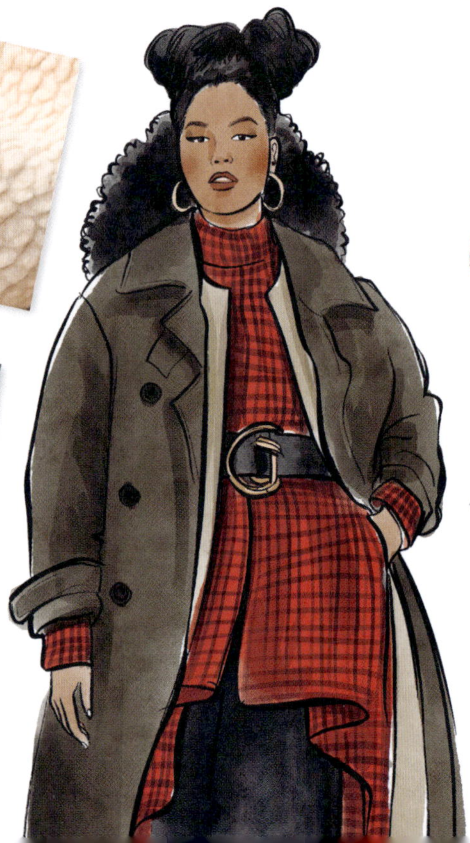

Belts are your secret weapon! Use them to cinch and define a layered outfit.

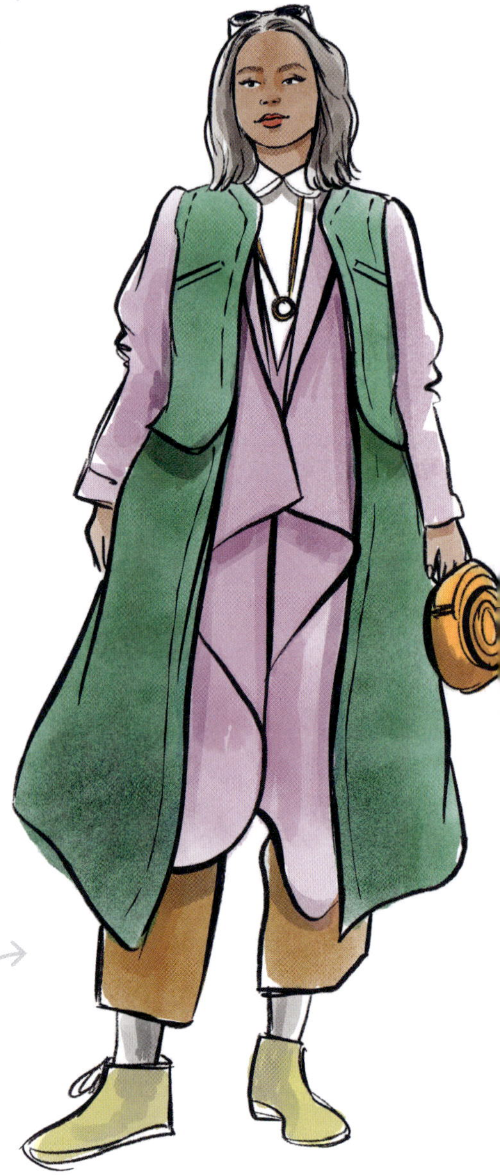

Pile on different hues to create visual interest.

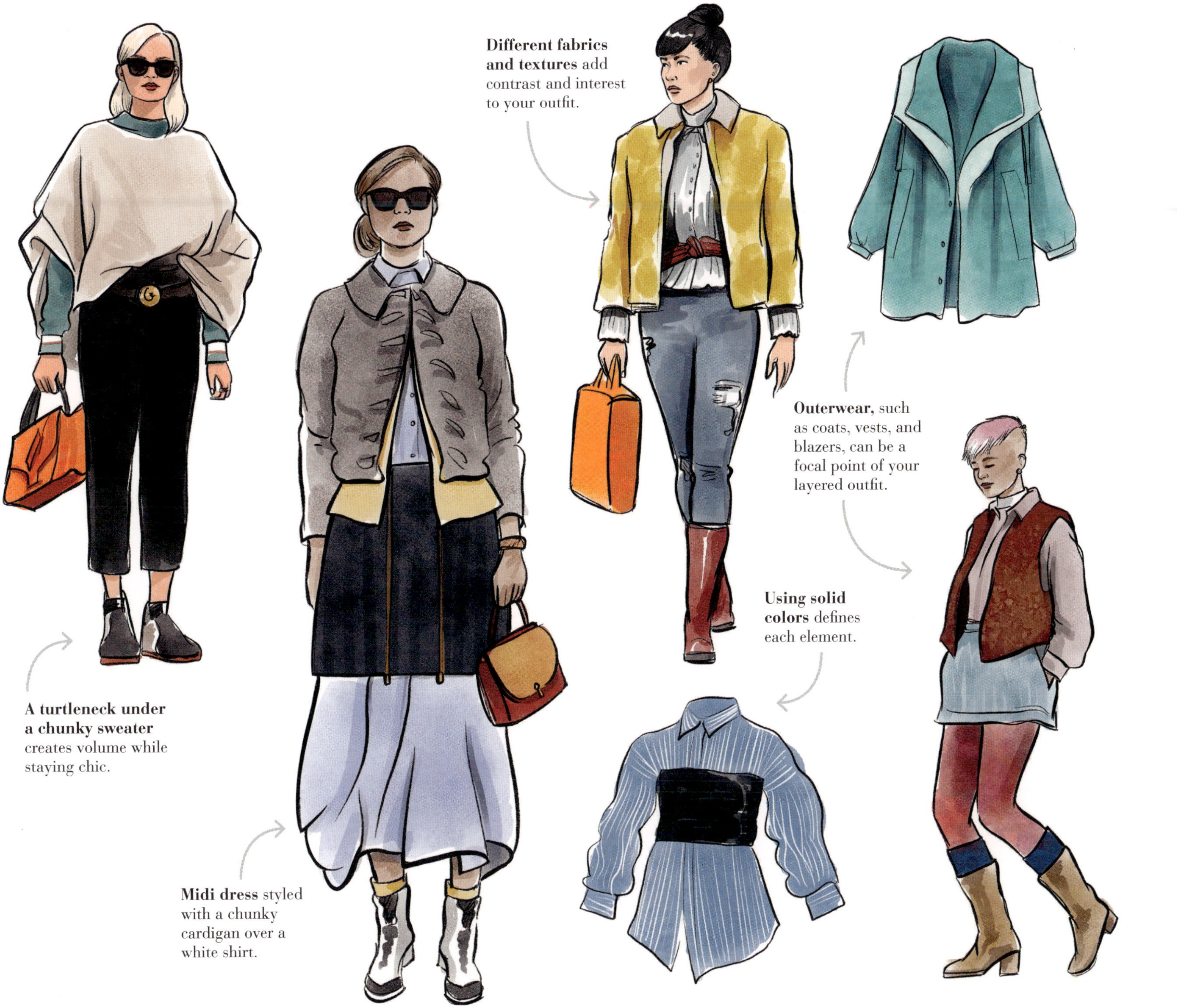
Different fabrics and textures add contrast and interest to your outfit.
Outerwear, such as coats, vests, and blazers, can be a focal point of your layered outfit.
Using solid colors defines each element.
A turtleneck under a chunky sweater creates volume while staying chic.
Midi dress styled with a chunky cardigan over a white shirt.

Complete this model's look. You could combine her leather jacket with a flowery dress. Experiment with different textures to add depth and interest to your ensemble.

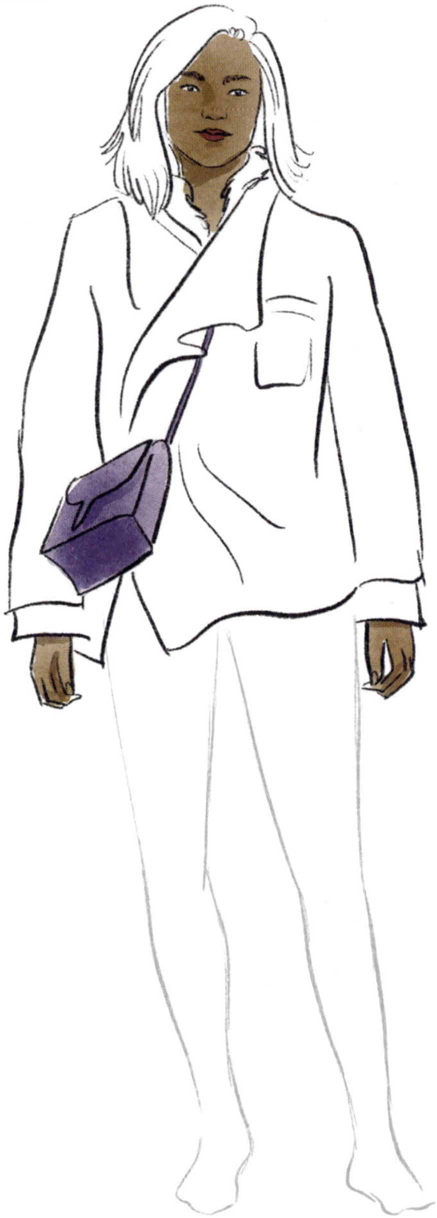

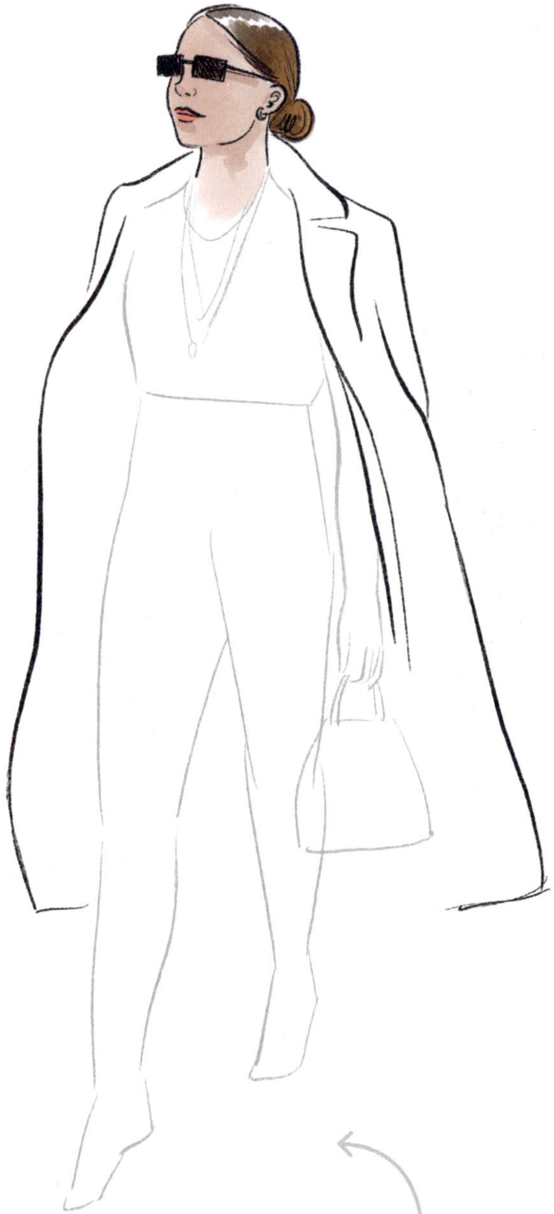

Trace as many layers as you like under this model's oversize coat. Play with complementary colors, or try a monochromatic approach.

Now design your own layered look!

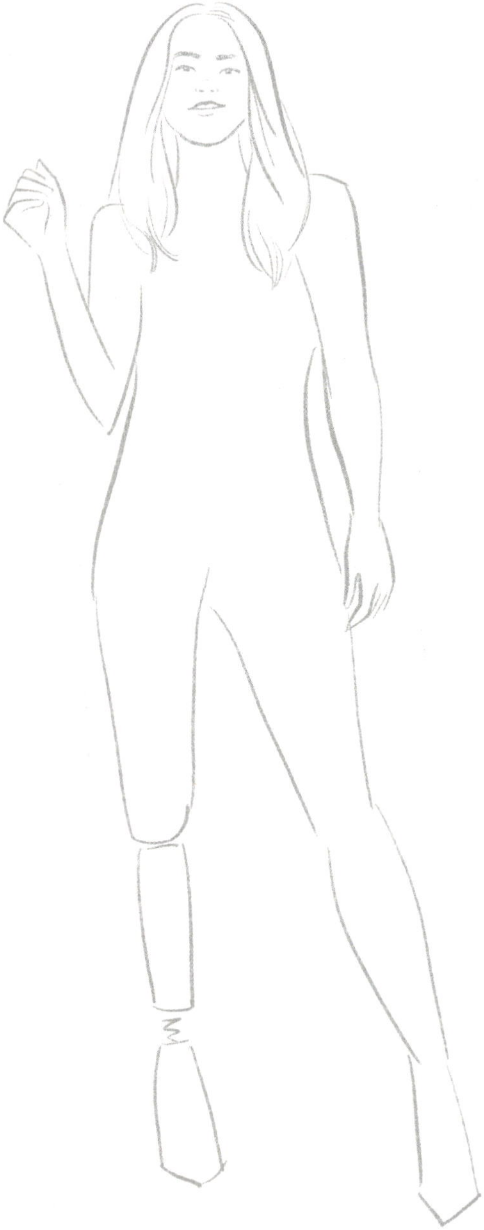

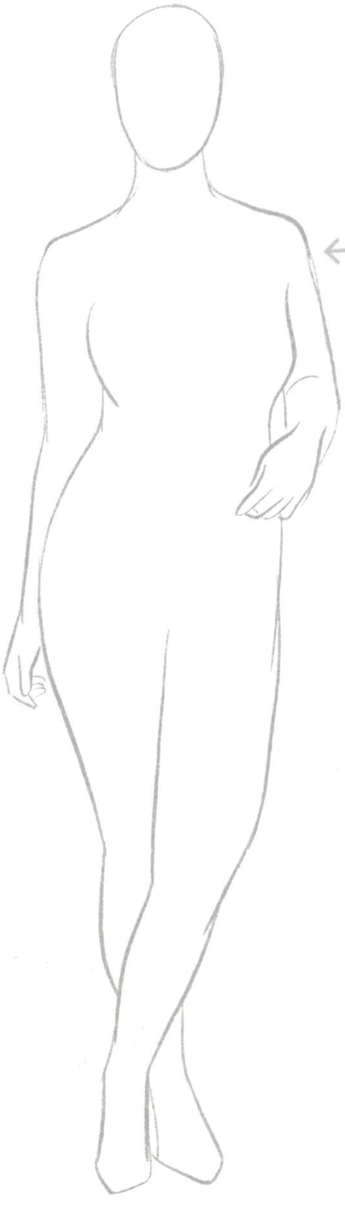

Design a multilayered outfit for this model. Remember to pile on the accessories as well as the clothes!

Layer up your jewelry, too!

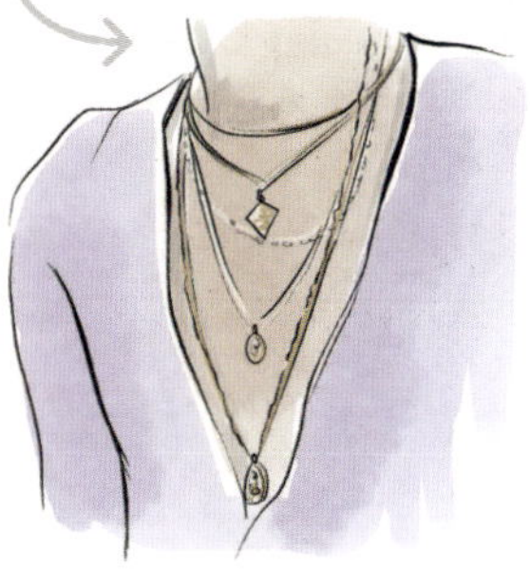

Artisan Crafts

Today's TikTokers' obsession with handcrafted pieces and DIY fashion shows us the power of Artisan and Craft fashion. These looks celebrate the beauty and skill of handmade production, showcasing the diverse techniques of different cultures and communities. This fashion style takes a modern, ethical approach to address the industry's long-standing reputation for cultural appropriation in favor of genuine co-creation and appreciation. A new generation of designers have set out to support the livelihoods and traditions of local artisans, who create high-quality and sustainable garments with care and attention to detail.

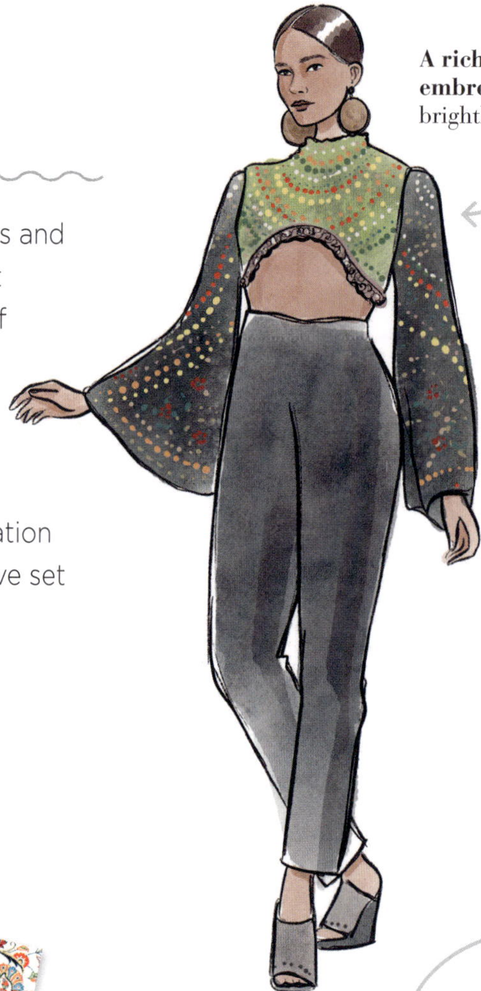

A richly embroidered, brightly colored top.

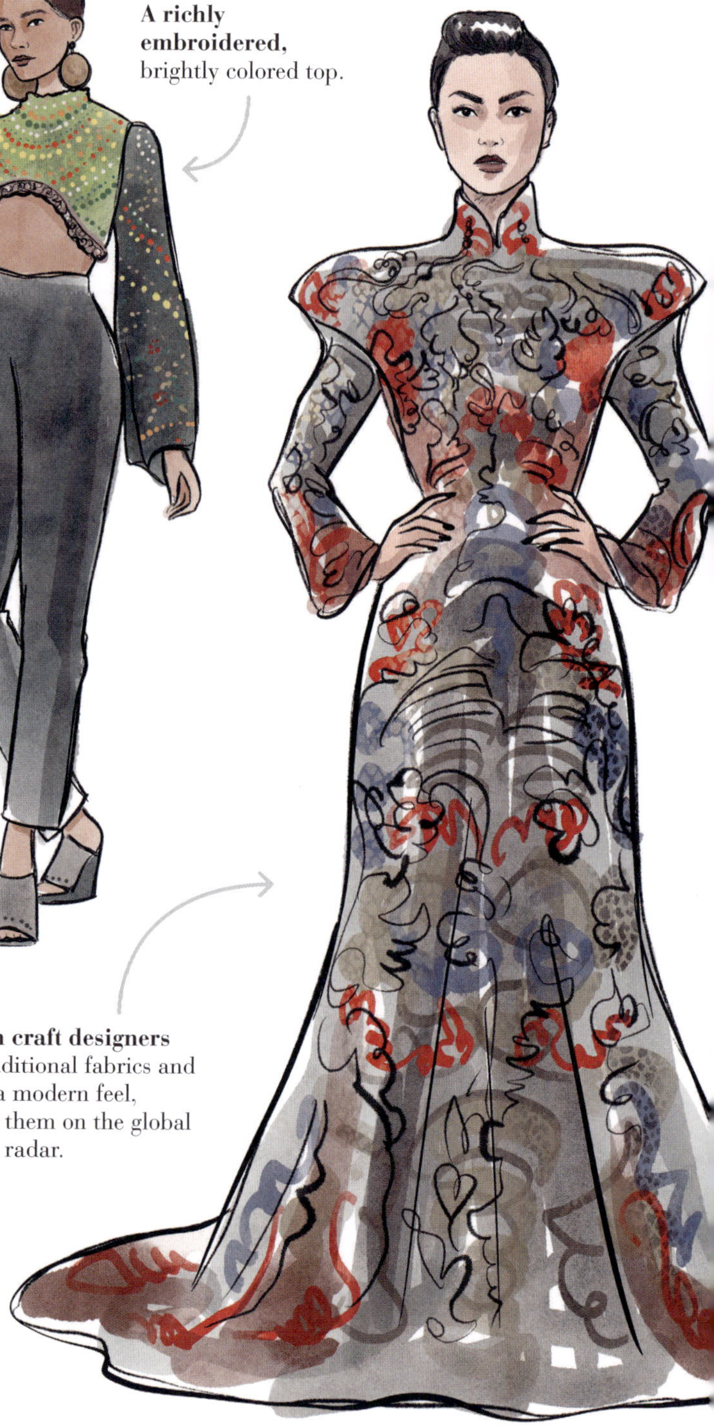

Artisan craft designers give traditional fabrics and motifs a modern feel, placing them on the global fashion radar.

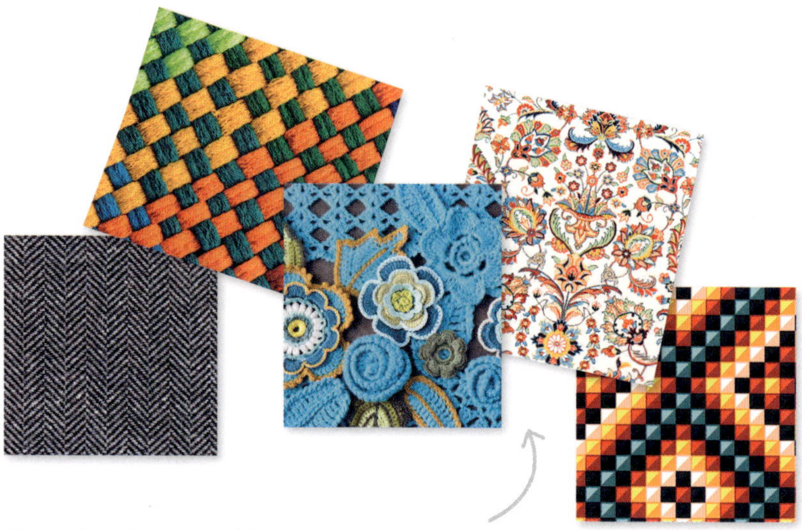

Natural and sustainable materials, such as cotton, wool, or silk, often feature in Artisan Craft fashion, decorated with beads and embroidery.

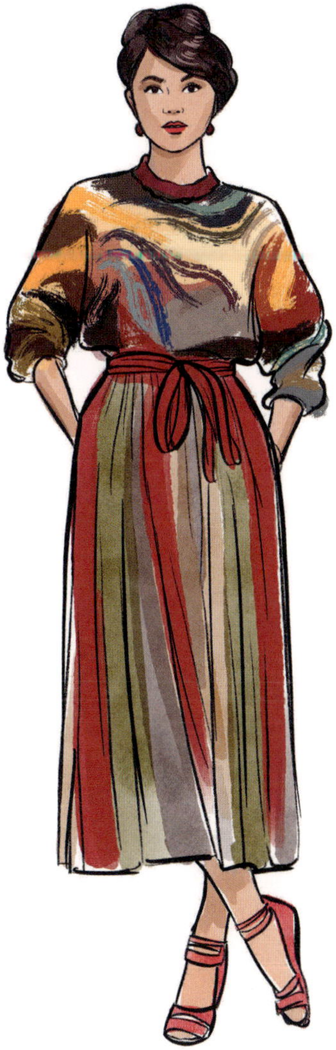

Gorgeous earthy tones and materials bring an artisan feel to a modern cut.

Natural dyes on handwoven fabrics celebrate ancient techniques while feeling contemporary and comfortable.

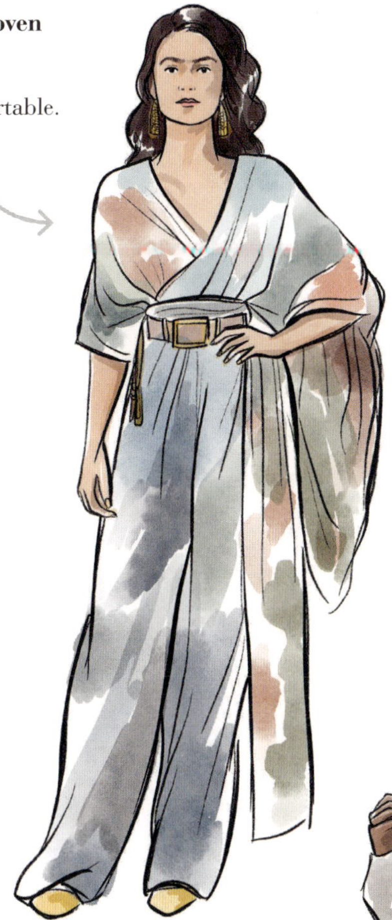

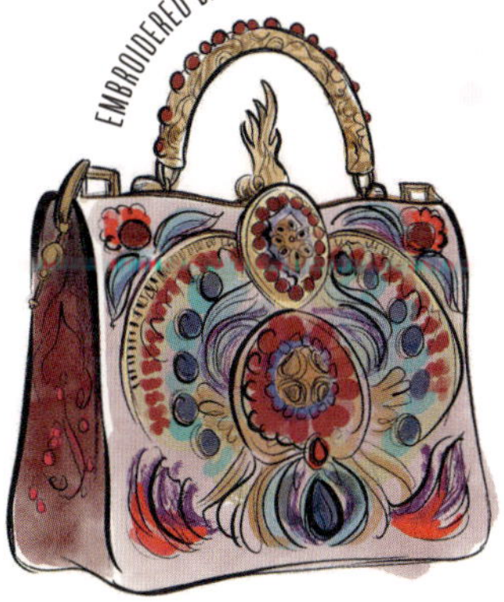

Traditional draped skirt mixed up with a street style look.

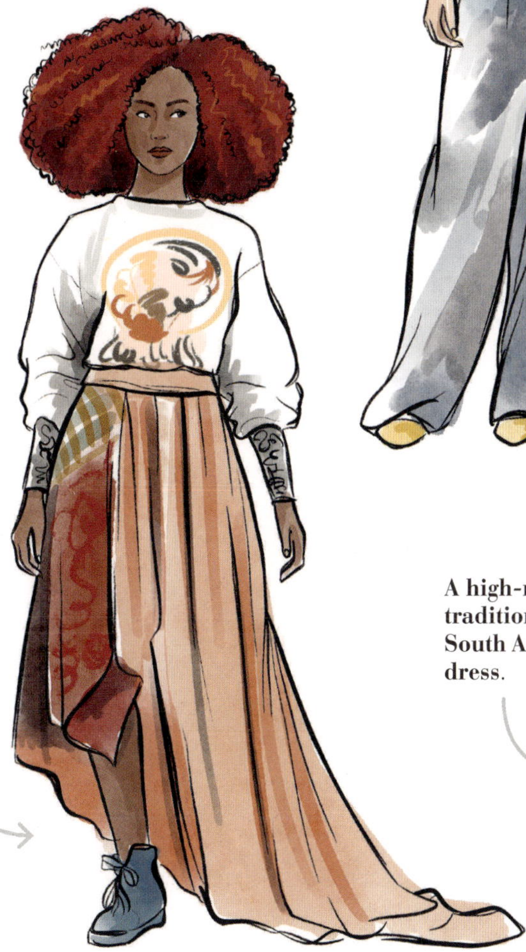

A high-necked traditional South Asian dress.

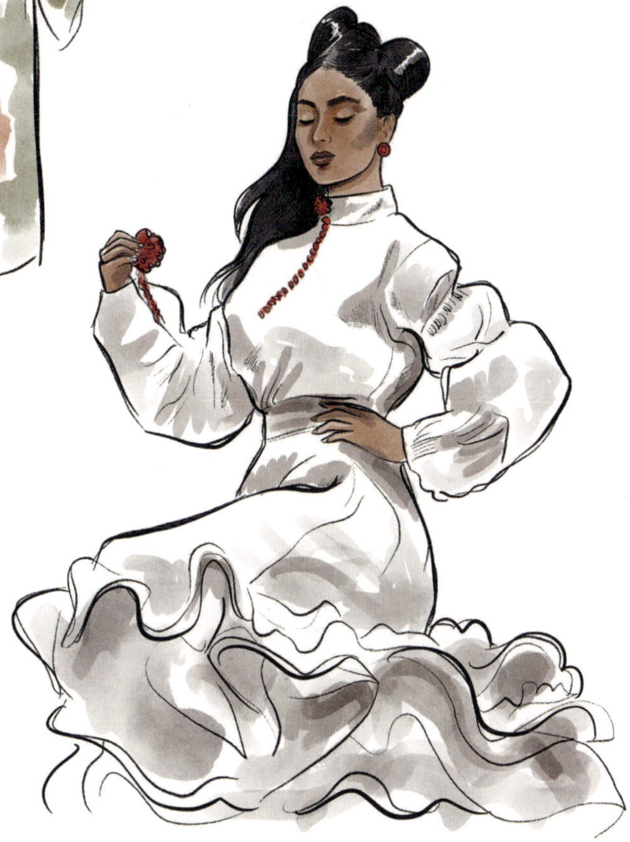

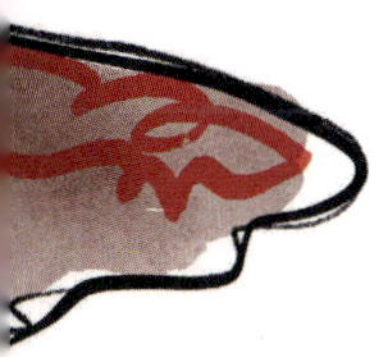

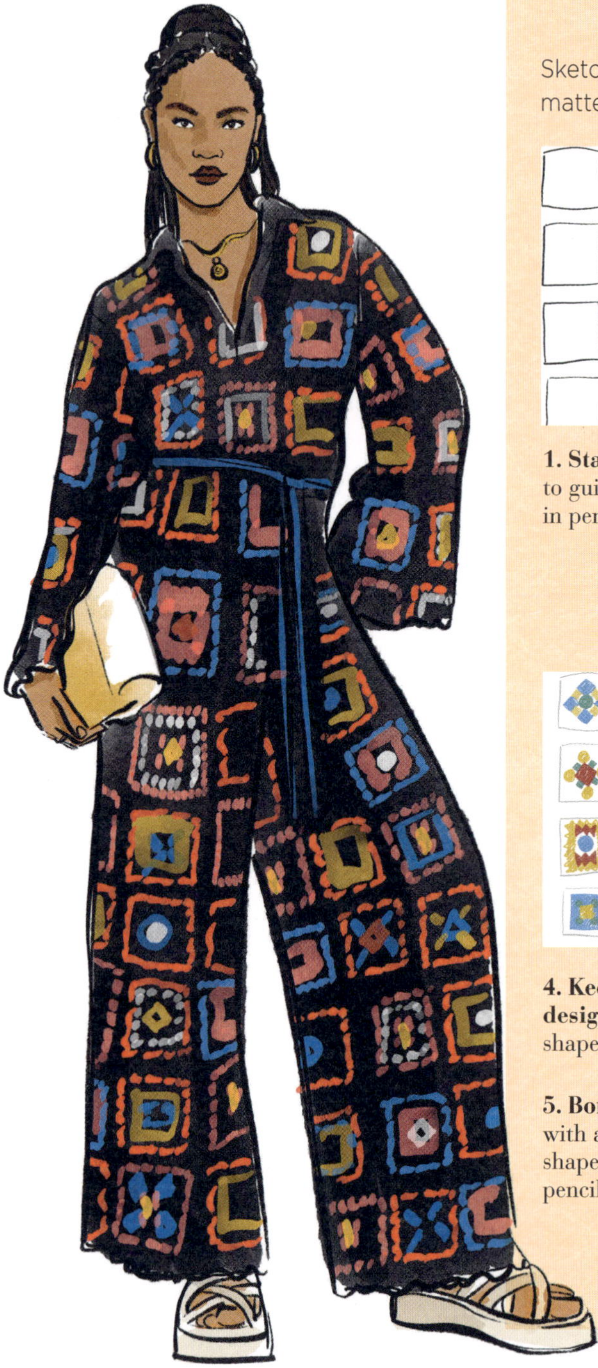

CREATING YOUR OWN PATCHWORK PATTERN

Sketch out a design or play with arrangements until a pattern emerges. Precision matters, but so does spontaneity—allow your creativity to guide your hands!

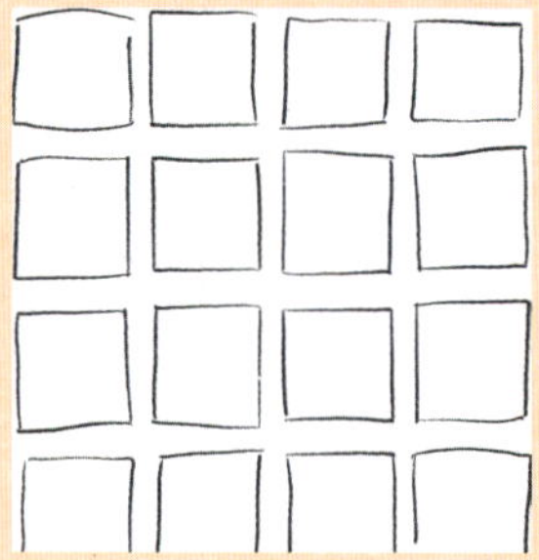

1. Start by tracing a grid to guide to your pattern in pencil.

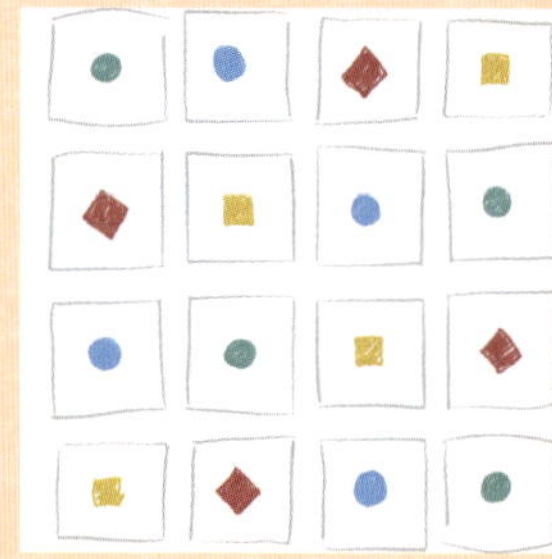

2. Draw a small, colored shape in each square. There is no rule here, but if you want to create a sense of unity in your design, replicate the same shape at regular intervals.

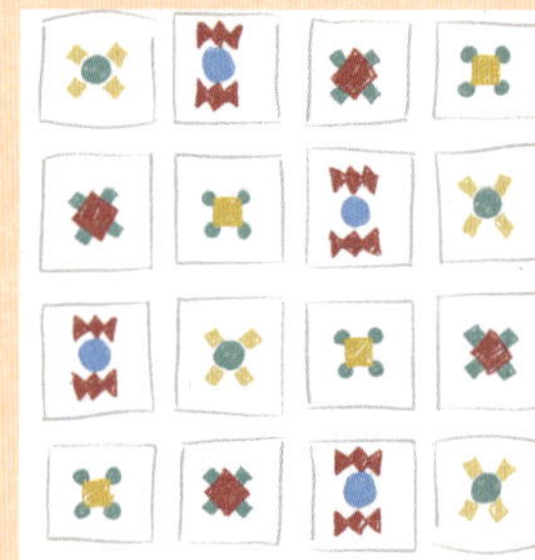

3. Add geometric shapes around each shape. You can use different ones for each shape or square if you like!

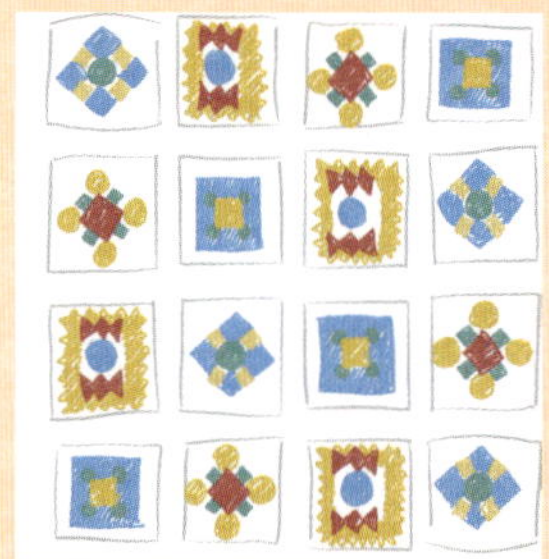

4. Keep building up the design with different shapes and colors.

5. Border each square with another series of shapes, and erase your pencil lines.

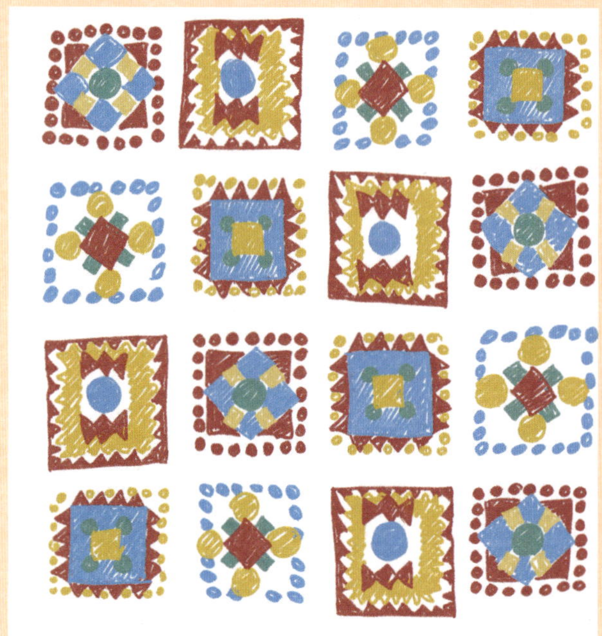

Intricate stitching in bright colors draws on the embroidering techniques in traditional Mexican dress.

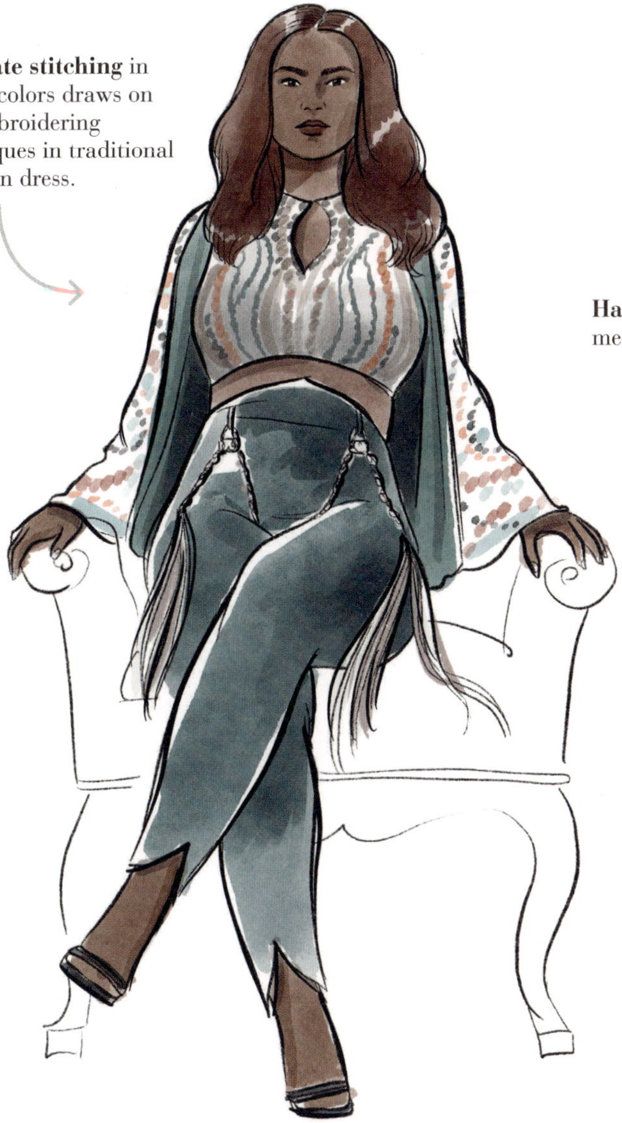

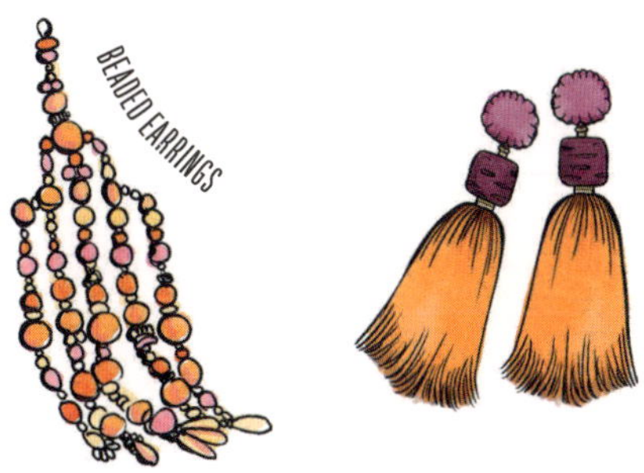

Haute couture meets Alpine lace.

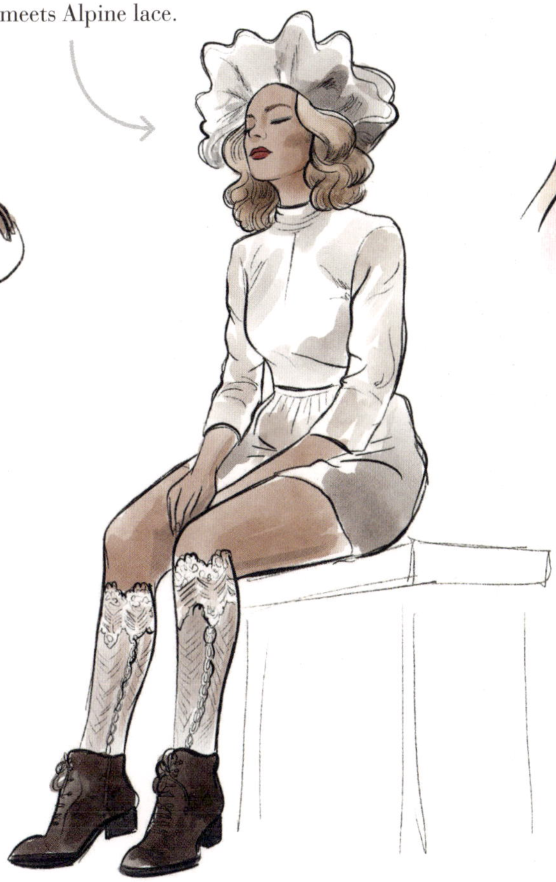

Imaginative new takes on traditional jewelry create modern, futuristic looks.

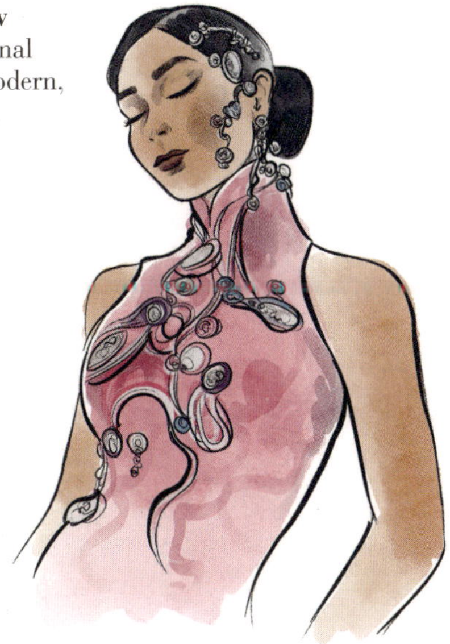

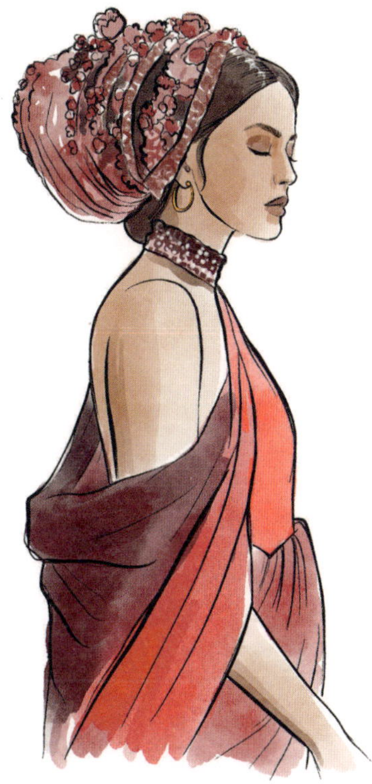

Statement accessories like this crocheted and embroidered headpiece and choker dress up a handwoven, draped style.

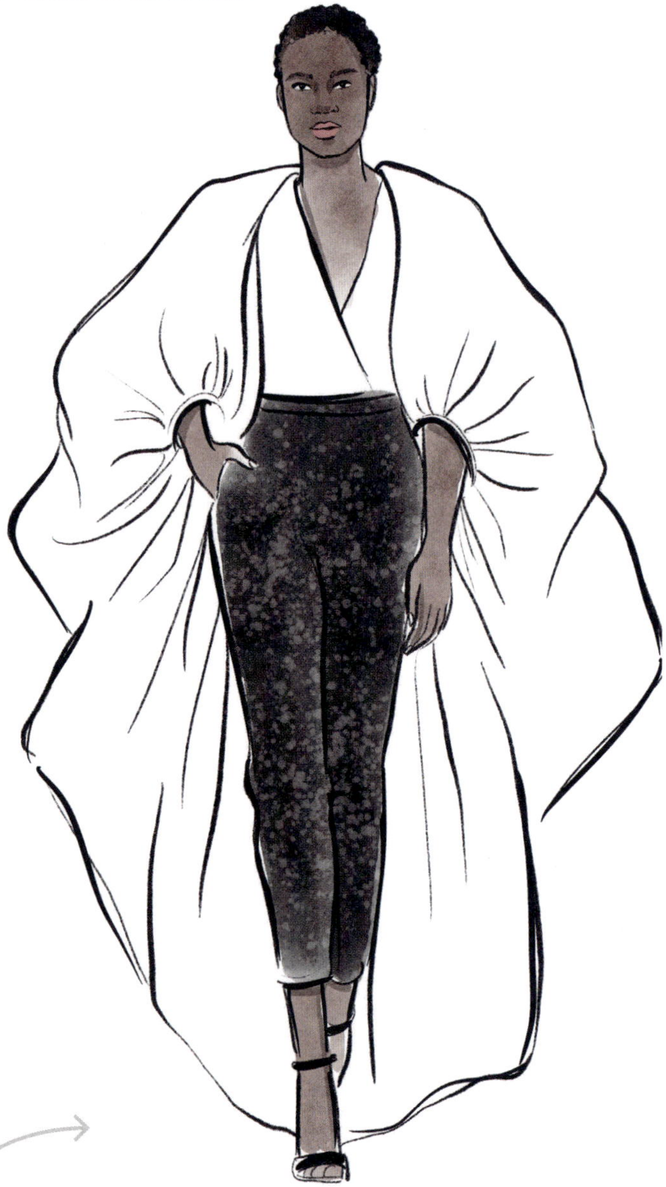

In 2021, Chloé reinterpreted a traditional poncho by designing a striped cashmere blanket on top of a puffer jacket in recycled eco-nylon. Add some texture and color to this model's poncho coat using traditional geometric patterns and vivid colors.

Can you create a beautiful embroidery pattern for this floating dress?

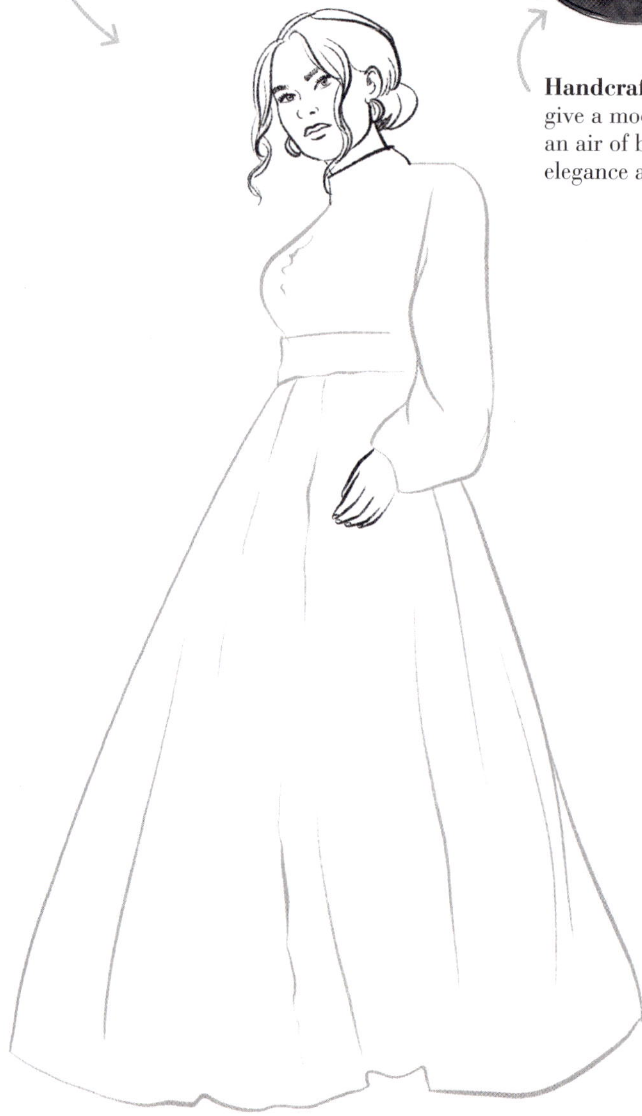

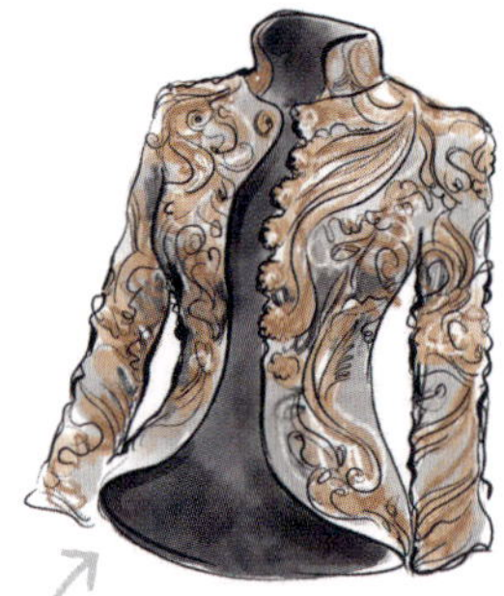

Handcrafted details give a modern jacket an air of baroque elegance and luxury.

Now design your own Artisan Craft looks. What cultures and techniques will you look to for inspiration and celebrate in your outfits? You could incorporate patchwork, tassels, crochet, quilting, lace—the possibilities are endless! Think about how the textiles are made, and how their unique character will shape your garments.

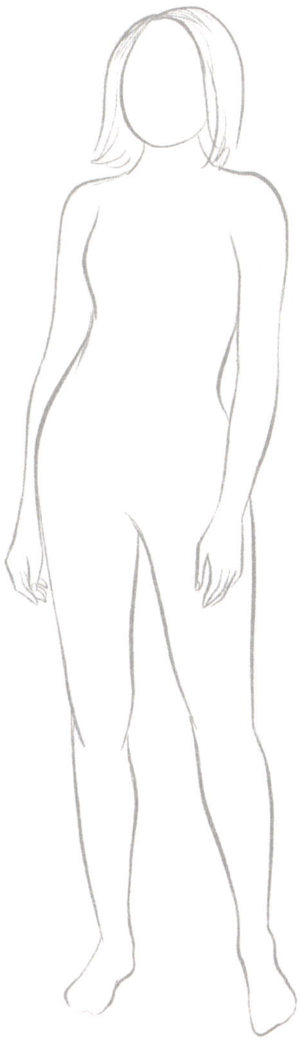

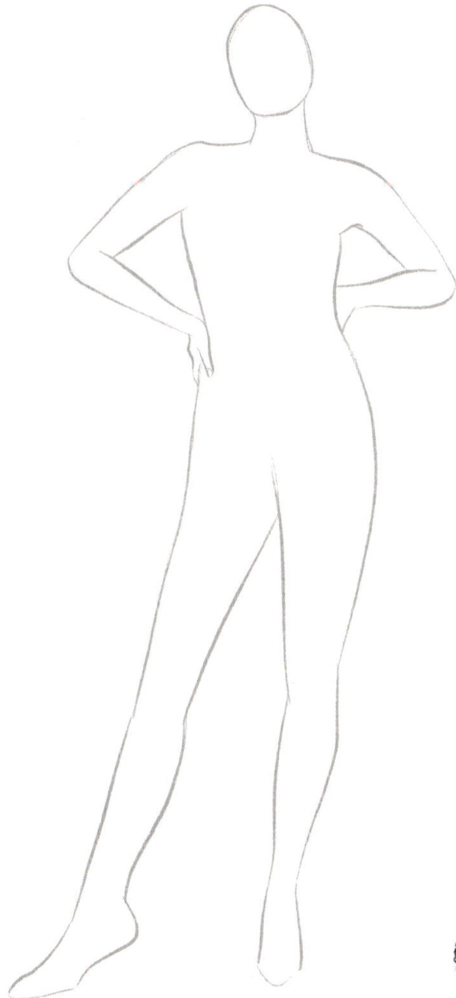

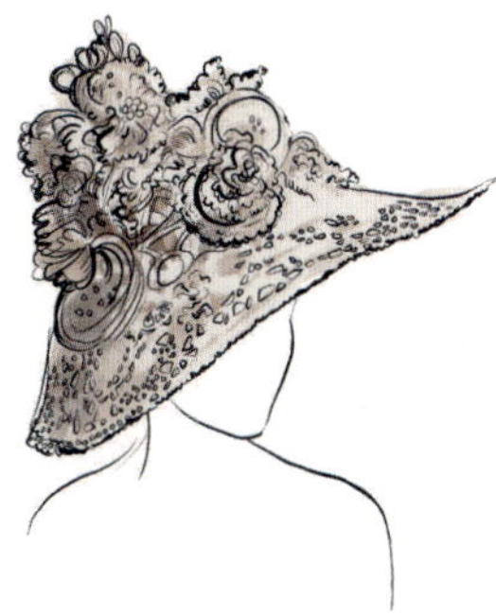

A statement hat constructed of delicate Alpine lace.

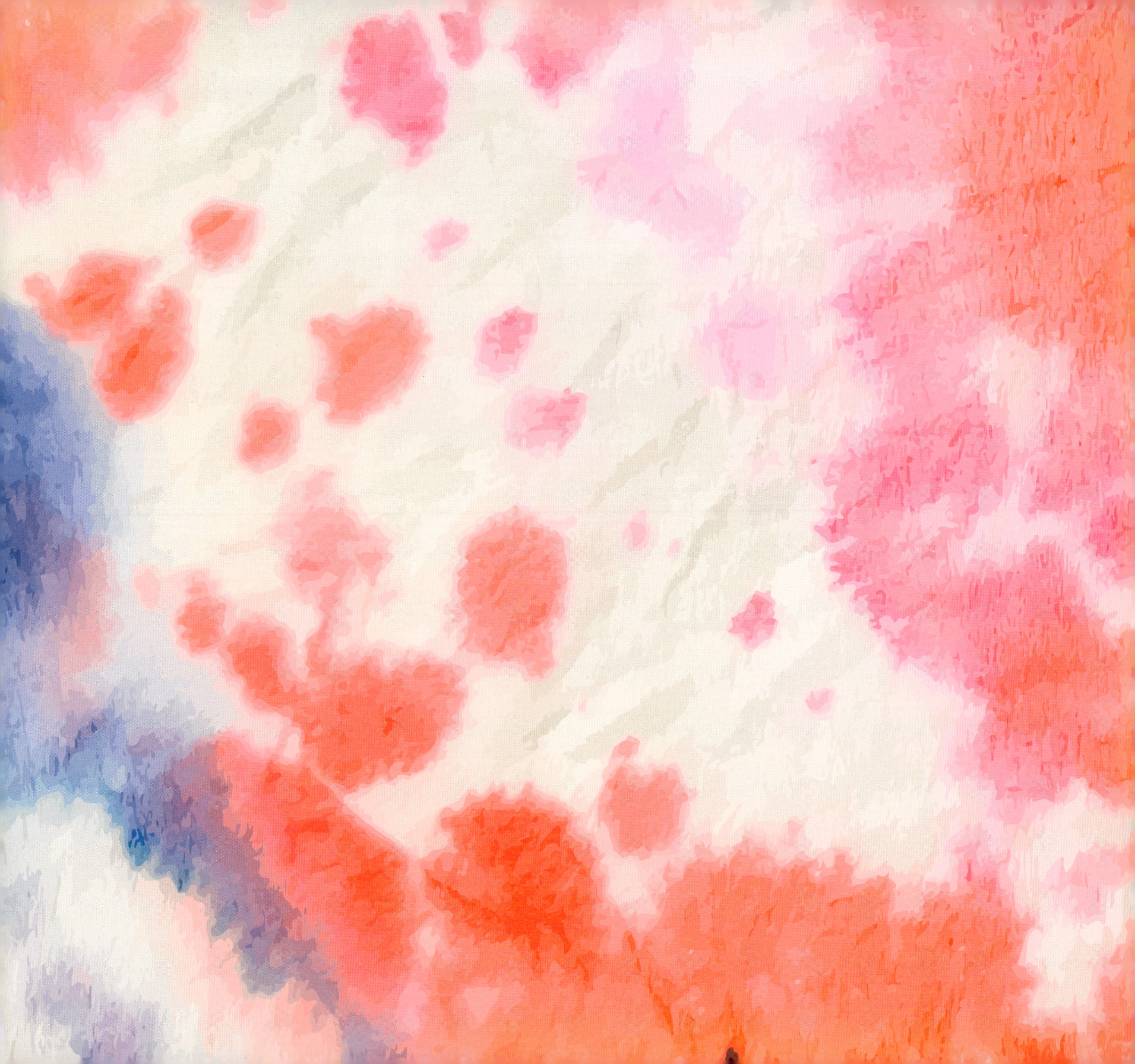

PART THREE

STYLE JOURNAL

Use this section to keep a visual diary of the styles you love from season to season. Fashion can reflect the trends and influences of the times, as well as your own personal taste and expression. Explore different colors, fabrics, and styles to suit every season, and record your favorite looks throughout the year!

Spring

Spring is the perfect season to inject some new life into your wardrobe and try out new styles. Experiment with layering as a practical and fun way to deal with the changing weather. Classic pastel tones like lilac, mint, lemon, and peach celebrate the soft and sweet colors of spring and will feel like a breath of fresh air after the dark winter season!

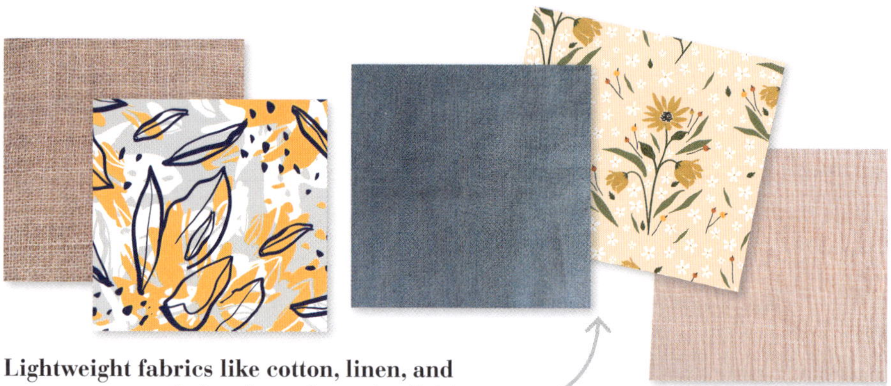

Lightweight fabrics like cotton, linen, and rayon are great choices for spring attire. Pairing cotton tops with jeans or linen pants creates casual spring outfits.

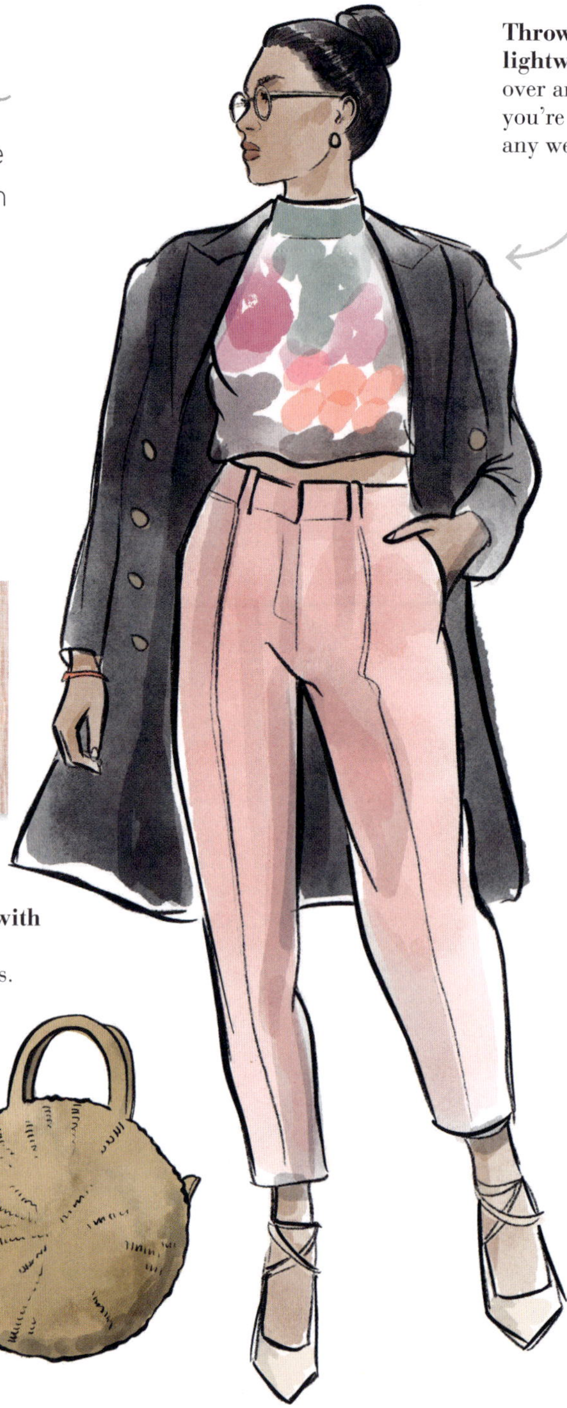

Throw a lightweight coat over an outfit so you're ready for any weather!

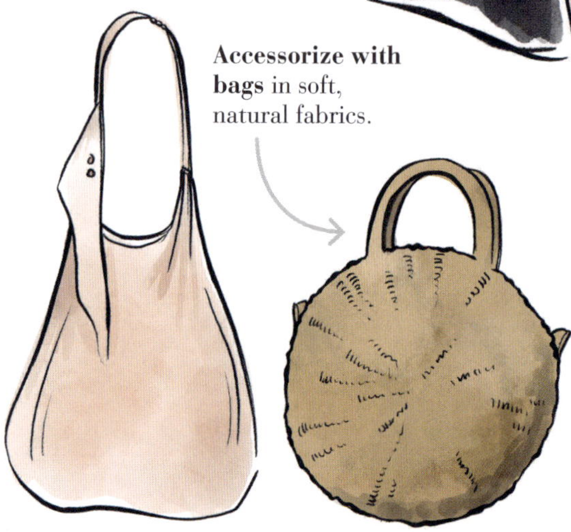

Accessorize with bags in soft, natural fabrics.

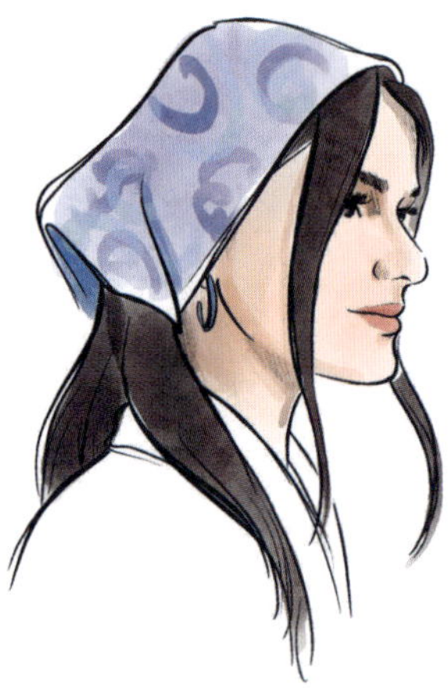

Pastels are perfect for a spring look.

Design your own spring collection! Look back at your favorite styles for inspiration.

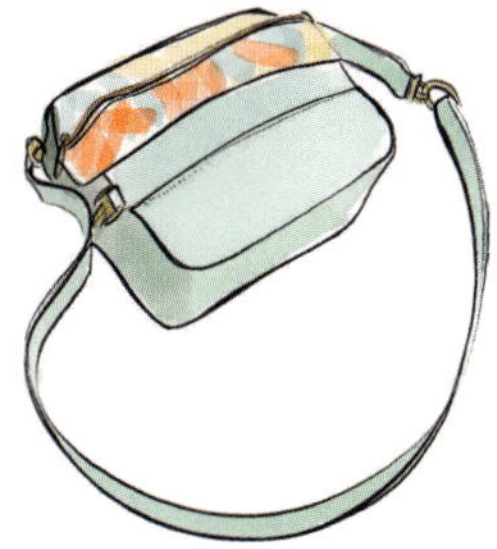

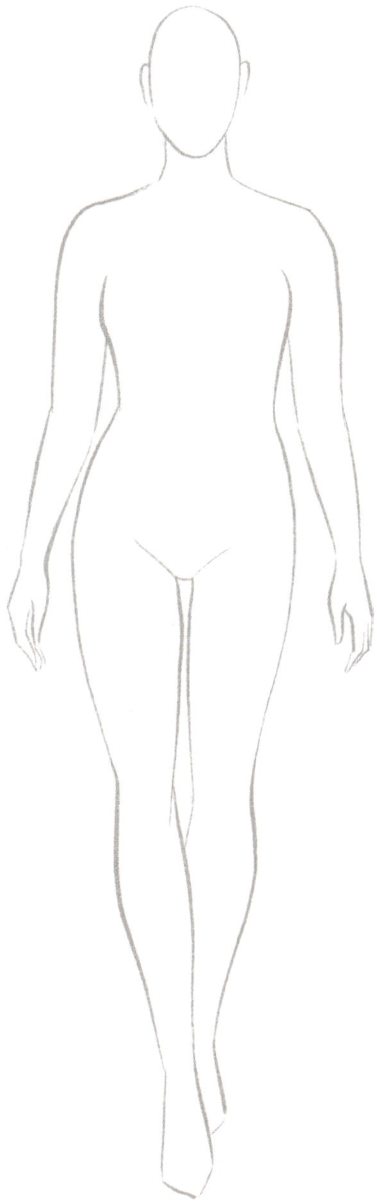

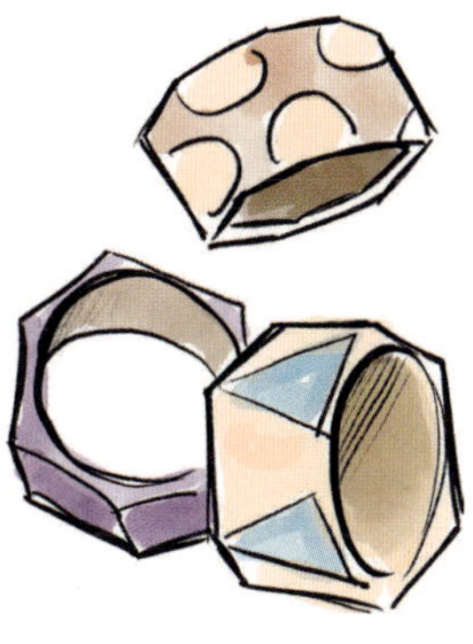

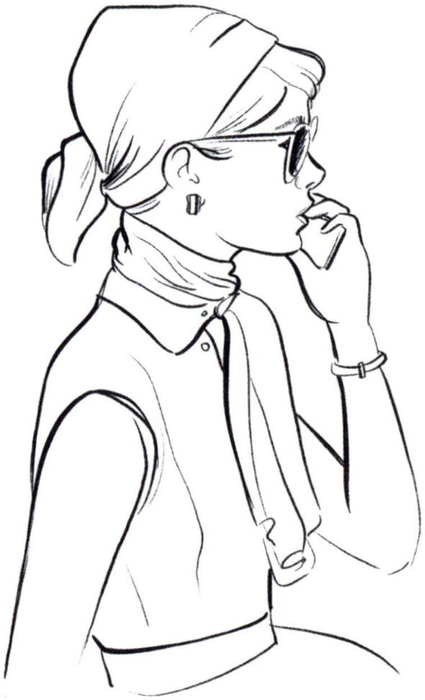

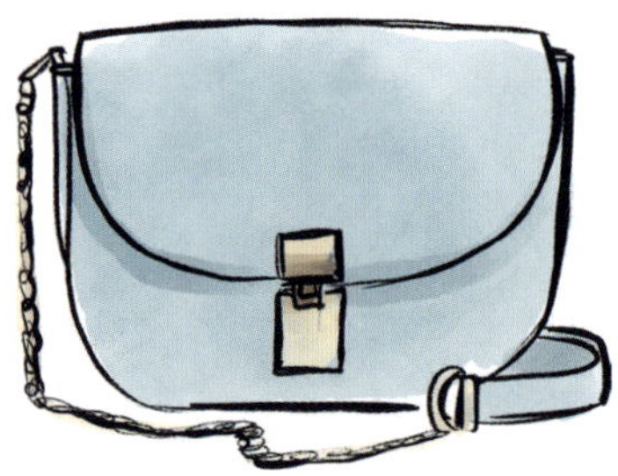

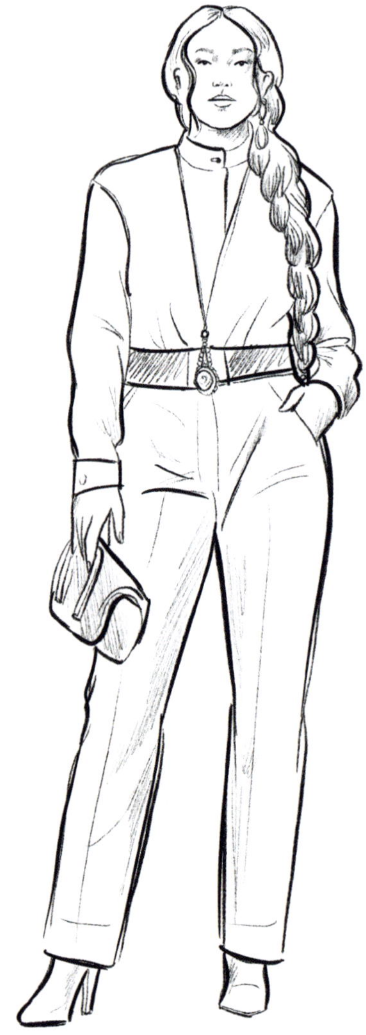

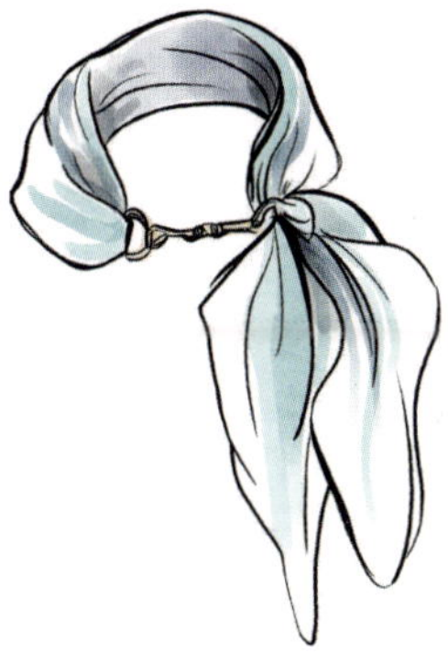

STYLE JOURNAL

DATE:

LOCATION:

INSPIRATION:

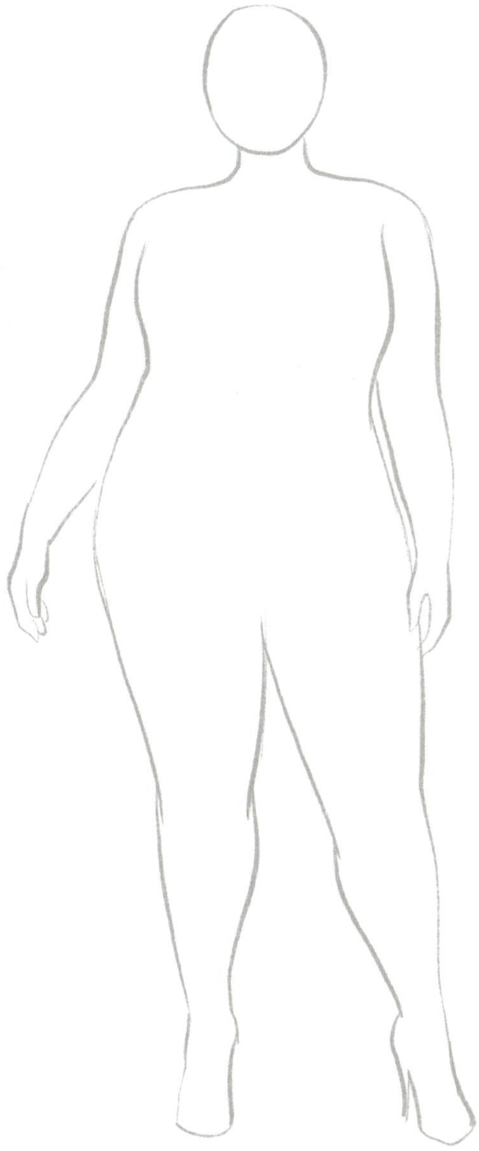

Summer

A summer wardrobe should always be fun and colorful! Pick bright and cheerful hues, such as white, yellow, pink, or blue. They will reflect the light and make you look fresh and radiant. Accessorize your outfit with sunglasses, hats, or jewelry to add some of your own personality to the look.

Beachwear and sunglasses are essential!

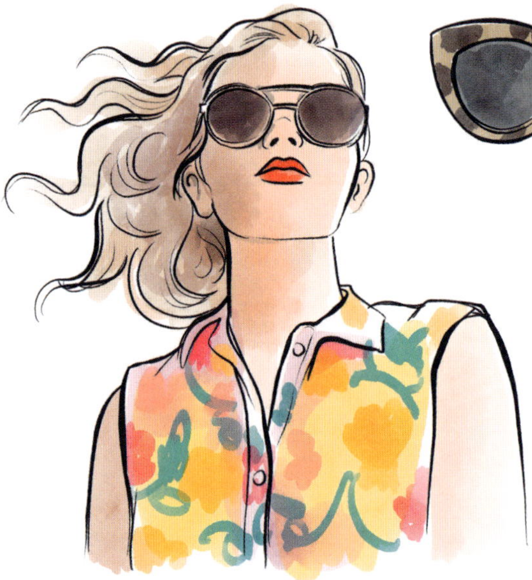

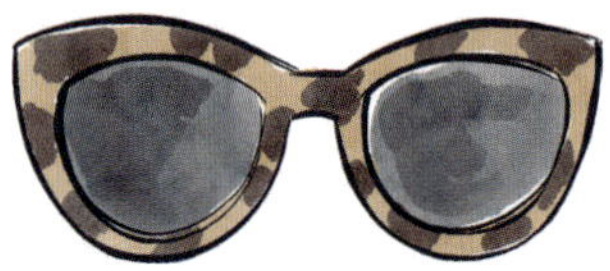

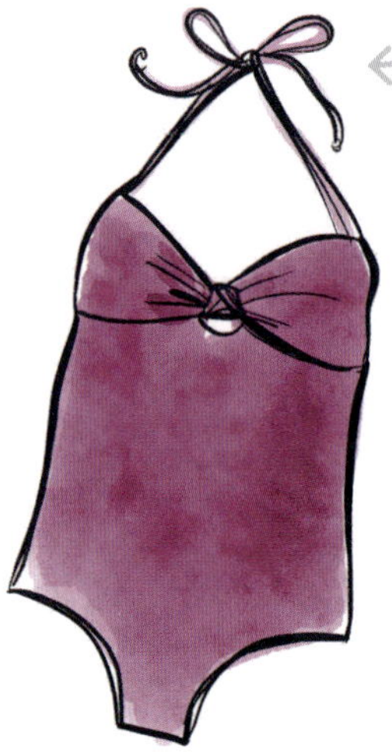

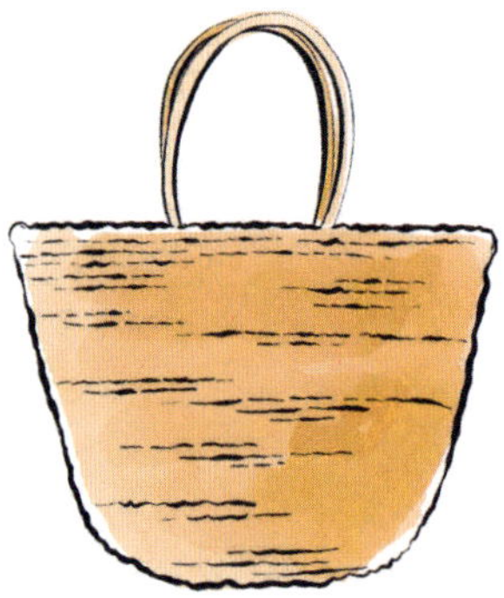

A tiered dress in a bold print shouts summer.

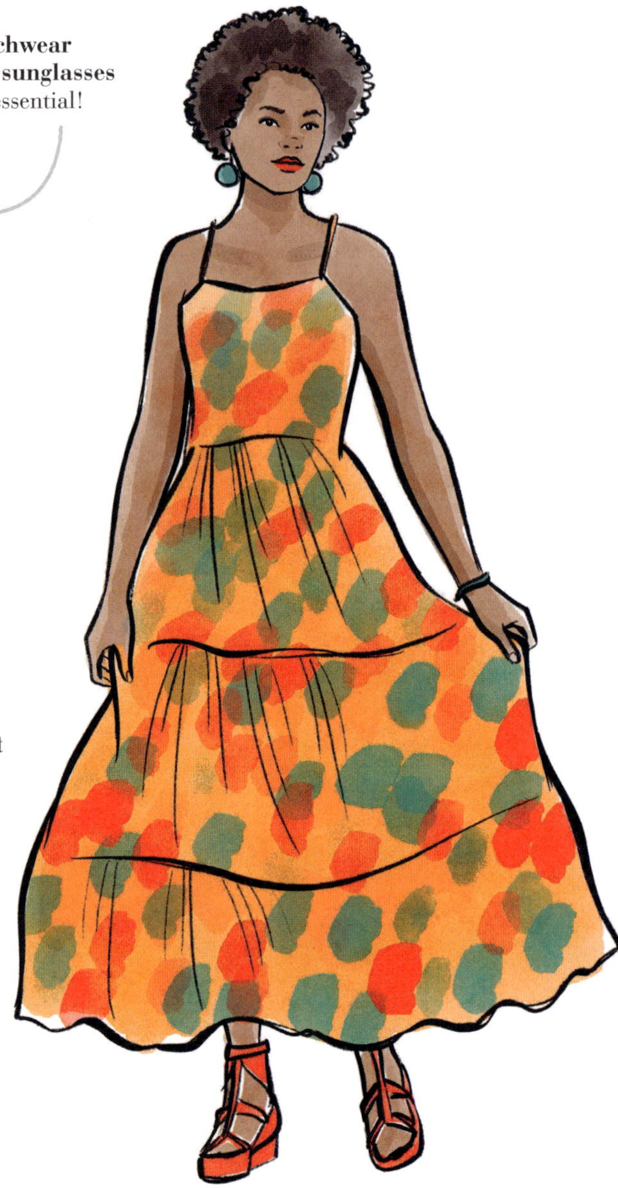

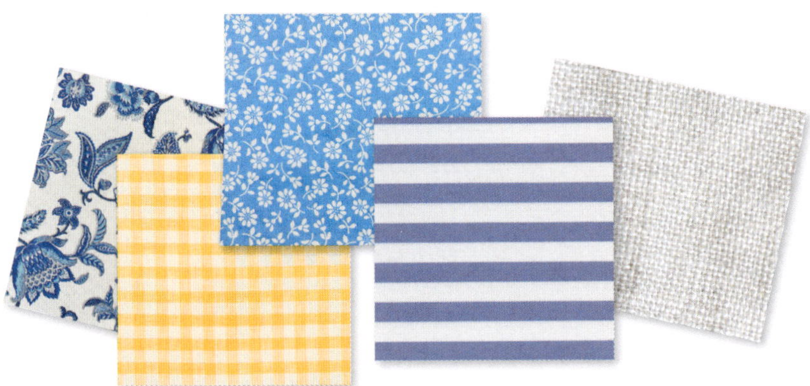

Floral prints, stripes, and gingham are great for summer, especially in lightweight fabrics like cotton.

Create your own summer looks, inspired by your favorite outfits from the book. Don't be afraid to use bold colors—take another look at the color wheels on pages 28 and 29 and experiment with complementary or analogous colors that work well together.

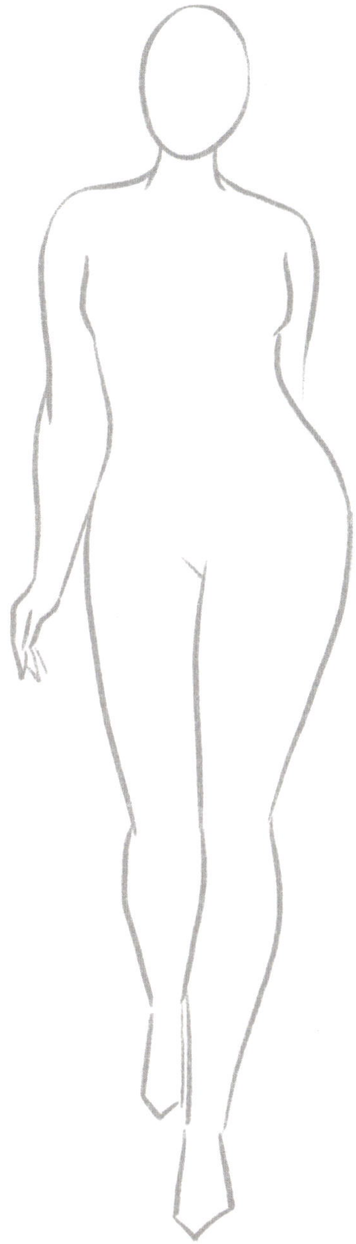

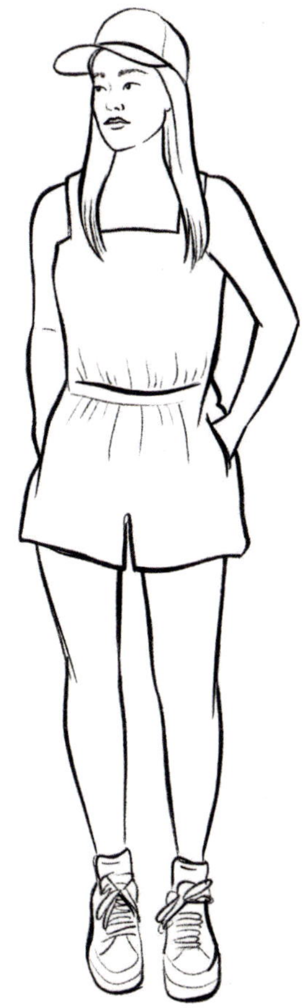

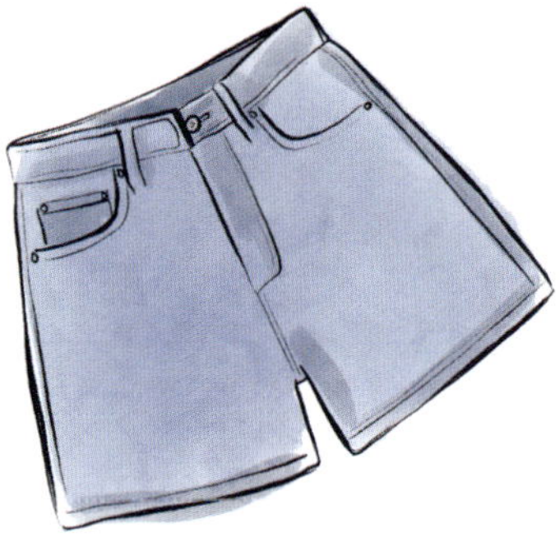

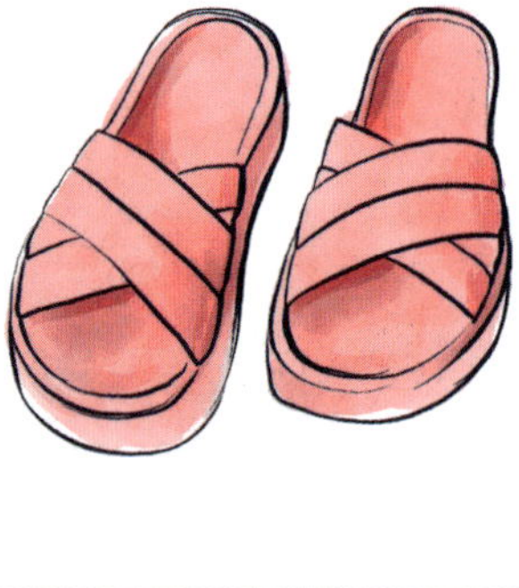

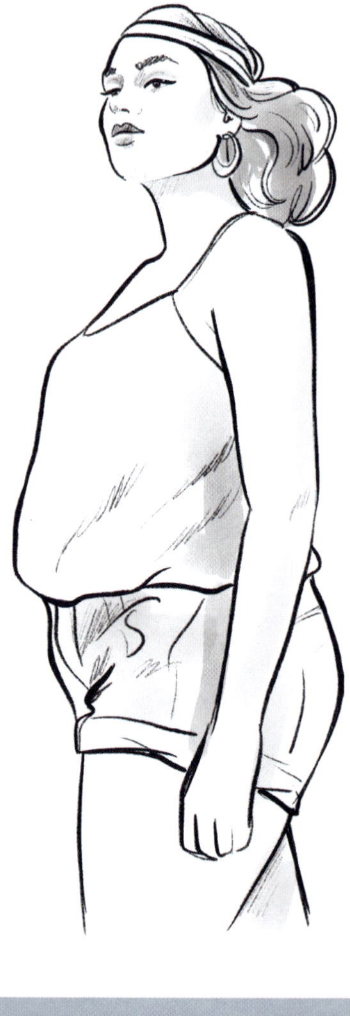

STYLE JOURNAL

DATE:

LOCATION:

INSPIRATION:

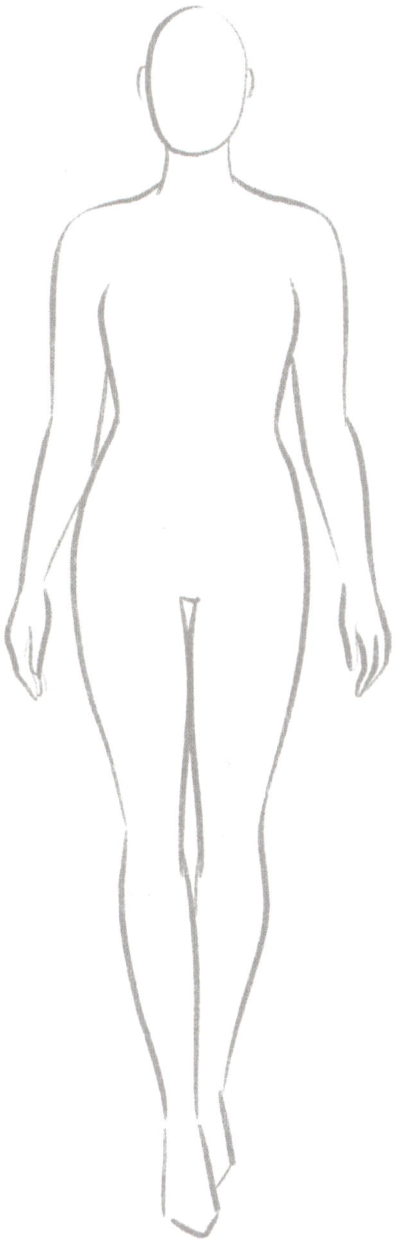

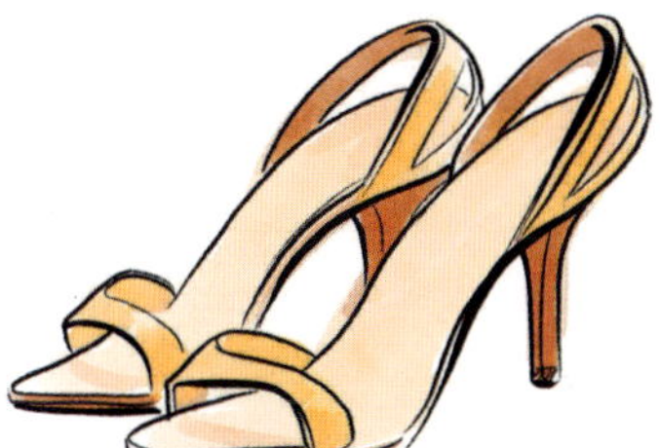

Fall

Fall is all about warm fabrics, rich and earthy colors, and layers and accessories that help an outfit adapt to the changing weather. A great way to elevate simple fall looks is to throw a long cardigan over whatever you're wearing. For an outfit that's both cosy and eye-catching, try mixing different materials and textures together. A faux leather bag is a nice way to add different layers to your look, too.

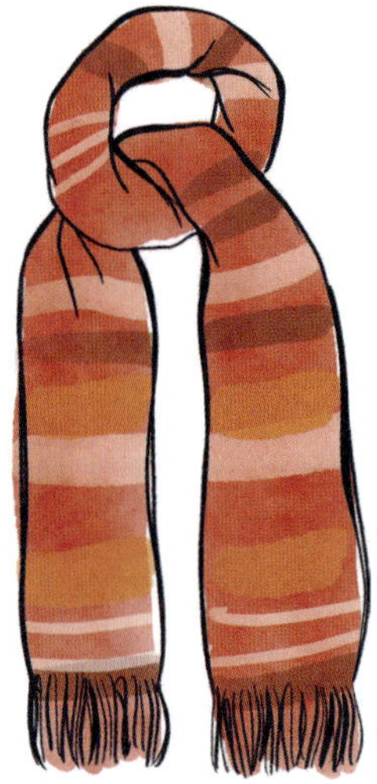

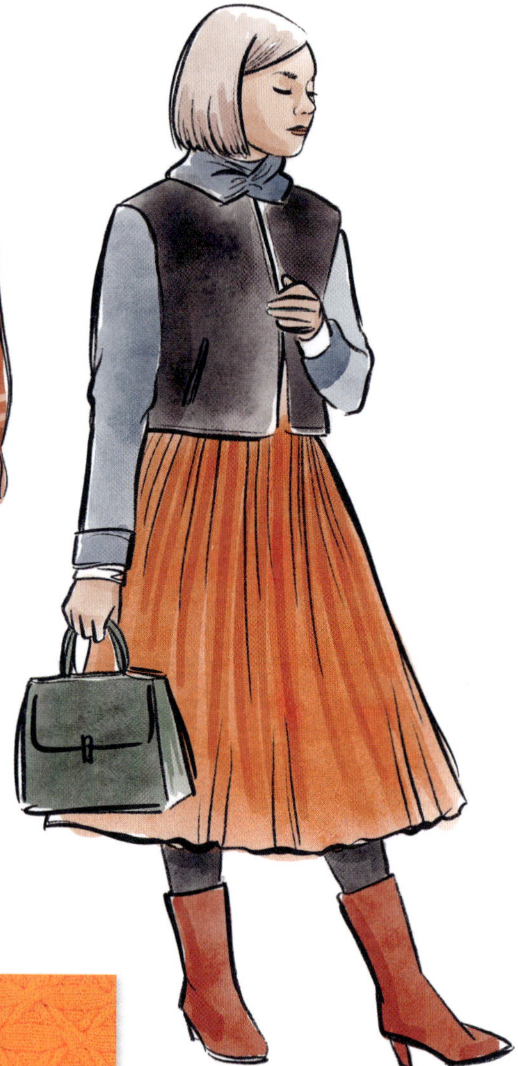

A cosy, burnt orange sweater to layer in your fall outfit.

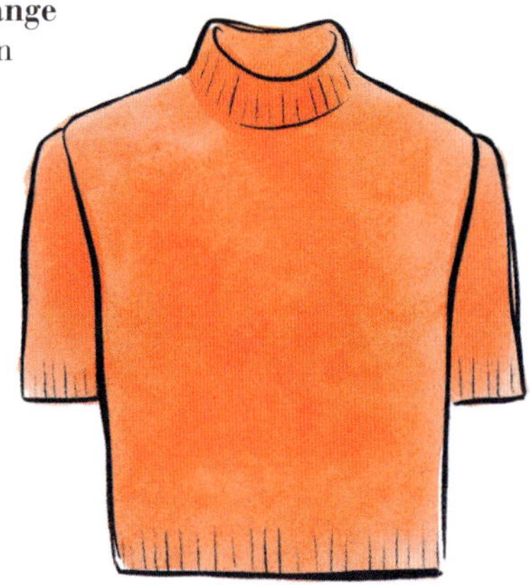

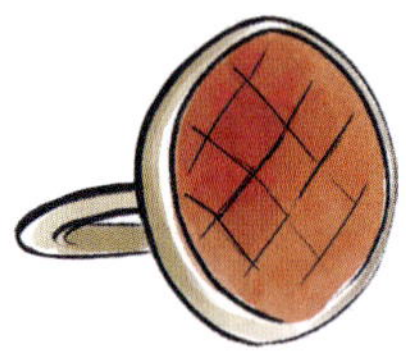

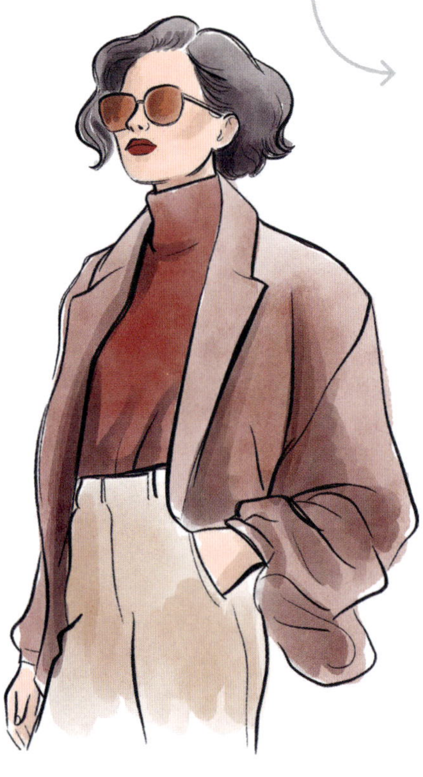

Thicker fabrics like wool and corduroy will prepare you for the fall chill. Include patterns like plaid in earthy colors.

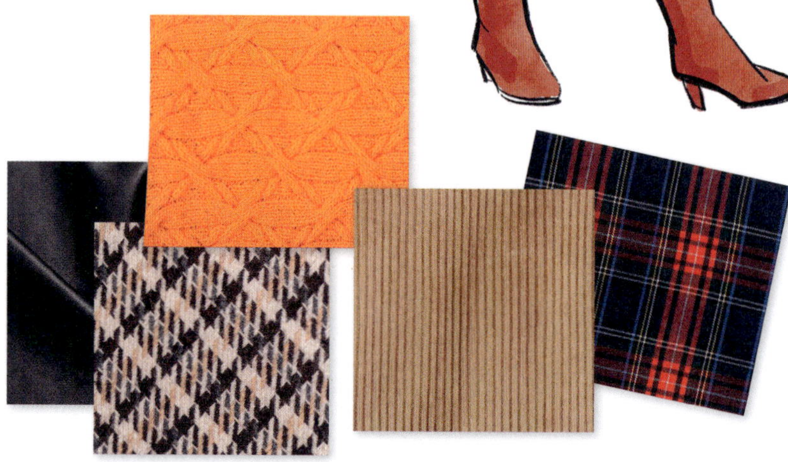

What style inspiration will you draw from for your fall wardrobe? Why not add a trench coat to whatever you're wearing—you can choose from different colors, lengths, and fabrics to suit your preference.

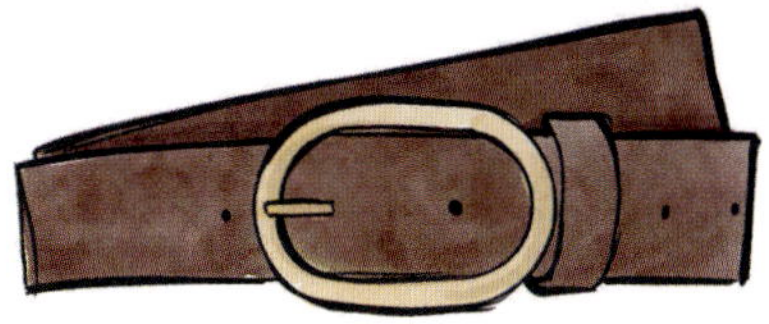

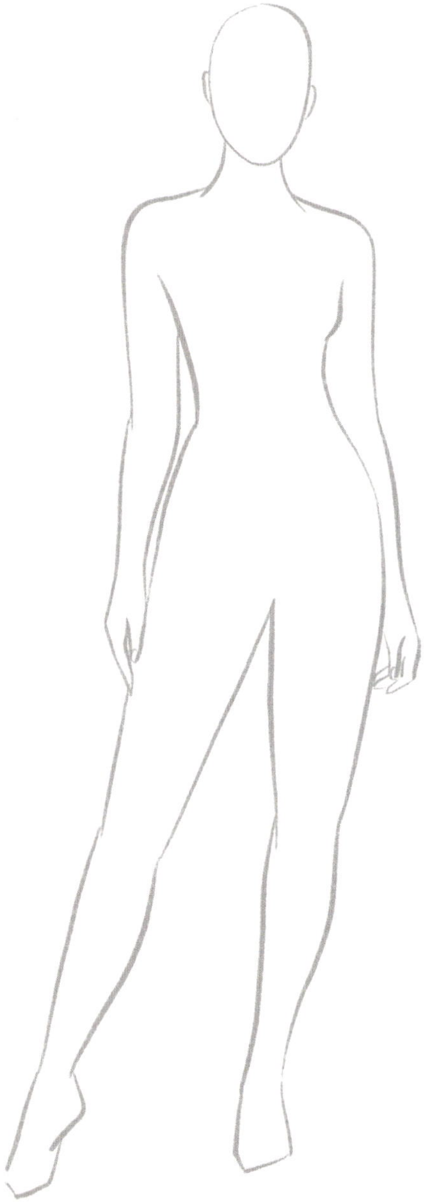

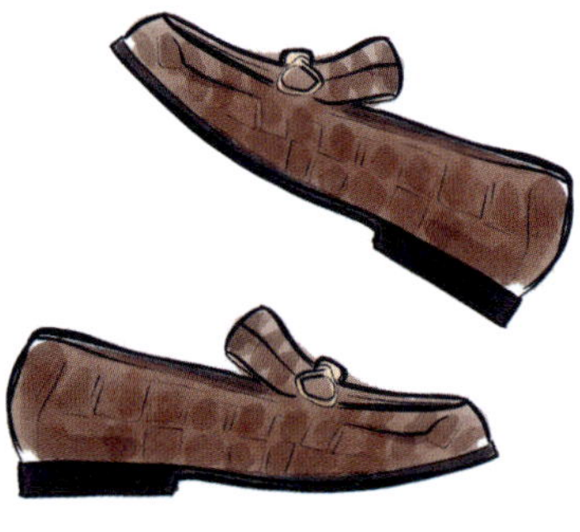

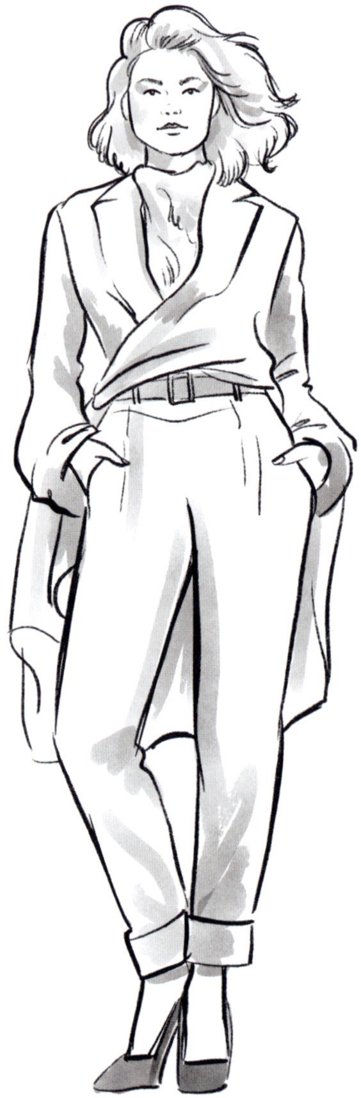

STYLE JOURNAL

DATE:

LOCATION:

INSPIRATION:

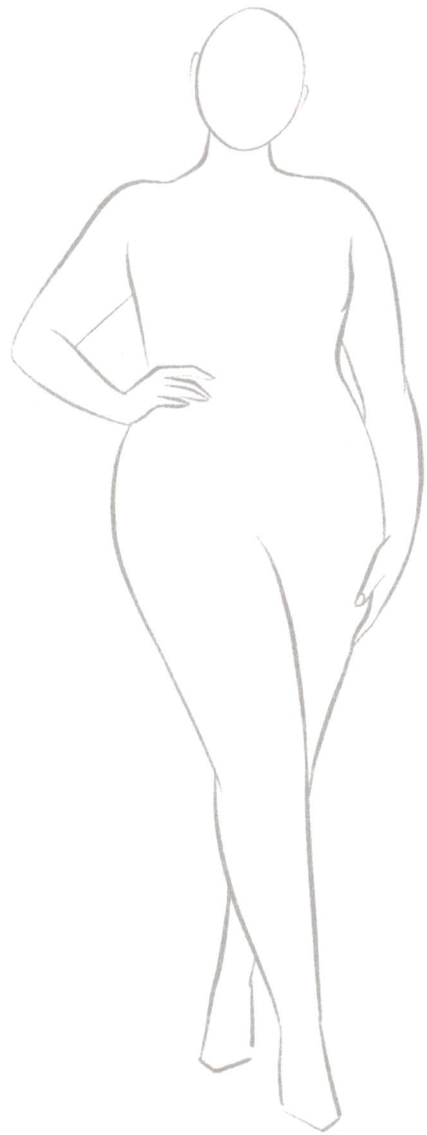

Winter

Winter is a season that requires some special attention when it comes to dressing. You want to stay warm and comfortable, but also look stylish and sharp. It's the ideal season for layering multiple garments on top of each other to create different looks and styles.

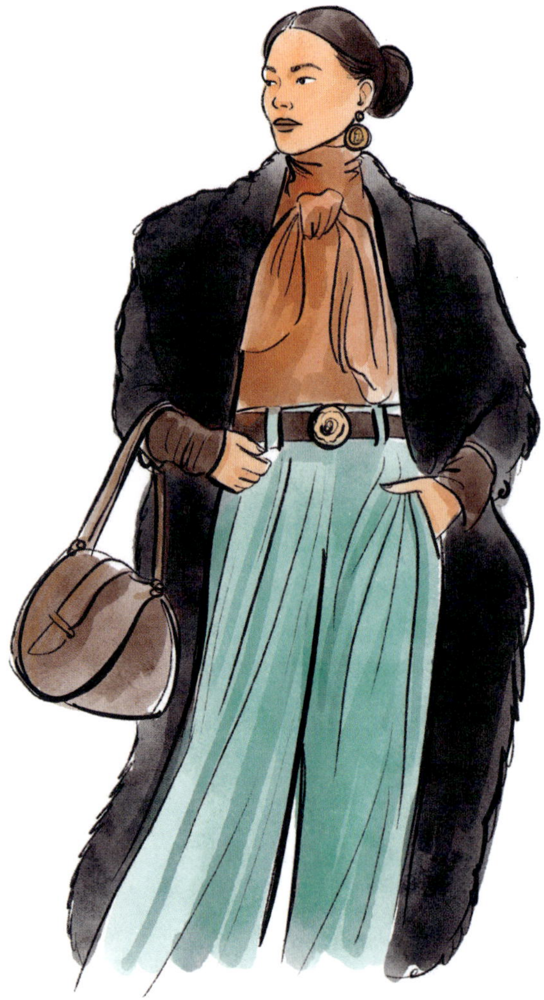

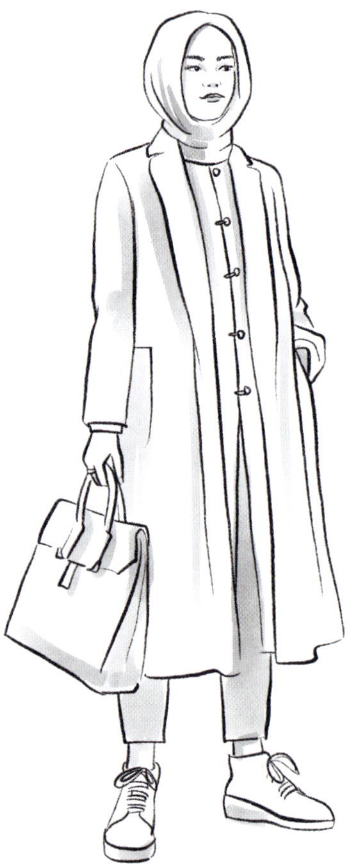

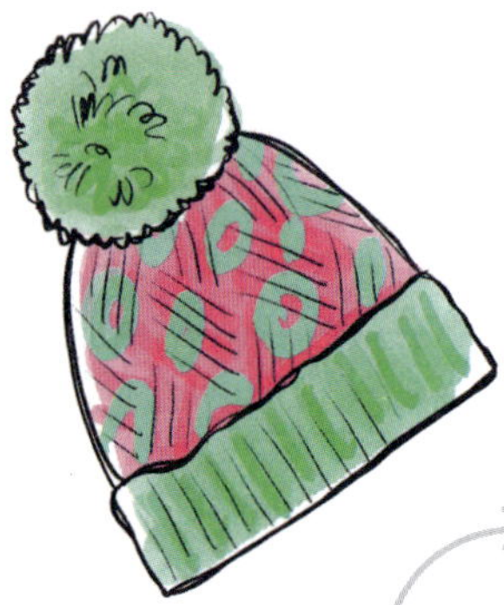

Patterned, knitted accessories add a fun touch to a winter look.

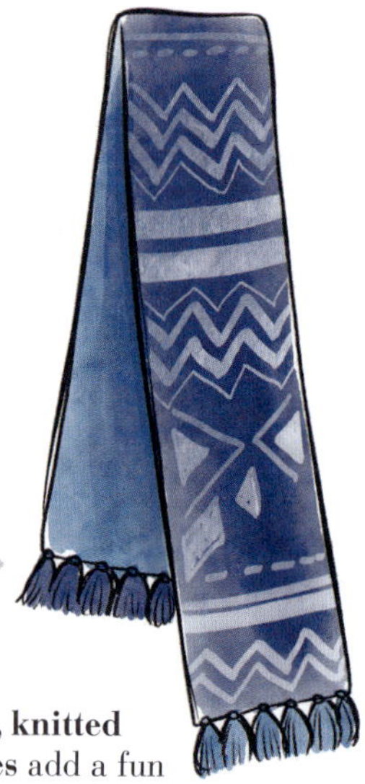

Layer rich fabrics like wool, velvet, and faux leather over each other. A classic houndstooth or cosy knit pattern will add visual interest.

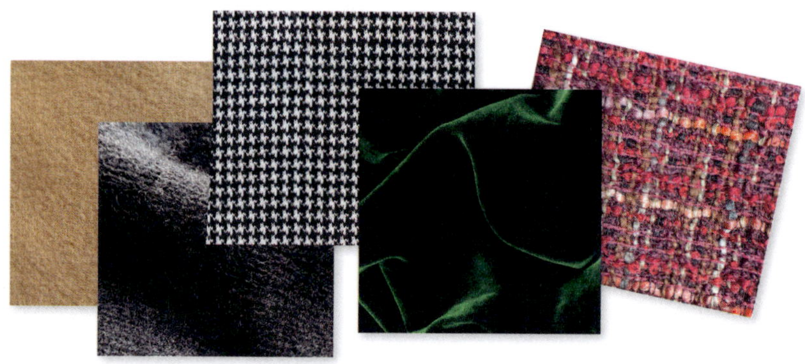

Create your own winter outfit inspired by your favorite looks from the book. Look through the Visual Glossary to find your perfect coat!

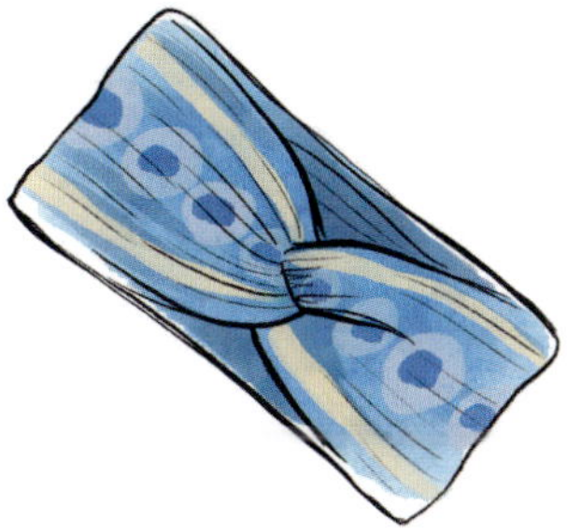

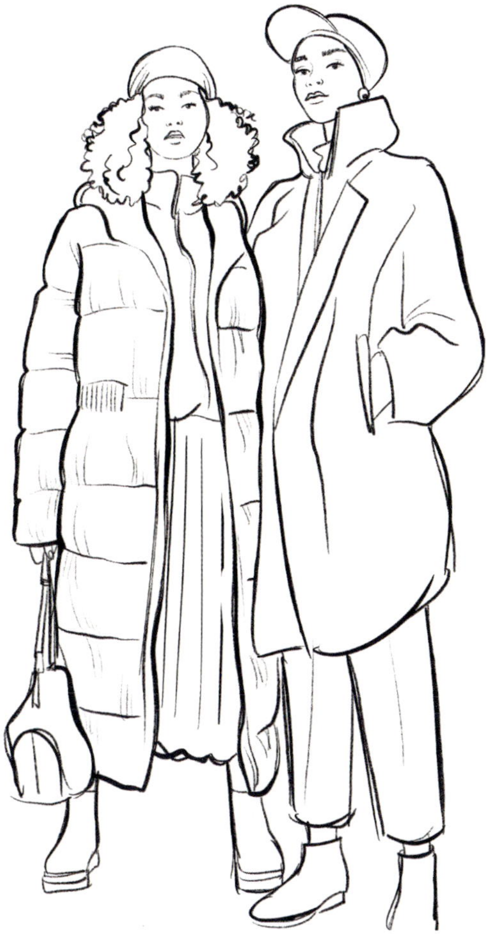

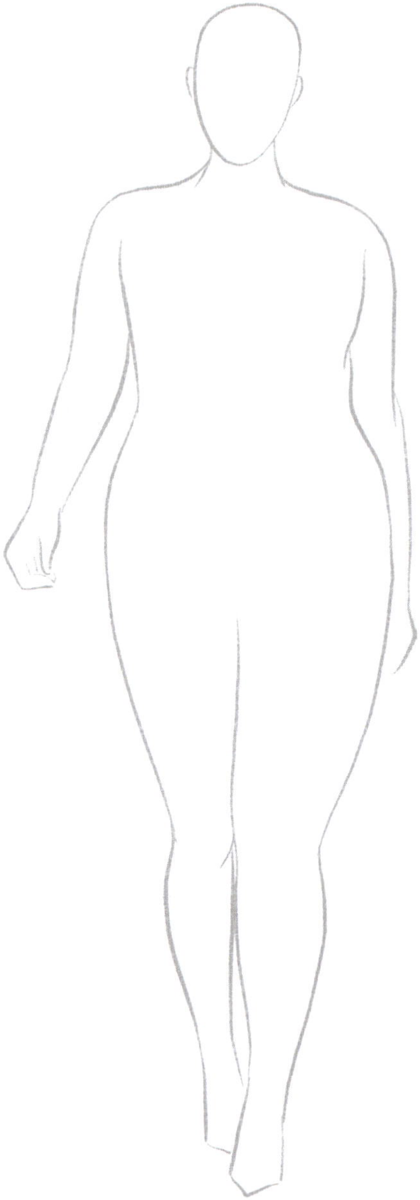

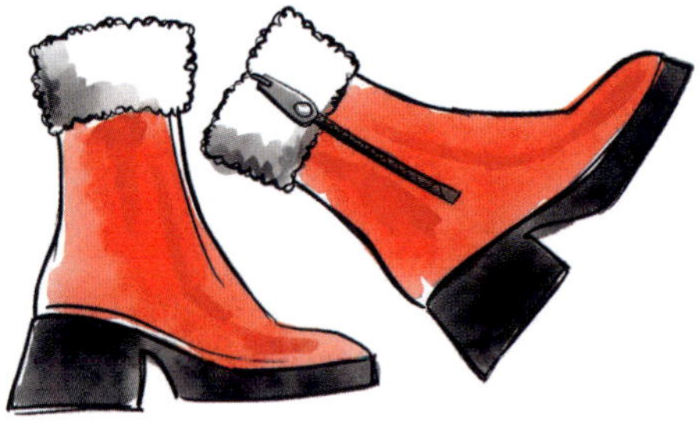

STYLE JOURNAL

DATE:

LOCATION:

INSPIRATION:

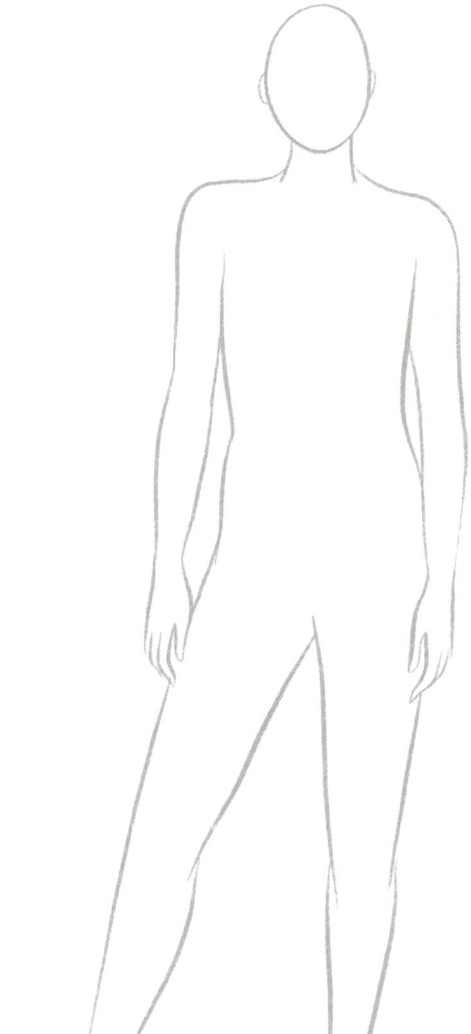

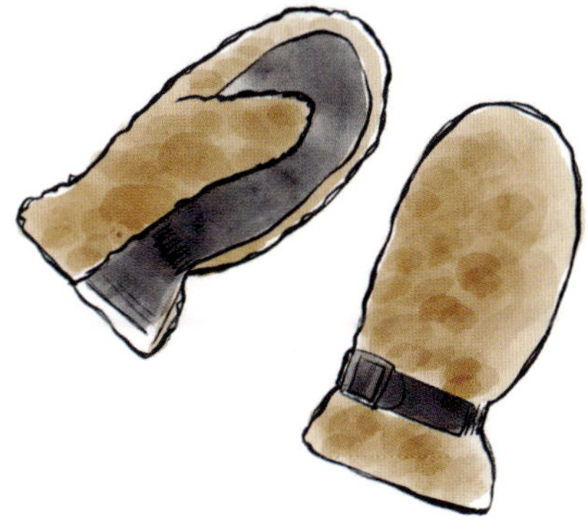

Chloe Takahashi

Chloe Takahashi is a fashion illustrator based in New York City. She is originally from Japan and has an international following.

Chloe has a unique background—she used to be a finance geek, and worked in investment banking for her earlier career. In 2019, she decided to pursue her passion for art and fashion, and made a career change to become an illustrator. After growing her Instagram community, she founded the online fashion illustration school "Chloe Takahashi Art Class," where she teaches the fundamentals of line drawing and coloring in depth, along with secret tips accumulated over the years.

She collaborates with fashion, beauty, and other renowned brands, editorial, and retailers, creating custom illustrations for their campaigns, installations, and consumer products. She also engages in live drawing at runway shows, brand activations, and corporate events.

Website: chloetakahashi.net
Instagram: @chloetakahashi_illustrator

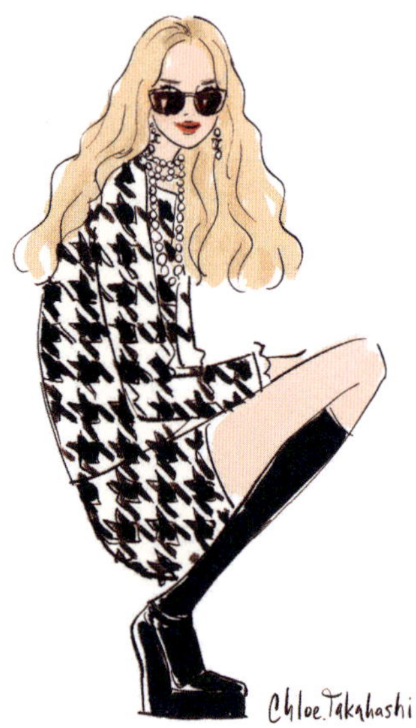

Justine Lecouffe

Justine Lecouffe is an illustrator, designer, and storyboard artist from France, currently living in Ireland. Her work focuses on digital illustration, graphic design, and motion media. It often features powerful women and contemporary themes, making it a good fit for clients in the fashion, jewelry, and cosmetic sectors.

While she likes to sketch in pencil, Justine's illustrations are executed digitally using natural-style brushes for an organic, textured look. She tries to create impactful illustrations, but with gentle lines. Flowing hair, detailed patterns, and intricate linework are highlighted with dashes of color—sometimes subtle, sometimes bold.

Justine has worked for a broad range of publishing, lifestyle, and editorial clients, among them Chanel, Apple, Aston Martin, the National Trust, the NHS, Redbull, Nivea, and Pandora.

Instagram: @justine_lcf

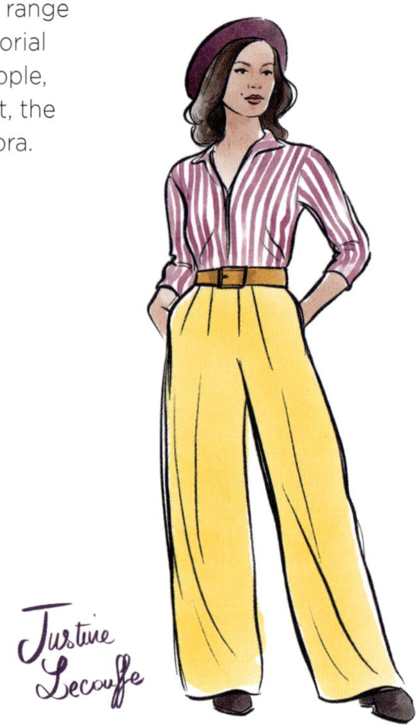